PIVOT

A MEMOIR

PIVOT

A MEMOIR

MACHAELLE WRIGHT

PERELANDRA
CENTER FOR NATURE RESEARCH
JEFFERSONTON, VIRGINIA

PIVOT
Machaelle Wright
FIRST PRINTING

This book is manufactured in the United States of America.
Cover design and special touches: James F. Brisson, Williamsville, VT 05362
Copyediting: Elizabeth McHale, Readsboro, VT 05350
Photo of MW: Clarence Wright
Ocean City photo courtesy of Allison Auriemma
Page design, formatting, and general Queen of Quark:
Machaelle Wright

Computer rescue: Beth Shelton
Readers & Proofreaders: Jeannette Edwards, Beth Shelton, Clarence Wright
Food: The kitchens of Claire's in Warrenton, VA and Foti's in Culpeper, VA.
Food delivery service: Olivia Duvall and Clarence Wright

This book was formatted, laid out and produced using:
Quark XPress 15 software.

Published by Perelandra, Ltd.
P.O. Box 3603, Warrenton, VA 20188

Library of Congress Control Number: 2018956050
Wright, Machaelle
PIVOT

ISBN 13: 978-0927978897

ISBN 10: 0-927978-89-X

2 4 6 8 9 7 5 3 1

Contents

For nature
For David
For Perelandra
For my Cottage family

PIVOT

A MEMOIR

Pivots

A PIVOT OCCURS WHEN a person who has been traveling on a familiar, well-defined life path makes a sudden voluntary or involuntary turn that untethers the individual from that path and propels him or her onto a new and often unrelated path that uproots the individual from his or her previous world.

My first pivot was involuntary and occurred when I was fourteen years old. Involuntary pivots may result from a tragedy where life as the person previously knew it no longer exists. Natural disasters such as earthquakes, tornadoes, hurricanes and floods can force an involuntary pivot. Manmade disasters such as war or abandonment, imprisonment or slavery can also force a pivot. Often involuntary pivots are closely linked to survival. To understand the extent of the uprooting caused by the pivot that I was forced to take, you need to understand something about my life that led to Pivot One.

Chapter 1

Upperco, Maryland
1950–1960

UNTIL I TURNED FOURTEEN, I had a life that appeared to fit easily and seamlessly into the immediate world that surrounded me. As far as I know, we weren't viewed as outcasts or overly odd. Okay, it's true that there were times in school when I was touched by anti-Semitism from a few teachers and a handful of students. But my father, who was raised an Orthodox Jew, was so focused on assimilating that he forgot to tell me I was from a Jewish family. As a result, I recognized people were sometimes being mean or made strange accusations without provocation, but I didn't understand why. (I'm looking at you, fellow third grader who shall remain nameless. When you came up to me in class to call me a "dirty kike" and shouted that the war was my fault, I actually didn't understand what the hell you were talking about. So I wasn't insulted or wounded in the way you had hoped. Just deeply confused and embarrassed. But in response to the only word I understood— "dirty"—I used more soap in my bath that night. Do hope you grew out of all that nastiness.)

I came from a well-to-do family. I heard that Isadore (my father) was making $90,000 a year. This was the late 1950s. Translated into 2017 dollars, he was earning $736,583 annually. Looking back I'd say we lived very comfortably. But at the time I didn't think we were rich. As I said, we fit into the immediate world that surrounded us. We lived in Upperco, Maryland, horse country. This pricey world absorbed money and kept horse owners from living the kind of ostentatious, glittery lifestyle that we associate with the word "rich" today.

My father, all of my parents' friends and most of my classmates had horses. We all rode, trained, hunted and show-jumped. I started riding around age six or seven. I began competing in hack classes (walk, trot, canter classes) around age nine. My father trained me with an eye toward making me into a steeplechase jockey, even though that was something I did not want to do. I went to school with kids who won national championships on the horse show circuit. Isadore had a horse that won Maryland's Triple Crown one year: champion hunter, champion green hunter and champion show jumping. That horse was loaned out to a rider on the U.S. Equestrian team another year. The four walls in our den were filled from ceiling to about three feet from the floor with lines upon lines of ribbons that my father won—awards for first place, second place, third place and fourth, plus championship and reserved championship ribbons. Our dining room decor included multiple displays of silver trophies (all needing polishing every few weeks), and we had an oil portrait of the horse that won the Triple Crown hanging in our living room. You could say there was a horse motif in my home.

Isadore gave me my own horse when I started to ride at age six—a big, standardbred bay that stood 16-1/2 hands tall. (One hand equals four inches. From the top of his shoulder to the ground measured sixty-six inches.) I named him Freedom. I'll let you come up with all the psychological implications behind the name on your own. But before you get too far down that road I'll just say that, at the time, I thought it would be clever if horses from the same stable had related names. We would start with Freedom and perhaps the next horse could be named Liberty, the next Democracy, and so on. No one else saw the cleverness in my scheme so it stopped at my horse with the name "Freedom." The horse that won the Triple Crown? His name was "Himboy." I liked my idea better.

Freedom was well-trained (Isadore trained him), loved to jump (he'd jump the pasture fence on his own when he wanted to join me on the lawn) and had an endearing, nutty personality. I loved him and I feel certain he trusted and liked me back. He was my pal. He was voice trained, which meant that when riding I only needed to tell him what I wanted him to do and he'd do it. And he had a calm, quiet, consistent disposition. Except for his size, he was a perfect horse for a young rider. Isadore started me on such a big horse because kids who began their riding career on ponies invariably had difficulty adjusting to the strides and gaits of a larger horse when they outgrew the pony and had to trade up. Isadore avoided that awkward stage and the subsequent loss of training time with me by putting me on Freedom first. During the first few years while I was learning to ride I was in constant fear that I was going to be killed if I fell off this horse. It was a long way down to the ground.

Nothing about horseback riding felt like a fun sport or hobby to me. Fox hunting season covered the fall/winter weekends and horse show season lasted from spring through summer and into early fall. During the week, horses needed to be worked out, kept fit and trained. We would travel to horse shows as far south as South Carolina and north to Madison Square Garden in New York City and Toronto, Canada. Then there were the fall awards dinners and winter after-hunt parties. To be honest, it felt like a profession. A serious and sometimes dangerous profession. Bones were broken, skulls were cracked and horses were injured. Isadore had two serious jumping accidents. In one he broke his collar bone when Himboy lost his footing going into a jump, flipped over in mid-air and landed on his back on top of Isadore. In the other he broke both his arms. (You don't want me to describe that one.)

The first jump I ever took was over a four-foot-high gate. For a first jump, that's high. Normally a rider in training starts with a little two-foot-high jump to get the feel for it. On the day of my first jump, we were trail riding miles away from home. When we came up on a fence and gate that blocked the trail, Isadore didn't feel like getting off his horse to open the gate, as was his usual habit. He told me we were going to jump it. I froze. He instructed me to "Just sit up there, give the horse his head and let him take the jump. He's smarter than you anyway." Isadore jumped his horse over the gate first ensuring that Freedom would follow. He was right about Freedom knowing exactly what to do. However a 1,600-pound horse landing from a four-foot-high jump is a little jarring. Since I had not jumped before I wasn't expecting such a hard jolt, but I managed to stay with him. I was exhilarated. First, I survived. Second, I discovered that jumping a horse was fun. To literally feel Freedom focus his attention and collect his body in preparation for that jump was amazing and something I can still recall today. I spent the rest of the ride feeling proud of myself.

I competed in my first show a few weeks after my first jump. It was a local affair and primarily for young riders. Isadore entered me in the beginners class, a hack class. About thirty competitors were in the ring at the same time following the judge's shouted instructions. We were to walk, trot, canter, then stop. Back our horses up about six or eight steps, stop again, walk, then hand gallop (a speedy canter). Stop, turn around and do the same routine in the other direction. We were judged on riding and horse skills.

Much to my surprise, I made it past the elimination round and into the top ten. We were then put through an abbreviated version of the earlier round. When it came time for the final canter, I had Freedom's reins too long and he couldn't pick up what lead I wanted him to take. (I know, I've got you staggering around in horse-talk tall grass. But I'm not going to describe any of this rudimentary riding stuff any more than this. If you care, Google "English horseback riding, cantering lead.") Anyway, Freedom began his canter on the wrong lead. I passed Isadore about halfway around the ring and heard him say in a low voice, "Wrong lead." After two or three strides, Freedom automatically switched his lead to the correct one.

When the awards were announced, Freedom and I came in second. I was thrilled. I was beat out by a seventeen-year-old kid who had been competing on the national circuit for years. Second place seemed pretty good to me. After all, it was my very first class and I got a ribbon. But when I looked over at Isadore, I could see that he was not pleased. When the judge pinned the ribbon on Freedom's bridle, he admonished me for making that mistake with Freedom's lead. He said I should have known better. My first class and I was the recipient of an embarrassing public dressing down by the judge.

This was the moment when I realized that in everyone else's eyes I was Isadore Small's daughter. I felt an air of expectation and responsibility surround me. Apparently as Isadore's daughter, I had a reputation to uphold. People expected me to meet some pretty high standards when it came to riding because I was Isadore Small's daughter. Isadore was a well-respected horse trainer and riding instructor. Riders from all around consulted and trained with him. He primarily dealt with experienced riders. I was the only person who had started training with him from the beginning. Obviously the last person to make such a rookie mistake in a class was Isadore's daughter. (Two hack classes later I beat that guy.)

There's nothing cheap about having horses on this level. Back then probably the least expensive thing was the horse. These people trained their own horses for hunting, show jumping and sometimes flat and steeple racing so they didn't have to pay big bucks for an already-trained horse.

To give you an idea of what I'm talking about: Isadore paid $50 for Himboy. He watched the horse racing at a nearby track one afternoon. As Himboy was coming down the home stretch he suddenly bolted, threw his jockey and jumped the inside rail. Isadore liked the way the horse took that jump. So he offered the owner $50 to take Himboy off his hands and the owner was grateful to finally get rid of that "impossible" animal.

As for the cost of a well-trained horse: Freedom had never had a saddle on him when Isadore bought him for $100. Several years later, a woman came up to me at a horse show where we were competing and offered $36,000 cash for Freedom. (That's $294,633 in today's economy.) She was an older woman and wanted a quiet horse with a good temperament for fox hunting. My father told her the horse was mine and the decision was up to me. I told her no. I loved my horse.

Aside from buying horses, there's the land for grazing and training, the stables, the feed, the bedding straw and hay, the tack (saddles, bridles, halters, shanks, lunging lines, special girths, special bits, special stirrups…), the vet bills, the farrier bills, the riding clothes and boots imported from England, the membership fees for fox hunting and entrance fees for showing, the training rings and jumps, costs for transporting horses to and from shows and hunts and, if you were lucky, a stable boy to clean out the stalls. We were lucky. My father had a stable boy. (Actually, I was lucky. I didn't have to clean out the stalls.)

So I went through these early years steeped in the world of horses and not wanting for anything material. With a $2 weekly allowance, I personally was not drowning in money. However, if I felt I needed something, I was expected to sit down with Isadore, present my case and convince him that this was a legitimate need. Once he agreed, he tended to go big. He worked in the clothing industry and dealt in large volume. Once I requested socks and he gave me 12 dozen pairs of quality white cotton socks. (That's not a typo. He actually gave me 144 pairs of socks.) I asked for a jacket and he gave me five car coats—six if you count the reversible car coat as two. One year I said I needed pencils for school and he gave me a box of twelve dozen #2 round, yellow pencils. I looked at the boxes and figured I would never live long enough to get through all those pencils.

Being an only child, I had my own room complete with a double bed, two lamp tables, a big dresser, an even bigger chest of drawers, a desk, three chairs, two windows, a blue shag carpet and a framed charcoal, limited-edition drawing of a white stallion rearing up on its hind legs while lightning streaked across the night sky behind him. The picture was my mother's idea of what one hangs in a girl's bedroom. I found it scary, even threatening. Maybe it was actually prescient.

We had a maid who stayed with us during weekdays for a couple of years after we moved to Upperco. I adored her. We used to sit in the kitchen together eating fried chicken. She would eat the chicken—bones and all—and tell me the bones were good for you. Something about the bone marrow.

I didn't realize until years later that my parents had a racist streak and they allowed me to disrespect this woman. I wasn't a brat around her, but my parents had a strict rule that I was not allowed to call any adult by their first name. Even when family friends encouraged me to use their first name, my parents would jump in and say that I was to address them properly: Mr. or Mrs. with their last names. ("Ms" didn't exist then.) This rule extended to every adult—except our maid. I was told to call her "Elsie." Just plain "Elsie." If she didn't feel I was disrespecting her it was because I was only five or six years old and she was a truly fine and understanding person. She gave me a pass on my questionable manners. (For the record, I'd like to publicly apologize to you, Miss Elsie, for my rudeness. I'd love to show you the full respect you deserve and call you by your proper name, but I don't think I ever knew your last name. The best I can do now is "Miss Elsie." I know you've passed on but I feel it's never too late to apologize.)

If we stopped this picture of my early years at this point, I think we'd all agree that I had an easy, well-structured life. But there was also an underbelly of cruelty and abuse that came with this life.

The Path to Pivot One

My mother, Dorothy, was an alcoholic. Back then I didn't know the word "alcoholic" so I just saw her as a drunk. She began drinking socially when I was about four years old. Then she went from part-time social drinking to full-time drinking when I was five and we moved out to Upperco. She drank from mid-morning until she stumbled to bed at night.

She was an angry drunk. From my perspective, there was nothing funny or charming about her when she was drunk, which was daily. She often smelled like a combination of stale booze mixed with a sour body odor, her eyes were always blood-shot, her speech was slurred, she was erratic in her behavior and actions, she could be sarcastic and mean, and she lied constantly. She seemed to enjoy humiliating or hurting others by playing odd pranks on them. Everything about her drinking screamed *wrong* inside me. She embarrassed me. I felt deeply that this was not the way a mother should act. This was not the way a woman should act.

She hated children and being a mother. Since I was her only child I became her primary target by default. I don't recall her ever speaking to me about anything other than the day-to-day chores she wanted me to do. There were no mother-daughter conversations. There was no laughter between us. I didn't tell her about my day nor did she ask about it. I also didn't ask about her day. I don't recall ever overhearing her having a discussion with a friend about life, ideas, differing opinions or current events. Her preferred subjects were any and all gossip and TV soap operas. I honestly do not know if this woman was intelligent. She had a quick temper and she was impatient, especially with me. Periodically, while I was in school, she would amuse herself by tearing apart my room looking for my diary and any damning evidence she could use to prove to Isadore what a terrible child I was.

She also didn't like me to touch her and would always tell me my hands were too cold and clammy. Actually, I don't remember her ever hugging me. We didn't do typical mother-daughter things together like shopping because she didn't enjoy being around me. She would go shopping by herself or with a friend and purchase the clothes she wanted me to wear. I had to wear them whether I liked the clothes or not. Sometimes I lucked out and I'd get some nice wool skirts or a sweater. (But then there was that frilly blue printed dress that I truly couldn't stand and had to wear to school fairly often.)

She hated cooking. Each meal was accompanied by a chorus of slamming cabinet doors, banging pots and pans and cursing. The odd thing is that she was a good cook. When she finished cooking a meal, she served it by slamming the plate down in front of me. I'd like to say I was able to calm her down by helping her prepare meals but she wouldn't allow anyone else in the kitchen.

It was my job to wash the dishes each night and clean the kitchen. Normally this was fairly uneventful since she sat in the living room drinking while I worked. At one point in one of my classes, I had been taught how to "properly" wash dishes. (Dishwashers weren't available yet so washing dishes in a sink full of sudsy water was still a human endeavor.) Glasses were to be washed first, next silverware, next plates, and then pots and pans last.

One night Dorothy walked in and saw that I had changed my routine to match what I had learned in school. I don't know why but she exploded with anger. From what she was yelling, it sounded like she was personally offended that someone had taught me another way to wash dishes. She seemed to be taking it as some sort of personal attack or insult. To punctuate her point, she picked up a large cast-iron skillet that was sitting next to the sink waiting to be washed and hurled it at my head. I managed to duck, thus saving my head. But the skillet hit the oven door knocking off a sizable chunk of enamel and leaving a large dent.

I didn't say anything to Dorothy and she stormed out of the kitchen. I picked up the pan and got back to washing the dishes my way. But as I stood at the sink I could feel that things had changed. She meant for that heavy pan to hit my head. I now knew for sure that I could be in serious danger. I was eleven years old and I could have died that night.

She got a perverse kick out of abusing me during meals. She would tell me to put my hand over a steaming hot plate of food to feel the heat and then when I did that she'd slam my hand into the food. Or she would tell me to smell the food and then shove my face into the hot food. If I hesitated or resisted she'd insist, even threaten. She yelled at me if I made a face or said ouch. She yelled at me if I showed her that I had gotten burned. She yelled at me for eating too slowly, then she'd yell at me for eating too fast. She forced me to eat everything she served on my plate even if it was too much food. When I had to eat more quickly, I would stuff food into my cheeks to chew and swallow (or throw away) later. If she spotted me doing this she would reach over and squeeze my cheeks to force the food back into my mouth saying, "Eat, dammit." Sometimes I had to leave the table to throw up.

Often she'd serve food that she knew I didn't like. I am lactose intolerant but she always gave me a big glass of milk with meals, which made her feel like a good mother but made me nauseous. I hated the smell and taste of anchovies but she always threw them on top of my salad. And I couldn't stand braunschweiger liver sausage sandwiches but she couldn't stop serving them to me. I once made the mistake of feeding the sandwich to my dog, Chris. Apparently she didn't like it either and dropped the sandwich out in the open for Dorothy to see. I was chased up the stairs to my room and beaten with a hairbrush.

She extended her abuse beyond meals. When I finished riding I would lie down on the living room floor to relax my back. Dorothy would sometimes sneak up, step on my hair so that I couldn't move my head and spit in my face. And then there were the many times when I'd be walking through the house, usually on my way to my room, and Dorothy would jump out of nowhere to put me through some physical or verbal test. If I reacted or didn't pass her tests according to her standards, I was sent to my room for the rest of the day.

And where was Isadore while all this was going on? He was working in Baltimore or traveling. He took frequent business trips that kept him away during weekdays. When he was around, Dorothy continued drinking but she somehow managed to not smell, look or act as drunk. When not on a trip he would come home from his office, change his clothes and go to the stable until dinner. Everyone knew that if they wanted to see Isadore, don't bother stopping at the house first. Just go directly to the stable. Even with him around, Dorothy was still pretty angry about that cooking thing, but she managed to move around the kitchen a little more quietly. As far as I know, Isadore never asked why the enamel was missing from the dented oven door. He had one requirement: Put dinner down in front of him on time. If she met this requirement, all was well.

I had fears and concerns about Isadore, as well. Generally, he was a strict disciplinarian. Around the horses, he had lots of rules: I was never to ride by myself. I was not to sit on a horse without someone present. I was not to fool around when riding or tending the horses. I was *always* to wear my riding helmet. There were more rules but you get the idea. We didn't talk unless he was giving me riding instructions. If I looked frightened about something or I looked like I was going to cry, he would say, "Keep it up and I'll give you something to cry about."

And then there was his infamous "Isadore Small dumb-shit look" that he used on people whenever he decided they were being stupid. His friends talked about getting hit with Isadore's dumb-shit look. As a child I tended to live up to his definition of stupid rather frequently. His stare was cold, intense and threatening.

At other times he made comments about my physical appearance and changing body for the amusement of others, which I found humiliating. At night, if I was lying on the couch watching television, he would walk by, grab my knee and squeeze tight with his fingers causing sharp pain. My whole leg would go numb. I don't know why he did that, but he did it fairly frequently and always thought it was funny.

And then there was the strange unease I felt around him. Except for when I was riding, there was always this weird icky vibe that I picked up from him. I never felt safe or comfortable in the house with him. I kept as much distance as possible and for as far back as I can remember I always made sure I was fully dressed around him. Years later I found out he had sexually abused his daughter from a later marriage.

How did I respond to this abusive environment? Avoidance. Since Isadore was away working or at the stable so often, my main concern was with Dorothy. I tried to avoid her as much as possible. With both Dorothy and Isadore, I made a point to behave, follow orders and remain quiet. I didn't talk back or yell or strike out. My goal was to keep my head down as much as possible. Be invisible. Family friends commented to my parents about how well mannered, well behaved and quiet I was.

I had a second response that was equally important: *I endured.* I endured Dorothy, Isadore and their abusive environment. According to the dictionary, "endure" means "to tolerate, bear or put up with without giving in or up." I may have felt confused, frightened, intimidated, under attack and in danger—but I also felt a strong sense of my own existence that was not connected to these two people. Internally I felt my own presence and from this I could feel strength. The attacks were like glancing blows—sometimes serious glancing blows—that landed on the surface but did not sink in or compromise what I felt about myself inside. I could feel strong pain, anger and fear but these feelings didn't consume me nor were they absorbed by the person inside. I don't know how else to describe this but suffice it to say that my parents never took away what I felt inside. I did not give them permission to diminish me. I realize now that to endure is a natural part of my personality. It must have been included in my "birth package" and is just there inside me to draw on when needed. When I've had to deal with something or someone unpleasant, endurance automatically provides the underlying foundation for my response.

I didn't think to reach out for help or talk to anyone about my situation because both of my parents insisted that our home life was no one else's business. I followed orders, remember? But how my friends described their family life didn't match my experiences at all. Consequently I didn't want to talk about what was going on in my home. I was young, I wanted to fit in and I didn't want to seem too weird.

SCHOOL PROVIDED RELIEF and I poured everything I had into it. It gave me a predictable schedule and there were kids I could talk to and laugh with. Just as importantly, I didn't feel danger lurking around every corner. I don't know how the schools in Baltimore County were rated as a whole back then, but the two schools I attended in Upperco (elementary and junior-senior high school) seemed to be quite good.

Not all my teachers in elementary school were anti-Semitic, and those who weren't provided support and encouragement. They must have seen some leadership qualities in me because in third grade I was appointed to the safety patrol (a year ahead of the other kids), and in fourth grade (two years ahead of previous appointees) I was given the job of heading up the school's Red Cross program to put together and provide aid boxes for overseas school kids. In both endeavors I tried my best but generally felt I was in over my head and only managed to hit the mediocre mark with the kind help of a couple of teachers.

My junior-senior high school had more students, larger classes, more activities and more opportunities to spend time away from home. I joined the band, I played sports and I joined the cheerleading squad. (Yes, I was a junior varsity cheerleader.) My major school fear was not being able to open the combination lock on my locker (which caused recurring nightmares for years).

Classes were challenging and I had to put a lot of time and effort in to keep my grades up. I consistently got As and Bs and one C. The C drifted around my report card from class to class. I wanted to make the Honor Roll in high school, but to do this I had to get rid of my roving C. It took five years for me to finally catch that sucker and beat it into a B.

Gradually I noticed something about school that raised questions for me: I seemed to be working a lot harder than most of the other kids in my class who were getting the same or better grades. I couldn't figure out what secret they knew about learning and taking tests. I always felt like I had somehow missed the introductory class where kids were told how to successfully navigate through school. It was frustrating and sometimes seemed unfair that I was never able to discover "the secret." I had no choice but to keep working hard. Twenty years later I found out I am dyslexic.

Back when I attended school, teachers weren't trained to recognize or to help kids with learning disabilities. I certainly didn't know anything about it and the term "learning disability" was not something I would have thought to apply to myself. Because my teachers and I assumed I was "learning able," I was left to figure stuff out on my own. Like so many kids who have struggled with dyslexia, I wanted to be invisible in class. I kept repeating silently, "Don't call on me.... Don't call on me.... Don't call on me." I confused letters and words and I read more slowly than my classmates. I also confused my right/left directions, had a terrible memory and would go completely blank when taking a test.

By necessity I leaned more towards out-of-the-box thinking, so I considered various ideas for overcoming class challenges. I had trouble maintaining focus on whatever I was trying to learn. I played around with this problem and found that if I added a little extra challenge to the exercise, making it slightly more difficult, it would be easier for me to hold focus. Essentially I made things more interesting. For example, I was placed in an advanced algebra class in eighth grade. Numbers and letters were floating and swirling all over the place—across the blackboard, my textbook pages and my homework papers. It even seemed like numbers and bits of formulas were flying around in mid-air. I had to figure out some way to anchor those babies. To make things more interesting, I began writing algebra formulas using Russian Cyrillic letters and Japanese numbers.

I was now doing algebra in code and this made it not only interesting but fun. More importantly, the algebra formulas remained anchored in place. I'm sure my teacher felt I was a little odd—I certainly would have felt that way had I been in his shoes—but suddenly I was able to keep up with the class. To his credit he said I could continue as long as I wrote the final answer in English and drew a box around it so that he could find it quickly. If I got it wrong, I had to translate everything pertaining to that formula and problem back into English so that he could see where I went wrong. I got a B+ in that class which, considering what I was dealing with, was nothing short of a miracle

I learned to count in Japanese from my eighth grade teacher's Japanese wife. She came in one day to talk about Japan, teach us some simple phrases and how to count. I was completely taken by the two of them together and for the remainder of the year I secretly wished they would adopt me. Well, there was no talk of adoption. I don't think he even singled me out in class in any special way. But he did give me—along with the rest of the class—something very important.

Each morning he wrote a quotation by a wide range of famous people (dead and alive) on the board. These quotes showed me that there were some very interesting people beyond my bubble who said or wrote things worth considering. Every morning I looked forward to the new quote. I copied it onto a 3x5 note card and then filed it—alphabetically according to author—in a small metal card box. I have to say that "Anonymous" was really prolific. Two of my favorites that I remember:

He who knows not and knows not he knows not:
he is a fool—shun him.
He who knows not and knows he knows not:
he is simple—teach him.

He who knows and knows not he knows:
he is asleep—wake him.
He who knows and knows he knows:
he is wise—follow him.
Confucius

Learn from the mistakes of others.
You can't live long enough to make them all yourself.
Eleanor Roosevelt

I WAS PROBABLY THE ONLY KID in my school who did not look forward to summer vacation. From mid-June until the first Tuesday in September, avoiding Dorothy became my full-time occupation and preoccupation.

During those three months Dorothy drank, sunbathed, drank, weeded her flower beds, drank, crashed her way through the kitchen while fixing dinner, then drank some more while watching television. I don't know when she went to bed but it was pretty late.

Isadore maintained his normal schedule: drive to his office each day or leave for the week on a business trip, come home, change into his "stable clothes," go to the stable for a few hours, come back to the house for dinner, watch television, fall asleep on the couch, wake up and go upstairs to bed.

I was expected to go to bed before Isadore. When Miss Elsie was still with us, I would ask her to come with me in the bathroom while I washed my hair. I wasn't allowed to take a shower so I had to lean over the tub and stick my head under the faucet. That meant that my back was to the door and I couldn't hear anything because my head was under the running faucet. I always had the creepy, scary feeling that Dorothy was going to sneak in and hold my head under the faucet until I drowned.

Logically, now that I've gotten older, wiser and more experienced, I don't see how that would work. The water would have to come out of the faucet with the volume and force of a fire hose. But I was a kid living with a drunk and I was convinced Dorothy could pull off the deed. So Miss Elsie would sit on the toilet, towel in hand and talk to me. I lost my protection after she left us and I had to come up with a new plan. The bathroom door didn't have a lock so I started propping things against the door that would be knocked over with much noise if someone tried to sneak in. Problem solved. To label me paranoid only works if I wasn't in actual danger and this fear was all manufactured in my head. The point is, I was in danger and I knew it. I just never knew which direction the danger would be coming from.

The key to spending long summer hours alone with Dorothy was to stay out of sight as much as possible—avoidance. I got up around 10 A.M. By then, if he wasn't on a trip, Isadore had left for work and, with a little luck, Dorothy was outside working on her suntan and having her first round of drinks of the day. Before she left, Miss Elsie taught me how to scramble eggs. Each summer morning I would add toast and voilà, I had breakfast. There was always a pitcher of orange juice in the refrigerator but I dared not drink it. Dorothy added vodka in with the juice.

After breakfast I got on with the task of disappearing. Living in the country meant long hours of solitude. There wasn't a neighborhood full of kids to melt into. We only had two neighbors' houses within sight. In one house lived an older couple whom I barely knew and felt shy about visiting. The other house had a gaggle of kids—six to be exact. One girl was in my class but during the school year we socialized in different groups. It was an active, chaotic home and when I felt up to handling the chaos, I would go there for a few hours. The kids laughed a lot, ran around the house (literally), yelled at one another, gossiped, called their parents by their first names—and ate cold pizza for breakfast. Sacrilege.

Most of the time I stuck to myself. I stayed in my room and read books or wrote in my diary. From the time I had learned to write I kept a diary. Along with recording my thoughts, ideas, dreams and fantasies, writing became my substitute for parental guidance. Granted I was talking to myself but the exercise made the issues and challenges I was facing clearer. If I had a particularly tricky problem to solve, I drew a vertical line down the paper and labeled one column "yes" and the other column "no." Then I would list all the benefits and good points I could think of in the yes column.

The problems were listed in the no column. Whatever column was the longest and had the most points listed was my answer.

I hid my diary and its key to keep Dorothy from finding it when she tossed my room. She was in search of any and all damning evidence but mostly she wanted to find that diary. My most successful hiding spot involved one of my foam-rubber pillows. I discovered that when I poked a small hole into the side of the foam rubber, the opening would lead to a series of "tunnels" that wove throughout the pillow. I could stretch out the hole, stick in my diary and move it through the tunnels to the middle of the pillow. I changed my own sheets so Dorothy didn't notice that my pillow was heavier or lumpy. For extra security I hid the diary key inside the hem of my window curtain.

In the early afternoons, I headed outside to wherever Dorothy wasn't. I liked climbing trees and observing the world from on high. I frequently pretended I was an Indian scout on the lookout for soldiers en route to attack my village. (I had no idea why I came up with this scenario. Back then most kids would choose to be the soldier on the lookout for marauding Indians.)

And I invented a game that could keep me occupied for hours. The challenge was to move through our woods without making a sound. No leaves crunching or twigs snapping. My goal was total silence. After hours upon hours of practice I reached my goal. A lot of that success had to do with how I put each foot down and rolled it slowly sideways. It was perhaps an odd little game but I liked the challenge. You just never know when you'll need to move silently through a woods.

I later learned two things that perhaps explained my summer obsessions: (1) Native American children had a game where they would spot a deer and try to move through the woods silently to get close enough to tap the deer on the butt. It helped them develop hunting skills. (2) I found out that I was one-quarter Native American. Dorothy was half Hopi. Her mother was full Hopi. Because my grandmother died giving birth to Dorothy (she was sixteen pounds at birth), and because my grandfather travelled all over Arizona to make a living as a well driller, my mother had to live with her Hopi relatives on their reservation. When she was five, my grandfather remarried and came back for Dorothy.

As an adult my mother spent as much time and effort distancing herself from her childhood as my father spent distancing himself from his Jewish background. She rarely talked about her experiences, and the tiny bits of information I did learn I picked up from overheard conversations she had with friends. I first found out about her Hopi background accidentally when I ran across an old photo of an Indian woman with an infant in a cradleboard on her back. Written on the back of the photo was "Dorothy—4 months." I asked Dorothy about the picture and she confirmed the child was her. That's about the sum total of what she told me about her Hopi childhood. I, on the other hand, thought that being one-quarter Native American was great and special and magical.

When I wasn't practicing my Indian deer-hunting skills, I spent a lot of time with Freedom. In secret I challenged Isadore's rules. I wasn't supposed to groom a horse by myself. But during the summers, I groomed Freedom nearly every day. To save steps, when I finished with one side of him, I'd duck under his belly to get to the other side. This isn't an unusual move for those who work around horses but for me it was forbidden. It could be dangerous if a horse kicked out while I was crossing beneath him. With Freedom I felt I could take a chance.

But I would have really gotten in trouble if Isadore knew what else I was doing. After Isadore left for work, I would go to Freedom's stall to see if he was still sleeping. This horse was so laid back that if he was lying down in the straw I'd pat him a little. He'd raise his head to look at me then rest his head back in the straw. I would slide on top of him until he stirred a little to let me know he wanted to get up. Listening to the sound of his breathing and feeling its rhythm was comforting.

Once he got up I'd feed him a little, talk to him while I groomed him and then lead him out to the pasture. I found that little touch of rebellion and my flirt with potential danger exciting, even if it was with the world's safest horse. Neither Freedom nor I ever tipped off what shenanigans we were up to when Isadore wasn't around. A couple of times when he commented on how good the horse's coat looked, I just said, "You're right. Must be that new feed he's getting now."

The summer when I was eleven or twelve, Dorothy told me that she needed to get some money to buy seat covers for her car. She decided she would collect the glass bottles lying in the roadside ditches. The idea was to cash them in at the grocery store for two cents a bottle. I was enlisted to help by driving the car—something I didn't know how to do—while she sat on the hood looking for bottles. When she spotted one she'd shout "Stop" and I'd hit the brake, usually so hard that it propelled her off the hood. I actually didn't do that on purpose. Really. I had just never operated a car before. (Okay. If I'm to be totally honest I'd have to admit that I didn't mind seeing her fly off the hood.) After a few days I got the feel for the brake and steering wheel. She was able to slowly slide off the hood and land on her feet and I was able to keep the car on the road. Luckily it had an automatic transmission. When we collected enough bottles, she'd drive to the grocery store, cash them in and come out with a whopping $2 to $3 for her efforts. I came out of the summer knowing how to drive—something that was soon to come in handy.

I later overheard her telling a drinking pal about her bottle collecting. It was clear the endeavor had nothing to do with seat covers. She was trying to embarrass Isadore by letting people see her cash in the bottles. She'd tell them that Isadore was no longer giving her any money and she needed the bottle money to put food on the table. Of course, none of this was true. When the story got back to Isadore, he clearly was not pleased. She told him that this was nothing more than an experiment to see how much people gossiped, how quickly it was passed around and how quickly it would get back to Isadore. The story that Isadore heard did not include that I now knew how to drive.

Dorothy's drinking intensified. The summer between seventh and eighth grades she changed my routine. Now each day she dropped me off at the swimming club that was about ten miles away. I met new friends, I swam, I ate hot dogs. It was great. She spent the day in some bar with her drinking buddies and at the end of the day she'd return to pick me up. As soon as I saw her sitting in the car looking at me I knew she was drunk. All the way home I paid attention to her driving and let her know when she was heading off the road or going too fast.

One evening after she picked me up she drove to a restaurant instead of going home. Well, it was a restaurant with a bar and a bunch of her friends. I had dinner at a table by myself while she and her friends drank and had a boisterous time. I saw a side of her I had not observed before. She was clearly enjoying herself and everyone seemed to be totally charmed by her.

We headed home about 11 P.M. She drove down a quiet, country back road that crossed some railroad tracks. As we were nearing the tracks, I could hear a train coming with its whistle sounding full blast. The closer we got the faster she drove. I told her to slow down, that we needed to stop. But that only made her go faster. The train was starting to cross in front of us and still the car picked up speed.

I looked at what was happening and suddenly realized that she was deliberately aiming to crash into the train in order to kill us both. I had to try to stop her and the car. The long, front bench seat gave me unobstructed access to her side of the car. I reached over with my foot and found the brake pedal. Her foot was on the gas pedal and I had to get her out of the way quickly. So with all the strength I had, I punched her in the face one time with my fist and knocked her out. Then I kicked her foot off the gas, slammed on the brake and grabbed the wheel. We stopped about ten feet from the tracks and I sat there staring at the train as it finished passing by. I got out and walked around the car shouting and shaking with an anger and fear beyond description.

Once I stopped shaking, I just wanted to go home. I pulled and pushed Dorothy across the seat to the passenger side, got behind the wheel and drove home. When we arrived Dorothy was still out so I left her in the car, went upstairs to my room and cried myself to sleep.

The next morning Dorothy was dressed and ready to drive me to the swimming club as usual. It was as if nothing had happened. I suspect she didn't remember anything about the night before and that she assumed the large welt on her face was caused by another one of her drunken accidents. I don't know what went through her mind when she woke up and found herself in the car in our driveway. In all these years, I have never changed my opinion that she was aiming to kill us both. Because I had no idea what triggered her that night, I increased my protective vigilance when I was around her.

As the new school year began, Dorothy's erratic behavior became more public. Fox hunting season started and with that the weekly after-hunt parties that my parents hosted at our house resumed. My job at these affairs was bartending. I sat behind a table with the liquor bottles lined up and filled drink orders. It wasn't difficult. They all tended to drink Scotch on the rocks or Canadian Club and ginger ale on the rocks. Any drink more ambitious than this the people had to fix themselves. I didn't mind the parties or bartending because it gave me a chance to people watch up close.

I don't know how Dorothy felt about those parties. She seemed to enjoy most of the company, but some of the people, along with their children, clearly annoyed her. Keeping her under control could be tricky especially since Isadore expected her to cook the meal for the fifteen to twenty guests each week. The food wasn't elaborate—usually spaghetti or chicken cacciatore, which she started in the morning in the slow cooker and let simmer until it was time to serve. Still, I knew how much she hated cooking.

Things started to unravel quickly at one of the parties. Dorothy was about three hours late serving the meal. A friend of hers went into the kitchen intending to help but she made a big mistake: She asked Dorothy when dinner might be ready. I don't know what Dorothy had been doing up to that point (besides drinking), but she exploded as soon as the question was asked and flung her martini glass across the kitchen. A remarkably obnoxious, spoiled seven-year-old kid was standing at the kitchen doorway checking to see what the commotion was about. The martini glass hit him in the head. I have no idea if that was on purpose or just collateral damage. She hated that kid.

She continued screaming and started running through the house knocking over and tossing furniture. Isadore chased after her and managed to catch a dining chair in mid-air that was headed toward the glass doors of a large cabinet that held some of Isadore's trophies and the family china. He finally caught up to her as she was headed back into the living room. By this time everyone had gathered their coats and were heading to their cars to escape the wrath of Dorothy. Isadore tackled her and the two of them landed on the floor in the living room in front of where I was sitting.

She was screaming insults at him and, to control her flailing attempts to hit him, he sat on top of her and pinned down her arms with his knees. She was calling him every name a sailor could think of, and he was bleeding from some face scratches and crying. I sat on the couch frozen from fear and shock, staring at the scene just in front of me.

I had no idea what to do. Isadore sat on top of her until she passed out while I continued to sit very still on the couch. I must have gone into shock because I have no memory of what happened next or how the night ended. I know I woke up the next morning in my own bed remembering what Dorothy did and the scene of both of my parents on the living room floor in front of me. When I went downstairs for breakfast it wasn't hard to notice that there was a new level of tension between Dorothy and Isadore. Outwardly our daily rhythm returned to "normal" and neither one of us ever mentioned that night.

Two weeks later they both sat me down and announced that they were divorcing. They asked if I understood what they were saying and I said yes. End of discussion. No further details or plans were given me.

However, not long after their announcement I overheard them arguing about me and where I would live. They weren't fighting about who wanted to keep me or who loved me more. They each made it clear that neither one of them wanted to keep me. My mother declared she didn't want me around her. And my father kept shouting that he had to work and wouldn't know what to do with me so she had better take me. This went on for about a half hour while I sat at the top of the stairs trying to absorb what I was hearing as I cried silently. It both broke my heart and confirmed what I already suspected about how they felt about their daughter.

Shortly after their announcement, the day before Thanksgiving to be exact, Isadore got a call from his attorney. Dorothy was in his office demanding to sign the divorce papers. Isadore told him to let her sign them. And with that, Dorothy disappeared and never returned to Upperco. Isadore was left with the task of figuring out what to do with his thirteen-year-old daughter. I guess this was Dorothy's way of winning the argument.

For me, life returned to fairly normal rhythms. Isadore hired a woman to clean the house and cook weekday dinners. I continued going to school and riding. The only thing missing was Dorothy's drunken presence, abuse and anger. Although I had no idea what might happen next or where Dorothy was, I now felt relief. I still had my home, my room, my horse, my dog and my school schedule. I figured if I just let the divorce dust settle a bit, life would go on and all would be well.

Within the first month of our new life, Isadore decided to farm me out. I was sent to live with a classmate and her family. I wasn't overly upset by this turn of events. Life with Isadore was beginning to feel oddly quiet and lonely, and I looked forward to being a part of a "real" family.

Unfortunately I moved into another mess. The husband and wife were estranged but living in the same house. The four kids had sided with the mother and no one was speaking to the father. He ate dinner with us while the rest of the family ignored him at the dining table. Then he retired to the den and read for the rest of the evening.

Sometimes I joined him in the evenings. He was an engineer, he was smart, he talked about interesting things and he seemed pleased to have my company. He'd tell me his stories and teach me about things from his world. I never figured out what was going on between him and the rest of the family but towards me he was very kind.

I lived with this family for a few weeks and was beginning to feel settled in. One Saturday Isadore showed up unexpectedly (to me at least) and told me to pack my stuff right away. He was taking me back to our house. When I asked him why, he just told me to go upstairs and pack my things. That's when I looked around and noticed something really odd. Normally there was all sorts of activity going on around the house, especially on Saturdays. Now everyone had disappeared. It was like the place had suddenly become a ghost house. I suspected the relationship between the wife and her husband was about to take a significant shift but because no one was around to explain or even to say goodbye, I left feeling I had done something wrong.

No matter the reason, I was grateful to be back home and back in my room. But that only lasted a week or two before I was farmed out again. This time it was to friends of Isadore's. He fox hunted with the husband. The wife had been an elementary school teacher but was now a stay-at-home mom with an infant son.

I wasn't sure why they agreed to my moving in because the house was rather small and they had to give up the only spare room to me. I found out that Isadore was paying people room and board for taking me in so I figured this was a way for the couple to have extra income now that the wife wasn't working. Because she had been a teacher and liked kids, I had great hopes that whatever I had done wrong at the first house would not be a problem for her. I was determined to succeed in this new home.

It took a couple of weeks but eventually I began to relax. They bought ice cream in five-gallon buckets and I was encouraged to eat as much as I wanted. Dorothy rarely had ice cream in our freezer so I thought I had now entered heaven. I still went to the same school but I had to stop my extracurricular activities in order to ride the bus to my new home. About every two weeks Isadore would call to see how I was doing and if I needed anything. The conversations were always utilitarian, short and to the point.

All seemed to be going well until one weekend when the wife traveled with the baby to visit some friends. That left me in the house with the husband. He spent the evening drinking and, long after I had gone to bed, he entered my room and began sexually molesting me. When he first started kissing and touching me I was asleep. But I woke up pretty quickly. At first I was confused and tried to figure out what was happening. I could tell from his breath and slurred speech that he was drunk, and I thought he may not know what he was doing. It even crossed my mind that he was confused and thought I was his wife. No matter what, I knew I had to stop this man before he raped me. I didn't try to fight him. Drunk or not, he had the physical advantage over me so I felt slugging him or trying to push him off me was just going to make matters worse. Instead I talked. I tried to engage him in a conversation in the hope that he would realize what he was doing and stop. I talked about his wife and baby, but he continued to molest me. I kept talking until finally I persuaded him to leave my room. When I could no longer hear him moving around in his room, I figured he was asleep—and I felt I was temporarily safe as long as I stayed awake and alert. I spent the rest of the night feeling both ashamed and frightened. I couldn't figure out what I had done to encourage this man.

When the morning finally came and I collected enough courage to walk out of my bedroom, I found that the husband had disappeared. That day I wrote a long letter to a close friend telling him what happened and asking what I should do. The wife returned from her trip in the afternoon and in the evening the husband acted as if nothing had happened. I took my cue from him and pretended all was well despite my heightened levels of concern and vigilance. Having the wife back in the house gave me a little confidence that I was safe.

My friend wrote back right away. He had discussed my situation with his mother and together they felt the best thing to do was get a lock for my door and tell my father what happened. I didn't do either, at least not right away. Instead I started piling things against my door at night knowing that the clatter alone would wake up everyone in the house should he come in again. I refocused on my classes and spent the evenings studying in my room—and eating ice cream. The only time I saw the husband was during dinner. He avoided eye contact and only spoke to me when necessary.

The wife must have noticed a change in me because one afternoon while I was at school she went into my room looking for clues and answers. I had left my friend's letter on the dresser and she read it. There was enough information in that letter to tip her off that something had happened while she had been away. When I got back from school that afternoon, Isadore and the wife were waiting for me. They told me to sit down. It was clear they were not at all happy with me. Isadore was holding my friend's letter. One thing I had hoped to avoid was an embarrassing public confrontation about this mess. That now appeared unavoidable.

The wife told me that she read my friend's letter and wanted me to explain what this guy was referring to and why he was telling me to get a lock on my door. I had barely begun speaking when she abruptly stopped me, left the room for a few minutes and came back with her husband. I could tell when he looked at me that he was really angry. His wife said I was to start over and to say what I had to say directly to his face.

I didn't think this situation could get worse. Everything I feared and hoped not to have to face was right in front of me. Now I had to describe in detail a scene that I found deeply embarrassing and I had to do it in front of my father, this wife and her husband, the perpetrator. When I started speaking again I could not make eye contact with anyone and I started to shake. Once I got the whole story out the husband stood up and declared in a rather loud, forceful voice that I was a liar. Then he stomped off. Isadore told me to pack my stuff. I was going home.

When I got in the car, I didn't know if the wife or Isadore believed me. Nothing was said by either one. Once again I felt defeated and like a failure. But at least I was going home again and would be back in my own room. After unpacking, I curled up in bed wishing I could disappear forever. I certainly never wanted to leave my room again.

Later that evening the husband stopped by. Apparently Isadore wouldn't let him in the house so they stood talking at the front door. I sat by an upstairs window listening. Isadore told the husband that he had contacted his lawyer to determine what should be done. The husband begged him to not take it any further. His marriage was shaky and his wife was pregnant again. Isadore told him the lawyer advised that he not press charges because at the trial I would be expected to testify. That ordeal may just "add to my trauma." It was clear from how the husband groveled, pleaded and apologized that he knew exactly what he had done. When it was over, he thanked Isadore and left.

I now knew two things: Isadore believed me. And he stood up for me: He got me out of that house immediately, he called the lawyer and he told the husband not to come to our house again. Suddenly, I could feel a shift. Instead of dealing with strong head winds I now had the wind—well, a gentle breeze—at my back.

The next day I still felt like I wanted to hide and wanted to stay in my room instead of going to school. I just needed a little time to gather my courage to face the world again. But that morning I discovered that I now had a new challenge to deal with. While I was being boarded out, Isadore was busy getting back into the dating game. His newest love came into my room to tell me I needed to get up and get dressed. It was better if I resumed my normal schedule right away. Since I already found the whole situation confusing, I had to consider that maybe she was right. She was an adult and a woman and surely she might know something about such matters. So I reluctantly got up, got dressed and caught the bus for school. I said nothing to my teachers and friends about what had happened.

Isadore's new love was barely an adult. She was just six years older than me. So it wasn't so much that I was looking at a potential mother replacement as a new sister. And that was fine with me. She was friendly, young, perky and, despite her youth, maybe she could help create my new family. She moved into Isadore's room that day and began taking on the role of mistress of the house.

It didn't take long for me to see that there was a problem. This girl didn't want to create a new life that included any of the pieces left over from Isadore's old life. She wanted Isadore all to herself, she wanted to create her own family with him and she wanted his money. I needed to go. She began a campaign to get Isadore to see me as a devious liar and someone set on making the two of them unhappy.

I could regale you with the details but suffice it for me to say that Isadore may have been brilliant when it came to equestrian and business matters but with people and family relationships he was an idiot. When she told him I was saying things I hadn't said and doing things I hadn't done, he believed her without question—no matter what I said in my own defense. I felt like I was back in the house with a sober Dorothy. I had learned how to deal with Dorothy and how to anticipate her craziness. This girl was a mystery. When it came to me, she lied, manipulated, yelled, argued, pouted and demanded that Isadore do something about me. When it came to the two of them as a couple, she was sweet, sexy, lively, coquettish, gave him much pleasure and she made him laugh.

He didn't spot anything in her conduct that would verify what I was telling him about her. (I would not call Isadore a proficient observer when it came to people. Years later when I questioned him about Dorothy's drinking, he said he hadn't ever noticed her drunk.) When I tried to talk to him, he would just accuse me of having a lousy attitude that needed changing.

Dorothy had this weird little passive-aggressive game she played on Isadore each morning at breakfast. She didn't have to cook anything for him because his breakfast consisted of a single chocolate-frosted donut. I used to look at that donut with great desire and envy. It was his morning coffee that was her target. He only drank half of whatever volume of coffee she poured in his cup each morning. If she filled the cup full, he drank half and left the other half. If she poured half a cup, he drank a quarter. No matter what she poured, he only drank half. It was their odd daily breakfast routine.

Well, I started using a variation on this game with Isadore. I could see I had no standing or sway with him, thanks to his girlfriend. He blamed me for everything that was wrong, especially for the trouble I was causing with his girlfriend, and told me I had to change my lousy attitude. I was on to the girlfriend and I knew I wasn't causing the problems. So I decided to see just how far he was going to go with this. Every time he accused me of having a lousy attitude, I would up my game and make sure there wasn't anything even remotely lousy about my attitude. I became a textbook example of a model kid.

The immediate upside was that I could see that the girlfriend had to work much harder to discredit me. Each time Isadore confronted me, I would figure out how to raise my game even higher. The whole situation was crazy and seemed unstoppable.

Finally, when I was about an inch away from sainthood, Isadore upped his game. Along with telling me I had to change my lousy attitude (I swear to you this was the only term he used), he began threatening to take something away from me if I didn't change. Now I wasn't only being admonished for something I hadn't done, I was also being punished for the phantom offense. I was never able to convince him that I was not the one causing the trouble and that I was not doing or saying the things I was being accused of. In the era of my young years, children had little, if any, credibility in the eyes of adults.

Life staggered on. Isadore continued courting his girlfriend while I avoided them as much as possible and finished out my school year. Between my horse, my dog, my studies and my room, I was relatively content. I had my world and I tried not to look at Isadore acting like a teenager who was discovering girls for the first time. Geez.

Isadore's difficulties about me with his girlfriend were escalating. From what he was saying, I could tell he had decided that I was the cause of it all. He told me that if he could get me out of the house long enough for them to get married and to get settled, all would be well. Then I could rejoin them.

Even at my ripe old age of fourteen, I knew his plan was nuts. He never understood how much she didn't want me standing between her and his money. At the time, I didn't know how much money he was making. I just knew we were "very comfortable." However, the girlfriend had been his secretary (ahhh...the plot thickens) and she knew about his plans to purchase the company he was currently working for. This promised to bring in loads of new money. She really needed to get me out of the way.

A week before school ended, Dorothy popped back into the picture. Isadore told me that he had talked to her on the phone and she now wanted me to come live with her. For six months she had not contacted me and I had no idea where she had gone. I was under the impression that Isadore also didn't know where she was. Now he was telling me she was living in Ocean City, Maryland (a resort town where we used to go on vacation) and wanted me to live with her. I was to leave for Ocean City right after school ended.

I didn't believe Dorothy wanted me to live with her. If she did, it was most likely a passing phase. She probably sobered up enough to realize that she had abandoned her daughter and was now feeling guilty about it. But it's also quite possible that Isadore knew where she had been all along and called her to say he needed her to take me off his hands. It is possible that heart-breaking argument I overheard when my parents fought about who was going to be forced to take me after the divorce was still playing out and this was Isadore's way to win. I never found out who initiated that call. I asked Isadore if she sounded drunk when he talked to her and he assured me that she sounded fine.

THE DAY I LEFT UPPERCO was beautiful—a warm, sunny, mid-June day. I was to be driven to Ocean City by one of Dorothy's old drinking friends. While I waited for her to arrive, I walked around the property with Chris. My most vivid memory of that day is the colors: the different greens of the pasture grasses and tree leaves, the clear blue of the sky and the bright white of the few fluffy clouds. It sounds romanticized, doesn't it? But I remember thinking to myself: *What an unusually perfect day.*

Freedom was grazing in the pasture so I headed over to the fence to say goodbye. He came to me and stood there while I rubbed his head and told him what was happening, that I had to leave. I was about to tell him that I would be back when I literally felt a new reality descend and surround me. Suddenly, without any doubt or question, I knew. I looked out across the pasture and said softly, "I'm never coming back here." I leaned against the fence and watched Freedom grazing near me until my ride arrived.

Isadore helped me load my stuff in the car: one suitcase large enough to hold both summer and school clothes and a large box with a framed picture, a photo album, books, the metal box with the quotes I had collected, a small record player, several LP albums including my four favorites (Benny Goodman, Andrés Segovia, Gershwin's *American in Paris,* the soundtrack from *Oklahoma)* and the encyclopedia set that my grandparents had given me. (I left behind 134 pairs of socks, four car coats and ten-dozen pencils.)

He handed me a slip of paper with Dorothy's address written on it and a $20 bill, "Here. In case you need anything for the trip." I thanked him, gave Chris one last pat and that was it.

As we drove down the driveway, the scene I saw beyond the car window was surreal. I had ridden up and down that driveway for years. We passed by the ring where I had schooled horses nearly every day. Now it suddenly all looked and felt as if these places had never been a part of my life. I didn't belong. I was leaving a stranger's house that I had just been visiting for a while.

PIVOT ONE

Chapter 2

Ocean City, Maryland

1960

FOUR HOURS AFTER LEAVING Upperco, we arrived in Ocean City, Maryland, a resort town located on the Atlantic Coast. In 1960, its hotels and motels extended from the southern inlet to about forty blocks north. Beyond that the dunes and beach stretched undeveloped to the Delaware line. Dorothy's apartment was on 36th Street, the northern edge of town.

Dorothy greeted us as we drove up. She looked the same except for her frosty-blue lacquered fingernails. And now she had a boyfriend trailing behind her. She didn't seem drunk so I allowed a little hope to rise, thinking maybe she wasn't drinking as much and maybe she actually had changed her mind about having a daughter. The boyfriend helped me haul my suitcase and box into the bedroom that Dorothy indicated would be mine, and I unpacked my stuff while she caught up on the Upperco gossip. After a couple hours of laughing, drinking and boasting to her boyfriend about her "beautiful, wonderful child" (which embarrassed me to my core), the party broke up. My chauffeur headed back to Upperco, and Dorothy announced that she and the boyfriend had a dinner date. If I got hungry, there was food in the refrigerator that she had picked up for me that day. As the two of them left, she told me she'd be home early and I was not to let any strange men into the apartment. She did not return to the apartment that night. In fact she disappeared again for over three months.

With that, I was fourteen years old, alone and faced with the task of figuring out how to survive.

I had lost nearly everything: my home, my room, my horse, my dog, my friends, my school, my teachers, my life trajectory and the future I had begun to think about, my sense of familiarity about my life and the world that surrounded me, my source of financial support and with this the confidence that I would receive the food, shelter, clothing and medical care I needed to grow into adulthood. I had lost my roots and I no longer knew where I belonged. All of these things had created a sense of stability and a safety net while I was living in Upperco.

Although neither one of my parents would ever come close to winning a "Parent of the Year" award, their mere presence and the position they held gave me hope for what might be possible. Maybe at some point these two people would realize I was worth knowing and caring about. With Pivot One, I also lost my parents and that hope. The only things I had left were the contents of my suitcase and box—plus myself.

And there's the key. The single important thing I had left was me. Upperco had given me the skills and training I needed for surviving and building my new life alone. Of course, at the time I was not aware of what I was bringing to this new situation. I thought I only had two practical skills: ironing handkerchiefs and scrambling eggs.

But I came away from Upperco with much more. I knew how to be alone, how to think for myself and how to problem solve. I knew how to entertain myself, how to make myself smile and how to be pleased with my accomplishments and not look to others to be pleased for me. I knew the effort, patience and determination it took to train, to develop a skill, to aim for a goal and do what was needed to achieve it. I knew how to drive. I knew how to protect the things that were important to me. I knew how to sense and avoid danger. I knew how to make myself invisible. Thanks to Dorothy and Isadore, I knew something about what not to do and how I did not want to live my life. Thanks to Miss Elsie, Freedom and Chris, I knew something about love. And above all I knew how to endure.

It took three days for me to realize that Dorothy wasn't coming back, that I was in a bad situation and I needed to make some moves. I couldn't just sit in that apartment and wait for something to happen. First, I found a payphone and tried to call Isadore to let him know what was going on and to ask for help. This seemed like a logical first step. I called twice but each time his soon-to-be wife intercepted the call, told me he wasn't available and that I was to stop bothering them. The cost of the calls was eating into my $20 so I eliminated calling Isadore as an option. I inventoried the food in the refrigerator and determined I had enough for sandwiches to last about three days—if I ate sparingly. I poured the gallon of milk and the pitcher of Dorothy's special orange juice down the drain.

It sounds as if I was calmly and methodically assessing my situation and figuring out what I needed to do to survive. Like I was going through some mental checklist. First of all, I didn't know what I needed to do to survive. There was no checklist. I was trying to figure that out on the fly. Truth be told, I was seriously scared. Suddenly finding myself alone in a new town where I had no home, family or friends felt dramatically different from the time I spent alone at Upperco. And I felt threatened. I didn't know what awaited me outside that apartment door. I was deeply disappointed and angry that Dorothy had not changed and had now roped me back into her mess. I couldn't understand why she told Isadore she wanted me to live with her only to disappear on the first day of my arrival. Why was she doing any of this?

The strongest motivating force that got me moving was the fear of starvation. I really, *really* did not want to sit in that strange apartment alone and slowly starve to death. With each passing day, my fear seemed less a hypothetical and more a reality. Survival became basic and uncomplicated. I needed money to buy food and I needed a job in order to get the money to buy food. In order to get a job I needed to be sixteen years old and have a work permit signed by a parent. In reality I was just fourteen years old and did not have a parent around to sign a work permit. Luckily I had gone through a growth spurt at Upperco and was now 5 feet 9 inches tall. In my youthful naiveté I thought my height would convince people I was sixteen. Apparently I was under the impression that the older people are the taller they are. But just in case my height wasn't convincing enough, I decided to magically become sixteen. For the benefit of my future employer's job application, I went from being born in 1945 to being born in 1943. I solved the work permit problem by forging Dorothy's signature on a note that I wrote stating that I was giving "my sixteen-year-old daughter, Machaelle Small, permission to work." Finally, relying on my egg-scrambling skills and recognizing I was in a resort town with an abundance of restaurants and coffee shops, I decided my best bet was to seek a waitress job.

The next hurdle terrified me. I had to leave the apartment and start introducing myself to strangers. But even though the world outside was a huge unknown, I still didn't want to starve. So I sucked up the courage, walked out the door armed with a forged work permit and headed off to find a job for which I was the wrong age, had no experience and no real skills. I also wasn't aware that I was seeking a job in Ocean City at the wrong time. Every spring an army of college and high school kids descend on the city to nail down their summer jobs. I was starting my search at the end of June and employment openings would be hard to find.

The apartment was on 36th Street so I started walking south toward the center of town looking for any "Help Wanted" signs. Finally on 23rd Street I spotted a "Waitress Wanted" sign in the window of a tiny coffee shop that was part of The French Quarter Motel. I stuffed my reticence into my back pocket and walked up to the reception desk. I don't think I could have been luckier that day. Their one waitress had called in that morning to tell the manager she found a better job and quit. It was about 10:30 A.M. by the time I walked in and the lunch rush hour was fast approaching. The manager needed me for the job as much as I needed the job, and he seemed willing to ignore my obvious inexperience and confusion while I filled out my first job application. I fabricated any information I felt would stand between me and the job.

But we hit a snag when the manager asked me for my social security number. "My what?" (I had no clue what a social security number was.) That's when he got a little concerned and asked me what was I doing in Ocean City. I could tell I was about to lose this job and I couldn't let that happen. Out of desperation I made up a tall tale that contained flashes of truth: My parents had just divorced, my father was out of work and my mother was not receiving any money from him to help support us. We came to Ocean City a few weeks ago so that my mother could find work. She had a job now but it didn't pay enough. So I needed to work as well. We forgot that I needed a social security number. But I promised faithfully to get a card immediately, if only he would let me have the job. Please. (I wasn't above begging.)

That was a lame, weak tall tale but it was the best I could do on the spot and under pressure. Looking back I'm sure any manager could see right through it. But the lunch rush was coming and he was pressed enough to overlook everything except my deep desire to work in his coffee shop. He accepted my promise to get the card (which took two weeks to arrive once I found out how to get one), paper clipped my forged work permit to my application and gave me the address of a nearby uniform shop. A little after noon I walked into the coffee shop proudly wearing my new pink waitress uniform (which cost me most of what I had left of the $20) and reported for duty—if only I knew what that duty was.

The French Quarter Motel was one of Ocean City's smaller motels. To say that the coffee shop was also small is not an exaggeration. It held six four-seater tables plus a U-shaped counter that seated eight. The grill was behind the counter and was manned by Bob, an ancient-looking short-order cook. This was his last job before retiring after a stellar, lifetime career in the short-order cooking business. As far as I was concerned, the man was a genius. He knew what he was doing and he could flip eggs and pancakes by tossing them in the air and catching them in the pan. (He let me try it once and my pancake landed on the floor.) The minute he saw me he suspected this was my first job. With remarkable kindness he decided to be my mentor. Besides, he needed an able waitress as much as the manager.

One might say that the first lunch rush was trial by fire. Any experienced server worth his or her salt could have handled that rush effortlessly. But I needed lots of help. The customers could see right away that I was nervous. A couple of them asked if it was my first day on the job. I didn't dare tell them it was my first day on *any* job. Once I admitted that I had just started at noon, they did everything they could to make my job easier—and their dining experience successful.

I wanted to do a good job and serve everyone properly. But a good server needs to have a first-rate memory, efficient movement and excellent organizational skills. Well, I had a lousy memory (dyslexia) and didn't know what I was doing. I was dashing around trying my best to get each order to the right customer, but it usually took me about eight trips. Sometimes I missed and a customer would kindly deliver the plate I had just served at their table to the right person sitting at another table. Bob was also helping. He anticipated my needs, caught me in mid-flight, spun me around and headed me in the right direction.

I think my intent and efforts endeared me to Bob and the customers. Also, I suspect what I was doing was nutty enough that I became the coffee shop in-house entertainment. No one could believe what they were witnessing. Whatever the reasons, the atmosphere in the French Quarter coffee shop from day one was both friendly and helpful.

I managed to make $8 in tips that first afternoon. That was enough for dinner (Bob cooked a couple of hamburgers for my dinner) and I still had money left over for the next day. At noon I had less than $1 in my pocket. I ended the day with a meal and about $5 in my pocket. I was coming back from the abyss. When I thought about it, I found it hard to believe that just three days prior to starting my first job I was packing and getting ready to leave Upperco.

I walked the thirteen blocks to and from work six days a week. The coffee shop was open from 9 A.M. to 3 P.M. but my workday started at 8 A.M. and finished at 4 P.M. After a week of some serious training and extraordinary patience on Bob's part, we were becoming a rather okay team—if you ignore the fact that I wasn't the best waitress in the world and Bob was still doing his job plus half of mine. I was learning, but it was going to take more time.

During the third week on the job, my legs from the knees down started aching badly. I assumed it was from working and that there was nothing to worry about once I got used to being on my feet all day. But the pain not only persisted, it got worse. Bob and the manager insisted I see a doctor.

I thought the more logical thing for me to do was call our family doctor in Upperco. I had been his patient for nine years and he had all my records. I placed the call in the motel office but it didn't go well. He didn't want to talk to me. He only wanted to talk to one of my parents (he didn't care which one).

I didn't understand the reasoning behind his stand. From my perspective he was a medical doctor who knew me and my history. Would he just please listen to me and give me some direction that might help? No. And with that, he hung up on me. I was shocked. I was under the impression that as our family doctor my health mattered to him. He had treated all my childhood illnesses. Now that I didn't have parents it seemed he no longer cared.

You know how people talk about society being built for right handers? The default position or setup for anything that requires human hands is for a right hander. Left handers rightfully tend to get annoyed by this. Well, after my conversation with my now former-family doctor I was beginning to get the idea that society, at least American society, had another default position. It gave the advantage to adults over children. Important societal structures were set up for adults to use, not kids. I know options for kids in need have improved, but back then the world operated by and for adults. Children were dragged along for the ride and, if they lived with parents, were provided for and given what they needed. Parents and home buffered kids from an adult world that operated with adult rules and regulations. However, if you were a "throw away" kid and on your own, you were missing the prerequisite adult and had to deal with the adult world unbuffered.

We closed the coffee shop and Bob (my surrogate adult) drove me to a local doctor. I was diagnosed with "growing pains." I was growing too quickly and my joints and bones needed time to catch up. I had measured 5 feet 9 inches for about a year so I didn't understand what he was saying. Why would I have growing pains if I was currently not growing? However, he was the doctor and I accepted his diagnosis with gratitude for the help. He said my problem was temporary, but my waitress job was stressing my joints and causing more pain. I would have to quit and get something less strenuous. He asked where my parents were so that he could send the bill. I gave him my address and told him my mother would be paying it. Of course that was a lie but at least it gave me time to get the money together to pay the bill myself.

When we returned to the coffee shop I assumed I would have to tell the manager that I would need to quit and why. This was a major blow. I was about to lose the security that waitressing gave me and would now need to start over and find a new job. As it turned out, my luck hadn't run out after all. The life guard came in on a break and I told her my news. She said she had wanted the waitress job when it first opened up because she could make more money, but I got it before she could apply.

My mind started clicking. I had taken Red Cross swimming lessons at Upperco and was considered an excellent swimmer. My skills qualified me to take the Lifesaving Course even though I was too young at the time. The French Quarter swimming pool was not large and I felt I could guard it well. By the time the manager returned, the pool had a new guard and the coffee shop had a new waitress with superior skills to my own. As for my new lifeguarding career: I only had to rescue two children who had slipped through their inner tubes. When parents asked if I could give their kids lessons, I didn't hesitate to say yes. I knew those Red Cross lessons by heart and this gave me the opportunity to make extra money.

The remaining two months of summer turned out fine. I was making enough money for meals with a little left over for savings. I liked my job, the pain in my legs gradually lessened and I was getting a great tan. Because I was still working at the same motel, I was surrounded by people I knew and felt safe around.

I tried to call Isadore a couple of times but the calls were still intercepted by now-wife #2. I wrote him a couple of letters asking for help but she intercepted them, as well. She sent back some seriously nasty notes calling me some seriously nasty names and accusing me of some seriously nasty deeds. She always ended by telling me to stop bothering them and to leave them alone. Taking a bus back to Upperco seemed like a bad option and a bad idea. It would most likely be a wasted trip, I'd just end up losing my job, losing the money for the ticket and I'd still be on my own.

I found out that Dorothy was working as a hostess at one of the hotel lounges and living with her boyfriend. I went to her a couple of times, mainly to tell her that the landlord was looking for the rent. But also, I hoped she'd do something or say something that would let me know that she wanted to help me. She did not ask if I was okay or if I needed anything. Instead, she just told me to go back to the landlord and tell him that she would be by in a few days with the money and that she'd see me then, as well—something that never happened, of course.

Neither one of my parents was coming to the rescue and summer was coming to an end. That meant my job would soon be over and school would begin. The landlord informed me that by the end of September, Dorothy and I had to be out of the apartment—and that he was still waiting for the rent. I had been able to stall him with the promise of Dorothy coming with the money, thus warding off an eviction. Now he had lost his patience.

Co-workers told me that there was one high school (Stephen Decatur High School, in Berlin, Maryland) about seven miles away. To get in, Dorothy would have to register me. Rather than try to deal with her, I got one of my co-workers (my surrogate adult) to drive me to school and help me to register. I think the woman behind the desk was stunned that a kid was asking to attend school. Together, the three of us got me registered. If I did not know the answer to a question or if I thought the real answer, particularly about my parents, might cause a problem, I simply made up a more acceptable answer. I took the papers that needed a parent's signature and told the woman I would return the signed papers shortly. The next day I returned the forged papers and I was officially registered.

At the end of the summer, I found another apartment on the lower floor of a converted house on 38th Street. The owner didn't want the building to stand vacant for the winter. I paid a portion of the first rent and told my new landlady that my mother would be coming by with the rest. She didn't buy my story about Dorothy and I could feel the rug starting to slowly pull out from under me.

I really wanted that apartment. It was small, it was only two blocks from the other apartment so I wouldn't have far to haul my stuff and it was cheap. I said everything I could think of to prove to her that I was quiet, neat, reliable, responsible and more than willing to be a winter watchdog for her building. I didn't tell her I was just fourteen. Now she believed I was telling the truth and said I could have the apartment rent-free if I was willing to stay without utilities. At that point, electricity was the least of my worries. So with much gratitude, I accepted her offer and she returned the money I had just given her. I now had my own place right on the beach, facing the ocean and the price was right.

The next hurdle was money for food during the winter. The Stowaway Motel (next to the French Quarter) stayed open year-round. During the summer, I became friends with the daughter of their manager, and she convinced her father that I really needed a job—any job. The day after Labor Day (after the pool closed), I was working at the Stowaway as a switchboard operator. Need I mention that I had no experience and had no clue what to do?

The switchboard was a maze of trunks and lines servicing about two hundred rooms, a lounge, several restaurants and a coffee shop. After a brief training on my first day, I spent the rest of the week trying to keep up with the calls while managing to disconnect and replug everyone into the wrong lines at least once. The motel was totally booked, thanks to a large bankers' convention, and I found myself in the middle of another trial by fire. But my luck was still holding. Most of the time they were drunk and never quite sure of what was happening to them on the phone. Due to the general booze haze hovering over the Stowaway that first week, I didn't get any complaints while I learned my new job.

The day the bankers arrived for their convention was the same day the prostitutes arrived for the bankers. The woman in charge (I guess she was the madam) was at the front desk signing everyone in and chatting with several people on staff who seemed to know her. Apparently she and her ladies were preferred regulars for "special occasions" at the motel.

At one point, I casually glanced over at her while they were talking and could not stop myself from staring. She was wearing a pair of sunglasses with frames the shape of rhinestone-studded butterfly wings that covered three-quarters of her face. As you might imagine, I had never seen anything like that. She spotted me staring, smiled and said a warm and friendly, "Hello."

She and her ladies were actually quite nice to me during that week. They were considerate, kind, polite and friendly. I think they knew how young I was and had decided to take me under their protective wings.

With my new job and apartment, I was set for the winter. I even had enough money saved to buy some supplies: deodorant, toothpaste, shampoo, toilet paper, hand soap, dish soap which doubled as clothes soap (I washed my underwear and blouses in the sink), several boxes of inexpensive candles for the winter nights and several boxes of sanitary napkins. My work shift at the Stowaway started at 4 P.M. and ended at 11 P.M. The manager didn't want me walking home alone in the dark so when my shift ended he would drive me to my apartment.

School started the second week in September that year. Even though I was entering a new school with new staff and students, I looked forward to going. Sure it was a new building and I had no idea where my classrooms, gym, locker rooms and the cafeteria were located but that wouldn't take me long to figure out. Just follow my classmates.

I don't know why I felt so strongly about going to school. It just seemed like the right thing for me to do. I also don't know why I was so determined to do the right thing. Here I was: fourteen years old and on my own with complete freedom. I could do anything. My only limitations and expectations were the ones I set for myself. I certainly didn't have to resume my education if I didn't want to. Like so many kids who find themselves tossed out or abandoned and on the streets, I could have lived rough. But for some reason

I chose to get a job, support myself and go to school. Except for that lying and forging thing, I was an exemplary teenager.

At the time I didn't consider my stories to be lies. I saw them as survival. I was doing what was needed in order to live. As much as I feared starving to death, I also feared being picked up by the authorities and thrown in a reform school or foster care. I had already experienced living with two families and that didn't turn out too well. I didn't want to go through that again. I'd rather take my chances on my own. No matter what, I knew that to remain on my own I couldn't attract the attention or interest of anyone in authority. I needed them to assume I was a normal kid with a parent. It wasn't that difficult to keep this facade up. As long as papers, permissions and report cards were signed on time and returned to the school with a consistent signature, nobody asked questions. Plus, I was an above-average student, I handed my assignments in on time and I did not become a behavior problem. They had no cause to pay attention to me. I was invisible.

But going to school was important to me in other ways. My post-Upperco summer and its challenges had mentally and emotionally exhausted me, and I knew from previous experience that school could provide a sanctuary from the stress. Since coming to Ocean City, I was constantly having to figure out what to do and then how to do it.

It wasn't just a matter of doing the "right thing." I had to first find out what the right thing was for each new situation and just about every situation I faced was new. What were the rules of this adult game I was now in? I had to make decisions. What would I do and what would I not do? Although I found it necessary to lie at times and forge Dorothy's signature, there were certain things I chose to *not* do. I did not steal and I did not cheat. If I agreed to do something I did not go back on my word. Thanks to Dorothy, I was not tempted to take up drinking and smoking, nor did I sell sex for a quick buck. (Dorothy did not smoke but she always smelled like stale bar cigarettes. I don't think she provided sex for money. She had a loose reputation and that was enough to make me not want to go in that direction.) I was determined to not become my mother.

Stephen Decatur High School gave me the structure, direction and relief I had hoped for. For seven hours a day all I had to do was respond to its pre-set schedule and expectations. After school, I went directly to my job, did my homework between phone calls, went straight home after work and to bed. I did not have to figure anything out. I have to laugh when I hear kids announce, usually defiantly, how they can't wait to get out on their own and have their freedom. They have no idea how much effort it takes to figure out life, especially if they are unsupported and dropped into the middle of it too soon.

Three weeks after school started, Ocean City was slammed by a major nor'easter—three days of heavy rains and hurricane-force winds. The town was evacuated and many of the buildings were destroyed or heavily damaged. I worked with a couple of friends around the clock, helping to rescue stranded people.

At one point we were told to go to one of the rooms at the Stowaway and help a couple who had decided they wanted to watch the storm and now were in desperate need of rescuing. Their situation was serious. The ocean-facing wall in the room was glass and was now ready to crash in on these two. About six of us had to hold the wall up against the strong winds while they got out.

When I was finally able to return to my apartment, I found that the ocean had been through at least once, and my possessions were strewn over the surrounding beach. The record player, which I had stored high in a closet, was untouched. I lost my encyclopedias, the majority of my clothes, plus the toilet paper and boxes of sanitary napkins I had stocked in for the winter. I found my four favorite record albums, the framed picture and my metal box still holding all the collected quotes. The apartment building was wet and sandy but structurally undamaged. My landlady arranged to have it cleaned right away. She also decided to leave the electricity on for a little while to help dry out the structure, giving me access to electricity and heat for a month.

The Stowaway was not so lucky. It sustained major damage that included losing its roof and had to close for the winter while being rebuilt. I was now without a job. The school which was seven miles inland from the coast was undamaged and we were able to return to class two days after the storm.

A week later I was unable to get out of bed. Once again, my legs were in terrible pain. I assumed it was a delayed reaction from the storm. Holding up glass walls in a hurricane is strenuous. The next day the pain got much worse, my knees were swollen and I got scared. One of my friends who noticed I was absent from school stopped by to see if I needed anything, saw the difficulty I had walking and took me straight to the hospital.

I stayed for three days in the ward while they ran tests—they suspected polio. I hated being there and was impatient to leave so I could continue putting my life back together. There was some concern among the staff about how I was going to pay the bill. Neither parent could be found or reached (wife #2 intercepted the call the hospital made to Isadore and hung up on them). Luckily for me, the doctors felt that they couldn't toss me out until they found what was wrong.

As it turned out, I had rheumatoid arthritis. I could go home with medicine (which they gave me), rest, and within a week or so, the pain would lessen and I could resume my normal activities. I hobbled back to school the day after I got out of the hospital.

My legs did get better as promised, but I soon found that living near the ocean, especially in the winter, was not the best environment for someone with arthritis. After the pills ran out, I wasn't able to refill the prescription and the pain returned, but not as bad as before. I was still able to move around—stiffly. As long as I could get from point A to point B, I felt I was still in the game.

The rest of the winter—which was only getting started—was one survival test after another. Because of the storm damage, there would be no new jobs available in Ocean City until spring. I would have to make my savings of around $200 last over the next six or seven months.

This meant rationing my meals. I calculated that if I ate one meal every three days, I would be able to keep that rhythm up until spring. Otherwise, I'd run out of money ahead of time and not be able to eat at all. I won't pretend it was easy. In fact it was scary—

the winter, the darkness, the cold, the aloneness and now the food rationing. Sometimes I got so hungry I just cried. Once it got so bad, I had to knock on a neighbor's door and beg for food. She gave me a can of chopped kale. (I've had a soft spot in my heart for kale ever since.) A classmate who was fortunate enough to have one of the few remaining coffee shop jobs periodically stopped by with a cooked hamburger. And every once in a while, I got invited to a friend's house for dinner. Other than this, I maintained my eating rhythm by buying a hot lunch at school every third day.

In November, the electricity was turned off and I had to spend the rest of the winter in the cold while doing my homework by candlelight. I now had no heat, lights, refrigerator, stove or hot water. I felt lucky to have running water even though it was ice cold. I could wash clothes in the sink, flush the toilet and I learned to take the world's quickest shower.

A couple of times that winter, Dorothy appeared unannounced on my doorstep. I hated seeing her. My existence still irritated her so she would sweep in, express her anger by wrecking the place and then leave for another three months. I had no idea why she bothered coming. She never said anything. Once she showed up while I still had electricity. I had set up my record player and was listening to the Andrés Segovia classical guitar album. It was my favorite and I found the music soothing.

As Dorothy left she went over to the player, picked up the arm and scratched the needle across the record. I was shocked. What the hell did she do that for? It was so deliberate and cruel. I yelled for her to get out and spent the rest of the evening trying to make the scratch magically disappear by rubbing it with a soft cloth. Of course, that didn't work. I played the record with the scratch for years before I was able to replace it.

I confided in a couple of my friends what was happening to me, and they tried to figure out ways to help. A couple of them told their parents about me, and I remember hoping that somebody would invite me into their home to be a part of their family. This was when I learned that I was no longer Isadore Small's daughter. Now I was Dorothy Small's daughter. Dorothy had become notorious and was known by all the regulars around town. Once the summer season ended, Ocean City's population went from a quarter of a million people down to about 150. Out of this 150, two groups formed. One was the fun-loving, bar-dwelling, hell-raisers who appreciated and welcomed Dorothy's charm. The other was the family oriented group. My friends' families were part of the latter group. But they knew about Dorothy and felt that getting involved with one of her problems—me—was bound to be messy. They would invite me for an occasional meal but that was as far as it went.

At the same time, Dorothy was telling her friends that I was her daughter. This wasn't at all helpful because I was now becoming known among the hell-raisers. Sometimes her male friends would assume "like mother, like daughter" and come around to try their best to "hit on me." Annoying and scary as this was for me, it didn't take much effort to convince them that they'd have to go back to Dorothy. Because I was living in an apartment and going to school, her friends assumed she was fulfilling her role as a parent, which included supporting me.

The bottom line is that Dorothy was not inclined to correct their assumptions or offer me any help, financial or otherwise. Twenty years later I found out that while I was in Ocean City, Isadore sent Dorothy monthly checks for $100 to cover my expenses. I never saw those checks and I know she never gave me any money or used the money for rent. You could say I was supporting her. I've wondered if this was why she agreed to take me in the first place. She walked away from the marriage with no settlement or alimony. Was she using me to gain some financial support for herself?

My tenth-grade experience at Stephen Decatur was blissfully dull except for a couple of classes I really liked. Miss Moore, my English teacher, was everyone's favorite, mine included. About mid-year she announced an assignment that I thought was completely nuts. We were to write a lengthy paper on how we saw our lives fifteen years down the road. What were the goals we wished to achieve by then? Where were we living? Were we married? Did we have children? Did we go to college? What was our profession? Our politics? Our religion? I thought the woman was mad. We were young. How in the world could we write about those kinds of life issues and goals now? We were given three weeks to map out the blueprint for our future.

Here's why I had a problem with the assignment: I couldn't see or imagine a future for myself. It was a blank. When I looked ahead in my mind's eye, all I saw was impenetrable darkness. I lost my future when I left Upperco. I lost the sense of my life's trajectory. I was now mainly concerned with getting through the day and looking forward to my next meal. Based on everything I had experienced and witnessed since coming to Ocean City in June, I couldn't begin to imagine what more was going to happen in the next fifteen years and where it was going to lead me.

On the day the assignment was due, my classmates handed in papers that looked to be thirty to forty pages long. They clearly knew where they were headed. I handed in one sheet of paper with my handwritten assignment filling the front side and half of the back side. I didn't and couldn't answer any of her questions. (I still thought her assignment was nuts.) Instead I described how I wanted my mind to be like a mound of sculptor's clay that was molded and shaped by my life's experiences as I went along. I ended with the hope that my mind—my clay mound—would never be glazed and would remain forever soft and workable so that it could continue to be shaped by my experiences throughout the whole of my life.

I assumed I would flunk the assignment, and when she handed the papers back I braced for the F. I got an A+. An honest-to-god, big red A+. I couldn't believe it. Then she asked me if she could read my paper to the class. I can't explain how much this moment in the sun meant to me and what a strong boost of encouragement it gave right at a time when I needed it the most. Miss Moore remained my favorite teacher.

As the end of the school year approached, I started looking around for my next summer job. A place called Frontier Town opened that spring not far from the high school. It was a replica of an old frontier fort, and all employees had to dress up as cowboys, cowgirls or Indians. The "Indians" turned out to be Native American families who traveled around the country for these kinds of summer jobs. I was hired as the cowgirl in charge of the Penny

Candy Store. (It was called "Penny Candy Store." The name was written on a big sign that hung above the door. I can't tell you how many people came in each day and seriously asked, "How much is the candy?") Several weeks after I started, I changed jobs and became the teller in the town bank.

Most of the boys and men who worked there lived in the bunkhouses. There was a separate house for the marshal/manager, his wife (the rodeo trick rider) and young son. The wife invited me to sleep on their sofa when they found out that I was losing my apartment in Ocean City and had no place to go. So for the summer, I was tucked away and safe.

Working at Frontier Town was fun but also disorienting. I had just come through a year of dealing with Dorothy and friends, Isadore and wife #2, new apartments, food (or lack thereof), money (or lack thereof), hospitals, school, cold, darkness and storms. Now I was living in a Wild West fort, working in a fake bank, getting robbed every hour on the half hour, hustling bandits out the back window so they could escape the law and getting accidentally shot in gun fights. In the quiet times, I weighed little vials of ground-up brass nails that the kids had collected from the panning stream and handed them wooden nickels in exchange. All this make-believe stuff became my new reality. It gave me new friends, a sofa to sleep on, food and a wage. (We were paid every two weeks with silver dollars given to us in draw-string pouches. The local grocery store loved seeing the Frontier Town workers come in with all those silver dollars.)

As the pressure around survival lifted, the strains of the past year surfaced. I was nervous and unsure of myself with my new family and friends. I felt as if people considered me an odd duck and I'm sure, in some ways, I was. I was constantly afraid the people who were helping me would get tired and toss me out. So I would either not respond to them out of fear of making the wrong move, or try to do something I thought would please them and end up feeling I had only managed to get in their way. Then there were times when I had difficulty simply pulling myself together and would forget to comb my hair or put on a clean shirt or iron my cowgirl skirt and vest. I could be a rumpled mess.

When I told my new family that I knew how to ride, they suggested I ride one of the horses in the mornings before work. There was even an old English saddle in the tack room that I could use. Well, the horse they gave me to ride wasn't Freedom and was in need of a bit of training but that was fine with me. I was just glad to be back on a horse again. I rode about four times a week and I felt the horse was responding well to the consistent workout. We were beginning to know one another.

One morning I was jumping him and, while we were in mid-air, I leaned down to the left to see if he was staying tucked as we went over the jump. I saw something swinging and realized it was the girth. You know, the belly strap that holds the saddle on. Now I was in mid-air with a completely free saddle that had begun to slip in the direction I was leaning. I pushed down on the stirrup on the opposite side to bring the saddle back up to center but I overcompensated and now the saddle was slipping the other way.

The horse landed and took a stride which made the saddle slip even more, so I decided to bail out. I landed on my feet facing him just in front of his right shoulder. At that point, I was fine and all was well. If only the scene could have stopped there. As the horse cantered by me, his right shoulder hit my right hip and spun me around. Unfortunately my left leg was firmly planted on the ground and when I spun, my left upper leg torqued in the direction of the spin and the lower leg remained planted. I dropped to the ground in sharp pain. I had torn my knee badly and could not flex it or straighten out my left leg or put any weight on it.

I was taken to the hospital (again) and told that because of my arthritis, surgery to repair my knee had been ruled out. I would need to wear three ace bandages on my knee until my leg straightened out. And I was to see a doctor weekly to have my knee drained and receive ultrasound treatments for six to eight weeks. I could continue working but I would not be able to put any weight on my left leg.

I went back to work that day. For the rest of the summer I hopped—and I endured the pain. I hopped down from the manager's house to the bank. I hopped to lunch and I hopped back to the manager's house at the end of the day. (How long did it take you to assume everyone called me "Hopalong" that summer?) The owners paid all my medical bills so I was able to receive my weekly treatments. Even though the doctor saw me hopping, he never suggested I use a cane or crutches, and I did not consider the aid because I was young, dopey and it didn't cross my mind. So I continued hopping. My right leg became quite strong. By the end of summer my left leg straightened out and I began to walk again—gingerly.

I found out that the girth broke because the leather had dry rotted. When I cleaned the saddle, I didn't notice the dry rot because I didn't know what dry-rotted leather looked like.

I didn't see Dorothy all summer. A couple of times, I tried to get in touch with Isadore to let him know what was happening and again was put off by wife #2. Once she called me at work just to tell me she and Isadore were getting a divorce (which wasn't true) and that it was all my fault. I had had enough of this woman, stopped her tirade in mid-sentence and told her something comparable to "shove it!" I slammed the phone down and hopped back to my fake bank—feeling satisfied.

My job at Frontier Town would end on Labor Day, and now I needed to find another place to stay for the winter. My pay for working from 10 A.M. to 10 P.M., six days a week, was $49 (after taxes). After expenses, I was only able to save about 150 silver dollars for the winter. I found a room in Ocean City at the Spanish Main Motel on 14th Street. The place was owned by a friend of Dorothy's who assumed he would get the rent from her. I didn't tell him differently.

Living at Frontier Town had left me out of touch with what jobs would be available for the winter, so I moved into the room and got ready for school believing that I could find something for the winter after school started.

You're not going to believe this. During the first week of school, a monster hurricane ripped through Ocean City. Most of the city was evacuated—again. My motel was on bay side and had a reputation for being hurricane-proof, so I stayed.

I watched the first half of the storm from my window and then took a walk around the area during the eye of the storm. I had never experienced a hurricane eye before. The sun came out, there was no wind, the air was fresh and dry, there was a calm but eerie quiet.... The damage around me was all there was to indicate that we were in the midst of a disaster.

As the winds began to pick up again, I returned to my room for the second half. In the bay just outside my window, I watched a fifty-foot yacht sink. When it was over, the motel had suffered no damage, fully living up to its reputation. But the rest of the city was a mess, and any chance I might have had for getting a winter job got washed away with the storm.

I was living in a motel room with a kitchenette, heat, lights, hot water and even a television that received just one channel. A big step up from the previous winter. But I wasn't going to be able to earn any money and the prospect of spending another winter eating once every three days depressed me. The first year, I didn't know what to expect from such a regulated meal rhythm. Now I knew full well what that felt like. Also, my new landlord's wife discovered that her husband was having an affair with Dorothy and was pressuring him to toss me out of the motel. Without money coming in, all I'd be able to find would be another unheated, unlit place—if I was lucky. The hurricane had done a great deal of damage to most of the buildings. I didn't know how I was going to do it, but I had to solve this problem fast.

Then I remembered: One of my employers at Frontier Town told me that his daughter went to a Catholic girls' boarding school in Pennsylvania. I knew nothing about boarding schools or Catholic schools, but somehow I knew that if I could get into this place, I'd have the solution to my problem and I'd be safe.

I called the man to get the name and address of the school, and he offered to call them for me and set up an appointment with Admissions. He called back that day to tell me the nuns would see me and my mother the following week. (What he did not tell me was that admissions to the school had been closed for the year, and he had to push hard to get them to see me.)

It took several days to track down Dorothy and several more days to persuade her to come with me to McSherrystown, Pennsylvania. On the day of our trip, she showed up drunk, leaving me no alternative but to drive. We set out for Pennsylvania, the kid behind the wheel and the mother trying her bleary best to read the road map.

Just as we pulled into the Academy driveway, Dorothy passed out. By this time, nothing was going to get in the way of my having that interview. I pushed her over onto the seat and parked the car so that no one could see her. Then I went in for my appointment.

The nuns were expecting Dorothy to be with me so I quickly made up one of my cockamamie stories—something about my mother becoming ill on the trip and walking to a drug store in the village to get some aspirin. She would be joining us as soon as she could. But she hoped they wouldn't mind getting started without her so that their time wouldn't be wasted. (I found out later that in their phone conversation my ex-employer had also warned the nuns about Dorothy and they suspected what was really going on.) I gave them the copy of my transcript that I had gotten from Stephen Decatur and, without missing a beat, we went right into the interview.

Saint Joseph Academy sounded like everything I could ever possibly want. At least, it was everything I needed at that moment. A warm bed, hot shower, three meals a day and an education. I was totally smitten by the kindness of these nuns. I had read *The Nun's Story*, so I knew nuns were good, kind, loving, gentle...your basic, all-around, perfect women dedicated to God. And at the moment these women were proving it. When asked who would be paying my tuition, which was $2500 yearly, I told them my father would. I had no idea how I would get him to pay that tuition, but this was something I could deal with later.

I was taken on a tour of the school, introduced to some of my future classmates, measured for uniforms (my first new clothes since leaving Upperco) and told to report back in two weeks. It wasn't until I felt secure about being admitted that I told the nuns I wasn't Catholic. (I didn't dare tell them my father was Jewish.) To my relief, they told me it didn't matter, that about twenty-five percent of the girls were non-Catholic. I would not have to take any religion classes, but I would be expected to join the girls for Mass on Sundays.

I left McSherrystown feeling relieved and happy about the turn of events. I was also amazed at my success. I wasn't sure I could make this happen but I knew that if I failed I would be back in Ocean City and just surviving again. I had to give it my best shot. Dorothy "came to" during the trip back to Maryland. Even though I was furious at her and didn't talk to her for the rest of the trip, I did not let her spoil my moment.

For the next two weeks, I continued going to classes at Stephen Decatur, talked to my friends about the Academy and managed to keep from being thrown out of the motel by promising faithfully that I would be leaving permanently in two weeks anyway. I didn't have to worry about packing my things until the last minute. Since arriving in Ocean City, my possessions had dwindled dramatically. Everything but my record player now fit into my suitcase with room to spare.

Dorothy promised she would drive me to Pennsylvania, and, lo and behold, she showed up more sober than I had seen her in a long time. Together, we left for Saint Joseph Academy. My mind-clay was about to receive a lot more sculpting.

Chapter 3

McSherrystown, Pennsylvania
1961–1962

SAINT JOSEPH ACADEMY was founded in 1854 by the Sisters of Saint Joseph who were, in turn, founded in Le Puy-en-Valay, France in 1650. It started out as an orphanage but by my arrival in 1961, it had long since functioned as a school. At the time it consisted of two brick buildings. The smaller building included the dormitory and classrooms for grades one through eight. The larger one included the chapel, student dining room and separate dormitories for each of the high school grades—plus three small private rooms and a double room for the exclusive use of senior class members. The convent wing was off the large dining room and included the Academy kitchen, the nuns' dining room and their private sleeping quarters. That area was off-limits for the students.

The Sisters also founded a women's college, Chestnut Hill College, in Philadelphia in 1924. This was their major source of pride and it was where the younger nuns at the Academy hoped to teach someday. The older nuns had already put in their time at the college and were assigned to the Academy so that they could ease into retirement. The place had a way station feel to it.

When I arrived in early November, there were about eighty girls from grades one through twelve boarding at the school. The junior class, the largest in the Academy's history, consisted of sixteen students. Four were day students who lived in McSherrystown and could go home each night, much to our never-ending envy. Two of the day students and I were the non-Catholics in the group. (Here's a useless bit of information that I found intriguing: Out of my class of sixteen, four of the girls were named "Diane." I've always thought it an unusually high ratio of Dianes.) Because the junior dorm was filled to capacity, I was given one of the two remaining private rooms. The nuns told me that my good fortune was because I was non-Catholic, and they didn't want me to be disturbed on weekday mornings when the girls in the dormitory got up early to go to Mass.

My room was tiny, with a high ceiling and institutional-pink walls. It contained a single bed, a vanity with a lamp, one chair and a closet. It also had electricity and heat, but thanks to the century-old window, I never had to worry about the room overheating. On cold, windy nights, I remembered what I had left behind in Ocean City. On snowy nights, I could lie in bed and watch snow flakes blow through the cracks in the closed window and collect on the sill in little drifts. Compared to the previous winter, however, this room was heaven.

The prefect of the junior class (the nun in charge) was Sister Mary Agnes—or SMA, as everyone called her. She was in her 30s, friendly and properly rotund. The girls in my class really liked her, which said a lot. Because she was our prefect, she lived in a tiny room (cell) just outside the junior dormitory and up the hall from me. Her presence was calculated to keep us young ladies in line.

SMA took an interest in me and would come into my room at night to talk. I was the new girl and I felt she wanted to help me adjust to Academy life. But mostly, she encouraged me to talk. I soon trusted her, and not long after arriving at the Academy, I told her about the trouble I was having with my parents. She asked my permission to relate it to Mother Superior and assured me that they would help me with the situation. I had nothing to worry about any longer, she said—all I had to do was concentrate on my studies. I did not know how she could help with Dorothy and Isadore but I was grateful she wanted to try. She was the first person who actually listened to me and, as an adult, she might have a different take on the situation that I wasn't seeing. I dropped the problem in her ample lap and focused on learning the routine of the school.

I was required to go to Sunday Mass and from the first Sunday I attended, I became enchanted by the mystery and movement of that ritual. Bells rang. Everyone stood, knelt and genuflected in a synchronized choreography. The priest went through his dance in front of the altar while saying Latin prayers. Nuns and students responded in Latin. (This was pre-Second Vatican Council when new rules came down from Rome making the Mass more user friendly.) Colorful vestments, lighted candles, linen, gold, crystal—the makings of a magical mystery tour. As far as I was concerned, it was an elaborate ritual all wrapped up in code. I left that first Mass determined that I was going to learn the code in order to breeze through this thing as casually as everyone else in the chapel. It was obvious I'd need to go to more Masses. I also needed a Missal, a prayer book, which SMA was kind enough to give me.

However, the overriding motivation that got me out of bed at 4:50 A.M. for Mass had nothing to do with my well-intentioned desire to learn. It was Sister Edward Eileen and her damned cowbell. Eddie, as everyone called her behind her back, was one of the younger nuns—I'd guess she was in her early 30s. She taught math and science and was the prefect for the freshman class. She also had a sadistic streak and a general dislike for the students, except for her freshman girls whom she protected. She was given the job of waking the high school girls each morning after daily Mass, a job that gave her an opportunity to practice her sadism. She would come around to each of the dorms and private rooms, clang a rather large cowbell and yell "Benedicamus Domino," to which the girls would reply "Deo Gratias" (or various mumbled, unchristian-like utterances) and kneel by their beds, waiting for Eddie to start the morning prayers. If one of the girls was slow about getting out of bed, Eddie would stand over her and continuously clang that cowbell until the girl was kneeling properly on the ice-cold linoleum floor and ready to pray.

I have a lifelong habit of waking up easily in the mornings to even the most subtle sounds. Isadore used to let me know when it was time to get up by tapping a cigarette on his dresser. My room at Upperco was at the opposite end of the house but I never missed hearing that tapping sound. I considered Eddie and her cowbell an affront to humanity. (At the very least, I'm sure it's considered torture and against the Geneva Convention today.) I needed to do something about this situation or I would be driven mad. The only way I could stop Eddie from entering my room was to get up at 4:50 A.M. for Mass, thus showing her that I was already up, dressed and I had prayed (even though it was in Latin and I had no idea what I was saying). I began going to daily Mass not because I was suddenly moved by religion or driven to crack the ritual code. It was for survival—mine and Eddie's.

Daily Mass was quite different from Sunday Mass. First of all, I arrived at the chapel the first morning to find that I was the only student attending. It must have been an act of hope on the part of the nuns when they told me I could have a private room so that I wouldn't be disturbed by all the other girls getting up for daily Mass. Secondly, there were about fifty-five nuns living in the convent, and on Sundays they sat side by side in the back pews. The students sat in the front pews. On weekdays, the nuns sat in a pattern, spreading themselves throughout the entire chapel. It was a pattern that never changed, with the same nuns sitting in the same spots. When I showed up, one of the nuns indicated where I was to sit, and I became part of the pattern. Also, what took the priest forty minutes to say on Sundays only took him seventeen minutes to say on weekdays. I was now faced with Mass on fast-forward and my state of confusion on Sundays was magnified tenfold on weekdays. But I stuck with it and in about six weeks, I was able to fly through both a regular speed and fast-forward Mass flawlessly. I still didn't understand what was being said by the priest or what was being said in response, and I didn't know what all the choreography meant, but I looked like I knew what I was doing. Image really is everything. Most importantly, I was successfully avoiding Eddie Eileen.

NOT LONG AFTER MY ARRIVAL, SMA told me that Isadore was coming to the Academy to visit me. She apparently was dealing with my situation, as promised. But with this news about Isadore, I suddenly felt less safe. I wasn't sure if SMA really understood what I might be walking into. But I had accepted her help, I even gave permission for her to help, and now I felt I needed to move forward with her help—even though I didn't understand what she was doing. I trusted that she understood what she was doing.

Isadore arrived on a Friday evening with wife #2. A nun escorted them into the private guest living room and then sent SMA to get me. On the way, she kept telling me that everything was okay and that my troubles were finally over. Based on my experience, I was skeptical.

At first, just Isadore and I spoke. It felt more like a business meeting between strangers and he looked uncomfortable in this convent setting. He asked how I liked the school. I said fine. He asked if the nuns were okay. I said yes. Were the classes okay? Yes. There were a few more minutes of the same type of questions and answers. Then there was silence. He broke the silence by saying that eventually, when things got settled, he wanted me to live with him and for us to be a family.

Cue wife #2. She began screaming, literally screaming, that I would be allowed in *her* home over *her* dead body. I was a conniving, spoiled brat who wanted to break up their marriage and I was the real cause of the problems in the marriage. Her face got red as she ranted on and spit out her words. I didn't know what to do except sit there, look at her and absorb the assault. Isadore tried to calm her down, but she pushed his efforts aside, saying that he let me rule him. She got up, announced that she would meet him in the car and stormed out of the living room, slamming the door.

Isadore, noticeably confused, muttered something about coming back soon to finish our discussion. Then he left. No "Goodbye." No "Do you need anything?" He just left. I sat there trying to figure out what just happened. I felt like I had been in a boxing ring and had been pummeled around the head and chest by a fast barrage of well-aimed verbal punches.

SMA had been sitting in the office across the hall, eavesdropping, which I was grateful for. At last, someone else heard what these two people were saying to me and how they were saying it. She told me to go to my room, that I was not to worry. She and Mother Superior would deal with my father. For the next few days

I still felt rattled by the attack but I put my effort into just focusing on the rhythms of this new school and my classes.

A couple of weeks later, Isadore and wife #2 came again. SMA walked with me to the living room and, like a good boxing trainer giving her fighter encouragement between rounds, she was telling me all would be well. I entered the room ready for the next round. Right away, we went through the same routine as before. First, the stiff calm as he asked the very same questions about the school, the nuns and my classes. But as soon as he got around to my living with them, wife #2 started screaming again. This time I tried to stop her by telling Isadore the trouble I had been having with her—the phone calls I tried to get through to him, the letters I sent him but were returned by her, and the comments she made about Isadore not wanting me around. That was a mistake. What I said may have been true and saying it may have been the right thing to do but, in fact, it was a big mistake. Right away Isadore turned on me and fired his "Isadore Small dumb-shit look" at me. He said he would hear no criticism about his wife—especially from "a child." He shouted that if I didn't change my lousy attitude, if I didn't straighten up and start living a proper life, I would get nothing from him.

While this was going on, I experienced two different realities simultaneously. One was a calm running commentary going on in my head that was reporting on the situation unwinding in front of me and pointing out the absurdity of what Isadore was yelling. I even started to contemplate what Isadore meant by "proper." I didn't see much that was proper about his life so I wasn't sure what he was referring to. The other reality was me sitting there in the room absorbing yet another verbal pounding. My head was telling me that this was an experience, albeit a difficult experience—that I only had to wait out. But that inner encouragement didn't take away the fact that I was sitting through another rough verbal beating. Isadore wouldn't stop yelling. I braced myself because I felt sure he was going to hit me. Instead, he abruptly stood up and told me not to bother calling him until I decided to change my lousy attitude. (Always, it was my lousy attitude.)

They left together this time. SMA came into the room pretty quickly and told me to go to my room and not worry about anything. She and Mother Superior would handle my father.

I didn't understand why I was going through this exercise with Isadore and wife #2. I actually didn't want these two people as my family. I didn't trust either one of them, especially wife #2. Before I left Upperco I had come to the conclusion that she was crazy and it was safer for me to steer clear of her. I admit it would have been nice if Isadore had given me some financial support to make my life a little easier but other than this, I didn't want anything from him or his wife. I felt that it would come with too high a price. And then there was Isadore's constant "lousy attitude" accusation. I had no idea what he was talking about. Once I left Upperco I had no direct interaction with him. What did I do that added up in his head to "lousy attitude"?

I also couldn't understand what SMA was doing. What did "take care of the situation" mean to SMA and Mother Superior? These meetings were not something I would have wanted for myself. They were exercises in gratuitous torture. Getting tossed in a boxing ring with Isadore and wife #2 felt like punishment I did not deserve. But still I held out. Maybe SMA and Mother Superior knew something I didn't know.

The Christmas vacation was fast approaching and I needed a place to stay. The nuns would not let me go to Ocean City unless they knew for sure that Dorothy wanted me to be with her for the holidays. She had not contacted me since my arrival, and the nuns were having no luck in finding her. I tried to persuade SMA to just let me stay at the Academy over the break. Except for this one lone girl eating meals in the student dining room, I promised they wouldn't even know I was there. Knowing how to make myself invisible, I was sure I could deliver on that promise. As it turned out, the nuns were planning a big retreat for the holidays and a bunch of Sisters of Saint Joseph would be traveling to the Academy. Invisible or not, I was definitely going to be in their way. So SMA decided to try Isadore again.

My third round in the boxing ring was almost an exact replay of the first and second meetings. The stiff calm…then the screaming, the accusations, the threatening looks and a reminder about my lousy attitude. Finally Isadore and wife #2 stormed out, slamming doors on their way.

I sat there dazed for about ten minutes and just stared into space. If SMA and Mother Superior were "taking care of things," how could this still be happening? SMA didn't come in the room this time, so knowing the routine I headed up the stairs to my room. I was walking through the corridor outside the junior class dormitory when a classmate passed me and cheerfully asked how the visit with my father had gone.

I don't know what happened at that point. I think it's fair to say I snapped and started screaming, although I have no memory of this. When I regained awareness, I was lying on a bed in the dormitory. One of my classmates was sitting on top of me, slapping me in the face. I could tell from seeing the power in her arm that she was hitting me hard, but I couldn't feel anything. I could hear myself screaming but I couldn't feel myself scream. The girl who had asked me the original, innocent question was standing next to me trying to pin my arms down. Normally, she had a lovely South American complexion. I remember looking up at her from the bed and seeing her face drained and pale white. I was struck by how strange she looked with a pale complexion. I saw SMA rush into the room. She slapped me in the face and shook me hard by the shoulders. I stopped screaming. She told the girls to stay with me, that she'd be right back, and rushed out of the dormitory. She told me later that she had gone outside to try to stop my father before he left. (She didn't realize he had long since gone.) I think that if she had gotten hold of him that night, she would have beaten him to a bloody pulp—Bride of Christ or not.

By the time she came back, I was quietly sitting on the bed with the others attentively staring at me, ready to jump into action if I should "go crazy" again. I felt shattered. SMA told me to take my shower and get ready for bed. Then she brought me a cup of tea and told me, once again, not to worry about anything. I got the feeling from what she was saying that the phone calls with Isadore gave SMA and/or Mother Superior the impression that Isadore cared about my well being. Clearly SMA couldn't understand why he changed his attitude once he saw me. I could tell she was underestimating wife #2's role in this mess.

The next day, I attended Mass and classes as usual. Again I was numb and quiet, and grateful just to drift through the well-defined routine at the Academy.

After lunch SMA told me that she had talked to one of the parish priests about my situation and that he offered to talk to me. She suggested that I think about it. She did not want to push me, but she honestly felt I needed more help and this man could possibly give it to me. If, after seeing him one time, I wanted to see him again, she would arrange for me to have permission to leave the school grounds as often as was necessary. I didn't have to think about it. I was in an emotional pressure cooker and I knew I needed help.

That afternoon, I walked the three blocks to the Annunciation of the Blessed Virgin Mary rectory and met Father Lahout. We spent three hours together. Mostly, I talked and he listened. By the time the three hours were over, he had even managed to make me laugh. For the rest of the school year, we met an average of three times a week.

The subject of religion was not a major issue between us. He wasn't the type to notch his belt with the conquest of another convert. In fact, he rather enjoyed my Jewish background. But religion aside, he didn't hesitate to share with me his personal code of moral beliefs. And he felt particularly strong about the commandment to "Honor thy father and thy mother." He believed that my parents were as crazy as could be—but despite that, they were still my parents and I had to deal with them. I could not simply walk away from them. I, on the other hand, didn't understand why I couldn't just walk away from them. Hadn't these two people forfeited their parent-status rights? Surely in this big world I could find two better qualified surrogate parents to honor. But Father Lahout was telling me I needed to work with Dorothy and Isadore.

As I had no idea where Dorothy was, Isadore became the only parent we worked on. Father Lahout encouraged me to write letters to Isadore, explaining how I felt about being on my own so much, how I hoped we could become a family and that I loved him. (Truth was, I didn't think I loved him and I didn't hope we could become a family. But possibly, if I said it enough, maybe my thoughts and feelings could change. I had my doubts.) I wrote lengthy letters telling him how I felt about what was going on, then gave the letters to Father Lahout to check before mailing, just to make sure I didn't write anything unintentionally stupid that might cause an argument.

The letters were either returned unopened or opened and mailed back in another envelope with a letter from wife #2 telling me that my father didn't wish to speak to me. One letter did reach Isadore. I got a note from him saying he didn't know who was coaching me to write these things, but he was not impressed and I still had to change my lousy attitude.

The responses even got the good natured, kind-hearted Father Lahout angry. Wife #2 was beyond his comprehension and was reduced to an irrational obstacle to be worked around. I didn't have to honor her. But he felt I couldn't turn my back on Isadore. I still had to try.

I HAD SPENT THE CHRISTMAS vacation with one of my classmates and was preparing to do something similar at Easter when I got word from SMA that Isadore wanted me to spend the vacation with him in Baltimore, where they were now living. Although Father Lahout saw it as an opportunity to break the ice between us, he wasn't stupid. Nor was I. Something inside both of us said proceed with caution. He set up an escape route for me in case something drastic happened in Baltimore. Isadore's new apartment was across the street from Loyola College. (Isadore and wife #2 were living there temporarily while waiting for the completion of their new home that was still under construction.) So he gave me a letter and said if I needed help, I was to walk across the street to the college, ask for the priest whose name was on the envelope (a friend of his) and give him the letter.

I arrived in Baltimore to find that Isadore was away on a business trip and would not be back for two days. The idea of being alone with wife #2 concerned me a lot. But she treated me politely, sometimes even kindly. I relaxed a little, she relaxed a little and, before we knew it, things became mildly enjoyable.

During our second evening together, she confided to me how difficult the marriage was for her, how hard it was to live with Isadore. I listened to her until 2 A.M. She said some cruel things about him, but because of my own experience with him, I could only sympathize. She also told me it was Isadore who didn't want me living with them, not her, and that she was working on him to let me live with them the coming summer in the new house. I could have my own room, we would have fun buying new furniture and decorating it, etc., etc. We were like two sisters (we were nearly the same age) planning for a bright and exciting future.

The next day Isadore returned. It was Holy Thursday and I had gone to the cathedral down the street to see my first Holy Thursday Mass. By the time I got back, the atmosphere in the apartment had shifted dramatically. When I walked into the den after saying hello to them both, Isadore followed me in, slamming the door. He was enraged—totally enraged. It didn't take me long to figure out from what he was yelling that wife #2 had repeated the entire conversation from the evening before, but rather than tell him that she had said those things about him, she told him I said them. All of wife #2's friendliness had been a setup and I, like a schmuck, fell for it.

I think if it had not been against the law, Isadore would have killed me on the spot. Instead, he kicked me out of the apartment. He did not care where I went or how I got there—I just had to get out as soon as I got my things packed. Had I needed it, I wasn't given time to make a phone call or to make arrangements. He wanted me out of his sight immediately. I remember my hands shaking a lot as I packed my stuff. When I walked through the living room, I saw Isadore and wife #2 sitting at the dining table quietly eating dinner. Neither one of them looked up at me as I left. It was as if I didn't exist.

A student answered the main door at Loyola and I asked for the priest whose name was on the envelope. About fifteen minutes later, a priest with a puzzled look on his face appeared and introduced himself. I opened my mouth to explain why I was there but started to cry instead. So I gave him the letter and continued to cry while he read it. Apparently, Father Lahout had been quite thorough in explaining why I might need help. After reading the letter, the priest took charge of the situation. (I later found out that this friend of Father Lahout's was the director of the college, a man used to taking charge.)

The first problem was to find a place for me to go for the rest of the vacation. I had a list of several classmates' addresses and phone numbers, and he called until he found a family to take me in. Then he got the bus connections, gave me money for the ticket and the trip and, in about two hours, was seeing me off at the Trailways Bus Station.

I arrived in Dover, Delaware, in the late evening hours. I remember walking through my classmate's front door and hearing a bunch of door chimes sounding out the tune to "Bless This House." The priest had called after I was on the bus to let them know my arrival time and the condition I might be in because of the situation in Baltimore. By the time I got to Dover, my classmate, her sister and mother welcomed me with sympathetic, open arms. The first thing they did was feed me. Then we talked. We even managed to laugh a little. I remember the kindness, care and support they gave me that week. I arrived after that fourth round in the ring with Isadore feeling not only pummeled but pulverized as well. When we returned to the Academy, I was back to feeling human again.

THE OPTION OF VISITING ISADORE in his home was no longer viable—even in Father Lahout's mind. He conceded that the man was impossible—the wife even more so—and the best I could do now was to avoid giving them further opportunity to hurt me. But that still didn't mean to Father Lahout that I could emotionally turn my back on Isadore. Things could change. He was an optimist.

I, on the other hand, did not see how it was possible to turn my back on someone who had clearly already turned away from me. That commandment, "Honor thy father and thy mother" did not seem to apply to Dorothy and Isadore. I was beginning to feel that the hierarchy of the Catholic Church needed to get together and rethink what that commandment meant. What was the definition of "father" and "mother"? How wide could that definition stretch? Surely it should not include people like Dorothy and Isadore.

For the remainder of the school year, I continued to see Father Lahout three times a week. We'd sit in the rectory eating ice cream, talking about the crazy things that went on at the Academy, the trouble the nuns were having with some of the girls, the trouble the girls were having with some of the nuns, his family, his old seminary days, the history of languages (his hobby), surviving (my hobby), and my feelings about my parents and what was happening to me.

ONE MORE THING OCCURRED at the very end of my junior year that was to significantly alter the course of my senior year.

It was customary for the outgoing senior class to nominate the candidates from the incoming senior class for next year's student council president. All the high school students were marched into the auditorium to hear the senior class announce the candidates. At the same assembly and immediately after the announcement, the students would vote. This was different from what I had seen at my other schools and I found it to be more than a little odd. There was no campaigning—no posters, no promises, no speeches. In fact, there was no guarantee that the nominees actually wanted to be president of student council.

This year there were three nominees. In a surprise twist, the girl who was expected to be the next president and had been groomed for the job since she was a freshman was not nominated. In an equally surprising twist, I was nominated. I was stunned. I had no idea the seniors knew me, let alone liked me that much. But then we had the vote and, as they say in the political world, it was a shocker (at least to me). I won. I was the new student council president. I felt overwhelmed by this sudden wave of acceptance. (Now all I had to do was figure out what the student council president at Saint Joseph Academy did.)

My newfound pride in being lifted to this position of honor dimmed quite a bit when I learned later that week that the seniors had fixed the election with the sophomores, thus assuring my victory. The senior class was composed of six students that year. Sister Virgo Regina, their prefect, was very close to them and they to her. I did not believe that by nominating me, they were deliberately setting me up nor did they understand the trap I would be walking into. It's just that they knew some questionable things about the girl who was expected to win and were determined to make sure she was shut out of the process. In short, she hadn't passed the seniors' character test. Apparently even the new Jewish girl was a better choice as far as they were concerned.

Sister Virgo Regina (she was called "Virgo" behind her back) was also the prefect of the student council. She had been waiting for the day when the girl in question would become president. The girl was beautiful, smart, had a fantastic singing voice and rich parents who made some sizable donations to the school while their daughter attended. It was clear from the deference Virgo extended to her that she felt the girl would represent the Academy well. Instead, Virgo was now faced with the prospect of working with an interloper. She did not take the election gracefully. She got up during my in-the-moment, off-the-cuff "acceptance" speech where I was attempting to say thank you in a hundred different ways, told me to sit down and then announced that starting next year, no one could be nominated for president of student council unless she had been a student at the Academy for two full years at the time of nomination. I don't know how the other students felt but I took it as a not-too-subtle sign that this woman was not happy with the election results. She made no attempt to congratulate me or even to extend courtesy. She had clearly set the tone for my senior year.

Just as I was about to panic about where I was going for the summer, Dorothy popped back up. I don't know if she phoned the Academy first or if SMA tracked her down and initiated the call. Since I had not heard from her all year, I suspected that SMA found Dorothy first. I was told she was now living in Riverdale, Maryland, and had a new apartment all ready for me. I had hoped to go back to Ocean City to work for the summer but SMA and Father Lahout felt that was the wrong move for me to make on my own. I disagreed, but maybe they knew something I didn't know. Since I had no other offers or ideas, I had to go to Riverdale.

Two weeks before school ended, Mother Superior called me to her office. She told me that Isadore had not paid anything toward my tuition, and if the problem couldn't be solved before school ended, I would not be allowed to return the next year. She wanted me to talk to the Academy lawyer about the situation. Perhaps he could come up with a solution.

The result of the meeting with the lawyer was a letter—sent to Isadore from the lawyer on my behalf, threatening to sue him for non-support of a minor. (The lawyer discovered that the court had awarded Isadore custody of me at the divorce. I was surprised because I didn't think either one of them had been given custody of me.) Within a few days, Isadore sent a check for the tuition's full amount to the lawyer. Mother Superior gave me the news and told me I was now promoted out of the eleventh grade and accepted back for next year.

Chapter 4

Riverdale, Maryland
1962

THE DAY AFTER the senior class graduated, I boarded a bus and headed for Riverdale, a suburb of Washington, D.C. Dorothy had moved to Riverdale to start a new life. Why she chose Riverdale, I didn't know. She rented a one-bedroom apartment, bought a new car (through a deal with one of her new friends) and got a new job—as a bartender.

One of Dorothy's friends met me at the bus station and drove me to the bar where Dorothy was now employed. During the trip I learned that she was telling people that she had been in constant contact with me at the Academy, had wanted to visit me but I wouldn't see her, had sent me money and gifts but I never wrote or contacted her to say thank you. In essence, Dorothy had built a fantasy about her relationship with me and her role as a parent.

When I walked into the bar that night, I felt like Daniel in a den full of angry, bleary-eyed lions. It was clear from the disapproving stares that Dorothy's new friends considered me a rotten ingrate of a daughter who was taking advantage of this poor woman who was working her ass off to keep both of our lives together. Thank god they were drunk and I only had to deal with some seriously nasty looks. Otherwise, if they had been able to get off their bar stools safely, they may have formed a staggering mob and beaten me to death. I waited at a small table until her shift was over and she was ready to leave. I didn't try to talk to her friends or change their opinion of me. I could see Dorothy's lies had them all firmly hooked and they were being solicitous and rather protective of her.

To say that I was not exactly thrilled with the prospect of spending the summer with Dorothy would be an understatement. I knew

I was going to have to endure a lot just to get through the three months. Because of my experiences in Ocean City, I was not as stressed about the food and shelter issue. I was now sixteen and could work legally. I only needed to forge a work permit. I assumed I could get a job that would cover my food expenses for the summer and, with a little luck, I'd be able to save enough for my senior year expenses. I still had $30 left over from the $75 I brought with me from Ocean City. I didn't think this would cover my senior year. But Riverdale is a suburban community, not a resort town, and although it offered a few summer jobs, they were taken by the time I arrived in mid-June.

Dorothy worked nights, which left me alone in the apartment from early afternoon—she liked to arrive at the bar early to help set up for the evening (so she said)—until around three or four in the morning, when she would stumble in, totally smashed. She'd collapse on her bed, sleep late, take a bath, get dressed and then leave again for work. Except for those two or three hours in late morning, I didn't have to deal with her directly.

A couple of weeks after I arrived, she stopped coming home, staying away for weeks at a time. I solved my food problem by taking $20 from her wallet every time she showed up. Eating two meals a day, I could make that stretch for three weeks by loading up on cereal and spaghetti. I discovered that I could get two meals out of a pound of spaghetti pasta topped with a can of tomato soup—not necessarily a healthy diet, but a filling one.

I developed a daily rhythm of reading, writing, cleaning, walking and watching television—a quiet rhythm only broken when Dorothy arrived on the scene. Then there would be a flurry of activity with her yelling at me, slamming doors and cabinets, making messes throughout the apartment and dropping a pile of dirty clothes that reeked of cigarettes and booze in the middle of the bedroom floor before leaving again with an armful of clean clothes.

The tension of never knowing when Dorothy was going to blow through wore me down. Pretty soon, I couldn't eat without feeling as if I was about to vomit any minute. I found a doctor in the area (whose bill I charged to Dorothy), and he informed me that I had a spastic colon—a poor man's ulcer, he explained. He asked me whether either one of my parents had a drinking problem. When I said yes, he told me that he had seen a number of teenagers with spastic colons and each of them had a parent with a drinking problem. Apparently the stress from dealing with Dorothy (and Isadore) had built up to the point where I, too, had a spastic colon. He gave me some pills and sent me on my way with the advice that I needed to learn to relax. I had no idea what he meant by "relax."

Once it had been diagnosed and was no longer a scary mystery, my spastic colon provided me with a much needed barometer. In order to survive, I had to ignore the emotions that surfaced when faced with a difficult situation. If something scared me, it didn't matter. I still had to deal with the problem, and I did not have time to waste dealing with the fear. So I'd shove the emotion to one side and get on with figuring out what to do. Now my spastic colon could tell me that something was hitting me especially hard and I needed to pay attention to the emotions I had just pushed out of my way. I spent the summer (and the next few years) figuring out how to release the pressure and calm my colon. (Okay, I'll let you in on a not-too-tightly-held secret. I learned that, for me, one of the best and most effective pressure releases was cussing. Good old-fashioned, sailor-like cussing. Just let 'er rip and I can feel the strain, stress and pressure dissolve. We have to warn new Perelandra staff about it so that when I walk into the business offices frustrated and shouting, "Fuck a duck," they won't faint. A lot of people aren't used to hearing a woman in her seventies say such things. They're a little delicate.)

IN LATE JULY, I DECIDED to convert to Catholicism—just like that. I woke up one morning and the idea was sitting right there in front of me. That afternoon I found the nearest rectory and presented myself to a priest for instructions. In the course of trying to figure out who I was and where I came from, the priest began to suspect that I might be in an unusual situation and asked questions that had nothing to do with religion. Eventually, I told him about Dorothy and her drinking. He immediately suggested she might be an alcoholic (the first time I had heard the word "alcoholic" used in reference to Dorothy) and said he knew some people who might be able to help me. Would I mind if he sent someone to talk to me?

A woman arrived at my door that evening, explaining that she was the wife of an alcoholic and belonged to a group called Al-Anon, a division of Alcoholics Anonymous. She also explained that there was another division of AA called Alateen, for the teenage children of alcoholics, and that she felt they could help me. The kids were meeting that night, and she would be glad to drive me to the meeting and bring me back home. As she spoke, I could feel that this woman understood exactly what I was going through with Dorothy. I didn't have to explain anything to her—she just knew. That evening I went to my first Alateen meeting.

There were about twenty-five kids at the meeting who (as they say) welcomed me with open arms. Their first concerns had to do with my living situation and whether I was in need—food, clothes, different shelter, protection from the alcoholic parent. They decided (and I agreed) that I needed companionship and food. So for the next seven weeks, until I went back to the Academy, I was visited often, and all visitors came bearing groceries. I was included in group outings, taken to the movies and, of course, always given a ride to the meetings.

Ed, my adult sponsor, who had been sober for twelve years, visited the bar where Dorothy worked and, over several ginger ales, observed her doing her job and interacting with the customers. He concluded that she was indeed an alcoholic. No question about it.

Now Dorothy wasn't just a drunk, she was an alcoholic. From Alateen I learned the difference between the two. I learned about the disease—how it affected the drinker. Dorothy's unpredictable behavior became predictable and she was no longer a mystery. She was a by-the-book alcoholic and her behavior fit right in with the "normal" symptoms and patterns of other alcoholics.

I learned that the feelings I had toward her, which at times I felt were shameful for any respectable kid to feel toward a mother, were natural and shared at different times by everyone in the group. The anger, the shame, the disgust, the hate, the fear—under the circumstances, those feelings were expected and they were okay. I realized I was a "normal" by-the-book daughter of an alcoholic. The more I learned about alcoholic behavior and about my own responses to that behavior, the more I was able to protect and stabilize myself and keep from being swept into Dorothy's life as she stumbled and crashed through mine.

Finding our way while living with an alcoholic wasn't an easy order for any of us to achieve. We were all hurting and we needed the support of those weekly meetings. A couple of the kids who so feared being alcoholics themselves began to drink to disprove it, got into trouble and ended up needing to switch to the regular AA meetings. One thirteen-year-old girl came to the meetings faithfully but would never say a word. At first, we passed it off as shyness. Eventually, she opened up and told us that her alcoholic father raped her every time he got drunk. That same evening we got her away from him and placed into another home.

At last I found friends who understood what I was dealing with. Before, I tried to explain my situation to friends who came from stable, sober homes. They couldn't understand what I was saying. They could hear the words but they couldn't grasp the scope of what the words meant. It fell too far outside their own experience. With the kids from Alateen, my problems were familiar. They didn't go into a frenzy if I called to say that Dorothy had wrecked the apartment and was now passed out in the bathtub. They'd just come over right away and encourage me to pull the plug in the tub so she wouldn't drown. Everyone assumed that I had already considered letting her drown, so we didn't need to talk about that. To them, contemplating matricide in such situations was perfectly reasonable. When all was secured in the apartment, they would take me to their home to wait until after Dorothy left for work. Then we'd return and they'd help me clean up her mess.

TOWARD THE END OF SUMMER, I got a surprise call from Maizie, an old friend of our pre-divorce family. She and her family had known Dorothy and Isadore since before we moved to Upperco. They visited Upperco several times a year and we visited their home in Riverdale about as often. The fact that they lived in Riverdale might have been the reason why Dorothy decided to move there after leaving Ocean City. I was happy to hear from her until she told me that Isadore wanted to meet with me the next day at her house. She would be happy to pick me up. I asked if he was coming alone and she said yes. I agreed to the meeting. Her call puzzled me because it came out of the blue. How did she know where I was? When she said she would pick me up, she didn't ask for my address or directions. How did she know the phone number? Had she visited Dorothy at the bar? Did Isadore contact her and, if so, which one of them knew how to contact me?

By the time Isadore arrived at Maizie's house the next day my spastic colon had kicked into high gear. This whole summer was one stress too many and my colon had had enough. It just gave out. Now it seemed the slightest bit of trouble could trigger it. I no longer had any pills left and I had not yet discovered the benefits of cussing, so I endured the nausea.

I think the purpose of Isadore's trip was to assure me that he was working on the home situation and still wanted me to live with them. He felt that eventually wife #2 would come around. I didn't say much in response. I didn't trust him or what he was saying. I found it difficult to believe that he still didn't understand that his wife wasn't going to let me anywhere near their home or life. The conversation between us was stiff but relatively cordial in that no one was screaming. I answered his questions and I didn't challenge him. He was there for less than half an hour and as he was leaving he asked if I needed anything. I said I could use a new pair of shoes. When he had arrived I noticed he was wearing a brand new pair of expensive looking shoes, so I guess I had shoes on my mind when he asked the question. The truth was, I needed a lot of things. I hadn't been able to buy any clothes for about three years and I lost over half the clothes I had taken from Upperco, thanks to the nor'easter in Ocean City. (I was still shaking sand out of the three wool skirts that I had rescued from the beach.) I was probably the only girl in my class who was thrilled to wear a school uniform. Isadore handed me $20 and said, "Here. This should cover the shoes." I thanked him and he left.

On the way back to the apartment, I asked Maizie if she knew anything about my situation and what I had been dealing with. She said she knew I had been on my own. When she heard that things "didn't go well" in Ocean City, she and her husband discussed offering for me to live with them but decided it might be too disruptive for their family. (They had three children. The middle child and I were the same age.) I had been on my own and they didn't think I could settle into their home. Maizie's comments left me speechless. What could I say? I had hoped for so long that I could join someone's family. Apparently they figured that I had been "roaming the streets" and it had turned me into a feral cat. How could I be expected to make my bed each morning? As far as I was concerned, they made a terrible decision. It was also a decision that surprised me. They were supposed to be good friends with Dorothy and Isadore. Actually, Maizie and Dorothy were best friends. They had known me since I was a little girl. How could they make the decision they made? How could they leave me "on the streets"? I felt certain that had they just talked to me I could have convinced them that I was still civilized.

Maizie picked me up the next day to take me shoe shopping. I bought a pair of loafers one size larger than I needed. I reasoned that if my feet grew, I'd still have a pair of shoes to wear. (My feet didn't grow so I spent the next few years stuffing toilet paper in the toes of the loafers to keep them from flopping.) We were in a small shop that also carried women's clothing. A wool jacket and skirt display caught my eye on our way out and I went over to look at it more closely. When I turned to leave, Maizie said she would like to buy it for me as a gift. Honestly, I didn't know what to say. It seemed like such a kindness. If it was motivated by guilt, I didn't pick up on that back then. I took it as a simple and much appreciated gesture of kindness. She even added a nice blouse to go with it. (Okay. It was probably guilt.)

Chapter 5

McSherrystown, Pennsylvania
1962–1963

IN MID-SEPTEMBER, I arrived back at the Academy with my Alateen sponsor and a carload of kids from my group. It was an unusually warm fall day but I didn't let that stop me from wearing my new wool outfit for the trip. I had been assigned the same room as the previous year, only this time I was told that my luck was because the nuns didn't want me to disturb the other girls when I got up early for daily Mass. My friends helped me move my stuff into my room and then I gave them a tour. The nuns were smiling and gracious until one nun asked my sponsor how we all met. He explained Alateen to her. I could tell from her expression as she backed away from us and left that she considered Alateen rather scandalous. News about Alateen traveled among the nuns quickly and now several were glaring at us as we walked by. Apparently they thought I was cavorting with the low life. And anything connected with alcoholics was definitely low life.

I don't know what happened over the summer but, by the time school started, a dense cloud of crazy had descended over the Academy and had driven several of the high school nuns mad. Now, instead of being thrown into a boxing ring with Isadore and wife #2 pummeling me, I was on a battlefield with several of the nuns firing at me at will. To make matters worse, I lost my two strongest allies. SMA had been transferred over the summer to another school (probably Chestnut Hill College) and Father Lahout was being transferred to another diocese in a few weeks.

There were two nuns in particular who had been hit hard by the crazy cloud. One was Sister Virgo Regina (Virgo). She was not only prefect of student council. She was also prefect of the senior class, our homeroom teacher, evening study prefect and the new resident on our dormitory corridor. She taught us English literature, English, religion and world history (from a Catholic perspective). We were rarely without her, and I could barely escape her.

She was a nun with power. In fact, she held the number two spot, right behind Mother Superior. I don't know if she had been elected or appointed to this position or if it was based on her age (which was fast approaching ancient) or on her tenure as a teacher. However she got the position, she was given deference and respect by the other nuns. And she knew she had the power.

At the Academy, everything was assigned. We students didn't try out or compete for anything. We didn't ask to be considered for anything. Virgo assigned me to be the front-page editor of the school newspaper (I enjoyed this), represent the school in a speech contest (I lost), represent the school at the funeral of some bishop (weird) and play the Mikado in the high school play (doubly weird). She told me I "won" the male role because I was the tallest girl in the class. For me, memorizing the script, learning the songs, dressing up in an elaborate Japanese ruler's costume and singing solos on stage was a remarkable triumph over my desire to remain behind the curtain and invisible.

Virgo was still angry about my being elected student council president and established a pattern of revenge toward me that started as soon as I arrived back at the Academy. Three or four times a day she would set a trap designed to make it look like I was ignoring Academy rules. She would give me a list of duties to perform as student council president—dumb stuff, such as checking the dormitories after the final morning bell to make sure no one was hiding out. This struck me as odd because I didn't think there was a problem with girls cowering in some corner in their dormitory to avoid classes. There were only about fifty of us in the entire high school. A missing girl would really stick out and I didn't think I needed to go on a hunt. As far as I was concerned it was a phantom problem that originated in Virgo's mind. Every time I arrived back in my homeroom about five minutes after the late bell had rung, she would give me a loud and public dressing down and accuse me of breaking the very Academy rules I was supposed to be upholding. According to Virgo, I was setting a horrible example for the other students.

One morning after a particularly outrageous and loud dressing down that Virgo brought to a dramatic end by storming out of the classroom, my classmates surprised me by convening an impromptu secret meeting to discuss what was happening to me. They agreed that Virgo was acting unfairly and decided they would protect me as much as possible by warning me when she was getting ready to set me up—which drove her nuts because she couldn't figure out how I was avoiding most of her traps.

There was nothing I could personally do about Virgo. The Academy had a rule that prohibited any student from making a negative remark or lodging a complaint of any kind about a nun. If we had a complaint, we were to speak directly to the nun involved. Fortunately, I came into the Academy knowing how to deal with, duck and avoid an out-of-control woman, so I applied those skills to Virgo. I didn't give her permission to diminish me. She could set me up, she could yell at me, she could falsely accuse me of stuff but she could not take away what I knew to be true and she could never stop me from thinking, "That woman is out of her mind." Between this and the support I got from my classmates, I was able to keep my footing with Virgo throughout most of my senior year.

About the student council and my job as its president: When I was elected, I wondered what my position and duties would entail. Well, I was quickly learning that it had nothing to do with representing the concerns and needs of the student body to the faculty. Instead, I and the other members of the student council (appointed by their respective class prefects) were enforcers and I, as president, was the chief enforcer. The primary focus of the council revolved around the Academy's rules and detention slips—lots of detention slips. Every time I brought up suggestions to make the council more student-oriented, Virgo would tell me I was too new at the Academy to understand or respect its traditions.

The rules were numerous and, to me, seemed a bit arbitrary. No talking on the stairs or in the halls. No sassing nuns—to be enforced at the nuns' discretion. Sometimes a look qualified as sassing and a girl would get a detention slip. If two students from different grades arrived at a closed door at the same time, the student from the lower grade had to hold the door open for the upper class student. All students had to hold all doors for any nun. Each girl's uniform hem had to touch the floor when she knelt. A couple of the nuns were notorious for giving random hem checks. A girl would be walking down the corridor and a nun would come up beside her and say, "Kneel." If the hem didn't touch the floor, her uniform was too short. The hem was ripped out on the spot and the offending student was thrown into detention for a few days.

And, as student council president, I was responsible for the morals of the high school students. If a girl got pregnant—which happened twice that year—I had to go before Mother Superior and explain how and why it happened. Then I had to convince her that it was impossible for me to have personally stopped the dastardly deed. I was also responsible for the girls' smoking and drinking habits—habits that refined Catholic young ladies were not supposed to have. It didn't take long for me to realize the undeniable fact that I was not going to stop the majority of my classmates from debauching their way through their senior year, so I put my effort into keeping the nuns from discovering the girls' indiscretions. Except pregnancy. That I could not cover up.

THE OTHER CRAZY CLOUD victim who was hit especially hard was Sister Edward Eileen (Eddie). She taught the seniors chemistry and trigonometry. During my junior year, she exhibited a sadistic streak as well as a general dislike for the students. Now she upped her game and launched a campaign against the senior class in particular. Of course, she continued the morning cowbell routine in the dormitories. (I continued going to daily Mass.) Remember the rule about students having to open the doors for nuns? Eddie applied this rule whenever possible. We caught her numerous times waiting at closed doors for a senior to come by, just so we could open it for her. It was this kind of stupid stuff that I'm sure she felt was getting under our skin. But we didn't care. It was just weird Eddie being weird again.

As the first semester wore on, Eddie grew even more strange—and vindictive. One morning three seniors showed up for trigonometry without having done their homework. Eddie exploded and accused us all of being lazy and stupid, among other things. Then she announced that she was not going to waste her valuable time teaching a bunch of unruly delinquents and walked out of the class, never to return that year. Not just that one semester, but the entire school year. We needed to pass a trig final in order to graduate. We asked Virgo to talk to Eddie for us, but she would not interfere. So, we took over our own class and spent the rest of the year teaching ourselves trigonometry and helping one another out when we got stuck. We all got above C on the final state exam. Triumph over madness.

Despite her decision to not teach us trig, she was still willing to teach us chemistry. I loved chemistry and it seemed like Eddie loved chemistry as well. She knew how to teach it and I excelled in the class. Well, not the whole class. I excelled when it came to the lectures, the reading and the exams (which she gave weekly). I was a disaster in the lab. It would probably be correct to say that my dyslexia excelled in the lab. I kept blowing up my experiments no matter how hard I tried and how careful I tried to be. I was slow and methodical when it came to following a list of written instructions but I always ended up with a small fire, an exploded mess or an oozing overflow. None of the other students wanted to pair with me so I generally worked alone. When I blew up my attempt at distilling water, Eddie barred me from the lab. I was too dangerous. But in the classroom I had no problems. There is an underlying logic in chemistry that I loved and that was easy for me to understand. I was learning something special about matter, how it operated and how it interfaced with other matter to create new form. In her classroom I could tell she liked me. In her lab I could tell she considered me impossible. Outside the classroom I was still one of those despicable seniors that she hated so much. At the end of the year we were given a final exam and, much to my everlasting surprise, I was exempt from taking it. Those weekly test scores (I got 100% on all of them) added up to an exemption and I got an A for the year.

Eddie didn't restrict her wrath to seniors. She had an issue with all upperclass students. She could spot a weakness in a girl and she would pick at it, pick at it, pick at it every chance she got. One girl was mentally slow. Not enough for it to be a problem socially but she had difficulty keeping up in the classroom. Eddie pressed this girl mercilessly. She especially liked calling her "stupid" or "idiot" or "dummy." And she kept pointing out the girl's slowness in class. It was cruel and sometimes the girl would be reduced to tears.

Eddie especially liked pressing girls in the mornings—yelling at them, correcting them sarcastically for the slightest thing and constantly needling them. For some reason, and no one knew why, she decided to badger one of the junior girls every time we waited in line to be marched down to the dining room for breakfast. Eddie patrolled the line and when she came to this girl she would say nasty, demeaning things to her. We knew the girl to be quiet and friendly, and I never noticed a behavior issue. I never heard her say anything mean about anyone, including the nuns. She was just a nice, pleasant girl as far as we were concerned. She had taken Eddie's morning abuse for several weeks when, one morning, the nun tipped her over the edge and the girl attacked.

When I arrived on the scene in response to all the yelling for me to come quickly, Eddie was on the floor and the girl was beating her. Eddie was bleeding from the mouth but no one was jumping in to save her. Then I remembered I was the student council president and needed to do something. So I decided to follow the rules that Virgo had been hammering me about. As students, we were not to intervene in such matters. The senior-most student was to get the nearest nun to take care of the situation. Well, it was morning and the nearest nuns were on the other side of the Academy in the nun's wing. We were also not supposed to run in the hallway. So I told the girls I'd be back with help and *walked* from the girls' dorm, down three flights of stairs, down the hallway to the dining room, and across the dining room to the big wooden door that led to the nun's wing. I took a deep breath, rushed through the door panting as if I had just finished a three-minute mile and yelled into the convent for help. By the time I returned with a platoon of nuns, the girl had beaten quite a bit of sense into Eddie and now was quiet and calm again. Eddie was bleeding from several places in the face, but other than that there was no real harm done. The layers and folds of her habit had softened the blows.

The girl was expelled on the spot and taken to an "undisclosed location" in the Academy to wait for her parents to pick her up. Several of the students smiled at her or nodded their heads as she walked by as our way of giving her a thumbs up. A couple of hours later, we gathered to say goodbye as she got into her parent's car. She was smiling. And so were we.

DESPITE ALL THE INSANITY, I decided again to request instructions in Catholicism. I felt that the Church contained a truth, and I needed to know it. I also felt that it contained guidelines for living a life of purpose, integrity and strength. That appealed to me. My parents had clearly shown me what not to do but I could only rely on my own sense of right and wrong when it came to figuring out what I should do. I felt I needed to expand on my innate good sense. I was certainly aware by then that the Church had its share of crazies who I felt were only pretending to be Catholic (or even Christian). I considered this ground noise and was confident I would be able to set it aside. I was in search of something deeper, something beyond the externals—I was searching for the heart, the soul of the Church. Because Father Lahout had been transferred by this time, I needed to talk to someone else at the rectory.

Father Hartnett, a friend of Father Lahout, agreed to give me instructions. He felt differently than Father Lahout about the fourth commandment. He took one look at my parents and announced that the commandment didn't apply to everyone. I didn't argue with him because I tended to agree. He also had little patience for the nuns' strict regimen at the Academy and decided it would be good for me to get out more than for the required weekly visit for instructions. In light of the high level of craziness going on with the nuns, I didn't argue with him about the extra visits either. During one weekly visit we talked about religion, and during the other two visits we just talked—or ate ice cream or played basketball. My spastic colon was quite active due to the Academy stress and my time with Father Hartnett gave it and me a short-lived reprieve.

I managed to get Eddie in trouble by telling him about how she forced every Academy high school Catholic boarder to go to confession each Friday, whether they wanted to go or not. During the week the girls discussed what sins they were planning to confess. They knew it would seem suspicious if they all confessed the same sin so a fair amount of collaboration was needed. I knew from my conversations with Father Hartnett that this was wrong and no one should be forced to confession. He was not happy when he heard what she was doing and just said he would deal with Eddie.

The next time he was at the Academy hearing confession, he listened for Eddie to make her move outside the confessional with one of the students. When she did, he bolted out of the confessional and sternly told her to leave the chapel immediately. He also told her she was barred from the chapel anytime confessions were being heard. All the high school boarders were sitting in the pews waiting their turn for their forced confession and heard him. It was pretty shocking to witness the take down of a nun and it seemed to me like the girls had stopped breathing. They watched as Eddie, obviously embarrassed, collected her prayer book and quickly made her way out of the chapel. For weeks everyone gossiped about Eddie's banishment by a priest. Of course I knew nothing. How could this happen?

Isadore and wife #2 were back in the picture. Virgo had decided that I would not be allowed to return to Riverdale on vacations if it meant spending time with my alcoholic mother and my Alateen friends. So she contacted Isadore and suggested that he take me for the Christmas holidays. That started another barrage of letters from wife #2 and visits from them both so they could tell me what a disaster I was. I do not think Isadore and wife #2 understood that their letters to me were being screened by Virgo. If I had an exam coming up and their letters were too vitriolic, she held them until after I had taken the exam.

I didn't leave the Academy for any holidays that year. I spent them with the nuns—which, on the whole, they resented since it was the only time during the school year when they could be together as a convent without having us pesky students around. Most of the time they ignored me and I was fine with that. Each vacation I had to clear out of my room, making it available for nuns' guests and move to the elementary school dormitory in the other building. I was assigned a bed that had a life-size crucifix complete with painted blood coming from the head, hands and feet hanging on the wall behind the headboard. This was the dormitory for little kids. Some were as young as five. How could they sleep with that thing hanging over them? I knew there were other less gory renditions of the crucifix the nuns could have chosen. I found this one overly big and rather creepy. I half expected to wake up one morning and find Jesus off the cross and walking around the dorm drinking His morning cup of coffee.

WE WERE IN OUR LAST SEMESTER when I found out I had finally achieved my goal of making the National Honor Society. It took three and a half years to beat my floating C into a B, giving me the required grades. No one outside the Academy—no parent, no family, no friend—knew about this accomplishment that made me feel so deeply proud—but I knew.

It was assumed most of us would go on to college, not in pursuit of a career but to better prepare ourselves for our roles as wives and mothers. A liberal arts degree would surely land us a higher caliber husband. I didn't want to be a wife or mother anytime soon and I didn't have a career in mind. But I really wanted to go to college. I didn't feel ready to enter the larger society on my own. I was grateful to be able to withdraw from the confusion and challenges of the larger world and tuck myself away in the academic world. Perhaps if I had had less outside agitation while I was at the Academy I would have felt ready to step out. But I did not have my footing and I felt I needed more time. College would give me four more years to steady myself and to carve out my future.

The college that appealed to me most was Colorado College, a private, four-year, co-educational, liberal arts and sciences college in Colorado Springs. I liked everything, including the photos of the campus and surrounding mountains. I fell in love with the idea of being in an academic setting while surrounded by such natural beauty. Another plus that was equally important: it was far away from Dorothy, Isadore and wife #2. As with my junior year, I figured I could have a lawyer in Colorado threaten Isadore each semester and get him to pay my tuition and book costs. I could work part time during the school year and full time during the summers to pay for my other expenses. Between my grades (I was a member of the National Honor Society!) and my obvious enthusiastic desire, I felt I had a good chance at being accepted.

About a month before graduation, I got the letter telling me I wasn't accepted. Virgo explained later that she had attached her own letter to my application recommending that they not accept me. She told them that I had serious family problems and would have difficulty getting the money for tuition. I was furious. I glared at her, then abruptly turned and left the room before I said or did something I would regret. She was flat-out wrong, she had made a bad decision, she had overstepped her bounds, she had interfered where she had no business and she had pulled the rug out from under me in ways that I didn't think she could begin to understand. I spent the next few days quietly seething and reminding myself, "That woman is out of her mind." It was clear I needed to graduate and get away from Virgo.

I now had to scramble to prepare for my life after graduation. I needed a destination, a place to live and a job—all right away. I wrote to Ed, my Alateen sponsor, and explained the situation. Within a week I got a letter back from him letting me know I would be welcome to stay at the home of one of my Alateen friends. She and her family were happy to have me. Shortly, I got a letter from my friend verifying that she and her family were looking forward to my staying with them. They even had a room for me that they were cleaning out and fixing up. Life was starting to look up for me. I was still deeply saddened about Colorado College and wondered if my application had been rejected on its own merits and I honestly didn't meet their requirements or if it was rejected solely because Virgo had sabotaged me. I could take the first reason—I gave it my best shot and I came up short. But the second reason just made me angry all over again.

We didn't graduate from the Academy, we escaped. I almost did not escape at all since Isadore had not paid tuition—again. I went through the same routine as the year before with the lawyer and, once again, as Isadore was being threatened with a suit for non-support of a minor, he came up with the money.

WE HAD ONE MORE CRISIS at the Academy that almost caused Virgo to cancel our graduation ceremony. Some of my fellow classmates had used their senior year to take up smoking and drinking, especially when we were bused to our "brother school" for dances. The girls and their boyfriends would disappear and drink themselves silly. As student council president I decided it was my job to keep these girls from being expelled. After all, they were part of the group protecting me from Virgo and I felt to cover for them was pay back. Each time we came back to the Academy after being bused to a dance, half the girls were drunk and needed help getting up to the dorm. The tricky part was the nun standing guard at the front door to make sure everyone got home. More often than not, that nun was Eddie. My job was to go in first and distract her while those who were too drunk to walk were carried past her. I'd stand there like an idiot telling her about the wonderful time we all had at the dance, how terrific the music was and how well the boys could dance...on and on until the last girl was dragged by. None of this was a conversation I would choose to have even under the best of circumstances. Once the coast was clear, I'd smile, say goodnight and head up to my room.

I managed to keep the drinking sprees a secret until two days before graduation. The priests at our brother school found out about the dance activities from one of the boys who apparently was caught drunk in his dorm and decided to save his own neck by implicating others. Virgo was phoned and all hell started flying everywhere. I was called in and grilled. I told Virgo I didn't know anything about such activities. (Technically that's true. I only saw the aftermath.) After countless discussions between Virgo and Mother Superior, it was decided that for the sake of the parents, graduation exercises would not be called off. But Virgo announced that she would not be attending the ceremony.

For graduation we were each given five tickets for family and friends. Out of respect for the "honor thy father and thy mother" thing, I sent a ticket and a small wallet-size graduation photo (it was the most I could afford) to Isadore. He sent both the invitation and the photo back with a note saying something about my lousy attitude. Since she had not contacted me all year, I had no idea where Dorothy was and didn't try to send her a ticket. Instead I gave my tickets to my Alateen sponsor and the friends and family I would be staying with. It was a good move. My gang of five were genuinely happy for me and were determined to show it with appropriately timed applause and cheers when I was handed my diploma.

Virgo had one last parting shot for me. Remember I said I was the tallest girl in my class? This meant I was the last girl to leave the stage for the ceremonial exit march up the auditorium aisle. Virgo was standing in a doorway at the foot of the stage steps congratulating each girl as she came down. She gave them a hug and wished them the best of luck and God's speed. When I came down the steps, she looked at me, turned around and walked away. I was shocked. This woman really was out of her mind. She could not even express an ounce of decency or simple humanity toward me. I said to the back of her head as she walked away, "God bless you, too, Sister." She ignored me and just continued walking.

My friends quickly got my stuff packed into the car and we left Saint Joseph Academy as fast as possible. They took me out to dinner and we topped the celebration off with the most decadent desserts on the menu.

Chapter 6

Washington, D.C.
1963

TIME FOR A PARABLE: Once upon a time, there was an odd little horse jump that was part of an Olympic equestrian cross-country event. These events typically incorporate a four-mile course over natural terrain and include twenty-four to thirty-six jumps over logs, wagons, picnic tables, ditches, banks, and over or into large or small bodies of water—all with various designs, depths, heights and widths.

The course tests a horse's speed, endurance, bravery and jumping ability. On the Olympic level, the horses have to be exceptionally fit and well-trained just to complete the course. And the rider and horse have to be in sync with one another with a strong bond of trust established between them. Sometimes when approaching a jump the horse can make better decisions that overrule the rider's decisions and result in a clean jump. Conversely, the rider can overrule the horse and choose a better approach and exit line to a jump that will save time. (The competitors must complete the course within a time limit.) The horse and rider each have to know when to trust the other to take the lead.

One odd little jump was sitting in the middle of an open field. It was a brush jump in the shape of a donut that sat up on end (vertical to the ground) with brush bundled in a 360-degree circle leaving the center open, like a donut hole. Normally the hole is large enough to provide the horse and rider with plenty of room for jumping. But our little donut was skinny (narrow) and had an opening just large enough for the horse and rider with little room to spare. Its smaller size challenged the horses' visual perception.

On approach, a horse could sense that the hole wasn't big enough to jump through. This is where training and trust are tested. If the rider indicates that they are going to jump through that little hole, the horse has to trust that the rider isn't heading him into danger and that there is solid ground on the other side to provide good footing for a safe landing.

The designer of the course knew this might be a problem for some horses so he added an option. Off to the left, about 200 feet from the donut, was a labyrinth, about thirty square yards, that the rider could choose to move through if the horse didn't like the donut. However, the labyrinth had a trade-off. It certainly was a safer option but its pathways were narrow with 90-degree and 180-degree turns. The rider had to slow the horse down to a trot just to weave through the intricate maze. Between the slower pace and the complexity of the labyrinth, the rider could lose a couple of minutes or more off the time clock. When taking on the donut, that horse could jump through the hole and then continue on to the next obstacle without breaking stride or pace. But if the horse refused the jump, he received twenty penalty points and lost time as the rider and horse tried the jump again. If the horse refused the jump on the second attempt, he received another twenty penalty points. Four refusals over the entire course and rider and horse were disqualified.

The first horse and rider galloped across the open field at a fast clip. The rider steadied the horse to jump the donut but the horse refused, ducking out to the left. The rider circled the horse around and headed him toward the jump a second time. The horse refused again. So to avoid more than the already earned forty penalty points, the rider quickly headed the horse over to the labyrinth—the slower, safe route. When they exited, they galloped to the next obstacle hoping to make up for lost time.

The second horse refused the donut twice, as well. That rider also headed for the labyrinth and moved the horse through it as quickly as possible. The same thing occurred with the next three horses. Trainers from several different teams were standing on the hill off to one side observing how the horses reacted to our little jump. After the fifth horse refused the jump, the trainers phoned their team members who were waiting to start the course and told them to ignore the donut because the first horses had all refused to jump it. Go directly to the labyrinth. It'll save time and penalty points. And that's what they all did.

The little jump sat out there in the middle of the field with no takers until a late horse and rider galloped over the rise and onto the field. They moved directly to the donut at a fast, easy pace. The rider steadied the horse and then let the horse take the lead. Without breaking stride, the horse jumped through the donut hole then continued on at a fast clip to the next jump. No penalty points and no time lost. This horse and rider won the competition.

Most parables have a moral to their story and this one has several. But I want to use it as an illustration instead. When I have told the story to others in years past, it was to illustrate how I see people approaching and dealing with challenges in their lives. Most folks opt for the labyrinth approach. They like to be cautious and safe and prefer to maintain control (or the illusion of control) as they address the challenge. They don't mind the extra time it takes to reach a solution or conclusion. They know that eventually the problem will be straightened out and then they can move on with their lives.

My innate response to challenge is to jump through the donut. I trust that the hole is large enough and I trust I will be safe if I take the jump. I also trust that a safe landing awaits me on the other side even if I don't know ahead of time what that landing is going to look like. For me, the extra time it takes to navigate a labyrinth feels unnecessary. And to be honest, I just don't have the patience for dealing with unnecessary steps and wasted time. So why bother traversing a labyrinth when all I have to do is jump through the donut hole that's sitting right in front of me and then move on without breaking stride?

Trust is the necessary element needed when jumping through a donut. And it seems it's often the element that is missing when a person opts for the labyrinth. They don't trust that they will be safe should they choose the direct donut approach. They fear they will crash or fall. If they choose to try jumping through the donut hole while harboring these feelings, the horse will refuse the jump over and over until they either get the courage to jump or they finally opt out for the labyrinth.

By the way, I *do not mean* to imply that everyone *should* jump the donut. Both options are reasonable and valid approaches to life's challenges. Like the equestrian riders, I encourage you to know what's best for achieving success and then head directly for that option. Don't waste time trying to force yourself to move through the donut hole when everything inside you, as with the horse, keeps skidding to a stop in front of the donut saying, "Nope. Not gonna happen. I'm not jumping through that thing no matter how many times you want me to try."

All along, as I moved from Ocean City to the Academy and now to Washington, D.C., my natural inclination to jump through the donut and face every challenge head on had served me well. But at the end of my senior year I tried to alter my normal response and take the labyrinth. Colorado College was my labyrinth. Had I been able to attend, I would have spent four years getting my feet under me. It was clearly the slower, cautious, safe choice. And by this time, I really wanted to take that route. After years of difficulty and challenge, I felt it would give me four years to catch my breath and discover what "normal" people did before I was faced with going out into the world. It was an enticing option.

But it was not to be. Instead I faced a series of donuts as I moved through this final survival stage in preparation for the new life that would follow. It was to prove the most difficult stage because, for the first time, I was my own challenge and I would have to face myself head on. I needed to drop some of the important survival habits and skills I had picked up since leaving Upperco. I needed to see that they were no longer working for me or necessary. I needed to experience what could happen if I let fear consume me. Now I was about to make poor decisions that were fueled primarily by fear, and it nearly cost me my life.

AFTER GRADUATION AND OUR celebration dinner, we drove to the suburbs of Washington, D.C. With my new Alateen family I had visions of a quiet, stable life away from the insanity of the nuns, Isadore, wife #2 and Dorothy. That first night, as I got settled into my room, I could tell I was deeply exhausted. It wasn't just from the day. It was more like the stress from the last four years had caught up with me. I laid in bed for a couple of hours staring into space feeling bone-tired and lost. Finally, I drifted to sleep.

The next day I joined the family for breakfast. All were friendly and welcoming, but it didn't take me long to realize that something was wrong. These people were in crisis and there was no logical reason why they offered, at this time in their lives, to have me come into their home except to say that they wanted to help an Alateen in need.

The mother had just been downsized, losing the job she had held for over twelve years. She had been the primary breadwinner for the family and this turn of events hit her especially hard. She spent a lot of her day talking about the company injustices and how badly they had treated her.

The alcoholic father had just "fallen off the wagon," ending years of sobriety. He was now bobbing and weaving his way through a rather extensive drunken bender while everyone else in the house ignored him. He had lost his job as well and spent most of the day slumped in a chair in the living room drinking. He wasn't a nasty or destructive drunk like Dorothy. Instead he was quiet. The more he drank the more he went inside himself. He actually seemed to diminish in physical size, and sometimes when he walked through a room he looked and felt like a ghost.

The daughter, my Alateen friend, was in bed recuperating from serious leg surgery that wasn't healing well. She was in pain, depressed or angry most of the time.

There was an older daughter who had a drinking problem, was married to a guy who liked to use her as a punching bag, and she was pregnant with a second child that she didn't want. She came over to the house frequently to add to the general level of depression, complaints and tension.

I guess you could say that my new home situation motivated me to move fast and get a job. At least I would be able to help out a little and pay the family room and board. I landed a job on my first interview—skip-tracer and collection agent with a small Washington collection agency, another job for which I was highly unqualified. I was still only seventeen and needed a work permit. But this agency didn't seem to care about permits. I guess I seemed eager and intelligent enough to learn the job and to them my age wasn't an issue. Besides, I would be eighteen when my next birthday rolled around and then I'd be officially legal for working.

With training I became a decent skip-tracer, but once I found the culprit I bought any story he or she had to tell me. I was a total pushover and the person knew it right away. I usually managed to bring in just one or two $10 checks each week—most of the time the checks bounced. Wes, the owner of the company, was about to fire me when, in a panic, I convinced him that his office was not set up well and needed a complete house cleaning and reorganization of all files and information. He agreed. I was now the new "girl Friday."

In actuality, Wes was not overwhelmed with my initiative nearly as much as he was interested in keeping a young, female body around. He pursued and, thinking he might be the "right" way out of the mess I found myself living in with the Alateen family, I accepted his pursuit. Looking back, I think the more accurate way to describe what I did is to say my fears about how I was going to pull my life together caused me to panic and I looked for the nearest person to save, protect, hide and provide for me.

Wes seemed to fit the bill. He was older. Thirty-six. Stable and settled. Son of a Protestant bishop (the bishop was deceased). College educated with a law degree. Taught history in college while he was going to law school. Spent several years in Europe working with the foreign service. Loved classical music. Wrote poetry. And not at all coincidentally, looked a little like Isadore.

We married in September. Since I was not yet eighteen years old, I needed a signed permission from a parent. Because we were to be married by a judge, I did not want to risk forging the permission. Now I was dealing with "the law" and a judge might suspect the forgery. I sent the permission paper to Isadore with a note saying I needed him to sign it. I did not explain what I was doing nor did he ask any questions. He simply signed it and sent it back.

The wedding ceremony took place in a judge's chamber during a court lunch break. It was rather convenient timing since Wes was in the courthouse that day going through a trial—a total surprise to me. He took me to the courtroom in the morning, saying that he was on trial for twenty counts of telephone harassment in connection with his work as a collector. The lawyers were accusing him of calling folks in the middle of the night and threatening them with bodily harm if they didn't come up with the money they owed. He told me it was nothing to worry about. These kinds of things happen in his line of work, he said. But as I watched the morning session, this didn't look like an insignificant legal annoyance that was a natural part of a bill collection business. It seemed the prosecutor was determined to make sure Wes was found guilty.

When the trial broke for lunch, I asked Wes what was going on. He assured me that it was all a mistake and that there was nothing to worry about. I overlooked what I thought I was seeing and figured that since Wes was a lawyer, he and his attorney knew what they were doing. He had assured me that all would be well and I believed him.

A different judge married us. I could tell he had some reservations about our union. Actually it didn't seem like he approved, but he performed the ceremony anyway. His receptionist was our witness. Wes had not bought a ring so the judge loaned us a spare wedding ring that he kept in his drawer for just such situations. At the proper moment in the ceremony, Wes slipped the ring on my finger. We were pronounced husband and wife, and then the judge asked for his ring back.

After a quick sandwich—our wedding reception—we went back to the courtroom. The trial continued to go badly for Wes. By the end of the day, he was pronounced guilty and quickly taken out of the courtroom to jail. His lawyer gave me the keys to Wes' car, a slip of paper with his mother's address written on it and said I was to go to her house. I wasn't sure what was happening but I felt my new husband was making sure I would be safe.

The address Wes had written led me to a stately, older house with a well-landscaped front yard and stone walkway in an upscale neighborhood in Northwest Washington. I was anxious about just showing up out of nowhere but I didn't know where else to go. I rang the doorbell and after a couple of minutes an older woman answered. I asked if she was Wes' mother and when she said yes I told her my name and who I was. I showed her his handwritten note and I could tell she recognized his writing. I explained that her son was in jail and that I was his new wife. After I showed her the marriage certificate, she politely invited me to come in.

I sat in the living room with her and explained the best I could what had happened in court that day. To be honest, a lot of it was a blur. She told me that Wes had given me her address because it was where he had been living the last few years. We talked for a couple of hours about the situation, trying to piece together what was happening. Then she took me upstairs to his "room"—a beautiful converted attic apartment with enough open space to create a bedroom, a living room, an office and library. She said I was welcome to stay there. She left me alone to settle in and rest a bit, saying as she left that I could join her for dinner, if I liked. I accepted and thanked her.

I have to say, I found his mother to be a gracious, kind, highly intelligent, quiet woman. I'm not sure I could have been as welcoming if a stranger with a similar story had just dropped into my life from out of nowhere. Apparently, in our relatively short time together, she had come to the conclusion that, if she let me stay, I wasn't going to rob her or slash her throat.

So there I was on my wedding night in a lovely but strange apartment, in a stately but strange house, in a new but strange part of Washington and with a kind, elderly woman whom I had met for the first time just a few hours before. Wes had been sentenced to eight months in jail, the maximum they could give him. It seemed I would be in limbo in this house with his mother for the next eight months while I waited for his release. There was no question in my mind about remaining loyal to him. He was my husband as of noon, he was in trouble, and I was going to help him out of this mess. I was determined to uphold my duty as a wife.

The common ground that his mother and I shared was our desire to find out how we were going to get Wes out of jail. While she made phone calls to see what kind of assistance we could get,

I went through the papers in his desk in the attic apartment looking for something that might help. What we began to discover stunned us both. Her son and my husband led a double life. He used two separate names and had different personalities with each name. She and I knew the same person, the one who used the name he was given at birth. As that person, Wes was calm, intelligent, thoughtful and considerate. The second person, the one who was in jail, went by the name Almus Chase and was a shady, violent man who liked to threaten and con people. Almus Chase was well known by the D.C. police. In fact, they already knew Almus and Wes were one in the same person. The judge had been surprisingly harsh in his ruling the day we were married because he knew the police had been anxious for years to get Almus Chase behind bars. As his mother and I dug deeper, we learned that Wes had set up phony businesses in Baltimore and Chicago in partnership with other lawyers, signed legal papers and opened phony bank accounts locally and in San Francisco all under the name of Almus Chase. We also discovered there were warrants out for his arrest for bad checks, forgery and assault. About two weeks after Wes went to jail, his mother started getting phone calls from lawyers, bankers and partners—all strangers and all asking where to find Almus Chase.

Over the next few weeks, I grew quite fond of his mother. She was sincere, honest and she had a first-rate mind. She was the head of education at the National Council of Churches, the largest ecumenical body in the United States, that was headquartered in Washington. She was well-respected, well liked and in line with her position at the National Council of Churches, she knew a lot of the local and national leaders around Washington. She was an accomplished woman in her own right. But now, in a surprising twist in her life, her son was in jail. I could see how deeply this situation drained her. Yet it didn't stop her. She was his mother and she was determined to do everything in her power to help him. So we worked together as a team focused on our mutual goal.

With Wes' arrest, the collection agency folded. I had to find a new job and I had to do it quickly. Wes' bank accounts were empty and I had no source of income. A chain of lumber yard/home improvement stores needed cashiers, but after the personnel testing, I was told that I was overqualified. (This was a first. I don't know how I suddenly became overqualified for a job.) However, they happened to have an opening for a secretary in their home improvement department, and the job was mine as long as I passed the bonding requirements. (Bonding? What was that?) They told me I had to take a polygraph test in order to be bonded.

I panicked. I figured that if they were fussy enough to require a polygraph test for a secretarial position, they would probably not want anyone in their employ who had a husband in jail. That didn't seem fair to me. I needed a job and I knew I wasn't planning to steal their money or building supplies. So I decided I would lie about Wes.

That may sound like a remarkably stupid move because now I had to pass a polygraph test with a lie. But listen, it worked. In the interview, when they asked about my husband, I made up some story about his being in Rome at the Vatican II Council as part of the American Protestant lay delegation. He'd be gone for eight months (the exact period of Wes' jail term). This story was not as outrageous as it now sounds. At that time, the Second Vatican Ecumenical Council was being held in Rome and there was a Protestant lay group attending from the United States. Wes was the son of a bishop. His mother was the current head of education at the National Council of Churches. Why wouldn't he be chosen to attend something like that? When it came time for the polygraph test, I had convinced myself that it was fact, not fiction, and I passed the test.

I started work the next day as a secretary for the head of the home improvement department—another job for which I had no experience and few skills. But I had heart and determination.

EVERY THURSDAY DURING my lunch hour, I visited Wes in jail. For me, it meant formalities with the guards: signing in, answering questions, getting searched (pat-down, not strip). Then I joined a small group of women who were also waiting to visit their men. We were escorted down several corridors. Steel doors were opened and then banged shut and relocked after we passed through. Every sound, including our footsteps, echoed. In the visitors' room, I was separated from Wes by a wall. I sat on a metal chair, looked at him through a tiny diamond-shaped window just large enough to show his face and spoke to him through a phone. When my half hour was up, a guard would hit the back of my chair with a stick. Then I'd leave and drive back to work.

During the first two visits, Wes was considerate and our conversation was easy. Then he started asking me to convey messages and transfer papers from his desk to business partners and lawyers, all of whom were strangers to me. Everything had to be secret. He devised codes based on characters from the different stories in *The Canterbury Tales* so that he could send coded instructions to me in letters that would be read by the guards. Each character represented a course of action I was to take.

But things got complicated and Wes started to go downhill fast. The people he thought would help him were reluctant to get involved with his mess. Each time I conveyed this to him, he got more irritated with me. If I would only do exactly what he was telling me, he wouldn't have these problems. Unfortunately for Wes, I was doing exactly what he was telling me to do and still no one wanted to get involved with him.

Finally, one Thursday he exploded. He started shouting at me, telling me that he didn't want to see me again. To punctuate his point, he picked up his chair and slammed it against the window that separated us. Guards grabbed him. Other guards quickly hustled me out of the room and into an office. An older guard sat down with me, handed me a cup of coffee and told me that it was evident to them that Wes had been mentally deteriorating. He suggested that I get this man out of my life as soon as possible. I thanked him for his kindness and advice but, in my mind, I dismissed it. I was determined to be a loyal wife.

A week before Thanksgiving, I met my new sister-in-law for the first time. She was a few years older than Wes and held an executive position in the New Jersey penal system. She listened intently as we brought her up to date on Wes' situation and what her mother and I had been trying to do to help. We talked about the mysterious double life that Wes had been leading as Almus Chase. The string of bogus businesses and bank accounts. His mounting bills that were now streaming in daily. I told her about my final violent visit with him at the jail and what he said about my not coming back. Later that night, she came up to the attic apartment to say one thing to me: "If you were my daughter, I'd tell you to leave this man and start your life over." The jail guard saying the same thing didn't have the impact on me that she had. As they say, she had "skin in the game." She loved her brother.

A week later, I left my mother-in-law's home and moved into a rooming house in the heart of D.C., just off DuPont Circle. I also saw a lawyer who had been recommended to me and started divorce proceedings.

I STILL HAD ONE PROBLEM to address. As far as my boss and co-workers were concerned, I had a husband in Rome. They were always asking how he was, when he would be coming back. I had to do something now that this man wasn't going to be in my life. So I killed him off. I called the office and told my boss that Wes had died in a car accident in Rome. I would have to fly to Rome to make arrangements for the body. He gave me two weeks off. During that time, the company newspaper ran a sympathy note to me. By the time I returned to work, everyone knew I was a widow.

Five months after we got married, Wes was released from jail early and had returned to his mother's house. I assumed his mother found someone to help her get him released. He convinced his mother that he wanted to talk to me to try to smooth things over, so she gave him my phone number at the rooming house. It was not a conciliatory call. He told me I was the cause of his present situation and that if it was the last thing he did, he would destroy me—he would kill me. He sounded like he meant it.

The first thing he did was get me kicked out of the rooming house by calling the landlord numerous times throughout the night, telling him he would keep calling if I wasn't evicted. I found another rooming house around the corner the day I was kicked out. I did not give my new phone number out to anyone.

Next, he found out where I was working from his mother (still unsuspecting about his motives) and went after my job by calling my boss, identifying himself as my husband and threatening to continue calling until I was fired. My boss didn't tell me about the phone calls at first, assuming it was just some weirdo playing a sick prank. After all, my husband was dead. Then one day, he called me into his office and played a tape of several of the calls. It was my dear, departed husband all right, making all kinds of pornographic suggestions about my moral character (some I didn't even understand). We were joined by several company executives who asked me straight out if this man was my husband. I said yes—and I was fired immediately.

I was boxed into a corner now and I knew there was no way I could continue my lies. The embarrassment, shame, humiliation and fear I felt when my boss and the company executives confronted me was enough to scare me straight. I retired the Rome story and lying forever.

I got another job as a receptionist for a small business machine company, and Wes got me fired from that in a matter of two months. At first he only used telephone harassment. When that didn't work with my supervisor, he escalated to dirty tricks. I was sitting at my desk answering phones when four men from the local Rescue Squad rushed through the door looking for the dying receptionist. The Rescue Squad didn't take kindly to false alarms, and it took a lot of fast talking by my supervisor before they were convinced we knew nothing about the false report. Again, I was fired immediately.

My next job was with *The Washington Post* newspaper as a copy desk girl in the classified advertising department. This time I anticipated Wes' skip-tracing moves and did a better job covering my tracks so that he wouldn't be able to find where I was working.

He changed his tactics and began to follow me in his car as I walked down the street. A couple of times when I was crossing the street, he ran the car through the crosswalk and tried to hit me. There was no question that he truly meant to kill me. I was being stalked by a mad man. I asked the police for help, but they could not/would not do anything unless Wes physically attacked me. The police reasoning struck me as insane. I was in danger but the police couldn't help me unless Wes actually beat me up or ran over me. Now the police had me boxed in as well.

THE JANUARY PRIOR TO WES' release from jail, I had gone to my local church, St. Matthew's Cathedral in Washington, and asked to be baptized Catholic. After one session, the priest was convinced that I already had instructions and could be baptized a week later. A co-worker from the home improvement company stood up for me as godfather, and later I celebrated by eating a pint of ice cream alone in my room.

As a new Catholic, the Cathedral became the focal point of my life, outside of my job. I went to three Masses on Sunday: the first one was the "real" one where I received communion, the second Mass was solely for the purpose of getting a good seat for the third one, which was a High Mass. I loved to listen to the choir. The music was superb. I went to confession every Friday (it was voluntary and not forced) and the special prayer services held throughout the week.

Now, with my fears of being killed and not getting any help from the police, I felt I had no place to turn but the Church. I walked to St. Matthew's rectory and requested to see the priest who had baptized me. I was told that he was hearing confessions and that I should come back in two hours. I knew that if I left the rectory, the man following me in the car was going to kill me. So I said it was an emergency and couldn't wait.

When Father Ruppert came in, he was furious that I had gotten him out of the confessional. I told him my story. I told it to him straight. No lies. I told him I thought I was going to be killed if I didn't get help right away. Could he help me find a safe place to stay? (Wes had already located my rooming house.) We had not spoken privately since he baptized me and he didn't know anything about me except that I had received Catholic instructions at the Academy. He listened but I could tell he thought I was a mental case and needed to be ushered out of the rectory quickly. He said there was nothing he could do. I'd have to get help from the police.

When I left the rectory, I felt I had run out of time and options. I could think of nothing else to do and I was convinced I would be dead shortly. In an odd way, I was calm. I wasn't even worried. The frantic stress I had felt as I walked into the rectory was now gone. I accepted that I was about to die and I was at peace with it. (In case you think I'm exaggerating about the threat—which is fair since everyone I reached out to about this assumed I was exaggerating—Wes was arrested for murder a year later. He was put away for life for killing the husband of a woman he wanted. He shot the fellow five times in front of a roomful of witnesses.)

I was a block from the rectory when I heard my name being called. I looked around and it was Father Ruppert calling after me. For some reason he decided to check out my story and, right after I left the rectory, he called a friend of his who worked in the police department. She told him that my story was true and that the guards at the jail believed this man to be dangerous. The police had been watching him for weeks now that he was out. She suggested he tell me to go to a nearby YWCA. They were sure I'd be safe there.

After a three-day stay at the YWCA, complete with hours of fitful sleep and nightmares, and after a few months' stay at a girlfriend's apartment, I found a furnished efficiency apartment in a high-rise building that was located three blocks from work and five blocks from St. Matthew's Cathedral. The building had security and a rooftop swimming pool. With my salary from *The Washington Post,* I could afford the rent—if I was careful. It was a touch of heaven. Again I covered my tracks so that Wes would not find me—at least not easily. Since I could not legally sign a rental contract because of my age, I sent the papers to Isadore for him to co-sign. He quickly sent them back signed and without a note.

Around this time I discovered that the lawyer I had hired for the divorce had been contacted by Wes and, without telling me, he was now representing Wes' interests instead of mine. Yet he was still billing me monthly and filing papers in my name that favored Wes' interests. I may have been young and naïve as far as lawyers were concerned, but this didn't seem right. Something was wrong. So I contacted another lawyer who was well known and respected in the Catholic community. He said he couldn't advise me because that would be unethical. The other lawyer was still "officially" representing me. I called the first lawyer from the receptionist's desk in the second lawyer's outer office and fired the bastard. Then I returned to my new lawyer's office to resume our meeting. He said he was sure that the other lawyer had acted unethically and, with the proof I had, I could file a complaint with the D.C. Bar Association. He told me what to do and what to say. I did exactly what the second lawyer advised and, after a few months of meetings and investigations, the first lawyer was disbarred in D.C., Maryland and Virginia. I, an eighteen-year-old young woman, took down a sleazy lawyer. Power.

I HAVE A LITTLE PLAQUE hanging in my house that says, "Do not start with me. You will not win." I can honestly say to you that at the end of this eighteen-year-long road that led up to the involuntary pivot and included the four years of struggle resulting from that pivot, I emerged unbroken, proud, strong and determined. I finally felt I had my feet under me and I was ready to hold my own in the larger society. I also realized that my home, where I belong, truly is where I hang my own hat. I learned that lying had dire consequences. It was no longer a useful tool for me, nor would it work and, more importantly, it was no longer needed. I had become a scrupulous practitioner of truth. Finally, I learned to respect my fears and the power they can hold over me. It was my job to keep them from overtaking me and sending me in the wrong direction. By jumping through the donut instead of taking the labyrinth, it took nine tough months instead of the four college years to *finally* bust through the end of my post-pivot survival time. I emerged carrying my banner high (in my heart and mind) that reads:

Do not start with me.
You will not win.

Chapter 7

Forrestine Gump's Washington
1963–1966

FROM THIS POINT ON, everything changed. Moving out of the post-pivot survival years and into the post-pivot building years felt like someone somewhere had flipped a switch. One day I was fighting for my life and the next day I was surrounded by normalcy. Dorothy, Isadore and wife #2 receded far into the background and went silent. I guess they were now interested solely in their own lives and didn't feel the need to pretend I was included. There were no phone calls, no correspondence, no contact. At age eighteen, I didn't exist to them and they didn't exist to me. Wes lost interest and disappeared. I didn't hear anything about him until the TV news reports on the murder. Even in the newspaper, in the part dealing with his background and history, his marriage to me wasn't mentioned. It was as if our paths had never crossed. The only leftover from the marriage was the divorce, which was finalized after the required waiting period was completed. The Church annulment came through long before the civil divorce because Wes had been married (legally and in the eyes of the Church) prior to me, thereby making my marriage to a divorced man "null and void."

I know it's cliché and these words are used too often, but for me they are an accurate description of the early building years: The dark clouds lifted, the sun came out and the sky was blue again. The survival years had felt stormy and heavy as I addressed one challenge after another in quick succession. My sense of a future had disappeared. When I tried to look forward, all I saw was black. For over four years I kept my head down and my focus on whatever was immediately in front of me. With the start of the building years, I lifted my head and my gaze. It wasn't something I thought about or planned or even encouraged myself to do. It just happened. One day I looked out to the horizon, a horizon that was there for the first time in years. I didn't know where I was going but at least now I could see there was a future for me to step into.

Along with my new apartment, I acquired a cat, whom I named Eloise, and bought a couple of house plants. I was actually living like a regular person. I had furniture (the apartment was furnished); I had a small kitchen with a stove, refrigerator, dishes, pots and pans; I had hot water—year round; in the winter I had heat and in the summer I had air conditioning; and there was a laundry room in the basement. I still had my metal quotes box, the framed picture from Upperco, my portable record player and the four LPs, including my scratched Andrés Segovia album. (After my many moves, the picture frame finally fell apart exposing a name plate on the back that read, "The Rugged Individualist.") I bought a small, used portable Singer sewing machine and began building my wardrobe. And I became friends with my neighbors, so I felt a little protected.

Father Ruppert introduced me to four women who quickly folded me into their group. For being in their twenties, they were impressively accomplished. One was William Fulbright's administrative assistant for his Senate Foreign Relations Committee, one was a government geologist, another was an artist and graphics designer who had just been hired to head a new department at National Geographic, and the fourth was the administrative assistant for the lawyer who handled Lyndon and Lady Bird Johnson's communications "empire." We would meet three or four times a week at the end of the day and discuss whatever topics didn't fall under the heading "Confidential" or "Classified." The level of discussion and gossip was pretty high and often involved tales from work trips abroad, the antics and adventures of individual senators and congressmen, White House and POTUS rumors, and National Geographic intrigue and adventure. Throw in some mentions of rocks, earthquake studies, communications law, newspaper lore and the ever-present wistful promise of someday having time for a date and you have our dinner conversations.

At St. Matthew's Cathedral, I was invited to join a men's group called Apostolic Action that had been set up to provide emergency assistance to anyone who came to the rectory for help. The men decided they wanted to include a couple of women to protect them from any false sexual accusations that might arise and to help with women's emergencies. Eileen and I became the group's first female team members and protectors.

I was a member of Apostolic Action for nearly three years. It was headed by a priest who knew how to lead a strong, cohesive team and, just as importantly, how to keep the group funded. Each year the twelve of us handled around 700 cases. We worked at the rectory in the evenings in shifts and dealt with basic survival problems—the nuts and bolts of helping people through a crisis: men and women needing a place to sleep, people needing jobs, some needing medical care, most wanting money.

We had a list of cheap rooming houses in the area where we could send people for one or two nights while we helped them find something more long term. If they needed to eat, we sent them to Sholl's Cafeteria on 20th Street NW where they could get free meals. If they needed a quick job, we sent them to the *Post* to stuff inserts in newspapers. For medical care, we sent people with serious problems to the emergency room and those with less serious problems to a doctor in the neighborhood who didn't charge those who couldn't pay. For folks with obvious mental problems, we worked to get them help or institutionalized. (PLEASE do not ask me about the woman who claimed the Rockefeller family was stealing sand from in front of her family's seaside home in New Jersey and shipping it to Saint John Island, an Island in the Caribbean that happened to be owned by the Rockefellers. She wanted us to help her sue them and she wanted her sand back.) Several times we worked with the Immigration and Naturalization Service to help get people back to their home country—or to keep others from being deported.

When I started working with Apostolic Action, I was eighteen. Because of my own survival years, I didn't find other people's survival issues alien. Now that I was on the other side, the assistance side, I was pleased to put in my time at the rectory. I knew something about how they felt. Sure, there were problems that were beyond my experience. Some people had been in survival mode many more years than I had been. When I wasn't sure how to help, I had the Apostolic Action men backing me up. Also the group met each week to go over cases. It didn't take me long to learn the ropes. If a follow-up was needed as a result of our discussion, we would find the person and give them the additional help. Sometimes we followed up just to make sure the person was okay.

My job at *The Washington Post* was interesting, challenging and felt important on both a large and small scale. It was a tiny part of the overall machinery that consisted of hundreds of other well-defined jobs that had to work in concert in order for the paper to be published daily. We all had the same goal: get *The Washington Post* printed and delivered each morning. I was eighteen years old when I started on the copy desk in the classified advertising department. I was promoted twice in less than a year. I was making a good salary—for a young woman. I was learning that I could do good work and hold my own in the adult job market, and I saw myself working at the paper for a long time.

The *Post* wasn't just a local city newspaper. It had a national and international reputation. It was normal to bump into the likes of Herblock (who had already won two of his three Pulitzer Prizes for his editorial cartoons), Ben Bradlee (then managing editor and later known for his role in guiding the *Post* coverage for Watergate and the Pentagon Papers), and Katherine Graham (the publisher). Actually, Mrs. Graham and I were frequent elevator companions. There was a service elevator close to my desk and Mrs. Graham's office on the floor above me. My fond memory of her is that she didn't pull rank when I stepped in the elevator. She'd just say hello, ask what floor I wanted and push the button for me.

The classified advertising department included 300 women sitting at desks in one huge, open room. They answered the phones, typed up the ads and sent them to the copy desk by way of a conveyer belt system that ran beside the desks. This was the era of manual typewriters and cradle phones so there was a distinctive sound of clacking and ringing that went on all day. (At the end of the day, I'd leave work and hear the sounds in my head for hours.)

The department functioned within a framework of three major deadlines each day: (1) the deadline for ads running the next day, (2) for ads running the following day or future dates, (3) for killing (canceling) or correcting an already running ad. Deadlines were not negotiable. If something needed to go down to the composing room (via a pneumatic tube connection) and we missed the deadline by less than a minute, the guys in composing room would reject it and shoot the tube back to us immediately. If this annoyed us refined young ladies on the copy desk, we'd stuff someone's leftover lunch sandwich into the tube and send that sucker back down just to let them know we were not happy.

Besides processing ads, we kept a running daily ad-line total. This may sound trivial, but it was one of the more important things the copy desk supplied. First, there was the ongoing, never-ending competition between the *Post, The New York Times,* the *Los Angeles Times* and the *Chicago Tribune* that included who had the most ad lines at the end of the year. Then there was some rule or regulation that required daily newspapers to have a certain ratio of ad lines to news lines. Normally ad-line totals could be projected weeks in advance based on past years' records and sent to the newsroom so that they would know what kind of space to expect each day. But if a big story broke and the newsroom wanted more column space, classified advertising needed to provide more ad lines to go with it. Conversely, if it was an unusually big ad day that took us over our projection, the newsroom had to come up with additional articles to balance the extra ad lines. (Harry, dig out that piece you wrote about horse manure versus hog manure in gardening. It's running tomorrow.) This is where negotiations between the two floors (advertising and newsroom) could get fierce. It wasn't unusual for my supervisor to toss me into the fray by sending me to Ben Bradlee's office with a list of extra line totals we could offer him. I would negotiate a solution that Mr. Bradlee could accept or, if what he wanted was impossible, I would flat out say no. He could be tough, rough, loud, profane, pushy and demanding, but he knew when I was not going to back down. He'd just dismiss me with an "Okay" and I would leave. (Personally, I think this is where my youth worked for my supervisor and me. We knew

Ben Bradlee wasn't going to steamroll and squash a "sweet, young girl.") So my time with the great Ben Bradlee was spent over line fights.

With my second promotion, I became head of the one-person customer service department in charge of 5,000 classified contract advertisers. These were the agencies and businesses who advertised frequently and had special-rate contracts: real estate offices, employment agencies, technology companies, etc. It was my job to decide how much money would be credited back to them for our errors. Some of the errors made me question the level of sobriety in the composing room. Remember, this was the pre-computer era and everything had to be set manually. One morning I got a call from my contact at H.G. Smithy Real Estate about one of their ads that read "H.G. Shitty Real Estate." The other realtors in the city had been calling them all morning to let them know the new company name was boffo. Another company's apartment rental ad read, "wall to wall floors." (I thought it was a good selling point.) Telefunken, a German technology company, was suddenly named "Telefucken" in very large type across the top of their multi-column ad. (They didn't seem to have an American sense of humor about this.)

When I got the customer service desk, the job was over six months behind on processing complaints. My first challenge was to get the job caught up, which I did in about two months by applying new organization and ergonomics, professional trust and common sense. What took my predecessor a half day or more to accomplish now took me about two minutes. Everybody was happy—the customer, the *Post* and me. I authorized an average of $10,000 monthly in credits and I didn't have to spend $30,000 worth of man-hours to do it. The *Post* was happy enough to give me a surprise bonus for my improvements.

WASHINGTON, D.C., IN THE 1960S provided a historical backdrop to my new life. It was an exceptional time for the city. Some have called it the decade of extreme events and emotions, and I agree. It left a deep impression on me that continues to influence my thinking about government, politics and social justice to this day. I lived in Washington from 1963 to 1973, so my decade of extreme events and emotions started with the March on Washington and ended with Richard Nixon's Watergate scandal.

Working for the *Post* and receiving the city's three daily newspapers on my desk each day made it easy to keep up with what was happening. I even had cold-war intrigue in the mix: The rear of the *Post* building and the rear of the Soviet Embassy were separated by a narrow alley. The array of large antennas on the embassy roof made us question: Were the Soviets spying on the *Post?* Were the vases of plastic flowers sitting on the tables in the cafeteria bugged? Were we *Post* employees going to be snatched one day as we walked home and whisked off to the Soviet Union never to be heard from again? We treated the intrigue with humor (sometimes we spoke directly into the plastic flowers in order to "assist" whoever might be listening). But for me, it was tinged with a quiet concern that I wouldn't admit to openly. I just wasn't sure what those Soviets were up to.

Added to this were the inside stories I heard from my friends whose bosses had close connections to the White House and Congress. And then there was the simple fact that I was living in the White House neighborhood. In short, I was in the thick of things.

I call my ten years in Washington my "Forrestine Gump Years" because I was surrounded by national and international newsworthy events and the people who drove those events as I moved through my regular day. This was my home town. It just happened that my neighborhood was in the center of the action. All I had to do was walk down the street and I could witness history—or be snatched by the Soviets.

My Forrestine Gump Years Begin

The huge March on Washington for Jobs and Freedom (its official title) took place on August 28, 1963. News of the march scared the crap out of most of Washington's white residents. They were convinced the marchers were going to riot and rip the city apart. The Sunday of the march, most of the white residents living in the central part of town had evacuated the city. I needed to get across town for a meeting and had to drive down 16th Street to Constitution Avenue to get there. This put me right in the middle of the march activity. Hundreds of buses were parked on both sides of 16th Street. Thousands of African Americans were walking down the sidewalks toward the Mall where the main event was being held. They looked like they had just come from church. I didn't think these people, dressed in their Sunday best, were planning to rip apart the city. It was obvious that the white residents had panicked and convinced themselves that trouble was all that could come from this event. In the end, Martin Luther King, Jr. delivered his famous "I Have a Dream" speech and 250,000 Americans showed the city and the country what an important, inspiring, nonviolent march with a massive crowd in attendance looked like. I did not stop and join the march. To be honest, the size of the crowd intimidated me. Not joining in is a decision I still regret. But I remind myself that I was just seventeen then and I was alone. It was easy to become overwhelmed by the sheer magnitude of what I was seeing. The truth is, that march was safe and I wish I had been braver.

On November 22, 1963, three months after the march, John F. Kennedy was assassinated. I was working at the home improvement company at the time. One of the supervisors came to our office to tell us that Kennedy had been shot and had died. I thought it was a setup for some weird joke and kept waiting for the punchline. When I saw others in the office crying, I knew it wasn't a joke. A president, *my* president, had been assassinated. This reality was alien to me and I couldn't get my head wrapped around it. I was part of the youth generation who had been challenged to think about our country and inspired by Kennedy to try to do something to help. We sat in the office for about a half hour trying to absorb what had happened. Then our boss told us all to go home.

As with the rest of the country, we felt deep shock, pain and loss. For us in Washington, the Kennedys were also our neighbors, members of our family. Their daily rhythms were a regular part of the city's rhythms. Now everyone just stopped and for three days the city was silent. I had recently moved to the first rooming house near St. Matthew's Cathedral and could hear the cadence of the drumming and the sound of the horses hooves as the funeral procession, which included 220 foreign dignitaries, walked from the White House to St. Matthew's Cathedral for the Requiem Mass. Hearing the sounds directly and not from the television coverage only served to further impress on me that this event had actually happened.

For the next few weeks until Jacqueline Kennedy was able to move to her new home in Georgetown, Lyndon Johnson commuted from his house on 52nd Street in northwest Washington to the White House. Each morning and evening I heard the motorcade's sirens as it sped through an intersection a half block from my rooming house. And each time I listened for sounds of disaster. It was tricky for the motorcade to maneuver through the intersection without cars screeching and swerving to get out of the way. There must have been something about that intersection that distorted the sirens' sound, confusing the other drivers. There were times when I saw Johnson's limo slam on its brakes just to avoid a major collision. I was certain our new president was going to be propelled through the windshield. For me, the potential for another disaster only added to the pain and concern I felt during those early days after the assassination.

On February 11, 1964, the city got a much needed change. The Beatles' first U.S. concert took place in Washington. This was two days after their appearance on the Ed Sullivan Show and the concert in D.C. was attended by over 8,000 screaming, crazed fans. I didn't attend nor did I care about the Beatles. Their early music drove me nuts. (If they wanted "to hold her hand" so damn much, why the hell didn't they shut up about it and just reach out and hold her hand?) I had my own concert experiences that were not as loud. I saw Joan Baez, Harry Belafonte and Miriam Makeba several times. They refused to allow tickets to their concerts to sell for more than $5 so they drew big crowds, too.

Around this time, a friend surprised me with tickets to another concert that was also sold out: Andrés Segovia. The audience overflow was seated in several rows on the stage behind Segovia. My first-row stage chair was about ten feet from him. At first I was disappointed to be seated behind him but I quickly realized what an extraordinary experience it was to watch him play from that close proximity and from that unusual angle. I recently ran across a couple of reviews of later Segovia concerts held in D.C. that describe perfectly my memory of the one I attended.

Louise Sweeney, a reviewer for *The Christian Science Monitor,* wrote about a 1980 concert at the Kennedy Center:

> A hush is what Segovia loves. Andrés Segovia, the great Spanish guitarist, is happiest when the audience becomes so caught up in his music that 3,000 people in a concert hall are as quiet as feathers falling on velvet.
>
> It happened here in Washington the other night when Segovia played a sarabande and allegretto by Handel. As one poignant, gold note followed the other at Kennedy Center Concert Hall, a capacity audience sat as quietly as if listening to a whisper that would change their lives. When Segovia finished the Handel, the applause burst like cymbals from the red velvet seats of the orchestra up to the crystal chandeliers of the top balcony.

And Joseph McLellan, a reviewer for *The Washington Post,* wrote on March 8, 1982:

> Andrés Segovia walked slowly across the vast, empty stage of the Kennedy Center Concert Hall last night—the careful walk of a very old man. But when he sat down with his guitar, the years melted away. His fingers showed none of the stiffness visible in his walk. They rippled out arpeggios, or launched a melody, glittering through a cloud of chords, all the way to the back of the enormous hall with every note beautifully formed, perfectly audible. It was, even with a large audience, a private ceremony for two lovers.

I celebrated my concert moment by finally replacing that old, damaged Segovia album with a new one.

On July 2, 1964, President Johnson signed the Civil Rights Act, which ended segregation in public places; banned employment discrimination on the basis of race, color, religion, sex or national origin; and enforced the constitutional right to vote. Civil rights leaders had pushed for this bill for years. To initiate debate on the bill, Johnson gave what many believe is his greatest speech.

> ...rarely at anytime does an issue lay bare the secret heart of America itself...rarely are we met with the challenge...to the values and the purposes and the meaning of our beloved nation. The issue of equal rights for American Negroes is such an issue. And should we defeat every enemy, should we double our wealth and conquer the stars, and still be unequal to this issue, then we will have failed as a people and as a nation.

When it was signed, the remaining echo of sadness from the assassination was replaced with relief and joy throughout the city. At the signing, President Johnson presented one of the first pens he used to Martin Luther King, Jr.

Racial tension in the city had been simmering for many years. Up until 1960, Washington was a small southern town. The arrival of the Kennedy family and its administration moved the city in a cosmopolitan, international direction. But for the residents, there remained a longstanding problem. D.C. did not have home rule. (It still doesn't have home rule.) This meant that Congress controlled everything when it came to running the city. We had a majority African American population living and working in Washington, and many congressional Southerners and their sympathizers did not want those citizens to vote or to take charge of their own city. The congressional committees that controlled the District's budget and made the city's decisions were run by white men; therefore, the laws and services favored whites. For example, the approval for building permits for essential stores such as grocery stores was controlled by Congress and skewed to the white communities. The black communities had fewer grocery stores, lower food quality and higher prices.

Of course, the signing of the Civil Rights Act did not magically wipe away racism. My heart was with the civil rights struggles that were ongoing around the country but my feet were squarely planted in my new life in Washington. My participation in civil rights consisted of consciousness-raising efforts such as singing "We Shall Overcome" about a thousand times at different gatherings around town. (I doubt if anyone's conscience was ever raised by this.) St. Matthew's Cathedral supported a small group of priests who traveled south to participate in voter registration and the civil rights marches. I helped with that support the best I could but I never considered traveling south to join the front lines myself. As for Washington, the underlying racial tension continued to simmer, and the city exploded in 1968.

In October 1964, just prior to the presidential election, there was a big shakeup at the White House and as a result the communications lawyer my friend worked for became a close advisor to President Johnson. The White House and President had to know where the lawyer was any time, day or night. My friend, his secretary, became their personal GPS tracking system. If the President needed him, the White House would call my friend for the relevant information or phone number. (Life has gotten so much easier in situations like this with real GPS tracking and cell phones.) If I was in the apartment at the time a call came in, I had to go into the bathroom, shut the door, run water in the tub and continuously flush the toilet so that I couldn't hear anything that my friend said. (And now you have an example of the finest security technology available in the 1960s.)

In November 1964, I was eighteen and eligible to vote for the first time. Thanks to the Civil Rights Act, District residents were allowed to vote that year for the first time, as well. Voter turnout was huge. I registered and then voted for Lyndon Johnson. (Barry Goldwater, his opponent, scared the crap out of me. I thought he was going to drop a bunch of nuclear bombs as soon as he got into office.) I worked in the newsroom the night of the election answering phones and giving out the results. It was a crazy scene. The updated results came through the teletype every half hour on twenty-foot long runs of paper listing each district across the country. We'd spread the sheets on the floor so that everyone had access to the latest information. The phones rang constantly. The calls were primarily from Hill staffers wanting to know if their guy had won and if they, the staff, still had a job. That night I also learned that Shirley Povich, the famous *Post* sports reporter, was a man. When I answered his phone and said "*She* wasn't available at the moment," the person on the other end gently informed me that she was a he. It was obvious the caller couldn't believe an employee of *The Washington Post,* did not know who Shirley Povich was. (Well, I didn't. So get over it.)

On November 27, 1965, there was another big march on the Mall—the March on Washington for Peace in Vietnam. It was organized by SANE (the Committee for a Sane Nuclear Policy) and 250,000 protesters attended. The city was starting to become old hat at this and didn't evacuate. I was aware of the war because of what I was reading in the newspapers but I didn't attend the march. I still believed that our president knew what he was doing. (Stop laughing.)

IN JUNE 1966, I MADE A MAJOR personal decision. One minute the thoughts surrounding this decision had not entered my mind. The next minute, I decided I *must* travel to Europe. I didn't know why; I only knew that it was important that I go.

My initial plan was to request leave without pay and travel throughout Europe for a month. Precisely which month was negotiable, depending on the most convenient time in light of my job. Because I already had two weeks paid vacation due me, I was only asking for two additional weeks without pay. Since I would be traveling to Europe and not to some nearby beach, requesting the extra two weeks seemed reasonable. I now had over $1000 in savings and, if I was careful, I could pay for the trip's expenses and keep my apartment. I was sure one of my friends would be willing to take Eloise for a month.

The next day I explained to my boss what I wanted to do. He thought about it for a whopping two seconds and said no. There wasn't anyone who could take over my job for a month. Suddenly I had become indispensable. I tried to explain how I thought we could pull this off but he didn't want to hear it. I said, "Fine" and walked out.

When I returned to my desk, I ripped apart my wall calendar and taped the individual months on the front of my filing cabinets. Then I closed my eyes and tossed my pencil dart-like. The pencil marked January 7, 1967. I made a new decision. On January 7, 1967 I would be departing for Europe—for a year.

That week I told my supervisor my plans and asked him not to repeat them to our boss. The *Post* required that I give two weeks' notice and that was what I planned to do. In December, I would tell the man who couldn't survive without me for a month that in two weeks I would be leaving my job. My supervisor happened to not like our boss very much either so he was more than willing to go along with the plan. We decided that I should begin training someone, giving us over five months to get my replacement ready. We picked one of the women on the copy desk whom we both felt had what it took to keep up with the job. She was pleased to hear the news and she also agreed to keep my secret.

On December 10, 1966, I passed a major milestone. It was my birthday and I was now twenty-one. *I was legal.* I was an official adult. I've noticed over the years that many young people celebrate their twenty-first birthday by getting legally drunk. All I could think about when I became twenty-one was that now I could sign my own contracts—finally. It was the last hurdle I had to deal with since leaving Upperco. First I wasn't sixteen and couldn't legally work. Then when I pretended to be sixteen, I had to forge the permission paper to make it legal for me to work. When I became sixteen, I no longer needed to pretend but I still needed to forge. When I became eighteen, I could work legally without the forged permission paper. But I still had to get my rental contract co-signed by Isadore because I was too young (and, I assumed, too irresponsible) for contracts. Now I was twenty-one years old and I could legally work and sign my own contracts. Happy birthday to me.

Something unexpected and weird happened that day, as well. I received a gift—a pearl necklace in a satin lined leather case—from Isadore with a handwritten note that read, "For 12/10." (That's the sum total of what he wrote.) We had not spoken in years and I had not received a birthday call, card or gift from him since leaving Upperco. I had no idea what to think about this turn of events. Did it mean he was seeking a thaw in our relationship? Did it mean that he, too, thought his daughter becoming twenty-one was special? Did it mean he was breathing a sigh of relief and was no longer legally required to pretend he was my custodian? I put the pearls in a drawer, sent him a thank you note that was polite but neutral in tone and decided to wait for him to make the next move, if there was to be a next move. I did not hear from Dorothy that day but she hadn't acknowledged my birthday since I was about twelve. Also she didn't know where I was living any more than I knew where she was living.

I had two nice surprises before leaving my job in January. At the company Christmas party, I won a small travel-size camera. I had never won anything in a drawing before so I suddenly felt charmed. Even though Mrs. Graham didn't know I was leaving when she handed me my prize, I still felt it was a sign that she would approve—and I was to take lots of photos. Clearly the gods were cheering me on.

The personnel department provided the second surprise. When I gave them my two-week notice, they said that when I returned from my trip I should stop by. If there was an opening, they would like to consider me for the newsroom. Now, that was a shock. It wasn't easy getting hired into the newsroom. Generally interns had to have a degree in journalism. I didn't have any college experience. I said I'd be sure to stop in and left feeling honored and appreciated.

Chapter 8

My Gap Year Launches
1967

I FARMED OUT ELOISE, gave up my apartment and job (with more than a little trepidation), resigned from Apostolic Action, said goodbye to my friends (who thought I was crazy but cheered me on all the same), and on January 6th, I departed for Europe with my new passport, $1,500 in travelers checks, two suitcases and a copy of *Europe On $5 a Day.*

Here's what I knew about Europe when I left: nothing. Well, maybe a little more than nothing. I knew there was a big clock in London. I knew the Eiffel Tower was in Paris. I knew the Vatican was located in Rome. I knew how to say "yes," "no," "thank you," "please" and "open the door" in French.

I knew nothing about art. A friend decided I needed a quick art tutorial to prepare properly for Europe and dragged me for my first visit to the National Gallery of Art. It was a painful experience. I spent about two hours getting yanked from one huge room full of paintings to the next. "These are the schools of paintings." "These are the big-deal artists everyone should know." "This is the most popular artist." "These are the artists no one cares much about." "Look at that exquisite brush work!" On and on it went. By the time we finished I was exhausted, nauseous and had a headache. I left for Europe still not knowing anything about art.

I was equally knowledgeable about history. I knew there had been a second world war but thought that happened fifty or sixty years prior. Way before my time. (It actually ended just twenty-one years prior to my departure.) I knew that German Nazis had killed millions of Jews including, most likely, members of my family.

(Many years later I found out that sixteen family members in Poland and Russia had not survived the Holocaust.) This was about the extent of what I knew about history.

I was about to enter one of the world's greatest centers of culture, history, science and politics and the best I can say for my preparedness is that I was a clean slate. Because I already had a fair amount of experience stepping forward into the unknown, I was nervous but not overwhelmed. It was all new and everything was sure to be an adventure (said I many times to myself).

> Note: I kept a journal on the trip and I put together an extensive scrap book soon after returning to Washington. The following account of my Gap Year, which I embarked on fifty years ago, is brought to you courtesy of these two sources combined with my memory, Wikipedia and Google.

SS *American Press*

One of my co-workers at the *Post* told me that the most cost-efficient transportation for crossing the Atlantic was by freighter. On December 12, 1966, I purchased a first class eastbound ticket for $207 on the SS *American Press,* departing at New York City's North River Pier 59, "on or about" January 6, 1967, at ("call to confirm time") for Liverpool. There was no arrival date on my ticket. I was told we would be sailing for approximately ten days. Obviously I wasn't traveling on a luxury liner where the ship's primary business and schedule revolves around its passengers. This freighter's primary business revolved around the safe delivery of printed matter and parcel post to Ireland. The schedule was set accordingly. I just happened to be tagging along for the ride.

On Friday, January 6th, I showed up at Pier 59 an hour before the confirmed 2 P.M. departure time. Here's a bit of history about Pier 59 that I did not know that day. The *Titanic* was destined for this pier when she sank. The *Carpathia* dropped off the *Titanic's* lifeboats at Pier 59 before going back south to Pier 54 to unload the passengers and survivors that she had rescued. I don't think this would have been especially soothing information to know when I departed from Pier 59. Sometimes ignorance really is bliss.

One of the ship's officers greeted me, helped me to my room and gave me a brief tour of the main deck, including the location of the all-important officers' dining room. After leading me back to my room, giving me the meal schedule and telling me to make myself comfortable, he left. (He didn't mention the *Titanic.*)

I decided to do as I was told and concentrate on making myself comfortable. Otherwise, standing alone in a strange room on a big boat in the middle of wherever would have overwhelmed me and frozen me in place. A huge gift fruit basket and telegrams from several of my friends were sitting on the desk. That helped me to feel not quite so alone. My first-class room (the only class they offered) and my home for approximately the next ten days was large, with two beds, two dressers, a sink, a desk and chair, two closets, two portholes, and a large bathroom with toilet and shower. The beds had a wooden frame that extended above the mattress about four inches, which I assumed kept passengers from rolling out while on the high seas. The decor was freighter chic—all the necessities and no frills.

We departed sometime after 2 P.M. That's when I was first hit by the strangest thought: I was actually leaving my country. I didn't know how to process that thought, that realization. I decided to ignore it and just let this "sensation of strange" take care of itself. I knew this was the first of many times I would not know how to process something. I was two hours into the trip and already I had experienced a number of firsts: my first pier, my first ship, my first fruit basket, my first telegrams, my first experience moving out to sea, my first departure from my country. In a couple of hours I would be off to my first meal on a ship. Time for a nap.

I reported to the dining room at the appointed hour. There were about twenty officers already seated, some eating, some waiting to be served. The overall atmosphere was both friendly and focused. The ease and familiarity of their comments to one another made it clear they had worked together for years. It was also clear some had a job to do getting this ship out to sea and were not about to linger over their meal. When I walked in they pointed me to the table assigned to passengers. I was surprised to discover that there were only two other passengers. I was also surprised to discover that I was the only girl on board. We three passengers introduced ourselves and proceeded to have a pleasant supper together. They had previously traveled by freighter and spent most of the time telling me about their past sea adventures. I can't tell you any more about these gentlemen because this was the last time I saw them for the rest of the trip, except during our mandatory emergency lifeboat drill. The first couple of days they stayed in their rooms. After that I was told they were seasick and did not want to come out of their rooms. (So much for hardened sea voyagers.) I had the passengers' dining table to myself until several officers joined me.

What I can say something about are the meals. Because this was a freighter, I had assumed the food served at each meal would be the same for everyone. At breakfast, for example, we'd all be eating scrambled eggs. No other options. Instead it was like a restaurant with a menu that included a bunch of options. The menu changed daily and I could pick as many options as I wanted.

Sunday, January 8th
BREAKFAST
Fresh grapefruit ~ orange juice
Rolled oats ~ assorted dry cereals
Eggs to order: scrambled, fried, boiled, poached
Plain or tomato omelette
Grilled ham, fried potatoes
Hot griddle cakes ~ buttered toast
Coffee ~ tea ~ milk
DINNER
Table celery ~ plain olives
Chicken noodle soup with saltine crackers
Roast tom turkey, dressing, gravy, cranberry sauce
Beef steak and kidney pie
Boiled ox tongue with barbecue sauce
Bacon and tomato sandwich
Candied sweet potatoes, mashed white potatoes, garden peas, fresh cauliflower
Banana cream pie
Coffee ~ tea ~ milk

SUPPER

Combination salad
Soup of the day (chicken noodle)
Grilled sirloin steak to order, fried onions
Steamed frankfurters, sauerkraut
Welsh rarebit on toast
Baked potatoes, steamed rice, baked squash, fresh lima beans
Cookies ~ vanilla ice cream with chocolate sauce
Coffee ~ tea ~ milk

This is probably the closest we came to a luxury liner experience. In essence, we ate our way across the Atlantic Ocean. (I did not eat the boiled ox tongue with barbecue sauce. I have my limits.)

After dinner that first evening, I was invited to have a cup of coffee with Captain Rappel, our commanding officer (I wasn't sure if I was supposed to salute) and several of the other officers. They seemed genuinely pleased to have me on board. They told me the ship's three critical rules: I was to stay on the main deck and under no circumstances was I to venture below deck. It might be dangerous. (It might be dangerous?) I was not to enter the ship's pilot house unless accompanied by an officer. It was against regulations. Finally, don't skip any meals. I needed to keep food in my stomach. If I got seasick I needed something in my stomach to throw up.

I left the dining room and stood by the deck railing watching the New York City skyline recede and the American shore slowly pass by—very slowly pass by. We were still in some river somewhere and it seemed like we were just drifting. At this speed, I figured we would reach England around March. When I awoke the next morning, we were out to sea.

The ship's activity quickly settled into an easy rhythm. While the officers and crew got on with their jobs, I wrote in my journal and sketched whatever part of the main deck drew my interest—on colder, windy days, whatever I saw out my portholes. We had a small flock of seagulls that hung out on the mast and stayed with us the entire trip. Apparently they were hitchhiking to England. I spent the first few days sleeping a lot thanks to the ship's gentle rocking. I was on the world's largest water bed. I also followed instructions and ate.

For the lifeboat drill, it was all hands on deck, including the crew. Once I saw the crew, I understood the captain's warning that it might be dangerous for me to venture below deck. They may have been fine fellows (I'm giving them the benefit of the doubt), but they looked like a bunch of guys that the shipping company found passed out in a back alley from a two-week bender. They stared at me a lot—and I inched closer to the officers. Once the drill was over, they quietly disappeared again below deck.

The dining room was the central gathering place for the officers when they weren't on duty. Several had daughters around my age so it didn't take long before I was surrounded by a bunch of overprotective fathers who kept warning me about the things I needed to watch out for during my trip. I'm not sure any of them would have felt easy about their daughters leaving for Europe for a week, let alone a year.

They each had tales from their twenty to thirty years' experience at sea and during the long stretches of boredom in the afternoons they talked and I listened. They became my teachers and I was their willing student. It seemed like there were specific things they wanted me to know. I needed to understand that the sea and its power were not to be taken lightly. And a good tugboat captain was worth his weight in gold. To emphasize their points, they told me about the time they were docking at a pier without the aid of a tugboat. The freighter was slowly moving into place when it was hit by a strong water current that slammed the ship against the pier, wiping out the entire pier. As the lessons became more advanced, I was taught to plot an exact fix using two celestial bodies, the horizon, a sextant and some math. (I couldn't begin to explain it to you today. Thank god for GPS and Google Maps.)

On the third day, I was escorted to the pilot house and asked if I'd like to take whale watch duty for an hour each afternoon. I spotted dolphins from time to time but didn't see any whales. I was also taught to steer the ship and shown how to stay on course. Periodically I was the ship's helmsman for about a half hour. There was an instrument next to the wheel that showed when the ship moved on (or off) course. All I had to do was keep the needle between two lines. I proved to be quite good at doing this, if I don't mind saying so myself.

On the fifth day, the sea got choppy. I was told there was a major storm about 1,000 miles ahead of us, and depending on the route they needed to take to avoid the brunt of the storm, we may be docking in either Liverpool or Southampton. They'd let me know a day or two before we docked. I didn't care. It was still England.

Our ship's rocking increased as the waves increased. Now I understood the purpose of the wooden frame around my bed. I had to devise new storm skills: wave walking, wave showering and wave souping. With wave walking, I relied on momentum and gravity. If I was walking toward the bow, it was now easier to move when the ship was on the down side of a wave and leaning toward the bow. While the ship was on the up side of a wave and leaning back toward the stern, I'd stop walking and wait a few seconds for the ship to rock forward again. In essence, I walked downhill "with the wind at my back" instead of trying to walk uphill "against a strong headwind."

Taking a shower became tricky. The hot water and cold water were stored in two separate tanks so when the ship leaned one way, the shower water was all cold. When it leaned in the other direction, the water was all hot. I had to step away from the shower during the two extremes and then step back under when the ship was in the middle of its roll and both hot and cold water could mix again.

In the dining room, each chair was anchored in place with a big chain hooking it to the floor. The dining tables had a short wooden edge (similar to the bed frames) that kept dishes and food from sliding off. Cups were half filled. Soup was served in bowls with flanged rims. For wave souping, we placed a finger beneath the rim and moved our bowl up and down opposite the ship's movement to keep the soup from sloshing out.

I was determined not to get seasick (despite several medium bouts of queasiness). I knew the officers had a pool and were betting on when I'd go down. No matter how I felt, I showed up for every meal. I was not going to let the storm take me down and no one was going to win that pool. Stubbornness and sheer determination kept me on my feet.

The men assured me that a freighter was safer in a storm than a passenger ship. A freighter's schedule wasn't set in stone and they could slow down, change their route or anchor in a nearby port to wait out a storm, thus reducing damage to the ship or its cargo. Passenger ships tended not to slow down in order to keep to their schedule, which apparently was set in stone. Even in serious storms, they tended to maintain speed and crash through the waves. To prove their point, the men described the serious damage that passenger ships had sustained during past storms.

After three days, the sea had settled down quite a bit and Liverpool was again our destination. I saw the first signs of land in the distance when we passed the coast of Ireland. Two days before docking, a smaller boat approached and moved alongside us so that a new guy could board. He was the pilot who would take the ship into the Port of Liverpool, through the locks and to the dock. (I was told that he didn't have to board so early but he really liked the pie on our ship.)

The news about our sister ship that had sailed out of New York three days before us wasn't good. They couldn't avoid the storm and took a direct hit. The ship sustained damage and the crew mutinied. (You read that right. They mutinied. A modern-day mutiny.) They were now docked at some island port for repairs and would be sailing out once they hired a new crew. They would be arriving in Liverpool about a week behind us. (What was that you guys said about freighter safety?)

The ship's purser met with me after lunch to give me a tutorial on British currency and to exchange several of my traveler's checks. Welcome to the world of pounds and shillings. It had its own logic that did not in any way resemble the logic behind U.S. dollars and cents. This was going to be a challenge. Along with the tutorial and a few currency-identification practice drills, he gave me a British currency pamphlet complete with photos. I felt I would be referring to this throughout my entire stay in England. He also gave me the address of Parry's, a small hotel that he recommended in Liverpool. They had good breakfasts.

Docking at Liverpool turned out to be an impressive process to watch. There was nothing simple or ordinary about the procedure. The pilot, the officers, the crew, the tugboats and the port crew all worked together to get this huge ship docked. Three big tugboats maneuvered us through a series of locks, raising the ship about seven feet per lock, just to get us to the Liverpool docks and pier. I already had an appreciation for tugboat pilots, and with the port's intricacy and tightness, I now understood why we also needed our expert, pie-eating pilot on board. It took us hours to move through the locks and to finally get docked at the pier.

While I was packing, getting my passport checked and preparing to depart, I remembered how alien and odd everything felt when I first arrived on the *American Press.* Now here I was getting ready to step on dry land again and I didn't want to leave. I had been adopted by these men, my room truly had become my home and I still had some fruit left in my basket. I was already homesick. I thanked everyone I could find and got off the ship as quickly as I could. I had to keep my feet moving forward if I was going to get on with this trip. Once I disembarked, I found a taxi waiting at the dock. The cabbie asked in a wonderful English accent, "Where would you like to go, love?" He called me "love." Yep. I was going to be just fine.

Chapter 9

Liverpool to London

PARRY'S HOTEL WAS A NARROW, converted three-story row house. The owner met me at the door and could not have been friendlier. He helped me haul my suitcases to my room and told me about a small restaurant down the street where I could go for dinner. My room was pleasantly simple—and cold. For warmth, I would need to pump a shilling (14¢) into a small space heater. When I came back from the restaurant, I pumped the first of many shillings during my stay in England.

I left New York with no itinerary. I wanted to see where the trip took me. But because I needed to be careful about money, I also wanted to apply logic to my travels. That way I would not waste money backtracking and zigzagging all over the place. So from Liverpool, where was the next logical city to aim for? London, of course. My next question: When would I depart from Liverpool?

Mr. Parry assumed I would be leaving for London right away. Throughout my trip across the Atlantic the officers had been telling me not to bother spending time in Liverpool. There was nothing to see. I found myself defending Liverpool. Surely the Liverpudlians would create an interesting home city with a few sites worth a tourist's visit. It seemed unfair, even rude, to say there was nothing worthwhile for me to see. According to Mr. Parry, I had already seen Liverpool's finest: the Port of Liverpool. After the hotel breakfast, which lived up to its advance billing, I set out to walk around the city and prove everyone wrong.

The day was grey, overcast and cold—really cold. A friend at the *Post* had warned me about the unusual winter cold in Great

Britain. I had checked the *Post*'s international temperature chart for weeks and the daily range for London seemed pretty "normal" to what I experienced in Washington. But now I found myself colder than I had felt in a long time. I think the humidity made the cold sink through my body and settle into my bones. I could actually feel cold bones inside my slightly warmer body.

I walked around. I went into a pub for lunch. I walked around some more. Then I came to the conclusion that they were right. It wasn't that Liverpool was a nothing city. (I was determined not to give up my protective fight for the Liverpudlians.) It's just that on this particular day everything was grey and average feeling while lacking promise, interest—and warmth. I returned to the hotel and told Mr. Parry I would be leaving for London the next day.

London

The train trip took about three hours. When I got to the Euston Station in London, I consulted my copy of Frommer's *Europe On $5 a Day*. If you're not familiar with this book, let me say a few things about it. Back in the late 1950s and early 1960s Arthur Frommer and his wife, Hope, felt that if we Americans were willing to travel like most Europeans whose income was much less than the typical American income, Europe would be open to more people (like myself). This is precisely what I wanted to do. I wanted to travel like the Europeans, not the Americans. Frommer's book, which quickly became the bible for most travelers, had a chapter on each major European city (Liverpool was not included) and described its hotels, restaurants, tours, museums, galleries and other attractions, all with an emphasis on economy and simple quality. In short, *$5* gave me a starting point for each city. After that, it was up to my feet and walking shoes. However, for me *$5* had a downside. It had great information that I could read in the evenings but I did not want to haul that 550-page book around all day. The first thing I did when I got to a new city was buy a street map.

From Euston Station, I called and booked a room at a bed and breakfast in a private home in a residential area of London. Traveling in January was working in my favor. I suspected it would be a lot more challenging to find a room in any of the places listed in *$5* during tourist season.

The cab dropped me off in front of a large home that, at one time, must have been an elegant, upper-middle-class family home. The woman who now owned and ran the place was gracious and not British. From her accent I thought she might be German. She led me to my room—another frigid room—and showed me how to operate the space heater. I was going to need more shillings. This woman, friendly though she may have been, had an obsession that drove me nuts. She was a firm believer in fresh air. Each morning after I headed out, she would come into my room and throw open the windows. I'd lose any warmth left over from heating the room the night before. When I returned in the evening I'd have to close the windows and start cranking the heater again. I asked if she would mind not opening my windows but she insisted it was much healthier to have fresh air—lots of fresh air. I backed off, thinking that perhaps this was a British custom I'd just have to get used to.

The upside to this was that it got me up and out right after breakfast. Why linger in a refrigerator. Each morning I hopped on a red double-decker bus and rode into the center of the city. I loved that ride so much that I never bothered to figure out how to use the London Underground. It gave me a chance to experience how Londoners went about their everyday life. The people on the bus were polite and considerate, not just to me but to one another, and the fellow who took our ticket money was always cheery and called all the girls and women "love."

Okay, this will give you an idea about how much I didn't know about London in 1967. I thought Piccadilly Circus was an actual circus with clowns and lions and high-wire acts. I headed there first because I wanted to see the circus. In actuality, Piccadilly Circus is a noncircular traffic interchange that links several major streets in the middle of London. It had lots of traffic, lots of pedestrians and lots of neon signs advertising Coca-Cola, Wrigley's Spearmint Gum, Air India, shops, theaters, businesses and restaurants. No lions or clowns. That was a bit of a let down.

Next, I walked to Trafalgar Square. Maybe this would be more interesting. I found a big open square with a tall column, Nelson's Column, lots of pigeons and more pedestrians.

I needed to regroup and get off London's "Circles and Squares" tour. But this raised the question: What kind of tour was I on? Trying to wrap my mind around all the history that surrounded me would only give me a headache. So I knew I wasn't on a history tour. I wasn't interested in pursuing a nightlife and sitting around in pubs all night. I didn't care about fancy food, although many would argue that there is no fancy food in Great Britain. I didn't find the food boring, which I think illustrates well that I did not care about fancy food. I wasn't drawn to shopping, even though there was not a shortage of stores. I guess the truth is I was not drawn to shopping because I didn't care about fashion. So what did I want from this trip? I walked over to St. James Park (it was near Trafalgar Square), found a bench in a quiet spot and sat. Time to think.

I sat on that bench for a couple of hours but didn't spend one minute thinking about my pressing questions. As soon as I sat down I started looking at the park. I observed. I observed the subtle winter colors and the winter rhythms of the trees and bushes. I imagined how they might look in the summer. I watched birds fly from tree to tree to bush and back. The ducks that waddled by. The flower gardens that were down for the winter. The walkway that cut through and the occasional person hustling along to some appointment or others out for a leisurely stroll. The more I looked, the more detail I saw. The more detail I saw, the more fascinating the park became. It was as if I was looking at a large mosaic. I thought about my painful introduction to the National Gallery of Art and my friend saying with unrequited appreciation, "Look at that exquisite brushwork!" Here in St. James Park, as I observed the winter detail and its patterns, I could say with awe and appreciation, "Look at that exquisite brushwork!"

I came away with the answer to my questions: What kind of tour was I on? What did I want from this trip? Well, now I knew I did not want to be dragged around London by guidebooks and expectations. I wanted to observe. I wanted to watch patterns form and move around me. My time in London was going to revolve primarily around quiet observation. If I was going to see the things that made London the city that it is, I would have to take the time to look. I'd let the city and its people show me what it's like to be a Londoner. No guide book, including *$5*, was going to give me this kind of insight or experience. I was going to become the new "London Lurker."

I knew I'd have to move indoors each day before frostbite set in. As the "Indoor London Lurker," I would only visit the galleries, museums and public sites that intrigued me. And I would stay for however long I felt interested and engaged—not a minute more. Otherwise, boredom and disinterest would override my ability to observe and I'd just be wasting time.

With my new direction and resolve, I felt freed. I stayed in London for two and a half weeks and using my street map to plot daily walking routes, I saw more than I thought possible. It would be fair to say that I managed to consider every major site in London but most of them did not pass muster. Still I left London with special memories that have lasted fifty years.

BIG BEN: Yep, it's a big clock all right. I synchronized my watch with Ben and stood there long enough to hear the half hour, three-quarters hour and hour chimes. I thought, "How special is this? I'm actually setting my watch to Big Ben."

PARLIAMENT AND THE HOUSE OF COMMONS: Because there wasn't a crush of tourists waiting to get in to the Visitors' Gallery, I was able to stay for about three hours listening to the day's debate and observing the action. I'm not going to pretend I understood what was going on. I hardly understood what was being said. The Minister of Power answered the first twenty-two questions. Next the Minister of Technology answered the twelve questions, followed by the Chancellor of the Exchequer, the Minister of Housing and Local Government, the Secretary of State for Commonwealth Affairs, The Secretary of State for Foreign Affairs, the Secretary of State for Defence, the Minister of Transport, the Secretary of State for the Home Department, the President of the

Board of Trade, and the Minister of Land and Natural Resources. Finally, the Prime Minister, Harold Wilson, answered the final twenty-eight questions. We visitors were given an Order Paper that listed the day's scheduled questions. Even with the cheat sheet, I didn't understand the questions or the answers. Example: "To what extent gas supplies from the North Sea are being held up by foreign companies refusing to agree to the British Government's price per therm; and what steps he [the Minister of Power] is taking to get over this difficulty." Members would grumble, mumble, groan, challenge, shout disapproval and voice approval while the Minister was talking. The Ministers and Prime Minister would sometimes have to shout over the racket and take on the dissenters. I was watching a British free-for-all. Then the noise would die down to a low-level grumble that sounded like everyone's stomach growling in unison. It would pick up again when the next slightly controversial statement was made. (And our elected officials think our press conferences and town halls are grueling. Good lord.)

WESTMINSTER ABBEY: Founded in 960 A.D. It is huge, ornate, with incredible chandeliers and stained glass windows. It contains burial sites and memorials for the famous and long-dead—kings, queens, Geoffrey Chaucer, Henry Purcell, Oliver Cromwell, Isaac Newton....It's also the site of every coronation since 1066 and most royal weddings since 1100. On the overcast day I visited, it was dark inside and I kept wishing I could turn the lights on. One thing in particular that caught my attention was King Edward's Chair. It has been used at every coronation since 1308—and it looks it. It's weathered, distressed and looks like some royal scamps carved their initials into the wood. Despite my decision not to get lost in history, I left the Abbey impressed by longevity and began to understand just how young America is. If a building dates back three hundred years in London, the Brits would consider this contemporary housing not worthy of special notice. We consider our buildings that date back a hundred years as something so special that we set it up for tours and include a souvenir shop.

ST. PAUL'S CATHEDRAL: Consecrated in 1300. Also huge but less cave-like than the Abbey and with an impressive, ornate, gold-gilded ironwork screen. Funeral services held there included Lord

Nelson, the Duke of Wellington and Sir Winston Churchill. There were memorials for Florence Nightingale, Samuel Johnson, Lawrence of Arabia, William Blake and Sir Alexander Fleming, among others. It also held the peace services marking the end of the First and Second World Wars.

THE TOWER OF LONDON: The first foundations were laid in 1078. I joined six others for a Yeoman Warder tour. For an hour we were given the history of the Tower, led up and around different towers, past living quarters, down into dungeons, past the Crown Jewels and onto Tower Green where, we were told, many beheadings had occurred.

This is where we met the Royal Ravens, a group of six ravens (actually six plus a spare making it a total of seven) who didn't appear to be concerned about our presence. According to superstition, if the six Tower ravens are lost or fly away, the Crown will fall and Britain with it. To ensure that the birds don't fly away, the flight feathers on one of their wings are clipped. During World War II, only one raven survived the bombing during the Blitz, so Prime Minister Winston Churchill ordered more ravens to be brought in, in order to bring the flock back up to the necessary six. According to our Yeoman Warder, each Tower raven is enlisted as a soldier of the Kingdom and issued an attestation card (enlistment card). As is the case with soldiers, the ravens could be dismissed for unsatisfactory conduct. (Attacking tourists or serial pooping on tourists' heads may be considered unsatisfactory conduct.) At the end of our tour we were allowed to wander around on our own. I chose to watch the ravens. I thought about the long history, the superstition and the expectations that were placed "on the shoulders" of these birds. Should they decide it's time to move on to another city (they'd have to take a bus because of their clipped wings), perhaps get a new mate and start a family away from all the tourists, they'd be responsible for the fall of the Crown and Britain. No pressure there.

THE CHANGING OF THE GUARDS, or how American pragmatism crashed into British pageantry: I had never before witnessed anything like this. The ceremony dates back to 1660 and I suspect it has changed very little since then. Traffic in front of Buckingham Palace was stopped as a band and regiment of about 100 military men led by two horsemen and followed by about eight horsemen marched up the street to the Palace. They were dressed in long, grey winter coats and those tall furry "beaver" hats. The drum major was wearing a gold, white and red brocade outfit (that defied description) and led the band with a long gold staff. Everyone was marching in a precision that said, "We practice this a lot." This is the regiment that is "collecting" the two guardsmen who were about to come off duty. In the meantime, as they paraded through the Palace gate, they were met by a second band and regiment who marched in from a different direction and were there to "drop off" the new guards. The regiments and bands marched around in the Palace courtyard, changing direction and tempo while remaining in perfect precision and not bumping into one another. Somewhere in the midst of all this pageantry the four guards swapped out. To be honest, there was so much going on that I never saw the actual changing of the guards. But at a certain point each regimental group accompanied by their band, drum major and horses left Buckingham Palace and headed back to wherever they came from. Once they cleared the street, the traffic started up again. The whole ceremony lasted 45 minutes. I thought:

1. They do this every day? (Every other day in the winter.)

2. There is no way on God's green earth that we Americans could pull something like this off on a daily basis with all the traffic stopped in the middle of the day in New York City or Washington, D.C. Open warfare complete with guns and live ammunition would break out from our inconvenienced drivers and pedestrians.

3. The precision of the marching showed me these guys really cared about what they were doing and it was their honor to participate in this. I suspected that for us, the American drive for independence and individuality would take over and the unified precision would evaporate into the ether as we moved to the beat of our own drum.

4. Dear Brits: You could make the changing of the guards more time efficient if you just had the two new guards walk up to the guards waiting to go off duty, tap them on the shoulder and say, "We're here, fellas. You can go to the pub now." Think of the inconvenience, money and time you'd save if you eliminated the horses, bands and full regiments complete with those uniforms that are currently required just to switch out two people. The three-century old ceremony you have in place seems a bit over the top—when witnessed by a young, inexperienced American traveler.

This was also my first experience of American tourists in action. They spoke and dressed loudly, jostled one another for better positions, took a ton of photos, complained about not being able to find a bathroom and made other assorted comments that had little to do with what was happening in front of them. I moved toward the quiet end of the crowd and dedicated myself to not traveling as a typical American tourist.

LONDON THEATERS: I discovered that I could purchase standing room or balcony theater tickets for about £1 ($2.83). I took full advantage and saw five first-rate London plays in five beautiful theaters. Before each play began, everyone stood and sang "God Save the Queen." At intermission, those who paid regular price for tickets were served tea in a china cup and saucer. We cut-rate ticket holders could purchase our own tea in a less-than-elegant ceramic mug in the lobby. At one of the theaters, a fellow on staff made an announcement during intermission. He started at one end of the lobby and walked slowly to the other end, loudly and carefully delivering his little speech. I had no clue what this man was saying. I hoped he wasn't saying, "Attention theater patrons. The theater is on fire and everyone will have to file out of the building in an orderly fashion. Thank you." I waited to see what everyone else did and since they were returning to their seats, I assumed he said, "Intermission is over and the play will begin shortly." (It was my first exposure to cockney.)

THE DICKENS HOUSE AND THE OLD CURIOSITY SHOP: I spent hours in Charles Dickens' house and discovered I had a passion for reading manuscripts and letters handwritten by famous dead people. *Pickwick Papers* and *Oliver Twist* were written while Dickens resided at that address and many of the original pages were displayed in glass cases. So here I was in his home, reading original manuscripts in his handwriting, complete with his editing and changes. I felt the generations between us come together and connect, giving me a sense of closeness with the author. He wasn't just another famous dead guy. He was right there in that room sharing his work with me. I half expected someone to enter the room and serve the two of us tea. At closing time they had to toss me out of the place. I celebrated my new passion by walking to The Old Curiosity Shop (yes, there actually is such a place) and purchasing a copy of Dickens' (you guessed it) *The Old Curiosity Shop,* complete with a red faux-leather and gold tooled cover to add a touch of elegance to my unsophisticated eye.

CARNABY STREET: How do I describe Carnaby Street? Back in Washington, I had heard and read articles about London's famous Carnaby Street. In the 1960s, it was *the* center of mod fashion. Even though I wasn't drawn to that style, I wanted to see what the fuss was about. With all the publicity and fame, I expected to find a sizable "Carnaby Boulevard" similar to New York's Fifth Avenue. Instead I found a tiny side street that was too narrow for cars and ran just one block long. My first reaction: "Are you kidding me?" How in the world could this small, cobblestone, alley-sized pedestrian street make such an international splash? It was lined on both sides with tiny shops and boutiques featuring fashionable hippie attire—casual, colorful but with designers' labels. I was determined to purchase some inexpensive thing from Carnaby Street and went on a hunt that proved to be more challenging than I had expected. Carnaby Street was not cheap. I ended up buying a plain white handkerchief—useful, inexpensive and wouldn't take up much room in my luggage. However, my real keepsake (and the primary motivation for my purchase) was the psychedelic printed paper bag the handkerchief came in. That was pure Carnaby Street. After fifty years, I have no idea what happened to the handkerchief, but I still have that bag.

LONDON FASHION: The "older" generation—those over thirty—wore what I would call conservative British fashion. The women wore sensible shoes, wool skirts, sweaters and dresses while the men wore tweed jackets, wool vests and wool trousers. The exception was the Financial District where the men wore blue suits, vests with pocket watches, bowler hats or top hats. I guess it was their uniform. The younger generation of girls, of which I was officially a member in age but not style, wore miniskirts. That wasn't a surprise to me because it was also the fashion in the U.S. at the time. However, these girls took that fashion a step further and wore winter minicoats with their miniskirts. Their legs were bare except for nylons (not thick tights) and exposed to the winter elements. I thought they were crazy. I was trying to keep from freezing and looked like a nun who had the misfortune to join a convent from the Middle Ages. I wore a long black all-weather coat, black boots, a black scarf, black gloves and a black hat. (Black: the color that goes with everything.) I wasn't trendy but I wasn't getting frostbite.

I'D LOVE TO BE ABLE TO REPORT that I was becoming a hardened, seasoned world traveler but truthfully, I got hit with a serious case of homesickness on the day I arrived in London that lingered throughout most of my stay. Despite the many kindnesses I had experienced from the Londoners, I was alone—completely and entirely alone. In the middle of my walks, I'd suddenly realize that there wasn't one person in London who knew me. It was a strange feeling. If I let these feelings overwhelm me, I either had to throw in the towel and head back to Washington where life was familiar and I had friends or I had to suck it up and move forward with the rest of my trip. I could tell that my time in London was coming to an end and ahead I'd face not only new countries with new customs but new languages, as well. I suspected that the feeling of isolation would only become more pronounced as I took my next steps but hoped that over time it would dissipate.

Before I left Washington, a friend (John) gave me the telephone number of an American family he knew in London. He assured me that they would be pleased to have me call and that, most likely, they'd want to show me around London. I had just a few days before I was planning to leave so I thought I would get over my shyness and phone to say hello and pass on John's good wishes. The most gracious, welcoming woman answered the phone and urged me to come over that afternoon so that she could take me out to lunch. (I found out later that John had already written to her about me.) I was completely swept up in this woman's friendly vortex and headed to her place right away.

John's friends, Mary and Peter, were "upper crust" Americans living in a British "upper crust" apartment in the middle of London. Peter worked for *Newsweek* and I believe he was its editor in London. When I entered their apartment, I entered a new British-American world. The apartment was huge with large rooms, high ceilings and a friendly, relaxed but elegant American decor. After a tour, Mary whisked me away for lunch at Marks and Spencer—a large department store that was commonly referred to as "Marks and Sparks." It felt similar to the huge, fancy stores in Washington. Except for the dead rabbits complete with fur and heads hanging from a clothes line at the meat department. That was different. We had a pleasant lunch and then I accompanied Mary as she did some shopping in the store. She didn't buy a rabbit.

Mary talked about what it was like for them to live in London. They had lived there for several years and, for the most part, loved being there—but they missed their old friends and family. I was invited to dinner that evening so that I could meet their daughter. Karen was a few years older than I and was living and working in London on her own. During dinner, after I had regaled them with stories about my landlady's fetish for frigid fresh air, Karen offered for me to stay in her old room until I left London. Before I knew it, Karen and I had collected my stuff and I was moved into an exceptionally nice (warm) bedroom in an exceptionally nice (warm) apartment with an exceptionally nice (warm) family. It was impossible not to be at ease with these people and not be overwhelmed by their kindnesses and inclusion. My sense of isolation didn't gradually dissipate over time. Instead, it disappeared in a proverbial New York minute.

Before leaving, I imposed on Mary one final time. When I packed for my trip, it was for a year that included all four seasons. Consequently, I was hauling around an entire wardrobe—plus the journal, plus *$5*, plus camera and film, and now my Dickens' book and the Carnaby handkerchief and bag. This was a mistake—a big mistake. The two suitcases were too bulky and heavy for me to deal with alone and I was going to have to depend on strangers at every stop to help me get to my next hotel or train. (This was before there were suitcases on wheels.) So I packed what was essential for winter into my smaller suitcase. I'd purchase a few inexpensive items for the following seasons as I went along. My smaller bag was now only half full and, more importantly, I was able to carry it on my own easily. I asked Mary if I could store my monster suitcase with the rest of my clothes in their storage. Once I got back to Washington and had an address I'd send her money to ship it to me. I understood that this request fell under the category "pain in the butt" but Mary agreed, and together we hauled the monster to her storage area.

I DEPARTED LONDON WITH a newly developed appreciation for "deep age." It was not that the people were old. It's their buildings and traditions (and yes, their history) that sometimes made me stop in my tracks. Westminster Abbey was founded in 960. St. Paul's Cathedral was consecrated in 1300. The first foundations for the Tower of London were laid in 1078. The Changing of the Guards and Royal Ravens date back to 1660. Carnaby Street was constructed in 1685. In comparison, we were a young nation. Columbus sailed the ocean blue in 1492, more than 500 years *after* Westminster Abbey was founded. Jamestown, our first permanent British settlement, was founded in 1607. Our Declaration of Independence was signed in 1776. Our Constitution was signed in 1787. When I thought about deep roots I now thought about London. The only thing we had that could be called "deep roots" was the history and remaining traditions of our Native people.

My visits to Westminster Abbey and St. Paul's Cathedral led to a decision that I made for the rest of my trip. These cathedrals were constructed for a reason. They were places of worship and they addressed the needs of their community and country. When I visited them I looked at their architecture and thought about the famous people who were buried there but I didn't understand how the architecture connected with the cathedrals' function. I was looking at the buildings as history and art museums, which disconnected me from the buildings' original purpose. I decided I would try to attend a service or mass in each cathedral I visited after I left London and experience the buildings come alive. I wanted to see form married to function.

As for the Londoners, I left with appreciation and gratitude for their friendliness, kindness and courtesy, even toward a stranger and novice traveler such as myself. They gave me a sense of safety that I had not experienced in the United States and I felt myself begin to relax and open in new ways. I was also impressed with their patience and care when it came to upholding and continuing tradition—i.e., maintaining their deep roots.

Chapter 10

Amsterdam

I HEADED TO THE LONDON train station for the start of a three-stage trip to Amsterdam. I decided to take the overnight train and ferry for the adventure and convenience—it would get me to Amsterdam by mid-morning and I wouldn't be "dumped" out in the middle of a new city late in the day. On the evening of January 26th, I was on a train heading to Harwich.

At Harwich we boarded a ferry, my first return to water travel since the *American Press.* I'd like to say it was my return to the sea but this was a ferry and not a big ocean freighter and we were crossing the English Channel and not the Atlantic. No matter. I was going to be on something that was floating on water and that made me happy—until I boarded the ferry. As I said, this wasn't a freighter. It was a mini-version of an ocean liner carrying a bunch of passengers who were determined to party their way across the channel. I felt like I was on a child's toy. I stood on the deck near the railing watching the water as well as all the human activity swirling around me for about an hour. I even managed to find a buffet for a late dinner. Finally I retired to my berth. When I awoke early the next morning, the ferry was docked in Hook of Holland. After a quick visit back to that buffet for breakfast, I left the ferry, moved through passport control and walked over to the waiting train that was headed for Amsterdam.

It sounds like I knew what I was doing but I was actually figuring everything out on the fly. *$5* provided the details for setting up the trip and purchasing the right tickets. For the ins and outs of how to navigate my way through the trip I followed signs, watched crowd movement and applied a little logic at each juncture.

En route to Amsterdam we passed several large farmhouses with thick thatched roofs. (Thatched roofs keep the rain out of the house? Really? Answer: yes.) I later learned that the barn and family livestock occupied the center section of those large houses. The farmer could fall out of bed, get dressed, open the bedroom door and say hello to Bessie.

It was close to noon when I arrived in Amsterdam. No question about it, Amsterdam was not London—and the Netherlands was not Great Britain. One city was not a lesser version of the other, they were just different. I was now in the land of guilders, not shillings. I exchanged some money at the train station, bought a street map, consulted *$5* for places to stay and decided on a small hotel within walking distance from the station. I didn't call ahead because I didn't feel like tackling a new phone system, so I set out with my suitcase and street map in hand in search of Ruyschstraat. The walk gave me a chance to look around and get a feel for the city. I had a feeling I was going to like Amsterdam.

My off-season luck was still holding. Before I knew it, I was checked into another cold room with a coin-operated space heater. (Guilders. I need more guilders!) I had settled in and was on my way out the door when the hotel manager stopped me and asked me to join him in the dining room for a moment. (I just got to this city. Did I do something wrong already? Was I about to be deported?) He sat down with me and told me he had some sad news to pass on. Three U.S. astronauts (Gus Grissom, Edward White and Roger Chaffee) had died in a flash fire during a test aboard their Apollo I spacecraft at Cape Kennedy earlier that day. He thought I would want to know and said he was sorry about the news. This conversation struck me in several ways.

1. He made it a point to tell me because he thought it was something I'd want to know. He didn't just decide to mind his own business, as we would say, and assume that I would not care.

> 2. The tragedy had occurred about twelve hours before he talked to me and yet he was already informed about it. News travelled faster than I had expected and people in Europe were more informed about our news than I had imagined.
>
> 3. He seemed genuinely sorry that this accident had occurred. It mattered to him that these three astronauts had died.

We talked over coffee for about a half hour and then I left to walk and think—and to find lunch.

Amsterdam is a beautiful city with its canals and bridges adding a special touch. There was little boat traffic on the canals but a lot of bicycle traffic on the streets and canal bridges. In London I nearly killed myself looking in the wrong direction for oncoming traffic at intersections. In Amsterdam, it was the bicycles that would present a threat to my life.

That evening, I mapped out Amsterdam into walkable sections and identified the sites that I might be interested in seeing. The first was the Rijksmuseum but this wasn't because I had some sudden driving desire to visit a big museum. According to *$5* and just about everyone else at the hotel who had an opinion that evening at dinner, I'd be crazy if I didn't visit the Rijksmuseum. Why in the world would I be in Amsterdam in January if it was not to visit the Rijksmuseum? It was fantastic! It was amazing! It was important! I didn't tell them about my spotty art gallery history and I think they just assumed I was "culturally normal" and would never want to miss the Rijksmuseum. I'd love it, they declared.

THE RIJKSMUSEUM: The next day I walked to the Rijksmuseum and had a remarkable afternoon experience. This museum was laid out in a chronological order that helped art idiots like myself see how art developed over the centuries. It didn't force me to jump around between randomly placed eras making the art (and me) feel disjointed and disconnected.

When I got to the Vermeer and Rembrandt exhibits, I spotted two essential elements that they added to painting in the 17th century: lighting and movement. For lighting, the main subject of the painting was lit from a source within the painting itself. For example, a woman working in her kitchen would be lit by sunlight streaming through the window in front of her. Prior to this, paintings looked a bit "flat" because the lighting in the painting was uniform. Also, and just as importantly, there was now movement. The people in Rembrandt's paintings were painted in motion and not posed or static.

The big-deal painting that everyone told me I absolutely had to see was Rembrandt's *The Night Watch* (1642). As I moved through the galleries I kept an eye out for it and hoped I wouldn't miss it. How would I face everyone if I had to tell them I couldn't find it? Well, *The Night Watch* was impossible to miss. This massive painting is 11'11"x14'4" and took up one entire gallery wall. The room itself was dedicated solely to this painting. A few spotlights provided a soft light around the painting in the otherwise dark room. I sat in one of the chairs that were placed around the perimeter of the room and read the information sheet that the museum provided. It emphasized the painting's movement: the "lively figures in a group portrait" and pointed out the guardsmen getting into formation (they looked like a bunch of rowdy drunks) and the captain telling his lieutenant to start the company marching. Then it drew my attention to a young girl in the foreground that was described as the company's mascot. (Wait. What? Really? Military groups had children as mascots?)

Another bit of information caught my attention: During World War II, *The Night Watch* was rolled into a cylinder and moved out of Amsterdam for safekeeping. This was the first time I had read anything about the massive effort to save artwork during the war. And now I was facing an actual painting that had been rescued and protected. I have to admit the size of the painting helped drive home the amount of time, care and effort it took to save Europe's art. They weren't going to just slip *The Night Watch* in a briefcase and store it behind a sofa for safekeeping.

I was joined by a class of about thirty children who looked to be about ten years old. They entered the room quietly and sat on the floor in front of the painting. Their teacher talked as he pointed to different parts of the painting and the children raised their hands to ask a question (as opposed to just shouting out the questions). I imagine if I had understood Dutch I would have learned a great deal about *The Night Watch.* Instead I observed the kids. What struck me was how quiet and orderly they were. They didn't whisper to one another, squirm around, laugh or giggle about who knows what. (Did the teacher point out the child mascot and threaten to put any unruly kid into military service if they did not behave?) They stayed there for about forty-five minutes, then they got up and quietly filed out. I left *The Night Watch* gallery thinking: There really is such a thing as a quiet classroom of kids who pay attention during an art lecture.

After my afternoon at the Rijksmuseum I had a whole new feeling about galleries and art. I saw that paintings were snapshots or windows into history—like looking at old family picture albums. I was more interested in the dishes and food that were set on a 17th century dining table. The layout of their kitchens and the containers they used for their milk. The things that were sitting on the floor or hanging on the walls. I didn't care about the fine points of painting techniques. It was the historical snapshot that held my attention. I was observing how these people lived and I liked thinking about the questions a painting raised. I wanted to know if the family was paid for that little girl's service as a mascot. What made them say, "Sure, no problem. Take little Lucy as your mascot"? Did she stay with the company and go near battlefields? What was the point of a child mascot? Was this something like the superstition surrounding the Royal Ravens? If they didn't have a child mascot, would they experience disaster on the battlefield?

The dinner conversation that evening centered on everyone's experience at the Rijksmuseum. No one knew anything about poor little Lucy's story except that Lucy's face was thought to resemble Rembrandt's wife, Saskia, who had died the same year Rembrandt painted *The Night Watch.* Now I had a new question: Was my little Lucy included in the painting solely as a memorial to Saskia or did they really have child mascots for the military in the 17th century? No one knew the answer and Google didn't exist in 1967. I needed to have a cup of coffee with Rembrandt and get a few questions answered and several things cleared up.

ANNE FRANK HOUSE: The next day I visited the Anne Frank House. It was a grey, bitter cold, rainy day, which provided an appropriate atmosphere. I knew only a little about Anne and her life. Of course, I had heard about Anne's diary but, to be honest, when *The Diary of a Young Girl* was published, I was too busy with my own survival to read about her tragedy. This afternoon was going to be my first direct exposure to the Nazi persecution, deportation and extermination of Jews during the war. At the Rijksmuseum I had looked at paintings as windows and I was standing on the outside looking through the window at a snapshot of a moment in history. At the Anne Frank House I would be walking in history from inside the painting itself.

I stood in the rain in front of the House at 263 Prinsengracht looking at the building. It was typically tall (four stories) and typically narrow (three windows wide). It was built in 1635 as a merchant's house and had a canal running in front that provided easy delivery of supplies. Over the centuries, different companies owned the building and had their shops set up on the ground floor. Anne's father, Otto Frank, owned Pectacon, a wholesale company selling herbs, pickling salts and mixed spices used in the production of sausages. In 1940, Pectacon owned the building.

After days of wondering about all the skinny, tall houses in Amsterdam, I finally learned the reason: The cost of building sites along the canals had always been extremely high. To compensate for the narrow sites, these row houses stretched a long way back from the street. What they lacked in width they made up for in length. Because of their length, there was a lighting problem. (No electric lights back in the 1600s.) Only the front wall and back wall had windows that could provide some light. To solve the problem, the structure was divided into two separate buildings (fronthouse and backhouse), each with their own windows that allowed light to enter into all the rooms. The two buildings were connected by a passageway on the second floor. At the Frank house, there was an inner courtyard between the fronthouse and backhouse where Anne's favorite chestnut tree grew.

When I entered the house, the ground floor where the Pectacon shop had conducted business was empty except for a sign with an arrow that indicated I was to proceed up to the second floor. To do this, I experienced my first set of "Dutch steps"—a narrow, steep staircase that we might call a glorified ladder with a railing. Back in the 17th century the Dutch must have had small feet. I climbed up the stairs on my toes.

On the second floor a new sign pointed me to the documentation section that was "manned" by one elderly woman at the reception desk. She quietly welcomed me, handed me a four-page brochure and said I was invited to explore the house on my own. Aside from the receptionist, I was the only other person in the house. According to records, in 1967 the Anne Frank House received 100,000 visitors. However, on this day in January 1967, they received just one visitor. Maybe it was the cold and rain that kept others away.

The documentation section was comprised of two rooms. The one we were standing in had a display on one wall with a general overview of the persecution of the Jews during World War II. The other wall had information about the Anne Frank Foundation and stated its aims: "The Foundation strives to promote a better understanding between peoples and individuals." There was a display case containing items connected with Anne and her diary. Even though I couldn't read Dutch, I looked closely at the pages to get a feeling for her handwriting and the girl behind the writing.

The second room contained a model of the backhouse. (Anne called it the Achterhuis, which translates as "Secret Annex.") Along another wall were photos and displays about the Netherlands and Amsterdam during the war. The Frank family had fled Germany and immigrated to the Netherlands in 1933, after Hitler and the Nazi party came to power. Despite the Netherland's policy of neutrality, German troops invaded in May 1940 and Jews were once again in peril. By 1940, 140,000 Jews lived in the Netherlands with about 79,000 of that number living in Amsterdam. By the war's end in 1945, the Nazis had deported 107,000 of those Jews to death camps. Only 5,000 survived the camps and returned home. However, over 20,000 survived in hiding throughout the Netherlands. Starting with the invasion in 1940, Otto Frank secretly worked to prepare the backhouse for hiding his family.

On July 5, 1942, Margot (Anne's older sister) received a notice ordering her to report for relocation to a work camp. Otto knew that notices for the rest of the family would be arriving shortly. The next morning (July 6) the Frank family moved from their apartment on the Merwedeplein into their hiding place at 263 Prinsengracht. One week later, they were joined by Hermann van Pels (the Jewish butcher who helped Otto set up Pectacon), his wife Auguste and their son Peter. They, too, had just received relocation notices. Fritz Pfeffer, a dentist and family friend, joined them four months later. They were now a community of eight.

They were able to remain in hiding thanks to five of Otto Frank's employees and friends (Bep Voskuijl, Johannes Kleiman, Victor Klugler, Miep Gies and her husband Jan Gies) who provided a steady stream of food, cigarettes, supplies, news and morale boosts throughout the two years the eight were sequestered. This group of helpers was the only connection the occupants had with the outside world and they each knew that, if caught, they could face the death penalty for sheltering Jews.

After leaving the documentation section, I turned right and entered the passageway connecting the fronthouse with the backhouse. The combination of the sounds of my footsteps and the rain hitting the roof and windows; the stark, chilly house that had been stripped bare by the Gestapo after the arrest in 1944; and my newly informed thoughts about the Holocaust melded together to create a haunting atmosphere. Standing against the wall opposite me was the tall revolving bookcase that still held some of the company's ledger books and concealed the entrance to the backhouse. The brochure stated that I could open the bookcase. It creaked as I carefully swung it on its hinges towards me. I stepped through a roughed out opening in the wall and found myself looking at a second wall with a wooden door that was about five feet in front of me. I was standing between a double wall. Otto had shortened the passageway by five feet by adding the bookcase wall that hid the original wall with its door to the backhouse. With a building this long, who was going to miss that five feet?

(I was seriously beginning to like this guy. I appreciated that he understood the danger when Hitler came to power and in 1933 he got his family out of Germany and settled in a country with a neutrality policy. I appreciated that he again recognized the danger when the Germans invaded the Netherlands and started preparing the backhouse right away. He transferred control of his business and its building to Victor Kugler to make it look "Aryan," to prevent it from being confiscated as a Jewish-owned business, and to protect his family while they were living in the backhouse. Now I appreciated his cleverness with the double wall and swinging bookcase. He wasn't afraid of the word "prepare.")

I opened the wooden door and entered the Secret Annex.

With no furniture, the rooms looked stark. Anne's mother, father and older sister had shared the larger bedroom that I was now standing in. I found the penciled growth lines marked on the wallpaper recording Anne's and Margot's growth during the years they were in hiding. Fritz and Anne Pfeffer (whose presence annoyed the hell out of Anne) shared a connecting room that was about a third of the size of her parent's room. Pictures of movie stars, the British royal family, friends, members of Anne's family, her teachers and famous pieces of art and sculpture that Anne had collected or clipped out of magazines were pasted on a wall in her room.

The door to the bathroom was in Anne's room. The toilet and washing facilities had to be used sparingly and carefully until after the shop on the ground floor closed for the day. Otherwise workers in the shop and warehouse area who did not know the family was in hiding would have heard the flushing toilet, running water and people walking around above them.

Next to the bathroom was another Dutch staircase that led to the third floor and a single larger room that served as Mr. and Mrs. van Pels' bedroom, the communal dining room, living room and kitchen. It was also now bare except for a round cast-iron stove that had been used for cooking and burning trash. They could safely use that stove because the neighbors knew that Pectacon's operation included a laboratory and this would account for smoke coming from the chimney.

Peter's tiny bedroom was next to another steep staircase that led up to the fourth floor attic. I tried to go up there but the trap door at the top of the stairs was locked. I was able to look though the cracks between the trap door and the attic floor to get a sense of what the space looked like. It was an unfinished attic with a wooden floor, wooden rafters, dust, cobwebs and a window.

I didn't hear any other sounds in the house, indicating I was still alone. I wanted to stay longer to get a feel for the place so I sat on the floor in the communal room in front of the stove. I was hoping the stove, which had not been fired up since 1944, would somehow warm me. I sat there and listened to the rain. It didn't take long for me to feel danger closing in around me. The atmosphere in the room now had an air of urgency and felt heavy. The walls around me seemed like they, too, were closing in and the room appeared smaller. I suspected that this must have been similar to what the occupants felt every day. I don't know how long I sat there.

On August 4, 1944, a group of German police, led by an SS officer who was operating on an anonymous tip, stormed the Secret Annex and arrested the eight occupants along with Johannes Kleiman and Victor Kugler. Miep Gies and Bep Voskuijl were detained and questioned but not arrested. They returned to the building the next day and found that the Germans had removed all the valuables from the Secret Annex. Anne's diaries, notebooks and her loose sheets of paper were scattered on the floor. (Apparently the Germans didn't consider them valuable. Bad decision.) The two women collected Anne's writings along with the family photos that were also thrown around during the ransacking and Miep kept everything in a drawer in her apartment for safekeeping. Victor Kugler and Johannes Kleiman were jailed at the penal camp for enemies of the regime. After seven weeks, Johannes was released because of poor health but Victor was held in several work camps until the war's end.

The eight Secret Annex Jews were deported on the last transport to Auschwitz in September 1944. Some were gassed at Auschwitz, Anne's mother died of starvation at Auschwitz, others were transferred to work details, and Anne and Margot were transferred to Bergen-Belsen. In early 1945, a typhus epidemic spread through the camp killing 17,000 prisoners. Margot and Anne died of typhus in February 1945. Bergen-Belsen was liberated on April 15.

The girls almost made it. Out of the eight, only Otto Frank survived and returned to Amsterdam to Miep's apartment. As a gesture of respect, Miep never took Anne's diary out of the drawer. She had intended to return it to Anne after the war but gave it to Otto after the Red Cross confirmed that Anne and Margot had not survived. To this day, the person who betrayed them to the SS has not been identified.

When I finally stood up to leave, one word jumped to mind and has stayed with me for over fifty years: Why? Why had any of this happened? Why had these parents and their children been killed? Why had parents with their own children persecuted, arrested, tortured and killed these families? It was the beginning of a long quest to find the answers to these questions. But no matter what I read or what I find out, for me it all boils down to one word: Why?

I left the Secret Annex, closed the bookcase again and returned to the woman at the reception desk. I thanked her for allowing me so much time to explore and experience everything on my own. She surprised me by asking, "Dear, are you Jewish?" I said, "Yes." She clasped my hand, gave it a small squeeze and said, "I'm pleased you came." This was the first time I felt welcomed anywhere as a Jew. The irony was that had I been a teenager and one of the occupants in the Secret Annex, the Nazis would have classified me a Jew (two Jewish grandparents and a Jewish father), and I, too, would have been arrested and deported to Bergen-Belsen. Now I was standing in this house and feeling welcomed for the first time precisely because I was a Jew. I thanked her again and with that, I left the Anne Frank House and walked out into the rain.

I didn't want to go back to the hotel and talk to anyone about my experience. (In fact, I haven't shared this experience with anyone until now.) While walking, I came across a Chinese restaurant. A Chinese restaurant in Amsterdam! I was so enchanted by my discovery that I went in and had a wonderful dinner—all for $2. (Try figuring out a menu for Chinese food that's been translated into Dutch! Oy.)

De Wallen (the Red Light District): The next afternoon I felt I needed a distraction and decided to visit Amsterdam's famed Red Light District. It was recommended in *$5* and was also touted as safe. I asked the hotel manager if he thought it would be safe for me to walk around the district. He told me to wait, then left the front desk and walked into the dining room. He came back with two young men—two American soldiers who had been staying at the hotel. They agreed to be my escorts that evening.

This 1.6-acre area in the heart of Amsterdam (located not far from the Anne Frank House) was built around a harbor and dates back to the late 13th century. It has gone through times when the trade has flourished and times of regulations and prohibitions. In 1967, prostitution was legal and flourishing (it was said).

Brian and Bill, my two army escorts, and I headed out to De Wallen after dinner. We walked down a narrow street and sidewalk with a canal on one side and building after building after building of houses that were only two windows wide with large glass storefront windows on the first floor. Behind each window sat a working lady dressed in a few clothes that I assumed were meant to be provocative or alluring. The thing that intrigued me about these women was that they didn't seem to be paying any attention to the pedestrian traffic. (Perhaps they looked at me and my two escorts and deemed us to be useless gawking tourists and not worth their attention.) Some of the women were reading, some were knitting, some doing needlepoint. I would not have been surprised if some were writing out a grocery list. If a woman had been hired, all we saw was an empty chair with the open book turned over or needlework sitting on the seat. It seemed like the theme for my time in Amsterdam was windows. Now I felt I was looking through a window (literally) at a short story. Each woman had her own story, some beginning with the woman sitting there in her chair and others beginning with just a book laying open on the chair.

The challenge, or perhaps threat, to this adventure was the younger women who were standing in the doorways and calling out to potential customers. They did not like the fact that I was walking down the sidewalk in De Wallen and they let me know it. They called out what I assumed to be Dutch insults and made various threatening hissing sounds. At the same time, they were attempting to entice my two escorts to come over and talk business. I think that had I not been accompanied, one of the girls would have stepped out from the doorway and tossed me in the canal. Business transactions in De Wallen were serious and apparently I was a threat. Never mind that I was wearing my medieval-nun finery and not at all alluring to any sane passing man.

The next morning at breakfast, Brian and Bill joined me for coffee. They had their own business transaction to discuss with me and it had nothing to do with the De Wallen activity we saw the night before. They were on leave and were due to be shipped back to the States in a few weeks but wanted to use their leave time to see Europe. They rented a car in Germany and drove as far as Amsterdam when it dawned on them that the cost of gas was more than they had anticipated. They would need a third person to share the cost. In two days they were planning to leave Amsterdam and head south to Tangier (Morocco) where living expenses were cheaper and the air warmer. Did I want to be the third person?

One thing in particular attracted me about this proposition: the promise of warmer temperatures. I had spent a month dealing with the cold and taking a break from winter sounded good. I asked them for a little time to think about it but indicated that I was leaning toward yes. I was intrigued at the idea of traveling to Tangier. I had not considered going to North Africa so this was potentially a new opportunity and adventure. We agreed to meet again at dinner.

That afternoon I told the manager what Brian and Bill had proposed. My first question was whether the manager felt it would be safe for me to join them for such a long trip. I had not picked up any "weird vibes" from them the night before or at breakfast. But I wanted to double-check my instincts. They had been at the hotel for about a week so I wanted his opinion of Brian and Bill. He felt I would be fine. He also had not picked up anything strange from them, which was why he had asked them to escort me to De Wallen. And he reminded me that if things got questionable, all I had to do was get out of the car and continue on my trip by myself. But he cautioned me not to go to Tangier alone. (Since I wasn't planning to go alone, I didn't ask him to explain the caution.) I asked if a third of the cost of their gas expenses was more economical than the cost of train tickets. (I had no idea how much gas cost in Europe.) He assured me sharing the gas cost would be cheaper. In short, he thought that what these guys offered was a good deal for me, especially if I wanted to go to Tangier.

Joining up with Brian and Bill was a major change in how I assumed my trip would unfold. I had planned to visit one city after another in a logical and sequential order and now I was about to throw all that to the wind (as they say). But I had also come to Europe without a set itinerary because I wanted to see where the trip led me. It looked like it was about to lead me to Tangier. I told the guys that evening to count me in. We decided to leave Amsterdam in two days. That would give us each time to prepare for the long trip to Algeciras, Spain, and from there we'd take the ferry to Tangier.

As usual I was nervous about moving on. And I was sad about leaving Amsterdam and the hotel. I liked the city and its beauty a lot, even in the cold winter. My main memory about the hotel, besides the helpful manager and the camaraderie I experienced in the dining room, is the shower. We had to pump a guilder into a little box installed on the outside next to the shower door in order to get five minutes worth of hot water. Otherwise, we'd be taking a cold shower. In an effort to get warm, some people wanted to linger under the hot water. When they went over the five-minute timer, they'd have to open the door a little, stick out their arm and pump in another guilder for the next five minutes of bliss. The competition and crowing rights revolved around how much you could accomplish in the shower for just one guilder. The challenge for women was the extra time it took to wash their hair. I came in with an advantage. Thanks (?) to my winter in Ocean City when I had no hot water, I knew how to take a lightning fast shower that included washing my hair for just one guilder. I was recognized by the others as a champion with a rare gift.

Throughout all the time I spent walking around Amsterdam, I did not see anyone wearing wooden shoes.

Chapter 11

1,623 Miles to Tangier

WE LEFT AMSTERDAM early in the morning to begin our mad dash to Morocco. We drove through Belgium and into France, skimming Brussels and Paris. (Mental note to self: return to both cities later.) We passed through Versailles, Orléans, Tours and Bordeaux, stopping only for gas, food and a night's rest.

From Bordeaux we crossed the Pyrenees Mountains and entered Spain, stopping in San Sebastián, Burgos, Madrid and Seville. The drive through Spain included dodging oxen, mules and horses pulling wagons, along with a constant parade of pedestrians. At times the landscape was desolate with no sign of human life or activity. Except for that fifteen foot tall stone statue of Jesus with outstretched arms standing by itself on a cliff overlooking the road in the middle of nowhere. There had to be a story that went along with that statue that would explain why it was there. But we just zoomed on by.

For me the big story was in Madrid where I had my first experience eating paella. (Real Spanish paella, made in Spain! How classy is that?) For Bill and Brian the big story was their new bota bags (Spanish canteens used for carrying wine) and their many attempts to drink wine from the bags without squirting it all over their faces and dribbling it down their shirts.

Five days after leaving Amsterdam we pulled into Algeciras, a port town at the southern-most tip of Spain. We were now one ferry ride away from Tangier. After booking rooms for the night we walked to the port to purchase our ferry tickets. Tomorrow we would be in North Africa.

In the hotel dining room that evening, we met several people who were also headed for Tangier. Brian and Bill struck up a conversation with two American college girls, Heidi and Ann, and ended up inviting them to join us for the trip. We were now a gaggle of five—two guys and three girls. Safety in numbers.

The thirty-two mile ferry ride crossing the Strait of Gibraltar took about an hour. We passed the Rock of Gibraltar, something I had heard about in school, of course, and here I was looking at it. This moment, as I was connecting a little pre-knowledge with the actual physical reality, felt special—special enough that I took a photo as we slowly passed by. The day was sunny, the temperature pleasant and the water calm. Life was feeling pretty good. As we neared Morocco, we could see the Tangier skyline. We docked at the Port of Tangier and walked off the ferry right into a section called the Medina, old-town Tangier.

Tangier

Wikipedia's introductory description of Tangier is this: "The history of Tangier is rich, due to the historical presence of many civilizations and cultures starting from before the 5th century B.C. Between the period of being a strategic Berber town and then a Phoenician trading centre to the independence era around the 1950s, Tangier was a center for many cultures. In 1923, it was considered as having international status by foreign colonial powers, and became a destination for many European and American diplomats, spies, writers, artists, traders and businessmen."

I didn't know any of this when we arrived. Since Morocco was in North Africa and not Europe, Tangier wasn't included in *$5.* So I was flying blind and didn't know what to expect. In fact, no one in our group knew what to expect. We had each been lured to Tangier by its promise of warmer February temperatures. The city lived up to its promise—it was about 65 degrees when we arrived.

My first impression: We had landed on another planet, the land of the dirham (Morocco's currency). What I saw before me was so completely outside my normal frame of reference that I am certain, at first glance, I experienced sensory overload. It was all coming at me at one time and I had difficulty taking things in—the different sights, sounds and smells. Everything looked beige—and sandy. The people had deeply weathered faces with expressions that seemed to say they weren't pleased with life. It was going to take a little time before I could say, "It's not that this city is lesser than the others. It's just different."

The folks in Algeciras had recommended a hotel and we set out to find it. As we walked along the narrow, twisting streets and alleyways, the five of us each studying our maps and trying to figure out how to get to our destination, a kid came up to us and in a low, conspiratorial voice said (in English), "Ya wanna buy a diamond?" We told him we weren't interested in purchasing diamonds but the kid pressed on. He had what looked to be a diamond ring and scraped its stone across the shop window we were passing, scoring the glass. "See. Real diamond. Ya wanna buy a diamond?" Again, no. He was singling out Heidi, Ann and me for his sales pitch when Brian and Bill piped in with a stern "No." With that, the kid ran off. About two minutes later, we were approached by another child diamond merchant who asked the same question: "Ya wanna buy a diamond?" After saying no, another glass window was scored with whatever he had in his hand as proof that his diamond was real. Eventually, at least six or seven plate glass windows had been scored, all by different kids and each asking the same question, "Ya wanna buy a diamond?" I was beginning to wonder how often shop owners had to replace their front windows when it dawned on me that the diamonds, along with the scratches, were fake—of course. As a group of five, all looking at maps and street signs with quizzical, lost expressions, we looked like American tourists and easy targets. Which we were.

We were completely lost. With all the twists and turns, it sometimes felt like we were doubling back on ourselves. This is when we met Nizar, a twelve-year-old boy with an abundance of good-natured chutzpah. He wasn't selling "diamonds." He was selling tours. Since we had no clue how to find the hotel on our own, we hired Nizar for a couple of dirhams (about 40 cents) to lead us. He was happy to help—and eager to earn a little cash. We were now being led through the Medina labyrinth by a twelve-year-old sprite. He led us to the hotel, helped us book our rooms and even bartered a deal for Heidi, Ann and me to share one room and split the charge three ways. We thanked Nizar and paid him his two dirhams, then headed up to our rooms.

After our first street adventure, we girls agreed that we liked the idea of the five of us staying together. I had noticed that as we walked along in the street with one kid after another trying to sell us diamonds, we gradually moved closer together. We were like a school of fish that swims and changes directions en masse in a tight bubble. Our sum was more protected than our individual parts. Now at the hotel, I appreciated not rooming alone.

We had about fifteen minutes to settle in and catch our breath before screwing up the courage to go back downstairs to meet up with the guys and head out in search of lunch. And who should be waiting for us outside the hotel to offer his services? Nizar told us he knew the perfect place for us to have lunch. (Is this kid good or what?) We negotiated the price for this next leg of his tour service and headed off into the disorienting confusion of the Medina.

He had us walking up, down, in and out of a maze of narrow streets, steps and corridors that somehow ended at a second-floor restaurant. Nizar talked to the fellow at the door and got us a table. (How much ya wanna bet the restaurant was run by his uncle or father?) Then he translated the menu for us and recommended several dishes. I decided to go with one of Nizar's suggestions. I mean, what the hell. I certainly didn't know what I was doing and, to be honest, as I looked around at what others were eating, it all looked good and everyone seemed happy.

I ended up experiencing one of the most amazingly tasty meals and, to this day, I still recall the smell and taste. Chicken bastilla: saffron chicken with sweet spices, covered with a layer of fried almonds sweetened with orange flower water, wrapped in a baked paper-thin warqa (filo shell) and topped with powdered sugar and cinnamon. (Good lord, I sound like a cooking expert. I took notes as Nizar translated the menu.) I ended the meal with mint tea—really tasty mint tea. Not that watered down stuff I was familiar with in the U.S. Now, instead of feeling like I had dropped onto another planet, I was beginning to feel like I had entered heaven. And I thought, "It's not that this city is lesser than the others. It's just different—*really* different."

When we finished lunch, we found Nizar waiting for us outside the restaurant. He asked what we wanted to do next, as if we'd know. We agreed it was time to walk around the Medina and get a feel for Tangier. To no one's surprise, Nizar assured us he could help with that. We knew we were being hustled by this kid but he was so good at it and we were so dumb about Tangier that we couldn't resist his charm or his hustle. Besides, we felt we were getting a good deal with him.

After another negotiation, we set off and spent the afternoon walking around the Medina looking at the architecture and archways that framed picturesque scenes. The men walking past us were wearing beige or brown berber djellabas (long cloaks with a hood and wide sleeves). We saw fewer women on the street but the ones we saw were also wearing layers of long clothing in muted shades of brown or tan. Between the buildings, the Moroccan clothing and the cobblestone streets, we were literally surrounded by different shades of brown, beige or white with just a touch of color here and there. It was an odd, monochromatic experience.

After a couple of hours, we cried "uncle" and told Nizar we needed to call it a day. At the hotel, he agreed to meet up with us the next morning and we five weary travelers headed to our rooms for a quick rest before a late dinner in the dining room. It was another fine meal but not as good as lunch. To my surprise, my four companions decided to continue their evening at the hotel bar. I begged off and told them I wanted to make notes in my journal and go to bed. (I can't imagine why spending an evening in a bar didn't interest me.)

The next morning at breakfast my companions looked a little rough around the edges from the night before. (Silly kids.) But they were game for the day. The previous evening they had heard about camel rides being offered. When we met up with Nizar (who was outside waiting for us, of course) and negotiated for his services for the day, we headed off for the camel rides.

Just outside the Medina stood three smiling men, each holding a camel on a short rope. The camels didn't look too excited to see us. Ann and Heidi got on the animals first while Brian, Bill and I stood back and cheered them on. They sat on the camels for about five minutes while we took photos. The camels may have looked bored but the girls were happy. However, by the time they got down, I had decided I wasn't going to follow suit.

1. It was a classic tourist trap.
2. This tourist trap, as with most such traps, was pricey.
3. It wasn't a "camel ride." It was a "camel sit" atop a stationary camel.
4. I had ridden too many horses to feel like I needed to experience sitting on top of another tall, four-legged animal for a quick photo op.
5. If they had offered a camel trail ride into the surrounding hills for about a half hour or so, I would have gladly paid the money. That would have been an experience—and adventure.

Bill and Brian begged off as well. The men were kind enough to let me pet one of the camels at no cost. As I was stroking the camel's neck I noticed that he was watching me. I couldn't tell if it was a wary look or a weary look. (Camel expressions differ from horse expressions.) I spoke softly to it and then stepped back pleased with my experience and relieved the camel did not spit at me.

Next on Nizar's tour: a Tangier open market. By now we knew that Tangier's open markets were a big deal. They were the traders' and local small producers' Mecca. Gourmet cooks and chefs from all around, including Europe and the U.S., came to these markets for spices and specialty foods. Moroccans stocked up for the day's meals and debated the day's news and gossip over lunch.

Nizar led us to a large, busy market. Everyone seemed to be arguing and bartering, which added to the general hubbub. The sights and sounds combined with the tsunami of smells crashed in my head and once again nearly froze my senses. At first it all seemed like a cluttered, noisy, chaotic mess with stuff thrown about and hanging everywhere. But the more I looked at it the less cluttered and noisy it became.

There were food stalls with different meats, cheeses, olives, teas, coffee beans, fresh vegetables and fruits, all neatly displayed. There were racks of bottled olive oil. Tooled pointy leather shoes in every color. Intricately designed silver jewelry and hammered brass trinkets. At one stall the guys could have purchased their very own djellabas—to go with their bota bags. There were several stalls with ground spices heaped in red, yellow, black and gold mounds that gave off different smells as we walked by. And there were baskets of unground spices. The smells from the bakery stalls with the freshly baked bread loaves were incredible. If we wanted something other than food, there were baskets, kettles, tin cups, buckets and wash tubs of different sizes hanging down from ropes strung along the overhang, making the market appear to have bangs. On the ground beneath the tables were stacks of pots, pans, utensils and pottery for cooking along with pottery plates and bowls. We five seemed to be the only ones slowly wandering around and gawking. Everyone else was there to take care of their day's business.

Along with the smells of spices and breads there were some amazing smells coming from cooking carts and stalls. Each person specialized in one cooked item. Nizar talked us into eating a market street lunch. I didn't see anyone passed out or writhing on the ground from food poisoning so I thought I'd give it a try. Besides, why would the fine Moroccans want to poison one another? (Said I, cheering myself on. For a cautious and cowardly food eater, this was a major leap of faith.)

I steered clear of the stuffed camel spleen sausage and the steamed sheep head. I even backed away from the stuffed sardines that looked and smelled good but I don't like sardines. (And I, like you, wondered how in the world you stuff a sardine.) I played it safe and settled on aubergine fritters: a fruit that was sliced, dipped in sweet smoked paprika batter and deep fried. I ended up going back for seconds, thirds and even fourths. The other four were more adventuresome and made choices that I didn't want to hear described. At least nothing looked like a steamed sheep head.

When we finally decided to move on, I can honestly say I was reluctant to leave all the sights, smells and sounds. It was as if my sensory system, which had been overwhelmed initially, had adjusted and was now somehow attached to the market. I felt glued to the place. Maybe it was the aubergine fritters.

Nizar led us around the Medina some more and included a walk through the casbah. (There really is a casbah! I kept expecting Bing Crosby, Bob Hope and Dorothy Lamour to come dancing out of the shadows any minute.) Finally we were back at the hotel. Since we would be departing the next day, we thanked Nizar for his fine tours. We even added a little to the day's negotiated price. We wished him good luck, said goodbye and then watched while our Tangier sprite skipped off. (One thing I noticed: The whole time Nizar was with us no other kids tried to hustle us. Was there an honor code among the army of Tangier child hustlers?) We again had dinner in the dining room. And once again, my companions stayed up late in the bar. (Silly kids.)

At breakfast the four weren't interested in food, just strong Moroccan coffee. I wasn't sure how they were going to hold up for the ferry ride but when I suggested we stay an extra day, they declined. Ann and Heidi needed to travel north to Paris right away and the two guys needed to get on with the next leg of their trip. I was the only one with the flexibility that came with the luxury of time.

After purchasing our ferry tickets, we had about an hour to kill. The only thing the five of us wanted to do was sit in the square, drink mint tea and people watch. Even this seemingly unadventurous activity in Tangier turned out to be an adventure with an element of danger. At one point the tinny sounds of someone playing a flute-like instrument (pungi) caught our attention. In the middle of the square, about thirty feet in front of us, a man (in a brown djellabas, of course) was sitting cross legged on the ground playing his pungi over a round, open basket. Before long a snake poked its head up from the basket. My first question to the others: "Is that a real snake?" Answer: yes. My second question: "Wait. Is that a cobra?" The snake continued rising out of the basket, stood erect about two feet in midair and displayed its hood. It was a cobra. We were being entertained by a snake charmer and his highly venomous partner. In a sane and appropriate response, the hair on my arms stood up.

The man continued playing his pungi, which to my ear sounded incredibly annoying. I was convinced the snake was telling this guy, "Hey, stop playing that damn flute. I'm trying to sleep here." After several minutes of standing up in midair, swaying, lowering back down into the basket and then rising again, the snake started to leave its basket. (Freedom. I want my freedom.) The man encouraged it back with his bare hands and quickly slammed the lid on. All was safe again (if you believe a six-foot cobra was incapable of escaping a flimsy looking basket with a half-cocked lid) and the people standing around the snake charmer applauded and tossed coins. It was a perfect coda to my Tangier experience.

Anybody wanna buy a diamond?

Chapter 12

Algeciras to Genoa

We arrived back in Algeciras a little after noon. Ann and Heidi left immediately for France. Bill, Brian and I sat down at a cafe for lunch and to plot our next moves. In Amsterdam we had agreed that I would ride with them to Algeciras and that we'd tour Tangier together. They were now headed east to Barcelona and invited me to continue on with them. They still wanted someone to split the cost of gas.

I wasn't sure I wanted to continue with them. During our trip to Tangier, it was obvious that Brian and Bill enjoyed the coquettish charm that had been extended to them by Ann and Heidi. But I wasn't Ann or Heidi, and the guys seemed disappointed (even a little annoyed) by that. Somehow in my youth, I missed the instruction manual for developing girlish giggling and innocuous conversation skills. I knew that Brian and Bill were going to have to get over their disappointment if we were to share the next leg of the trip.

There was another issue I had been thinking about: Overall, I did not feel their company was unpleasant. Rather, it was American. While riding in the car from Amsterdam, I watched the French and Spanish countryside pass by from within an American bubble. Even though I tended to be quiet during the trip, I was still surrounded by an American conversation going on between two American guys. In essence, I was an American tourist in an American bubble that separated me from the outside European reality. I realized it was the trade-off I made by accepting their offer in Amsterdam and opting for a convenient, money-saving mode of transportation. But now I was starting to feel it was time to re-enter the full European reality.

I looked at a map and thought about what I wanted to do next. I wanted to go to Barcelona (the next logical stop from Algeciras). And see the Riviera and Monte Carlo. Then I wanted to head to Italy. We three quickly came to an agreement. I would ride with them to Barcelona (where we would stop for about three or four days) and Monte Carlo (where we would stop for another three days). Since we would be traveling along the coast after Valencia, I would be able to see the Riviera as we drove along. (It was still February and I didn't think I would be longing for a quick dip in the sea.) When we entered Italy, they agreed to drop me off at the train station in Genoa. From there they would head north and I would take the train to Rome. I had one other request. Once we stopped in Barcelona and Monte Carlo, I suggested we go our own way. I wanted to experience those cities on my own. We'd meet up when it was time to leave. They didn't have a problem with this.

After lunch we left Algeciras for Valencia, the halfway point of the 500-mile trip to Barcelona. While the rest of the western world was going nuts over the Beatles, the BeeGees and the Rolling Stones, Spain was embracing El Cordobés, their top matador. He was young, he was famous, he was unorthodox, he was good looking and his picture was plastered on posters all over the country. We traveled through several towns that had bullfighting rings—and more posters of El Cordobés. Back then it seemed like bullfighting was to Spain what baseball was to America.

We debated about stopping to see a bullfight but I resisted—unless it was to see El Cordobés. Actually, I wanted the bullfight to be divided into two parts: (1) El Cordobés' performance, and (2) the killing of the bull. Then we could buy a ticket for just the part we wanted to see. I didn't want to see an injured, bleeding or dying bull. (I clearly did not grasp the spirit of a bullfight.) But El Cordobés' fame was based in part on the fact that he had killed so many bulls. I decided I would just stick with looking at his posters.

Valencia is the third largest city in Spain and has a history that goes back to 138 B.C. when it was founded as a Roman colony. It has been a player throughout western history ever since. I didn't care. I wanted to eat and go to bed.

From Valencia to Barcelona, we traveled along the coastline with its remarkable vistas of pebble beaches and the Balearic Sea. (How could anyone relax on the beach with all those pebbles?) I spent much of the ride fantasizing about living in a small house on the coast with its rocks, cliffs, beaches and sea. (I'd figure out how to live with the stoney beach.) Maybe I could become a writer and support myself by publishing a bunch of novels. Or maybe I would find a sunken treasure worth millions and I could live a life of leisure in my little coastal house. A girl can dream.

Barcelona

When I think back to Barcelona, one word comes to mind: fun. We found a small *$5*-recommended hotel on La Rambla in the Gothic Quarters (the old city) with views of the city's ports. My room was small, simple and clean. I was happy. The main focal point in the hotel was the dining room where the guests gathered for meals and made plans for what to do next. The ring leader was Josephina, our maître d' and sole waitress. (It was still mid-February and despite the 60 degree temperature, the hotel was only partially occupied. Just one "Josephina" was needed.) She was happy to fill the diners in on what was happening in the area and the things she felt sure we'd want to do.

By the time we departed Barcelona, I had walked around the Gothic area, explored side streets (that's where the shops and cafes are), visited a replica of the *Santa Maria* (that ship was truly small), appropriately marveled at what was billed as the world's largest color fountain and stared at the famed Sagrada Familia, a church that was designed by Antoni Gaudi back in the late 1800s and was still under construction. The church looked like someone hovering in a helicopter had poured buckets of wet cement all over the exterior, giving it a downward, anti-gothic, melted look. I thought it was weird looking. But I think I was a group of one. Everyone else raved about the beauty and brilliance of the Sagrada Familia architecture. They are expecting to complete the church in 2026. (It still has that drippy cement look.)

On her afternoon off, Josephina led a group of us to Tibidabo, a mountain in Barcelona that has, as you might imagine, spectacular views of the city, its port, coastline and the sea. We rose to the top of the mountain on a funicular, a cliff railway. (Two trams attached to a cable provide a counterweight to each other. The down tram lifts the up tram.) At the top of the mountain was the Sagrat Cor church. Sitting right next to it, and the main reason for our ascent, besides the view, was the Tibidabo Amusement Park, Spain's longest running amusement park.

The park opened in 1905 and many of the original rides and fun houses were still functioning in 1967. I especially remember the House of Mirrors where we laughed ourselves silly. And a sharp shooting booth with its line of moving metal duck targets. Brian and Bill had joined our group for the mountain trip and Brian taught me how to shoot a rifle. I then went on to surprise myself by demonstrating a previously unknown hidden skill while onlookers declared that I might have a promising career in the French Foreign Legion.

The next morning, Josephina said we had one more thing we needed to see for the full Barcelona experience: Bodega Del Toro. At first I thought she was talking about bullfighting. But she was actually referring to a club with some of the finest flamenco dancing in Barcelona that just happened to be within walking distance of the hotel.

That evening eight of us spent three hours at the Bodega Del Toro watching a non-stop performance of flamenco dancing. We were sitting around three small tables that were right next to the foot-high riser where the dance troop performed. We were practically on the stage. One member of our group had long blonde hair and, at a certain point, the lead female dancer pointed her out and performed a number that paid tribute to her blonde hair. Apparently blondes were revered in Spain. Sometimes one dancer performed, sometimes several, sometimes there were up to eight men and women, all pounding their hearts and feet out. At times wood chips from the stage would fly out over us. We left the club with temporary hearing impairment but with no wounds from the flying chips. I thought about Maurice Ravel. I felt I had just witnessed his inspiration for Bolero.

After four fun-filled days of living the Barcelona life, we bid our fond farewells to Josephina and departed for Monte Carlo.

Monte Carlo

If my word for Barcelona is "fun," my word for Monte Carlo is "money." As one might expect, our travel expenses were now higher than in Spain or Tangier. But I'm not referring to that when I say "money." As soon as we pulled in, it was clear that Monte Carlo was a showcase for wealth. Not the gaudy, glitzy kind of wealth we associate with the nouveau riche or Las Vegas but a more subdued, classy kind of money. Old tax-dodging money from Europe's finest royal families, political leaders and industrialists. Hell, the town's trash collectors wore black suits, white shirts and black tie. This pretty much said it all about the place. I'm not even going to discuss the yachts that were moored in the harbor. Everything was spotless, beautifully landscaped and perfectly placed. (If someone littered in Monte Carlo, I was sure the police would chop off the offender's hand.)

We found a small, reasonably priced hotel with a perfect view of the harbor and with rooms that felt like an oasis. (They included bathrooms complete with shower and toilet!) At the front desk, we were handed copies of their well-designed, artistic brochure that gave us a short history of the town and a list of activities that were available to us. The banner across the brochure read, "the country of everlasting holidays." It also included a welcome from the royal family:

> Gifted by its eternal summer, the Principality looks out o'er the glad waters of the dark blue sea. Suspended between blue of heaven and blue of sea, it is a heartening example of public virtues—a state with rulers dedicated to the arts of peace—whose subjects quarrel with

> none—an urban setting retaining grace and dignity—a resort of fashion, welcoming with equal warmth people of all races and degrees of fortune—a sun-dial state which counts only shining hours.

(The royal family needed a good copyeditor.)

I announced to the guys that I would be in search of Monégasque (the fancy name for Monaco nationals, subjects of His Serene Highness the Sovereign Prince) who were disobeying the royal family's decree to "quarrel with none." If found, I'd report them and perhaps get a reward. Barring that, I looked forward to experiencing the "equal warmth" that was to be extended to people of "all degrees of fortune." I assumed I was on the very low end of Monaco's fortune scale.

Monte Carlo is not that big so it was easy to walk around and explore. There's a royal palace on a cliff that had its own daily changing of the guards ceremony. After seeing the routine at Buckingham Palace, I have to say this ceremony at Monte Carlo was the height of subtlety. And apparently they had picked up on my recommendations on how to streamline the changing of the guard ceremonies. Two new guards marched up to the guards they were relieving, saluted and the four switched positions. We now had the two new guards standing in front of the little red-and-white chevron-striped sentry boxes while the two old guards marched off. It took about two minutes. There were no horses, no bands with fancy-dressed drum majors, no marching regiments, no tall beaver hats. To emphasize the simplicity of the moment, I was the only person watching. Thank god I didn't blink.

Besides gawking, there were two other things I wanted to do: visit the Casino de Monte-Carlo (and gamble $1) and eat a real French meal at a nice Monte Carlo restaurant. I did both. I visited the Casino in the late afternoon thinking the dress code might be more relaxed during those early hours. When I paid my entrance fee, I was told that there wasn't a dress code as long as I stayed in the main room and away from the private rooms—the ones with the tuxedo and gown crowd. I bought a $1 (5 franc) chip and wandered around the room for over an hour watching how the different games were played. I knew nothing. I didn't even know how to play Black Jack. Luckily, the casino provided a small brochure listing the various games and their rules. After drifting around, reading and observing, I decided to try my luck at the roulette table. I put my 5-franc chip down on something. I can't remember on what. And I experienced that heightened gambler's moment of hope. (I could win a fortune. I could get my little house along the Spanish coastline.) The wheel spun, the ball dropped and I lost my $1.

Next, I headed for a real French dinner. We had an unusually warm evening and I spotted a restaurant not far from the Casino with tables set up in a courtyard surrounded by gardens. Here it was late February and I was eating dinner outside. My waiter spoke English, as I was sure everyone did in Monte Carlo, and I told him I wanted to experience a typical French meal. I admitted it would be my first. He suggested I leave it to him. He seemed nice and, after all, the brochure stated that he would treat me with grace, dignity and equal warmth. I didn't think he'd deliberately poison me so I accepted his offer.

For the appetizer, he brought a whole artichoke. I had no idea what to do with it. Luckily, the woman sitting at a table near mine had been eating her artichoke when I sat down. I would sneak glances as she gracefully ripped off one leaf at a time, dipped it in a bowl of something that looked like melted butter, gently pulled the white end through her teeth and then delicately placed the remainder of the leaf in another bowl. I set out to emulate her. The artichoke dismantling went pretty well but I don't think I was as graceful about it as that woman. The waiter helped me uncover the artichoke heart and, with that, I finished my first course. The artichoke tasted perfectly fine but I felt it was an awful lot of work with, what I considered, relatively little reward.

The main course was a fresh fish complete with head and tail. Now I had this fish staring at me from my plate. I had to ask my waiter for help—again. In anticipation, he was standing nearby. He showed me how to remove the head first and then he opened the fish lengthwise in two halves. He removed the spine and talked me through the final deboning. I picked up the tail with my fingers and slowly pulled the tail toward where the head had been. I ended up with a fish tail and skeleton in one hand and a deboned, de-headed fish on my plate. I could not have been more proud when the waiter tapped my shoulder and said, "Good."

I was able to get through the rest of my meal without needing any further tutorials. But one other thing I learned: The Monégasque take a long time to serve and eat a meal. My French meal was an enjoyable evening-long endeavor. (Unfortunately it didn't turn me into a life-long lover of fish.)

After three nights in Monte Carlo, it was time to move on. I don't know what Brian and Bill did with their time but I felt my experiences were well worth the time (and money) spent. I was a little reluctant to leave my perfect room (complete with bathroom), but it really was time to move on.

A SHORT NOTE ABOUT BATHROOMS: The Monte Carlo hotel and its bathrooms were worth obsessing over because it was the first and only time I had a bathroom in my room. This was luxury at its finest. Throughout the rest of my trip, as was the normal European custom, I had a small sink in the room. Each floor had two or three toilet rooms down the hall and a shower room nearby. I became the queen of washing myself, my hair and my clothes in a sink.

And while we're at it, Monte Carlo was also the only place where the toilet paper was close to what I was used to in the U.S. The rest of the time I either experienced stretchy, flimsy crepe paper, or small sheets of paper that had a glossy, wax-like surface, or long strips of newspaper. I never understood the logic behind the waxy, glossy version. I considered collecting toilet paper samples from each city as weird souvenirs from my trip but decided against it because I didn't want to have to explain it to the custom's official at the airport.

Chapter 13

Genoa to Rome

IT TOOK A LITTLE OVER two hours to drive along the coastline from Monte Carlo to Genoa, Italy. Bill and Brian dropped me off at the Genoa train station a little before noon. We wished one another luck, bid our farewells and off they drove toward Germany. I was pleased to be on my own again but it had been a while and I had lost my edge since leaving Amsterdam. Standing in the station, figuring out the train schedule to Rome, exchanging money into lira and purchasing my ticket felt like a first-time experience. However, I pressed on. By 12:40 I was sitting in a second class car with four Italian women as we departed for Rome.

The trip took almost six hours and included a memorable incident provided by Enrico, a young Italian who stopped by our compartment to check our tickets. He started getting a little flirty with me and wanted to know if I needed help finding a place to stay once we arrived in Rome. Unfortunately, I didn't understand any of this because I was clueless when it came to Italian and he didn't speak English. I only suspected this was what he was saying based on his hand gestures and elaborate charades performance.

He "solved" our language problem by going to one of the first-class cars and talking a German businessman into following him back to our compartment. That conversation must have been interesting because after he seated the German on the bench opposite me it became clear that the German wasn't sure why he was there. Enrico made the assumption that the German and English languages were close enough and we'd be able to converse. Instead the German and I just stared at one another and tried not to laugh.

Neither of us understood what Enrico wanted from us. Finally the four women joined in and tried to get across to the German that Enrico was offering help. The German, thinking he was being asked to help me, respectfully declined—which I was relieved about. He wished me good luck (at least that's what I assumed he said) and returned to his first-class sanctuary.

Between Enrico and my compartment mates, I finally figured out that Enrico had a relative who had an inexpensive pensione in Rome. He would be glad to walk me there and introduce me, if I wanted to try it out. I realized we were going to be arriving in Rome a little late in the day and since the four women seemed to be vouching for Enrico and indicating I'd be fine if I accepted his help, I replied "yes" and "thank you"—in English. Everyone seemed satisfied that I had made the right decision and we settled in for the rest of the trip. It was clear that my compartment mates would be looking out for my best interest while we were on the train together. They even shared their bread and cheese with me. I was no longer traveling in an American bubble.

By 8 P.M., I was sitting on my bed in a pensione that was located right in the heart of the city and within easy walking distance to just about anything I might want to see—all thanks to Enrico. Once he walked me to the pensione and introduced me to the Signora, an elderly woman who I suspected was his aunt, he was off and I didn't see him again. After staring into space for about a half hour trying to figure out what just happened between Genoa and Rome, I decided to head out into my new Italian world in search of dinner. I found a small restaurant around the corner and had the first of many Italian pasta dishes.

The next morning the Signora came to my room with a breakfast tray and introduced me to my first cappuccino and a plate of Petit Beurre cookies. I fell in love with both and started an obsession with Petit Beurre cookies that lasted for years. Serving breakfast in my room was something I had not expected but I wasn't going to argue about it. In my newly acquired second language that consisted of one word, I said "Grazie" about four times. (I wanted her to know how much I appreciated her breakfast.)

If Barcelona's word was "fun," and Monte Carlo's word was "money," I'd have to say Rome's words were "large and touristy." I spent time mapping out the city and over the next two weeks visited the usual must-see sites: the Spanish Steps, the Trevi Fountain, the Victorio Emanuele Monument, the Pantheon, the Colosseum and the Roman Forum. I walked down Via Nazionale, Via del Corso, Via Emanuele. I sat in parks, checked out about five famous piazzas and watched the changing of the guard at the Quirinal Palace. Here's my take:

THE SPANISH STEPS: Meh. A popular hangout for American and European hippies.

THE TREVI FOUNTAIN: Big, pretty, impressive, liquidy and surrounded by many tourists tossing in their coins. They say that currently an estimated 3,000 Euros (3,361.05 U.S. dollars) are thrown into the fountain each day. And in 2016, an estimated $1.5 million was thrown into the fountain. The money subsidizes a supermarket for Rome's needy.

THE VITTORIO EMANUELE MONUMENT: Huge, white and, in a city filled with large things, its size seemed a bit over the top.

THE PANTHEON: Ancient, mysterious, architecturally fascinating, with 21-foot thick walls and an oculus open to the sky. *(Da Vinci Code* fans know what I'm talking about.)

THE COLOSSEUM: Over its 1,900-year history it has been damaged by time, earthquakes and stone-robbers. In its heyday it held about 65,000 spectators who gathered to watch gladiatorial contests and public entertainment spectacles. Now the floor of the Colosseum was filled with the remnants from early medieval public housing. It was also surrounded by a large assortment of Italian men and boys who roamed around asking tourists if they speak English. The tourists who made the rookie mistake by saying yes were offered a variety of legal and illegal services. I found the best way to deal with them was to pretend I didn't speak English and ignore them.

THE ROMAN FORUM: According to my guidebook, this was the ancient center of Roman public life, but its history and true significance were lost on my young, uneducated mind. I just thought it looked like the Italians brought in trainloads of marble chunks and old columns, dumped them in this big space, then stood back and announced, "We shall call this the Roman Forum." (In Italian, of course.)

CHANGING OF THE GUARDS AT THE QUIRINAL PALACE: As with many things in Rome, the presidential palace is huge (1,200 rooms) but I was there to see the changing of the guards ceremony. In comparison to London, it seemed a smidge on the casual side with its single marching regiment that tried mightily to stay in step. After the guards successfully changed, the regiment spilled out of the main entrance and marched up the street. No bands or horses. Just a few police on motorcycles to accompany them.

VIA NAZIONALE: Rome's famous street for shopping. I bought a pair of the world's ugliest shoes solely because I believed no one would ever buy them and I felt sorry for them. They deserved a home. Plus they were good walking shoes.

Many miles of streets that included piazzas, obelisks and parks: I stopped in one park to eat lunch and watched two little girls (they looked to be about six years old) chasing one another and playing. They exuded joy, innocence, over-the-top cuteness and spirit—so much so that when they skipped close to me, I held up my camera and indicated I'd like to photograph them. They stopped right away and struck a perfect camera pose complete with broad smiles. I thanked them and they skipped off giggling.

If it seems like I'm rushing you through Rome, it's because I am. Some cities speak to us and we can develop strong attachments to them. Other cities just don't speak our language. Every city I visited up to that point spoke to me in special ways. But generally speaking, Rome wasn't one of them. Lord knows, I put in the time, mileage and effort to find things I could care about but had limited success. Except for the Pantheon, my new ugly shoes and the little girls in the park, I found just two additional points of interest that touched me in special ways: the Church of Santa Cecilia in Trastevere and St. Peter's Basilica.

Out of the more than 900 churches in Rome, I chose to visit the Church of Santa Cecilia in Trastevere. (Trastevere is a district in Rome.) It was constructed in the fourth century and tradition has it that it's built on the site of St. Cecilia's home. It's a smaller church that's a bit off the beaten path so I felt I was going to have a quiet, relatively tourist-free experience.

When I entered the church I was the only "civilian" there and a group of nuns were in the choir loft rehearsing. (One important point: Saint Cecilia is the patron saint of musicians.) I sat in one of the pews in the center of the church and listened. I don't know if I can adequately describe what I heard without using words like "heavenly" and "saintly." The women's voices were clear, clean and perfectly blended. The acoustics in the church added a remarkable resonance. I kept thinking, "I can't believe I'm hearing this." There were times when my sense of reality was floating in the air around me and I actually wondered if I had somehow been transported to some different level. Was something otherworldly going on here? I stayed for as long as the nuns rehearsed. When they finished, they left the loft so quietly I could barely tell they had moved. I sat there for a while, not wanting to break the mood.

THE VATICAN: Being a fairly recent convert to Roman Catholicism, I felt St. Peter's Basilica represented the heart of the Church. For me this wasn't a tourist stop. Rather, this stop was personal. In 1967 the pope was Paul VI, a fact that I found a bit disappointing. After his predecessor, Pope John XXIII, with his forward thinking, sense of reform and charisma, Pope Paul VI felt flat and conservative. So it wasn't the pope who drew me to the Vatican. It was its history, tradition and symbolism that drew me. I had yet to hear about the sordid underbelly of intrigue and scandal that was also part of the Vatican's history so I went there with an unsullied sense of purpose.

I visited St. Peter's four times. The first time was my "tourist trip" and I walked around with a guidebook in hand. I have to say that out of all the places I visited in Rome that made me feel this city was large and touristy, the Vatican was the largest and had the most tourists. There were groups of guided tours being conducted all over the place, all in different languages. It felt more like a spectacle than a church.

They say it's the largest church in the world and to prove it there are small brass markers embedded in the marble floor of the nave that show the comparative lengths of the world's other large churches. I had to stop and think for a few minutes as I read the markers and realized that each of those cathedrals (including Westminster Abbey) could easily fit inside St. Peter's. Here are some specs about the Vatican that I found impressive:

Total length: 730 feet

Total width: 500 feet

Interior length including vestibule: 693.8 feet, more than ⅛ mile

Total area: 227,070 square feet (5.7 acres)

Internal area: 163,182.2 square feet (3.75 acres)

The magic of the Vatican's architecture revolves around its remarkable proportion, dimension and scale. You just don't realize how big this thing is, especially when you first walk in, until you walk up to what appears to be a life-size statue and realize it is about five times larger than a regular human. Or watch someone else walk up to a statue and see how dwarfed they become as they get closer to the statue. Each aspect of St. Peter's is perfectly proportioned and all the pieces weave together in a way that belies their size.

To me, this is even more remarkable because so many different artists, sculptors, architects and builders worked for 120 years to complete St. Peter's and yet they all remained faithful to the overall sense of scale and proportion. For example, the Papal Altar sits beneath Bernini's *baldacchino* (a pavilion-like bronze structure) that stands 98 feet tall. (That's almost ten stories tall.) It's held up by four bronze twisted columns and it takes five people standing hand to hand with outstretched arms to encircle one column. The ten-story *baldacchino* points up to the massive dome with its interior height of 390 feet. (That's thirty-nine stories.) There are four medallions at the base of the dome, each depicting an evangelist. Saint Luke is holding a quill pen that measures about seven feet long. That's just the quill. The four medallions appear relatively small, but I estimate (based on the length of Luke's quill) that they are about fifty feet in diameter.

I must have spent over a half hour looking at Michelangelo's *Pietà.* He was just twenty-four years old when he completed that work. I was fascinated by the nuance and softness in the marble. How does someone pull something like that out of a big chunk of marble? I felt that if I touched Mary's arm, it would feel real. (I was fortunate to see the *Pietà* close up, undamaged and intact. Just five years later, in 1972, some crazed geologist attacked the statue while yelling "I am Jesus Christ." Swinging his hammer he smashed Mary's arm completely off from the elbow down, chipped a chunk out of her nose and damaged one of her eyelids. Now restored, the *Pietà* is on view in its regular spot at the Vatican and is protected in a bulletproof acrylic glass case.)

As is tradition, I dutifully touched the toe of the bronze statue of Saint Peter. Because so many people over the centuries had followed that tradition, there were hardly any toes left on his right foot to touch. The poor man was virtually toe-less and in dire need of surgical transplants.

I visited a portion of the Vatican Treasury and bored myself to death, so I cut it short. But I came away with one question: How many poor people could be fed for a year if the Vatican sold off just one gold or crystal cross or one fancy chalice from its treasury?

To wash away my disgust, I went to the Vatican bar. Yes, there is an Italian bar in the Vatican. In 1967, it was located just off the hallway leading to the treasury. (Now I think it's located somewhere on the Vatican roof and billed as a "rooftop café.") I was told it was open to the public so I opened the door and walked in. There were about twenty priests in there. They all turned and shot me a rather menacing "what the hell are you doing here" look that felt vaguely familiar. Where had I seen looks like that before? Oh, yes...Dorothy's drunken friends in the Riverdale bar. I was older now and I wasn't about to let these men intimidate me. I had been assured that the bar was not only open to the public but "public" also included individuals of the female persuasion. I walked up to the bar, ordered a double espresso and took my time drinking it. Then I turned, shot the priests a look of my own and left. The espresso washed away the treasury disgust but the bar gave me clerical disgust.

There was one more thing I wanted to see: the Sistine Chapel. Maybe I was becoming overly tired at this point because when I entered the Chapel and looked up at that 44-foot high ceiling and around at the walls, all I could think was, "This is really noisy." It was as if the walls and ceiling were shouting. There were murals of naked and clothed people, clouds, angels, rocks, lightning bolts, pedestals and columns painted everywhere. I couldn't imagine how anyone could calm their mind and focus in there. If you prayed, did you have to shout just to get beyond the room noise and have your prayers heard?

The tourists who were already in the Chapel were draped all over the place. Along each long side wall was a row of wooden benches. A number of people were lying down on their backs studying the ceiling. Others were lying on the floor. (Ah, the clever tourist solution for avoiding "Sistine Chapel neck strain.") I found a bench space, laid down and stared at the ceiling for a while.

Then I sat up and stared at *The Last Judgement,* the mural behind the altar and the other murals covering the side walls. I wasn't sure about the meaning or significance of what I was looking at and I wasn't sure I cared. That was the problem. I was aware that I was looking at something that was judged to be extraordinary and famous—Michelangelo and High Renaissance art at their finest. But I couldn't get past how loud and active that room felt. (Art experts are now clutching their chests and keeling over in a dead faint from the heresy and shock of what I'm saying. Have heart, folks. My knowledge and appreciation for art developed over time. At age 21, this was my starting point. Now, relax. I know a bar where you can go to have a nice, relaxing espresso.)

My first Vatican trip presented an interesting challenge. How was I going to convert this enormous, touristy spectacle of a place into a functioning, personal house of worship? What I saw that day was an ecclesiastical gawk-fest and had nothing to do with the actual purpose behind the building for the simple layman. My solution: There were side chapels off the nave that offered daily

Masses. I decided I would go to Mass at the Vatican and experience a small part of the building in action.

I attended two morning Masses, each in a different side chapel. Both were in Italian with only about thirty others attending. The chapels were calm and quiet. We couldn't hear the tourist commotion going on in the nave. It was a peaceful experience and it felt special to receive communion at the Vatican. The one odd thing I remember is that the priest in each chapel had to climb up on a short stepladder to reach the tabernacle. It was a reminder that in order for the regular day-to-day operation to occur, they still had to deal with the unusual enormity of the venue.

For my final visit to St. Peter's, I attended the big Easter Mass and had to make an overnight train trip back to Rome from Florence for the event. From the daily Mass in a side chapel to the Easter Mass in St. Peter's Square, I saw the Vatican function in its two extremes—the small parish church and the large, international, ceremonial church.

Earlier I had stopped by the Church of Santa Susanna, an American church run by Paulists, to say hello to one of the priests, a friend of Father Ruppert. When I got up to leave, he surprised me with a ticket to the Easter Mass that would allow me to be one of about two hundred people seated near the altar. He told me to arrive an hour early in order to have time to make my way across St. Peter's Square, enter the Vatican and present my ticket. I would be led to my seat.

I don't think this priest had ever attended the papal Easter Mass. An hour before the Mass was to begin there were about 200,000 or more people packed in the Square. The only way I could get to the Vatican entrance was to skirt the crowd and move along the edges under the colonnades. I almost made it. I produced my ticket at the appointed spot and was being led to the seating area when a huge roar went up from the crowd. The Pope and a rather large entourage were making their way toward the altar that was set up on risers in the Square. At that point I wasn't allowed to move to my seat and ended up standing behind the French choir. I was still closer to the altar than 90 percent of the people in the Square.

For me, the experiences that I walked away with from Easter Mass were the enormous, attentive and tightly packed crowd; the French choir; the logistics required to pull off a Mass in such a big venue (it was like doing card tricks in Yankee Stadium); and the Easter blessing that the Pope gave in about twenty different languages. As he spoke each language, a cheer went up from different groups in the crowd. When the blessing was delivered in French, my choir cheered along with their fellow Frenchmen. It seemed that as each group responded to the blessing in their language it somehow united the crowd and gave it its unique identity. Funny how that happened. Everyone had been given a voice.

It had been over two weeks since I arrived in Rome and I could feel my time there was coming to an end. One significant change at the pensione resulted in my gaining a roommate. My room was a double, which I had to myself until the Signora asked if I would mind if an American student joined me. That's how I met Karen. She had been in Italy for several months studying art.

Over the next few days she talked about a massive art restoration project that was going on in Florence. There had been a huge flood in November that had done a lot of damage, especially to Florence's art. Karen had already been accepted to join the crew that was restoring damaged old books and manuscripts. She and her friend Daniele wanted to leave in a few days and would be hitchhiking north to Florence, stopping at Orvieto, Siena and Pisa along the way.

She explained that hitchhiking in Italy was more efficient if there were three people traveling together—two girls and one guy. An Italian male driver would stop for this group thinking that the female who wasn't attached to the fellow would be fair game for the driver. Once the driver tipped his hand as to which girl he was attracted to, he was told that girl was the guy's fiancé. Out of Italian respect, the driver would back off and all would be well. The hitchhikers got their ride and the driver saved face. He even came out looking gallant.

With that, she asked if I would like to join them on their trip to Florence. I'd be the much-needed third person (again). It sounded good to me so I said yes. I was headed for Florence, as well, and their plans coincided with what I wanted to see along the way. I figured that this would also give me an idea of what it was like to hitchhike, something many Europeans did. I could decide later if I felt comfortable hitchhiking alone. (By the way, Europeans call it "auto-stopping.")

While we were still in Rome getting ready to leave, Karen gave me some pointers about navigating Italy as a lone female traveler. For example, a woman should never walk between an Italian man and the wall of a building. He'll crowd the woman against the wall and then take the opportunity to grab her breast. (That charming move had already happened to me in Rome.) When the woman sees a man walking toward her, she should gravitate toward the street, leaving the man to walk next to the wall. If he can't corner her, he can't grab anything.

Karen also talked me into not traveling any further south than Rome. The things that had annoyed me about the men in Rome would only be amplified the further south I got. And she warned me away from Sicily. Like Tangier, it was best for a single woman to travel there in a gaggle.

Much to my relief, Karen spoke Italian and she helped me unlock the mysteries of the Italian menu. I was now ordering more interesting meals.

One thing I noticed in Rome's restaurants was the German tourists. It was hard to miss them. First of all, the men all dressed the same—grey trousers, blue blazers, blue shirts and blue or blue-striped tie. The women didn't adhere to a national uniform. But the other thing that was hard to miss was the obnoxious habit the German men had when they wanted to get their waiter's attention. They would bang their knife multiple times on their water glass making a rather loud clanging. It was clear that the Italian staff took this as an insult and would often take their time getting to the German table. The clanging also annoyed the others in the restaurant and patrons would shoot some pretty menacing looks at the Germans, yet they never seemed to take the hint and cut it out.

Chapter 14

Rome to Florence (a.k.a. Firenze)

SINCE THIS WAS MY FIRST auto-stopping experience, I let Karen and Daniele, veterans of auto-stopping, plot out the trip. As long as we ended up in Florence, I was happy.

I have to admit that Daniele's presence on our trip put me more at ease by adding an element of safety to the adventure. When I met him in Rome, I liked him right away. He was a tall, quiet American with a sly sense of humor who had been studying in Italy but I can't remember what he was studying, other than Karen. He and Karen had a relationship that they seemed to float in and out of rather casually.

We had to make one stop before leaving Rome. Karen insisted we visit the Etruscan Museum. At the museum, those two spent their time looking at the sculpture and pottery while I walked off in search of something more interesting. (To my mind, if you've seen fifty Etruscan pots, you've seen them all.)

First I had to find out who the hell the Etruscans were. According to the museum's brochure, the Etruscans lived around the Mediterranean and in Italy in the 8th and 9th centuries B.C. They began as agricultural tribes but over time they became craftsmen, traders and navigators. They also developed an advanced level of dentistry. I found several display cases of different dental instruments and gold dental prostheses. What especially caught my attention were the Etruscan dental tools, many of which were nearly identical to modern dental tools. This raised a question: You big-time, modern-day dentists can't come up with a technology that dramatically improves upon what the Etruscans developed? Really?

By noon we were on a bus heading out of Rome. I've long since forgotten the name of the village where we got off the bus to have a late lunch and to walk to the first prime auto-stopping road that would head us to Orvieto, our destination. We had a ride within twenty minutes—a fellow in a tiny Fiat 500. We squeezed ourselves in and we were off. The driver hinted that he might like to spend some time with Karen, so she became Daniele's first fiancé. By the time we rolled into Florence, Daniele's fiancé was pretty evenly divided between Karen and me. Since Karen tended to be chatty and spoke Italian, she kept the drivers entertained.

Orvieto

Although we stopped at Orvieto primarily to see the cathedral *(Duomo)*, I have to say the town itself was equally worth visiting. If you could picture in your mind the perfect, picturesque Italian village, it would be Orvieto. It is situated on the flat summit of a volcanic rise with steep, vertical rock sides giving the appearance of a village sitting on a big rock pedestal. It looked like someone had sawed off the mountain. From the town's perimeter we could see out over the valley for miles. My new friends, the Etruscans, established themselves there first and the village became a major center of their civilization until the third century B.C. If in real estate location is everything, I have to say the Etruscans nailed it at Orvieto.

The large, green and white horizontally striped Duomo towers above the rest of the town. It was begun in 1290 and was completed in 1591. Just about every major Renaissance architect, sculptor and artist worked on it. What caught my attention, besides the stripes, was the completely open and uncluttered nave that led to the altar. Not a pew in sight. I couldn't figure out if worshipers had to stand for an entire Mass or if they hauled out chairs and benches for each service. To my mind, hauling the furniture around would get tedious quickly so I was inclined to think everyone stood. After the big cathedrals and churches I had already visited, with their many rows of pews on either side of the main aisle,

I have to admit this Duomo with its wide open space from the doors to the altar was visually restful, even peaceful.

By the time we finished wandering around, it was getting late. We booked a couple of rooms and found a little restaurant for dinner. Daniele regaled us by reading about the "secret" labyrinth of caves and tunnels that lie beneath the town. Orvieto is sitting on soft volcanic rock that, I assume, makes it fairly easy to dig. And dig is exactly what they did. There were more than 1,200 tunnels beneath us. It must have looked like a honeycomb down there. My question: With all those tunnels, what keeps the town's buildings from collapsing down into them? Some of the tunnels provided an escape route for the villagers to use when needed. Following the passageways, they could emerge again at a safe distance away from the town. The tunnels included underground galleries, cellars, more passageways and cisterns. Unfortunately, but understandably, tourists couldn't just wander around down there on their own and when we were there, no guided tours were scheduled.

Montefiascone

Just to the west of Orvieto and one short car ride away lies the town of Montefiascone. My travel mates said we absolutely had to go there and taste the table wine. There was a famous legend behind the wine that was named *Est! Est!! Est!!!* Some say this story is apocryphal but it and a number of its variations have been around for centuries.

The legend: Back in the 12th century (or 10th century, depending on the legend's version) a German bishop traveling to Rome to meet with the Pope sent a servant ahead to find the villages with the best wine for the bishop to enjoy. The servant would scrawl *Est* (Latin for "There is") on the door of the inns where he was impressed with the quality of the wine they served. The bishop would then know in advance where to stop. Legend has it that the servant was so impressed with the wine being served at a Montefiascone inn that he enthusiastically scrawled *Est! Est!! Est!!!* on the door. And the rest, as they say, is history.

I didn't know anything about wine (and still don't) and only had half a glass so I can't give a reasonable opinion about *Est! Est!! Est!!!* I don't think the other two knew much about wine either. But knowing the legend made that wine spectacular for the three of us. We left Montefiascone for Siena feeling satisfied that we had taken the time to have the *Est! Est!! Est!!!* experience.

SIENA

By around 3 P.M. and after two more rides, we were sitting at an outdoor restaurant in the Piazza del Campo in Siena, the fan-shaped town square, drinking cappuccino and eating pastry. It was a warm, sunny day and I chose to return to the restaurant after we visited the Duomo (another Romanesque, green and white, horizontally striped cathedral). I drank more cappuccino, basked in the sun's warmth, read about Siena's history and watched children chase pigeons in the piazza.

Siena was first settled by my new pals, the Etruscans, who resided there from 900 B.C. to 400 B.C. At first, the surrounding land could not be farmed but the Etruscans reclaimed it through their use of irrigation—giving them grains and fresh vegetables to go along with their clean, straight teeth.

We spent the night in Siena and prepared for the last leg of the trip the next day. I was confused because I had not seen any road signs along the way for Florence. When would we start to get close to Florence? Karen just looked at me. When she realized I was not kidding, she explained that there had been road signs all along our route. I had been looking for the "wrong" name of the city. We weren't going to Florence. We were going to *Firenze,* the Italian name for its own city. Silly me. (Auto-stop tip #1: Know the name of the town you are trying to get to.) The next day we would be making a quick stop in Pisa, presumably to see if the Tower was still leaning, and then we'd get our final ride(s) to Firenze.

I did not think we could complete this auto-stopping trip fast enough for Karen. She had a major challenge with her backpack—a monster backpack that must have weighed over seventy pounds. She wasn't that big of a girl. I don't know what she had stuffed in that thing but I'm pretty sure it included large art books. She was planning to work in Firenze for a few months so I suspected it held everything she owned. To get the backpack on, she'd have to set it on a chair seat, squat down in front of the chair and slip her arms through the straps. Then we'd have to help her stand up. We only lost her one time. We were sitting on a low stone wall next to the road waiting for the next car to approach so that we could give them the distinct opportunity and honor of stopping for us. At one point as we were chatting about nothing, Karen started to slowly tip over backwards off the wall. We tried to catch her but that pack made it impossible. Luckily she fell on soft ground. It took the two of us to get her back upright.

On this first trip, I learned an important tip about auto-stopping gear. As I said, every fellow who stopped for us was driving a Fiat 500. Compared to the Fiat 500 models that are now sold in the U.S., the 1967 European version was a matchbox on wheels. Karen had her monster backpack, I had a regular suitcase (that was much lighter than the backpack) and Daniele had a duffle bag. The suitcase was the most cumbersome luggage because it kept its shape and was tricky to fit in tight spaces. Karen's pack was challenging simply because of its size and weight but at least it could be squished a little for an easier fit. Daniele's bag had the most flexibility for stuffing into small cars. To fit into our various Fiat 500s, Karen sat in the back on my suitcase. (On its side, not standing up which would have required us to cut a hole in the roof for her head.) Daniele held her backpack on his lap and I held Daniele's bag on my lap. Auto-stop tip #2: Travel small and definitely travel light.

Auto-stop tip #3: The town the driver lives in is included on his car license plate in an abbreviated form of two or three letters. If the auto-stopper knows how to read the abbreviation, he can pick out the cars going in his direction. As a car approaches, the auto-stopper gestures to let the driver know he knows where the driver is headed and it happens to also be where the auto-stopper is headed. The driver's anonymity is busted and he'll usually stop.

Pisa

Guess what? The Tower was still leaning. I learned that we were now in the area in Italy where a town's Duomo, Baptistry and Bell Tower were built as three separate but architecturally related buildings. The Leaning Tower of Pisa is the bell tower that goes with Pisa's Duomo and Baptistry complex. It looked like an eight-tiered wedding cake created by a team of drunks. On the morning we arrived at the complex there was an Italian movie crew filming what looked to be a grade-B ancient Roman story complete with white horses ready for battle and soldiers carrying spears while sporting some useless looking Roman battle armor. They were using the Duomo-Baptistry-Tower complex as their backdrop. From casual observation, it didn't look like anyone on the crew knew what they were supposed to be doing. There was a lot of aimless wandering around going on.

To add to the general air of confusion, there was a sizable crowd of students staging a sit-down demonstration in the middle of one of the streets just a block from the Tower. From their signs and what was being chanted, Karen figured out that they were protesting the antique facilities at the university and that it was a demonstration organized by the communists and socialists.

Our driver for our third ride of the day, a fellow named Paolo, joined us for the quick stop at Pisa and then offered to drive us to Firenze. He seemed to have nothing else planned that day and I think he saw us as an adventure. We weren't complaining and I have to say Paolo, who spoke English, was entertaining.

Chapter 15

Mud Angels

WE ARRIVED IN FIRENZE on Friday, March 17. Pepe, a friend of Karen's, had invited us to stay at his place for a few days while he was out of town. Paolo helped us locate the address and dropped Karen and me off in front of the building. She and Daniele needed to take a break from one another so he headed off with Paolo to find a pensione. Karen and I were met at the door by Pepe's apartment mate, Nerio, who had been expecting us and invited us in. After a long and rather crazy day, I was finally in Florence.

Up to this point, I had a foolproof routine for familiarizing myself with each new city and plotting out my walks. I was a tourist and I was there to observe, experience and learn. But I was on the outside looking in. From the moment Nerio opened the apartment door, that routine changed. I was no longer a tourist. I was about to experience Florence from the inside, as a fellow participant in the city's daily rhythms. There were two reasons for the change: Nerio and the 1966 Arno flood.

The day after we arrived, Nerio and I began dating. Since I did not speak Italian and he didn't speak English I'd say our mutual attraction was against all odds. The night we arrived, Karen, Nerio and I went out to dinner and Karen served as our translator as we got to know a little about one another. He was twenty-eight years old and was in his last semester of law school at the University of Florence. Prior to that he had lived in France for several years and taught French. I never understood that. One would think that the

French who lived in France would be able to find a French person to teach them French. But this school apparently felt it was better to hire an Italian. (I think it was a private school so perhaps having an Italian on staff was considered prestigious.) I told him, through Karen, that I had worked at *The Washington Post.* He was familiar with that paper and the *International Herald Tribune.* He asked me questions about why I decided to travel to Europe and I had to admit that I didn't know. I only knew I had to take the trip. I was attracted to his calm, quiet nature. What he saw in me remained a mystery.

The one thing that pulled me up short was his political affiliation. He was a communist. I had been taught in school that these were people you stayed away from. They were enemies, enemies of the state. Nerio didn't seem like an enemy nor did he sound dangerous. He explained he wasn't a "red communist," the party that was aligned to the Soviet form of communism. In fact, he had nothing good to say about the red Soviet communists. He was a "yellow communist," the party that fashioned itself after the Chinese form of communism. (Leave it up to the Italians to color code their political affiliations.) Pepe, his roommate, was a fascist but not the Mussolini-type fascist. All this political slicing and dicing just left me confused. I made the decision to remain calm about Nerio's political affiliation and, instead, see where our mutual attraction was leading.

Two days after Karen and I arrived on the scene, Pepe returned from Bologna. He came waltzing into the apartment singing loudly and dressed in a long black cape, tails, striped tee shirt and top hat. He was also well on his way to being smashed. I've always felt this was the only way to meet Pepe. He spoke beautiful English and immediately offered, as any fine Italian gentleman might, for Karen and me to stay with him in his room. We respectfully thanked him for his generosity and declined. (It was time to get serious about finding a pensione.) Although he didn't show it often when in a social setting, Pepe had a serious side and was studying engineering at the university. I was fascinated by the contrast between these two apartment mates—Nerio, the quiet, calm, yellow communist and Pepe, the crazy, outgoing, anti-Mussolini fascist. Yet they seemed to get along well.

Karen checked in with the restoration team at the Biblioteca Nazionale (the National Library of Florence) the day after we arrived and was scheduled to begin working right away. They gave her a lead on a family-owned hotel where a number of restoration workers were staying. The day Pepe returned, she and I headed to Via Osteria del Guanto, 6 and the Albergo Imperiale. The hotel was down a one-block long side street that looked more like an alley but its location could not have been better. It was a block from the Uffizi Gallery, Palazzo Vecchio and Piazza della Signoria. The hotel rooms were simple and clean—and the price was right. We could each have a single room for $100 a month. They catered mostly to restoration workers and I suspected they lowered the price of their rooms out of consideration for them. Besides, at that time there were hardly any tourists in Florence clamoring for hotel rooms. Karen's upcoming work schedule somehow qualified us both for rooms at the reduced price. I told them I wasn't sure how long I would be staying but it didn't seem to matter. By that afternoon, she and I were settled into our respective rooms.

The Albergo was nestled in a medieval building that had an unusual interior architecture that gave the hotel an endearing charm all its own. My room number was 11. One would think it would be located between rooms 10 and 12. Not at the Albergo. The door numbers were random, not sequential. Along one hallway the room numbers might read 6, 4, 18, 8, 3, 22. During World War II the building had sustained serious damage. Some of us decided that the doors were recovered from the rubble and as Osteria del Guanto, 6 was rebuilt and the hotel restored, the old doors were installed with no attention paid to the numbers that were nailed to each door. The door that fit was the door that got installed. There was also another more colorful story: We were told that during World War II the hotel was a brothel. The confusing door numbers added a layer of privacy and security. Angry wives couldn't barge in on their philandering husbands and police could not target individuals because they couldn't locate the offender's room fast enough, thus allowing the lady of the evening and her offender time to escape. It was useless to tell someone, "Meet me at the hotel. I'm in room 11." Eventually I'd have to send out a search party to find the person as they wandered around looking for number 11.

Actually, room 11 wasn't between any other room numbers. To get to my room, I walked down a hallway (past the shower room and toilet rooms) to the end, turned left, walked a bit further down a dark hallway and up a short flight of stone steps to my room at the top. It was the only room down that hallway. It had a double bed, a dresser, a small closet, a portable bidet and a sink. Its window overlooked the hotel's large courtyard where the owners, who also resided at the Albergo, kept their pet box turtle.

The Albergo was owned and operated by the Lorini family. Three generations resided there: the paternal grandparents, the parents and their two children (ages 9 and 12). They all pitched in to keep the place operating—except for the grandfather. Unless his job was to flirt with every girl who walked into the office, he didn't have much to do. I'd say the grandparents were in their late 70s. The grandmother helped at the desk while Signor Lorini, her husband, told every girl who walked in that he wanted to run away with her and take her to the forest. Then he would waggle his eyebrows up and down to show he was "serious." His wife ignored him and tended to refer to him as *"Il vecchio stupido"* (the old fool). There was a doorway that led from the office to the family quarters and nailed above the door was a foot-tall wall sconce of the Blessed Mother. Signor Lorini kept his can of snuff hidden from his wife behind the Blessed Mother. We residents enabled his snuff habit by not telling his wife where the can was hidden. (She probably knew and was just ignoring him—the old fool.)

The back of a restaurant butted up against the Albergo on the other side of the courtyard. At 9 A.M., one of their chefs would go about his tasks while singing opera—loudly. He did this every morning except Sundays when the restaurant was closed. Luckily for all of us he had a good voice.

It was also lucky that he was so punctual about beginning his day because I learned quickly not to depend on the accuracy of the Palazzo Vecchio bells. These bells have a history. Palazzo Vecchio's construction began in 1299 and it has functioned as the city's town hall since. The bells were rung to alert the Florentines to danger or to call them to assemble for speeches and announcements in Piazza della Signoria, the piazza directly in front of Palazzo Vecchio. (The bells were an early form of instant messaging.) During World War II, the bells were silent until August 11, 1944, when they were rung to signal the Florentine partisans to rise up and help liberate Florence from the Nazis. In November 1966, church bells rang out across the city to alert the townspeople that Florence was about to be flooded, giving people about twenty minutes time to protect themselves and their property. (There is some debate about the Palazzo Vecchio bells. Some say the bells were silent and others say that definitely the bells rang out that night.)

The Palazzo bells were manned by human bell ringers and rung every hour and half hour. Since Palazzo Vecchio with its 312-foot-tall bell tower was right around the corner from the Albergo Imperiale, I couldn't miss hearing those bells. But the bell ringers were either perpetually drunk or did not know how to count. At 8 A.M., the bells might be struck ten times or seven times or sometimes even eight times, if we were lucky. It was a crap shoot. The bottom line: The bells woke me up every morning and the opera singing told me when it was 9 A.M. and time to get breakfast.

The Italian bar that was considered by the Florentines to be one of the city's finest was only a half block from the Albergo. I went there each morning not because of its reputation or its proximity but because of its pastry. Just inside the door was a long self-serve counter filled with an endless variety of freshly baked petit fours (those small pastries we might get at a wedding). I would choose three or four (or five), go to the bar and order a cappuccino, sit at one of the small cafe tables and read the *International Herald Tribune.* The bar ran on the honor system. When I left I'd tell them how many pastries I ate, how many I was carrying out with me and how many cappuccinos I drank.

Apparently I was driving my friendly bar keep nuts each time I ordered *"uno cappuccino."* One afternoon he leaned over and said softly, *"UN cappuccino, non UNO cappuccino."* I smiled. Correction noted. I tried to speak Italian as much as possible and that sweet, well-meaning experience I had with the bar keep was something I experienced from many Italians. They were encouraging, even grateful, if I just gave it a shot. Sometimes the women would hug me and say, *"Bene, bene, molto bene!"* I also became adept at the international language of hand gestures. And I bought a pocket Italian/English dictionary that I kept with me at all times. If I couldn't get something across, I'd look up the key word and let them read the Italian translation. If their answer bounced off my head, they'd take my dictionary and point to their key word. You'd be surprised how much communication two people can accomplish that way. In time I could have a conversation in Italian as long as the person I was conversing with was willing to mentally conjugate my damn verbs correctly and gender-identify my nouns. Essentially I was speaking "pigeon Italian" but that didn't seem to matter. It was still *"bene, bene, molto bene!"*

During my first two weeks in Florence I settled into a relaxing, relatively gentle rhythm. After breakfast, I walked around and observed. The Florentines and the army of rescue workers had done an amazing job cleaning up and rebuilding the city in the four and a half months since the flood. The streets' cobblestones had been relaid. There were no piles of debris. And no mud. Life was moving forward. But as a reminder, there were flood photographs displayed at all the news stands. Hotels, restaurants and shops were still shuttered. The water line on all the buildings' walls indicated how deep the water had been. Via Osteria del Guanto had a water line that was over fifteen feet high. Piazza della Signoria and Palazzo Vecchio (less than two blocks away from the Albergo) were on higher ground and there the water mark was three feet high.

The flood killed 101 people. They said it could have been much worse had it not been for the fact that many Florentines were out of town on November 4 on holiday. Still it was considered the worst flood in the city's history since 1557.

The flood timeline:

- On November 3, after a long period of steady rain, the Levane and La Penna dams in Valdarno began to discharge more than 2,000 cubic meters (71,000 cu ft) of water per second toward Florence.

• On November 4, at 04:00, engineers, fearing that the Valdarno dam would burst, discharged a mass of water that eventually reached the outskirts of Florence at a rate of 60 kilometers per hour (37 mph).

• At 07:26, the Lungarno delle Grazie cut off gas, electricity and water supplies to affected areas.

• By 08:00, army barracks were flooded.

• By 09:00, hospital emergency generators (the only source of electrical power remaining) failed.

• Landslides obstructed roads leading to Florence, while narrow streets within city limits funneled floodwaters, increasing their height and velocity.

• By 09:45, the Piazza del Duomo was flooded.

• The powerful waters ruptured central heating oil tanks, and the oil mixed with the water and mud, causing greater damage.

• Florence was divided in two, and officials were unable to immediately reach citizens of the city past the Piazzale Michelangelo.

• At its highest, the water reached over 6.7 meters (22 ft) in the Santa Croce area.

• By 20:00, the water began to lower.

City officials and citizens were unprepared for the surge of water and the widespread devastation that it caused. There were virtually no emergency measures in place, at least partially because Florence is located in an area where the frequency of massive flooding such as this is relatively low. In fact, approximately 90% of the city's population were completely unaware of the imminent disaster.

When it was over, 5,000 families were left homeless, 6,000 stores were forced out of business and over 10,000 cars were destroyed. Approximately 600,000 tons of mud, rubble and sewage severely damaged or destroyed numerous collections of books, manuscripts and fine art, including the

> famous Cimabue *Crucifix* that hung in the Basilica di Santa Croce. It is estimated that between 3 and 4 million books and manuscripts were damaged or destroyed, as well as 14,000 movable works of art.
>
> ["1966 Flood of the Arno," Wikipedia, n.d.]

The scope of the disaster was so great that it took days for me to wrap my head around what had actually happened. I was surrounded by constant reminders of the flood. Each church had a water mark and the murals that had been submerged were covered or in the process of being covered with protective gauze. Most of the museums were closed for repair and restoration. I ended up walking around the city's streets letting the reality of the flood gradually sink in. Sometimes I would walk over to the river wall and watch the Arno as it gently moved along. On November 4, the river had to rise up at least twenty feet before crashing over the walls and bursting into the city. I'd think, "Really? That river way down there did all this damage?"

EACH EVENING AT 6, I met up with Nerio at his apartment and we would head out to dinner. Since both of us were on a tight budget we usually walked the three blocks to the University Mensa, the student cafeteria that had all the food choices anyone could possibly desire. Because it was part of the university and meal prices were greatly discounted, people (including tourists) couldn't just walk in off the street. However, restoration workers and guests of the students were welcome.

The University of Florence is composed of twelve schools: Agriculture; Architecture; Arts; Economics; Education; Engineering; Law; Mathematics, Physics and Natural Sciences; Medicine and Surgery; Pharmacology; Political Science; and Psychology. It was established in 1321 as the Studium Generale and recognized by Pope Clement VI in 1349. The first Italian faculty of theology was established by the Pope in Florence. It was finally named an imperial university in 1364. Due to politics and city power struggles, the university was moved to Pisa in 1473, then back to Florence, then back to Pisa. The modern university in Florence dates from

1859. Alumni include Italian presidents, two popes, several prime ministers, architects, astrophysicists, botanists, immunologists, philosophers, poets, physicians (including Napoleon's personal doctor), judges, philosophers and soon-to-be alumnus Nerio.

Nerio had quite an international group of friends. Besides the Italians, there were fellow students from France, Sweden, Greece and Turkey. Some spoke English but not everyone knew all the languages represented in the group. A lot of translation accompanied their discussions. I tried to translate my American into English. Nerio and I did not speak directly to one another during these dinners because there was too much noise and confusion, especially as the group's discussions heated up. If I was questioned about anything or I added something to the conversation, I depended on those who understood English to translate my words into Italian, French, Swedish, Greek and Turkish. For us to converse, Nerio and I needed quiet, no distractions, strong focus and my Italian/English dictionary.

Most of the group's discussions revolved around the war in Vietnam and America's role in it. It didn't take me long to see that these people were well read and well informed about what was happening in the world. They read several newspapers daily. Not just Italian papers but papers from around Europe. The English-speaking students and I read the *International Herald Tribune* daily. Additionally, they were listening to lectures and speakers at the university discussing Southeast Asia politically, economically, militarily and culturally. They had a body of information that I had only begun to suspect existed.

Before I arrived in Florence, I had already changed my opinion about the war and I no longer naïvely held to the belief that my president was right, no matter what he said. The University Mensa group believed that the war in Vietnam was wrong and America's role in it was immoral. They had differing ideas about what could be done, but overall they were appalled by the destruction and the number of people, Vietnamese and American, being killed and wounded. They held the firm belief that we Americans were being lied to and they discussed much larger casualty numbers than what I was reading about. They and their families had experienced war just twenty-two years before and the students held strong opinions about what war could and could not accomplish. They were not opposed to war in general and believed that America's role in World War II was moral. It's just that they didn't find anything moral about our role in Vietnam. By this time, I agreed.

(It would be nice if I could tell you that the Mensa group was just a bunch of young people spouting off about things they knew nothing about but that would not be the truth. Not long after I returned to Washington, the American newspapers and TV news reports began to provide information that shredded into little pieces the administration's stories about Vietnam. I was now hearing the same numbers and getting the same information in Washington that I had already heard in Florence.)

You'll never guess what the second most discussed topic of conversation was. Feminism. The Mensa group introduced me to Betty Friedan's *The Feminine Mystique* and was astounded that I had not heard of the book. It was published in 1964 and was on the *New York Times'* Bestsellers List for weeks. I told them I had been a little busy during that time.

This is where we bumped heads a bit. They made assumptions that I was a young, white American woman (astute deductions so far, based on obvious evidence) who came from a privileged family and who had been taught to expect the things that Betty Friedan wrote about when it came to jobs, marriage, motherhood and housewifery. Had I continued living in Upperco, had we remained a family, and had I managed to survive Dorothy and Isadore, I felt certain that I would have been struggling with the issues Friedan described in her book.

But at twenty-one years old, I had already been on my own for eight years and had supported myself (as best I could) during that time. I didn't do too badly. I was traveling in Europe on money I saved from my own earnings and not on family money. Yes, I knew about pay inequality and had bristled when someone said to me, "Well, you know, honey, men are paid more because they are the primary wage earners and heads of their households." To which I would think (and sometimes say), "What the hell am I, chopped liver? I'm the sole wage earner and head of *my* household."

I tried to explain that my life had been a little different and that many of the points they were talking about from Friedan's book simply didn't apply. I had already "evolved" in a number of key areas. I was not an unhappy, frustrated, angry housewife and mother trapped in her home with her condescending husband, nor did I plan to become one of those women.

Part of the problem I had with the Mensa group was that I was not willing to give them many details about my life or experience. It felt raw and too complex for a multi-language, multi-translated discussion so I told them just enough to get across that I didn't have to rush out and buy *The Feminine Mystique* in order to better myself. To their credit, once they got over the shock of my not knowing about this book, they seemed to accept that my circumstances might be different and they backed off.

But this didn't stop them from discussing the book in general. They were aware of and sensitive to the inequality and unfair plight of women around the world who were trapped in their lives, whether it be privileged or poor.

My relationship with Nerio reflected his sensitivity to women's issues. He didn't attempt to dominate me and I felt he respected me as a peer. It made for a very different interaction with a man that I had not experienced previously. At times I had to laugh at myself because I would do or say something that sprang from old habits or what I was used to seeing in the U.S. And in all fairness, every once in a while old habits would spring up in Nerio, as well. (Ah, change, evolution and growth can be so much easier on paper than in practice.)

From the Mensa discussions I learned something else. Citizens of the United States may choose to isolate themselves and our country from the rest of the world but the citizens of the rest of the world are not isolating themselves from us. They continue to keep up with what is happening in America. At times they can be way ahead of us about something, as I saw with the war in Vietnam. As my post-Europe years have rolled by, I have made it a point to also listen to what knowledgeable Europeans are saying and thinking about us and world events.

A few years back, I was listening to a report on NPR about a special election being held in Sri Lanka. As part of the report, they interviewed a street vendor for his take on what was at stake in the election. First of all, the Sri Lankan street vendor spoke perfect English. He proceeded to outline the political, economic and social situation from several points of view and summarized how one set of points was more helpful to the country and its people than the other points.

When the report was over, I found myself staring at the radio. This street vendor from Sri Lanka was more knowledgeable and articulate about his election than anything I had ever heard from our experts, talking heads and voters about policy and elections in my own country. To this day (and much to their annoyance), I hold everyone, myself included, to the Mensa and Sri Lanka standard when it comes to national and global awareness.

TWO WEEKS AFTER ARRIVING and just about the time when I was thinking about how much longer I should stay in Florence, Karen caught up with me and asked if I'd like to work on art restoration. They were woefully understaffed in the sculpture division and would be grateful for any help—on a volunteer basis. They didn't have any money. She didn't have to go any further. I quickly said, "Yes. Count me in." The next day I reported to work at the Uffizi and officially became a "Mud Angel."

On November 4, as soon as the flood waters began to recede, thousands of young people (mostly students) from all over Italy and Europe rushed to Florence to do whatever was needed to help the Florentines and to save the art, books, frescoes, carvings, statues and other priceless pieces. Giovanni Grazzini, a journalist covering the disaster for the Italian daily *Corriere della Sera* was the first to call those volunteers "Mud Angels." The initial wave of Mud Angels cleaned the city of refuse and mud. They rescued works of art and books from flooded rooms and out of the mud. They had no electricity, no running water, no drinking water, no hot water, no hot meals, sometimes no meals at all because food was in short supply and, for the first week, no rubber boots. The days and nights were bone chilling cold and they were wading, sometimes waist deep, in thick mud, sewage and naphthalene (heating oil) while dodging floating cars and livestock carcasses. Many workers slept outside in sleeping bags or just leaned against the interior walls of the buildings they were working on. Mudslides and debris had cut Florence off from the outside and it took days for a large truck filled with rubber boots to reach the city. After three weeks, medical problems began to surface and a number of the first-wave Angels were encouraged to evacuate. (Not all did.) As some left, more volunteers from around the globe poured in and the rescue, recovery and restoration continued without pause.

I had not heard the name "Mud Angel" until I was researching the flood for this book and discovered a bunch of articles about the week-long 50th-anniversary remembrance of the flood that was held in Florence in 2016. For the first time, the Angels were invited back to be honored but I suspect a fair number of us, myself included, never heard the call. Even so, thousands showed up. Essentially the city rolled out the proverbial red carpet for the Angels. Discounts for lodging and meals were provided. Special Angel Masses were said. Free tickets to all the museums were handed out. There were Mud Angel processions, parades, lots of conversations and tales from the flood days. They even unveiled a new Mud Angel postage stamp. It was a remarkable gesture of appreciation that made me smile just reading about it. Even without attending, I felt thanked.

By the time I became a Mud Angel in March 1967, the initial rescue efforts were completed and the primary focus was on restoration. There were large teams of experts and volunteers (including Karen) tackling the three to four million damaged old books and manuscripts that needed to be dried out, cleaned, disinfected and restored page by page. I had a chance to visit Karen at the Biblioteca Nazionale to see the operation. There were drying pages hanging all over the place from clothes lines. To me, considering the number of damaged books, their task seemed impossible.

Other teams were addressing the damaged paintings. Moisture caused the panel paintings on wood to buckle, crack, develop blisters and chip. Rice paper was applied to slow the drying process and to keep paint chips from falling off. For canvas paintings and frescoes, similar problems were occurring and the teams applied sheets of gauze to the damaged areas.

Then there was the marble street team that consisted of about eight people when I joined. Immediately after the flood, Palazzo Davanzati had been set up as a "marble hospital" where experts worked on the smaller pieces that could be transported to the Palazzo. I don't know how many experts were over there because we rarely saw them. They were a bit of a mystery.

The street team worked on the marble that could not be moved, like ten-foot tall statues, 350-foot-long marble walls, plaques and reliefs. Our immediate supervisor was Anthony, a British fellow in his mid-twenties. He wasn't appointed or hired by anyone. He just saw a need that no one was addressing and stepped in to do something about it. As Anthony tells it, he was part of the first wave of rescuers. But after several weeks, he noticed that no one was paying attention to the city's statues and marble buildings. In the beginning, the early workers had rinsed off as much mud as they could but took the cleanup no further. Something more was needed.

The X factor that made all the art restoration so challenging was the naphthalene (heating oil) that floated on the surface of the flood water. Remember, the flood occurred in November and everyone had just had their oil tanks filled in preparation for winter. The rushing water was so forceful that it literally blew apart those tanks all over Florence and a massive amount of oil was released. When the oil hit any marble, it didn't just coat the surface. It absorbed into the marble and left a deep, dark brown stain on the surface. I'm going to give you a disgusting visual that I feel best describes how marble looked after it was hit by that oil. Imagine a lovely, large white marble statue of a young girl holding a lamb in front of you. Now imagine a giant cow that is suffering from diarrhea suspended above your beautiful white statue. Try as she might to keep everything held in, the cow suddenly explodes and releases an avalanche of dark brown poop all over your statue. When you wash the poop off, you'll find a dark chocolate brown stain that cannot be washed off. Ick. (Welcome to the world of Florence's marble Mud Angels.)

No one had ever dealt with naphthalene damage. Think about it. When the previous monster flood hit Florence in 1557, the city's marble was submerged under a mix of water, mud, wood ashes, maybe a little candle wax and some livestock carcasses. There were no petroleum products floating around. In 1967, there was so much other art that needed immediate attention thanks to the oil damage that everyone ignored the marble with the ugly cow-poop stains because they didn't know what to do about it anyway. New procedures to address the oil problem needed to be developed for each area of the restoration, including marble.

Enter Anthony. He didn't let a little thing like not knowing what to do hold him back. He stepped in, talked to the folks at Davanzati about the problem and began to carefully experiment to see what could be done to restore marble back to its original state. In short, how do we deal with the oil that was not only sitting on the surface but absorbed into the interior of the marble mass as well? Other important questions: Was the naphthalene that was inside the marble mass damaging the integrity of the marble itself; and, if so, would that lead to deterioration over time; and, if so, how much time did we have to solve these problems before the statues and church walls crumbled into big heaps of dust? Finally, how could we accomplish all this without scratching or breaking the marble's protective patina (the polished surface that I liken to tooth enamel)?

Just as I arrived on the scene there was a major breakthrough in solving these problems. A British professor from the University of London discovered that if we mixed a chemical he called "Sipolite" with talc powder and packed this mixture on marble, the Sipolite would draw oil to the surface and the talc would absorb that oil. The professor flew in to show us how to mix the Sipolite and talc and how it was to be applied.

However, there was a downside. In order for the mixture to adhere to the marble, it had to be applied thinly, about an eighth of an inch, and by hand. This meant that one application was not going to do the trick. When the talc dried, we had to brush it off and apply the mixture again. That had to be repeated four or five times before the oil was drawn out and the marble was once again its original color. Packing the mixture on every marble surface that had been submerged in the flood and doing it four or five times was beyond daunting. But we were young and determined.

My first assignment was to join a small group headed to Santa Maria Novella to pack a courtyard wall. Consecrated in 1420, Santa Maria Novella was the first great basilica in Florence and considered one of the more important churches. By the end of the week, we had finished packing a rather long wall up to the six-foot-high water mark twice. We left knowing it was going to need to be packed again.

PIAZZA DELLA SS. ANNUNZIATA: Robbin (another American Mud Angel) and I lugged the packing supplies—Sipolite, deionized water (a process of purification that removes ions from water), talc powder and buckets—to Piazza della SS. Annunziata to pack a well. It was a beautiful day and we pretty much had the piazza to ourselves. The church, Santissima Annunziata (founded in 1250), anchors the piazza. It is flanked on one side by the Spedale degli Innocenti, the first orphanage in Europe. Original Della Robbia terra-cotta reliefs glazed in their distinctive blue and white colors were set into the wall above the orphanage's portico pillars. Each round relief depicted a child, presumably an orphan. They were installed around the mid-1400s, and there I was in 1967 looking at them in situ. I wasn't looking at them detached from their original purpose in a museum somewhere. As I stared, the chasm between 1450 and 1967 narrowed and something connected. I had first felt this connection that could span centuries with Charles Dickens in the Dickens House. It was something I would experience many times in Florence, including with the Della Robbias in Piazza della SS. Annunziata.

Oh yes, right...the well we were sent to pack. (It wasn't hard to get distracted.) There was a large marble relief panel inset on each side of the square well. We packed each panel, ate lunch on the steps of the well, brushed off the dried talc and packed it again.

UFFIZI: The Uffizi is one of the largest and best known museums in the world and it was located in my backyard, adjacent to the Piazza della Signoria. It was begun in 1560 for Cosimo I de' Medici to accommodate the offices of the Florentine magistrates, hence its name. *(Uffizi* means "offices.") The top floor was originally made into a gallery for the Medici family and their collection of Roman sculptures. By the 18th century, the Italian Renaissance collection had expanded to all fifty rooms. The flood waters had damaged the ground-floor rooms along with the books, statues and art collection that had been displayed there at the time, so it was closed to the public. (But not to Mud Angels.)

It was home base for Anthony and if we needed him we always knew to check the Uffizi first. A lot of different restoration was going on there because of the wide range of damaged art. The story goes that Leonardo da Vinci, and later, Michelangelo walked the halls at the Uffizi "for beauty, for work and for recreation." Here I was walking down the same hallways but I was walking down them for restoration.

During my initial exploration (actually, I was lost), I discovered the marquetry restoration room. (Marquetry is inlaid pieces of varicolored wood set in pieces of furniture.) This huge room was filled floor to ceiling with 6x6-inch cubby holes that were about six feet deep. Each cubby hole held long, narrow strips of wood of a particular size, wood type and natural color. One little old Italian man, who apparently was *the* wizard of wood marquetry restoration, meticulously matched, carved and shaped bits of wood to fit in the missing and damaged spaces in the furniture that was brought to him. The marquetry was so fine and so detailed that the finished patterns looked like paintings and not like an inlayed wood mosaic.

When I located Anthony, I was assigned to clean a marble bust of Servius (whoever the hell he was). The bust, along with a number of other statues that were being worked on, was sitting in the Uffizi basement. I was given new tools for the job, courtesy of those mysterious experts at Palazzo Davanzati: toothpicks, a handful of cotton swabs, some Q-tips, a squirt bottle of deionized water and a safety pin. Servius had been washed right after the flood. Now I had to finish the job. Unfortunately he had a curly beard and curly hair making it challenging to remove dried mud and assorted gunk from deep within those crevices. My other challenge was the one bare light bulb we were all working under, making it difficult to see into the crevices let alone clean them out. At one point Anthony came by to check my work. I told him the toothpicks, cotton swabs and Q-tips were the wrong tools for the job. He agreed, but this was all we were being given to work with. We talked about how much more effective dental tools would be and I told him I knew where we could get some dental tools. We'd just have to go to Rome, bust into the Etruscan Museum and snatch a bunch of their old dental instruments. They were just sitting there collecting dust and I was certain the Etruscans wouldn't mind. He walked away saying he may have to consider that.

It took the better part of four days to get Servius cleaned up and presentable. When I finished, Anthony asked if I'd like to go on the payroll. They could offer me $100 a month. I'd have to commit to working five (sometimes six) days a week, ten hours a day. That was the best they could offer. (Such a deal.) I said yes right away. My Albergo expenses would be covered by that $100 per month. At 625 lira per dollar (in 1967), this gave me a hefty sounding monthly salary of 62,500 lira. Staying in Florence and doing something I found rewarding was barely going to eat into my personal traveling cash. At the beginning of each month I collected my salary at the Uffizi from some overwhelmed and confused guy who worked for the government. Because we were paid in cash, I always suspected we were doing something illegal and were getting paid under the table. But maybe it was just that the Italians didn't want to keep track of us or deal with all that extra paperwork.

I've used the word "rewarding" to describe the work but this doesn't adequately cover what it meant to me and to the other Mud Angels I spoke with. We felt we were saving Florence and an important part of the world's history. There was no question or debate about it as far as we were concerned. It wasn't hard for me to grasp that Florence was the center of the Renaissance and that a lot of the history, government, culture and art that we talk about and take for granted today flows from this era and city. I'm usually lost when it comes to history but in Florence I found myself immersed in the Renaissance. I was walking the same streets, crossing the same piazzas and entering the same buildings as Michelangelo, da Vinci, Botticelli, Donatello, Brunelleschi, Dante, Savonarola and the Medici family had done before me. So working as a Mud Angel gave me a unique opportunity to touch history and sculpture in a deep and personal way. It was a commitment of the heart. (You can take a moment to appreciate the irony here. I, the one who tried to keep history at arm's length, was now saving history.)

Being on the payroll meant I had to adjust my schedule with Nerio. I was now working later in the day and needed to shower off the layer of talc dust before meeting him around 8 P.M. for dinner. I usually had both weekend days free and used Saturdays to recoup from the previous week and prepare for the next.

Sundays became my R&R day. In the morning I went to Mass at San Marco, the 15th-century Dominican home of Fra Angelico, the workaholic who left his mark by painting a fresco in each friar's cell. (I imagined his fellow Dominicans saying something like, "Hey, Angelico, I'd like to spruce up my cell. So when you get a chance, how about painting one of your pretty pictures on my wall.") What really drew me to San Marco on Sundays was not the frescoes or even its beautiful church but, rather, its courtyard. After Mass I'd go across the street, get a cappuccino and buy a copy of the Sunday *International Herald Tribune.* Then I'd go back to the courtyard, sit on the stone wall, lean against a pillar, sip coffee and read. It was a remarkably beautiful, peaceful setting that no one else seemed to know was there.

I met up with Nerio in the afternoon and we'd spend the rest of the day together. The weather was now quickly turning spring-like and much of our time was spent walking and sitting in different parks. Sometimes friends invited us to their apartment for dinner and we would play Twenty Questions in multiple languages. Once Nerio took me to a restaurant that specialized in serving tiny birds, complete with head. He said it was a delicacy. I don't remember the name of the bird but I saved its tiny wishbone as a trophy for the courage it took for me to eat a bird's head.

I needed these weekends to give my hands time to recuperate from the chemical burns I was getting from the Sipolite. All of us marble Angels had a red rash on our hands and wrists that could get pretty raw if we had a heavy packing week. At least our hands weren't bleeding. I asked Anthony if we could wear rubber gloves but he said they had already tried that. The Sipolite ate through the gloves. I felt this begged a question: If the Sipolite was eating rubber, what was it doing to our hands? No one knew—yet. Our hands also needed the weekends to recuperate from a week of pounding out thin layers of the Sipolite mixture on the marble. By Friday, my hands were red and in pain. By Monday, they were only a little red and were ready for more pounding.

There was another break the weekends provided. Generally speaking, the Florentines treated the Mud Angels very well. They were hospitable, friendly, helpful and appreciative. It was easy to tell who we were because we were the dusty, smelly, dirty foreigners walking around with buckets. But sometimes we'd walk by an older person and we'd hear the person hiss at us as we passed. Or see them stare angrily at us. A few times men spit at us.

We could not figure out what was going on with these people. In our minds, we were working to save their history and art, and in the process their tourist industry. For a long time I thought it was solely because we were dirty. There's this thing in Italy called *Buona Figura* (good appearance) that describes the need for Italians to appear smartly dressed and neat at all times. Here we were in our work clothes creating little clouds of talc dust as we walked by. I always felt our dust and dirt may have been too much for the older generation to bear. On the weekends when I wasn't dressed in work clothes or creating dust clouds, I never heard a hiss or dodged spit.

As I've thought about this over the years, I think it was probably due to something else that makes more sense. The Florentines were hit hard by the flood personally. They lost a lot—their homes, their possessions, their shops and their livelihoods. We Mud Angels were not paying attention to the needs of the city's residents. If we thought about it, which was rare, we assumed the government and other rescue organizations had taken care of them. We were focused on saving the art. Most people understood what we were doing. But some people were still hurting and they were angry. I read later that in 1967 the mayor of Florence had said publicly, "Enough talk about losing the Cimabue *Crucifix*. We need to talk about helping Florence's Christians instead." The people should come first, not the loss of some 500-year-old painting that had become the world wide symbol of the flood's destruction. I think our dusty presence reminded those who were still hurting that art was continuing to receive the lion's share of attention. The chasm between the two groups was not resolved or even recognized by the restoration people I met while I was there. We remained focused on the art.

When I read what the mayor had said, I felt it was a bit tone deaf. Florence has the largest Jewish community in Italy whose history goes back over 700 years. It includes an internationally recognized library of holy books and illuminated manuscripts, a school and two synagogues. The Great Synagogue of Florence is one of the largest synagogues in south-central Europe. The flood water in The Great Synagogue and library rose to over six feet, damaging and destroying ninety Torah scrolls and 15,000 holy texts. Back in 1967, the word "Christian" did not cover the full population of Florence. I suspect it excludes even more today.

THE BASILICA DI SANTA CROCE: After I went on payroll, Robbin and I were transferred from the Uffizi to Santa Croce where we spent the next six weeks working first in the loggia on the south side of the church and then helping to pack whatever was needed inside the church.

The Basilica is the principal Franciscan church in Florence. Its groundbreaking occurred in 1294–1295 and the church was consecrated in 1442. At 377 feet in length, it is the largest Franciscan church in the world and features sixteen chapels. Legend has it that Santa Croce was founded by Saint Francis himself.

It contains some of the most highly regarded Renaissance art. (This paragraph is dedicated to those art history majors who clutched their chests and keeled over at my description of the Sistine Chapel. I told you things were going to look up.) A few of the artists represented in the church who you might recognize are Cimabue, della Robbia, Donatello, Gaddi, Giotto, Andrea Orcagna, Rossellini, Vasari and Veneziano. The basilica is also the burial place for Michelangelo, Galileo, Machiavelli, the poet Foscolo, the philosopher Gentile and the composer Rossini.

Because of this, Santa Croce is sometimes called the Temple of the Italian Glories. Due to being out of favor with Rome, Galileo was first buried in the basilica in an out-of-the-way spot in the back of the church (in a cupboard under a staircase—oh wait, that was Harry Potter) but eventually he was brought out and placed in his own fancy tomb in the nave of the basilica.

Dante, the statesman, poet, language theorist and political theorist, has a cenotaph in Santa Croce. (A cenotaph is an empty tomb.) Dante was born in Florence but was exiled around 1301 as a result of some pretty weird political intrigue, fights and alliances. He loved Florence but he was never allowed to return. He died in Ravenna and was buried there. Once they woke up and realized what they did, a number of attempts were made by the Florentines to have Dante's body returned to Florence for burial in Santa Croce, but the people of Ravenna said no. Finally, in 1829, a cenotaph was created for him and installed in its current prominent spot in the basilica. That tomb was empty when it was installed and has remained empty ever since. If the people of Ravenna ever agree to return his remains, this is where he will be laid to rest. (Nothing like being prepared.) In 2008, the Municipality of Florence officially apologized for expelling Dante 700 years earlier. (Oops. Our bad. Sorry about that.) In 2015, a celebration was held in Florence to honor the 750th anniversary of Dante's birth. But still the body remains in Ravenna.

Something else in Santa Croce bears special mentioning: Giotto's frescoes. At the beginning of the 14th century, Giotto, the workaholic from San Marco, was the most important artist of his time. He was commissioned by two of the wealthiest Florentine families to paint the basilica's Bardi and Peruzzi Chapels with frescoes. Over the centuries, the frescoes have taken quite a beating. The most obvious is the white-washing that was done in the mid-16th century by Vasari that resulted in the frescoes being covered over. Vasari felt the church's original gothic style that included the frescoes was no longer in fashion. (Let's get rid of these damn frescoes and cover the walls in a nice egg-shell white.) Much of the original Giotto paint has been restored but there are still frescoes that are framed in that white-washing or have strips of the white-washing running through portions of the painting. The visual begs the question: What idiot did that? Even though they had not been hit by the flood waters, we Mud Angels were careful not to harm the Giotto frescoes in any way. They had already endured enough.

Santa Croce was the bullseye for the worst of the flooding with water rising over twenty-two feet deep there. On the north side of the church near the Pazzi Chapel, there is a fairly large courtyard in the center of the friars' cloister. In 1967, the Franciscan friars who served the church lived on the second floor. Here's the sad story we Angels were told: One old friar was the keeper of the keys and in charge of opening the church doors each morning at 6 A.M. He walked along the second-floor walkway under the cloister's portico, entered the church through a second-floor door and made his way down the steps to the ground floor. There he unlocked and opened the doors. On November 4 at 6 A.M., there was no water inside Santa Croce even though the piazza and streets outside were flooded. In an act of utter and complete detachment from reality, our keeper of the keys had not noticed that the entire courtyard he had just walked around was completely filled with water (from photos it looked like a gigantic, fifteen-foot-deep swimming pool) or that it had risen so high that it overflowed the second floor walkway and he had to trudge through about six inches of water. If he glanced at the courtyard at all, he didn't notice the water. And apparently he didn't notice that his feet were submerged in some cold, nasty water either. Many felt that Santa Croce would have been saved from the flood had he not opened the doors and let the flood waters rush in.

The damage to the church was devastating. It took two days to get the receding water out of the church, and two months and an army of young volunteers to get rid of the thick layer of mud. The water mark in the nave was nearly nine feet high. Everything in the church that was below that mark was either damaged or destroyed. Pews were tossed all over the place. Santa Croce's museum, Museo dell' Opera, is at a lower elevation and in 1966 Cimabue's *Crucifix* (c. 1288) and Vasari's *Last Supper* (painted in 1546) were submerged in thirteen feet of flood water for over ten hours. Because of its size (14'3"x12'7") it took ten men to carry the *Crucifix* out of the museum. By that time, the already heavy wooden crucifix had taken on so much water that it had grown three inches, doubled its weight and lost 60 percent of its paint.

While I was working in Florence, Cimabue's *Crucifix* was considered completely destroyed. Many considered it the greatest loss for Santa Croce, Florence and the art world and despite the mayor's frustration, it quickly became the symbol of the flood's devastation. I didn't hear anyone talking about trying to restore it back then, but ten years later (1976) the restored *Crucifix* was returned to Santa Croce and is now hanging out of harm's way in the church's Sacristy.

The Last Supper by Vasari (he of white-washing fame) was painted in 1546. It too had suffered tremendous damage from being submerged for over ten hours. After they dried it out and protected it with sheets of Japanese mulberry paper, it took another forty years to acquire the technology and expertise to accomplish the whole restoration. In 2009, restoration was begun. In November 2016, as part of the 50th anniversary celebration, the five-panel painting (measuring more than 8x21 feet) was returned to Santa Croce and remounted on the museum wall—higher. It has become the symbol of the city's resurrection.

Robbin and I were assigned to work in the Santa Croce loggia located along the northern (left) exterior wall. There were two sarcophagi and a series of 15th-century plaques, all of which had been submerged. To work on the first sarcophagus we had to build a makeshift scaffold using the pews and risers that had been moved from the church to the loggia. It was three "stories" high starting with two pews, then one riser balanced on the backs of the pews, then two more pews and finally a board supported on the back of those pews. Even when I added my 5'9" height to this, I was still unable to reach the top lid. So we worked on the sides, the bottom and pillars. It wasn't exactly the most stable scaffold and there were days when the spring winds were so strong that we had to come down and work inside the church.

By the time we finished cleaning and packing (and packing and packing and packing) the first sarcophagus, we had discovered a pleasing surprise. The carvings on the front included two family coat of arms. The shields had originally been painted, the top half yellow and the bottom half blue. The color was faded but it was still there. No one was expecting this and when Anthony told Davanzati about it, several of the "mystery experts" came over to see for themselves. While they pointed and examined and gushed, Robbin and I stood to one side and made quiet comments like, "Get a grip. It's just some faded color."

The second sarcophagus came with a story: Back in 1478 (Sunday, April 26, to be exact), members of the Pazzi family (rivals to the ruling Medici family) mounted a *coup d'état* to overthrow Lorenzo and Giuliano de' Medici. The plan was to assassinate them in the Duomo during Mass in front of 10,000 people. They were successful in killing Giuliano, stabbing him nineteen times, but Lorenzo, though wounded, escaped. Consequently the coup failed and the conspirators were captured and executed.

One might think that would be the end of it but apparently this punishment wasn't enough. In a classic case of overkill, the entire family was tossed out of Florence, and their lands and property were confiscated. Their name and their coat of arms were wiped out forever. Their name was erased from public registers, and all buildings and streets carrying the name "Pazzi" were renamed. Anyone named Pazzi had to take a new name and anyone married to a Pazzi was barred from public office. In short, the city hit a massive Delete button. Robbin and I were told that this second sarcophagus contained the remains of the Pazzi who killed Giuliano. He wasn't allowed to be buried in the Pazzi Chapel nor could he be buried inside the church. His sarcophagus was relegated to the far side wall of the loggia.

The flood waters had seeped into that sarcophagus from the top and the lid had been removed for drying out. That meant that the Pazzi body was exposed to certain curious young American Mud Angels. I climbed up and found the 489-year-old bones had been swept up into a pile. There was no discernible body structure, just a heap of bones.

Each day we worked in the loggia we had to deal with another challenge—perhaps it was more an annoyance than a challenge.

The loggia was enclosed by a twelve-foot-tall wrought-iron fence topped with five-inch iron spikes. Even though the loggia was over 300 feet in length, there was just one gate for entering and exiting.

Guess who showed up daily at 1 P.M. rattling his keys? The now infamous keeper of the keys. What astonished us most was that he still had the keys. Besides opening the doors and flooding the basilica, his duties also included closing the gate to the loggia during lunch, thus locking us in. He didn't reopen the damn gate until 3 P.M. There were times when we couldn't stop what we were doing. We tried to explain, bribe and sweet talk this friar into being a little reasonable but reason wasn't his strong suit. We considered jumping the guy and ripping the keys out of his hands but he was old and looked too frail to survive our attack. So every day the fool locked us in. The best solution we came up with was to climb the fence—and try not to get impaled on our way over the top.

For lunch we stopped at our local bread shop, then our meat shop and then our cheese shop to buy the pieces needed to make sandwiches. My inexpensive lunch meat of choice was *mortadella.* It tasted like our bologna. I stopped eating it when I found out that *mortadella* was horse meat and I felt like I was eating Freedom. Sometimes we'd take our sandwiches and head on over to the Galleria dell'Accademia where Michelangelo's *David* stands and watch American tourists deal with a seventeen-foot tall naked man. It could be entertaining. Anyway, it was good lunch entertainment.

There was another hot spot for lunch: Palazzo Vecchio. Florence's town hall dates back to the 13th century when its construction began. Michelangelo's *David* (1504) originally stood outside the entrance to the Palazzo but was moved to the Accademia in 1873 to protect it from damage. A full-size replica of *David* now stands outside the entrance. (That's a good thing since every once in a while the people of Florence rise up about something and invariably someone tosses rocks or buckets of paint on the *David* replacement as a protest that has nothing to do with the statue.) Inside the Palazzo, in the far corner of the first courtyard, stairs led down to the best kept secret in Florence: a tiny restaurant that only served pasta—heaping plates of the best and least expensive homemade pasta dishes in town. A simple Pasta Bolognese cost 100 lira (14 cents). It had been especially set up for construction workers and Mud Angels. Tourists not allowed.

Not long after we finished the second sarcophagus, Robbin was assigned to help with the efforts going on inside the church. I worked on the row of fifteen marble plaques along the back wall of the loggia. Many were over 500 years old and all had been submerged in the flood waters. I had deionized water for washing and the Sipolite mixture for packing but I had nothing for removing the thick layer of hardened vehicle exhaust and pollution that had built up over the decades. It created a coating that left the plaques black and could not be penetrated with any of my tools.

One morning while walking to work I spotted a bent, rusty, square nail in the street. I picked it up, examined it and decided it might be just what I needed to get through that hard black coating. I chose a tiny hidden spot on one of the plaques for testing and, after soaking it with the deionized water, I gently rubbed the flat side of the nail over the coating. As the nail broke through the crust and more water was added, a thick paste formed. I kept rubbing until I got down to the surface of the marble. I looked for any signs of scratching but could see nothing. (A scratched or damaged patina can eventually destroy marble sculpture.) The paste had protected the marble.

I asked Robbin to look at the test spot and she agreed that there was no sign of damage. So I carefully moved forward with the nail. It was pretty obvious that I had to be doing something different because these plaques were turning from a dull black back to the original color of the marble. Anthony heard about it and stopped by to find out what I was doing. When I showed him the magic tool, he nearly fainted. But I urged him to look at the marble's patina for scratches. He even went back to the Uffizi to get a magnifying glass. He examined all the plaques I had completed and found no scratching or other damage. With that, he gave me the okay to continue. His last words: "We won't be telling Davanzati about this."

It took two weeks to finish the plaques. Working by myself gave me a chance to feel the rhythms of the neighborhood around me. Each afternoon I was joined by an elderly woman who stood on the church steps next to the loggia and tossed bread scraps to the pigeons. Normally there weren't a lot of pigeons that hung around the church. But as soon as she started walking across the piazza toward the steps, hundreds would flock in and swirl around her waiting for their treats. When the postman came by to deliver mail to the residents across the street, he called up to their open apartment windows. Then I'd watch the women lower baskets on ropes for their mail. Add to this lovely picture the dusty girl in the loggia cleaning old plaques with a bent rusty nail. Life felt good.

Enter the flasher: I was locked in the loggia (again) when I heard a weird noise behind me. I turned to see what was going on. There, standing about five feet from my ladder, was a middle-aged man dressed in a three-piece suit with his fly down and his erect penis jutting out. With the gate locked, I felt trapped and had to quickly come up with a way to deal with the situation. While he was busy moaning and masturbating, I picked up my deionized water bottle and aimed it at his penis. I sprayed his penis and pants as much as I could and then said sharply, *"Chimico."* (That's "chemical" in Italian.) He got a panicked, horrified look on his face, clutched his penis with both hands and slinked over to the other side of the loggia. He sat over there for about twenty minutes holding himself, rocking back and forth and moaning, only now his moans were not derived from pleasure.

Before I sprayed him, I had noticed a breeze blowing through the loggia. I knew that as soon as the water hit his skin it would start evaporating. In his panic, he was going to think I had indeed squirt a chemical on him. I returned to my work with my back to him, but I remained on high alert and listened for any movement in case I had to hit him with the "chemical" again. After about twenty minutes there was quiet. I glanced over and he was gone. Then it hit me. "Hey, wait a minute. Are you telling me that some guy in a three-piece suit climbed that fence topped with spikes just to flash me?" The gate was still locked so his only option was to come over the fence. (No pun intended.) When the keeper of the keys returned I shot him a look and fired off a hand gesture that I felt certain he would remember for a long time. He floods churches and puts young women in danger. Again, could we discuss jumping that old man and taking away his keys?

I was proud of the plaque technique I had developed with my trusty nail and the results. I suspected those old plaques had not looked that good in a very long time. On one of the plaques I chose to leave the upper left corner untouched to show a before and after contrast. And it was my "signature." Those plaques were cleaned courtesy of one Machaelle Small. (Over the fifty years, I suspect the new pollution and car exhaust buildup has wiped out my work. But for one, brief, shining moment...)

With the plaques completed, I joined the others inside Santa Croce. The church was a beehive of restoration activity with attention being paid to paintings, marble and the floor. In the far corner just inside the front doors, a German crew was slowly drying out a 30x30 foot area of the floor with massive gas heat blowers. There was a lot of concern that the floor could collapse into the lower catacombs and weaken the church foundations if it dried out too quickly. The Germans donated the huge blowers and the experienced crew to go along with them to address the tricky floor problems. In the midst of all the activity, tourists (individuals and groups) would wander through and stare. Honest to god, I actually heard an American man say loudly, "Where the hell is the bathroom in this place?" What is it with us Americans and our toilet fetishes?

About this time, our British professor from the University of London met with us to pass on some unsettling news. Further tests with the Sipolite showed that it destroyed human white blood cells. We needed to stop mixing and applying it with bare hands. He suggested that we now use wooden boards as paddles. We could sling small amounts of the Sipolite mixture onto the marble and smooth it out with the boards. We tried his suggestions for two days then came to the conclusion that he had never tried to pack vertically standing marble. Being the young, invincible minded, dedicated people that we were, we went back to applying the mixture with our hands. In a nod to the professor, we mixed the Sipolite and talc in the buckets with the boards. We'd let the white blood cells and chemical burns sort themselves out.

There was a new guy on our crew who was being trained to pump the Sipolite tanks to the right pressure for spraying into buckets with the talc. All was going well until suddenly we heard an ominous sound and looked over at this guy. He had over-pumped a tank and it was getting ready to explode. On top of that, it was sitting about ten feet away from a Giotto fresco. The Sipolite would destroy the fresco. There wasn't enough time to get the tank out of the church before it exploded so a couple of us grabbed the guy and forcibly sat him down on top of the tank. His butt kept the explosion low and away from the fresco. His first day on the job and he gets Sipolite blasted up his ass. But the fresco was undamaged.

After a week, Robbin and I were sent to the cloister courtyard that had been completely flooded on November 4. There was a larger-than-life-size marble statue of a nude man standing just inside the entrance. It had been submerged and we were to clean it. We started packing at the top of his head and worked our way down—until we got to the guy's penis. Neither one of us wanted to pack that thing. We were facing an impasse and the only solution was to play Rock-Paper-Scissors. The loser had to pack the penis. My scissors won out over her paper.

NOT LONG AFTER WE BEGAN our work on the sarcophagi in the loggia, Hubert Humphrey (my country's vice president) came into town to deliver a big speech to the fine folks of Florence. He had been traveling around Europe trying to mend frazzled relations and drum up support for America's role in Vietnam. I read about his efforts and was aware that the trip wasn't going well. Apparently I knew something that the U.S. government didn't know (or chose to ignore): No one in Europe supported that war or our role in it. Humphrey was on a fool's errand. As he spoke in each city, his reception became more and more dicey. Now he was due to speak at Piazza della Signoria on April 23 and the students at the university were gearing up for a big protest, buzzing with discussions, posters, flyers and planning.

I had this cockamamie feeling that it was my duty as an American citizen to attend his speech in support of the man who was my vice president, even though I no longer supported the war or our policies in Vietnam. Nerio warned that I might be in danger. A lot of police would be present and they had a reputation for swinging batons at the slightest provocation. I felt that because this was a public event and not some private speech, I had the right to be there. I was not going to participate in any violence so they better not hit me. (This is where the same invincibility mindset that led me to ignore my white blood cells had kicked in again. Ah, youth.) Even though I had no idea what I was doing, I wasn't going to back down.

Nerio did the next best thing. He got me to agree to a plan that was designed to protect me. On the evening of April 23, Nerio and his friends met at his apartment. As soon as I got there I saw that everyone was taking this protest very seriously. They were dressed in old clothes and busy deciding what identification cards they would carry in their pockets. From the day I met him until the day I left Florence, Nerio always wore a dark blue suit, blue shirt and dark blue tie—his version of *Buona Figura.* Now he was dressed in old khaki slacks, white shirt, and a khaki raincoat. He and the others were prepared for the possibility of blood, water canons and arrest.

The plan was for me to join them for the walk to Piazza della Signoria. When we got there, Nerio would peel off from the others and lead me to a safe spot. Then he would join the others and I would be on my own. When we arrived, the piazza was already full of students and ringed by police standing shoulder to shoulder, all holding batons. My "safe spot" was off to one side and just outside that ring. I still had a clear view of the balcony at Palazzo Vecchio where Humphrey was due to speak. Before he left to join the others, Nerio said something to the guard standing directly in front of me. I didn't hear what he said but I suspected it was something like, "This is my friend. She's American and she just wants to hear the speech. Don't beat her." My approach was to smile, be friendly, ask the guard how he was and, in general, flirt a bit so that he wouldn't club me with the baton he was holding. It worked. We spent the next hour smiling at one another. Every once in a while a loud roar rose from the crowd on the other side of the piazza with some pushing and shoving that resulted in swinging batons. Humphrey never did appear. He didn't even come out on the balcony. We were told that the speech was cancelled due to security concerns.

When I got back to Nerio's apartment, everyone was there except for one fellow, the student from Sweden. He had been hit hard over the head and had been airlifted back to Sweden for surgery. His skull was fractured and they feared other serious internal injuries. Thus ended my very first protest march against the war in Vietnam.

BY THE TIME ROBBIN AND I finished cleaning and packing the naked guy standing in the Santa Croce courtyard, it was mid-May. Florence was hit with some major summer-like heat. Tourist season was slowly starting and Robbin accepted a job on the other side of the Piazza di Santa Croce at Ennio's Santa Croce Leather Factory. It was a job that didn't include talc powder, chemicals or heat (the shop was air conditioned). After knocking off the dust from the morning's work, I would walk over and visit with Robbin during lunch just to sit in cool air for a while.

Ennio's was one of the largest, if not *the* largest, leather shops in Florence. Being right on Piazza di Santa Croce it was in a prime location for tourists on foot and in buses. (Visit Santa Croce and then pop on over to Ennio's to stock up on your lifetime supply of leather wallets, gloves, belts, purses and anything else that could be leather-ized.) When the shop got busy, I'd sit behind the counter and watch. Some Americans assumed I worked there and, with a little encouragement from the Ennio's staff, I started to function as an employee. It was pretty easy to sound like I knew what I was talking about because all I had to do was chit-chat with the English speaking customers when they came up to the counter, add up their purchases and, in Italian, tell the Signora who manned the cash register their total. Being able to talk to American tourists in English and then give the Signora the information she needed in Italian made Robbin and me valuable to Ennio's. They asked if I would like to work on Saturdays. I said sure. I'd make a little extra money and, as I keep pointing out, it was air conditioned.

One thing I couldn't understand was why the American tourists never figured out that Robbin and I were American. You'd think they would recognize the ease with which we were speaking their language. They'd actually say to us, "Wow. Where did you learn to speak English? Your accent is perfect." And I'd respond, "Berlitz. The three-week course."

In early June, Anthony sent me on what I considered to be another special assignment: Casa Buonarroti or, as I called it, Mike's House. Technically, it was "Mike's Sorta House." Michelangelo owned the property but never lived there. He left the place to his nephew, Lionardo Buonarroti and it was his son, Michelangelo the Younger, who converted the place into a museum dedicated to Mike. It features the sculptor's letters, drawings and studies, the preparatory models he made for his sculptures, and his first two sculptures: *Madonna of the Steps* and *Battle of the Centaurs.* (These pieces are reliefs—that is, the subjects of the sculpture project out from the background and the piece is mounted on a wall and not freestanding.)

Because of the flood, the museum was closed to the public. There were workmen on the ground floor repairing and rebuilding whatever was damaged. I worked by myself on the first floor (in our American vernacular we would call that the second floor). The *Madonna of the Steps,* the *Battle of the Centaurs* and a casting of Michelangelo's *Dying Slave* were in my room. I was to dust the reliefs and then clean the *Dying Slave.* I couldn't believe they were letting me touch these pieces. Because Anthony didn't warn me to not whip out my bent rusty nail, I had to assume that he trusted me to work on them with the proper care and respect.

Actually the reliefs just needed a gentle dusting, but it gave me the opportunity to look at these pieces up close over a longer than normal period of time. My touch broadened how I "saw" the pieces. It was what I imagine a blind person experiences when they explore an object with their fingers, only I had the benefit of sight to go along with it. His very first sculpture, The *Madonna of the Steps,* was sculpted around 1491 when Michelangelo was seventeen. Even though it was a relatively simple relief sculpture, I made sure I took as much time as possible to dust it—and examine it.

The *Battle of the Centaurs* (1492) with its mass of nude men and their intertwined arms and legs jutting out from the background took more time. I came out of my experience thinking, "If you want to understand something about how a piece was sculpted, clean it." With the *Battle of the Centaurs* I began to see and understand Michelangelo's approach to his sculpture. It was his second piece and he was only about eighteen when he completed it, but in the *Battle of the Centaurs* he broke from tradition and began to develop his signature *"non finito"* sculpting technique: the smooth figures of the foreground rising out from the rough-hewn background. I was able to see how he worked with his chisel while I cleaned the rough background.

The final piece I worked on was *Dying Slave* (created between 1513 and 1515). It wasn't the original but it came with its own story. It seems that when Napoleon was mucking about in Italy in the late 1700s to the early 1800s, he decided to take *Dying Slave* as a little seven-foot-tall souvenir. The Italians weren't happy and demanded that he return the statue. Instead, he sent a casting of the statue to Florence—as a gift. (What a guy.) The original *Slave* is currently in the Louvre in Paris. I had nothing to compare the casting with since I had not seen the original, but to me the casting, with all its detail and nuance, seemed to be a quality copy. I worked on it for about three weeks.

Over the years I've come across three of Michelangelo's quotes that describe what I recognized and felt as I worked on *Dying Slave.*

> "Every block of stone has a statue inside it and it is the task of the sculptor to discover it."
>
> "I saw the angel in the marble and carved until I set him free."
>
> "Carving is easy, you just go down to the skin and stop."

With the rough-hewn background I could clearly see how he approached and freed the *Dying Slave* from the marble block. I have to say that I didn't think the *Dying Slave* was dying. I thought he was in a state of peaceful sleep. As I worked on him, I had to remember that this was a statue in order to stop myself from falling in love with it. *Dying Slave* is young, handsome and naked.

WHEN I FINISHED WORKING at Casa Buonarroti it was late June and hot as hell. With the heat came what looked to be a major setback with the marble that we had packed. The heat drew more oil from deep within the marble to the surface and dark brown splotches began to reappear everywhere. While we worked we had no way of knowing if we had removed all the oil except to pack until the surface was no longer brown. However the prolonged period of high heat drew the rest of the oil to the surface. Everything was going to have to be repacked. To say this was a blow to the marble Angels is probably understating it. But many stayed on and began repacking right away.

I had been working for about four months by then and I didn't think my hands could take much more. Besides, I was feeling I needed to make a decision about Florence: stay and set roots or leave. My relationship with Nerio was fine but I could see that our language and cultural barriers were going to get in the way if we tried to move it to a new level any time soon. Neither one of us talked about or desired marriage but there were other options we could have chosen. I had a gut feeling that any step forward with Nerio would be temporary and that there wasn't a future for us.

I had another feeling I was dealing with, as well. I don't know what happened but as we moved into summer I felt Italy close in around me and I was beginning to feel claustrophobic. I can still recall the sensation but I can't explain what caused it. I'm sure the heat didn't help. The thing is, I really loved Florence. All I knew was that if I stayed I ran the risk of being driven mad.

I talked to Nerio about my decision and he supported my gut feelings about both our relationship and how I was feeling about Italy. I decided to leave in two weeks. I spent much of that time preparing to auto-stop through the rest of my trip and saying goodbye to friends and to Florence. As strongly as I felt about my decision to leave, I was also sad and I knew it was going to be tough.

When I resigned, Anthony thanked me for my work and walked with me to the Uffizi so that I could collect my last paycheck. I told the folks at the Albergo Imperiale my plans. Signor Lorini had just two weeks to take me away with him to the forest. I said goodbye to the folks who worked in my favorite bar across the street and were kind enough to pass on a few Italian lessons along with their pastries. Of course I had to say goodbye to everyone in the Mensa group. When I told the people at Ennio's I was leaving, they would not let go of me. More American tourists were coming into the shop every day and they needed their star Berlitz graduate. So I said I would work each day for one week but for shorter hours.

Florence has a huge open market that had been wiped out in the flood but was now back and bustling. I went there to find my perfect auto-stopping bag. I chose an Alitalia flight bag with a shoulder strap that was the size of a medium duffle bag. Then I concentrated on what I was going to carry in that bag. I packed and unpacked and packed it again until I got it just right—bare essentials plus a bungee cord I could wrap around the bag for support and also use as a clothes line, one bar of the most amazing clothes soap that Italian women used when washing their clothes by hand and a light travel mug. I tossed out my copy of *Europe on $5 a Day* (which gave me a wonderful sense of freedom). I would rely on what I had already learned about European travel and add common sense. I knew that to travel simply and like the Europeans, all I had to do was go to the center of a town and look up. The hotels that catered to Europeans were a floor above the ground-level shops.

I needed to add one more touch to my Alitalia bag to help ensure my auto-stopping success. Most American travelers stuck an American flag decal on their backpacks. Because of our role in the Vietnam War there were a lot of bad feelings toward Americans that often resulted in stranded American auto-stoppers. The smarter Americans stuck a Canadian flag decal on their pack. I found the perfect addition for my bag in the marketplace: a five-inch-tall decal of Donald Duck enthusiastically sticking his thumb out as an auto-stopper. I decided that a little humor would help.

I packed all the stuff I would not carry in my Alitalia bag into my old suitcase, took it to the post office and shipped that baby back to a friend in Washington. Life was quickly becoming simplified and manageable.

I spent my last week in Florence walking around the city revisiting the places I had worked and the spots I had grown to love. The marble that Robbin and I cleaned fared better in the heat than other marble and showed fewer brown spots. We were a formidable team. I met Margaret, another Mud Angel who was getting ready to leave Florence, and we walked over to Palazzo Vecchio to take the most snapped tourist photo. We just couldn't leave without taking that dumb shot. We took turns striking silly poses in front of the fake *David* statue at the entrance to the Palazzo. Like the tourists' shots, our photos were to be our "definitive proof" to family and friends that we had made it to Florence. However, Margaret and I made one little mistake. I took the photo of her with my camera and she took the photo of me with her camera. I now have the definitive proof that Margaret was in Florence. I have no proof that I was there.

On the Saturday of my last weekend, I attended the Calcio Storico Fiorentino finals match. It is a team sporting match that is a combination of soccer, rugby and wrestling. But in all honesty, it's a free-for-all. It originated in Florence in the 16th century and is played in historical costume. Even though this is an event that happens each year, the match held in June 1967 was special. Most of the costumes had been destroyed in the flood and a bunch of women put forth a herculean effort to replace them in time for the June match. Normally the match is held in Piazza Santa Croce but this year, in honor of what it meant to the city, it was played in Piazza della Signoria in front of Palazzo Vecchio. There was a lot of buzz about this match and the bleachers were packed. The Calcio Storico Fiorentino held in 1967 was a clear signal that Florence was coming back from the flood.

The match was played by a bunch of men dressed in bright costumes that looked like they were designed by the same guys who designed the "uniforms" for the Vatican guards. Apparently the 16th century was a bit flamboyant. In the piazza, an eight-inch layer of dirt and sand was laid and bleachers were set up all around the perimeter. The two teams, led by a bunch of medieval drummers, marched in behind their banners. Trumpets were sounded, the crowd cheered and eventually the match began with the firing of a cannon.

The official rules of the Calcio Storico were first published in 1580. Each team started with twenty-seven players and no substitutions were allowed for injured or expelled players. It was a wild mixed martial arts match that included punching, kicking, tripping, hacking, tackling and wrestling in an effort to tire the opponents' defenses. However it often descended into an all-out brawl. (I'm not sure how they distinguished the actual match from a brawl.) Each team tried to pin down and overwhelm as many players as possible. Once there were enough incapacitated players, the other teammates swooped up the ball and headed to the goal. For centuries, the game's violence resulted in severe injuries, including death. Early on, in order to encourage wagering, bulls were released onto the playing field in hopes of adding confusion and tipping the game to victory for the favored team. However due to the many fatal injuries, bulls, sucker punches and kicks to the head were eventually banned. More than one player attacking an opponent was also forbidden. Any violation led to being expelled from the game.

Goals were scored by throwing the ball over a designated spot on the perimeter of the field. There was a main referee, six linesmen and a field master (all in medieval costume). The game lasted fifty minutes with no timeouts. I never did figure out who won. It was hard to follow fifty-four players running around, punching, tackling, grabbing one another around the neck, head-butting and kicking. I was told that there was a winning team (more likely it was the last team standing) and that this team won a complimentary dinner. That was it. Just a dinner. In the old days, the winning prize was a Chianina calf (an Italian breed of cattle).

On Sunday I went to Mass at San Marco and sat on the wall in the courtyard drinking cappuccino and reading the paper as usual. I was going to miss this gentle, peaceful routine. I met Nerio for the afternoon and that night he took me out for a special send-off dinner. We crossed Ponte Vecchio, the beautiful stone bridge that I had crossed so many times, and went to a tiny restaurant that had a total of about eight tables. It looked like I was the only "foreigner" there. The place was lively and friendly and the food was excellent. Toward the end of our meal a man came into the restaurant playing a concertina and singing for us.

Just as I was thinking, "Oh, how pleasant," the patrons in the restaurant started yelling at the guy and telling him to get out. The owner came over and firmly escorted the guy to the street. I had no idea what was happening. Nerio explained that the guy was a known "red communist" and this little restaurant was for "yellow communists" only. Adding insult to injury, the concertina player was singing a red communist song just to taunt them. Again, the political color coding.

I never could match up Nerio's political and social beliefs with what I had been taught about communism. To me it seemed closer to what we now call "populism," the belief in the right and ability of the common people to play a major part in governing themselves. But one thing I can testify to is that the Florentines take their political colors seriously.

I had decided to take the train out of Florence to Bologna and from there I would begin auto-stopping. Leaving Florence was going to be hard enough and I didn't want to add the new challenge of auto-stopping by myself on top of it. Nerio and I also agreed that he would not accompany me to the train station. Neither one of us wanted that moment of final separation and closure in public. Sunday evening he walked me back to the Albergo and we said goodbye at the hotel door. Cut quickly. Separate. Don't prolong the agony. Pain. I watched until I could no longer see him as he walked down the street.

The next morning I walked to the train station with my comfortably light, perfectly balanced Alitalia bag, bought a ticket for

Bologna and boarded the train. It was comforting to hear the Italians conversing around me.

That morning Signor Lorini met me as I was leaving the Albergo to try one last time to get me to run away with him to the forest. I kissed his cheek instead. He handed me a letter that I had received that morning and on the train I opened it. It was from Bruce, the friend in Washington who was taking care of Eloise, telling me that Eloise had died. She got sick suddenly and there was nothing the vet could do, so they put her to sleep. I had checked in several times during the trip and he wrote back saying she was running around, playing and eating normally. The vet told Bruce that her illness was something that just happens.

I spent the train ride to Bologna staring out the window while quietly crying—for Eloise, Florence and Nerio. A woman sitting near me asked if I was okay and, in my pigeon Italian, I told her that I had just received news that a dear friend had died.

Update

Italy has made improvements to prevent the river from flooding Florence again. They raised the walls along the Arno and increased its depth under two central bridges where it narrows, easing the river's flow through the city. In the 1990s, they built a dam on a northern tributary to the river and started work on dozens of retention basins on tributaries downstream in the densely populated area between Florence and the Pisa coast, where the Arno flows to the Tyrrhenian Sea. But like everyone else, Italy has had budget problems and constructing the rest of the needed improvements has essentially stalled.

The flood brought a lot of change and innovation in conservation and restoration practices. Restorers learned how to save frescoes without detaching them from walls and how to preserve manuscripts using historic materials and techniques. In marble restoration they learned about Sipolite. The special charms and excellent results of a bent rusty nail have not been passed down. (Until now.) Today Florence's post-flood response is considered a great achievement of international collaboration and laid the foundations for Italian excellence in art conservation. But they say 25 percent of the damaged pieces from 1966 are still waiting to be restored. It is slow, painstaking work and innovations are still being discovered to meet new challenges. The word that best characterizes the Florence restoration experts: patience. The words that best characterize the Mud Angels: dedication and heart.

The Albergo Imperiale has morphed into a three-star hotel called Hotel Fiorino Florence. The address remains the same: Via Osteria del Guanto, 6. It's still family run but I don't know if they are talking about the Lorini family or another family. Though still in its medieval building, the hotel has been completely modernized and now the rooms include private bathrooms, air conditioning, flat screen TVs, WiFi and a complimentary gluten-free breakfast served in their cafe or, weather permitting, out in the courtyard. In creating the new hotel, I suspect they removed the old endearing charm that I found at the Albergo Imperiale: the random room numbers, the snuff box behind the Blessed Mother wall sconce, the turtle in the courtyard and, of course, Signor Lorini.

Chapter 16

Hitchhiking with Donald Duck

I LOVED AUTO-STOPPING. It gave me a freedom that I had not experienced up to that point on the trip. I didn't have to pay attention to train schedules or meld with others' traveling plans. I also didn't have to pay attention to logic and efficiency when choosing my stops. Auto-stopping came at no cost so it didn't matter if I retraced my steps. Now I could look at a map, point and say, "I want to go there."

To be honest, after my time in Florence, I was physically and emotionally spent and I did not want to continue my trip as a tourist, a visiting sightseer. I wanted to move forward as a traveler, a wanderer, experiencing the rhythms of a European summer. Obviously, I didn't want to experience the kind of summer I had just left in Florence with its hellishly high heat. I was heading to the Alps.

My first task was to gain some confidence about auto-stopping solo. When I traveled from Rome to Florence with Karen and Daniele, I deferred to their experience and let them pick the routes as well as the stops along the way. After Bologna, it was up to me and my judgment.

BOLOGNA, ITALY

I stayed one night in Bologna, the city famous for its twenty-four miles of porticoes. The afternoon I arrived I walked to Piazza Maggiore, spun around in a circle looking at the porticoes that surrounded the piazza and wondered, "Do the residents of Bologna even own umbrellas?" The only time they would be exposed to the elements was when they crossed the streets. Then they could duck under cover on the other side of the street.

Milan, Italy

Milan is 125 miles from Bologna. I played it safe and chose the Autostrada (highway) as my route. Surely there would be plenty of people leaving Bologna and driving to Milan. It's against the law to hitch on the Autostrada itself but auto-stoppers could stand along the shoulder of the entrance ramps.

When I got to my first ramp, I found a queue of about fifteen fellow stoppers. The protocol was to walk to the end of the line and wait your turn. Some of the stoppers had been standing there for two or three hours. Most of them were American students, an easy deducement on my part based on their dress and appearance—torn jeans, t-shirts, sandals and backpacks with American flag decals. I was dressed in slacks, a plain shirt and wearing my ugly shoes from Rome. Plus I had a bag with "Alitalia" printed in large letters across the side along with my Donald Duck decal. I watched as the drivers passed us by and it appeared to me they were avoiding American hitchhikers.

To test my theory, I separated myself from the crowd by walking further up the entrance ramp and standing alone. This still gave the students first crack at the oncoming cars. The next car passed by us all. A second car passed the gaggle. As he approached me, I read his license plate and saw he was from Milan. Using international arm and hand gestures, I let him know that we were both headed to the same place, and he stopped.

Three things served me well once I got into the car. When he asked me questions (in Italian), I could respond with my pigeon-Italian. When he asked me what I had been doing in Italy, I told him I had been working on the flood restoration in Florence. My tenure as a Mud Angel seemed to carry some currency. The third thing was Donald Duck. My decal made him smile. It took about two and a half hours to get to Milan. He dropped me off in the center of the city and pointed to a European hotel that he said was not expensive. I thanked him, headed right to where he had pointed and booked a room for the night. When I finally sat on the bed, I took a deep breath and smiled. My first venture into solo auto-stopping was a big success.

Milan is a big, bustling, beautiful city, but it was not where I wanted to be. I needed to get away from big cities.

Aosta, Italy

The next morning I decided to head 115 miles north to Aosta, a small Italian town near the French border at the base of the Italian Alps. I walked to the Milan Autostrada on-ramp and again took my place away from the other auto-stoppers. I got a ride right away. My new driver was passing through Aosta. After a pleasant two-hour ride, he dropped me off close to the center of town. I bought a street map at a news stand and began my search for a hotel.

This is when I stumbled upon a secret that European travelers knew about. European hotels are located in old buildings, often in medieval buildings, and they are on the second floor above the building's street-level shops. (This isn't the secret.) When I asked for a room in Aosta, I said, "I'd like a small room for one." Well, the magic passwords were "small room." When constructing a hotel, they often ended up with space left over, usually at the highest point in the hotel. Instead of leaving it empty, they made it into a small room and rented it out at a discounted price. The fellow at the desk did not know I didn't know what I was talking about. (I think he was charmed by my Italian.) When I said "small room," he assumed I was in on the secret and booked me into their small room at half-price.

You might be thinking that small rooms were nothing more than converted closets. They were usually about 8x10 feet (sometimes smaller) with a single bed, small table, wooden chair, night stand and lamp. Normally they had a sink with running water but sometimes I'd find a water pitcher and pan. The nearest toilet and shower rooms were one floor down. I don't know how the other rooms were, but in the small rooms I often found beautiful handcrafted touches like handmade quilts, sheets and pillow cases trimmed in lace and handmade lace curtains. If I had a pitcher and pan they were hand-painted with symbols and scenes from the locale. To me these rooms were special, and from Aosta on I always requested the small room.

After a late lunch, I sat on a hill outside the restaurant with my mug of cappuccino looking at the mountains that surrounded the town. A large lorry pulled up to the front of the restaurant. It caught my attention because it turned into the restaurant at a fairly fast clip. It was full of empty five-gallon wine jugs. When he stopped at the door, the wooden panel on the right side gave out under the shifted weight and the entire load of glass jugs crashed onto the asphalt pavement. There was now a mountain of broken glass. The driver jumped out, looked at his disaster and started yelling, waving his arms, jumping and stomping around, then yelling some more. He kept this useless routine up for a good twenty minutes. People from the restaurant came out to see what had happened. Everyone watched as he kept gesturing and yelling, *"Cosa fare!"* (Literally this means "What to do?" But in these kinds of situations when accompanied by wild arm gestures and assorted cries of anguish, it means, "What the hell!?" or "What the f**k!?") While he continued his dance of woe, people began picking up glass and several waitresses came out with brooms and large trash cans. All the while, I sat on my hill quietly sipping my cappuccino and thinking, "Italian men. They're crazy."

Aosta is a little town with all sorts of history going back to pre-Roman times. It has its own collection of ancient arches, towers, walls and palaces. Even though it is in Italy, the town was more French. Its street names and shop signs were French. There were outdoor cafés. More often than not the residents spoke French even though they were fluent in Italian. I found the town laundromat: two large cement reservoirs set into the ground with a sizable and fast-moving stream flowing through them. Women washed clothes in the lower tank and then moved to the upstream tank with fresh water for rinsing. The river flushed out the rinse water and sent it into the wash tank, which was, in turn, flushed out as the river flowed through it and continued on.

Despite the interesting sights and rhythms of the town, I kept looking up at the mountains. That's where I wanted to be. After three days in Aosta, I hit the road again. Destination: Chamonix, Mont Blanc and the Aiguille du Midi Cable Car. To get there, I needed a ride that would take me through the Mont Blanc Tunnel.

The Tunnel

The Mont Blanc Tunnel is a seven-mile long highway tunnel that passes almost directly under the summit of the Aiguille du Midi Mountain. At its center point, the tunnel lies 4,577 feet beneath the mountain's surface. It was completed in 1965 and because it dramatically reduced travel distances, it quickly became the preferred north-south route for drivers.

The tunnel entrance is sixteen miles away from Aosta. Just about everyone driving north was headed there so I caught a ride right away, this time with a businessman who was heading to Germany. Once we entered the tunnel, it took us about twenty minutes to shoot out the other end into Chamonix, France. In the middle of the tunnel, we had driven over the border between Italy and France and, for the first time since March, I was in a new country with a new language and new food.

Chamonix, France

Chamonix is located in the valley at the base of Mont Blanc and the Aiguille du Midi. With 7,500 residents, it felt more like a village than a town. My ride had dropped me off near the center of town and it didn't take long to find a hotel and to check into a new small room. This time my room had a skylight instead of a window with a view of the Aiguille du Midi and a long, skinny water falls that started about halfway up the mountain. It looked like a silver white ribbon winding its way through the green pine trees.

I loved the cafés, the small restaurants and shops, the planters full of flowers along the sidewalks and my room with its skylight. But the real draw for me was the Aiguille du Midi and its cable car. In 1967, this was the highest cable car in the world. (I think now it's the second highest.) It rose 12,605 feet to the Aiguille du Midi summit. The day after I arrived, I bought a bottle of mineral water and two sandwiches, grabbed my hat, two layers of sweaters and my wind breaker and headed to the cable car station.

The ascent to heaven took about twenty minutes. I watched the village of Chamonix get smaller as the cable car quickly rose. It was actually a two-stage journey. At the Plan de l'Aiguille, a little over halfway up, we changed cable cars and continued on to the top station and its terrace. Once there, I walked around the terrace and looked out at the seemingly endless French, Swiss and Italian Alps. I then moved one of the terrace chairs next to the railing. And that's where I sat for the next five hours.

I had never seen or experienced anything like what I saw from that terrace. I could see the summit of Mont Blanc, the highest mountain in the Alps, close by. I could see miles and miles of jagged snow-covered mountains no matter what direction I looked in. I watched clouds moving above and below me, some bumping into mountains and some skirting around them. I watched eagles and hawks soaring over the valley below. It was a remarkable panorama. And it was an unforgettable experience to see my world, my planet, from that perspective.

Luckily the air temperature that afternoon was a comfortable 50 degrees. When the temperature began to fall, I took the cable car back down to Chamonix. The next day I repeated the experience and returned to the mountain terrace for another afternoon of quiet observation and wonder.

I decided to spend one more day in Chamonix before moving on. The village was an Alpine picture with its railing boxes full of flowers and the Arve River that ran through the middle of town. I walked around gawking at the beauty. Since their primary tourist season was winter, there weren't a lot of visitors when I was there in July. I had a late lunch at an outdoor café with tables sitting next to the Arve River and I stayed there for several hours drinking coffee. No matter where I looked, the mountains were always right there as the dramatic, ever-present backdrop rising high above the tops of the houses.

The next morning, I headed for Geneva, Switzerland. It was only about fifty miles and an hour's drive from Chamonix so I could not have been more relaxed about getting a ride. Besides, with my auto-stopping "uniform," my bag with its friendly Donald Duck decal and my continuing good fortune when it came to catching rides, I had come to the conclusion that it was easier to auto-stop solo. I still agreed that central and southern Italy required a group of three to keep some Italian male drivers under control. But in my travels now, I often watched while drivers passed by groups of two or three but then stopped for me, a group of one. These drivers were often businessmen or married couples. I think by traveling solo I seemed safe. The businessmen wanted a little company and, as long as they could converse in English or Italian, we had pleasant conversations. The couples stopped out of concern. They would warn me about the dangers of auto-stopping alone and made sure they dropped me off in a safe place. I always thanked them for their concern but felt that if these were the kind of people who would stop for me then I couldn't be safer.

Geneva, Switzerland

My Geneva ride dropped me off in the center of the city at Pont du Mont-Blanc next to a sixteen-foot diameter flower clock that not only worked but showed the correct time. They say that 6,500 flowering plants and shrubs are used for the clock face. While I was admiring the beauty and wonder of the clock, I was hit with my usual wave of pragmatism. Just how many people did it take to keep the clock's plants perfectly trimmed so that the hands could move unimpeded? When the seasons changed, the flowers were changed out for 6,500 new temperature-appropriate plants. Without question, the flower clock was beautiful and attention grabbing but it sure seemed like a lot of work just to say to the world, "This is Geneva and we want to make sure you know we are famous for our time pieces."

The other attention grabber, which was equally hard to miss from where I was standing, was this monster water jet, the Jet d'Eau, on Lake Geneva. It sends water 460 feet in the air and they say it can be seen when flying over Geneva at 33,000 feet. The nozzle is just four inches in diameter, and 130 gallons of water per second are jetted through it at a speed of 120 mph. At any given moment there are about 1,800 gallons of water in the air. (A warning sign told us not to stand downwind or we'd get drenched.) It was originally installed in 1886 further down the lake and used as a safety valve for a hydraulic power network. In 1891, it was moved to its present, more central location after it was noticed that crowds kept gathering to see it.

I needed to stop staring at the clock, the water jet and the lake with its extremely calm swans slowly swimming about and go find a room. In Florence, a couple of Mud Angels had recommended I try to get a dormitory room at the University of Geneva. During the summer when most of the students were on break, vacant rooms were rented out at a lower cost than the city's hotel rooms. Once I bought a street map, I discovered that a university residence was just a few blocks from where I was standing.

What dominates my memories isn't the residence building or my room but, rather, the students. The students I met were attending the School of Translation and Interpreting. Languages were flying through the air everywhere. Each night a group of students met in a lounge just outside my room to socialize in what sounded like a thousand different languages. They wrapped me into their group right away. (I think the fact that I spoke English provided them with an opportunity to practice that language.) When I arrived, I was not aware of the school's international reputation or that many U.N. interpreters were graduates from there. But I caught on right away that these students were serious about languages. They were required to master five languages and speak them fluently, and they were not allowed to speak their native language while on campus. This meant the only ones who could talk to me in English were the non-English speaking students. I met one student from Kansas. I just looked at her and asked, "How did you get here from Kansas?" (Translation: How does a girl in Kansas wake up one morning in 1967, and say she'd like to go to Geneva and learn a bunch of languages?) Well, she couldn't answer me in English. Instead she answered in another language to a student who was studying English. That person translated her answer for me. (And I thought the multi-lingual conversations in the Florence Mensa were tricky.) They could flip in and out of languages in a nanosecond. I felt lucky just to keep up in my own language.

During the days, I walked around Geneva and found the city to be both tranquil and exciting, as well as beautiful. Perhaps it was the swans that gave it its tranquility. As I walked along the north shore of the lake and looked south, I could see Mont Blanc, just forty-three miles away. The only touristy thing I did was take a tour at the Office of the United Nations in the Palais des Nations. I was convinced world peace would permeate my body and mind, and I'd leave knowing how to achieve it. I guess I don't need to point out that this didn't happen, and I left the tour feeling just as much in the dark as when I came in. However, I did take away a feeling of hope.

Each afternoon I took a break and headed to my most important find in Geneva—Tea Rooms. These were small shops located all around the city (the precursor to Starbucks) that served excellent coffee, as well as tea and small sandwiches. For me the important attraction was their wooden newspaper racks with an extensive selection of international daily papers hanging on wooden dowels. I could choose any paper at no charge, lift its dowel off the rack and take it to my table. I could stay as long as I wanted, which was lucky since I read several U.S. papers, the *International Herald Tribune* and several London papers. They really should have been called "Reading Rooms with Tea."

After another late afternoon walk and another stop by the lake to watch the swans, I headed back to the dormitory and my new multi-lingual friends. Sometimes one of them would show up with a guitar for a group singalong—in multiple languages. This was the closest I would get to a college experience.

At the end of the week, the students held a dance and I was invited to come along. It was to welcome back the Israeli students who had just returned after fighting in the Six Day War. I was hoping to meet some Israelis and to have a chance to ask questions about the war and their country. Well, I soon realized I was at a dance and not a conference. The Israeli fellows were primarily interested in picking their evening's sex partners. You know how to discourage a soldier with carnal desires? Ask him to explain the war he just fought in and describe his country's politics.

I had struck an easy, relaxing rhythm in Geneva. But after a week, I knew it was time to move on. I bid farewell to my friends and hit the road, aiming for Zurich. I was 170 miles from Geneva so I divided the trip in half and stopped in Murten, a tiny village eighty-three miles down the road.

Murten, Switzerland

Murten was founded in 1159, but they've discovered archaeological evidence that indicates the area was settled around 8200 to 5500 B.C. It has been the scene of many battles over the centuries as one faction after another took over the town. The surrounding Swiss population spoke French, but the majority of the 4,000 Morat residents spoke German.

The tiny village looked like a Swiss movie set. After I checked into my new small room, I walked along each side of main street (all three blocks of it), taking in the sights: the medieval buildings, the troughs filled with flowers, the window boxes, the fountain, the shops, the cafés—and the Tea Room. At one end of the street stood a huge medieval clock tower with an archway at the base large enough for single-lane traffic to drive through. The whole place was the epitome of Swiss charm.

Despite the pull to stay in Murten for the rest of my life, I got back on the road the next morning and headed to Zurich.

Zurich, Switzerland

It's a good thing I didn't settle for life in Murten because I would have missed Zurich and Lake Zurich. In my quest to experience a European summer, I discovered my all-time top, favorite swimming beach: Mythenquai at Lake Zurich.

Most Americans head to their nearest coastal beaches in the summer to swim. The rich go to Nice and Monte Carlo. When I think about swimming, I think about Lake Zurich and Mythenquai. The lake itself is about half the size of Lake Geneva, extending out for 25 miles with a depth of 161 feet to 446 feet. (Lake Geneva is 45 miles long with a depth of 507 feet to 1,020 feet.) The maximum depth of the swimming area at Mythenquai is thirteen feet. The beach includes a long stretch of sand and a huge grass lawn. The water quality? When I was there it was sparkly clean. They even advertised that the water was potable and that with a little purification they fed it into the Zurich water system. For me, it was a joy to swim in, once I got used to the somewhat exhilarating water temperature. I stayed in Zurich for ten days and swam there nearly every day. I topped off my swimming days at a nearby Tea Room to eat, drink and read.

My newest small room was in a hotel located near the Landesmuseum, the Swiss National Museum. Since I could practically roll out of bed and land at the museum entrance, I decided a visit would be in order. Because it was a cultural history museum, it had a wide range of exhibits. Two things in particular stood out to me. One room held an entire apothecary from the early 1700s, complete with equipment and labeled bottles. The cabinets and shelving were a beautiful, deep rich wood. I couldn't figure out the uses for most of the equipment and the bottle labels were a mystery, but I decided that had I lived in the 1700s, I would have felt comfortable walking into that apothecary for help, and I probably would have felt confident about the help given.

The second Landesmuseum highlight was the huge ceramic tiled, two-seater wood stove from 1620. It was about eighteen feet tall and maybe twenty feet long, with intricately designed hand-printed, glazed tiles. Obviously it had been used in a well-to-do, large residence with large rooms and high ceilings. The center section contained the firebox. On each end and about eight to ten feet away from the center firebox was a ceramic seat with a smaller stool in front for heating bums and feet without frying said body parts. There's a possibility that I appreciated this stove because of my winter without heat in Ocean City. It was July when I saw the Landesmuseum stove yet I felt strangely comforted by it.

As a city, Zurich was a beautiful city of contradictions. It was reasonably large with a lot of activity but it never felt overwhelming. It had that Swiss old-world charm just about everywhere I walked, mixed in with the city's modern business buildings. In short, Zurich was large without feeling large. It was bustling without feeling chaotic or frantic. It was active, yet felt quiet and peaceful. At the end of my afternoons, I sat along the lake watching the swans, ducks and lake boats while soaking in the city's ambience that surrounded me. I felt relaxed, rested and, after ten days, ready to move on.

Auto-Stopping to Liechtenstein

Up to this point, my auto-stopping had proceeded without a hitch. (Pardon the pun.) I was confident in my skills and grateful for the kindnesses shown me by the drivers. But auto-stopping to Liechtenstein provided both challenge and magic. The morning I departed Zurich I walked to the road leading to Liechtenstein. One of the first drivers to come along stopped. When I told him where I was going, he said, "You're on the wrong road. You need to be on the other side of the lake." He drove me over to the other side and said, "Here you go. Good luck, young lady." With that, I was now on my way to Liechtenstein, just sixty-eight miles away.

My first ride dropped me off about fifty miles down the road. I noticed that this road, although scenic, was light on traffic but I felt confident someone would come along. Surely people would need to drive from Zurich to Vaduz (Liechtenstein's capitol) regularly on business. I sat on a short stone wall and waited—and waited and waited and waited.

Here's where things became magical. On the other side of the road, in front of a small family chalet, an elderly gentleman was sitting on a lawn chair reading a book. For a while we ignored one another. I'm sure he was aware I was sitting on the wall, but he just continued reading his book and I continued looking down the road for an approaching car. His vantage point was higher than mine and after about forty minutes, he started signaling to me to get ready because a car was coming. Apparently the cars were turning off because no one approached. Then my new auto-stopping pal would throw up his arms in good-natured frustration and we'd sit back down until he signaled again. By now, we were both laughing. (He reminded me of Signor Lorini.)

I needed to think. What was I going to do if no one stopped? I didn't know where I was. There was no village around me and no road signs pointing to one. I didn't know how far I was from Liechtenstein. This was probably the shortest distance I needed to cover as an auto-stopper but here I was stuck in the middle of beautiful, green, idyllic Somewhere. There wasn't even any near-by protection (tree cover or an old abandoned barn or shed) if I needed to sleep out overnight and try my luck the next day. If this had been 2017, perhaps I could have used a cell phone and called Uber. At least I wasn't alone and still had my auto-stopping pal.

After about another hour, he walked to the chalet. I assumed he had gotten bored. About fifteen minutes later he returned to his post and waved for me to join him. When I climbed up the bank to him, he pantomimed an invitation to join him and his family for lunch. That was a surprise. I tried to indicate that I didn't want to intrude but he persisted, took hold of my arm and started leading me to the chalet. I have to admit that I wondered what I was walking into. (Headline: Young American Traveler Kidnapped by Rogue Swiss Family Cartel.)

Well, instead of members of some shady cartel, it was just one remarkably friendly, kind family. When the grandfather escorted me in, I saw a younger woman setting an extra place at the table. Lunch was a buffet of assorted cheeses, breads and sliced sausages. Introductions were made all around and that's when we discovered that we had no language in common. Three languages are spoken in Switzerland: French, Italian and German, depending on the location. This family spoke Swiss German and a little Italian. For me, common sense, hand gestures and pigeon-Italian reigned. There was the grandfather, of course, his daughter, her husband and their teenage daughter. We were joined by the grandmother who had been napping. She came downstairs to "meet the American." I was the first American she had ever seen, so I was told. She spent much of the lunch smiling and staring at me. Their young daughter and I discovered we had another possible language bridge—high school French. But it was a language neither one of us had excelled in. Our classroom French tended to boil down to, *"Ouvre la porte."* (Open the door.) We both tried to work *"Ouvre la porte"* into as many sentences as possible. The lunch was filled with a lot of teasing, laughing and good food.

When it was over, they stopped me as I was about to head back out to the road. "No, no. We'll drive you to Vaduz. It's only twenty miles away" (they said in multiple languages with multiple hand gestures). I hardly knew what to say. I tried to indicate that I didn't want to inconvenience them but they would not hear it. After saying my goodbyes to the grandfather and his wife, the husband, wife, daughter and I piled into their car and headed for Vaduz, Liechtenstein.

These people could not stop being kind to me. Once we arrived in Vaduz, the husband stopped at a hotel that he thought would be safe for me and we all walked in together to book my room. Actually, the husband took over the whole booking process. He told the guy at the desk that I was the daughter of one of his business associates and got me a good deal on a room. Once we were given the key and were heading up en masse, he explained what he had said and that if there were any questions I was just to say that my family knew his family. We were now co-conspirators. The hotel had a dining room and I invited them for coffee/tea/wine and a pastry before they headed back to the chalet. To my delight, they accepted. How in the world do you say "Thank you" and "I appreciate all that you have done" and "I will always remember this afternoon" in bad French, pigeon-Italian and English? As soon as they departed, I knew I was going to miss them.

Vaduz, Liechtenstein

My arrival in Vaduz coincided with the week leading up to a royal wedding. Photos and posters of the happy couple were plastered everywhere. The streets were festooned with garlands and streamers. Flowers were all around. There were special postcards and stamps to mark the occasion. Royal flags and banners were hanging from the buildings. People from all around the country (all ninety-nine square miles of it) were flocking in with tents and trailers. I didn't know about the wedding until after I arrived and I was sure that I had been lucky to get the family's help booking a room.

The Crown Prince Hans-Adam van und zu Liechtenstein was marrying Countess Marie Kinsky von Wchinitz und Tettau. According to several newspaper reports:

> Forty-thousand visitors (twice the population of Liechtenstein) poured into Vaduz and just on the wedding weekend alone they consumed 40,000 pork sausages, 20,000 veal sausages, 130,000 pints of beer and 20,000 pints of Vaduz wine. The guests included one queen, four crown princes, two crown princesses, twenty-two "regular" princes and fourteen "regular" princesses, a duke, a duchess, seven countesses and six counts. Prince Philip did not attend. He sent his regrets—he had a polo engagement. Rumor had it he was miffed that one of the attending crown princes was not marrying Princess Anne. It was also reported that the fire department hauled off ten truckloads of drunks to a woods to sleep it off. One German fell off a bus, yelling "I don't want to go home. There's more beer." Because of the presence of Queen Anne-Marie of Greece, four Greek hotel employees had to spend the week in jail. A few photographers were mauled. But all in all, everyone, including the Greek "prisoners" and the wedding couple, had a grand time.

Update: From 1989, Hans-Adam van und zu Liechtenstein has served as Liechtenstein's current ruling prince. He is still married to Marie. They have four children and fifteen grandchildren. I guess fairy tale weddings leading to long marriages can happen—in Liechtenstein at least.

Vaduz Castle (12th century) is sitting on the side of a mountain that overlooks the village and is the official residence for the royal family. (No visitors, please. Thank you. Go away.) I had heard that the world's largest collection of DaVinci paintings was kept in a climate controlled room in the castle basement, but no one could see them in order to maintain the climate control. It was also said that these works were in the best condition of all his paintings.

Each day after an early dinner, I spent the rest of the evening in my room, on my bed, crying. I could not stop crying and usually cried myself to sleep. I had no idea what was making me cry. I was surrounded by celebration, I had arrived thanks to the kindness of a terrific Swiss family. My trip was proceeding well. I was enjoying the hell out of my European summer. But each evening in Vaduz, I cried. It wasn't just quiet, little sniffles either. I was sobbing into my pillow. And I couldn't stop.

Later, back in the States, I talked about this with a friend of mine who was a child psychologist. He said it made sense to him. I, on the other hand, couldn't find anything in it that made sense. He knew a bit about my early life and suggested that I had not cried enough as I went through all the challenges. Once I got to Europe and relaxed, it was inevitable that I would make up for lost crying time. I had cried from time to time during those early years but because I was so busy keeping my head above water, I often didn't have time to cry, at least not often enough. It was a luxury I couldn't afford. Whether or not his explanation was accurate, it made more sense than anything I came up with and I decided to accept it.

Three days before the wedding, the festivities started to hit full stride and I was beginning to feel like a wedding crasher. Thankfully, I had stopped crying. It was time to move on—again.

Innsbruck, Austria

It took two rides and about three hours to travel the eighty-seven miles to Innsbruck, the halfway point en route to Salzburg. I took a quick walk around the center of the city, declared it to be another beautiful European town, spent one night (in another small room) and moved on. Was there a lot to see? You bet. Did I want to see it? No. My favorite memory: Innsbruck had a nice Tea Room.

Salzburg, Austria

I only needed one ride to travel the final 115 miles to Salzburg. Along the way, we traveled from Austria, then crossed the border into Germany and finally crossed back into Austria before arriving in Salzburg. Once I left Amsterdam, the border and passport checks had been, shall we say, casual. There were always checkpoints manned by utterly bored guards and most of the time we were just waved through. Even though everyone else seemed blasé about borders, I still thought it was amazing that in two and a half hours I had crossed two international borders and traveled through two countries.

When I arrived in Salzburg, the hills actually were alive with the sound of music, thanks to the annual Salzburg Festival (a five-week long international music and drama festival). It was another big celebration that I didn't know about until I walked into the middle of it. The festival provided the city with its latest opportunity to proclaim that in the 18th century, Salzburg was the birthplace of Wolfgang Amadeus Mozart. There were posters and signs about Mozart's birth as well as festival events everywhere. Clearly, it was time for the concert series part of my European summer.

The first thing I checked out was the Felsenreitschule. (Don't you just hate it when a word has too damn many letters in it? *Felsenreitschule* literally means "rock riding school." Back in the 1700s, it had been used as a summer riding school.) For us Americans, it's the concert hall where, in *The Sound of Music,* the von Trapp Family performed during the 1938 Salzburg Festival and from where they made their escape. Because of the movie, there had been quite a bit of hype about this hall. When I stood in front of it, I had just one thought: "Is that it?" I expected something larger. Grander. Worthy of a big-time movie. Reality crushes hype again.

I picked up information about the festival events from my hotel and saw that there was an outdoor concert scheduled for the next afternoon in a park near the Felsenreitschule.

The next day I found the park, paid for a ticket and chose a seat about ten rows from the front. The orchestra was already seated and warming up. I can't remember the name of the concert they played (it was probably Mozart) but I remember that it was magnificent. To be sitting outdoors in Salzburg surrounded by this music was indeed special. The concert had four movements. During the first movement, I noticed that while the orchestra was playing, not one person in the audience moved. It seemed like people weren't even breathing. All we heard was the orchestra and a few bird twitters. In between each movement people stood up, shuffled their feet, repositioned their butts on their chairs, coughed, sneezed and whispered to one another. When the conductor raised his baton to start the next movement, the audience was silent again. I may not remember the name of the concert, but I do remember the self-discipline and etiquette the audience demonstrated that day.

The following afternoon there was an organ recital at the Salzburg Cathedral. The cathedral is known for its Baroque architecture and for the medieval font in which Mozart was baptized. It also has a 4,000-pipe organ and that was something I wanted to hear. To boot, the organ master was going to play Bach's "Organ Toccata and Fugue in D Minor." If you've watched any scary vampire movies set in Transylvania, you've probably heard this music. Especially when the unsuspecting, cute blonde heroine is running up the dark driveway in a thunderstorm towards the creepy house on the hill. The beginning of this Bach piece is always played to warn us that the little sweetie is about to die. (If only she would listen to the music and take the hint!) Prior to that afternoon in Salzburg, most of the organs I had heard "live" were those home organs with the obnoxious programmed rhythm beats. This cathedral experience was bound to be different.

It seems like I have difficulty finding the words to describe special musical moments in European churches. There was the soft "heavenly" experience I had while listening to the nuns' choir at the Church of Santa Cecilia in Rome. At the other end of the spectrum, there was Bach's "Toccata" in the Salzburg Cathedral. When they crank up a 4,000-pipe organ to unload Bach's "Toccata," you've got to hold on to body parts that are about to vibrate off. Of course, hearing it in a cathedral with its exceptional acoustics adds that much more to the sound. My chest, legs and arms were literally vibrating. (But interestingly, my ears weren't hurting.) The music filled the cathedral with depth, drama and majesty. I had the feeling the organ master couldn't wait for this recital to unleash that organ and set it free. I left the cathedral thinking, "Well, I've definitely heard Bach's 'Toccata.' Nothing is ever going to compare with this."

Every afternoon and evening for the next month different operas, dramas, concerts and recitals were scheduled. For not having heard of the Salzburg Festival prior to my arrival, it's fair to say that I was now in the thick of something very big and feeling what it had to offer was over my head—and wallet. With the organ recital and outdoor concert, I felt I had my special experience and taste of the festival. I was happy to move on.

Salzburg to Munich, Germany

My hotel in Salzburg was above a sausage shop. The morning I left, I stopped in and bought a couple of sausages and a small bottle of mustard for lunch during the next leg of my journey. I stuffed the package in my bag and set off for the eighty-nine mile trip to Munich.

The fellow who stopped for me was driving a white Jaguar with white leather seats. My initial reaction was to decline his ride because I felt I wasn't dressed well enough for his car. I was afraid I might get it dirty. He would have none of that silliness and told me, in English, "Come on. Get in." Still, I wasn't going to eat my sausages smeared with mustard in that car.

Although German, he spoke fluent English and we conversed for much of the trip. He had been on a solo three-week hiking trip and I was the first person he had talked to since coming out of the mountains. He was soft spoken, thoughtful and curious. He asked me questions about my trip and what I had been doing. We talked about the restoration work in Florence for quite a while. When he asked about my plans in Munich, I told him I would be getting the bus to Dachau. I wanted to visit the concentration camp.

Our free-flowing conversation hit a wall right then. We rode along quietly for about fifteen minutes. Then I was hit with a combination of total naiveté and courage that overwhelmed my otherwise good sense. I wanted to take advantage of the opportunity to ask this man, the first German I had met, some questions. I explained that I was from a Jewish family and that I was having trouble understanding why Jews were hated so much during World War II. Could he explain what happened? I said I wasn't interested in blaming anyone for anything. I felt that if he saw that I was being sincere, he would explain things and help me understand. (I was so young.)

In my head the war had occurred a lifetime ago, at least my lifetime ago. It was another era and it was history. Here I was asking a German man in his mid- to late-thirties these questions. It didn't dawn on me that he had been alive during the war and that perhaps his father had fought for the Mother Country. I also didn't know that in 1967, the Germans were not discussing the Holocaust even among themselves, let alone with a young American Jewish girl. It wasn't old history to them and was best left unspoken. Over the years I've read a number of books about the rise of anti-Semitism that led to the Holocaust and how the Germans in the post-war years have had to move through their own slow process just to get to the point where they could honestly look at and think about the Holocaust. Even now, not every German has moved forward about this. They still have their share of Holocaust deniers.

But there I was, in a white Jaguar with white leather seats, thinking (in my youthful zeal) that honesty and sincerity would carry the moment and he would feel free to open up and explain the Holocaust to me. Finally he said quietly, "I can't answer your questions." And with that, my good sense resurfaced and I dropped it. We were quiet for the rest of the trip to Munich. He drove me to the center of the city, and when I thanked him and got out he said, "Good luck with your trip."

Munich to Dachau, Germany

I hated Munich. It was a big, congested city and, at this point, I was a little nervous about being a Jewish girl in Germany. On top of that, the hotel I chose didn't have any small rooms, so I was back in a regular-size room at a regular-size price. After tossing out my sausages, which I felt certain were no longer safe to eat, I had an early dinner, walked around the city for about an hour and then retired to my room. Tomorrow I would catch the bus to Dachau.

The next morning I learned something else important about Germans. You do not, I repeat, *do not* bend or break their set routines, even if it is by mistake. Follow the plan. I had boarded London buses from the rear and, without thinking, I boarded the Munich bus to Dachau from the rear. When it arrived and both doors opened, no one had exited using the rear door. So I figured we could use both doors for getting on the bus. Well, the people standing in the aisle were not too happy with me when I realized my mistake and apologized to every single one of them as I worked my way to the front to pay. They acted like I was there to commit a crime. At the very least, I was an irritant in their well-ordered morning. Good grief. (And I hadn't even asked them to explain the Holocaust. What was their problem?) I finally maneuvered my way up to the driver, paid for my ticket and found a seat. Thank god it was only nineteen miles to Dachau. Any longer and I wasn't sure I would arrive alive or in one piece.

Dachau Concentration Camp

My memories of the Dachau Concentration Camp Memorial Site are like individual snapshots mounted in an album. Let me take you through my memory one snapshot at a time.

1. Walking down the city street to the Memorial
Dachau Concentration Camp is located in the town of Dachau. It wasn't out in some isolated field like so many of the other camps in Eastern Europe. It was less than two miles from the center of the old city. Residents of Dachau walked by as they went about their day. The fence surrounding the camp was mostly barbed wire and they could easily see inside the camp. My first questions: What the hell, people? Did you not notice what was happening? Didn't you think people in that camp were getting awfully thin? What did you think when ashes rained down on you from the sky?

2. The Memorial museum
The museum was located in what used to be the camp's administration building. Most of what was on exhibit is a blurred or blank memory, except for one exhibit. Page after page after page of prisoners' records were displayed in glass cases and on the wall behind the cases. Each page included the name of a prisoner, his home address, other pertinent information, his medical information and his head lice history. Did a prisoner have no lice, just a little lice, an average amount or a heavy amount? The lice checks occurred on a regular basis and the results were recorded showing the progression of an individual's infestation. Obviously, the Nazis were meticulous when it came to keeping records. I was surprised that the Germans were willing to exhibit those innocent looking but damning records for all to see.

3. The main grounds
From the museum, I walked outside to the roll call area and looked out at the camp that stretched in front of me. Next question: Where's the camp? All I saw was a five-acre, fenced in barren landscape with two watch towers and two newly constructed barracks.

According to my guide map, there were supposed to be two rows of barracks with sixteen buildings lined up side by side in each row. Instead the grounds were empty (except for those two barracks) and covered with a thick layer of light-colored gravel and small pebbles. Low cement curbs outlined the rectangles where the other thirty barracks had once stood and a small concrete tablet with the original barrack number was sitting on the gravel inside each rectangle. My first impression: empty, scrubbed, an uninterrupted five-acre sea of pebbles.

4. The barracks

The two new buildings were constructed just before the camp opened as a memorial site in 1965. They were built according to the original barracks' specifications: 330 feet long by 33 feet wide. The main difference between the missing old structures and these new buildings was that the replicas included modern construction standards with foundations, cement floors, tightly fitting windows and locking doors. One of the replicas was left empty. Why? I don't know. The other included the original interior layout: the three-tiered bunks, a large day room, tall windows, a long U-shaped eating table with stools, wooden lockers for prisoners' belongings, one large washroom with wash basins designed for use by several prisoners at a single time and one narrow communal toilet room with ten flushing toilets sitting side by side. (No stalls.) The barracks were divided into two sections. Each section included these rooms and furnishings and housed ninety men. Each barrack held a total of 180 prisoners.

At this point, if you know anything about the Holocaust and concentration camps, you are probably thinking that the Dachau barracks were pretty posh in comparison to the other camps. And they were. The Dachau Concentration Camp was built in 1933, just a few weeks after Hitler came to power. It originally housed political prisoners and it was to be a showcase prison to demonstrate to the outside world what a humane and considerate bunch Hitler and his Nazis were. The Jews and the Final Solution were not yet in Germany's plans. Hitler had some pretty high-ranking and well-positioned enemies who were imprisoned at Dachau—

clergy, members of opposing political parties, professors, professionals and the educated. The Nazis certainly did not want outsiders thinking they were forcing these well-regarded people to live in squalor.

5. The small crematorium

If I hadn't known where I was going (which I did, thanks to the map), I would have missed this area altogether. Through a gate at the far end of the camp that led to the main place of remembrance and cemetery stood a small one-room cabin surrounded by a stand of trees. It housed the camp's first crematory oven. About fifty feet away was the larger crematory building with its four ovens that had been added in 1942. They were the original buildings and ovens, not replicas. The crematoria had been saved from demolition by a group of survivors back in the 1950s.

For some reason, I was drawn to Dachau's first crematorium. The cabin floor was concrete and the oven was brick. There were some artisan touches in the brickwork indicating that the men who constructed the oven were skilled and took pride in their work. One of the cast iron doors had the logo of the Topf Company, proud maker of that oven as well as the ovens used at Auschwitz and Auschwitz-Birkenau camps, Buchenwald, Mauthausen-Gusen camps, Mogilev ghetto and the Gross-Rosen Concentration Camp.

The oven's six cast iron doors were swung open. Two medium-sized openings, one on the far right and the other on the far left, were used for loading fuel. Two smaller openings below the oven's main chambers were for removing overflow ashes. Bodies were placed in the two main chambers. Several bodies could be burned at one time, depending on the size of the corpses.

During the early years of the camp, only the small crematorium with its one oven was needed. The corpses of those who died from old age, torture, overwork, execution or disease were burned on the orders of Heinrich Himmler in an effort to prevent the spread of disease and the contamination of ground water. In the final two years (1943–1945), this oven plus the four ovens in the large crematory building ran 24/7.

I stared at the oven for the longest time—at least thirty minutes or more. I couldn't believe I was actually looking at a concentration camp oven where real bodies had been burned. This wasn't a movie and it wasn't a photograph. Right in front of me was a real oven with a real and tragic history. Of course the human ashes inside the oven had been removed but there was still what looked to be a film of grey ashes coating the two main chambers' interior bricks and the concrete floor directly in front of the oven. As I struggled to wrap my head around what had occurred just twenty-three years prior, the oven seemed to grab my focus and lock it in, as if to say to me, "Don't ever forget what you are seeing. This is what humans can do to one another."

When I was finally able to break my focus, I made a silent promise to always remember (like so many Jews before me and since). That oven was now permanently imprinted in my brain and I knew I would always be able to touch it, see it, recall it. (Over the years, this memory has served as a caution and a warning of dangerous times as I've watched citizens, politicians and governments—nationally and internationally—spin out of control. Sadly, it's especially relevant these days.)

When I returned to the main camp, I looked out over the empty landscape with its endless sea of pebbles and whispered, "What the hell happened here?"

Dachau's history is divided into two defining periods: the "clean camp" years and the "dirty camp" years. To understand the camp's role and its impact on the prisoners as well as the residents in the town of Dachau, both periods need to be considered.

The "Clean Camp" Years: 1933–1942

Dachau was not designed or built as a death camp. As I've written, it was the first concentration camp to be set up in Germany and it was built to imprison Hitler's political opponents and dissidents. It was also the first camp to be under the supervision of Heinrich Himmler. (He would soon control the entire concentration camp network in the German Reich.) By early 1934, the full twenty-acre Dachau compound (which included the five-acre fenced prison) had become Himmler's model concentration camp. Besides the "posh" barracks, the 1,000-feet by 2,000-feet prison area included grass, planted flowers, a tree-lined main road down the center of the camp, an infirmary, a library, kitchens, a canteen, a laundry, a barrack for imprisoned clergy, a chapel barrack and a brothel barrack. The larger compound outside the fenced area included an herb garden, a large vegetable garden and greenhouse, hutches for rabbits, kennels for guard dogs, more kitchens, the crematory area, the camp commandant's house and an on-site training facility where many camp officials received training. (Eighteen of the concentration camp commandants and officials, including Adolf Eichmann and Rudolf Höss, commandant of Auschwitz, started out in Dachau.)

The prison camp was originally built to accommodate 5,000 inmates. The camp was expanded in 1938 to accommodate a total of 6,000 inmates. (The prisoners provided the labor for the expansion.) The prison population now included Jehovah's Witnesses, Gypsies, homosexuals, the mentally and physically disabled and repeat criminal offenders. During the clean camp years, relatively few Jews were imprisoned in Dachau. Still thousands of Dachau prisoners died of disease, torture, malnutrition and overwork. Thousands more were executed for infractions of camp rules.

German physicians performed medical experiments on the prisoners at Dachau, including testing new medications, high-altitude experiments using a decompression chamber, and malaria and tuberculosis experiments. Hypothermia experiments were conducted to determine if individuals immersed in freezing water could be revived. For hours at a time, prisoners were submerged in tanks filled with ice water. Some prisoners died during the process. Prisoners were also forced to test methods of making seawater drinkable and of halting excessive bleeding. Hundreds of prisoners died or were permanently disabled as a result of these experiments.

From the start, Himmler's SS frequently took German and foreign officials on tours of the Dachau camp. In testimony before the Nuremberg court in 1946, General Von Eberstein stated:

> I can only repeat that everything was scrupulously clean, the sanitary installations that I saw were in excellent order, that in peacetime the prisoners were well nourished and, as I saw during the war, on the average their food was like the food of every German outside.

The "clean" impression was created by extensive preparations prior to visits. When a delegation was expected, the prisoners had to make sure that their barracks and other key buildings such as the kitchens and infirmary were spotless. The grounds had to be perfectly landscaped and flower gardens well maintained. Prisoners considered dangerous were kept out of sight, and visitors met only with carefully selected inmates.

Dachau Concentration Camp was never a secret to the townspeople. Residents saw the prisoners on a daily basis when they were brought to town to work in factories or to build roads and a new cemetery. New inmates arrived regularly at the train station in the center of Dachau and walked the two miles through the town to the camp. The townspeople tried to help the prisoners in any way they could. They sent packages of food and medicine, which the Nazis claimed they distributed to the prisoners. The townspeople risked being arrested in order to give food to the prisoners while they were working. Pharmacies slipped free medicine to the working prisoners and the town dentist secretly provided dental care.

Starting in 1941, camp conditions worsened. Thousands of Soviet prisoners of war were sent to Dachau, then executed at a nearby rifle range. In 1942, construction began on Barrack X, the large crematoria with its four ovens.

In 1942, with the implementation of Hitler's Final Solution to systematically eradicate all European Jews, thousands of Dachau Jewish prisoners were moved to Nazi extermination camps in Poland, where they died in gas chambers.

The "Dirty Camp" Years: 1943–1945

Beginning in 1943, as the Nazis crammed more prisoners into Dachau, the townspeople began to disconnect from the reality of the prison and its prisoners and backed away from their support.

In the summer and fall of 1944, to increase war production, satellite camps (work camps) under Dachau's administration were established near armaments factories throughout southern Germany. Dachau alone had more than thirty large subcamps in which over 30,000 prisoners worked almost exclusively on armaments. Thousands of prisoners were worked to death.

After January 1945, thousands of survivors from the eastern death camps were brought to Dachau, causing a dramatic deterioration of conditions and an outbreak of typhus. Almost half of the deaths in the Dachau camp occurred in the final five months of the war.

According to the last roll call taken by the Nazis on April 26, 1945, three days before its liberation, there were 67,665 registered prisoners in Dachau and its subcamps. Of these, 43,350 were political prisoners, 22,100 were Jews, and the remainder fell into various other categories. There were 30,442 prisoners in the main camp, a facility that was built to hold 6,000 prisoners. There were an additional 37,223 in the subcamps surrounding Dachau. Additional prisoners from other camps arrived at Dachau after the final roll call and the official count by the U.S. Seventh Army at the time of liberation was 31,432 surviving prisoners in the main camp.

When the United States military entered Dachau on April 29, they found emaciated prisoners, stacks of bodies and more than thirty railroad cars filled with decomposing bodies that had been brought to Dachau from one of the eastern death camps.

General Henning Linden, who arrived only hours after the liberation, toured the camp with representatives of the underground prisoners' organization and reporters from *Time-Life,* the New York *Herald Tribune,* and the Associated Press. He filed the following report [Dann, 1998, 15f]:

> We went through a small crematory, outside of which were shoes and clothing...we saw several stacks of dead bodies...each looking like a human skeleton with the skin stretched over it. We visited rooms in barracks, where bunks were stacked five and six high in a room twenty by thirty [feet], where fifty men were quartered

> in so-called hospital wards that were nothing more than a concrete barracks floor with straw strewn on it...living skeletons were lying in ragged, dirty clothing and bedding. The outstanding picture I got from my inspection of this camp was the barbaric, infamous systematic effort of the camp routine to degrade the human to a point where he bordered on the animal. I would strongly recommend that all German citizens within marching distance of this concentration camp be forced to walk through [it], to the end that the German people could know and realize what form of government and philosophy they have been supporting during the Nazi regime.

The liberators made sure that the residents of Dachau were marched through the camp. The townspeople could not understand how the prisoners could have starved to death since they said they had regularly sent food packages to the camp. On May 8, 1945, nine days after the camp was liberated, a group of Nazi elite from the town was forced to tour the crematoria. Some fainted when they viewed the bodies. Some cried and many shook their heads. Most of them turned away to avoid the scene.

SO THE ANSWER TO MY FIRST question on the day I visited Dachau ("Did you townspeople not notice what was happening?") is complicated. If we are referring to the clean camp years when the camp was kept spotless; the prison population size was reasonable; the inmates considered respectable and under control; and the torture, death, executions and medical experimentation were kept out of sight, they would answer "Yes. And we tried to help the prisoners as much as we could." If we are referring to the final dirty camp years (1943–1945) when the camp housed over five times more prisoners than it was designed to accommodate, when prisoners resembled walking skeletons, when many more executions and cremations were taking place each day and the ovens were burning continuously, they would (and did) answer, "No. We had no idea what was going on. How could we know?"

From 1945 to the present, the camp's evolution has reflected Germany's national struggle to face what happened and its efforts to erase all evidence. The camp has gone through several phases since liberation. For two years, the American military used the camp for arrested Nazi functionaries and SS. In 1948, the camp was returned to the Bavarian State and converted into housing for refugees and the homeless. In 1962 the Bavarian government and CID (Comité International de Dachau) agreed on a memorial at the camp site. In 1965 the Dachau Concentration Camp Memorial Site was opened to the public.

The 1967 camp I saw was unchanged from the camp that opened in 1965. It clearly reflected the clean camp mentality. Evidence of torture and murder were missing, except for the crematoria. Traces of life and history that did not fit into the message that the memorial site wanted to convey to visitors had been removed. In 1959, former camp elder Oskar Müller noted that the Bavarian authorities were constantly trying to destroy as many relics of the camp as they could. He wrote to a friend:

> It is quite obvious: The motivation for this stance [of the Bavarian authorities] is the intention to spread the cloak of silence and oblivion over the last period of German history. The persecutors of yesterday who are once again setting the tone fear the presentation of historical truth, they fear those documents that reveal their shameful deeds.

Dachau had been deliberately reduced to a sterile, shallow image: a barren, grey-white pebble landscape surrounded by a high barbed wire fence and watchtowers, a museum, two newly constructed barracks at one end and the crematoria at the other. And we mustn't forget those meticulous records on display in the museum that seemed to say, "See how organized, caring and responsible we were with our prisoners." As Volkhard Knigge, director of the Buchenwald memorial site in the 1990s, stated: "The minimization of remains is a prerequisite for the maximization of possibilities for creating new meanings." [Knigge, 1996, 207]

Even before I arrived, I had already (and accidentally) entered the German people's national struggle with how to face their war's atrocities and present them to the outside world. It had started with the fellow in the white Jaguar who closed down our conversation when I asked a question about the Holocaust. However, at Dachau, where I was surrounded by the clean camp mentality, I was still able to pick up that something was askew with what I was seeing. I was supposed to be looking at a concentration camp yet that was not at all what I saw. The only thing that felt true that day was the crematorium. Overall, I'd say that the attempt by the Bavarian government to corral and control my perceptions of the Dachau Concentration Camp had failed.

Today, thanks to the increasing distance from the war years, the relentless efforts of the survivors and their relatives for the camp to reflect truth, and the increasing desire of young people to know the truth, the camp's full history is being brought forward. Over a million people visit Dachau annually. (In 1967, there were 150,000 visitors.) This increase in interest has pressured the government to preserve, document and restore the camp's true history. Today Dachau has trees and lawns, as it did while it was an active concentration camp, and it has been transformed into a multi-media information and learning facility that includes displays, lectures and discussions that cover the dirty years. However, many agree that if the camp is to serve its full potential as a cautionary tale, it still has a way to go. The evolutionary wheels of consciousness can sometimes move slowly but they do move forward.

Herrshing, Germany

When I left the camp, I knew I needed to get out of Dachau (the town) and go someplace where I could be quiet and think. According to my map, Herrshing was just 28 miles south and less than an hour's drive away. I could easily make it there before dark.

By 8 P.M., I had arrived in Herrshing, checked into my new small room in a small hotel and was sitting in a small restaurant eating a meal with German sausages. I needed for life to feel small. I was not able to think that night. In fact, I felt lucky just to be breathing.

Herrshing is on the eastern shore of the Ammersee Lake, a large lake that is ten miles long and about three miles wide. It has a lakefront promenade and that's where I headed the next morning. I needed to walk. When I got tired, I sat on a bench and stared at the lake. Then I'd walk some more. This was my rhythm for two days—this and eating German sausages. Even though it was still August, I could feel the season changing. Fall was fast approaching.

By the end of the second day, I knew that my time as a European wanderer was ending. I had three more things I wanted to do: visit Ludwig II's castles, see the church in Wies and spend time in Paris. I estimated that this would take about three to four weeks to accomplish. Sitting next to the Ammersee Lake I made the decision to return to Washington in four weeks. I wanted to find an apartment, get a job and get settled for the winter. I wanted to be home for the holidays. I wanted to go home.

I wrote to several friends back in Washington to let them know when I was returning. I asked one friend if I could stay with her until I found a job and an apartment. I told her I would remain in Herrshing for a couple of weeks to give her time to respond to my request. Email would have been so much more efficient but Steve Jobs was still banging around in his parents' garage then and I had to rely on Express Air Mail. By the end of the first week, I received a response telling me I was welcome to stay with her.

I received a second letter from Bruce, the friend who had taken care of Eloise. He offered to fly over and join me for my last two weeks. He'd rent a car and that way we could take a final spin around Europe, he could see a little of Europe as well and then he could help me get back home.

It was obvious that Bruce wanted to make the trip. He was independently wealthy and often traveled on a whim. I felt it was only fair to agree to this plan since he had taken care of Eloise and then dealt with her illness and death. I didn't have the heart to tell him I didn't need help getting back home. He didn't realize that Donald Duck and I were doing just fine by ourselves. But I wasn't opposed to one final spin around the continent. I knew it was time for me to go home but I also knew it was going to be a little tough leaving Europe. Traveling for the final two weeks with Bruce, someone from back home who spoke only English, might ease the transition. And since Bruce was gay I knew I wouldn't have to fight off unwanted hands. With a lot of assistance from the woman at the front desk, I called Bruce.

By the end of my second week in Herrshing, my endgame plans changed as we agreed on a schedule, timing and cities to visit. In two weeks I would meet Bruce at the Lufthansa terminal at the Frankfurt Airport. He would pick up the car at the airport and we would head to Vienna, then Venice and finally Paris. After two weeks of traveling, we would drive back to the Frankfurt Airport and leave for Washington on Lufthansa. All rather neat and organized. Donald Duck and I now had two weeks to continue traveling on our own.

LUDWIG'S CASTLES IN BAVARIA

NEUSCHWANSTEIN CASTLE: The three castles I wanted to see were clustered in southwest Bavaria. I first aimed for Neuschwanstein Castle, which was a little over an hour away from Herrshing. A German family on vacation and on their way to the same castle picked me up. I have to admit, their young son's excitement about seeing a castle was infectious.

Neuschwanstein Castle is a huge white structure perched atop a large, rugged hill and framed by a forest of evergreen trees. As we walked up the path together, I expected to hear Jiminy Cricket singing "When You Wish Upon a Star" and see Tinker Bell flying out to sprinkle us with fairy dust. You're probably familiar with this castle. It's frequently used in television ads for a fantasy ambience, it has appeared in several movies such as *Chitty Chitty Bang Bang* and *The Great Escape,* and it was the model for Disneyland's Sleeping Beauty Castle.

Construction began in 1869 and was privately funded by King Ludwig II of Bavaria as a private refuge. He wanted to live out his idea of the Middle Ages in his medieval knight's castle. Had it been completed, the castle would have had more than 200 rooms. But no more than fifteen rooms and halls were finished when Ludwig died and construction was halted.

The finished rooms were big, lavish and opulently appointed—lots of gold leafing, wood panelling, tapestries and over-the-top extravagance everywhere. I had trouble believing medieval knights had once lived like this. What interested me most were the technical innovations that Ludwig incorporated in the castle. It had a battery-powered bell system for ringing servants and another battery-powered system for lowering and raising a massive chandelier. It also had telephone lines, but I wasn't sure who he would have called. The kitchen was equipped with an oven that turned the skewer with its heat, which automatically adjusted the rotation speed. The hot air was used for a central heating system. There was running warm water and the toilets automatically flushed.

Ludwig was castle obsessed. He had three different construction projects going on at the same time. They completely drained his resources and left him so deeply in debt that a court counselor needed to warn Ludwig that he was insolvent. Ludwig handled the money crisis by threatening suicide if his creditors seized his palaces. Even though he was buried in debt, he insisted on continuing his castle projects. In June 1886, the Bavarian government decided this guy was out of control and needed to be ousted. Ludwig, who was staying at Neuschwanstein at the time, led a one-day standoff when a deposition commission arrived to take him into custody. The next night, he was forced to leave the castle and was placed under the supervision of one Bernhard von Gudden. On June 13, both died under mysterious circumstances and were found in the shallow shore water of Lake Starnberg. At the time of Ludwig's death he had slept only eleven nights in his medieval knight's castle.

By the time I left Neuschwanstein Castle I had given King Ludwig II of Bavaria a new name: Crazy Ludwig. And his castle was now Crazy Ludwig's Place.

HOHENSCHWANGAU CASTLE: Hohenschwangau is just over the hill and a thirty-minute walk from Neuschwanstein Castle. It was the official summer and hunting residence of Maximilian, his wife Marie of Prussia, and their two sons, Crazy Ludwig and Otto (the later King Otto I of Bavaria). When King Maximilian died in 1864, Crazy Ludwig succeeded him to the throne and moved from the "children's annex" at Hohenschwangau into his father's bedroom. His mother moved into another suite of rooms and continued living at Hohenschwangau until her death in 1889. Crazy Ludwig hated his mother and only enjoyed living at Hohenschwangau whenever she was away. When Ludwig's grandfather, Ludwig I, died in 1868, a large sum of money was freed up, thus allowing Crazy Ludwig to begin his castle-building spree. In 1869, he began building Neuschwanstein. It seemed a rather elaborate solution to his need to get away from his mother.

Unlike Neuschwanstein, Hohenschwangau had an atmosphere of both a castle and a home with its smaller, warmly appointed rooms. That's not to say Hohenschwangau was a hovel. It had its share of elegance and wealth on display, including ninety large murals depicting scenes from the history of Schwangau (the village where these castles are located) and medieval German romances. The composer Richard Wagner was a family friend and spent time at Hohenschwangau. He had his own piano in the music room and often played his works for young Ludwig. The two developed a close friendship and artistic tributes to the composer and his works are present throughout Crazy Ludwig's castles.

LINDERHOF PALACE: Since it was only 28 miles away, I still had time that day to visit the third castle, Linderhof. Many people leaving Hohenschwangau were headed to Linderhof, so it was easy to hitch a ride. This was clearly my all-time castle-hopping day.

Linderhof Palace is the only castle of his that Crazy Ludwig lived to see completed. (Hohenschwangau had been completed by Ludwig's father.) The palace was inspired by Versailles, only on a smaller scale. The grounds, gardens and fountains are spectacular and have a distinct Versailles flavor in their landscaping.

As I toured the palace, I saw a few unusual touches that I felt reflected Crazy Ludwig's eccentricities. For example, the Hall of Mirrors had a carpet made of ostrich plumes and an ivory chandelier. (We won't discuss the elephants they killed for that chandelier or the ostriches that had run around naked for that rug.)

The center table in the dining room sat on a dumb-waiter platform and could be lowered into the kitchen below. Crazy Ludwig liked to dine alone. Really alone. He didn't even want to see any servants. So the staff would lower the table, set it in the kitchen and then raise it back up to the dining room. Here's where Crazy Ludwig lived up to his madness. The table was set for at least four people because he used to talk to imaginary people like Louis XV, Mme de Pompadour or Marie Antoinette while he was eating. So I guess technically he didn't dine alone.

In the gardens, I visited one of Ludwig's more interesting structures, the Venus Grotto. This is an artificial cave complete with large fake boulders and stalactites. It has an underground lake and a golden swan-boat that was built along the lines of Wagner's *Tannhäuser.* When he needed to get away (and what mad king doesn't need to get away from time to time), Ludwig used to be rowed around the grotto lake in his golden swan-boat. Now I had a visual I didn't especially want to have in my head but it was definitely a fitting way to end my Crazy Ludwig castle-hopping day.

En Route to the Wies Church in Germany

When I left Linderhof my head was spinning (probably from all that gold leafing) and I had come to the conclusion that I didn't care that much about 19th-century castles and Crazy Ludwig's obsessions. It was still early evening and there was plenty of daylight left so I decided to get out of castle country and head north toward my final stop, the church in Wies. It was only 25 miles away but I wanted to travel a secondary road and stop at one of the small villages along the way for the night.

My first ride dropped me off about ten miles up the road. All was fine while I waited for another ride when a dark, menacing thunderstorm with some serious thunder and lightning quickly pushed over the hills and loomed over me. I was in the middle of nowhere with no buildings around me and I figured I was either going to die from a lightning strike or drown from the torrential rain that I was sure was only minutes away. I was in serious trouble.

It had just begun to rain when a fellow stopped his car and asked if I needed help. I told him I was trying to get to the next village but wasn't having luck. He said it was just a few miles up the road and he could drive me there. He asked if I had a place to stay for the night and, when I said no, he offered to take me to a friend's home. They had a room they rented out and he was sure they would welcome me. I was a little nervous about accepting this offer since I had no idea what kind of situation I was getting myself into. But I figured I had just two options: accept his offer and take a chance or stand outside and die in a storm. I chose the offer.

He was right about the family. They welcomed me into their home with proverbial open arms. I felt like a wet cat that had come in out of the storm. They showed me to the room and even provided a meal in their kitchen. After a day of looking at Ludwig's castles, I was happy to be surrounded by the simplicity and comfort of a real home. I went to sleep listening to the storm rage outside.

The next morning the family invited me to join them for breakfast. Since everyone spoke English, I asked why so many Germans spoke English. They explained that they were required to learn English after the war. (To my credit, I didn't ask them to explain the Holocaust.) They asked about my trip and my life in the United States. We had a long, leisurely, enjoyable breakfast together and, when it was over, I thanked them for taking me in the night before, paid my bill and headed to the Wies Church.

Wies Church

The Wies Church is near Steingaden in Bavaria and its official name is The Pilgrimage Church of Wies. That sentence, although factual and boring, doesn't come close to describing what I found when my ride dropped me off in front of the church. First of all, the church was located in the foothills of the Alps and surrounded by cow pastures. There were no other buildings around. Just fields, fencing and some peacefully grazing cows and horses. My first question: Why did they plunk a big church in the middle of a cow field? It was a picturesque location, but it didn't make sense.

So why was it sitting in a field? In 1738, the hamlet of Wies is said to have been the setting of a miracle in which tears were seen on a simple wooden figure of Christ mounted on a column that was no longer venerated by the monks of the nearby Abbey. A wooden chapel constructed in the field housed the statue for years. However, word got out about the Christ with tears and pilgrims from around Europe began to flock to the little chapel. The Abbot decided to construct a larger, proper sanctuary. In 1745, he commissioned the architect, Dominikus Zimmermann, and said to him something like, "Dominikus, do your thing right here in this cow field." The church was finished in 1754 and, to Zimmermann's credit, it was immediately recognized as one of the most remarkable creations of Bavarian Rococo around.

Some of the Mud Angels had told me that the Wies Church was considered to be a masterpiece of Rococo art (an art movement that emerged in France in the late 17th and early 18th century), which is why I wanted to visit. I had seen examples of Rococo architecture, art and design during my travels, and I had just seen many examples at Neuschwanstein and Linderhof. I found it all to be excessive and visually confusing. To me it was gold-leafing and swirls gone mad. I wanted to give Rococo one final shot by seeing what was considered the best, the Wies Church.

So many times during my European trip I found myself confronted by something that was beyond any experience I had had up to that point. In those initial moments, my brain felt frozen, as if not sure how to process whatever I was facing and all the brain gears had temporarily locked. I learned that if I just stopped, held onto the moment and gave my brain time to adjust, I could begin to see what I was looking at, smell the scents wafting around me, taste what was in my mouth, feel what I was touching and hear the sounds I was listening to.

When I entered the church, I experienced one of those frozen moments. I had to stand there for a few minutes and let my brain adjust to what I was seeing. After about fifteen minutes, I sat in one of the pews and slowly moved my gaze around the church and up to the dome's oculus, taking in the movement, the light and colors. I fear my words cannot begin to express the remarkable beauty, balance and harmony that I saw. I kept thinking, "So *this* is how Rococo is supposed to look."

When I visited, I didn't know the story of the teary-eyed wooden statue of Christ and I'm pretty sure I didn't notice it when I was there. If I did see it, I must have assumed it was just another element of the church's art. Consequently, I missed my miracle and wasn't healed of any ailments, something many pilgrims claimed they had experienced when they visited the church in the cow field.

ZURICH, SWITZERLAND—AGAIN

When I came out of the church, I still had over a week before Bruce's arrival. I was only three hours away from Zurich, the perfect place to spend my final days as a solo traveler.

I needed three rides to get to Zurich that afternoon. Once there, I returned to the hotel by the Landesmuseum, booked their small room again and headed out for dinner. It seemed like years had passed since I had left Zurich for Liechtenstein.

I had hoped to swim at the Mythenquai again but the daytime temperatures were just struggling into the upper-60s. We had two warmer afternoons, and I and a number of other people headed to the Mythenquai for a fall swim. At least the water was warmer than when I first visited.

The only significant thing I did (besides frequenting different Tea Rooms) was think. I walked along the lake promenade, watched the water birds and swan activity, and spent hours sitting on benches and thinking, mostly about the trip. I was struck by the fact that it was drawing to an end. When I started out in January, this trip was a blank. Now all the blanks, except for Vienna, Venice and Paris, were filled in. I think the smartest thing I did was to arrive with no itinerary and just let the trip unfold on its own in real time. Instead of remaining faithful to some pre-set schedule, I responded to whatever rolled in front of me. This gave me adventures that were well beyond anything I could have imagined prior to leaving Washington, D.C.

I thought about how it started on the SS *American Press.* Then London, Amsterdam and the Anne Frank House, Tangier and its food, Barcelona, Monte Carlo, Rome and the Vatican, the Church of Santa Cecilia and the nuns, Florence, the Albergo Imperiale, the Aiguille du Midi and its terrace, Salzburg and the Salzburg Festival, Dachau and the Wies Church.

I thought about the people I met along the way, starting with the officers on the freighter and the family in London. I thought about the many kindnesses extended to me—the shopkeepers, the elderly woman at the Anne Frank House, the hotel manager in Amsterdam, the many people I met in Florence. I thought about Nerio and how I experienced love while having my social consciousness raised at the same time. I thought about Signor Lorini and his hidden snuff box. I remembered the family who drove me to Liechtenstein, the family who took me in out of the storm and the families who picked me up as I auto-stopped because they wanted to make sure I was safe. Throughout my trip, I found the Europeans to be gracious, friendly and kind (except perhaps those bus riders in Munich). They gave me the kind of environment I needed to blossom and to come into my own.

I thought about some of the many things I had learned along the way. I came to Europe knowing zilch about art and history. Now I had worked in a major historic art restoration program as a Mud Angel. I had touched, dusted and cleaned works by Michelangelo. I walked along the streets of history. I visited buildings that had been built long before my own country was founded. I had a new appreciation for age and what defined age, as well as tradition from experiences like the Changing of the Guard at Buckingham Palace, the ravens at the Tower of London and Easter Mass at the Vatican. And the crematory oven at Dachau was forever burned into my memory.

My Europe trip was now a rich, deeply hued, complex part of my life's tapestry with colors that have not faded over time.

The Final Leg: Frankfurt, Germany

When it was time for me to leave Zurich, I decided to take the train to Frankfurt and not gamble my luck with a 184 mile auto-stopping adventure. I left a day ahead of Bruce's arrival, spent the night in Frankfurt and took the shuttle bus to the Lufthansa terminal. Pat myself on the back: I met Bruce on time.

It felt a little odd to be waiting at the airport for his arrival. I felt like a European resident meeting a visitor from the States. His plane was on time and before long he came through the door leading to the greeting area where I was standing.

He was hauling three suitcases. After the requisite hellos and hugs, I asked him why he had three suitcases. He explained they were each only half full so that he'd have room for his purchases along the way. (I was now on a European shopping trip. Ugh.) He looked at my Alitalia bag and asked where the rest of my luggage was sitting. When I told him that bag was it, he just stared at me. Right there in the middle of the airport I could feel a culture clash beginning. (Europe had changed me.)

It didn't take long for us to pick up the rental car and start heading south in the direction of Vienna. (First we had to consult the map to figure out how to get out of the airport and on the Autobahn.) Bruce's job was to drive and my job was to pay attention to the map and road signs. (I had the more challenging job because reading in a moving car made me car sick. But I soldiered on.) En route, Bruce talked about the many things that had happened in Washington while I was gone. It sounded like I hadn't missed much. I talked about my time auto-stopping. It pleased me when he said he was open to picking up auto-stoppers on our trip. About two hours into the drive, we stopped at a small town for lunch. Over lunch I said that it was going to be a long drive to Vienna so I suggested we break it up with an overnight stay in Salzburg. We had a new agreed-upon plan.

On the way back to the Autobahn, we stopped for gas. The fellow pumping gas asked a question and I answered yes. Bruce asked if I now knew German. (He had an edge in his voice, as if he was annoyed that I might have learned something during my trip.) When I told him I didn't, he asked how I knew what that guy was saying. I pointed out that the guy was standing next to our gas tank with a gas nozzle in his hand, asking a question and gesturing. I said, "What do you think the chances are he was asking the German equivalent of 'Fill 'er up?'" I told him my newly acquired language was a mix of body language, gestures and common sense. (I didn't tell him about my pigeon-Italian.)

As we were turning onto the ramp leading back to the Autobahn, we stopped for our first auto-stopper—a young fellow en route to meet some friends in Salzburg. We were now a traveling band of three. His name was Brandon, he was just eighteen and he was from Ireland. He had been traveling around the continent for a couple of weeks and this was the last leg of the trip before returning home. I was grateful for Brandon's company and diversion. It kept me from punching Bruce when he complained about things being different "over here."

Salzburg, Austria—Again

It took three more hours to drive to Salzburg. We dropped Brandon off close to where he needed to go and headed to the center of town to find a hotel. We had just gotten out of the car when Bruce said, "All right. Do your thing. Find us a place to stay." That's when I knew that Bruce and I had different ideas about how these two weeks were to go. I thought we would be working together as a team as we wove our way through the different countries. Bruce assumed I would be his personal travel agent. I would book his hotel rooms, choose the restaurants and map out travel routes for him. There was a little problem with this, other than the fact that I had no intention of being a travel agent. Bruce wanted to travel as an American and first class. He liked expensive hotels with private bathrooms and Michelin-star restaurants. They didn't have to be five star but they needed to be at least two star. (His idea of roughing it.) I was operating on a tight budget and I had to make sure I had money for a plane ticket back to the States. Besides, I preferred to travel as a European. I told Bruce I needed to make more modest arrangements for myself. I pointed to a hotel sign above a shop and said, "I'm going to check in at that hotel. If you want to come along to see about your own room, fine. If you want something fancier, you'll need to find it on your own." Struggling to carry his three suitcases (he was concerned about theft if he left them in the car), he followed me up the stairs to the hotel on the second floor. I booked the secret small room and he booked one of the larger rooms. The shower and toilet rooms were down the hallway for both rooms.

For dinner he invited me to a nice two-star restaurant near the hotel that had been recommended to him by the fellow at the desk and even offered to pay for my meal. (I think he was afraid I was going to drag him to some back-alley soup kitchen.) He suggested we stay an extra night in order to see a bit of the city and maybe do a little shopping. (He was serious about loading up those suitcases with souvenirs.)

The next morning I joined up with Bruce for breakfast and shopping. Normally shopping isn't my favorite activity but I have to admit that Bruce made it an adventure. He wasn't interested in souvenirs sold to the masses. He had money to spend. He wanted to look at items that expressed the unique craftsmanship of the area. Plus he liked that the people working in these high-end shops spoke flawless English.

After watching Bruce shop for about an hour, I told him I'd meet him back at the hotel for dinner and headed out to walk around Salzburg. The festival had ended, the crowds had thinned out and the streets felt quieter now. There were still signs everywhere reminding me that Mozart had been born in their fine city. Salzburg was not going to let me or anyone else forget that.

I was impressed by the beauty of the town no matter what street I walked along or which direction I headed. During World War II, fifteen allied bombing strikes destroyed over forty percent of the city's buildings. It's bridges and the cathedral dome were destroyed but much of its Baroque architecture remained standing, making Salzburg unique among other European cities in its architectural style.

I stopped at a Tea Room for a break and some reading. I was relieved to be back to my familiar routine. After thinking about the situation I now found myself in, I decided that Bruce probably was a good transition person for me, but I realized that my transition was going to be more difficult than I had anticipated.

I chose the restaurant for dinner that night. It was small and no Michelin stars had been awarded to it. To Bruce's surprise, he not only found the food edible but tasty, as well—and inexpensive.

Vienna, Austria

The drive from Salzburg to Vienna took about four hours, that's including lunch and picking up another auto-stopper. We dropped off this fellow at a small town about twenty miles before reaching Vienna. With the roles reversed and now being the one to pick up auto-stoppers, I could see why so many drivers stopped. The folks we picked up added something pleasant to the drive. (And they kept me from punching Bruce when he started complaining.)

I have to be honest with you. As soon as we arrived in Vienna, I felt overwhelmed by this city. It was elegantly beautiful and big—too big to just spend the two days we had planned. Its art, history, museums, theaters, government buildings all needed time. I made a mental note to someday return to Vienna and give it the time it deserved. (I have yet to check that off my mental to-do list.) You'll be pleased to know that Mozart got out of Salzburg and came to Vienna to work. (I didn't know if I was stalking Mozart or if he was stalking me.)

I walked to St. Stephen's Cathedral to see its architecture and fancy multi-colored mosaic tile roof. The Cathedral's bell tower contains a whopping total of twenty-three bells. They say that Ludwig van Beethoven discovered he was entirely deaf when he saw birds flying out of the bell tower as a result of the bells' ringing but could not hear the bells. It's fair to say that St. Stephen's offers a complimentary hearing test to anyone passing by at the right time. Just watch for the tower's birds. If they're flying and you don't hear anything, see a doctor.

I lucked out and stumbled on an outdoor concert. Bruce was busy shopping so I attended on my own. It was held in a park, which added to the magic of the setting, and admission was free. I have no idea what piece I was listening to but it didn't matter. It gave me my special Viennese experience and memory—an early-fall concert in a Viennese park.

Venice, Italy

It was a long drive from Vienna to Venice, lasting about six hours and ending with a short boat ride to St. Mark's Square where we were greeted by thousands of pigeons. I know this is going to sound crazy because everyone knows that one of the things Venice is famous for is its canals. I certainly knew that long before arriving in Europe and it was one of the reasons why I was pleased to get to Venice on this trip. Despite what I knew, when I arrived and actually saw the canals, I experienced another brain freeze. I could not get my head wrapped around the fact that there were no paved streets. Just water. There were sidewalks in the central area outside the shops and restaurants. But in some areas there were no sidewalks and the canal water lapped against the buildings. In my travels I had stepped off many sidewalks and crossed countless cobblestone streets. If I tried that in Venice I'd be splashing around in a canal (with a bunch of Italians yelling at me to get out of the canal). Amsterdam had canals but it also had streets and sidewalks running alongside and bridges for cars to drive over the canals. In the Venice that I saw there were beautiful bridges for pedestrians only. No cars.

So I spent my time in the city with water streets and observed the different ways people negotiated that reality. There weren't only tourists floating around in gondolas. There were plenty of motor boats of all sizes, small barges delivering supplies, long motor buses and shorter motor boat taxis. And they had traffic jams. There were waterway rules designed to prevent jams and to spell out who had the right of way, but apparently this could break down. I saw gondoliers expertly maneuvering to get out of the jams. If they didn't have any tourists sitting in their boat, they would trash talk the others and accuse them of creating the traffic mess. (Picture much arm waving, hand gestures and angry shouts of *"Cosa fare."*)

Bruce seemed to take the canals more in stride and didn't suffer from the same fascination I had. He liked the shops.

We took time out from our respective fascinations to explore St. Mark's Basilica together. St. Mark's had its groundbreaking in 978 and was completed in 1092. It houses a treasure-trove of art, most of which I wasn't interested in seeing. But the bright mosaics covering the upper levels caught my attention. They used something called "gold glass tesserae" (individual glass tiles used in creating a mosaic) as the background. This made the upper basilica appear to be shimmering and alive as the sunlight hit the gold tiles.

We ascended a spiral stone staircase (with very narrow steps) that led to the outside balcony and the basilica's three famous bronze horses. They had been installed on that balcony above the portal around 1254. In 1797, the horses were taken to Paris by Napoleon but returned to Venice in 1815. (Someone needs to have a chat with Napoleon and tell him to stop stealing large statues that happen to catch his eye. He also hauled off Michelangelo's *Dying Captive* from Florence and it's still sitting at the Louvre because France won't give it back. The guy was a kleptomaniac.)

After three nights and two full days, we left Venice to begin our long journey to Paris. It was a 525 mile trip so we decided to stop for the night in Geneva, the halfway point. We now had just seven days remaining in this two-week dash through Europe and we wanted to spend that time in Paris.

Paris, France

I usually shy away from large cities, but my six days in Paris were different. The city spoke to me. I loved the cobblestone streets laid out in patterns, the sidewalk cafés with their ham sandwiches on French bread, the bakery shops, the street markets, the gardens and parks, the Eiffel Tower, the Arc de Triomphe, Notre-Dame de

Paris, Montmartre and the Paris Metro. God, how I loved that Metro. It was my first metro experience. It was easy to navigate, it was inexpensive, it saved me a lot of time and I used it often. The point is, Paris and I got along just fine. I even enjoyed the Parisiennes. Unlike their reputation for being snotty toward tourists, especially American tourists, I found them to be friendly, helpful and kind.

I visited the Louvre but the only things I wanted to see were the *Mona Lisa* and the marble original of Michelangelo's *Dying Slave.* Overall I found the Louvre overwhelming. I committed an art-world heresy and walked out of the Louvre after about a half hour. I rescued myself at a nearby café.

My favorite museum was the Musée Rodin that was housed in the Hôtel Biron. In the early 1900s, Jean Cocteau, Henri Matisse and Isadora Duncan lived in the hotel. In 1908, the famous sculptor Auguste Rodin rented four ground-floor rooms to use as his studios. By 1911, he occupied the whole building. At that time the French government was planning to purchase the hotel, but Rodin negotiated a sweet deal with them. He announced his intention to donate all his works to the French state, including his drawings and his collection of antiquities, on the condition that the state kept his collections at the hotel and the Hôtel Biron would become the Musée Rodin. In exchange, Rodin received the right to reside there all his life rent-free.

Rodin's more famous sculptures—*The Gates of Hell, The Burghers of Calais, The Thinker* and *The Kiss*—were sitting at the Musée Rodin. I was especially drawn to his work because it reminded me of Michelangelo's sculpture. I later learned that I wasn't alone in this. During his lifetime, Rodin was often compared to Michelangelo. Rodin's subtle detail of the human body and how the muscles functioned was the same detail I had seen in Michelangelo's work. No matter what position the body was in, I could see the active muscles that were needed to hold that position, giving the sculpture body weight and authenticity.

Rodin and I also shared a Michelangelo connection. Rodin's inspiration for his *Age of Bronze* was drawn from Michelangelo's *Dying Slave,* which Rodin had studied at the Louvre. (Okay. For this alone I'll give Napoleon a pass for hauling the *Dying Slave* out of Florence.) At Mike's Sorta House, I spent three weeks up close and personal, cleaning the casting of the *Dying Slave* that Napoleon sent back to Florence in exchange for his grand theft.

One of my favorite spots at the Musée Rodin was the gardens. Rodin's large pieces *(The Thinker, The Gates of Hell, The Burghers of Calais)* were sitting out there. As I walked around the grounds, I could feel that these were the same gardens where Rodin had once walked. When I sat on a bench, I felt the gap close between my current time and Rodin's time when he lived at the Hôtel Biron. He was there, sitting with me on that bench as we looked at his sculptures together.

I'm not sure what Bruce was doing with his days but it probably involved shopping. The afternoon before we were to leave for Frankfurt, the shopping bug finally hit me and I walked to Galeries Lafayette, Paris' big department store. I wanted to get something that would make me smile and remind me of Paris and my trip. It had to be practical and not just something that sat around on a shelf gathering dust. I settled on a blue wool tweed suit. Perfect.

I needed to make another purchase at Galeries Lafayette. As I walked up the stairs to my hotel room the day we arrived in Paris, my trusty Alitalia bag fell apart. I needed to replace it to get home. I found a red-plaid cloth bag of equal size. That night I gently removed my Donald Duck decal from the Alitalia bag and gave the bag a fond farewell as I placed it in the trash can. As for Donald Duck, he was coming home with me.

The morning we left Paris we discovered that someone had hit a side window on the car and cracked it. It didn't look like the smasher was interested in stealing anything out of the car. It looked more like he just wanted to bust a window, which made the whole act that much more puzzling. We taped the window to shore it up for the trip and, with that, headed out of Paris for the 358 mile drive to Frankfurt.

During the drive, Bruce and I decided that we had been mad to drive a total of 1,784 miles and visit three major cities in just two weeks. It felt more like an endurance test. Even with that, Bruce said he was pleased with his experience and glad he came.

I suggested that the next time he traveled to Europe he plan to stay a few months. It's a whole different experience. (He may need to rent a U-Haul for all his purchases.)

Frankfurt, Germany and Home

Bruce already had his return flight ticket. The plan was to go to the airport early on the day he was due to fly out and I would buy my ticket on the same flight.

First we had to drop off the car and explain to the fellow that the window had been busted by some unknown person in Paris. He didn't seem especially perturbed by this. He explained that cars rented out of that airport often came back with some kind of damage. Because of the sticker on the back identifying the cars' country of origin (Germany), people took their anger about the war out on the cars. He made it seem like this was just something the Germans had to cope with.

At the Lufthansa counter, Bruce checked in, handed over his three now-filled suitcases and waited while I asked to purchase a ticket on the same flight. I hit a snag. (It was probably naïve for both of us to think I could buy a ticket on the spot.) The flight was booked and they had to put me on standby. Also, depending on the flight they could get me on, I would either be arriving in New York City or Toronto. From either location I would need to transfer to a Washington-bound flight. (Apparently knowing ahead of time where I was to disembark was not in the cards for my trip. On the *American Press,* I hadn't been sure if I'd be docking in Liverpool or Southampton.)

The other thing I discovered was that my one-way ticket was going to cost almost as much as Bruce's round trip ticket. (Color me miffed.) This seemed arbitrary and unfair. Of course I felt that my one-way ticket should be half the cost of Bruce's two-way ticket. Fortunately I had budgeted $500 for the return trip and that was enough to cover the $312.35 for the ticket. So for ten days at sea that included thirty meals and a lot of high-seas adventures, I paid $207. Now for $312.35 I would get two meals and spend eight hours in the air with, hopefully, no adventures. I was paying for the convenience of speed because it sure wasn't for the meals.

About a half hour before departure I was given a ticket on Bruce's flight (landing in New York City) and assigned a seat. It wasn't next to Bruce's seat, which was fine with me. I didn't feel like having a long, somewhat boring conversation as I headed back to Washington and a new life.

Chapter 17

Marching Through Washington
1967–1970

IT TOOK TWO WEEKS TO LAND a job and find a new apartment. After returning, I spent the first three days sitting on the couch in my friend's apartment, staring into space, rocking back and forth, making spit bubbles and murmuring, "Where am I?" Jet lag and I are not friends. By the fourth day, I knew I needed to get moving.

Europe truly had changed me. I didn't want to resume the life I had prior to departing. I still had *The Washington Post* offer to consider but I wanted to create a softer, quieter life. I didn't want to re-enter the world of a large daily newspaper with its constant sharp-edged, intense atmosphere. Beyond this, I didn't have any notion about the kind of job I wanted. It was time to search the Help Wanted listings for ideas and opportunities.

One ad intrigued me. The National Gallery of Art was advertising for a position in their Publications Department. It sounded like a sales girl job, which I was certain I could do. Plus working at the Gallery seemed like a logical extension of my time in Europe. There was one glitch: The job required a master's degree in art history. Even though I didn't have an art history degree let alone any other college degree, I figured I would apply anyway and hope that I could speak to someone about my time in Europe and my Mud Angel experience. I felt certain that actual hands-on experience would trump book learning. Besides, how much art education did a person need to sell a 5¢ post card? I'd give it a shot.

The interview was conducted by Mrs. Dundas, an elderly, well-dressed, sweet, soft-spoken woman who headed the Publications

Department. From my application, she knew that I had just returned from Europe and asked me about the trip as soon as I sat down. She wanted to know what historical sites, museums and galleries I had visited. I told her about my time in Florence and the work with the restoration program. She was concerned about my lack of art history education, and I told her my theory about the value of hands-on experience being greater than looking at photographs in a book. I could tell that I was asking her to step out of her box. I suspected that hiring new staff for the Gallery shop was normally pretty straightforward. (Is the person presentable? Is the person well behaved? Does he or she smell bad? Does the person seem halfway intelligent? Do they have an art history degree?) Yet it was clear that she felt my experience-over-books theory had some merit.

Then she asked the question that I was sure would be a deal breaker. How often had I visited the National Gallery of Art during my years in Washington? I told her I had come to the Gallery just once at the insistence of a friend who dragged me around the rooms for about two hours. I left nauseous and with a headache. I explained how things improved once I got to Europe and how much the Rijksmuseum had helped. (I think the fact that I knew how to pronounce "Rijksmuseum" meant a lot to her.) Assuming I had destroyed the interview, I thanked her for her time and started to leave. That's when she asked if I could start work Monday (three days away). Without hesitation, I said, "Yes."

When I got back to the apartment, I realized that in my excitement about being hired, I had not asked Mrs. Dundas a few vital specifics about the job. I called her right away and asked what time I was to report to work (9 A.M.) and how much the job paid ($100 a week). That was four times greater than my salary in Florence. I was rolling in dough.

Now that I had a job, I could look for an apartment. I didn't want to live in my old neighborhood near St. Matthew's Cathedral, *The Washington Post,* Dupont Circle and the White House. It felt too commercial and business-like. During the trip, Bruce had suggested I check out Capitol Hill, a middle class neighborhood that was family oriented and integrated. The Saturday before I was to begin my new job, I walked into a real estate office on the Hill and asked if they knew of any apartments for rent in the area. Timing really is everything. One of the agents had an English basement apartment in his home on 7th Street SE and the tenant had just moved out. He said he'd be happy to show it to me.

It was perfect. It had its own entrance, one large main room with a big bay window, a brick fireplace, a full kitchen and bath. I fell in love with it right away. It reminded me of the small rooms in Europe. It also had something else I liked—a walk-through closet. The back wall of the closet had another door that led to the family basement with a washing machine I could use. Also, I could have a corner space for storage. The rent was $90 a month. I went back to the office with the agent and signed the lease. (The first lease I had signed on my own!) I paid the first month's rent and deposit out of the money I had left over from my trip. He said I could move in any time and handed me the key.

At the end of two weeks, I had a job, an apartment and the promise of a simple, quiet life.

My new neighborhood was (and is) historic. Maybe it wasn't as old as the European towns and their buildings, but by American standards it was historic. In 1793, Secretary of State, Thomas Jefferson, named the area Capitol Hill. There actually is a hill, and the U.S. Capitol, the Supreme Court, the Library of Congress, and the Senate and House office buildings sit at the top of that hill. Walk a block beyond and you'll find tree-lined streets and 19th-century row houses along with shops, a bakery, restaurants and small bars. The Eastern Market, an 1873 public market where vendors sold fresh meat and produce in indoor stalls and at outdoor farmers' stands was on 7th Street SE, just two blocks from my apartment.

Over the next couple of months, as finances allowed, I furnished the apartment with pieces from a nearby used furniture store. Because of its size it didn't require much and everything had to serve more than one purpose: a narrow Napoleonic bed doubled as a couch, a side table opened to a four-seater dining table, two dining chairs, a small desk, a coffee table and a large reading chair. I was inspired by the room in Paris where I had stayed that last week. I loved its colors (blues and beiges), its furniture and its feel. It didn't take long to recreate that feel. Once I hung *The Rugged Individualist* (the picture from Upperco) and unpacked my metal quotes box, I was home.

I decided to learn to cook properly and let Julia Child and her book *Mastering the Art of French Cooking* guide me. I also learned to bake bread, grind coffee beans and make good coffee. I shopped at the Eastern Market, which felt like I was shopping in Florence. And I purchased a three-speed bicycle that became my sole mode of transportation.

Bike riding in Washington in 1967 required skill and caution. This was a few years before the convenience and economic advantages of urban biking came into fashion, so there weren't bike racks or bike lanes. I had lamp and sign poles for securing my bike to and I had that open space next to parked cars that created a narrow lane. As long as no one threw their car door open without first looking (which happened more than you might imagine), I was fine. Otherwise I would have to come to a screeching halt or just crash into the door and land in the driver's lap. On a good day, I might see one other brave biker. But most of the time, I was a lone maverick. I loved the freedom. I even enjoyed the weather changes. When it snowed, which wasn't often, I'd walk to work until the streets were clean and dry again. That only took a day or two, then I was back to pedaling.

My apartment was a fifteen-minute ride from the National Gallery of Art if I took the more direct route and cut through the U.S. Capitol grounds. The first day I showed up at the Gallery with my bike, I was given a parking spot inside one of the receiving and loading garages.

The Capitol guards got to know me and we would greet one another as I rode by. When I was scheduled to work on Sundays, I stopped by the bakery for chocolate chip cookies to share with my co-workers. The guards must have smelled the cookies as I passed by because they would stop me on Sundays for cookies that they claimed was the entrance fee to the Capitol grounds. I increased my cookie order on those Sundays. It was fair. People who had to work on Sundays needed a fresh baked chocolate chip cookie.

At the Gallery I joined a team, mostly young women, who manned the shop and assisted visitors with their purchases. There were hundreds of reproductions of the paintings available in postcard, 11x14 inch and poster sizes. Only the postcards were self-serve. A sample of the other reproductions was displayed on spindles around the room. The visitors would flip through the spindles and write down the stock number of whatever they wished to purchase. Then they would come to the main counter and present us with their lists. We pulled the items they wanted from a bank of drawers behind the counter, bagged everything and took their money. Sounds pretty simple, doesn't it?

But Americans are known for being independent, free thinkers who are prone to not want to follow a set routine. (The bus riders in Munich would be apoplectic.) This is where a job that could have killed us from boredom became challenging. A fair number of people did not want to be bothered with writing down stock numbers. So they would come to the desk and describe what they wanted to buy. Sometimes they knew the artist, sometimes not. Sometimes they would mix and match the artists with the wrong paintings. Sometimes they knew what room they had been in when they saw their painting, most of the time not. Sometimes they knew the name of the painting, sometimes they morphed that name into something completely unrecognizable. Salvatore Dali's *Last Supper* became *Dolly Madison's Last Dinner* by more than one person.

Often their descriptions were…shall we say, challenging. One woman nearly stumped us when she asked for a copy of "the painting with the peacock." We tried to figure out what painting had her peacock. After considering a number of possibilities, it finally hit one of us and he pulled out the reproduction of *Adoration of the Magi,* painted by Fra Angelico and Filippo Lippi in Florence between 1440 and 1460. You could not get more people, animals and things into this painting. There is an endless procession of people coming from Bethlehem and lining up behind the Magi to greet the Baby. There is an equally long procession filing away. Of course, Mary, Joseph and Jesus are in the foreground. People riding horses and camels are coming down the path to join the event. There are horses, donkeys and an ox in the manger and a dog lying on the ground in front of the Magi. There are mountains in the background and the city's walls angle toward the manger with a group of little weird, half-dressed dancing guys on one of the walls. And on the apex of the manger that sits behind the Holy Family and the kneeling Magi (and the dog) was perched one peacock. She smiled when she saw the print and we had one of our many high-five moments that always felt like we had just won a contest.

Some visitors did not understand the concept of a master painting. Women who wanted a nice picture for their living room wall would ask for a specific painting but then request that their reproduction be in colors other than the ones used in the original painting. (It had to match their couch.) Sometimes women would ask if we had Picasso's *The Tragedy* in green (from his Blue Period and painted entirely in shades of blue). Actually, this was the one such request we could accommodate. The shop sold some of the prints as laminated plaques that were ready for hanging. When *The Tragedy* was made into a plaque, the lamination yellowed the print and all the blues appeared as shades of green. Picasso didn't know it, but he ushered in another period—his Green Period.

Many people bought reproductions because they were so inexpensive. The postcards were 5¢ a piece and the 11x14s were 25¢. People would come up to the counter with a list of stock numbers for a hundred 11x14s to go along with the 300 postcards. I always wondered what in the world they were planning to do with all those reproductions. There had to be a black market that we didn't know about that was hungry for cheap art prints.

But every once in a while someone would ask for just one print. That painting had spoken to them and touched them in some special way. (I guess we could say the peacock spoke to the woman.) An elderly man who had the tan and rough hands of a farmer asked me for a copy of *The Farm* (Charles-François Daubigny, 1855). It's a painting of an old French farm with thatched roofs, a stone wall and a well-used wooden wagon, all in shades of tan and brown. It's very peaceful on the eyes. When I handed him the copy, he carefully held it, looked at it, gently placed it on the counter and said softly, "Yes, that's the one." I felt like I was sharing a special moment with him. Just remembering him makes me smile.

A surprising number of visitors did not understand the National Gallery of Art's purpose. Some people treated the Gallery as a cooling station. In the summer they would dash into the building with bare feet just to cool off, then quickly dash back out again without looking at any of the art. After seeing the Gallery's rotunda, some would ask, "Is this where Kennedy is buried?" (John Kennedy's body lay in state in the rotunda at the U.S. Capitol building before burial at Arlington Cemetery.) Shortly before I joined the National Gallery, the Louvre had loaned da Vinci's *Mona Lisa* for a special exhibit. According to the staff who survived to tell the tales, a half-million people flocked to the Gallery and stood in line to see this painting. They then stormed the shop to purchase their 25¢ copy of said painting. It got so crazy that they would just throw their quarters on the counter or at the staff, bag their own print and rush out the door. The staff couldn't ring the sales up on the cash registers fast enough so every fifteen minutes one of them would scoop the quarters into paper bags to be counted after the Gallery closed each day. One man asked, "What is this building used for when the *Mona Lisa* isn't here?"

My favorite place to work was Kiddie Land. The Gallery offered special tours for groups of kids from local elementary schools. After their tour, they were led to an area outside the large shop that had been set up just for them with prints of the paintings they had seen on tour. I liked to watch their reactions and listen to their comments. Every kid bought a copy of Gilbert Stuart's portrait of George Washington. I knew all their mothers would be taping that print on their refrigerator door that night. The boys bought prints of Copley's *Watson and the Shark* because they believed the naked body in the water was a girl and this was their first naked-girl picture. (In actuality it was a fourteen year old boy named Brook Watson. I didn't want to destroy the boys' fantasies by saying anything. And listening to them debate the issue was pretty amusing.) One boy walked up to me and asked in a rather defiant tone, "What's so special about this stuff? All they had to do was follow the numbers." It took a few seconds for me to figure out what he was talking about. Then I realized he thought the artists painted by number. I said, "Oh, you have to understand. These guys were the ones who figured out what numbers went where on the canvas." He bought that and I could tell he now had a better appreciation for what artists did. On the other hand, this kid was a boy after my own heart. I certainly could relate to his feelings about art and the hoopla that surrounded it.

There was always one kid in each group that held back and did not pick any prints. These were the kids with no money to spend. It broke my heart to see them standing quietly to one side and just waiting. Half the experience of coming to the Gallery was to leave with prints of the paintings they liked. So with each group, I would call the quiet kid over and tell him that I couldn't keep up with the purchases his classmates were making and I needed help. Would he like to pack the prints in bags and earn $3 while I rang up sales. Each kid brightened up right away and eagerly accepted the job. I gave them a one-minute tutorial on sliding prints in a bag without dog-earing them. After that, my new assistant and I functioned as a well-oiled team. (They took their job seriously and made a point to bag the prints carefully.)

When the final four or five kids were still picking out prints, I gave my assistants their $3. By that time, they had seen what everyone bought and had decided just what combination they needed to buy for the maximum number of pictures totaling $3. They had become smart shoppers. Often the teachers would thank me, but it was the look on the kids' faces that meant the most to me. And when they left with their class, their walk had a little bounce to it.

The most expensive painting at the Gallery was *Ginevra de' Benci* by Leonardo da Vinci. At $5 million, this was the highest purchase price of any piece of art at that time. I know this because it wasn't unusual for someone to come rushing into the shop and ask, "What's the most expensive painting in this place?" We'd tell them *Ginevra de' Benci* and they would leave the shop to go look at it.

Often it was the only painting they looked at. Or they would just buy a 25¢ reproduction of *Ginevra* and leave the Gallery to continue their sightseeing without seeing the original.

There's a weird little story behind da Vinci's *Ginevra de' Benci.* Not long after I began working at the Gallery, John Walker, the Gallery's director, gave a talk to the full staff describing how *Ginevra* got to the Gallery. And he introduced us to "Bird."

Ginevra was painted between 1474 and 1478. No one is quite sure what happened to the painting for the next 200 years until around 1700, when she came into the possession of the royal family of Liechtenstein. During World War II, the family hid her from the Nazis in a monastery. As Soviet troops approached, the prince smuggled her into his castle in Vaduz for safe keeping. He concealed her in his wine cellar. (Is any of this starting to ring a bell?)

Twenty years after the war, Prince Franz Joseph let it be known that the family was willing to sell *Ginevra de' Benci.* You already know why. He needed the money to pay for his son's wedding that was to be held in Vaduz in the summer of 1967. Somebody had to pay for all the beer and sausages.

Bidding was fierce among galleries around the world. Italian syndicates jumped in, determined to return *Ginevra* to her homeland. John Walker personally negotiated for the painting. He told few people about the negotiations, he gave the portrait the code name of "bird" and he locked all of his *Ginevra* correspondence in a safe. It was the art world's best kept secret. In February 1967, it was announced that the National Gallery of Art had won the bid. There was a lot of excitement (and jealousy) in the art world because this was to be the only da Vinci to hang outside Europe.

Now they had to figure out how to transport *Ginevra* from Vaduz to the Gallery in Washington safely and without attracting the attention of art thieves. Secrecy was key and they decided to go with the quiet, understated approach. She arrived in Washington in a suitcase—a grey, American Tourister suitcase. (At this point in his talk, Mr. Walker showed us the suitcase, inside and out.) Although nondescript and ordinary in appearance on the outside, its lining had been replaced with Styrofoam designed to buffer the painting while in transit and act like a Thermos, safeguarding it from the atmospheric conditions outside.

As befitting her $5 million price tag, she flew first class. Her companion was Mario Modestini, the art conservator who had verified that she was indeed a real Leonardo. *Ginevra* had her own ticket and traveled as Mrs. Mario Modestini, the conservator's wife. (I don't know if they served *Ginevra* her meal, but her extra bag of peanuts might have been appreciated by Mario.) All anyone saw on that seat was a grey suitcase with the seatbelt strapped around it. They did not know what it contained, of course, and they did not know that the interior of the suitcase was constructed to maintain a temperature of 44 degrees during the flight. It was fitted with a gauge that showed the interior temperature and humidity. Just prior to boarding, Modestini sent a coded telegram to John Walker: "The bird flies." (I felt that out of all the careful arrangements they had made, this coded message was the weakest part of their plan. I couldn't imagine any art thief worth his salt not figuring out right away that "The bird flies" meant *Ginevra* is on the move and we now know what plane she is on.)

Not to miss a good marketing angle, American Tourister took out an ad in *The New York Times* that read: "This $5,000,000 da Vinci masterpiece flew the Atlantic in American Tourister luggage. Isn't this the kind of luggage you should travel with?"

By the holidays in 1967 and the new year, I was well settled into my new apartment, my new job and the rhythms of my new life.

My pre-Europe gang had broken up and gone their separate ways. When I met with them right after coming back, it was clear they weren't interested in hearing anything about my trip. My experiences, thoughts and ideas no longer fit in with their lives and interests. We had each simply moved on.

On Sundays I attended Mass at the local parish church on the Hill. In comparison with the churches and cathedrals I had visited in Europe, this church was a bit of a letdown—boring architecture, inside and out. I suspected I just needed time to get used to the fact that I was no longer in Europe. After a few weeks I did settle down around this and the church's architecture stopped irritating me.

However, there was another irritation that would not go away. The priests serving at this small church were mostly older, ultra-traditional and performed their jobs in a tired, detached manner. It seemed they had long ago lost enthusiasm about the religion or their calling. It especially showed when they gave their sermons on Sundays. They chose to speak about obscure topics that had nothing to do with daily life or the world around us. I don't think these guys ever read a newspaper or listened to what parishioners were telling them in confession. The priests were dutifully giving their weekly sermons and it didn't seem to matter to them that nothing they talked about touched the lives of the listeners.

Converts to Catholicism are known to be a different kettle of fish from what we call the "Cradle Catholics." We converts consciously chose the religion and, at times, could be critical, even rebellious, if we felt the Mass and sacraments were not being handled with the proper care and consciousness. When I attended St. Matthew's, I had a confessor. This was a priest who I went to for confession regularly and with whom I developed an ongoing relationship through the sacrament of confession. The experience gave me emotional and social building blocks that added to my personal growth. One time when my confessor was out of town, I had to go to another priest at the cathedral. When I entered the confessional, I noticed he was sitting there with his light on reading his daily prayers. After I knelt, he continued reading. I waited a few minutes and he just kept reading. Finally I said to him, "Look. I'll be sitting in a pew right outside. When you decide you're ready to hear a confession, let me know." With that, I left the confessional. A few minutes later, he came out and asked me to re-enter the booth. I was sure he had never before experienced a parishioner refusing his services based on his conduct.

Another time a different priest heard my confession and, at the end, he gave me a typical, rote penance: "Say two Our Fathers and ten Hail Mary's." I said, "No." He looked at me and said, "What do you mean, no?" I told him that his penance had nothing to do with what I had said in my confession and I was refusing that penance. He asked what penance I felt would be acceptable and, after a little thought, I told him what I thought a relevant penance would be. He agreed and told me to "go do that." (We converts can be so demanding.)

I'm pointing this out to show you that many converts tend to be serious about the new religion that they consciously choose and don't accept tedium or lack of thought as part of that practice. For me, ceremony had meaning and contained a truth. Both the priest and the parishioner were required to consciously participate in order to touch deep into that meaning and truth.

Even before I left for Europe, the American Catholic Church had started leaning toward being more liberal. Priests didn't just read about the Civil Rights Movement in the papers; they were actively participating in it. They were supporting the anti-war movement, as well, and debating hot topics like birth control and divorce. By the time I moved to Capitol Hill, there was an even stronger lean to the liberal side of issues. To my mind, the parish church on the Hill belonged in some bygone era. I was going to have to do something about this—soon.

I was fast becoming friends with the family living above me. Paul was a real estate agent on weekends only. During the week, he taught French at Howard University (D.C.'s historic black university). His wife, Sara, was a stay-at-home mom with their two young children, Maddie (age 3) and Charlie (age 6). It wasn't unusual for the kids to poke their heads through the closet and come in to tell me about their day. I was like their personal basement troll and I loved it when they showed up.

Because of my shifting schedule at the Gallery, I had a couple of weekdays off every two weeks. Sara would frequently stomp on her living room floor above my apartment as an invitation to join her for coffee and some spirited conversation. We'd spend the afternoons discussing, arguing, debating and challenging one another. Sara was seven years older, had been born and raised in Boston, and had attended Catholic University before marrying. She was smart—really smart—and I felt she should have been teaching somewhere. She was fluent in French (it was her first language as a child) and she wrote poetry, usually in French. Because she was a college graduate and I was a non-college non-graduate, our discussions tended to include debates around Sara's "learned-journal facts" versus my "common sense and street-smart facts." We took on any and all topics: religion, literature, education, the women's movement, war, anti-war, nonviolence, economics, politics, Congress.... No matter what, we each had opinions and were ready to defend those opinions when needed.

One inevitable topic was the Vietnam War. Vietnam was a daily presence in Washington. The war and the public's opinions about it were white-hot topics. It seemed like everyone was asking: Why are we there? How did we get into this war and who got us into it? Why are young men dying over there? What did we hope to gain from this war? Were we being lied to by the President (Lyndon Johnson), his cabinet members and Pentagon officials? (The answer to that last question was yes.)

In the fall of 1967, anti-war protests and demonstrations were occurring nationwide.

- On October 16, protests were held in thirty cities across the U.S. and over 1,400 draft cards were burned.
- On October 20, protest leaders presented draft cards to the Department of Justice.
- On October 21 through October 23, 50,000 people gathered at the Lincoln Memorial on the National Mall for "The March on the Pentagon to Confront the War Makers." Up to 35,000 participants marched to the Pentagon while others chose to engage in acts of civil disobedience around the city. One group wanted to "capture" the State Department and close it down. Police were waiting in the hallways of the State Department with semi-automatic rifles ready to gun down any protesters who entered the building.
- On October 27, The Baltimore Four, led by Father Philip Berrigan (a Josephine priest and World War II veteran) and accompanied by three others, occupied the Selective Service Board in the Customs House in Baltimore, Maryland, and performed "a sacrificial, blood-pouring protest," using their own blood mixed with poultry blood. They poured it over draft records as an act meant to protest "the pitiful

waste of American and Vietnamese blood in Indochina." They then waited for the police and were arrested.

• On December 4–8, New York City held "Stop the Draft Week" demonstrations that resulted in 585 arrests, including the arrest of Dr. Benjamin Spock, the pediatrician and author of *Baby and Child Care.*

["List of protests against the Vietnam War," Wikipedia, n.d.]

In Washington, protests were going on all around me. The irony was that I had moved to Capitol Hill in search of a quieter life. In reality, all I did was move from one end of Ground Zero to the other end. And Ground Zero was the National Mall, a 1.9 mile long park that has at one end the Lincoln Memorial and the White House. At the other end sits the U.S. Capitol. The George Washington Monument sticks up in the middle of the Mall. If you're going to protest the federal government and some misguided policy, the National Mall, with its history and symbolism, has been the prime place to do it since the 1850s.

I was asking the same questions everyone else was asking about that war. What were we doing there? I could not find any reasonable or logical answers. It didn't take long for me to feel the pull to join the protests. All I had to do was leave the apartment, bike seven blocks to the Capitol and join the protest in progress right there on the Mall. However, I didn't want to join in the crazy carnival atmosphere that was prevalent during some protests. I wanted to listen to the speakers, I wanted to be one of the numbers counted in the crowd and I wanted to learn the answers to my growing number of questions.

1968

This is the year people talk about, write about and make documentaries about. It's the year that everything blew up. I won't be reconstructing the Vietnam War for you. I'm not even close to being qualified for such an endeavor. Instead I'd like you see what 1968 was like through the eyes of a twenty-two year old young woman who experienced that year from Ground Zero in Washington and lived to tell her tale.

> • On Monday, January 15, a group of women's pro-peace organizations, including the "Women's International League for Peace and Freedom" and "Women Strike for Peace," joined together to confront Congress on its opening day with a strong show of female opposition to the Vietnam War. At age 87, Jeannette Rankin led the march of some 5,000 women. They were called the Jeannette Rankin Brigade. Even though it was happening just seven blocks from my apartment, I couldn't join in because I was scheduled to work. But I was aware it was going on when I pedaled through the Capitol grounds and had to weave my way around protesters, police and press.
>
> • The first phase of the Tet Offensive in Vietnam was launched on January 30, 1968, by the Viet Cong and North Vietnamese People's Army of Vietnam against the South Vietnamese Army of the Republic of Vietnam, the U.S. Armed Forces and their allies. It lasted until March 28. It was a campaign of surprise attacks involving more than 80,000 North Vietnamese troops striking more than 100 towns, cities, military and civilian command and control centers throughout South Vietnam. It was the largest military operation conducted by either side up to that point in the war and there were heavy casualties on both sides. It also was the first time that Saigon had been attacked.
>
> ["List of protests against the Vietnam War," Wikipedia, n.d.]

Enter Walter Cronkite. In numerous Gallop Polls over a thirty-year period, Walter Cronkite, the anchorman for CBS Evening News (1962–1981) was consistently named the most trusted man in America. I, along with many others, called him "Uncle Walter." With his half-hour live news show each weekday night, he became our ballast during these turbulent years and he was the person I looked to for the truth about what was happening in Vietnam. In mid-February 1968, Cronkite and his executive producer traveled to Vietnam to cover the Tet Offensive in a series of live reports titled "CBS Special, Report from Vietnam: Who, What, When, Where, Why?" Nearly everyone in the U.S. watched.

While he was there, Cronkite became troubled by what he was seeing in Vietnam and how it contrasted with what President Johnson and the generals were telling the American public. On February 27, he summed up his trip with a rare editorial report:

> We have been too often disappointed by the optimism of the American leaders, both in Vietnam and Washington, to have faith any longer in the silver linings they find in the darkest clouds. They may be right, that Hanoi's winter-spring offensive has been forced by the Communist realization that they could not win a longer war of attrition, and that the Communists hope that any success in the offensive will improve their position for eventual negotiations. It would improve their position, and it would also require our realization, that we should have had all along, that any negotiations must be that—negotiations, not the dictation of peace terms. For it seems now more certain than ever that the bloody experience of Vietnam is to end in a stalemate. This summer's almost certain standoff will either end in real give-and-take negotiations or terrible escalation; and for every means we have to escalate, the enemy can match us, and that applies to invasion of the North, the use of nuclear weapons, or the mere commitment of one hundred, or two hundred, or three hundred thousand more American troops to the battle. And with each escalation, the world comes closer to the brink of cosmic disaster.
>
> To say that we are closer to victory today is to believe, in the face of the evidence, the optimists who have been wrong in the past. To suggest we are on the edge of defeat is to yield to unreasonable pessimism. To say that we are mired in stalemate seems the only realistic, yet unsatisfactory, conclusion. On the off chance that military and political analysts are right, in the next few months we must test the enemy's intentions, in case this

> is indeed his last big gasp before negotiations. But it is increasingly clear to this reporter that the only rational way out then will be to negotiate, not as victors, but as an honorable people who lived up to their pledge to defend democracy, and did the best they could.

Many of us were stunned by what we heard. First of all, this was a different Cronkite than the man we had become accustomed to. Up until that point, he had avoided expressing any personal opinions on-air. With this commentary, he now cast serious doubt about the United States' mission in Vietnam. Following Cronkite's telecast, President Johnson is claimed by some to have said, "If I've lost Cronkite, I've lost Middle America."

After his Vietnam reports, Uncle Walter's nightly war coverage included something new. The government and the Pentagon had been giving the public daily casualty figures that begged belief. They suggested that we were on our way to a quick and successful outcome. The daily body count became the measure of success. Each day we were told by the administration that "our side" suffered minimal casualties while many hundreds, even thousands, of North Vietnamese had been killed. From his sources in Vietnam, Uncle Walter knew those numbers were deliberately and wildly inaccurate. Each evening he would describe (using a large topographically contoured map table) the daily actions and operations in detail and give us different casualty and body counts.

The American public's perspective of the war began to change. Of course, one reason was Cronkite's February visit and editorial when he declared the war to be a hopeless stalemate. It is generally agreed by all involved that during Tet, the Viet Cong had suffered a terrible defeat at a huge human price. But the psychological effect of the Tet Offensive, combined with the presence of some 536,000 U.S. combat personnel in Vietnam that year, made Americans rethink and ask again: What are we doing and why are we there?

Photojournalism was another major component of the Vietnam reporting. This war has been called "the living room war" due to the unprecedented level of press coverage. For the first time in American military history, journalists were given near unlimited access to combat zones in which American servicemen were fighting and dying. The result of this unbridled access is an abundance of documentary evidence of the war. Prior to the Tet Offensive we saw images of a clean, effective, technological war. After the Offensive, the coverage changed and now it emphasized the war's chaos, confusion and near collapse. Film footage showed street battles as they were being waged. Still photos became more graphic, showing the wounded, their blood, disconnected body parts and the dead. Eddie Adams' black-and-white photograph of "South Vietnam's police commander summarily executing a captured Vietcong guerrilla officer on a Saigon street" shocked the public and became a new tipping point for public opinion. It was published in all the major papers and quickly became the symbol for what was going wrong in Vietnam. (Since Vietnam, the military has imposed tight control over the media and no longer are they given near unlimited access to combat zones.)

What we were now learning from Uncle Walter, along with film and photo coverage, made many, myself included, scream, "Stop the goddamned killing—now." We were witnessing insanity and we were trying everything we could to stop it.

Large anti-war protests continued to break out across America and around Europe. Even at the National Gallery of Art, among all those art historians who normally discussed the fine points of Monet, the main topic of conversation was the war in Vietnam.

On the evening of March 31, 1968, Lyndon Johnson addressed the nation. The one line he spoke at the very end is what I remember: "I shall not seek, and I will not accept, the nomination of my party for another term as your President." This was stunning and unexpected. The new presidential election was to be held in the fall that year and it was assumed that Johnson would run again. Now the field was wide open for Eugene McCarthy and Robert Kennedy, two strong anti-war candidates.

I was relieved that Johnson was stepping down. I no longer gave him any benefit of doubt. I assumed he and his Secretary of Defense, Robert McNamara, and the commanding general leading the war, General Westmoreland, were lying every time they opened their mouths.

On Thursday, April 4, just four days after Johnson's announcement, Martin Luther King, Jr. was assassinated in Memphis, Tennessee. He was shot at 6:05 P.M. and Walter Cronkite announced it on CBS Evening News at 6:30 P.M. that same night.

Sara and Paul were out of town on a rare four-day trip and a young family member was taking care of Maddie and Charlie. When Uncle Walter gave us the news of the assassination, I went upstairs to see if she needed help. We put the kids to bed as if nothing was wrong. Sara called to say they had turned around and were on their way back to Washington. I told her I would stay with the babysitter until they returned.

The news about Dr. King travelled fast around the country. Robert Kennedy was in Indianapolis, Indiana, to give a campaign speech at a large outdoor rally when an aide told him about the assassination. Many on his staff urged him to cancel his speech because of concerns about a potential outbreak of violence once they heard the news. But he walked out before the crowd and told them, many of whom were African American, about King's death. In shock, some called out, "no" in disbelief. Many others cried.

Once the crowd quieted down, Kennedy gave a heartfelt impromptu speech. He spoke of the threat of disillusion and divisiveness at King's death and reminded the audience of King's efforts to "replace that violence, that stain of bloodshed that has spread across our land, with an effort to understand with compassion and love." He acknowledged that many in the audience would be filled with anger, especially since the assassin was believed to be a white man. For the first time in public he referred to the assassination of his brother, President John F. Kennedy, by a white man. Quoting the ancient Greek playwright Aeschylus, Kennedy said, "Even in our sleep, pain which cannot forget falls drop by drop upon the heart until, in our own despair, against our will, comes wisdom through the awful grace of God."

He went on to say: "What we need in the United States is not division; what we need in the United States is not hatred; what we need in the United States is not violence or lawlessness, but love and wisdom, and compassion toward one another, and a feeling of justice towards those who still suffer within our country, whether they be white or whether they be black." To conclude, Kennedy reiterated his belief that the country needed and wanted unity between blacks and whites and encouraged the country to "dedicate ourselves to what the Greeks wrote so many years ago: to tame the savageness of man and to make gentle the life of this world." He finished by asking the audience members to pray for "our country and our people." Afterwards, rather than exploding in anger at the news of King's death, the crowd dispersed quietly.

By 8 P.M., our Capitol Hill neighborhood was starting to boil and African American teenagers, including the next door neighbors, were out on the street yelling and looking for ways to express their anger. I was living in a neighborhood that was integrated in name only. Blacks and whites lived side by side but hardly spoke except for occasional hellos as we passed one another. Some blacks resented the migration of young white families with their higher income and greater opportunities moving into the neighborhood. Some whites looked at the blacks as property-value issues. There wasn't a lot of commingling. But there was a pretty solid veneer of courtesy and civility shared among neighbors. On the night of April 4, that veneer cracked and crumbled away.

During the evening of April 4, crowds began to gather at 14th and U Streets. Stokely Carmichael, the black activist and leader of the Student Nonviolent Coordinating Committee (SNCC), led a large group of SNCC members to stores in that neighborhood demanding that they close out of respect. At first the SNCC members were polite, but things went downhill fast and they began breaking windows. In a little over an hour, window-smashing and looting spread throughout the area. By the time order was restored around 3 A.M., 200 stores had their windows broken and 150 stores (primarily liquor stores and gun shops) were looted.

Sara and Paul made it home late that night and I returned to my apartment. We all hunkered down hoping, assuming, that things would settle down by morning. But this was not to be the case.

The next morning (Friday, April 5), everything was still dangerously tense. Paul decided he should go to Howard University to check on his students. The National Gallery of Art closed only on

Christmas Day and New Year's Day so I assumed they would be open, even though it was just one day after King's assassination and riots were still flaring up around the city. I was scheduled to work. (We needed to sell those prints of *Dolly Madison's Last Dinner.*) I felt that the six blocks down East Capitol Street onto the guarded security of the Capitol grounds and the final four blocks down Constitution Avenue to the Gallery would be safe. I hopped on my bike and showed up at the Gallery fifteen minutes later without incident. Guards and staff alike were pretty tense. There was concern about what to do should rioters storm the Gallery and go on a rampage to destroy paintings. We were told about the emergency lockdown procedure and what to expect should it be activated.

That morning Stokely Carmichael addressed a rally at Howard University, warning of violence. He was quoted by *The Evening Star* as saying,

> I think white America made its biggest mistake when they killed Dr. King last night...He was the one man in our race who was trying to preach mercy and forgiveness for what the white man has done.... Execution of this retaliation will not be in the courts but in the streets... We're going to die on our feet. We're tired of living on our stomachs.

He encouraged blacks to arm themselves, saying the killing of King

> ...made it a lot easier for a lot of Negroes—they know it's time to get guns now...Go home and get you a gun and then come back because I got me a gun.

After the rally, crowds walking down 7th Street NW and in the H Street NE corridor came into violent confrontations with police. With this, the lid got ripped off the city.

By midday, numerous buildings in that corridor and around D.C. were on fire. Firefighters were prevented from responding by crowds attacking them with bottles and rocks. Someone came into the Gallery and told us the Hecht Company building, just two blocks from the Gallery, was on fire. Several of us went outside and watched the black smoke rise as the building burned. The whole sky was hazy with smoke from the other burning buildings around the city.

Large, angry crowds with as many as 20,000 overwhelmed the District's 3,100-member police force. By early afternoon, President Johnson called in 13,600 federal troops to assist them. Marines mounted machine guns on the steps of the Capitol and Army troops from the 3rd Infantry guarded the White House. At one point, rioting reached within two blocks of the White House before rioters retreated.

At this point, discussions changed at the Gallery. Now the supervisors were concerned about our safety and considered imposing the lockdown early with all of us still inside. We had food available from the cafeteria, water, toilets and cushioned benches for sleeping. But with the arrival of the federal troops, the announced ban on the sale of alcohol and guns in the city (a classic case of shutting the barn door after the horse has escaped because of all the looting) and a curfew that was to be imposed at 7 P.M., things had settled down enough for us to leave for home at the end of our day.

I still felt fairly confident that my bike route was safe. Besides, how else would I get home? Buses weren't running. Cabs had disappeared. (Uber had not yet been "invented.") No one I knew at the Gallery lived on the Hill. Walking seemed too slow and made for an easy sniper target. Bicycles were silent and fast. I pedaled home with speed and determination. It was really eerie. There was no traffic on the streets nor were there any pedestrians walking on the sidewalks. As I passed through the Capitol grounds, I saw the Marines standing next to machine guns that had been mounted on the Capitol steps. The Capitol guards were present in large numbers and not up for any friendly banter as I rode past, but they signaled to the Marines that I wasn't an enemy.

When I turned off East Capitol Street onto 7th Street SE, I skidded to a stop. Parked on the street right outside my apartment was an armored military tank with a big gun sticking out its turret. A few soldiers were casually leaning against the tank and smoking. It was another one of those brain-freeze moments. I had never seen a tank before in real life and I certainly wasn't expecting to see one outside the apartment. I slow-pedaled forward and stopped between my apartment and the tank. I told the soldiers where I was going and they waved me on. That night I looked out the window several times just to verify that there was, indeed, a tank sitting out there and it wasn't my imagination. It made me feel both frightened and oddly safe at the same time. (I later learned that the tank was part of a seven-block radius of protection that was set up around the Capitol building during emergencies and crises.)

Saturday afternoon, we were still under riot conditions and evening curfew. Our neighborhood grocery store had been looted and its shelves were now completely empty. Across the street from the store, the Eastern Market was closed and locked down. We did not know how long the riots would go on and Sara wanted to shop for a supply of food. The large grocery stores in the suburbs had not been looted. She asked if I wanted to accompany her to get some food for myself. (You bet. Yes, I'm in. Let's go.)

The street was calm as we walked outside to the car, probably thanks to the tank—even though the crew seemed to be away taking a break. As soon as we closed (and locked) the doors, a teenage neighbor kid, who we had just seen casually walking down the sidewalk, took a flying leap and landed spread eagle on his stomach on the hood of the car. He pressed his face against the windshield and beat his fists hard on the glass while screaming at us. We were both scared silly but outwardly remained calm and just stared at him (probably in shock). We expected him to get off the car after he finished his protest but he wasn't showing any signs of stopping. His face was badly contorted against the windshield glass as he continued to beat his fists and yell. We couldn't understand anything he was saying. Finally Sara started the car, hoping he would take the hint and stop. When he didn't, she put it in gear and slowly inched forward. I guess he didn't want to ride with us to the suburbs on the hood of the car. He shouted a few more things that we couldn't understand, slid off the hood and continued strolling down the sidewalk as if nothing had happened. For much of the trip, the question that we couldn't stop asking was, "What the hell was that?"

On Monday, April 8, it was announced that the city was under control (whatever that meant). Twelve people had been killed,

1,097 injured, and more than 6,100 arrested. Over 1,200 buildings, with 283 housing units and 1,590 commercial establishments with 900 stores, had been burned and were either badly damaged or destroyed. The National Guard continued its presence after the rioting had officially ceased to protect against a second riot. On the morning of April 8, the tank outside my apartment pulled out.

Although Washington, Chicago, Kansas City and Baltimore had the largest riots and received the heaviest damage, riots had also broken out in 110 cities around the country after King's assassination. It was the greatest wave of social unrest the U.S. had experienced since the Civil War. And the occupation of Washington was the largest of any American city since the Civil War. The property loss caused by the D.C. riot was extensive and everyone was left with cleaning up the damage and rebuilding. Washington's inner city economy was devastated. With the destruction or closing of businesses, thousands of jobs were lost. On some blocks, only rubble remained for the next thirty years. In most neighborhoods, including Capitol Hill, life did not fully return to pre-riot days. We now had to move forward into a new reality.

After King's assassination, the media broadcast programs about his life and his nonviolent movement. Since moving to D.C. in 1963, I had become aware of what Dr. King and the many people in his movement were doing and accomplishing. I greatly respected their bravery as I watched news coverage of peaceful marchers being attacked by dogs, angry mobs and baton-wielding police and as they were being knocked down or slammed against buildings with water from high-powered fire hoses. The marchers bled, were knocked down and arrested, but they didn't attack back and they didn't stop marching.

I knew priests who had traveled to the South to participate in King's marches. They talked about the three-week intensive training they went through before they were allowed to join in. The people in the Civil Rights Movement weren't just a crowd of random individuals strolling down the street hoping to be treated as equal Americans. Nor were they angry gangs. They were well organized and well trained to present themselves peacefully and remain nonviolent, no matter what was done to them. I didn't think I had that kind of courage.

I thought about the genius of nonviolence, what it had achieved and what it meant for me. As I participated in the anti-war protests, I made sure I was supporting not just the push to end the war but the protest itself. I asked the question: Was this demonstration organized to be nonviolent in nature and intent? If it was encouraging or hoping for violent acts of civil disobedience, I'd step back. King and his legion of marchers had shown me that violent acts, even for a noble cause, would only put the participants on the same level as the perpetrators and set back public opinion and the cause.

I NEEDED TO FIND A NEW Sunday Mass. I couldn't procrastinate about this any longer. Despite everything that had happened in Washington and in our neighborhood, the priests at the parish church remained out of touch. In their sermons they did not mention King's assassination, the riots or the war. I had to find another Mass, one that was responsive to the reality swirling around us, and I had to do it fast.

Sara told me she had heard people talking about a Mass at George Washington University (GWU). I might want to check it out. The next Saturday I pedaled thirty blocks across town to the University's Newman Center and got information about the Mass.

Only one Mass was scheduled on Sundays and it was held at the student union building in the amphitheater that seated about 500. By the time Mass started, the place was packed. The priest saying the Mass was Father Jack Wintermyer. The homily that morning was given by an African American guest speaker who talked about the needs of the African American community in Washington, especially after the riots. He included contact information for anyone who wanted to help out.

The Mass itself was a carefully crafted, multi-media event that included live music, slides and film, all revolving around the homily theme for the day. The music was provided by a small group of talented musicians that included guitars, percussion and an amazing trombonist from one of the U.S. military bands. The congregation included families and their children, students, government workers and assorted individuals like myself. This Mass was alive, relevant and it spoke to me. My parish Mass irritation was solved.

IT WAS STILL 1968. The anti-war protests not only continued but intensified in the city and across the country. People were becoming angrier about the obviously fake assurances that victory was just around the corner. It was a war being waged out of sight so I guess the administration thought it would be easy to lie to us about it. Tens of thousands of soldiers were being sent to Vietnam each month and we still didn't understand why. All we knew was that the coffins being flown back to the States were increasing in number at an alarming rate.

The GWU students and the Newman Center were actively participating in the demonstrations. Now I was able to get more information about what was going on and I could join other Newman members attending the marches. I was no longer a lone individual in a crowd of thousands.

- In late April and early May, protests erupted on Columbia University's campus after students discovered links between the university and its institutional framework financially supporting U.S involvement in the war. The students occupied five buildings at the university for a week. They were violently removed by the New York City Police Department. Students were injured but not killed.

- In May, the FBI's COINTELPRO campaign was launched against the New Left. (I assumed we were the ones called the "New Left." I wondered who was the Old Left.) COINTELPRO (counter intelligence program) was a series of covert, and often illegal, projects conducted by the FBI aimed at surveilling, infiltrating, discrediting and disrupting American political organizations. FBI records show that COINTELPRO targeted groups and individuals that the FBI deemed subversive: anti-Vietnam War organizers, activists of the Civil Rights Movement (including Dr. King), the

Black Power movement, feminist organizations and a variety of organizations that were part of the broader New Left. FBI agents were instructed to "expose, disrupt, misdirect, discredit, neutralize or otherwise eliminate" the activities of these movements and their leaders.

• The Paris Peace Talks began in May—slowly. After thirty-four days of discussions to select a site for the talks, the U.S. and North Vietnam agreed to begin formal negotiations in Paris. Ex-Foreign Minister Xuan Thuy headed the North Vietnamese delegation at the talks. Ambassador W. Averell Harriman was named as his U.S. counterpart. The start of negotiations brought hope that the war might be settled quickly.

• Instead there were lengthy debates concerning the shape of the table to be used at the conference. The North favored a circular table, in which all parties would appear to be "equal" in importance. The South Vietnamese argued that only a rectangular table was acceptable, for only a rectangle could show two distinct sides to the conflict. Eventually a compromise was reached, in which representatives of the northern and southern governments would sit at a circular table, with members representing all other parties sitting at individual square tables around them. (The table-shape debates went on for months. How in the world was this war ever going to end?)

• On May 17, Father Philip Berrigan, his Jesuit brother, Daniel, and seven other Catholics entered a draft board office in Catonsville, Maryland, removed draft records and burnt them with homemade napalm in a lot outside the building in front of reporters and onlookers. In a statement they said:

> We confront the Roman Catholic Church, other Christian bodies, and the synagogues of America with their silence and cowardice in the face of our country's crimes. We are convinced that the

> religious bureaucracy in this country is racist, is an accomplice in this war, and is hostile to the poor.

They were arrested—again.

- May 12–June 19. As part of the Poor People's Campaign, several thousand demonstrators built and camped in Resurrection City on the Mall while they lobbied Congress for a $30 billion economic justice program. It was estimated that between 50,000–100,000 people attended over that five-week period. Days of heavy rain and mud ended the encampment after the Solidarity Day march on June 19.

["List of protests against the Vietnam War," Wikipedia, n.d.]

JUST AFTER MIDNIGHT on June 5, and after celebrating his victory earlier that day in the California presidential primary, Robert Kennedy was shot three times as he was walking through the hotel kitchen. He died the next morning on June 6.

When I heard that he had been shot, I felt like I had been kicked in the stomach. Literally. I was walking across the room in my apartment when I heard the news. I just stopped and bent over in sharp pain. I couldn't move for a few minutes because the pain was so bad. The whole world around me had just blown up again and gone completely mad. Whatever threads of sanity that had remained up to that point were now destroyed. It had only been two months since the assassination of Dr. King and many of us had not yet had time to recover from that shock and pain. And now this. Kennedy was considered by many to be the hope of both the anti-war and Civil Rights Movements.

The country stopped again as we mourned the loss of another Kennedy. Robert was buried close to his brother John in Arlington National Cemetery.

ON AUGUST 28, AT THE Democratic National Convention in Chicago, tens of thousands of anti-war protesters battled police in the streets, while the Democratic Party fell apart over Vietnam inside the Convention Hall.

One group, led by Senator Eugene McCarthy, the remaining Democratic anti-war candidate, challenged the assumption that the United States should remain in the war. As the debate intensified, fights broke out on the convention floor. Literally. Delegates and reporters were beaten and knocked to the ground. We, the viewing public, watched this scene unfolding on our televisions as it was happening. Eventually, the delegates who felt we should continue the war, led by Vice President Hubert Humphrey, won out.

Meanwhile, several thousand anti-war protesters gathered on the streets of Chicago to show their support for McCarthy and the U.S. withdrawal of troops from Vietnam. Chicago Mayor Richard Daley deployed 12,000 police officers and called in another 15,000 state and federal officers to contain the protesters. As you might guess, the situation quickly spiraled out of control, with the policemen severely beating and gassing the demonstrators, as well as newsmen and doctors who had come to help. From the convention podium, speakers announced that we were now living in a police state while Mayor Daley, who was sitting among the delegates, shouted back at the speakers.

The street riot was televised. As a result public opinion began to change again. For the first time, many Americans, who had up to that point remained quiet, came out in strong opposition to the Vietnam War. They, too, began to feel it was pointless and wrong.

In November 1968, Richard Nixon was elected President of the United States. During his campaign, he had stated many times that he would negotiate a quick end to the war, but I didn't hold out much hope that it would end soon. In Paris, they had barely stopped debating the table shape.

1969

I hadn't voted for Nixon nor did I agree with him about much, but in January I went to his inauguration to hear what he had to say. I also went to his inauguration because it was conveniently held in my neighborhood (the Capitol) and I wanted to see what an inauguration was like. Most of the time I watched the Secret Service guy who was standing in front of me speaking into his shirt cuff. I hoped he wasn't trying to be inconspicuous.

On Friday, March 28, Dwight Eisenhower died. In case you are not familiar with who he was and what he accomplished, he was the 34th President of the United States, from 1953 until 1961. He was a five-star general in the U.S. Army during World War II and served as Supreme Commander of the Allied Expeditionary Forces in Europe. He was responsible for planning and supervising the invasion of North Africa in Operation Torch in 1942–43 and the invasion of France and Germany in 1944–45 from the Western Front. He served as the sixteenth Chief of Staff of the Army from November 1945 until February 1948. From 1948 until 1953, when he became President of the United States, he was the president of Columbia University. During that time and at President Truman's request, he took an extended leave from the university to become the Supreme Commander of the North Atlantic Treaty Organization (NATO), and he was given operational command of NATO forces in Europe from 1950 until 1952.

I didn't know much about him, except for the bare basics: He was the U.S. president before John Kennedy and an army general. I hardly paid attention to the news of his death when I heard it at the Gallery that afternoon. To me it was just the death of another old famous Washington figure. When I got home, I found that once again our street was lined with posted notices telling everyone that there would be no parking on Sunday and Monday. (What now? Oh, right…the Eisenhower funeral.) Residential parking along our street was prohibited when something important was going on at the Capitol and each time I would gripe about the unfairness and inconvenience it created for the neighborhood. It was a bit silly because I personally wasn't inconvenienced. I parked my bike in the apartment. But out of some misplaced sympathy, I'd stomp into the apartment grumbling, "What do you expect these people to do? Eat their cars?" That whole weekend I was irritated by the signs every time I left my apartment.

On Sunday, Eisenhower's body was brought by caisson to the Capitol where he was to lay in state in the Capitol Rotunda until

Monday. The arrival ceremony was part of a highly organized military state funeral. The main funeral procession to the Capitol included the U.S. Army Band, the U.S. Navy Band and the U.S. Air Force Band, each with a leader, a drum major and ninety musicians. Of the seventeen companies, there was one from each of the four military academies; one each from the active Army, Marine Corps, Navy, Air Force and Coast Guard; one was a composite company of servicewomen; and seven represented all the reserve components of the five uniformed services. Each unit numbered four officers and eighty-five enlisted men, except for the company of servicewomen which was comprised of five officers and seventy-six enlisted members. Also marching with the military escort were the national commanders, or their representatives, of eight veterans' organizations. In all there were 2,394 military members marching down Constitution Avenue with the caisson.

A joint honor cordon of troops from the Army, Marine Corps, Navy and Air Force totaling another 640 members lined both sides of Constitution Avenue from 15th Street to the Capitol. A cordon of sixty troops lined each side of the steps leading to the rotunda.

After the caisson and all the participants were in position on the East side of the Capitol and after the escort units and honor cordon presented arms, the Army Band then sounded ruffles and flourishes and played "Hail to the Chief." At the first note of music, the fourteen-member saluting battery from the 3d Infantry, located on the grounds across Constitution Avenue from the Capitol, delivered a 21-gun salute, firing their rounds at five-second intervals. Following the salute, the Army Band played the hymn, "The Palms."

[B.C. Mossman and M.W. Stark, "The Last Salute."]

Except for the strange cars parked on my street, I wasn't aware of anything that was going on at the Capitol. That morning I went to Mass across town at the Newman Center, choosing a route that bypassed the funeral. When I got back to the Hill, I pedaled to Eastern Market for some shopping, returned to the apartment and fixed coffee and warm biscuits, my favorite Sunday snack. All the time I was out, I heard no sounds from the ceremony. No muffled drums from the three bands marking the cadence of the marchers. No shouted commands. No music from the bands. No footsteps from the more than 2,000 marchers or from the riderless horse and the horses pulling the caisson. Yet all of this was going on well within earshot.

I had just settled down with my coffee and biscuits when the 21-gun salute began. That I heard. It wasn't unusual for us Washingtonians to hear this kind of thing so I didn't pay any attention when the salute began. By the third round, I noticed that the sound was getting louder. As the shots continued, the sound became louder still. After the fifth or sixth round, I covered my ears and wondered what was going on. I felt like I was sitting in a tin can and the 3d Infantry was standing outside my door shooting at the can. The sound of the rifles became alarming. The shots were ricocheting inside my head and I wasn't sure how much more my eardrums could take. All I knew was that I had to get out of the apartment and I had to do it right away before my head blew apart. I grabbed my bike and, without thinking, quickly headed to the Capitol.

When I arrived, a policeman took note of my bike and motioned me to a prime spot on the sidewalk next to the rope that was corralling a large crowd. That gave me an unobstructed view of the ceremony. The flag draped casket (an $80 standard issue pine casket chosen by Eisenhower in 1966) had already been lifted from the caisson and was being carried up the steps, followed by the Eisenhower family and President Nixon and his family.

Ten honorary pallbearers and some guests were standing at the top of the steps. I recognized two men in particular: General Charles de Gaulle and General Omar Bradley. I looked at this line of distinguished elderly military men and for some unexplainable reason I felt I was witnessing an exceptional moment. There stood the surviving Allied leaders of World War II, and this was probably the last time they would be together. I don't know why I understood the significance of these men standing at the top of the steps. I only know the moment filled me with honor and awe.

NOTE: In the description of the Eisenhower funeral in my book, *Dancing In the Shadows of the Moon,* I have a number of things reversed. In actuality,

> I was watching the arrival ceremony on Sunday, March 30, and not the departure ceremony the following day, as I described in *Dancing*. I watched the casket as it was carried *up the steps* and not *down the steps*. After much research, pouring over old journal notes and combing through my memory, I can confidently say that what I've written in *Pivot* is the accurate description of what happened and what I experienced.

While the arrival ceremony continued inside the Capitol, the crowd outside waited quietly—very quietly. The crowd size filled the Capitol grounds. There was no jostling to get a better view and there was no whispering. People weren't shifting their weight or shuffling their feet. It was as if they were standing at attention, civilian style. Because many men and women, were wearing hats, I assumed this was primarily an older crowd who knew and respected Dwight Eisenhower and were deeply touched by his death.

The ceremony inside the Capitol lasted a half hour. Finally the family and dignitaries from inside began to file out and come down the steps to the waiting limousines. The line of cars slowly moved out the East entrance, which ran right beside me. For some reason, the line stopped.

Charles de Gaulle was sitting in the back on the driver's side of his limousine right next to where I was standing. His window was down, and while the car was stopped, we stared at one another. I was no more than five feet from him. He had a somber expression and at first I thought he was giving me a disapproving look because I had brought a bike to a funeral. But his gaze changed and I realized that he was no longer looking at me. He was now looking through me. There was deep sadness and what looked to me like despair in his eyes. This puzzled me because I couldn't figure out why an old soldier like de Gaulle would have such deep sadness about the death of another old soldier. (I was young.) I don't know how long we stared at one another. Oddly neither one of us turned our eyes away. At one point I thought I was picking up his pain and wanted to reach out and touch his arm but I knew I'd be shot on the spot if I tried that. The cars started moving again and the limousines finished departing. The crowd quietly broke up as most of the people moved toward the Capitol rotunda to pay their final respects. I headed back to the apartment and continued with my day with just one thought, "Boy, that was weird."

The next morning after the departure ceremony at the Capitol that transported the casket to the National Cathedral for the formal funeral, the no parking signs along my street were removed and our lives got back to some semblance of normalcy.

Stick a pin in this bit about the Eisenhower funeral. We'll be returning to it later.

Back in May 1968, the Agricultural Building at Southern Illinois University was bombed, resulting in $100,000 in damages while, at the same time, students took over five buildings at Columbia University. This was the prelude to 1969. Campus demonstrations were mostly peaceful, but some included burnings and bombings. Protesters at a number of the large universities took over campus buildings for periods of days, even weeks. More students researched their universities' connections with the government and pro-war corporations. What they found didn't make them happy and they wanted the universities to stop supporting the war through these quiet and morally objectionable associations.

Right after his inauguration, Nixon ordered the bombing of Cambodia, thus signaling that the war was widening, not winding down as he had promised. A new wave of protests fired up. In March, the FBI's COINTELPRO activity was stepped up. J. Edgar Hoover issued new directives to again order FBI agents to "expose, disrupt, misdirect, discredit, neutralize or otherwise eliminate" the activities of groups and individuals that the FBI deemed subversive. Anti-war groups were now in COINTELPRO's crosshairs.

My first brush with COINTELPRO occurred in the spring of '69, at the GWU Newman Center. When I arrived for a meeting, there was a guy in pristine clean white overalls crouched down behind the water heater. He had arrived saying that he was a plumber and he was there to fix a water heater problem. The puzzling part was that no one at the center knew of a hot water problem and no one had called a plumber. But maybe Father Wintermyer, who was out at the time, had called earlier. While several of us sat on the couch and watched, the "plumber" quickly finished his work, packed up his tools, declared that the water heater was now fixed and left.

When Father Wintermyer returned, we told him the plumber had been by and the water heater was now working. "What was wrong with the water heater?" When we said the guy was doing something to the back of the heater, he went over to take a look. The "plumber" had left a trail of dirty fingerprints on the back and all we had to do was follow the prints to a spot down low on the tank. He had installed a bug about the size of a pack of cigarettes. Apparently the FBI felt it was important to monitor the Newman Center conversations. From that point on, we obliged by sitting in that room from time to time and taking turns reading aloud the Constitution, the Bill of Rights and various passages from the Bible. When any of us passed through the room we would say hello to the FBI agent who was monitoring at the other end and ask how his day was going.

Although most protests remained loud and peaceful, frustrations about the continuation of the war rose and there were more incidents of violent clashes between the anti-war protesters, the police and pro-war demonstrators who, thanks to the new administration's encouragement, began to join in to show their support for Nixon and the war. They were small in number, older and carried signs declaring their undying support for their president.

Historians have said that the protests in '67 and '68 were primarily on moral grounds: the war was wrong, killing was wrong and it needed to be stopped. In 1969, the draft changed to include more college students. For these kids it was now personal. They did not want to be sent to Vietnam to kill or to be killed in this insane war.

Some could rightfully argue that because the war was not personal for me, I had the luxury to respond to it on larger moral grounds through nonviolent action. And I have to admit that if I was twenty and faced with the possibility of being killed in that war, I might want to burn something down, too. The bottom line: We each did what we did. And my participation included the moral issues of that war within the framework of nonviolent action.

I was by no means alone in this. I was surrounded by many—young and old, Quakers, Catholics and other pacifists, professors, congressional members who were against the war, family members of those who had already died or been wounded, alumni from the Civil Rights Movement. We were not personally at risk to being sent to fight yet we believed, we knew, that killing was wrong, this war was bad, we were being lied to daily, and hundreds of thousands of people on both sides were being killed for no valid reason. As protests became edgier in 1969, I felt I needed to better understand nonviolence as a concept and strategy in order to make good decisions about my participation in future demonstrations. In short, how do *I* help stop this war while, at the same time, maintain personal integrity?

About this time in the late spring of 1969, Averell Harriman returned to Washington from Paris and the Paris Peace Talks. He was scheduled to testify at the Capitol before the Senate Foreign Relations committee and word got out that he was going to say something "explosive." On the morning of the hearing, Sara and I walked to the Senate to make sure we could be present in the hearing room. Harriman's statement wasn't long but in it he clearly separated himself from the administration's policy and stated that the only people who wanted to keep that war going were the Americans. The Vietnamese, North and South, wanted to return to their rice paddies and continue with their lives. The Americans wanted the war to continue for political and economic reasons.

And there it was, finally. For the first time, I felt like I was hearing the truth. Harriman verified what so many of us felt in our gut. It was in the administration's interest to perpetuate the war. People were dying and a country was being destroyed for no valid reason. But the question remained: How do we get this war stopped?

I had been talking to Sara about my concern with the anti-war movement's increasing incidents of violent civil disobedience. Soon after Harriman's senate statement, she gave me a copy of a newly published book by Erik Erikson, *Gandhi's Truth: On the Origins of Militant Nonviolence.* This launched my educational journey into his concepts of nonviolence and nonviolent action.

Gandhi developed a particular form of nonviolent resistance or civil resistance called *satyagraha*, a Sanskrit word that means insistence on truth, loyalty to the truth or holding onto truth. He differentiates *satyagraha* from passive resistance in the following ways:

> Passive resistance has been universally acknowledged to be a weapon of the weak. It does not necessarily involve complete adherence to truth under every circumstance.
>
> *Satyagraha* must have three essentials:
>
> *Satyagraha* is a weapon of the strong.
>
> It allows no violence under any circumstance.
>
> It ever insists upon truth.
>
> Truth includes:
>
> Truth in speech, as opposed to falsehood.
>
> What is real, as opposed to nonexistent.
>
> Good as opposed to evil, or bad.

This was critical to Gandhi's understanding of and faith in nonviolence. He stated:

> The world rests upon the bedrock of *satya* or truth. *Asatya,* meaning untruth, also means nonexistent, and *satya* or truth also means that which is. If untruth does not so much as exist, its victory is out of the question. And truth being that which is, can never be destroyed. This is the doctrine of *satyagraha* in a nutshell.

For *satyagraha*, means and ends are inseparable. The means used to obtain an end are wrapped up in and attached to that end. Therefore, it is contradictory to try to use unjust means to obtain justice or to try to use violence to obtain peace. As Gandhi wrote: "They say, 'means are, after all, means'. I would say, 'means are, after all, everything'. As the means so the end…"

Gandhi used an example to explain this:

> If I want to deprive you of your watch, I shall certainly have to fight for it; if I want to buy your watch, I shall have to pay for it; and if I want a gift, I shall have to plead

> for it; and, according to the means I employ, the watch is stolen property, my own property, or a donation.

Gandhi rejected the idea that injustice should, or even could, be fought against "by any means necessary"—if you use violent, coercive, unjust means, whatever ends you produce will necessarily have embeded in them that injustice. To those who preached violence and called nonviolent activists cowards, he replied: "I do believe that, where there is only a choice between cowardice and violence, I would advise violence.... I would rather have India resort to arms in order to defend her honour than that she should, in a cowardly manner, become or remain a helpless witness to her own dishonour.... But I believe that nonviolence is infinitely superior to violence, forgiveness is more manly than punishment."

[mkgandhi.org]

In his autobiography *The Autobiography of Martin Luther King, Jr.*, Dr. King wrote about Gandhi's influence on his developing ideas regarding the Civil Rights Movement:

> Like most people, I had heard of Gandhi, but I had never studied him seriously. As I read I became deeply fascinated by his campaigns of nonviolent resistance. I was particularly moved by his Salt March to the Sea and his numerous fasts. The whole concept of *satyagraha* (*Satya* is truth which equals love, and *agraha* is force; *satyagraha,* therefore, means truth force or love force) was profoundly significant to me. As I delved deeper into the philosophy of Gandhi, my skepticism concerning the power of love [truth] gradually diminished, and I came to see for the first time its potency in the area of social reform.... It was in this Gandhian emphasis on love [truth] and nonviolence that I discovered the method for social reform that I had been seeking.

From Gandhi, I continued on to read about the nonviolent philosophy and actions practiced by others: Cesar Chavez, Dorothy Day, Leo Tolstoy, Thomas Merton, Albert Schweitzer, Albert Einstein and Dag Hammarskjöld. They each added to my understanding of *satyagraha* and I could see that the underlying concept of their own theories and actions included *satyagraha.*

I had to step back to think and regroup.

It was still spring but Washington was hit with an unusually early heat wave. During World War II, the British listed Washington as a hardship post because of its high heat and humidity. I had to make a decision about my means of transportation.

I loved riding my bike everywhere. I loved the freedom as well as the convenience. And with it I had special experiences. One morning I had to stop for a little old lady at a pedestrian crosswalk near the White House. As she passed in front of me, I realized it was Golda Meir, the Prime Minister of Israel. She looked like everyone's sweet, short, chunky grandmother. She smiled and said, "Good morning. Lovely day, isn't it?" I responded, "Good morning and yes it is! Nice to see you." She said, "Thank you" and walked on while I smiled and rode on. (Golda Meir just said hello to me!)

> Note: Golda Meir was elected Prime Minister of Israel on March 17, 1969. Former Prime Minister David Ben-Gurion used to call her "the best man in the government." She was often portrayed as the "strong-willed, straight-talking, grey-bunned grandmother of the Jewish people." I heard she also baked cookies for her cabinet meetings. I bet they were chocolate chip.

Then there was the time when one of my "special experiences" was a little too up close and personal. One late afternoon as I was riding through the Capitol grounds on my way home from work, things went a little haywire. We were having an exceptionally beautiful sunset and I watched it as I pedaled in front of the Capitol steps. At the same time, Robert Kennedy was coming down the steps and watching the sunset, as well. We were both looking up. He didn't see me and I didn't see him. As he stepped off the curb right in front of me I bumped into him.

That's the polite way of saying it. Picture this. I was coming up on his left. He had just stepped off the curb with his right foot creating a V-shaped scissor gap between his legs. My front tire went right into the gap. Between hitting the brakes and the force of hitting his body, my bike came to a sudden stop. His face was now about a foot from my face. His eyes teared up—I assumed from the pain I had caused his manhood. (Still being polite here.) He didn't say anything. I think he was trying to breathe. Being twenty-two, I wasn't overly sophisticated and didn't know how to deal with this delicate situation. For a minute or two, which must have seemed like hours to both of us, neither of us moved. The guards were running toward us but Senator Kennedy waved them off. They asked if he was okay and he managed to croak out a "yes." I said, "God, I'm so sorry.... Tough day, huh?" He gingerly stepped back so that he was no longer straddling my bike tire and said, "I've had better." He collected himself and walked toward his car—carefully. I stayed there until I was sure he could make it. Several months later he and his wife announced that they were expecting their eleventh child. I guessed I had not done any permanent damage.

Despite the adventure that only bike riding could provide, I was still faced with the coming summer with its heat and humidity. The challenge was the hill that I had to go up each night at the Capitol. I watched some riders successfully take that hill but they were on 12-speed racing bikes. My 3-speed Raleigh couldn't compete. Even just walking the bike up the hill in the summer left me sweaty and exhausted. I decided it was time to upgrade to a motor scooter.

I found a cycle shop not far from my apartment and headed over to see if I could make this happen. I didn't want anything fancy or big so I was pretty confident I had the money for something. The guys at the shop could not have been more helpful. Sure, they wanted to make a sale, but my little purchase wasn't going to make much difference to their day's final tally. They were happy to help a girl. (They reminded me of the officers on the *American Press.)* They steered me to a used Lambretta 150cc that they had just finished restoring. They assured me that mechanically it was in great shape. And the price was right. They even threw in a tutorial and training. I said yes, and we headed to an empty parking lot (thank god it was empty) so that they could teach me how to operate my Lambretta and show me what I needed to pay attention to.

After about an hour, I was declared ready to strike out on my own and was faced with the daunting task of getting the scooter to my apartment. I drove it in second gear all the way home. Sara let me park it in their small front courtyard, then she drove me back to the cycle shop so that I could get my bike. I was now the proud owner of two vehicles. It didn't take long for me to become an easy-riding scooter mama. I still had my freedom and I could still feel the wind in my face. (This was before face shields were required.) I applied butterfly decals all over my new helmet to signal to drivers that I was a girl and that I'd like them to not run over me. The Gallery allowed me to park my scooter in the same garage space I had used for my bike. All was well.

With the scooter I could participate in more Newman Center activities. The Center reached out to young draftees who wanted help applying for conscientious objector status. They suggested lawyers and the members offered support as the draftees went through the classification process. Often they felt overwhelmed and isolated. There was also a group of lawyers who were doing pro bono work on what I called "the insane cases." One evening I attended an informal gathering to raise money for the lawyers and to help with mounting legal expenses. Individual cases were presented and we could choose the ones we wanted to help support.

The draftee I chose to help had been called up and trained as a helicopter pilot. They were about to send him to Vietnam when he burned his draft card and refused to go. Why did he do this? He had a history of epileptic seizures and he felt flying a helicopter would be foolhardy. (I felt he had a good point.) At the time he was drafted, he had given the Army letters from his doctors stating that he was an epileptic and had suffered seizures for much of his life. Apparently the Army didn't want to hear this. They trained him anyway. They wanted him in Vietnam flying helicopters. In protest, he burned his draft card (which was illegal) and by the time I heard about his case, he had been sitting in jail for several months. It took a little time, but his lawyer eventually got him released and reclassified 4F.

There were a number of cases where guys were sitting in jail because they had burned their 4F draft cards during a protest.

That 4F classification meant they were physically or emotionally incapable of serving. So they weren't going to be sent to Vietnam anyway and their action was largely symbolic. But burning a draft card, no matter the classification, was illegal. So they sat in jail until the lawyers could move them through the legal process and get them released. As I said, these were the insane cases.

Three months after I purchased my Lambretta, some guy attempting to drive a Mercedes crushed it. (I'll call him Mr. Mercedes.) Luckily I wasn't sitting on it at the time. As is usual in these cases, Mr. Mercedes was trying to pull out from where he was parked and hit the gas pedal instead of the brake. In the process, he ran over the scooter that was parked in front of his car. Pitted against a Mercedes, my scooter didn't stand a chance. I found it crushed and in pieces with a note stuck on it telling me to knock on his door that was just a couple of houses away. When he answered, he was remarkably cheerful and invited me in right away. From the looks of his house, he was a guy with some money and, since it was 11 A.M. on a weekday, I assumed he had no need for a job. From his breath I could tell he had also been drinking. He thought running over my scooter was one of the most amusing things that could happen. He couldn't wait to tell his friends. I tried to impress on him that I didn't find this funny. (The fact that I was crying probably helped press the point.)

I wasn't sure what to do so I asked if he had insurance. Yes. Then I asked to use his phone and called the cycle shop hoping they could tell me how to handle the situation. My guys took over immediately and spoke to Mr. Mercedes. In short order, Mr. Mercedes and I were loading the remains of my scooter into the trunk of his car and he was driving me to the cycle shop. As soon as we pulled in, the cycle guys came out and dealt with Mr. Mercedes. He handed them his insurance information and any other information they needed. When Mr. Mercedes left, he was still happy. I think it was because we weren't reporting the mishap to the police. I suspected my Lambretta wasn't the only vehicle he had reshaped with his car and by not reporting it, I was saving him some grief. He seemed like the kind of guy who avoided grief in his life at all costs. Literally.

After about a half hour's wait while the guys called the insurance company and filled out paperwork, they presented me with the keys to a brand new 200cc Lambretta scooter. I wasn't sure how they pulled that off but I assumed Mr. Mercedes' insurance company paid for it. The guys assured me that everything was taken care. I thanked them several times and rode away on a shiny, new, more powerful Lambretta. (The moral to this story: Don't park a scooter in front of a Mercedes owned by a drunk.)

While I continued my tutorial on nonviolence, I read *Silent Spring* by Rachel Carson. Since I was familiar with how corporations had quietly teamed up with the military to provide weaponry, technology and support for the war while also providing themselves with a handsome profit, I wasn't surprised to read about corporate activity taken at the expense of the country's agriculture and environment. But the way Rachel Carson laid out the information in *Silent Spring* presented a clearer picture that both grabbed my attention and alarmed me. She focused on DDT and other poisons from insecticides and weed killers used in common products. She also addressed the use of sprays in agriculture, a practice that led to dangerous chemicals in our food source. Carson argued that those chemicals were more dangerous than radiation and that for the first time in history, humans were exposed to chemicals that stayed in their systems from birth to death.

I felt that *Silent Spring*'s information was important and that the situation Carson described was as serious for humankind as war. Both had to do with our survival. Environmentally I saw that as we destroy the planet, we destroy ourselves. I followed up *Silent Spring* by reading other recently published books on the fragile state of the environment.

My ongoing tutorial was now two-pronged: nonviolence as a concept and strategy, and ecology as a concept and strategy. It did not take long for the two prongs to merge and become one. I saw that ecology was a natural extension of nonviolence. And to address the challenges that ecology raised, to save the planet as well as humankind, one needed to apply *satyagraha:*

It needed to be a movement of strength.

It needed for there to be no violence (either enacted or in reaction) under any circumstance.

It needed to always insist upon truth.

Unfortunately, among the anti-war people I knew at the time, my ecology-as-nonviolence theory was acceptable to one person: me. Many had heard about the emerging environmental movement and Rachel Carson's *Silent Spring,* but ending the war was their most pressing issue. Anything else was a distraction and interference. The environment would have to wait. I disagreed. To honor my new commitment and understanding around the ecology-as-nonviolence theory, I bought a green and white ecology decal and stuck it on my new 65-mpg scooter. (It was a start.)

BEING A FIRM BELIEVER that human beings are capable of walking and chewing gum at the same time, I also remained active in the anti-war peace marches while I continued my exploration into ecology. There were two major demonstrations in Washington in the fall of 1969.

- On October 15, Washington joined in the Moratorium to End the War in Vietnam. There were large crowds—over 200,000 on the Mall in Washington and 100,000 in Boston.
- On November 15, the Vietnam Moratorium was held in D.C. With over 600,000 participants, it was considered the largest march in U.S. history up to that point. The march and all-day rally on the Mall ended a week of protests throughout the city, including a "March Against Death" from Arlington National Cemetery past the White House to the U.S. Capitol led by Dr. Benjamin Spock and the Rev. William Sloane Coffin of Yale. Eugene McCarthy, George McGovern and Charles Goodell, the only Republican to take part, were the featured speakers at the Moratorium. There were musical performances by Peter, Paul and Mary, Arlo Guthrie and Pete Seeger, who led the crowd in the singing of John Lennon's "Give Peace a Chance."

• The Moratorium was a huge coordinated anti-war effort that included smaller rallies, marches and prayer vigils held in cities and on 300 campuses across the country. The largest protest outside Washington was held in San Francisco, where an estimated 250,000 people demonstrated. Anti-war demonstrations were also held in a number of major European cities, including Frankfurt, Stuttgart, West Berlin, and London. The largest overseas demonstration occurred in Paris, where 2,651 people were arrested.

["List of protests against the Vietnam War," Wikipedia, n.d.]

This time the demonstrations included not just those who had marched before but many who had never raised their voices against the war. When I saw a large group marching behind a banner announcing that they were members of a teachers' union, I knew the anti-war sentiment had truly gone mainstream. There were labor union locals, teachers, students, librarians, engineers, scientists, doctors and health workers all carrying banners. Walter Cronkite called the Moratorium "historic in its scope. Never before had so many demonstrated their hope for peace."

However, *The New York Times* had a different take on the event. It described the crowd as "predominantly youthful" and "mass gathering of the moderate and radical Left... old-style liberals; Communists and pacifists and a sprinkling of the violent New Left." To make sure the American public knew he was not going to be deterred, Richard Nixon had his photo taken in the White House watching a football game while the Moratorium was going on outside his windows. He stated (and it was recorded on his secret tapes for posterity) that he wanted to "show the little bastards" what kind of man they were up against. (Boy, he sure showed us.)

By the end of 1969, over 45,000 Americans had already been killed and almost half a million U.S. men and women were deployed in the war. (Nixon kept the war going for another four years. Thousands more Americans were killed, along with perhaps a million Vietnamese.)

1970

On New Year's Eve, I watched newsmen on each of the three TV channels (life was much simpler back then) announce their prognostications about not just the coming year but the coming decade, as well. They declared the 1970s to be the "Environmental Decade" and used the word "ecology" in their comments and reporting for the first time. They were responding to the new information and reports from scientists and environmental experts about the state of our planet, our food, our water, our air, our soil and our health. I rang in the new year with hope and celebrated by reading Rachel Carson's *The Sea Around Us.* But I also knew that as long as that war continued the Environmental Decade was not going to get off the ground.

I was surrounded by plenty of people at the Newman Center who supported the concept of nonviolence but because they didn't take the time to learn about the concept, they were fracturing into different groups, each with their own version of nonviolence. It was a phenomenon that was happening across the country.

- There were those who supported the nonviolence that was taught and practiced by Martin Luther King and the Civil Rights Movement.
- Others looked to Gandhi and aimed their activism toward *satyagraha.*
- There were those who believed that civil disobedience that included property damage or destruction was acceptable as long as people weren't injured or killed.
- There was Joan Baez's "The Institute for the Study of Nonviolence" to promote social change through nonviolence. She had been a strong supporter of King's Civil Rights Movement, had participated in many of his marches, and was encouraging draft resistance at her concerts. (She also believed the cost of concert tickets were too high and would not allow tickets for her concerts to be sold for more than $5.) People traveled to her center in

California to learn about nonviolent social action (that did not include property damage).

- There were those who believed that Leo Tolstoy had the answer. He took the passive approach and believed that "pure nonviolence" meant that humans should not interfere with the lives of other humans no matter what the circumstance. One time, when asked about this, he stated that if his three-year-old grandson was running across the lawn toward their lake, he (Tolstoy) would not stop him from jumping in and drowning. He said that he could not know what the child's soul had intended. To stop the child risked interfering with the child's higher plans and the soul must be honored, no matter what. He sparked a lot of debate around this approach.

- Then there were those who used nonviolence as an excuse for their personal lack of discipline and common sense. These were the folks who were never on time and said they considered it violent for others to expect them to be on time. And there were those who felt it was violent to expect them to adjust their language to something more socially acceptable when speaking before a group that included sensitive segments of the population such as children and nuns. (Even I knew there were times when it was inappropriate to use salty language.)

I thought wrapping property damage into nonviolent action made no sense, especially after reading Gandhi's philosophy on means and ends. Because I was living in Washington, Joan Baez's center was too far away for me to even consider as an option. I felt that Leo Tolstoy's passive philosophy was the sure path to societal chaos and breakdown. (I also felt that Tolstoy was just too damn lazy to get his ass out of the chair and go save his grandson.) And I didn't have any patience for those who grabbed onto nonviolence as an excuse for the annoying habits they didn't feel like changing. I concentrated on Martin Luther King and Gandhi.

On May 4, the Ohio National Guard opened fire on a group of students at Kent State, killing four and injuring nine. Some of them had been protesting the war earlier and others were students who were standing in the crowd watching what was going on. The shootings shocked everyone, including the Ohio National Guard. The students may have been young but the Guardsmen were equally as young and had been placed in a tense situation that was beyond their training. Nationwide, the shootings were so unexpected and traumatic that it forced people to once again reconsider what was happening and what we were doing. It's fair to say that Kent State left a permanent scar on the country and it was another turning point in public opinion.

A week after the Kent State shootings, 100,000 demonstrators marched in Washington to protest the shootings and Richard Nixon's invasion into Cambodia.

August 6, 1970, was the 25th anniversary of our dropping the atomic bomb on Hiroshima, Japan. The bombing had wiped out ninety percent of the city and immediately killed 80,000 people. Tens of thousands would later die of radiation exposure. Three days later, the U.S. dropped a second atomic bomb on Nagasaki, killing another 40,000 people. Japan's Emperor Hirohito announced his country's unconditional surrender in World War II on August 15, 1945.

In 1970, the Japanese Embassy in Washington announced that they had put together a peace memorial and offered to make it available to any church or group to share for the anniversary. The only group that took them up on their offer was the GWU Newman Center. The Newman parishioners worked for two weeks to put together a Mass wrapped around the Embassy memorial. A member of Robert Kennedy's former senate staff heard about what Newman was planning and called to ask if he (the staffer) could participate at the Mass. The memorial was like a play in three voices. One voice presented straight history and gave the facts and outline leading up to August 6, 1945. The second presented the average Japanese family living in Hiroshima that day. (August 6 was a Monday and that morning the residents were going to work and helping their children get ready for school.) The third presented the American reaction to the news that an atomic bomb had been dropped, ending with the hope for peace by all. The play alternated between the three voices to present a broad picture of the event from the different perspectives.

At the Mass, in place of the homily, two parishioners and Kennedy's staffer, who were seated with the congregation, stood and started reading their parts. Slides were projected onto a large screen, giving texture to the readings. Where the play paused and we were being given time to think, the musicians added soft music that added more texture. It was a remarkable, tightly woven presentation and Mass. When the service was over, I saw the people do something I had not seen before or since. Instead of getting up and leaving the theater right away, as was our habit, everyone remained seated. No one spoke. We just sat there as if we were frozen in place and needed to take a little time to think about what had just happened. Finally, after about fifteen or twenty minutes, one person got up and quietly left the theater. Soon a few others followed. It wasn't a mass exodus, by any means. Eventually everyone left except for a handful of people who were still sitting in quiet thought. This was the most effective Mass I ever attended. After that morning, Kennedy's staffer commuted in from the suburbs each Sunday with his family to attend the Newman Mass.

That August, Father Wintermyer focused the remaining Sunday Mass homilies on environmental issues: food, air and water, and population. The homily on population was tricky because of the Catholic Church's position on birth control. If he gave the homily on the topic, he'd be in trouble—immediately. The archdiocese was already not too happy about the Newman Masses and each Sunday sent a spy from its office to sit with the congregation and watch for any transgressions. It wasn't hard to spot the spy. He was the old guy sitting in the back in his priestly finery taking notes. Each Sunday, we let the spy know that we knew who he was and why he was there by waving, saying hello and asking how his day was going.

The three Masses focusing on environmental issues had been well researched and were thought provoking. Father Wintermyer got around the birth control issue by inviting a guest speaker, an expert on the issues around a rising population and its environmental impact. When the guest mentioned birth control, it was in this larger context and Father Wintermyer could tell us that the expert's comments were not endorsed by the Church. Wink. Wink.

The fall of '70 was quiet, relatively speaking. Protest demonstrations continued in cities and on campuses outside Washington. In D.C., there was lingering post-riot racial unrest that felt more like the pot simmering rather than boiling over. Paul, my landlord, was having problems at Howard University. The students wanted to purge all the white professors from the university and replace them with black professors. To emphasize their point, they began doing things to make life difficult for the white teachers, things like pouring sand or sugar in the gas tanks of the professors' cars. Paul's students remained loyal to him and he stayed long after most of the other white teachers had left. But finally it happened. His car was one of the last to receive a dose of sand. That day Paul became a full-time real estate agent.

Our neighborhood felt tense, as well. The streets got loud at night with groups of kids roaming up and down shouting. During the day I had to be careful before stepping outside because now it was not unusual for a gunfight between two kids or between the police and a kid to be going on outside my apartment. At times it was like the wild west. It would have been easy for me to step right in the middle of the gunfire. My apartment was broken into but they only took the passport wallet I had bought in Florence and my passport. (For me, this was tragic because the passport had the border checkpoint stamps I had collected from all the countries I had traveled in, including the comically oversized and rare stamps from Vatican City and Liechtenstein.)

Shortly after I had moved into the apartment on 7th Street, a friend gave me a calico cat that he could no longer care for due to his job and work schedule. I named her Gretel and we quickly bonded into quite a team. She possessed an attitude that I fully appreciated. She did not suffer fools gladly. If she didn't like someone, she made it clear that the person was not acceptable. They needed to get out of the apartment and, preferably, off the planet immediately. I'm convinced that the robber only had time to steal my passport before Gretel pounced into action, hissing menacingly and chasing him out of the apartment. Paul installed a deadbolt lock on my door and between the new lock and Gretel, I now had a high level of security.

I WAS THREE YEARS into my job at the National Gallery of Art and I was becoming a little knowledgeable about the paintings. I even took an evening art history class at GWU. Unfortunately (or fortunately) the professor used slides and reproductions she had purchased from the National Gallery shop. Not only could I name the artist and the name of the painting, I could also tell her what collection the painting belonged to and its stock number. I didn't learn much from that class. But I received an easy A.

One thing I discovered while working at the Gallery was that my co-workers weren't interested in hearing anything about my time in Florence or my work with the restoration. I thought the National Gallery of Art would be an appropriate place for me to talk about it but the two or three times I brought it up in conversation were met with glazed eyes and that look of boredom.

There was one person who did talk to me about it: H. Lester Cooke, the Curator of Painting at the Gallery. I was sitting alone in the cafeteria eating lunch and reading when he sat down at my table and said, "You look interesting. Tell me about yourself." I thought that was an odd opening so I responded with what I thought was an equally odd answer. "My name is Machaelle Small. I'm half Jewish, Russian and Polish, quarter Irish and quarter Navaho. [I learned later I was Hopi.] I do not have a masters in art history and I'm here because Mrs. Dundas liked that I had worked in the Florence restoration program. I don't have fancy art-gallery clothes. I don't have any gold jewelry [something most of the female staff wore at the Gallery]. I don't really belong here and I'm twenty-three." Apparently I passed his criteria for "interesting" because, with this, we started a friendship that included many lunch conversations.

Lester Cooke was an interesting fellow in his own right. He was an internationally recognized art historian, writer and painter. He was the Curator of Painting at the Gallery from 1961–1973. Even though he was highly regarded in the art world, he wouldn't play the art-world games. He wasn't stuck up, he didn't speak with an exaggerated rich-man's accent, he didn't sport handmade silk ties or expensive tailored suits from New York City and he thought the art history degree rule was stupid unless you were giving tours at the Gallery. He had books in his office on palmistry, astrology and numerology. He loved opera. And he said he was part Cherokee.

He headed the Expert Opinions Section of the Gallery and was a well-known authority on fakes and forgeries. He was called the "Sherlock Holmes of the Art World" for his work in solving art mysteries of attribution. On Wednesdays he sat in an area set up as a lab near one of the remote Gallery entrances and examined paintings that owners lugged in for authentication and valuation. Usually he was alone in the early afternoons and would sit there singing opera at the top of his lungs. He loved the acoustics. I'd join him there for lunch. I once admitted to him that I really didn't care about brush strokes in paintings. That whole topic bored me. He asked what I thought about da Vinci's work. I said he seemed to have a habit of using homely women as models. He agreed, but what about the brush strokes? He could tell I didn't understand what he was asking and showed me something remarkable.

From his file cabinet he pulled out two x-rays, one of *Mona Lisa* and the other of *Ginevra de' Benci,* and set them side by side. X-ray use was (and is) a common practice when authenticating paintings. From an x-ray, they can see what's happening underneath the painting. Apparently canvas has always been expensive because it's not that uncommon for an x-ray to show an entirely different painting underneath that the artist just painted over. And sometimes what's underneath is more important and valuable than what's on top. Types of paper, materials, preparatory sketches, changes to the composition and other clues can be discovered with an x-ray to prove the nature and origin of a painting. X-rays also see different layers of paint and can reveal touch-ups and restorations that have been made. All of this provides the evidence needed for authenticity. Is this consistent with the known preparation and painting method of the artist? Are the hidden compositions similar to the style that the artist used?

The *Mona Lisa* x-ray revealed that the painting had been extensively touched up, repaired and restored over the centuries. The remaining original da Vinci brush strokes were mostly in the background trees. There I could see that da Vinci painted with such a fine hand that it was like looking at the smoothness of a photograph and not a collection of brush strokes. *Ginevra* was different. She had had very little restoration done. The major part of the work we see is pure da Vinci and the x-ray showed his same fine hand and brushwork throughout the painting. It also showed me why the Gallery wanted *Ginevra* so badly. She had been carefully protected in Switzerland and then in the castle in Vaduz over the centuries by the royal family of Liechtenstein. She wasn't just a da Vinci; she was an exceptional da Vinci. With this, Lester Cooke had changed my attitude about brush strokes.

He had some interesting side jobs due to his position at the Gallery as well. Lester was influential in the government-sponsored art programs, helping to select artists for the Environmental Protection Agency art program and serving as art advisor to NASA for ten years. When NASA asked Lester to head their project, he was told that the artists would be given behind-the-scenes access to NASA missions, including suit-up, launch and landing activities, as well as meetings with scientists and astronauts.

In his letter to the artists he wanted as part of the program, Lester wrote,

> NASA decided to ask artists to supplement the record after reviewing the documentation of the first few years of the Space Age. It was realized that important steps in the Space Age were missing. When a launch takes place at Cape Canaveral, Fla., more than 200 cameras record every split second of the activity. Every nut, bolt, miniaturized electronic device is photographed from every angle. The artist can add very little to this in the way of factual record. But, as [Honoré] Daumier pointed out about a century ago, the camera sees everything and understands nothing. It is the emotional impact, interpretation and hidden significance of these events which lie within the scope of the artist's vision. An artist may

> depict exactly what he thinks he sees, but the image has still gone through the catalyst of his imagination and has been transformed in the process.
>
> ["Hereward Lester Cooke," Wikipedia, n.d.]

I didn't see this letter back then and when he told me about the NASA art program, I didn't understand why it was needed since, as he stated in the letter, we had photography to document every nut and bolt. But in 1969, after Lester put together a large show for the Gallery *(Eyewitness to Space)* that presented the artwork from the program, its value was obvious. Next to many of the paintings and sketches were photographs documenting the same scene. Nuts and bolts were clearly evident. However, the paintings expressed something that the photos had not picked up—the atmosphere, tensions and relief that occurred during a launch, flight and recovery. They conveyed the human component of each moment.

He had another government assignment and this one seemed nothing short of insane to me. During the Civil War, the government sent artists to the battlefields to paint scenes from the war as part of the historical record. This has been done for every U.S. war since. Lester told me the artwork was stored somewhere in the bowels of some building and not shown to the public.

Around 1969–70, Lester teamed up with George, a close friend and one the artists who had been part of his NASA project for years, and headed to Vietnam. Over lunch one day, he asked if I wanted to go along. I just stared at him. In lieu of anything else I could think to say, I told him, "I can't afford it." (I also did not know if I could duck bullets and run from bombs fast enough.)

When he returned from Vietnam, he said he was pleased with the work they had done. However, the federal government was not so pleased and told him they would have return to Vietnam and do the assignment over. What he brought back was unacceptable. But the story he brought back was terrific..

When they arrived in Vietnam (the first time), they met up with George's lover, Michèle Ray, an ex-Coco Chanel model turned French journalist and photographer. In light of what Lester and George were there to do, meeting up with Michèle was smart. She was the only woman journalist who had met, talked with, and gone through action with both the Americans and the Viet Cong. Not long after her arrival in Vietnam, she had been captured by the Viet Cong and lived with them for three weeks. In that time she endured repeated severe U.S. air attacks with them. In her book, *The Two Shores of Hell,* she wrote that she found the Viet Cong to be kind, considerate and fiercely nationalistic. When she met up with Lester and George, she had no problem leading them into North Vietnam so that the two men could observe the war from that perspective.

They spent their entire trip in North Vietnam, documenting the war and daily life as experienced by the North Vietnamese. Lester's government contact for the program wanted Lester and George to go back to Vietnam and this time document the war from the South Vietnamese and our American perspective. I do not think the government destroyed the work they brought back from the first trip. It's probably all neatly filed in the catacombs that holds the rest of the artists' war records.

BY THE FALL OF 1970, I had been living in my Capitol Hill apartment for three years. During that time, I had forged a wonderful friendship with Sara. We continued our afternoon discussions and I was invited to join them for dinner once or twice a week. The children considered me the member of their family who dwelled in their basement. (I was the family troll.) I was included in evening discussions Paul and Sara had with a group of priests they had known since their Catholic University days. I suspected that I was included because I seemed to bring out-of-the-box thinking and ideas to the discussion and I wasn't afraid to challenge them, even though the priests, along with Paul, were each members of Mensa. I found my time with Paul and Sara to be comforting and intellectually challenging during these years of social upheaval.

But over the final months of 1970, the edges around this comfortable life began to fray. Sara and Paul bought a gun for protection and all I could think about was the possibility of rushing up the back stairs to help in an emergency and getting shot in the confusion because they thought I might be an intruder. Sara and I had several heated exchanges about the gun. I understood that primarily the gun was to protect the children, and I also understood that the neighborhood had become unsettled enough to warrant extra protective measures. At the same time, I felt we could sit down and come up with a different strategy that was equally effective. Something that wouldn't get anyone killed, accidentally or otherwise. For Sara, thinking about nonviolent options at that point was pie-in-the-sky thinking and she needed for me to just shut up. Until then I had felt safe in the house. Now there was danger and a strain that deeply saddened me and I was beginning to feel like a basement prisoner.

I didn't think about moving. I still loved my apartment and I had faith that Sara and I just needed time to let the dust settle and our friendship repair. In my mind, we had a strong friendship. An occasional strain in a friendship was normal. We would get over this hump and move forward to a new level of friendship that included this rough patch. I hoped.

In late November, Ed Guinan, a popular and charismatic Paulist priest working with Father Wintermyer at GWU, talked to me about a new community that he and a lawyer were starting. It was to be called the Community for Creative Nonviolence (CCNV). They wanted to start small with just five or six people who were interested in studying, teaching and promoting nonviolent action. Would I like to join? It was a perfect offer that landed in my lap at the right moment. Instead of thinking about these things on my own, I'd be part of a like-minded group. I found the idea of sharing, discussing and acting to be deeply appealing. He arranged for me to meet the lawyer and co-founder, Bill Durland, for coffee to get his stamp of approval. I thoroughly enjoyed my meeting with Bill and came away confident that this was a good next move for me. I had one thing to clear up. I told Bill and Ed that I had a cat and, if that was a problem for anyone, I would need to decline their invitation. They both assured me Gretel would be welcome. It was the Community for Creative Nonviolence, for Pete's sake. Of course my cat would be a welcome addition.

I talked to Sara about my decision and she agreed it was a good move for me. I gave them a month's notice on the apartment and started packing. Ed and Bill had not yet found a house so I spent December not knowing where I would be moving to. It was the month of waiting.

On December 10, I turned twenty-five. I was amazed at how much I had survived and how far I had gotten in the first-quarter century of my life. I don't know why but with this birthday I felt like I had graduated. I officially moved out of my girlhood phase and into a new phase, womanhood. I could now see myself as a woman—a young woman, but a woman nonetheless.

Chapter 18

Marching to the Woods
1971–1973

In early January, I learned that Ed had found a house for CCNV on Washington Circle, just three blocks from the Newman Center. I was moving back to the other end of Ground Zero. Because I now had furniture and Gretel, moving was more complicated. Bill Durland and his big family station wagon came to my rescue. I stuffed Gretel into a carrier and set her on the front seat next to Bill, then hopped on my scooter and we convoyed it to the new CCNV center.

Washington Circle is located on the northern edge of the GWU campus, five blocks from the White House. Three major streets intersect the circle: 23rd Street, Pennsylvania Avenue and New Hampshire Avenue. K Street runs in a tunnel underneath the circle. In 1971, the George Washington University Hospital was located on the south side of Washington Circle at the intersection of 23rd Street. Ambulances with sirens blaring added an extra challenge for motorists trying to get around the circle in one piece.

My new home was in a large, old brick house located on the corner of 23rd Street and Washington Circle, directly across from the GWU Hospital Emergency entrance. The house had the remnants of long-ago elegance, but a lot of restoration and money would be required to restore it to its earlier grandeur. There were huge rooms downstairs that could easily accommodate the center's meetings, classes and gatherings. There were four bedrooms upstairs, one small bedroom off the kitchen and another bedroom in the basement. There was one bathroom.

Six regulars from the Newman Mass made up the live-in core of CCNV—one priest (Ed), three young men, two young women—and a cat. My bedroom was upstairs and had a turret with windows overlooking Washington Circle and its park on one side and the hospital entrance on the other side. The room was larger than my apartment on Capitol Hill. I settled in and sequestered Gretel in the room for two weeks while she got used to the move. After two weeks she was ready to leave the bedroom and explore the rest of her new world.

With this, I began my adventure into community living. Our intention was to live a nonviolent, Christian lifestyle, continue our nonviolent activism within the anti-war movement and set up an educational program that would give classes on nonviolence. Before moving in, I had met with Bill several times to discuss the goals and future activities of CCNV. I was truly looking forward to this adventure and to being with other like-minded people. I was tired of trying to figure out these things on my own.

As you might expect when six people who hardly know each other move into a house together, things went downhill fast. Soon after we moved in, we struggled to find how we each fit together as housemates and as part of the CCNV team. Everyone arrived with their own history, their own habits and their own expectations. We had two things in common: (1) We were dedicated to the goals of CCNV. (2) We each had heart and the best of intentions.

But best intentions be damned. We still had to live together and address the problems of the day-to-day running of the house. One person couldn't cook without dirtying every pot and pan on the block—which drove that day's dishwasher into fits of frenzy and eventual mutiny. Another person couldn't cook at all and took us across the street to the hospital cafeteria every time it was his turn to prepare dinner. One person was a slob. Another couldn't stand the filth. I had lived an independent life, made my own decisions and supported myself for ten years. Several of my housemates had never lived on their own. Consequently, my life experience and their life experience did not easily dovetail. (At least I knew how to cook! But cooking for six people plus guests instead of just for one was a new experience.) We had regular house meetings where grievances were aired but habits were slow to change. In spite of this, we each continued to have heart and hope.

To add to our challenges, Gretel changed her rhythm and went into heat every two months (instead of every six months). She would take out her frustrations on anyone's leg, lap and especially bearded men's faces. I couldn't afford to have her spayed so I kept her in my room during her delicate times.

Early on, I could tell that my housemates were ambiguous about their feelings toward Gretel despite their assurances that she was a welcomed addition. It seemed like having an animal around was a new experience for these people and they weren't sure how to respond to her. To Gretel's credit, she didn't back away from anyone. She'd jump on their laps or lay at their feet and purr until each person caught on that it was okay to pet the cat and talk to her.

My enthusiasm about ecology as an expansion of nonviolence grew every day. I talked about our responsibility with nature, the destruction of nature being the destruction of ourselves, the quality of our existence being directly related to the quality of our link with nature. I wanted to stir up interest in incorporating an environmentally responsible lifestyle into our fledgling community. I was partially successful. But CCNV's activity was focused on the war. This was no time to deal with ecology. Flowers, butterflies, recycling and all that "frivolous stuff" would have to wait.

The person who was interested in hearing about my ecology-as-nonviolence theory was Bill Durland. Bill was an attorney, a peace activist, a student of nonviolence and firmly against the war in Vietnam. He was the person who organized the fundraiser for the attorneys who were working pro bono to get the draftees out of jail.

The idea for CCNV originated with Bill. He wanted to create a center to study, teach and promote nonviolence and nonviolent activism as it had been developed and practiced throughout history. He felt that it was important to not just be against something. Nonviolence needed to permeate all aspects of life. Once I talked to him about ecology, he agreed that the nonviolence umbrella had to include the environment.

As soon as we moved into CCNV, Bill started contacting local high schools and offering (at no cost) for CCNV members to speak to students about nonviolence. There weren't many takers. Those first few months I think we visited two high schools. One surprising thing I learned was how much these fifteen- and sixteen-year-old kids parroted their parents' ideas and beliefs. I thought that by that age they would be more willing, able and ready to think about life's issues and develop their own set of thoughts and beliefs. I was wrong. I made the mistake of comparing their development with my own. (Remember, Machaelle: Not every kid gets tossed out of their home and has to learn to think and fend for themselves.)

By early spring, Bill changed his approach and was now speaking to local college students. He invited me to accompany him and we discovered that we made a good team. Bill was the historically rooted professorial one and I was the practical one. I would apply what he was saying to current life by bringing it down to toilet paper, food, water and jobs.

I became Bill's typist because the CCNV person he had previously asked was a lousy and overly creative typist. I may not have been the fastest and most accurate typist but I had one skill over her. I corrected typos. She did not. She felt it was an act of violence to expect her to correct her typing mistakes. (This was the annoying era of manual typewriters, carbon paper and Wite-Out.)

It would not have been so bad if she had just left the mistyped words alone. Most of us can figure out that "morched" should have been "marched" when seen in the context of a sentence or within the flow of a thought. But when she knew she had just made a typo, instead of correcting it, she would change the word to match the typo. For example, "marched" with the typo "mor" might be changed to "morphed." She would then go on to finish the sentence in a way that correctly incorporated the word "morphed." "We marched to the top of the hill" could became "We morphed into a street gang and conquered the hill."

Bill liked to read his presentations. He'd get halfway through a sentence and realize it no longer resembled anything he had written or wanted to say. I have to admit, sometimes the end result could be quite funny. And her creativity was impressive. It just was not helpful. Several times he asked her to be more careful but it was to no avail. So I got the typing job—and a small paycheck from Bill for my efforts.

I was grateful for the extra paycheck. In December, while I was waiting to move into CCNV, Father Wintermyer told me about an opportunity that I might want to check out. The pastor of the Methodist Church that was close to the Newman Center had an idea for some unused space on the second floor of his church. When I talked to him, the pastor said he wanted someone to set up a handcraft shop in that space. He would not charge rent. He just wanted the space to be used well and reflect the spirit of the church. A handcraft shop sounded appealing. I told him I would give it a try and started setting up the shop right away. I soon realized this was going to be a full-time venture so I resigned from the Gallery. December 31 was my last day.

By the end of December my shop had a name, "The Garrett." When word got out, people started coming to the church with their crafts. I didn't have to find them, they found me. I had made the decision to keep 20 percent of the sales, which I felt was fair to the craftspeople and to me. That decision attracted lots of attention and I had people from all over the city showing up with some remarkable crafts that they left on consignment. The key to my success was the 20 percent. They were used to shop owners keeping 40 to 60 percent. To them, I was a godsend. They brought leather crafts, blown-glass animals and ships, macrame belts and purses, weaving, knitting, sewn clothing, paintings and pottery. Lots of pottery from several potters. I thought their workmanship was wonderful and felt good about selling it for them. It was a win-win-win for all: the church, the craftspeople and me.

By mid-January, I was fully stocked and ready to open. I decided to open The Garrett on Thursdays through Sundays (prime shopping days), giving me the other three days to devote to CCNV activity. A friend designed flyers announcing the shop and I plastered them on every bulletin board I could find around the GW campus.

Soon after opening, I met Clarence Wright. He came up to the shop with an armful of large black and white photographs he had taken, developed and matted for sale. Now photography was added to The Garrett.

I can't say sales were brisk those first few weeks. It was winter, The Garrett was new and I was tucked away on the second floor of a church. I had a wooden sandwich-board sign on the church's lawn with a big arrow pointing to the staircase leading to the shop but it didn't draw in hordes of customers. Still, those who did venture up were enthusiastic and always bought something. I felt confident that this was going to work. I just needed a little time to develop it.

When the weather broke for spring, I felt I needed to do something to introduce the shop to more customers. Instead of making people climb up the steps to me, I'd take the shop down the steps to them and set it up on the lawn next to the sidewalk. (Lesson: Customers love convenience.) The pastor gave me permission to use the lawn as long as it wasn't during church services on Sundays. With this move, sales greatly improved.

Sales jumped again when I added "user notes" with the pottery that listed ideas for how each piece could be used. People would pick up a bowl, tell me how much they liked the shape or colors and then say, "But I don't know what I'd use it for." Once they read the note they'd say, "Oh, yes. I can use it for that," and they'd buy it. I never did understand why so many people needed "use instructions" for something as obvious as a bowl or vase.

I had a steady stream of sidewalk customers. The craftspeople stopped by often to replenish my stock and collect checks. Even Lester Cooke stopped by from time to time and would buy something. Packing up everything and hauling it inside at the end of the day only to unpack it all on the lawn the next day got a bit wearisome but I managed to pick up some volunteers who helped with the lugging.

One person who showed up fairly regularly was Clarence Wright, the photographer. He was one of the three Paulist seminarians who assisted Father Wintermyer. They lived together in an apartment a couple of blocks from the Newman Center so The Garrett was in their neighborhood. When he could, he would show up at the end of my day and help me close up. Afterwards we'd go out for coffee. One thing led to another and we began dating. I found him to have an innate ability to heal the torn soul and damaged spirit of just about anyone. I was especially susceptible to his kindnesses. And he was intrigued with my strange life and free thinking. I had questions about the fact that he was a seminarian but that didn't seem to be an issue for him. I soon discovered that a lot of the seminarians, including two of Clarence's roommates, were also dating. It was a liberal time for the Paulists.

BETWEEN APRIL 19 AND 23, the Vietnam Veterans Against the War (VVAW) came to Washington for what they called "Dewey Canyon III" and held peaceful anti-war protests at Arlington National Cemetery, the Pentagon, the Supreme Court building and the Capitol. A thousand veterans challenged a court injunction and camped on the National Mall. Later that first day, the District Court of Appeals lifted the injunction.

On April 20, in the fastest reversal of an Appeals Court decision in the Supreme Court's history, Chief Justice Warren Burger reinstated the injunction. The veterans were told to leave the Mall by 4:30 the following afternoon. On April 21, many veterans were prepared to be arrested, but none were. The Park Police ignored the Court's orders. Headlines the next day read, "Vets Overrule Supreme Court."

On the morning of April 20, more than 1,100 veterans, led by Gold Star Mothers (mothers of soldiers killed in war), marched across the Lincoln Memorial Bridge to the Arlington Cemetery gate. When word was received that the marchers were coming, the gate was closed and locked. The Gold Star Mothers placed wreaths outside the gate and the group left. Later that morning, Reverend Jackson H. Day, who had resigned his military chaplainship a few days earlier, conducted a memorial service during which he said:

> Maybe there are some others here like me—who wanted desperately to believe that what we were doing was acceptable, who hung on the words of "revolutionary

> development" and "winning the hearts and minds of the people." We had been told that, on balance, the war was a good thing and we tried to make it a good thing. All of us can tell of somebody who helped out an orphanage, or of men like one sergeant who adopted a crippled Vietnamese child. Even at My Lai the grief of one of the survivors was mixed with bewilderment as he told a reporter, "I just don't understand it...always before, the Americans brought medicine and candy." I believe there is something in all of us that would wave a flag for the dream of an America that brings medicine and candy, but we are gathered here today, waving no flags, in the ruins of that dream. Some of you saw right away the evil of what was going on; others of us one by one, adding and re-adding the balance sheet of what was happening and what could possibly be accomplished finally saw that no goal could be so laudable, or defense so necessary, as to justify what we have visited upon the people of Indochina.
>
> ["Vietnam Veterns Against the War," Wikipedia, n.d.]

At the Capitol, VVAW members visited their congressmen to lobby against our participation in the war and to present a sixteen-point suggested resolution for ending the conflict.

On April 21, more than fifty veterans marched to the Pentagon, intending to surrender as war criminals. A Pentagon spokesman took their names and turned them away. For a second day, veterans met with and lobbied their congressional representatives.

On April 22, a large group of veterans rallied on the steps of the Supreme Court, saying that the Supreme Court should have ruled on the constitutionality of the war. The veterans sang "God Bless America," and 110 were arrested for disturbing the peace. Singing "God Bless America" on the Supreme Court steps was considered disturbing the peace. Later, once everyone settled down and came to their senses, they released the veterans who had been arrested.

The spokesman for VVAW during Dewey Canyon III was John Kerry, later to become a U.S. Senator, the Democratic nominee for president in 2004 and our Secretary of State from 2013 to 2017. In April 1971, he was a 27-year-old Vietnam veteran. As their spokesman, he testified on their behalf for two hours in front of the Senate Foreign Relations Committee. Word had spread that morning that Kerry's testimony was going to be important. People flocked to the Capitol and quickly filled the Senate hearing room. Unfortunately, by the time we at CCNV heard about it, it was too late to get in. We joined the millions of people around the country who listened to their radios, watched the testimony on TV or read the transcript the next morning in the newspaper. His testimony was raw, rough and deeply troubling, but his unvarnished words delivered in a calm, measured voice were what the VVAW needed to say and everyone needed to hear. War is bad enough, but Kerry and his fellow VVAW members were telling us that, for the Americans who were fighting it, the Vietnam War had gone completely off the rails.

He began his statement:

> I would like to talk, representing all those veterans, and say that several months ago in Detroit, we had an investigation at which over 150 honorably discharged and many very highly decorated veterans testified to war crimes committed in Southeast Asia—not isolated incidents but crimes committed on a day-to-day basis with the full awareness of officers at all levels of command.
>
> "It is impossible to describe to you exactly what did happen in Detroit, the emotions in the room, the feelings of the men who were reliving their experiences in Vietnam, but they did. They relived the absolute horror of what this country, in a sense, made them do.
>
> They told the stories that at times they had personally raped, cut off ears, cut off heads, taped wires from portable telephones to human genitals and turned up the power, cut off limbs, blown up bodies, randomly shot at civilians, razed villages in a fashion reminiscent of Genghis Khan, shot cattle and dogs for fun, poisoned food stocks, and generally ravaged the countryside of South Vietnam in addition to the normal ravage of war,

> and the normal and very particular ravaging which is done by the applied bombing power of this country.
>
> We call this investigation the 'Winter Soldier Investigation.' The term 'Winter Soldier' is a play on words of Thomas Paine in 1776 when he spoke of the Sunshine Patriot and summertime soldiers who deserted at Valley Forge because the going was rough.
>
> We who have come here to Washington have come here because we feel we have to be winter soldiers now. We could come back to this country; we could be quiet; we could hold our silence; we could not tell what went on in Vietnam, but we feel because of what threatens this country, the fact that the crimes threaten it, no reds, and not redcoats, but the crimes which we are committing that threaten it, that we have to speak out.
>
> I would like to talk to you a little bit about what the result is of the feelings these men carry with them after coming back from Vietnam. The country doesn't know it yet, but it has created a monster, a monster in the form of millions of men who have been taught to deal and to trade in violence, and who are given the chance to die for the biggest nothing in history; men who have returned with a sense of anger and a sense of betrayal which no one has yet grasped.
>
> As a veteran and one who feels this anger, I would like to talk about it. We are angry because we feel we have been used in the worst fashion by the administration of this country....

Kerry summed up his feelings with this:

> ...Each day to facilitate the process by which the United States washes her hands of Vietnam, someone has to give up his life so that the United States doesn't have to admit something that the entire world already knows, so that we can't say that we've made a mistake. Someone has to die so that President Nixon won't be, and these are his words, "the first President to lose a war.

> And we are asking Americans to think about that because how do you ask a man to be the last man to die in Vietnam? How do you ask a man to be the last man to die for a mistake?…
>
> ["John Kerry's 1971 speech," msnbc.com]

On Friday, April 23, the final day for Dewey Canyon III, over 800 veterans, one by one, tossed their medals, ribbons and discharge papers on the steps of the Capitol to protest the continued prosecution of the war. As a final act, the VVAW planted a tree on the Mall as part of a ceremony symbolizing the veterans' wish to preserve life and the environment.

Dewey Canyon III and Kerry's testimony resulted in congressional hearings held that week regarding atrocities committed in Vietnam and the media's inaccurate coverage of the war. There were also hearings on proposals to end our participation in the war. It was an intense week that demonstrated that as a strategy, nonviolence isn't for the weak. Dewey Canyon III was effective.

EIGHT DAYS LATER, we had a very different protest. On Saturday, May 1, Washington was again Ground Zero for three days of mass action by anti-war militants in what they called the "Mayday Protests." They declared that nonviolent political protests would not end the war and that more aggressive actions were needed. They were going to shut down the federal government. Their slogan was "If the government doesn't stop the war, we'll stop the government." Their official protest button had a picture of Gandhi with a raised fist. They said it would be a nonviolent mass civil disobedience campaign of blocking traffic at key intersections and commuter routes and closing down all the bridges connecting Virginia and D.C. so that two million government workers would be unable to get to their offices. (What could go wrong with that plan?)

Once more the Mall became a campground as 35,000 protesters camped near the Washington Monument, listened to rock music and planned for the coming action. Unlike the carefully planned, well executed and peaceful demonstrations that moved the antiwar ball forward the previous week, Mayday was a mess.

On Sunday, the Nixon Administration canceled the protesters' Mall permit. Park Police and Metropolitan Police, dressed in riot gear, moved through the park firing tear gas and knocking down tents, forcing out the campers and closing down the campsite. Over half of the protesters left the city and, presumably, went back home.

The 10,000 protesters who stayed announced that they would be shutting down the government starting Monday, May 3. Because of its location, the CCNV house was going to be in the thick of it. We were close to two major bridges linking Washington and Virginia. And 23rd Street was a major commuter route to Washington Circle. We were also across the street from the GW Hospital and close to the State Department, the Justice Department and the White House—all Mayday targets. After some discussion, we decided not to participate in the Mayday Protests. Despite the organizers' claims to the contrary, we assumed their activity would turn violent. We also didn't agree with their goal of shutting down the government. That was not going to stop the war. It was just going to infuriate two million people trying to get to work. To try to help keep the situation calm, we voted to serve coffee to commuters on 23rd Street who might be stuck in a traffic jam because of protests.

On the morning of May 3, I got out of bed early, looked out my window and saw a platoon of soldiers standing in formation and holding rifles with fixed bayonets. They were facing in the direction of our house. This didn't make me feel safe. It was another one of my brain-freeze moments. That just wasn't a sight I was expecting to see first thing in the morning. I think the bayonets bothered me most. Were they planning to spear people?

Overnight, the federal government had activated Operation Garden Plot (there's a charming name for a military operation), a previously prepared plan for dealing with major civil disorders in Washington. During the late night hours, 10,000 federal troops were moved to various locations in the city. At one point, so many troops were being moved into the area from bases along the East Coast that transports were landing at the rate of one every three minutes at Andrews Air Force Base, just outside Washington.

Troops from the Marine Barracks lined both sides of the 14th Street bridge, one of the main bridges targeted by the protesters. These troops were to back up the 5,100 D.C. police officers along with 2,000 members of the D.C. National Guard and federal agents that were already in place. Every monument, park and traffic circle (including Washington Circle) had troops protecting its perimeters. Marines, along with 4,000 paratroopers from the 82nd Airborne Division, arrived by helicopter on the Mall. One might say that by morning the federal government was "locked and loaded" and ready for the protests. Let the Mayday games begin.

I drank my morning coffee while I sat by my window and watched the police clash with protesters along with federal employees who were just trying to get to work. The police were not distinguishing between the long-haired, bandana-wearing, scruffy protesters in jeans and the people with short, combed hair wearing suits and dresses. One of the things that had impressed me during the years of protest in Washington was how restrained and disciplined the D.C. police were. I assumed that, in this case, practice really did lead to perfection. However on Mayday, the police snapped. From my bedroom window I could see that everything was out of control. If you were standing or walking on the sidewalk, you were going to be roughed up and arrested. By 8 A.M., 7,000 people in the city around Ground Zero had been arrested.

The protesters used hit and run tactics to disrupt traffic and cause chaos in the streets. President Nixon, who was watching from afar from his home in San Clemente, California, refused to give federal workers the day off, forcing them to navigate through the chaos, police lines and Mayday roadblocks. I'm not sure how much work the federal employees were able to do once they got to work since everyone's eyes were burning and watering from the tear gas, including my own and Gretel's. (The cloud of gas around us seeped through the walls of our old house and stayed with us for over a week.)

Vehicles were disabled and left blocking streets, as large groups blocked intersections. When traffic was blocked and not moving on 23rd Street, we walked up and down the line of cars with trays of coffee. A few drivers refused our free offer but most were happy that someone cared enough about their predicament to give them a little break.

While the troops worked to secure the major intersections and bridges, the police moved through the city making massive arrest sweeps and firing off more tear gas. There was no escaping the gas.

In Georgetown, the police herded protesters and onlookers through the streets to the Georgetown University (GU) campus. They lobbed tear gas over the university's main gate to push the protesters and the crowd back. Other forms of gas were used at GU including pepper spray and a gas that induced vomiting. Police helicopters dropped tear gas on the university's lower athletic field where protesters who had been driven off the Mall had camped the night before. Numerous people at GU were severely injured.

The GW Hospital Emergency entrance across the street from my window had a nonstop line of ambulances and cars delivering the injured. People arrived dripping blood from head wounds and face cuts. Others arrived frantically rubbing their eyes with handkerchiefs to try to get relief from the gas. It was nearly impossible to negotiate Washington Circle with all the traffic chaos. Ambulance sirens were useless. Drivers were stuck in the circle and could not get out of the way. One of our CCNV guys who had been serving coffee was now in the hospital. He had a history of bad back problems and, of course, a policeman struck him hard across the back with a baton just outside CCNV. (His crime: He was crossing the street while carrying a tray of coffee cups.) They carried him into the hospital on a stretcher. No ambulance needed.

Around noon, we heard that there was going to be a nonviolent Federal Employees for Peace rally in Lafayette Park (in front of the White House). We CCNV members (minus the guy in the hospital) decided to walk over and support it. Several Senators spoke eloquently about the need to end the war and called for calm in the city. But then the police arrived. They announced that the rally did not have a permit and we had five minutes to leave the park before being arrested. Most of the crowd remained. I considered staying but I had just started my period that morning and I did not feel like going through an arrest and holding process while needing to deal with that situation. I suspected I would end up experiencing an inconvenient, painful mess. So I left. The rest of my housemates stayed and were arrested along with everyone else in the crowd.

By the end of the day, it was reported that over 23,000 people had been arrested, including a bunch of construction workers who had come out to support the government. It was the largest mass arrest in the history of the United States.

The city's prisons did not have the capacity to handle 23,000 people. A temporary detention center surrounded by an eight-foot-high fence was set up next to RFK Stadium (then home of the Washington Redskins) and surrounded by National Guard troops. No food, water, or sanitary facilities were provided. (I made the right decision to leave.) Lawyers set up tables inside the fence to process "prisoners." Judges set up tables near the lawyers to quickly look over the paperwork and pronounce judgment. About half the number arrested were federal and city employees who had just been trying to get to work. Most of the 23,000 people, protesters and workers alike, were released as soon as they were processed. But it took several days to process all those people.

I stayed at the CCNV house answering phone calls from my housemates' worried families and waiting for the return of the CCNV felons. Within twenty-four hours, all but two had returned. The guy with the injured back was still in the hospital and needed to stay there for a few more days. The other person, a young woman who didn't live at CCNV but was closely linked with us and a frequent visitor, was lost in the D.C. jail system. It took a lawyer a full week to find where she was being held and to get her released. (Yep. I definitely made the right decision.)

A small group of Mayday protesters tried to disrupt traffic the next day but no one was in the mood for their antics. More arrests were made and everything just fizzled out. By Wednesday, the Mayday Protests were over. The troops who had been standing in the middle of Washington Circle with rifles and bayonets were gone. As far as I knew, no one got speared.

All those calls coming in to CCNV from worried families led me to think that Isadore also might be worried. On Tuesday, I called him to let him know I was okay. I had listed his contact information in my passport in case something happened while I was in Europe and someone needed to be notified. When I got back and was settled on Capitol Hill, I let him know my new address and phone number in case he needed to contact me. It seemed like the responsible thing for me to do. About once a year he'd call and we'd struggle through a short conversation. He was onto his third marriage and I felt it was now safer to be in contact with him.

My call after the Mayday Protests was weird. I guess I expected to hear some concern from him about my safety. Right away I realized he had heard nothing about the protests in Washington. I gave him a thumbnail description of what had happened and said I was calling to let him know I was okay, in case he was worried. He chuckled. He thought the protests were silly and it seemed to me like he thought my calling him was kind of cute. Thankfully, it was a brief conversation. I hung up the phone and reminded myself (once again) that I was a tightrope walker moving through life without a family's safety net.

I didn't try to call Dorothy because she was still MIA and I had no idea how to reach her. Besides, I did not want to describe the Mayday Protests to a drunk. Dealing with Isadore was enough.

Two weeks after the Mayday Protests, I spotted a guy with a large camera mounted on a tripod standing in the middle of Washington Circle. His camera was pointed at the CCNV house. Every time someone entered or left the house, he snapped a photo. COINTELPRO was back. When we realized what he was doing, we started waving hello when we walked in and out of the house. I think someone even took him coffee. At the end of the day, he came to the house, camera in hand, and knocked on the door. When I opened the door, he started snapping flash photos of me, Gretel, the living room and my two housemates who were sitting there reading. I asked, "Would you like to come in?" He responded a curt "no" and quickly left. We CCNV members and Gretel now had FBI folders complete with our photos. It seemed like Nixon and the FBI had problems with our name "Community for Creative Nonviolence." We wondered if the whole name disturbed them or was it was just the word "nonviolence." Or maybe it was "community." Or maybe "creative" sounded subversive to them.

They also tapped our phone not long after we moved in. We continued the tradition of reading the Constitution to them over the phone. The taps weren't high quality and sometimes interfered with our ability to hear a caller. We had to shout into the phone to the FBI to check the tap because it was making too much background noise. Sure enough, in a few minutes the line noise cleared up. I feel certain that technology has improved over the fifty years and these illegal phone taps are now much better for us legal citizens to deal with. Also, unless today's FBI photographer is Ansel Adams, I'm sure he won't be using a big camera and tripod to record potentially suspicious activity. In short, COINTELPRO and the FBI were not slick James Bond operations back in 1971.

In early June, Clarence traveled to Atlanta, Georgia, for the summer to participate in a pastoral counseling training program in an alcohol and drug rehabilitation center. Since meeting in the winter, we had grown closer and neither one of us was particularly happy about the separation. He phoned so often in June that we both realized it would be a lot cheaper if I flew down to Atlanta for a four-day visit over the July 4 weekend.

It was only for four days but I had a lot to do to prepare for the trip. I asked my housemates if they would mind taking care of Gretel. They had all relaxed with her over the months and I felt she would be fine while I was gone. They assured me that caring for her would not be a problem. I gave a tutorial on cat care, made sure there was plenty of cat food in the house and sat a new bag of litter next to her box.

I asked if anyone wanted to run The Garrett while I was away. To sweeten the pot, I offered the 20 percent I normally made from each sale. I had one taker who felt she had time in her schedule to do this. I showed her how to set up on the lawn and how to keep the sales records. I introduced her to the pastor, our host, and told him she was taking care of The Garrett while I was out of town. I even had a little time to introduce her to some of the craftsmen who showed up at the lawn with new wares. Everyone was fine with my trip.

Lastly, I pre-paid my portion of the house rent. I wanted to make sure my room was secured and that they understood I was committed to CCNV and would be returning.

I was ready to go to Atlanta. Bill drove me to the airport and saw me off.

Atlanta, Georgia—1971

After our happy hellos at the airport, Clarence told me that he wanted me to meet the other ministerial students who were with him in the pastoral counseling program. He arranged for us to have lunch together in the center's cafeteria the next day. So there I was seated at a big round table with about eight guys—Protestant and Catholic and from all around the country—listening and laughing as they regaled me with stories about their weeks in Atlanta and in the program.

At one point, a young woman walked across the cafeteria carrying a lunch tray. She was dressed conservatively in a business outfit. There was nothing remarkable about her except perhaps for the fact that most people would look at her and note that she was neatly dressed and well groomed. I noticed her because every guy at my table stopped talking and watched her as she crossed the room. It was obvious that they were mentally undressing her. I couldn't believe it. I said, "What the hell are you doing? Are you undressing her?" And this started a debate that lasted about twenty minutes. It was one female versus an all-male group of future ministers and priests.

My argument boiled down to their not having the right to undress her, mentally or otherwise, without her consent. She had every right to walk across a cafeteria without feeling that she was being mentally undressed by a bunch of men. Their argument boiled down to telling me this is a natural activity for men. And just because they were heading into their ministries didn't mean they were no longer "natural men." I pointed out that they believed leering was "natural" only because they and everyone around them throughout their lives had told them it was natural—

and repeated it as a mantra to the point where they assumed it was so. I asked if they were planning to mentally undress every pretty female congregant who came to them for help? I suggested that would be bad form on their part. They answered "no" in a tone that made it clear they thought I had taken the discussion over an unreasonable edge. I warned them their mental leering would not go unnoticed. Women sense when that kind of thing is happening. We had to drop the discussion because it became clear there would be no resolution. I was not going to buy the "It's natural!" routine and they thought I was being an unreasonable, uptight girl.

In light of the current avalanche of news stories about the widespread instances of sexual harassment and assault, combined with my fifty years of personal life experience since that Atlanta discussion, I would be better able to confront those men about their misplaced feelings of entitlement toward women. However, in 1971 that was the best I could come up with. The thing that hit me most that day was how easily they felt they had a right to objectify the young woman for their enjoyment (It's natural!) and how easy it was for them to take away her freedom and rights as a human being, as a woman.

Clarence and I continued the discussion that evening. He had said little during lunch but I could tell he was leaning to the "It's natural!" side. Because he was willing to listen that evening and consider what I was saying (something I gave him points for), I could see he was beginning to see how flimsy the "It's natural!" argument was.

At the end of the planned four days, we decided to extend our time together for another two weeks. I called CCNV and asked if they would be willing to continue caring for Gretel and taking care of The Garrett. No problem. They'd be happy to do this. Both Gretel and The Garrett were doing fine.

At the end of the two weeks, we decided to extend our time once more and return to Washington together in early September. I called CCNV again and told them my new plans. They were still fine about caring for Gretel and The Garrett. I told them I would send rent money each month to secure my room.

We needed to find a place to stay for the remaining two months and someone suggested the campus dorm apartments at Emory University. It was a good suggestion. We moved in right away. We decided to split the rent, which meant that I was now responsible for rent in two places. I needed a job. I spotted a "Typist Wanted" notice on a bulletin board in our building, got the job and started right away. It was for a professor who needed a paper typed by the end of summer. The only thing I can remember about that paper was that it was boring beyond words. But I diligently typed it. The other typist at CCNV, with her high degree of creative typing, could have made that paper much more interesting.

Clarence and I spent the rest of the summer carefully, and sometimes tentatively, weaving together the start of our partnership while he continued with the program. Free time often included shared dinners and maybe a movie with the others in the program. This gave us a tight circle of friends who supported our relationship. With the way things were unfolding, it felt like everyone and everything were saying "yes" to our partnership. I took that as a good sign.

There are a few things I remember about my time in Atlanta. (1) It was quiet. There were no protest marches. No chanting. No gun fire. No tear gas. No soldiers carrying rifles with bayonets. (2) Nearly every afternoon we had a thunderstorm. (3) Most of the streets and buildings in downtown Atlanta had the word "peach" in their names. (4) Underground Atlanta was special, and that summer they had an amazing group of gospel singers performing in one of the Underground clubs.

At the end of the summer, all the program's participants were given an evaluation form and encouraged to include their ideas for improving the program. I asked Clarence to get a copy for me. I had something to say—and it didn't have anything to do with men mentally undressing random women.

This program was not easy. I think it was the only program for pastoral counseling in the country at that time. The head of the program was a no-nonsense, straight talking, tobacco chewing, tobacco-juice spitting minister and therapist named Chuck. He attended a number of our get-togethers and that gave us time to talk and to get to know one another. I liked him and I think he appreciated my directness.

The program's setting, the Atlanta rehabilitation center for drug addicts and alcoholics, was challenging in itself. Addicts and alcoholics are not always easy to help. (That's an understatement.) The program structure was also challenging. The guys had to be on duty twenty-four hours per day and were rotated around three daily shifts. Lack of sleep became an issue. Each ministerial student was assigned a patient to counsel and assist. Not easy when the patient was usually smarter and more adept at manipulating a naïve young ministerial student. Everything had to be monitored and discussed with the program counselors. Also the participants went through their own private and group therapy sessions that were scheduled several times a week throughout the summer. And there was a weekly group session that included the patients that could sometimes get rough for all. There were times when it seemed some of the students were being ripped apart. On the final day, one of the ministerial students tried to commit suicide (he slashed his wrists) and was hospitalized.

To me, the program had a gaping hole that needed to be addressed. Most of the Protestant students were married and had brought their wives with them to Atlanta. While the program was ripping apart these guys each day, their wives (or significant others) were left with the task of dealing with the fallout. Sometimes the guys would go silent and not talk to their wives for days. Sometimes they would explode in anger over nothing, sometimes they would smoke pot for relief and sometimes they would just look to their wives to paste them back together and get them ready for the next day of challenges. These were all young women (in their early 20s) who were not prepared for the program's intensity. Marriages became strained. But their hearts were with their husbands and they wanted to help. Over the weeks, we women would meet at lunch and discuss what was going on. I suggested they talk to Chuck and ask for some kind of guidance on how to deal with this stuff. But those who did say something were told the program was for ministerial students and did not include wives.

I felt that Chuck and the other program counselors did not fully appreciate what was happening with some of these guys when they left the center each day. They could hold it together while at the center, but once they got home they fell apart. The stress and confusion the wives experienced as they tried to help was not being taken into consideration. For my evaluation, I described the wives' situation as best I could and suggested that something be set up in the program to assist the partners to better deal with the fallout. Perhaps a class on what to expect from their husbands and how to help. On the last day when I handed my evaluation to Chuck, he smiled (it was pretty cheeky of me to fill out an evaluation) and said, "I'll definitely read this." I felt confident that he would read it.

It was time to leave Atlanta. What began as a four-day weekend visit was to last thirty years. When we started dating, Clarence had been wrestling with whether or not he wanted to spend his life as a priest. He was less than a year away from ordination. When I arrived in Atlanta, he was still wrestling with this. By the end of the summer, he had made his decision to leave St. Paul's College and we had decided to continue our lives together.

WASHINGTON—1971

When we arrived back at CCNV, we were greeted with a frosty unwelcome that quickly turned to ice when they realized that Clarence and I were serious about our relationship. They knew we had been dating before Clarence left for Atlanta but, for some reason, dating was acceptable and forming a partnership was not.

Ed, the priest at CCNV, talked to me for over two hours trying to convince me that our relationship was nothing more than a figment of my imagination. When Clarence wrote the Paulists to let them know he was leaving, the head of the order wrote a letter back and referred to me throughout the letter as "the problem." (I wrote him back and informed him that my name was Machaelle and not "the problem." He didn't respond to my letter.) Others accused me of snatching Clarence away from the loving arms of the Holy Mother Church. A close friend refused to talk to me and would have nothing to do with me.

Many of the seminarians, whom Clarence considered brothers, shunned him. When he walked up to them to say hello they acted as if he wasn't there. It was really weird and painful to watch. I felt like I was observing a bunch of spoiled four-year-olds rather than adult seminarians. They were acting like no one had ever left the Paulist Order before when I knew it happened frequently. We learned that their reactions to Clarence's decision to leave forced each of them to question why they were staying. They didn't like being challenged. I thought they should have handled this better.

Clarence wasn't the only person they struck out against. With some of these fine, soon-to-be ordained men, I became the primary target. They couldn't conduct themselves politely toward me, couldn't say hello without an edge to it and they ended up casting most of the blame for the situation on me.

I took perverse pleasure over the next couple of years when those people who raised a stink when we returned found themselves in similar circumstances. A lot of the seminarian shunners left the order to get married to the women they had been dating and, in some cases, living with. The friend who had refused to speak to me fell in love with a priest, divorced her husband and moved in with the priest. Eventually they married. Clearly we had inspired everyone to project their personal insecurities onto us. (Lucky us.)

Gretel wasn't just pleased to see me when we returned. She was thrilled. Life in the Community for Creative Nonviolence had not been easy for her. Her food bowl had maggots. Her water bowl was empty. Her litter box had no litter even though the bag was sitting next to it. She had to use an empty box which, considering how fastidious she was, must have driven her nuts. And it seemed like my housemates stopped relating to her. She had spent her two months in the "Torture Prison Camp for Cats" (TPCC). It's a wonder she survived, and I felt guilty about how she had been treated.

While I was away, and while I was still paying rent, my room had been rented out to someone I didn't know. That individual thanked me by leaving a mildly trashed and dirty room. The CCNV folks said they didn't think I would mind if they rented it out to bring in some extra money. They were wrong.

When I checked The Garrett, I found a mess there as well. The minister was very angry with me. He felt I had just abandoned the shop. The CCNV person who was supposed to run it while I was gone had not passed along my messages to him about my arrangements for the summer. Plus, she only opened the shop when it was convenient for her. The craftspeople had not been paid and didn't know what was going on. Glass and pottery items had been broken and just left around. Records had not been properly kept. I had to notify all the craftspeople and make arrangements to pay them for anything that had been sold or broken. I have to say that once I explained the situation and apologized, everyone was willing to work with me to shovel The Garrett out of its mess.

I couldn't understand why the CCNV people bothered to tell me that they would be happy to care for Gretel and the shop when it was clear that they had no intention of doing that. I could have made other arrangements, especially for Gretel's care. And why did they rent out my room without saying anything to me first? Nothing was making sense.

The situation was so bad that Clarence and I decided to find a new place right away. By the second week after our return, we had moved to our new apartment and I was back on Capitol Hill. This time I was on 4th Street SE and not 7th Street SE, three blocks closer to the Capitol building and Ground Zero. I didn't care. Gretel and I were just pleased to get out of CCNV.

We spent the first ten months in our new place getting settled and financially stabilized. There wasn't a big calling in the Washington job market for an ex-seminarian with a bachelor's degree in philosophy. Clarence managed to land a job tutoring kids in a special education program, but they wanted a lot of dedication in return for a low salary.

I needed to get a job. We were moving into the cold-weather months and I would have to move The Garrett back up to the church's second floor. I had hoped to build a customer base over the summer so that those people would remember the shop in the winter and climb the stairs. Obviously that didn't happen and I knew I wasn't going to make it through another winter with the shop. In late October, I reluctantly closed The Garrett.

I convinced the shunners that I had completely sold out to "The Man" by landing a job selling human hair wigs door-to-door. How could I possibly do something this irresponsible? In my mind I was able to justify my new job by feeling that if a woman was already inclined to buy a wig, it would be better for the environment, her finances and her health (not to mention her appearance), if she bought one quality wig made with human hair instead of six cheap wigs made with synthetic fibers. That stretch of logic worked for me. Just as importantly, our combined salaries covered our living expenses and paid for our $135 a month apartment.

During the winter, we got together regularly with our remaining three friends, Bill Durland and his family and a couple of Paulists, "Wolfjaw" (priest) and Joe (deacon).

I don't know why Wolfjaw was given that name but perhaps it had to do with the fact that he was crazy, fearless and outrageous. He had spent several years in Paris (Montmartre) ministering to the prostitutes. Apparently they trusted him because he didn't try to get them to change their profession. By the time he got back to Washington, he had become a wine connoisseur. They served him a glass of red wine at the College dinner one night. He took a sip, spit it out, loudly declared it to be swill and threw the half-filled, crystal wine glass across the room.

One time when we were dining together at a restaurant on the Hill, he stood up on the seat of the chair and announced to everyone that this was a special evening for him (for no reason except that he was happy and a little tipsy), and they had all helped make it so. Then he thanked them for being present that night. Luckily everyone enjoyed him and we weren't tossed out of the restaurant. He taught Sacraments at St. Paul's College and he offered a Mass on Sundays that was outstanding. He knew how to read the mood of the congregation and married the Mass to that mood. We switched from the GWU Newman Mass to Wolfjaw's Mass at St. Paul's. One Sunday as we walked down the hall to the Mass, I noticed a bunch of crayon drawings on the hallway wall. Not on paper that had been tacked to the wall but drawn directly on the wall. I asked what that was and Clarence said matter-of-factly, "That's Wolfjaw's final exam. They had to draw sin."

Over our many dinners, we had long discussions about the current liberal movement in the Church, the human soul, spirituality and the afterlife. What did it mean for souls to be physical, to be on Earth? How did that affect things like our capacity to love? Was being physical confining to our true nature? What was the "nuts and bolts" process of death?

When it came to the afterlife, the discussion generally revolved around a debate: Is there an afterlife or not? I had already decided that there was an afterlife, so for me the debate was closed. I felt we human beings were much too complex (physically, mentally, emotionally) from a life of personal development and experience for us to get to the end and say, "Well, that's it. It's all over. I'll be dying now. Dump me in the ground and let the worms have at it." To die with no future to step forward into seemed like a colossal waste of a person's life.

Once I came to the conclusion that there was an afterlife, my thinking and questions focused on the practical matters of an afterlife. What does the afterlife mean? How do people continue on? Does everyone sprout wings like Christianity implies? Or does everyone just walk around? Walk around where? Do they eat? Do they go to the bathroom? Do they live in houses or clouds? In short, what did it mean to say there is an afterlife?

1972

In early January, we got a phone call from Wolfjaw. A psychic was going to speak at St. Paul's College that Saturday. He didn't know what she was going to speak about, but he felt we might be interested in hearing her. I didn't have to think about it twice before saying "yes." Hopefully I'd have a chance to ask her questions about the afterlife.

The psychic was a woman named Peggy Townsend. When we arrived, there were about thirty-five priests and seminarians in a conference room, seated three deep around a long table. Clarence and I were seated at one end of the table facing her.

I had no idea what to expect from this woman. I knew nothing about psychics—only that they did strange things, and I wasn't sure what the strange things were. I also expected a thin, wispy, old woman dressed in flowing white robes to come floating into the room. She was thin but she wore a wool pants suit, walked like a normal person and appeared to be in her late forties.

Even though she had been invited to the College by one of the priests, I wouldn't say she was welcomed with warm, open, loving arms. Many clergy came prepared for a fight. Armed with their Bibles, they attempted to blast holes in her role as a psychic and in her work by using Scripture. Unfortunately, they picked the wrong person for a scriptural fight. She happened to be equally versed in the Bible and quoted passages back to them that supported the role of the psychic within Christianity. I sat quietly watching her. She wasn't combative with these men. Instead, she did two things: First, she quietly, confidently and calmly matched their challenges point for point. She dodged nothing. And second, she opened some interior door and released a massive wave of gentle acceptance that touched everyone in the room. This calmed the clergy.

Once the men backed down from their Bible battle, she was able to move on. As if she had been reading my mind, she addressed the areas of death and life after death. I started asking her questions based on what I had been learning and thinking. Much to my surprise, she verified everything. And, for the first time, I entertained the notion that the stuff that had been falling out of my mouth in discussions wasn't just some creative fantasy on my part.

When the session ended, I went up to her and said quietly, "I think I need to see you privately." She replied simply, "I know," and set a time for the next morning.

My experience with Peggy Townsend had disoriented me a bit. All I knew for sure was that I needed to see her. I needed to find out what was happening to me. And I desperately wanted to take the opportunity to grab every iota of information she had on the afterlife and anything else she was willing to share.

That night, the temperature dropped below 0 degrees Fahrenheit. The next morning, we could not get the Lambretta started. The gas line had frozen. To facilitate our two work schedules, we had purchased a second scooter—a little 125cc Vespa. I wanted Clarence to be with me when I met with Peggy, but the Vespa could only carry one of us. I arrived at my appointment a little late and alone. I was about to apologize when I saw Peggy but she waved it off saying, "I know. I know. You had motorcycle trouble." (It was scooter trouble, but that was close enough, Peggy.)

We went into a small room and I sat in a chair directly opposite her. She asked me to uncross my legs and arms so that the energy could flow through me, and then she explained that she had spent most of the previous night meditating on what she was to say to me. She had felt that there was much to tell me. But every time she considered what to talk to me about, a steel curtain would drop before her. However, I was not to worry. She was going to try again with me there and see what came up.

She sat quietly with her eyes closed for about a minute, then she began to speak. Little things at first. Clarence had heartburn from the garlic I had put in the spaghetti sauce the previous week and wasn't telling me for fear of hurting my feelings. Other little things about our apartment decor and colors, including suggestions for small changes that would facilitate my internal process.

All the while, I said nothing. She said that the steel curtain had come down once more. So she decided to use another tactic. She asked that it be revealed to her what was to be said to me at that moment. Then she was quiet again. I was going crazy. I didn't know what she was doing and I didn't see any steel curtains anywhere. (I was ready to jump up with a sledge hammer and start busting through that curtain as soon as I spotted the damn thing.) I just knew that I had to keep my legs uncrossed and my mouth shut. (I had the hard part.)

Finally, she spoke. She explained that I had the potential to develop psychically in any area. (I had no idea what she meant by that.) It was all open to me. (All *what* was open to me?) But I had to understand a few things first.

- There would come a time in my psychic growth when my relationship with Clarence would need to become secondary if I was to continue moving forward. At that time, I should decide carefully if I wanted to continue my development. I could decide at any time to go no further.
- Also, there were two things that were preventing her from being fully open to me. First was my determined desire to know, to obtain knowledge about this new world of the unseen. This was blocking me, and it was essential that I learn to relax and trust that everything would simply flow to me once I relaxed.
- Second, there was a piece of the puzzle that was not yet a part of my consciousness, but that would shortly come to me. Without this piece, I could not understand the things she could tell me. But again, I was to relax. Once the piece was in place, much of what Peggy wanted to say would simply fall into place for me on its own.

The last thing: She cautioned me not to force any of my new awareness onto Clarence. When it came to these matters, he was less open and flexible, and I needed to respect his timing.

After twenty minutes the session ended. As I got up to leave, she hugged me and offered me her love and support. I could tell she wasn't just handing me empty social politeness. She meant it. I walked out of the room knowing I was about to embark on a new adventure—if only I could learn to relax.

I wish I could say that I followed the advice I got from her, that it was all a snap, that from the moment I left her, I was relaxed, open and calm, waiting patiently for the cosmos to smack me in the face with some missing piece. But that would be a lie. The best I could do at that time was to try to soften my diligent search for knowledge about things unseen.

Of course I told Clarence everything that happened with Peggy. She had been right about his heartburn. We agreed that if he ever felt I was ramming something down his throat, he'd tell me to back off. But except for one time, he had always found our discussions about such matters interesting and thought-provoking. The one time I had pushed was during an argument we had had when I tried to convince him that there were vampires somewhere in the universe simply because the word "vampire" existed. (For me, the word couldn't exist if the reality didn't also exist.) But after Peggy's warning, I decided not to shove vampires down his throat.

I didn't understand how my development in the unseen world could ever force my relationship with Clarence to become secondary, and, quite frankly, the thought of it scared me. We both ended up pushing this bit of information into the background, fairly confident that when it became an issue, we'd understand and somehow know what to do. (In five years' time, Peggy's warning in this matter proved true. The irony is that Clarence was the one who triggered the necessary shift in our partnership with the gift of a book in December 1976.)

Not long after seeing Peggy, Clarence talked about a book he was reading on reincarnation. *Reincarnation.* As soon as he started talking about the concept, I saw a huge, old, arched wooden door open inside of me and a wave of information washed through the door and into me. What I had been saying about the afterlife now took on a totally different dimension. A multitude of missing bits of information slipped into the mysterious gaps I myself had recognized existed in what I had been saying. I now saw life—both afterlife and Earth life—from the perspective of the many reflections of the soul rather than of just one reflection. Human beings and human life were much more complex than I had imagined.

IN THE SPRING OF 1972, Clarence and I decided to formally declare our partnership. We would invite family, old friends, new friends…all to come together for a celebration. The celebration would include a Mass and the theme would be the power of relationships. After the Mass, we would eat and play. In a generous show of support, Bill Durland and his family offered us their home for the gathering and helped with the planning.

Everything moved smoothly until we asked Wolfjaw to say the Mass. Much to our surprise, he refused. He would not say our Mass unless we made it a wedding Mass and had it registered at the diocese as a marriage.

We refused. As far as we were concerned, we had already created a valid, moral partnership based on no promises, no vows. We simply wanted to share and celebrate what we had already created.

I was particularly adamant in this instance. I had grown to believe that it was impossible to promise or vow today what I would do tomorrow. I had accepted Ivan Illich's premise that a vow was not something you took at the start and then hoped you would be able to live out its intent. Rather, taking a vow was something you earned after many years of demonstrating and living its intent. If we were ever to exchange marriage vows, it would have to be after living together as partners for—oh, maybe fifty years.

> Note: Who the hell is Ivan Illich, you ask? Ivan Illich [1926–2002] was one of the world's great thinkers and, coincidentally, a Catholic priest. He was a polymath—his knowledge covered a wide variety of subjects. His theories and controversial writings raised questions about western institutions from the 1970s. In seven books he addressed education *[Deschooling Society*, 1971], technological development *[Tools for Conviviality*, 1973], energy, transport and economic development *[Energy and Equity*, 1974], medicine *[Medical Nemesis*, 1976] and work *[The Right to Useful Unemployment and Its Professional Enemies*, 1978, and *Shadow Work*, 1981]. He was fluent in ten languages.

Back to our Mass: I felt that if we allowed this celebration to be turned into a Church-recognized wedding, we would be saying that we regarded our personal beliefs as trivial, to be disregarded and tossed aside at the slightest challenge from the Church. We would also be saying that the partnership we had created in good conscience in August '71 was no longer valid in our eyes and that we now wanted the Church to create a valid one for us.

Even though Wolfjaw was a good friend and supported our relationship, it was clear that he was not going to change his mind about saying our Mass. We reached out to a priest we knew through CCNV, Father Richard McSorley, an elderly Jesuit priest who founded the Center for Peace Studies at Georgetown University and taught classes on peace and justice. He said he would be happy to officiate at our celebration Mass. His reason for doing this revolved around St. Augustine (354–430) and the Just War Theory—a statement that would cause rational-thinking people to blink and say, "Could you explain that, please?"

Father McSorley believed that once the Church had accepted the Just War Theory, it went off the rails. (The Just War Theory is a doctrine to ensure war is morally justifiable through a series of criteria, all of which must be met for a war to be considered just.) For Father McSorley, war was never justifiable. He pointed out that it countered the commandment "Thou shalt not kill."

To divert attention away from this disastrous and controversial decision on war, the Church has spent centuries, starting way back when Augustine first spoke about it, regulating every conceivable detail of sex, sexual relations and marriage as a diversion. Anything to kick up enough dust to divert attention away from the fact that the Church was now sanctioning killing by stating that there were circumstances when "Thou shalt not kill" didn't apply and killing fellow humans was acceptable.

Nothing diverts people's attention like sex. As far as Father McSorley was concerned, he refused to accept the validity of the multitudinous canon laws on sex and marriage. Those pronouncements were faulty because, as Father McSorley believed, they existed solely for distraction. Once the Church reversed its stand on the Just War Theory, the dopey sex and marriage laws would drop away. The remaining laws would reflect the Church's true stand on the issues of sex and marriage. Until then, he was not going to pay any attention to any of those laws. He agreed with our stand about not registering the Mass as a marriage.

On June 6, 1972, Clarence and I had our partnership Mass at Bill Durland's house. Father McSorley showed up on his motorcycle wearing black jeans, a bright blue-and-white shirt that had a Hawaiian flair to it and a black belt with a huge silver buckle in the shape of a peace symbol. I invited Isadore and his third wife to join. He arrived from New York with a small kosher delicatessen in his trunk from Zabar's. Along with all the other food the others brought, we had enough to last everyone for two weeks. With seventy-five family and friends, old and new, we celebrated our partnership. And ate—a lot. For communion, Clarence and I served everyone a small square of homemade banana nut bread. (It reflected how we felt about the Church.) Wolfjaw joined us despite how he felt about saying our Mass. And Joe, Wolfjaw's friend, delivered a homily titled, "Saying Yes in a No Society."

The controversy surrounding our Mass pushed me into my next important shift in my relationship with the Catholic Church and my search for truth. When I first joined the Church, I looked within its structure for the essence of Christianity, for what I called the essence of truth. I was young and alone and I needed the guidance I found within the Church's structures. Later, when I focused on Christianity and its relationship with social issues that led, eventually, to the theories of a nonviolent life and action, I saw that the essence of truth was outside the Church walls, as well. Finally, by standing up to the Church and saying "no" to their demand to have a properly sanctioned and registered wedding, I saw that the essence of truth lay within myself. It wasn't in the Church and it wasn't floating around me. It was inside me.

By the summer of 1972, Clarence had changed his career path from teaching to electrician to technician. In between the first two jobs we bought a Ford Econoline van which Clarence outfitted as a camper with a ramp so that we could roll the Lambretta in and out. We set out for a six-week-long drive across Canada with our two cats, Gretel and our young black cat named Fred. By the time we entered Canada, both cats had become seasoned van travelers. But all the way up the East Coast to Maine they were in a contest to see who could caterwaul the loudest.

We drove and camped from Nova Scotia to Calgary, with a quick trip to the border of British Columbia just so we could say we made it all the way across the country. We were eaten alive by mosquitos in Thunder Bay and we dodged a snow storm in Calgary. We nearly lost Gretel on our way back in Montana when she decided to explore the town and didn't return for three days. We almost died in Montana from carbon monoxide poisoning. I was just drifting to sleep when Fred suddenly keeled over. We threw open the van door, laid him outside on the ground and massaged his chest until he came back to life. (The culprit was a dutch oven with hot charcoal bricks that we had in the van next to open windows. Apparently two wide open windows wasn't enough ventilation. Note to self: Don't do that again.) We spent the night in the parking lot of the Newman Rectory on the Ohio State campus in Columbus, Ohio, and were invited to join the priest for dinner. I worked really, really hard to contain myself as this priest kept ringing a little brass bell every time he wanted the woman serving the meal to come to the table. It seemed disrespectful and rude, not to mention unnecessary because she was right outside the room and able to hear him if he had called her name. I reminded myself several times that I was a guest and it would be bad form if I jammed that bell up his ass.

We made it back to Washington and returned to our apartment in time for Clarence to start his new electrician job.

THE WASHINGTON ANTI-WAR intensity began to dim. People looked to the peace talks in Paris for a resolution to this mess. But peace talks or not, the war continued to wage on in Vietnam. In the spring of 1972, the North Vietnamese launched their first major offensive since Tet, called the Easter Offensive.

- December 1972: The North Vietnamese left the negotiating table in Paris. Feeling that Hanoi had tried to embarrass him and to force them back to the negotiating table, Nixon ordered Operation Linebacker II. Our military dropped more than 36,000 tons of bombs on Hanoi and Haiphong in twelve days, exceeding the total dropped from 1969–1971. This became known as the Christmas Bombing.

- December: A massive protest was held in Washington and around the country to protest Nixon's Christmas bombing. Clarence and I stepped out of our apartment building and participated in the protest.

- End of December 1972: American and North Vietnamese negotiators reached an agreement in Paris. They had gotten past the shape of the conference table.

- January 20: Twenty-thousand people attended a "Plea for Peace" concert at Washington Cathedral on the occasion of Nixon's second inaugural.

- January 21: Members of the VVAW marched from Arlington National Cemetery to the Lincoln Memorial; 85,000 people attended the afternoon demonstration.

- January 27: A ceasefire and the Paris Peace Accords were signed. ["Vietnam War Timeline," Wolfe, Cold War Studies]

Fighting continued between North and South Vietnam until North Vietnamese troops finally captured Saigon on April 30, 1975. South Vietnam surrendered the same day. After thirty years of war, Ho Chi Minh's vision of a united, communist Vietnam had been realized. The citizens of Vietnam were now faced with rebuilding a country that had been devastated by a long war.

Life moved on more easily for us civilians in America. For veterans, recovering from the war's experiences and resuming life were daunting tasks that continued for many years. Most members of the anti-war movement disbanded and local chapters of protest groups closed their dsoors. CCNV changed its focus from anti-war protests to feeding and housing the homeless. I was no longer selling wigs. Bill Durland asked me to join him at Georgetown University to help put together a class for Father McSorley's Center for Peace Studies. Neither Bill nor I continued to have a connection with CCNV. We both had just moved on.

1973

In January, Clarence changed jobs again and went to work as a technician for the Xerox Corporation in Springfield, Virginia. Along with the job came a significant salary raise. We were beginning to live like grown-ups—money in our pockets, company benefits with health insurance and profit-sharing. We were also the proud owners of a van—actually, we were in partnership with the bank, just like grown-ups.

We were still living in the same apartment. Well, the apartment was the same, but the rent was now $150. The neighborhood was rapidly being converted into condominiums, and our entire apartment building (all four floors of it) was being taken over by an invasion of roaches seeking refuge from all the disruptive condo construction on our block. We had to think about moving.

While I was still working at *The Washington Post,* I read an article about "farmlets"—little farms that consisted of a small house on five acres of land renting for about $35 a month just outside the Washington beltway in the Virginia countryside. Xerox was located ten miles outside Washington, which meant that Clarence had a ten-mile commute in heavy, rush hour traffic. In a masterful stroke of logic, I figured that we could rent one of these farmlets (of course, for $35 a month), and as long as we stayed within that ten-mile radius from Xerox, it wouldn't add extra distance onto Clarence's commute and it might even eliminate some of the traffic. As a bonus, I could begin experimenting with and applying the principles of nonviolence to land.

I didn't have to work too hard to convince Clarence that my scheme was worth investigating. When the roaches started organizing into gangs and moving our furniture around the apartment, we both realized we were ready for a change.

As luck would have it, the woman I had worked for when I sold the human hair wigs had closed that company and was now a realtor. One gray, drizzly Saturday in late January, Clarence and I, along with our realtor, headed to the Virginia countryside to look for our $35 dream farmlet.

Things had changed since that article had been written. Instead of farmlets, we found subdivisions with homes selling for an average of $75,000. Our realtor told us renting would be an expensive and unsound financial move. Land on which to build a home would be our most feasible move. She had a list of ten possibilities for us to consider.

I was obsessed with one idea: We had to live in the woods. I did not know why, I just knew it and that's all I knew. We looked at all ten properties that day, most of them in subdivisions with one tree left standing on each parcel of land. (That was their idea of a wooded lot.) Dusk was fast approaching as we got to the tenth property. Actually, we had no intention of seriously considering this piece. It was fifty-five miles from Xerox. But the real estate blurb said it was a ten-acre wooded lot with two streams. We were driving around anyway. Why not take a look?

It was nearly dark, it was still drizzling and this lot was half a mile down a rural gravel road. I got out of the car, and as I looked into the woods from the road for about a minute, I was enveloped by an air of absolute knowing. I turned to Clarence and said matter-of-factly, "This is it."

He was stunned.

The first hurdle we had to get over was the fifty-five mile drive to Xerox. On our way back to the city, we timed the trip—one hour and ten minutes. By the time we got back to the apartment and our resident roaches, Clarence had convinced himself that since he didn't mind driving anyway, he would be able to put up with the commute.

The second hurdle was buying the property (ten acres for $11,000, a fortune for us) and getting a home built. We had no idea how to accomplish this. The realtor steered us in the direction of prefab modular homes. They were well-constructed and had a good reputation for holding up over time. I looked at the information she gave us and immediately spotted the home that I thought would fit well with our wooded property: a single story, three bedroom, two bath home with cedar-shingle exterior siding and birch wood interior paneling. (It did not come with roaches.) The house, septic field, well and driveway came with the whopping price tag of $27,000.

Our third hurdle was the bank and getting a loan. We were so naïve. Clarence was now making a good salary. Xerox was a solid and well-recognized company, not some "hippie" venture. And we had been together for over two years, which to us seemed long enough to prove we had a stable commitment. Surely a $38,000 mortgage would not be a problem. *Au contraire.*

From the bank's perspective, we were young (27), Clarence had not worked at Xerox long enough, we had no loan history except for our van and we had no collateral. I sat in the banker's office listening to the guy explain the problems to Clarence. (He wasn't including me in the discussion. In fact, he was ignoring me. I was just "the little woman.") I could tell this banker was standing between us and our new home, and I wasn't going to let that happen. I asked him if I could use his phone. (Sure, little lady. Just dial 9 for an outside line.)

I called Isadore. He and his money could possibly get us over this hurdle. While Clarence and the banker listened, I explained the situation. Could Isadore help us buy the land outright so that we could use it for collateral? When I told him the price of the land and the price of the house we wanted, he just chuckled and said, "Let me talk to that guy." I handed the phone over to the banker and for about five minutes Isadore spoke to him without the banker saying a word other than "yes" and "uh-huh" a few times. When the call ended, the banker turned to me for the first time in our meeting and said our loan would be approved and the property would be the collateral.

I don't know what Isadore said to the banker. From his amused reaction, I suspected that the $11,000 for the land and the $27,000 for the house was chump change to Isadore. I also suspected that he threatened the banker with bodily harm that would be delivered by some New York mobsters (he was friends with some of those guys) if the banker didn't approve our loan. Whatever it was, we were now over the bank hurdle.

We moved fast to get everything in order and sign the papers at closing before the banker changed his mind. We had to drive to New York to get the money for the property. Isadore gave us $11,000 in cash after talking to his accountant. (And this is how I met Isadore's accountant, Michael Slater, who later served as Perelandra's trusting and lovable accountant for over thirty years. Life's mysterious weaves.)

By the end of May, our home was ready and we could move in—as long as we didn't mind living there without power. There was a delay in getting the power lines to the property. But we had strong motivation to move. With the warmer weather and the increased restoration of old buildings on our block, the roach issue exploded. We boxed our belongings (including the *Rugged Individualist* and my metal quotes box), packed the van, grabbed our two cats and moved to the woods.

My Forrestine Gump Years in Washington were over.

Chapter 19

Decompression
1973–1976

WE LEFT D.C. BEHIND. We left the traffic, the noise, the coming heat and pollution. We left a roach-filled apartment and the acrid marijuana smoke that wafted up from the apartment below us. We left behind the people who accused us of selling out (again) by fleeing to the country and not staying in the city to fight the good fight. To them, that meant staying to fight for the cause of the common man. It did not include working for a big corporation like Xerox. And it definitely didn't include escaping from the reality of city life to the idyllic solitude of the woods. To give up the fight for decent food in the neighborhood Safeway for the chance to grow our own food in the country was the cowardly way out. In short, our move was a betrayal of our civic responsibilities.

Starting in late March, we spent every weekend camping in the woods and getting to know our new land. I named the small stream that ran through the property "Jonathan's Run," after a stuffed panda bear Clarence had given me our first Christmas. We hung a sign by the stream to make the naming official. We worked to clean up and repair the damage caused as the crew made way for the house, septic field and driveway. In early May, the house arrived in two halves on long trucks. Each half was slid onto the foundation and joined. Three weeks after its arrival, the house was ready—except for electricity.

The crew that showed up to start drilling the well brought an old man with them to douse for the best well location. He walked around the woods with a dousing rod made from a forked wooden branch and in short order, the branch pointed down to the ground. That's where they drilled our well—125 feet deep with a five-gallon per minute water flow. I later learned that drilling a well in our area was tricky. We are on a rock shelf that runs from Virginia to Tennessee. Only having to drill 125 feet down and getting a good water flow was next to a miracle, they said. I may have been a little skeptical about that old man with his magic stick as I watched him slowly walk around but he proved to be worth his weight in gold (as they say).

At the end of May, we had a new house, a driveway, a well and a septic field. Too bad we didn't have electric power for our house, well and septic field. To us that didn't matter. We were ready to move in.

Not having power for the first five months proved to be an odd blessing in disguise. We didn't have good power-free survival skills, but after five months of on-the-job training we became quite adept. Actually, all we had to do was walk into a local hardware store to find everything that was needed. We bought a transistor radio, one Coleman camp stove, three kerosene lamps, a gallon of kerosene, two five-gallon water jugs, two cinder blocks, one shovel and a toilet seat.

Each day Clarence hauled ten gallons of water from Xerox for cooking and cleaning. In the early weeks, we washed off in Jonathan's Run. By mid-summer the stream had dried up and Clarence had to haul in extra water. We'd shower in the tub holding a watering can over our heads.

We converted our refrigerator into an ice box. Every night on his way home, Clarence stopped at the 7-Eleven in town and picked up a ten-pound bag of ice. Thanks to the rotating bag of ice in the freezer, we had our ice box. (Clarence did this for five months, usually arriving at the store at 2 A.M. or later. The clerk—the same fellow every night—never made a comment like "Must be one hell of a party." Nor did he ask why Clarence was buying all the ice. We came up with a bunch of responses should curiosity ever overcome this guy, but alas, he remained curiosity-free.)

The shovel, two cinder blocks and toilet seat became our toilet. When needed, we'd grab the shovel, blocks, seat and a roll of toilet paper and head off to the woods in search of the perfect spot. Several times we considered building an outhouse but the guy at the electric company kept telling us that our power lines were only a week or two away. Building a structure seemed like a waste of money and effort. We hauled around our toilet for the full five months we were power free. The routine got old.

Clarence was working the late shift at Xerox and would leave home around 2:30 in the afternoon and return between 2 A.M. and 4 A.M., depending on whether or not he was working overtime. For a large chunk of my day, I was alone. My first order of business was to establish a life on the land. I settled us into our new home and helped the cats adjust to their new life. (It wasn't much of an adjustment for them. They loved living in woods.) Every day I spent a little time walking around the house and appreciating every inch of that place. It felt magical. Everything was new—the walls, the hardwood floors, the windows, the doors, the rooms and the promise of a new functioning kitchen, as soon as we got electricity. After a long journey that began in Upperco, I had a real home.

Each evening before sundown, I prepared the oil lamps, carried in water for the night and cooked a simple dinner for one. I grew to appreciate how much time-consuming work women had to do before the convenience of electricity. At night I read by lamplight, spent time with Fred and Gretel and together we listened to old-time radio programs—*The Lone Ranger, The Shadow, Burns and Allen* and several 1930s detective series.

During the days I worked outside while listening to the Senate Watergate Hearings. On June 18, 1972, *The Washington Post* published an article by Woodward and Bernstein with the headline, "Five Held in Plot to Bug Democratic Offices Here." The story reported that burglars had been arrested inside the offices of the Democratic National Committee in the Watergate office complex in Washington. The two reporters raised questions and suggested connections between Richard Nixon's reelection campaign and the men who were arrested. This set off a string of investigative reporting that lasted for two years as the Watergate story and Nixon's shenanigans were unraveled and revealed. It felt like the country was being run by members of a mafia. I had read each article as they were published. I knew, from my time working at *The Post,* that Katharine Graham, Ben Bradlee and the company attorneys would not have allowed the articles to be published unless they were verified up the yin-yang. There was too much at stake (like losing the newspaper and the company) if what they ran was incorrect. Based on the Woodward and Bernstein articles, I could tell that President Richard Milhous Nixon was heading for impeachment.

By the time we moved out of Washington in 1973, new revelations were still coming out, a number of high-ranking men in the Nixon Administration had been convicted and sent to jail, and all but the diehard Nixon fans knew that the president would be impeached. On May 17, 1973, the Senate Watergate Hearings began. It was the first step towards impeachment and it was a big deal. The hearings were broadcast live during the day on commercial television. At the start, CBS, NBC and ABC covered them simultaneously. Later the coverage was rotated among the three channels, while PBS replayed the hearings at night. I watched the coverage in D.C. from day one, found them riveting and continued listening to it each day in the woods. I clearly remember John Dean's "cancer on the presidency" testimony that began on June 25. It wasn't just what he said that held my attention, it was his voice. His deep, monotone, calm voice with its lawyer-like cadence that gave weight to his exceptional memory for detail and his exacting words. Nixon really was going down. And we hadn't even learned about the Oval Office tapes yet.

(On August 8, 1974, Nixon resigned. The 38 members of the House Judiciary Committee had voted to submit three articles of impeachment to the full House. In a classic Nixon move, he essentially yelled "You can't fire me! I already quit!" just before the vote. His vice president, Gerald Ford, was sworn in the next day. We had a new president and many Americans started breathing again.)

During that first summer, I landscaped around the house with plants that I transplanted from the woods. (Some of the fiddle ferns are still alive and well despite having to listen to the Watergate Hearings.) I tried to prepare areas for flower beds but I didn't know how to prepare soil or how to plant seeds properly. My initial attempts resulted in total failure. Seriously. Not one seed germinated. I thought that if I planted a single seed in one location and then another single seed a foot away, they would germinate and the resulting two plants would have plenty of room to grow. No seeds would be wasted. I had a lot to learn about planting seeds.

It was a quiet existence and I took full advantage of the solitude. There were no houses or neighbors within sight or sound. Rush hour traffic consisted of two cars going down the gravel road at 5:30 in the evening. Maybe a tractor would rumble by in the afternoon. I relaxed in a way I had not experienced since my year in Europe. With the quiet, I began to feel an energy pulsating from the woods. At night the feeling intensified to the point where I was uncomfortable walking in front of a window. Especially during a full moon. Whatever it was didn't feel hostile or creepy, and I didn't fear that I was going to be attacked. I was just surrounded by a strange and strong air of intensity.

As soon as we moved from D.C., I started thinking about different names for our home and land. One of my early choices was "If You Are Here, You Are Lost." Although it had a ring of truth to it, it didn't quite catch the right spirit of the place.

In 1968, I had read a science fiction book by C.S. Lewis titled *Perelandra*. The story focused on a planet named Perelandra, a planet that existed in perfect harmony and balance and had no human habitation. Eventually two men from Earth arrived—one embodied good, the other evil and destruction. The one could see the perfection in the planet and sought to move carefully and in harmony with it. The other was blind to the perfection and sought to alter the planet to his will and benefit, thus adversely affecting the planet's natural balance.

Despite the damage we caused when we moved in, I felt that our woods had not lost its perfection. I was convinced that once we helped the woods repair itself and return to its natural rhythms, perfection would be restored. But Clarence and I possessed the qualities of both men in C.S. Lewis' book. Our goal for living on the land was to move with the woods and not against it. However, most of the time we didn't know what that meant and operated according to our best guess. Because of the inner struggles we were experiencing, struggles similar to the ones described in the book, we named our land "Perelandra."

It was nearly November and the night temperatures were beginning to drop below 40 degrees when we finally got electricity. The holdup had been Danny, the inept employee at the power company who was supposed to get a signed right-of-way from each of the seven people who owned a portion of the woods. (We owned ten acres in a subdivided ninety-acre woods.) We needed their permission in order to bring the power lines down the gravel road because the lines had to cross through their properties. Danny wouldn't/couldn't do this. He also wouldn't/couldn't admit that he wouldn't/couldn't do this. Consequently, the many times he told us (starting in May) that the power lines were on their way and we'd have electricity in a week or two, he was lying. By October our patience had run out. Clarence got the names of the other property owners from Danny and drove to their homes to get their signatures. Once he delivered the signed permissions to the power company, the electric poles started going up and we had electricity in the aforementioned, forever-promised two weeks. We sent a letter complaining about how Danny mishandled everything and, as might be expected, the power company responded by giving him a promotion and "kicking him upstairs."

On the day the power was scheduled for hook up at the house, one of the guys knocked on my door to tell me they would be ready to connect the power in a half hour and that I should turn on one of the lamps to verify that we, indeed, had electricity. Well, in the five months that we lived there, we had managed to flip on most of the lamps and light switches out of habit. When the power finally came on, the entire house lit up, the refrigerator started buzzing and the well pump started. Good thing he told me to turn on the one lamp that I had been staring at for a good half hour. I may have missed the magic moment!

Our five-month off-the-grid experience got us over our city-folk concerns about living in the middle of nowhere without power. And we no longer had any rosy, idealistic urges to embrace the pioneer, back-to-the-land lifestyle of the 19th century. In 1973, E.F. Schumacher came out with a book titled *Small Is Beautiful: A Study of Economics as If People Mattered.* His phrase "Small is Beautiful" was used to champion small, appropriate technologies that were believed to empower people more, in contrast to the "bigger is better" technologies and lifestyle. For us, a simple, small lifestyle included the concept of appropriate technology. A little bit of electricity felt appropriate.

We were settled, we had electricity and apparently it was time to expand our family. We were joined by Jesse, an abandoned puppy who was very happy to meet some friendly people. She was one of three puppies and clearly the ringleader. I noticed her prancing about on our front lawn one afternoon. When I went outside, she insisted I follow her to the back of the house. Once there she barked and her two brothers, who had been hiding, came running out. For the next two days, we checked around for possible owners. No luck. We took her brothers to a local animal shelter to be adopted and officially invited Jesse to be part of our family. It was an unnecessary gesture on our part. After two days, Jesse had adopted us and was settled in. At first, the cats were curious, but not especially pleased.

According to our mailing address, we lived in Jeffersonton a town that was platted in 1798 and named for Thomas Jefferson. (They say that Jefferson rode through the town often on his way to Monticello, his home just outside Charlottesville. He would stop and baptize the town's children at a well located near the Methodist Church.) We were over five miles from downtown Jeffersonton and, if we moved our mailbox to the opposite side of the gravel road, we would have been living in Remington, Virginia. Our mailing address hinged on the post of our mailbox.

When I say "town of Jeffersonton" I use the word "town" loosely. When we moved there, the town center consisted of one small country store, a post office that was located in the country store, a brick one-room school house that was being renovated as a residence, a Baptist Church at one end and a Methodist Church and community center at the other end. I was told that at one time there were small shops lining both sides of the road but they had long since been taken down by the time we got there. The only remaining commerce was the country store. (Several years after our arrival, the store's owner was arrested for arson. He set the store on fire in an effort to collect insurance money. In the process, he nearly killed his wife and child who were sleeping in the back room at the time and needed to be rescued. All that remains of the store now is remnants of its old stone foundation and porch steps.)

We had three neighbors living down our road. Dottie, a single mother in her early 50s, lived with her two teenage children in an old farm house on thirty-five acres next to the woods. She was, shall we say, unique. She had a small collection of horses, cows and geese that frequently busted through her old fences and roamed around the neighborhood. Those of us who lived around her often had to return the escapees to her. She drove a school bus for the county and would use the bus to round up her animals and herd them back to her barn. So there she'd be, rumbling across the field in an empty school bus. Every time she stopped, the flashing red warning lights would go on and the "Stop" sign would swivel out. I always thought I was watching some bizarre Fellini movie when I saw her on a roundup.

Fred and Frances Garrison had a 125-acre farm just up the road from us. They had lived in their home their entire long marriage. In fact, the home had belonged to Frances' parents and she had been born there. Her two grown sons had been born in the same bed in that home. Fred and Frances were warm, friendly and quick to include us in their social gatherings. Each fall when they burned the huge brush pile they had been building over the year, friends and neighbors were invited to join them around the huge bonfire for homemade ice cream, singing (Fred played a mean fiddle) and pony-and-cart rides. They were easy to be around and generous with their offers to help us.

The Myers family lived directly opposite us (in Remington!) on a 350-acre cattle farm. They were an old German farming family of siblings: two sisters (Frances and Elizabeth) and three brothers (John, Nelson and Bernard). There was a fourth brother, Everett, but he was the black sheep in the family and no longer lived on the farm. His sin? He got married at age 54 and moved away, so they all stopped talking to him for a while. Their mother was still alive but she was an invalid requiring full home care, which they provided. Their father had died just before World War II. These are the neighbors I came to know the most. As a family, they were, shall we say...unique. When people asked us where we lived, we would tell them and they would respond, "Ah, yes. Next to the old weird Myers."

Their day started around 4 A.M., just as Clarence was arriving home from Xerox. They never changed their clocks for daylight savings time because, as they said, cows can't tell time. Each sibling (minus Everett) had specific, well-defined jobs. Elizabeth did most of the cooking—on a wood stove. Frances was the main gardener (they had a one-acre garden), helped with meals and answered the phone. (Elizabeth never answered the phone.) Frances and Elizabeth teamed up to do the canning. The "boys," as Frances and Elizabeth called them, divided up the farm chores. John, the eldest, was looked to as the leader and tended to be the one to make final decisions. Bernard took care of the vehicles and was the one who drove—very slowly. We always knew when we were following the Myers down the road. I don't believe Bernard ever shifted that car out of second gear. (John once told me that he stopped driving when Ford stopped making the Model T with the crank start. According to John, that was the best car ever made.) Nelson worked around the farm with the other two and was the family story teller. He had each minute detail of their stories neatly tucked away in his memory. When he started to tell a story, I knew we had to settle in for an hour or more. There was the time a ball of lightning came down the chimney, rolled across the living room and exited the open window on the other side of the room. He knew the date, the time and the path the lightning took as it rolled across the room. Clarence and I learned not to interrupt to ask a question. Once interrupted, they would answer the question, then Nelson would start the story over again—from the beginning.

Most of the time the three boys worked the farm together as a team. By the time we met them, they were up in years with ages ranging from the upper sixties to eighty. They had lived on the 350 acres across from us since 1912. They also tended 700 acres at the end of the road that bordered along the Rappahannock River. These three elderly men took care of about 300 head of cattle and 1,050 acres. (At times they made us feel like slackers as we worked to tend our ten acres.) Their farm, fences and outbuildings were well maintained. The sisters kept an immaculate house. Part of our getting to know the Myers was learning how they managed to do everything. Watching the boys unload 150 bales of hay off a wagon was like watching a team of three finely tuned, perfectly coordinated sloths. Every movement was in slow motion but perfectly timed and in sync with one another. Not one movement was wasted. The result was extraordinary efficiency without physical exhaustion or strain.

I looked at the Myers' farm as an antique repository that was stuck in time. They kept everything—just in case they might need it at a future date. They had all of their old wooden wagon wheels and leather harnesses neatly stored in one of the barns. They kept all the twine cut from each hay bale in large, tightly wrapped bundles that they hung on hooks in the barn. They had fifty-year-old cotton flour sacks folded and stored in a drawer in the kitchen. During World War II, the flour-sack material was used to make shirts, blouses, dresses and dish towels. They had the butter churning paddle that their father whittled from a chestnut tree in 1912 and gifted to their mother for their anniversary. When they found out that Clarence had an interest in photography, they gave him an old Kodak camera that was still in its original box.

They had gotten electricity in 1963, because their mother had become more incapacitated and having electricity would help them care for her. But they kept all their oil lamps and still used their wood cook stove daily. With electricity, they added running water, flush toilets and bought a blender for preparing food for their mother. They also had a television but the only things they watched each night were the weather report and one 15-minute nightly news program.

They canned all their own vegetables and neatly stored a two-year supply of quart jars on metal shelving in the basement that would outdo any Safeway in quantity and variety. They froze enough meat, poultry and fish for the year and kept it in large freezers in an outbuilding. If I remember correctly, the only things they purchased at the grocery store were sugar and flour. Each spring they fished at a spot close to where the Rappahannock River flowed into the Chesapeake Bay. They strung nets across the river and, according to Frances, it usually only took them just two or three days to catch enough fish to feed the five of them for the year. They had a hen house and fenced chicken yard for the chickens for eggs for the family and to sell to several country stores in the area. Once a year they killed chickens for the family freezer and spread the throwaway parts along the fence line that I had to walk by to get to their house. With the thirty or more vultures sitting on the fence after their feast, I felt like I was walking in an Edgar Allen Poe story. As I walked by, I'd say quietly, "Nevermore."

They ate the same food every day. They had fish for breakfast, meat and poultry for lunch, and meat (including groundhog) for dinner. Each meal was accompanied with cornbread and its own array of vegetables, which never changed. The only change in the daily menus occurred on Christmas Day. In honor of the special day, the sisters creamed the corn and Frances made a coconut cake that was the best cake, coconut or otherwise, I have ever tasted. Don't forget, she baked it in a wood stove. Maybe that was the secret to its perfection. A number of times I thought about inviting them to dinner at our place but always stopped myself. I was afraid that any change in their diet might kill them.

It is fair to say that the Myers took us under their wing. To them we were city folk and, without their attention and assistance, we might end up killing ourselves. (I was smart enough not to argue with them about that assessment.) I spent many late afternoons in the summer sitting with them on their porch, shelling peas, snapping beans and listening to Nelson's stories. Frances taught me how to make sweet pickles using their family's 125-year-old recipe. (She started her lesson at 7 A.M., an hour that I thought was uncivilized but she was already halfway through her morning.) They didn't do any decorating for Christmas, so we cut a small cedar tree from our woods and decorated it to give them a little touch of Christmas. It was clear from their reaction that they were moved by the gesture and invited us to join them for Christmas dinner. (That's how I knew about the creamed corn and coconut cake.) That spring, Frances gave me a rooted cutting from their fifty-year-old Christmas cactus. It's been forty-five years since I received her gift, making the combined age of the large houseplant that currently sits in my house close to 100 years old.

So why did everyone refer to these people as the "old, weird Myers," you ask? This is the best answer I can give you about that. They were different. They didn't join in social activities with the rest of the community. They did not have community bonfires or play instruments for singalongs. They belonged to the Baptist Church and attended services every Sunday (unless something needed attending to on the farm). But they returned home immediately after the service ended. They didn't stay for coffee hour afterwards. There wasn't time for socializing. Or marrying. Or having children. (Everett was the rebel.) Or anything else that was considered part of a "normal" life by the rest of the community. Consequently, they were considered outcasts and called "weird."

The x factor in all this was their father. He had been a hard-working, no-nonsense German who had instilled nonstop work habits in his children. In turn, his children deeply respected him and spoke well of him when I met them twenty-five years after the father had died. But in listening to others in the community, it was clear that he had rubbed people the wrong way and had ignited a few feuds along the way. Whatever he had done and whatever feelings the interactions between Mr. Myers and the rest of the community had inspired had been passed down to the next generation and lived on.

A perfect example of this was the Myers and the Garrisons. They lived next door to one another their whole lives and had gone to school together. But they had an ongoing feud that began with their respective fathers. I don't know what the original feud between the two fathers was about and I'm not certain the siblings remembered any specifics. (Nelson probably had the story cataloged in detail in his head.) Most of the time the best the two families could do was not talk about one another at all. By the time I stepped into the picture, a lot of their mutual feelings seemed to revolve around fences. All the Garrison fence lines were lined with large beautiful cedar trees. Fred told me he considered the trees a cash crop and took care to thin them out over the years so that they could grow properly. The Myers fence lines were clean, so clean they looked…well, Germanic. They believed the Garrison fence lines were poorly tended and an eye sore. They didn't appreciate the beauty of the cedar trees and considered them impractical. The Garrisons considered the Myers fence lines bare, sterile and devoid of beauty.

These two families could not have been nicer and more giving to us. They each had heart. But their styles for expressing their hearts were different. Where the Garrisons were gracious, warm and open to all, the Myers were a closed, protective family who were fiercely loyal and protective of one another and who reached out to others sparingly. The Garrisons were relaxed, trusting and well liked in the community. The Myers were cautious and fearful. They lived a tightly closed, self-sufficient life that reflected their concerns about and their anticipation of some major uprising of the poor (read blacks) in Washington. They were convinced that someday hordes of poor (read black) people would rampage the farm, steal all their food and ravage the land, leaving nothing but cattle carcasses and smoldering buildings. They were secretive about the food they had stored until they trusted the person. (Hell, they were secretive about having all those wooden wagon wheels and bundles of bailing twine.) The outbuilding with their six large freezers had double locks on the door. Their primary driveway had three gates you had to go through to get to the house. Everything was set up to suggest that strangers and the uninvited were not welcome. Yet once I was invited to their house and walked onto their land, I felt an air of peace and calm surround me. How they felt about the outside world was one thing, but the gentle environment they had created on their land and in their home was something different.

By the winter, I felt it was time for me to reach out to the rest of the community. I learned about a women's group that met each month at the Jeffersonton Community Center. That seemed like a good place to start.

I tried to join in but, to be honest, I nearly died of boredom. The first meeting I attended included a two-hour tutorial on flower arranging. I tried mightily to care but I didn't give a damn about flower arranging. (My preferred method: Stick the flowers in a vase, walk away and hope for the best.) The next couple of meetings were equally boring so I stopped attending. At least I got to meet some of my fellow Jeffersontonians.

Early one morning in the spring of '74, just when I was beginning to feel life and its rhythms were settling in around me nicely, something mysterious and alarming happened. I awoke to the sound of voices. Many voices shouted and called at me. Not *to* me but *at* me. There was no one in the bedroom except Clarence, who was sound asleep and showing no signs of being disturbed by a noisy crowd. I saw nothing that could account for the sounds. But what I was hearing was clear, strong and fairly loud, as if ten people were standing in the bedroom trying to get my attention. This went on for about fifteen minutes. Then there was silence.

Frankly, I was scared. Ever since I left Upperco, I had expected that someday I might lose my mind as a result of the pressures I dealt with growing up. But I didn't expect it to happen when things were going so well for me. Why now? I said nothing to Clarence about the voices, hoping that I'd never hear them again.

The next morning, the noisy voices happened again. There were no distinguishable words. Just a calling out as if trying to get my attention. I didn't feel threatened but I felt confused and scared. Still I said nothing to Clarence. I needed time to figure out how I was going to tell him that I would have to be institutionalized.

The third morning. Voices again. I was still concerned but now I was starting to get annoyed. Who the hell were these people and what did they want? And what were they doing in my bedroom? Was this going to be a morning ritual for the rest of my life? I couldn't figure out how Clarence was able to sleep through all that racket. Gretel was curled up on the bed and also showing no signs of hearing any noise. And Jesse, who barked at anyone who came to the door, was quiet. I had to face the fact that I was the only one hearing the voices. Damn. How disappointing.

Obviously, I was disintegrating fast and needed to give Clarence a heads up about my situation. He listened carefully while I explained what was happening and then, without missing a beat, he quoted a letter from the New Testament from St. Paul to the early Christians. Apparently, the early Christians had heard voices and questioned whether or not they were going insane. (I could feel their pain.) St. Paul's letter was assuring them that the voices they heard were of the Spirit and they were not to be afraid. (Easy for him to say.)

Well, I'm not a fan of St. Paul—not after some of his writings about the role of women. But when Clarence quoted the letter to me, I could feel that his words applied to me as well. I couldn't understand the stuff about the voice of the Spirit, but I paid attention to Paul telling these people that they weren't losing their minds. (Okay. Paul says I'm not crazy. I was willing to grasp at any straw.)

Clarence showed no concern about the voices. My declaration of insanity was being rejected, and I was going to have to deal with the voices from another perspective. He suggested that I meditate. I just looked at him thinking, "What a dumb suggestion. What was meditation going to give me?"

I'm not sure why he suggested this. It was something we had heard about but neither one of us practiced it. The only time I had heard the word "meditation" in reference to myself was two and a half years earlier, when Peggy Townsend suggested I learn to meditate. I didn't know what she was talking about then either, so I shoved it aside. Now Clarence was suggesting that meditation might be the way to find out what the voices meant.

I didn't have time to take a course on meditation or do a bunch of reading about it. I was going to have to wing it and see where it led. That afternoon, I went into the bedroom determined to meditate—whatever that meant. As soon as I closed the bedroom door, I heard one voice. (What is it with these people in our bedroom?) The voice told me to lay on the floor. I figured I had nothing to lose so I stretched out on the floor. Then the voice told me to relax. I relaxed the best I knew how. To be honest, unless a person has received training and knows what to do, they are pretty lost when first told to relax. But in the bedroom that afternoon, I gave it my best shot.

After about ten minutes, I was starting to drift off to sleep and thought, "Is this it? Is this meditation? Don't we normally call this napping?" The voice told me to relax my mind the way I did when I was a child and had wanted to "fantasize." Ah-ha! I knew exactly what the voice was referring to. I shut my eyes and repeated what I had done many times as a child. I relaxed my eyes and allowed whatever static I was seeing and feeling in my head behind my eyes smooth out and soften. In short order, I felt the familiar sensation of my body lifting and, at a particular point, I gently fell off a ledge into space. With that, the voice said that this experience was a form of meditation. What a pleasant surprise. Unbeknownst to me, I already had years of practice in meditation behind me. I was in familiar territory now and I felt comforted.

I was then instructed to recreate one of my childhood fantasies. I recalled a particular island I used to "go to" and, in a flash, I was once again experiencing that island, actually feeling the sand beneath my feet, hearing the ocean waves, feeling the breeze and smelling the sea air. After leaving Upperco, I didn't have time to indulge in these kinds of experiences. Life got too busy. Now it felt like I was returning to an old friend.

When I pulled myself away from the island and continued floating in space, the "voice" explained to me that it was important that I spend a portion of each day in meditation, that meditation wasn't just floating in space. It had numerous facets that were open to me, if I wished to learn them. All I had to do was say that I wanted to learn, ask for the help and get into the same quiet, relaxed state. When I thought about the gaggle of voices I had heard in the bedroom, the voice said, as if reading my mind, that I had not been responding to the more subtle hints, like the heightened woods energy I had been feeling, and I was being given something more obvious that could point me to meditation. A shouting gaggle of bedroom invaders seemed a bit over the top, but apparently I had a thick skull.

The "voice" stopped. I waited for it to say something else, but nothing came. So I said aloud, "I want to continue and to learn, and I ask for help." There was no reply and I wasn't sure if I had been heard.

The second day, I got into my version of a relaxed state, slipped over the ledge into space—and there was nothing. No voice. No island. Just space. That was puzzling—and disappointing—but at least I enjoyed floating around for a while.

The third day, I slipped over the ledge, only this time the space felt different. It felt like I had gone to a higher ledge before slipping over. Instead of empty space, I saw a small, wooden, one-room building with a window. I looked through the window and saw a group of people so out of focus that I could only make out that they were human. They were seated around a wooden table and sharing a meal. I remained outside the room watching through the window. Suddenly, I realized that I had come home—my real home—and these people were my real family. I didn't know who they were or where this place was but I knew, without a doubt, that this was my home.

A wave of homesickness and longing washed over me. I had a strong desire to walk into the room, join those people around that table and stay. Then I realized that I had left home to experience life on Earth and these people, my family, had supported my decision. Even though I didn't consciously know why I had made that difficult decision, I knew it was a sound decision.

My family turned to me, acknowledging my presence outside the window. Then something remarkable happened. They projected a huge energy wave of love to me. It was like one of those monster waves surfers always wish for. The wave rose high above me, then crested right over my head. The love-infused "water" cascaded down and washed through me with force. It was exhilarating. Acting on instinct, I added my love as an energy to the wave. Using intent and focus, I projected the wave back to them. It crested over their heads, cascaded down and washed through my family. Then they directed it back to me. After it cascaded over me, I added my love again and sent the wave back to them. This back-and-forth action was powerful and smooth, and the wave felt both exciting and comforting as it moved through me. I was surprised that I knew how to participate in such a powerful action. As we continued, the intensity of the wave kept increasing and I could feel pressure building in my body. Eventually it felt overpowering and I couldn't take any more. I was afraid I might explode, literally, and I began to sob.

It took perhaps another half hour for me to release from this experience and pull out of meditation. I felt rattled, confused and overwhelmed, and I couldn't stop crying. At Perelandra, a powerful thunderstorm had begun while I was in meditation and was now raging. The lightning and thunder cracked right over the house. I lay on the floor listening and thinking about what had just happened. I knew I had experienced my life not from the vantage point of Earth but from outside Earth. I now had an entirely different perspective about myself, my home and family. But I didn't know what to do with the experience, what it meant or why I made the decision to leave my home.

I continued through my day at Perelandra feeling fragile and like I had experienced something momentous as my normal day-to-day life swirled around me like nothing had happened. I remember walking down the driveway to get the mail and thinking that this must be what it's like on the day a close loved one dies and still the mailman, unaware of what has happened, delivers the mail as usual.

The fourth day, I returned to the bedroom, but this time I was more than a little nervous. Although the experience of going home was deep, I was frightened by its intensity and concerned about my ability to experience and deal with such strong intensity. My overriding question: Was I going to be able to survive meditation? When I slipped over the ledge, I once again asked for help.

Immediately, I saw a beautiful arched stone bridge. It was old and the large grey stones were weathered. I walked onto the bridge, leaned my elbows on the side wall and watched the river flow by. After a few minutes, I felt a presence next to me. I turned my attention to my left and saw a monk dressed in a long, brown, medieval-looking hooded robe. He was leaning on the wall and looking at the river also. He didn't say anything; he didn't even look at me. But I felt safe next to him and calmed by his presence.

We never did introduce ourselves to one another. I felt we didn't need to. I could tell he knew me and even though I didn't know his name, who he was or where he came from, I felt a warm friendship emanating from him. He never spoke out loud. I, on the other hand, spoke out loud to him. We laughed together—he even enjoyed my wise cracks.

Every time I saw him we started out by leaning our elbows on the bridge and watching the water flow by. Without speaking or looking at me, he began to gently transmit simple information and instructions. It was as if he transmitted his thoughts directly into my mind and I would suddenly have access to a body of information that was now present and a part of me. It was a gentle, quiet process. One moment I didn't know something and the next moment I understood something new.

He started by giving me the beginner's basics about meditation and I knew that this was the person who was going to help me, to be my teacher. He was going to teach me how to survive meditation. We met on the bridge each day for the next two years.

The monk said that at the beginning of every lesson, I was to clear my mind. At first I didn't know how to accomplish this and simply gave it my best shot. The monk observed a couple of my attempts, then took over. We spent months on the concept of word energy and how to clear my mind of thoughts and emotions. I saw how what I had assumed were subtle, harmless words could create distress and disturbance if I didn't "clear them out." I learned that it wasn't the word itself that was the problem, it was the intent behind the word. (It's the difference between saying, "Those Ikea instructions are a bitch to understand," and "Get out of my way, you bitch." The first bitch is harmless (yet accurate in its intent). The second bitch packs a wallop because of its intent.)

He had me identify a thought or emotion that was floating around in my mind, then pull from my head a word that described or was connected to the thought or emotion. I'd see the physical word, grasp it (using focus) and gently pull it out of my head. Then he instructed me to wrap it in brown paper, carefully tie string around the packet and throw the packet into the stream. Each time

I watched the packet float downstream and out of sight. Taking the time to watch the packet float away slowed down the process, but I understood that taking that time and watching the word disappear downstream was an important step for successfully clearing my mind. Once the packet was gone, I'd turn my attention back to my mind, remove another word and go through the same routine. After tossing away each word packet I could feel my head lighten, the static in my mind decrease and my brain waves smooth out. Finally, as the last word floated away, I felt the relief of a freed mind. With practice, I became more efficient at identifying the thoughts and emotions and finding the words connected to them floating around in my head. Sometimes the words were slippery little buggers that took a little time and patience to "capture" them, or I'd find them tucked away in the crevices of my brain.

We spent time on the "art" of coming out of meditation carefully so that I would experience a gentle touch down. He taught me how to protect myself from outside intrusions such as a phone ringing, the dog barking, someone walking into the house or knocking on the door. When intrusions occurred, it felt as if I had been tossed out of an airplane and was in a dead weight free fall. I'd hit "land" hard and end up feeling lightheaded and nauseous from the trip. I was shown how to quickly create an energy pillow beneath my body the moment an intrusion occurred to cushion the sensation of falling and soften the landing.

At one point, the monk explained that while in meditation, a person could request that they perform a service for someone in need. One day I decided to try it and requested to use my meditation time "in service." Immediately I found myself walking down an aisle on a train in Yugoslavia. There was no indication from any of the passengers that they saw me. The monk told me there was an Eastern Orthodox priest on the train and once I located him, I was to share my Going Home experience with him. I found the priest quietly sitting alone next to a window. I created a ball that contained the energy of my entire Going Home experience. (As I recalled the experience, I moved the energy of each recollection into the ball.) Using one of the techniques the monk had taught me about moving energy, I rolled the ball from my mind to the priest's. I watched the ball disappear (as if absorbed) into his head. Mission accomplished. Then I left. The monk explained that the priest had been in despair over his life, that the train was going to crash and that he might die. Had he died in that state of despair, he would have had difficulty moving through his death process. When I placed my Going Home experience into his mind, he was able to experience it and release his despair before death.

The next day at Perelandra, I was leafing through the newspaper and saw a tiny article in the back pages about an express train bound for West Germany that had crashed in Yugoslavia near Zagreb the night before, killing over 100 people and injuring another 150.

Another time I was standing in a crowd observing a large protest march in Liberia. Again, no one indicated that they were aware of my presence. As I watched the black protesters march by chanting, the white military showed up in full force and opened fire on the marchers. There was panic and screaming all around me. Protesters and bystanders were mowed down and lay dead or dying everywhere I looked. It was a massacre. One man who had been marching directly in front of me when the shooting began was now bleeding and falling to the ground. As he fell, he looked directly at me. He could see me. His face was bloodied and contorted from the pain, and there was shock and horror in his eyes. His body hit the ground hard.

Then I watched the scene play out before my eyes again—from the start to the man's body slamming against the ground. Each time his body hit the ground, the scene repeated, as if on an endless loop.

The monk told me that the protesters who had been killed had not released themselves from the massacre and were in a kind of limbo, reliving the horror over and over and over. Together, they were recreating the scene that I was watching. The man in front of me had been a respected tribal leader. No one was going to let go unless he let go first. The monk told me what I was to do. I reached out to the man and gently placed my hand on his arm to calm him as he fell to the ground. Then I knelt beside him and calmly and softly told him that he had died. That they had all been massacred. They all needed to let go and continue moving through their death process. They would be fine, once they moved on. The horror would end once they let go. With as calm a voice as possible, I kept repeating the information to this man, this leader. I don't know how long it took, but eventually the massacre stopped repeating. I stayed with the leader holding his hand until he completed his death process and was drifting away. As he drifted out of sight, the others followed.

The monk said that these service experiences were accomplished through a form of astral traveling—meditation that allows us to transcend time, space and location. I found this type of service deeply rewarding and for several months I requested to be of service every time I meditated. Each experience was different, but mostly they had something to do with the death process. I was learning a lot about the unseen complex activity and assistance that goes on around us all the time.

One day I decided to stop. As valid and rewarding as this work was, I could feel that it was not what I was supposed to be doing as a lifetime job. It was time to move on. But years later, I passed it forward. I developed the *Post-Death Process* for anyone who wishes to assist a friend, loved one or acquaintance through their death process. It includes in its foundation and steps the lessons and insights I learned from the monk on the bridge and from those months of experiences.

After telling the monk that I wanted to move on, I felt a change in my meditation. It was as if I was rising in an elevator that was moving through different levels of form or reality. Each level felt well beyond anything I had experienced up to that time. At the "top floor" I gently tipped over the edge and stayed there for about an hour. I only know this because I had the habit of checking the clock at the beginning of my meditation and again when I touched down and was ready to resume my day.

Later, the monk explained that I had entered a state of being that many on Earth refer to as "Void." Another way to call this state is "Oneness." "State of being" is probably the best way to describe what happened, because in Void I experienced nothing.

That's the point. It's a void. There was no experience to be had. There was no movement, no sound, no light, nothing to see. There were no forms or colors, not even black or darkness. There was no awareness, no thought, no emotion, no mental process, no words. There was nothing with which to engage my sensory system. I was no longer aware of or able to feel my body. I was no longer aware of my own existence. Zen refers to Void as "No Thing" and that's exactly what it is, no thing.

I never knew I was in Void until after I came out of it and reflected on what had happened—or not happened. People who write about Void can get pretty schmaltzy about the experience. In their books, they wax eloquent about the joys of Oneness. Maybe it's because I tend to be pragmatic but I don't see how anyone can spend time (actually there is no time in Oneness) in that state and then go on for page after page describing in flowery terms what Void is. How in the world can you describe a void and complete nothingness? I can only say what it isn't.

Every afternoon for about six months, my meditation consisted of riding the elevator through the different levels to the top floor and tipping over the edge into Void. I didn't know why I was experiencing this. To be honest (and sacrilegious), after spending my meditation time in service, I found Void boring. But I trusted the monk, I believed he knew what he was doing and I was determined to continue moving forward. At the end of the six months, I had a deep appreciation for what I had not experienced in Void: differentiation. I missed the joy of seeing the multitude of individual things that made up the world around me. I was happy to move on.

I'd like to be able to tell you that on this day the monk taught me X and on that day the monk taught me Y and on another day the monk taught me Z. But generally speaking this isn't how he worked with me. When he moved information and insight to me, I didn't experience a linear A leading to B leading to C thought progression from him. Instead he transmitted a "package" containing a body of information all at one time. Later, as I continued my day, I'd find myself thinking and moving differently. I knew the changes were due to my automatically accessing that package and drawing on the monk's lesson of the day.

Here's what I can say about the monk's lessons:

- The *average* life of a human being is much more expansive than we commonly accept and expect.
- With a little training, we can reach beyond the self-imposed box that has been created by our assumptions and expectations, and broaden our understanding and experience about life. We like to think this kind of expansion is only for the "special" among us. In truth, seeking to reach beyond the box is a normal component of human life. It's what we call "evolution." We just need to understand that stretching beyond our box may require new skills, training and practice to move forward *comfortably.*
- Things are happening around us and beyond our five senses all the time.
- Differentiation is wonderful.
- There definitely is life beyond death.
- There is no such thing as "afterlife." The life we experience after death is simply a continuation of our life.

One afternoon in the fall of 1976, the monk looked directly at me for the first time and I knew that the lessons had ended. It was time for me to move on—again. The monk, our bridge and our afternoons together hold a special place in my mind and heart. To say that I am grateful to him is an understatement. Although we have not met up again on the bridge, the monk lives on. I haven't been keeping what he taught me to myself. As with the *Post-Death Process,* what I learned from him is embedded in the different process steps, insights and information I've developed through my continuing work at Perelandra.

As I moved into this new world with the monk, my connection with the Catholic Church became more distant, more nebulous. The Church's attitude and teachings were not supportive of what I was experiencing (remember how the priests received Peggy Townsend) and what I was experiencing had more vital reality than anything the Church was offering me. Having found that the essence of truth was within myself meant that I no longer needed or wanted the clergy or the Church to act as middleman.

What finally kicked me into action came from the Church itself. A bill had been introduced in the New York State legislature that would guarantee certain civil rights for the homosexual community. With this bill, homosexuals would be protected from discrimination in housing and employment. The New York Catholic Archdiocese lobbied and campaigned hard and openly against this bill and was largely responsible for the bill's defeat.

Perhaps it was because of my post-Upperco childhood, but I felt strongly (and still do) that everyone should have the right to housing and a job. And while we're at it, throw in food, education and health care. At least this New York bill covered housing and employment. It was a start. I could not believe that the New York diocese was on a tear to prevent these people from receiving their basic human rights. And no other diocese in the country was stepping in to disagree with the New York position. I found the situation both sad and deeply embarrassing. And I was outraged. As far as I was concerned, the Church had crossed the line. I realized that if I remained a member of the Catholic Church I would be tacitly accepting the Church's position.

On June 12, 1974, I wrote to Pope Paul VI to inform him that I was resigning from the Catholic Church. I included my reasons and stated that I could not, in all conscience, belong to an organization that sought to deny human rights to anyone. The Catholic Church was too embarrassing for me to remain a part of and I tendered my resignation effective immediately.

Of course, we all know the Church and the Pope could not have cared less about my little letter and it probably ended up in some Vatican trash basket. But it was important for me to write my intent and formally cut ties. I had entered the Church (via baptism) with an act of clarity and intent, and now I felt I needed to leave the Church with an equal act of clarity and intent.

As soon as I signed the letter, I fell into a meditative state that lasted twenty-four hours. At first, I saw myself floating in space with my oxygen cord tethered to a spacecraft. Then the cord was cut and I was still breathing and free-floating. That was where I remained for twenty-four hours, gently free-floating in space. I experienced two strong, clear emotions. One was related to freedom. Now that the cord had been cut, I was free to move about in any direction. It was as if the whole universe was suddenly mine to explore. Nothing was beyond my reach, and it felt invigorating. The second involved responsibility. I was struck with the heavy realization that from this point on and for the rest of my life, determining and doing the right thing was entirely up to me and totally my responsibility. There was no structure or institution in my life to fall back on or to provide guidance. By the end of the twenty-four hours, I had fully accepted both my new freedom and my new responsibility.

IN 1974, I DECIDED to start a vegetable garden. I was convinced that somewhere in some dusty old government archives, there was an edict that stated that if a person owned property, that person was required to put in a vegetable garden. The Garrisons had a garden. The Myers had a monster one-acre garden. Even nutty Dottie had a garden. Everywhere I looked I saw vegetable gardens. Despite my earlier failure at planting flower seeds, I decided it was my turn to join the Jeffersonton garden movement.

The Myers took over my education from the start. They weren't about to leave me on my own. The boys gave a tutorial on tilling and loaned us their tiller to break ground. Frances showed me how to plant and, just as importantly, how to thin after the seeds germinated. (When I told her about how I had spaced out the flower seeds the previous summer, she rolled her eyes.) She steered me to charts that told me what to plant and when for our area. And she gave me the all-important class on properly using the insecticide Sevin®. (If you are a non-conventional gardener, you are now probably hyperventilating just from reading the word "Sevin®." Take a moment to catch your breath. It gets better.)

My first garden was a miniaturized reflection of the Myers garden. Where theirs covered one acre in a nearby field, mine was 30x50 feet and located close to our kitchen door. (It was a kitchen garden. Where the hell else would I put a kitchen garden besides close to the kitchen?) The rows were straight, thanks to the trick Frances showed me using string to mark the rows. Of course I fertilized using the commercial fertilizers Frances and the boys recommended. But you know what? With the Myers pointing me in the "right" direction, I had a lot of success that first year. To my surprise, seeds germinated, plants grew and we had plenty of vegetables. In late summer, Frances taught me the fine art of canning.

In the spring, I got the garden ready for the new season by repeating what I had done the previous year. Why argue with success? Everything was moving along just fine until I spotted the first signs of insect activity on my plants. This was the signal to leap into action with Sevin®. Just before spreading it I sat down in the garden and read the information on the back of the Sevin® bag. Because Frances had shown me how to use Sevin® the previous year, I didn't think I needed to read all that information then. Now I wondered what it said.

Here are the key points that jumped out and grabbed me by the throat:

- Sevin® kills over 100 insect pests.
- Use outdoors only.
- When applying as a wet spray, keep treated areas clear of people and pets until the spray dries.
- When spraying large areas, start at the farthest point and work back to avoid contact with the wet spray or dust.
- When applying as a spray or dust, wear rubber gloves, a face mask, long sleeves and long pants.
- Follow the recommended pre-harvest intervals (PHI) for treating edible crops.

  1 day PHI for asparagus

    (Translation: After application, wait 1 day before harvesting and eating asparagus.)

  3 days PHI for tomatoes and peppers

  7 days PHI for Irish potatoes

  14 days PHI for turnip and mustard greens

There was nothing in this information that made Sevin® sound even remotely safe. Actually, it screamed, *Toxic! Don't touch it and don't eat these vegetables!*

What really alarmed me was the PHI list, which was more extensive than the examples I listed above. If I can't eat a tomato for three days after dusting with Sevin®, who is to say that tomato is safe for consumption on the fourth day? What determined the line between unsafe and safe? And if I can't safely eat a tomato on day two after dusting, what happens when a bird or frog eats a Sevin®-killed insect on day two or a rabbit nibbles on a Sevin®-dusted spinach leaf on day ten? Do they die as well? By killing over 100 insect "pests," what kind of damage was I doing to the wildlife and to their natural food chain?

I stood up, walked out of the garden with the bag of Sevin® and tossed it in the trash can. That was the end of my gardening with Sevin®. But I still had the insect issue to deal with. If I wasn't going to use commercial insecticide, then the next obvious step was organic gardening.

Knowing nothing, I dove into the world of organic gardening right away and read as much information as I could find, which was considerable. In 1975, organic gardening was starting to be considered a legitimate practice among gardeners, thanks, in large part, to the Rodale Institute and its monthly magazine, *Organic Gardening.* I subscribed to the magazine two days after tossing out the Sevin®.

ORGANIC GARDENING CERTAINLY addressed my concerns about using commercial insecticides. Its focus on soil also raised questions about using commercial fertilizers. Building healthy soil as the key to better quality food made all the sense in the world to me. If I accepted that eating quality food had a beneficial impact on my body and health, why wouldn't the same principle hold true about healthy soil resulting in healthy plants?

But organic gardening also includes a huge array of hints, tips, ideas and practices—some of which, when tried, work and some of which don't. Reading volumes on organic gardening in an effort to find the magical combination of practices that would give me a strong, successful garden made me feel that not only would I not reach a respectable level of gardening until age eighty-five, but that I had no right to expect it before eighty-five. I was going to have to put in my time like everyone else.

Even though I was in the middle of the growing season, I worked with my soil first by adding organic matter between the rows to feed it. I read Ruth Stout's book *How to Have a Green Thumb Without an Aching Back: A New Method of Mulch Gardening* and began mulch gardening (covering the soil with 6–8 inches of hay or straw) to preserve moisture, cut down on weeds and provide continuous, gentle fertilizing from the decomposing mulch. The Myers and the Garrisons kept me supplied with bales of old hay.

The avalanche of information overwhelmed me and I needed to get organized. I set up folders for each vegetable I grew in my garden and filed all the articles I ran across pertaining to that vegetable. If my yellow squash plants were suddenly hosting a horde of squash bugs, I pulled out the yellow squash folder, looked at the articles on squash bugs and chose the remedy that seemed right for my garden. I kept doing that until I found something that worked. It was a crapshoot.

It quickly became clear that by making the switch to organic gardening, I gave up the simplicity of a conventional garden. If there was a bug problem, apply Sevin®. If the soil needed nutrients, apply a commercial all-purpose fertilizer. Organic gardening replaced that simplicity with a complexity and the need to understand the many elements that went into creating a vegetable garden. There were a thousand options and answers for everything. At times it just seemed like chaos. Everyone was doing something different. But its overriding principle remained simple and compelling: A healthy garden environment creates healthy plants that are, in turn, beneficial to eat.

There were some things I didn't like about organic gardening. I hated the uncertainty and the endless range of options. In 1976, I was into my second year of organic gardening and found that what had worked for me the year before no longer worked in the new season's garden. All the variables—soil, temperature, atmosphere, shade, sun, weather, water—kept changing. That was frustrating and annoying, though unavoidable. Nature was not going to stand still while I looked for answers. Because of the uncertainty factor, I could not get my feet under me and often felt I was spinning around in circles.

Then there was the yuck factor: the insect repellant method of grinding up a handful of the problem bugs or caterpillars in a blender and spraying that mixture on plants. Sure, that would repel insects. Who or what would want to stick around in an environment that included regular applications of a slurry made up of ground up members of your own species? It felt like genocide and I didn't have the heart or stomach for this. Yet in 1975, this was a popular organic gardening practice.

I was going to have to dive deeper into the world of organic gardening in order to build the base of knowledge and experience I needed to successfully navigate the information jungle and make the right decisions for my garden. But to be honest, after closing down the garden for the winter in 1976 and after two years of reading, thinking and hacking my way through the information jungle, I was getting a little weary.

When we moved to Perelandra, we had not been completely shunned by all the people we knew in Washington. One couple supported our move. In November, during one of our visits with them, the husband and I got into a discussion that lasted ten hours—nonstop. The husband taught philosophy at a nearby college and he enjoyed any and all chances to have a challenging discussion (read argument). For me, this ten-hour discussion was not planned nor was it about a topic I had given much thought to. In fact, I'm not sure I had given any thought to it. I had to leap in with both feet and just wing it.

I started the discussion off by announcing that a human being could be a hermit living on a mountain, tending a garden and still learn all there is to know about life and living. I talked about a garden being a key to the universe, and that it was an access, a doorway, to spiritual truth and universal law. The position that he countered with was that human beings were meant to be social and family oriented. There were crucial aspects of life that could only be learned through social interaction with other humans—particularly within the family structure. After ten hours, I knew in my gut that what I was saying about a hermit, his garden, life, truth and universal law were true. And after ten hours, neither one of us had budged from our respective positions. It was a standoff, and we were both exhausted. But for me, it had been a ten-hour marathon that soon proved to be important.

That December, I read an article about regressive hypnosis and became fascinated with the concept, especially regressive self-hypnosis. Suddenly, I felt compelled to learn to do this. I had to find out about all those past lives of mine. Since the monk on the bridge had not covered this topic, I was "gonna have to buy me some books" and teach myself.

The next Saturday, Clarence and I drove into D.C. to the *Yes!* Bookshop. While checking out the books on my latest interest, Clarence handed me two books and said, "Here, I think you'll be interested in these."

I looked at them. Two books on something called Findhorn—*The Magic of Findhorn* and *The Findhorn Garden.* I asked why I would find them interesting and he said, "They're about gardening." I thought, "Oh joy. More books on organic gardening. Shoot me." I stuck the books in with the others I had chosen, figuring "what the hell. They're paperback. They're cheap. I'll buy them and that way I won't hurt Clarence's feelings. If I get bored this winter, maybe I'll want to read them."

That evening, the only books I wanted to open were the Findhorn books. In the time it took us to drive back to Perelandra, I had completely lost my interest in regressive hypnosis. In fact, I never read the two books I had just purchased on the subject. I began reading *The Magic of Findhorn* and didn't stop reading until I finished it and *The Findhorn Garden* about two weeks later, just in time for New Year's Eve.

I couldn't believe what I was reading. Everything that I had said in that ten-hour argument was laid out in these books. I was being told that the energies I had felt around me at Perelandra weren't my imagination. And I was being told that if I applied myself, I could communicate with this intelligence and get the answers to my gardening questions. Instead of guessing and hoping for the best, I could ask nature directly what I needed to do to address a problem with the plants or an invasion of insects. Nature could guide me through the information jungle.

One week later, on a cold early-January night, I walked out into our woods, sat down on the ground and leaned back against a big oak tree. It was a clear night and I remember spending a few minutes looking up at the stars. I also remember it was really cold, yet somehow I was comfortable. Speaking out loud, I asked to speak to nature. I waited about thirty seconds for a response but felt and heard nothing. I had nothing to lose, so I plunged ahead and stated (again out loud):

> I want to do at Perelandra what they did at Findhorn. I want to work with the devas, and I want to work with nature spirits. [Two terms I picked up from the Findhorn books.] I invite all of you to make yourselves known to me. I am ready to learn.

To my surprise, I felt the nature around me immediately change and intensify in a way that can best be described in today's vernacular: Let the games begin! With this simple declaration, I had successfully triggered Pivot Two.

PIVOT TWO

Chapter 20

Nature's Classroom Begins
1977

ON PAGE ONE, I WROTE the following: A pivot occurs when a person who has been traveling on a familiar, well-defined life path makes a sudden voluntary or involuntary turn that untethers the individual from that path and propels him or her onto a new and often unrelated path that uproots the individual from his or her previous world.

Pivot One was involuntary. It happened. It was unexpected. For seventeen years I worked to figure out how to survive that pivot and then how to create a life that would fit into the larger world while, at the same time, remaining faithful to myself.

Pivot Two was a voluntary pivot. I consciously made the decision to declare my intent:

> I want to do at Perelandra what they did at Findhorn. I want to work with the devas, and I want to work with nature spirits. I invite all of you to make yourselves known to me. I am ready to learn.

I chose to walk through that new door. But this was the extent of my awareness or understanding about what I was doing. I didn't understand the scope of what I was declaring nor did I know the ramifications of what I was asking for, where it would lead and how fundamentally it would change my life. Instead of losing my home, my family and my support as I had experienced with Pivot One, I lost my sense of logic, my understanding of reality and my carefully constructed expectations about the world around me. I was thirty-one years old and everything I thought I knew about reality would be challenged and was about to be changed. This was much more than learning about what to do about cabbage worms or squash bugs.

Freshman Year: 1977

That January, I walked out of the woods, returned to the house, put myself into a quiet state and waited. *(I've made this declaration. Now what do I do?)* With that small action, I sealed my declaration by opening myself to whatever was to happen next.

Once again the response from nature was immediate. I had a "crowd of voices" coming at me, all talking at the same time. This was a different gaggle of voices than the ones that had started me on my journey to the monk in 1974. It seemed like this new crowd had been waiting for me to say "yes." Yes to what, I didn't know.

I remembered reading in the Findhorn book that when Dorothy Maclean described a similar experience, she asked the devas to speak to her one at a time. Having nothing to lose, I tried the same thing. Much to my amazement, they responded instantaneously. And from that point on, I received information from nature one "voice" at a time.

I didn't realize it then, but I was the one who called for that crowd response when I stated in my declaration: "I invite *all* of you to make yourselves known to me. I am ready to learn." Had I said, "I invite *each* of you to make yourselves known to me, and please speak one at a time," I would have avoided the confusing crowd babble. (Lordy, I had a lot to learn about nature and how to work in a partnership.)

Unbeknownst to me, my declaration initiated a major shift in my garden as well as within me. It was no longer a family kitchen garden. Now it was a nature classroom. I was the student and I was there to learn from nature within the context of a garden. It wasn't hard for me to consider that in this pairing, I was the dopey one. *(She who knows not and knows she knows not is a child. Teach her.)*

Pivot Two moved me from a human-dominant world in which nature was but a part, to a new world, a real-life parallel universe, that we happen to call *nature*. This universe is vast and operates according to its own laws, rhythms, patterns and cycles. It has its own unique intelligence that coordinates and holds it all together and keeps it moving forward. Nature's intelligence operates differently from human intelligence and contains a different driving force. Our intelligence is driven by our free will. The driving force behind nature's intelligence is balance. This is the new world I pivoted into that January night. I was now experiencing Perelandra on a whole new level.

The Findhorn books pointed me to this new world. But they did not provide a roadmap for entering and working with that parallel universe. From the lessons the monk taught me, I had an idea about how I might access nature's intelligence. Beyond that, I was flying by the seat of my pants (as they say) and I would need to embark on an intense period of discovery and development. The classroom that first year broke down into four major areas:

1. Understanding the enormity and complexity of nature's world and the depth and breadth of nature's intelligence.
2. Developing communication bridges and understanding between two different worlds.
3. Learning about nature's world.
4. Developing an equal partnership.

1. Understanding the Enormity and Complexity of Nature's World and the Depth and Breadth of Nature's Intelligence

One of my favorite facts about nature is this: In the *healthy* mouth of one human being, there are more bacteria present than there are people populating the planet. Let's think about that another way: There are over 7.5 billion people populating today's world. If each of these people were the proud owners of a healthy mouth containing 7.5 billion bacteria, then the collective mouths of all humans would house 48,750,000,000,000 billion bacteria. And yes, each of those bacteria have intelligence that, when accessed, can identify itself, tell us what it needs for balance, what is needed if it is currently not in balance and how this relates to the rest of a person's digestive system. (Does your mouth feel heavier from the weight of all those thinking, breathing, intelligent bacteria?)

At any given time, we can do a head count and fairly accurately find out how many humans are inhabiting the world. Everything else in the world, seen and unseen, is nature. As with the bacteria in our mouths, the presence of nature on the planet far outstrips our human presence. It is beyond any head count. Beyond even a reasonable guess. How many deciduous trees are there on the planet? How many birds? How many robins? How many insects in the rainforests? How many fish in the sea? How many different natural elements make up a meadow or a tundra? Or a handful of soil? How many different elements are present in one tomato plant? In short, when we set these two worlds side by side, we 7.5 billion humans are completely dwarfed by nature.

Now consider this: Every element in nature has intelligence. All of nature can be communicated with by humans and can give us information about what is needed for balanced growth and survival. Nature can tell us how it relates to and coordinates with its environment and with the larger world. My question became: What kind of information could Perelandra's nature give me? I was soon to discover the answer: *everything.*

I once asked nature to explain nature intelligence. (I figured I would go right to the source.) The following is an excerpt from nature's answer:

> *Intelligence is beyond the human brain. Consequently, it does not require form to provide a specific physical facility, such as the brain, for it to be present and to function. It only requires that there be a focal point (the form of a bird, a tree, a garden plant, a rock) through which its intelligence may flow. It does not need a central nervous system, a sensory system or a brain. Again, it needs only the overall form to serve as a focal point in order to flow. We have used the word "flow" twice now and this is a key to understanding intelligence. It is an organizing flow. It does not require that it be held, sorted, identified or catalogued. It simply flows.*

> *What all form (human and nature) has in common is intelligence. How it expresses its flow is determined by the unique qualities of the form. All form must have intelligence in order to exist because all form must be linked with and express its highest or soul dynamic. Intelligence is the organizing force that provides the movement of soul through form. If you could see and feel this dynamic, you would experience an active force moving throughout all creation that in size, scope and power would be beyond words—and, from the perspective of humans, beyond belief. How humans currently express and understand intelligence is reducing true intelligence to its smallest point.*

Learning about the enormity and complexity of nature's world and the depth and breadth of nature's intelligence is like being smacked in the face by a tsunami. But that isn't particularly practical when it comes to working with nature on a day-to-day basis. To get a handle on this new universe and to keep from feeling overwhelmed, nature and I reduced the universe to a manageable size. We focused on my garden and not the planet. I didn't have to consider nature in its larger global context, just in the context of my small garden. By doing that, we added practical organization and structure to the classroom.

2. Developing Communication Bridges and Understanding Between Two Different Worlds

When I walked *into* the woods that January night, the main thing I wanted nature to address was cabbage worms. How do I control cabbage worms? When I walked *out* of the woods, my focus had changed. Now I wanted to know what my garden would look like if I gave nature a free hand and set it up exactly as nature directed. What would it be like to work in a garden designed and managed by nature? I didn't consider anything I had learned in my first three gardening years to be sacred or inviolate, so I was perfectly happy starting over with a clean slate. Curiosity about experiencing a garden designed and managed by nature propelled me forward and whatever I harvested from the garden was now secondary to the classroom.

But how would I access nature's massive body of intelligence? The door was open, but what do I do after walking through it? How will I know what to ask and how will I be able to understand nature's answers? The Findhorn books didn't provide any practical help. I just had to buck up, take one small step at a time and see where it led me. My instinct was to keep everything simple. For my first step, I drew on what I had learned from the monk by getting quiet and clearing my mind. It seemed like the polite thing to do next was to explain "why I was calling this meeting." I said aloud, "I wish to enter the garden classroom with nature." Boom. I was connected with nature and we were in the classroom.

Up to that point, I had made two successful requests (the Pivot Two trigger and the request to enter the garden classroom) by articulating what I wanted out loud and in my own language. (Thank god. I didn't know how to nature-speak. I really didn't want to learn conversational barking.) Okay, I'll continue speaking in English and I'll speak out loud. Let's see where *this* leads me.

Although I prepared in much the same way to speak with nature as I had done to work with the monk, working with nature proved to be different. I was not in a meditative state while with nature. I wasn't trying to transcend time, place and levels of human reality as I had done with the monk. Now I was working with a partner who was constantly present all around me. No liftoff required. We just had the challenge of learning to communicate with one another in ways that took into consideration our differences.

Over the years, many have made the assumption that I hear nature in the same way I would hear a friend having a conversation with me. I call hearing my friend "outer hearing" and hearing nature "inner hearing." Outer hearing stimulates a person's auditory system. Inner hearing stimulates a person's consciousness and soul. The words are equally distinct. But with outer hearing, anyone passing within range of the conversation can hear what is being said. With inner hearing, only the person whose consciousness is being stimulated knows what is being said.

Inner hearing requires focus and an unfettered mind. With outer hearing a person can shout to be heard over noisy, competing distractions. It is easier to disrupt inner hearing with outside disturbances, and it is more challenging to keep one's focus during those times. It's also more difficult to hold one's focus during a lengthy session. In the beginning, my conversations with nature would last maybe thirty minutes before I would start to tire and my mind would wander off into the tall grass. With practice and experience, I was able to extend my nature-session time.

Along with inner hearing, I had inner feeling. It was a natural thing for me to feel energy shift and move around me. It's how I felt the heightened energy in the woods. Although I had had this ability throughout my life (it must have been included in my birth package), it had been further developed and sharpened during my time with the monk. Inner feeling was included with each of my experiences with him, making it easier to identify one level or action from another. It felt like everything came with its own identifiable vibration.

Lastly, I entered the classroom with visual thinking. It was and is one of the perks that researchers say can accompany dyslexia. Rather than thinking about something using a string of words, I tend to see thought played out like a movie inside my head or concepts presented in images. It had been a source of entertainment since I was a child. Now nature used this quirk of mine as another communication option. I would ask a question and rather than provide words for my inner hearing, I would see something play out. Then I would describe what I saw and ask if it was accurate.

Visual thinking is probably the most efficient of the three options when it comes to transferring large blocks of information quickly. It proves that old saying: *A picture is worth a thousand words.* Visual thinking that lasted no more than thirty seconds one morning in 1995 resulted in my seeing and understanding the principles behind the Microbial Balancing Program. A 452-page book was then required to teach the program to others.

Holding up my end of a conversation with nature was simple. Just speak. Whatever I wanted to know, I only needed to say it. No special translation required. To be fair, I was speaking American and not English. I thought this might be challenging for nature since some feel American, with all its slang, is pigeon-English. But it turned out to not be an issue. I also discovered that if I said everything aloud, it was easier to maintain focus. The words didn't wander around aimlessly in my head. And by hearing the words, I could listen to what I was saying and make sure it was what I had intended to say.

> A few words of wisdom from an old lady with a lot of experience at this nature thing: Enter the classroom with your own set of skills. Nature works with a person's native language and already-existing abilities and can't work with nonexistent or undeveloped abilities that a person wishes they had. Those aren't abilities, they are desires. I have seen more people waste time and fester in their own frustration when they insist on trying to work with nature in a certain way. Sometimes it's because they want to be seen by others as special. So they try to copy others whom they respect. It's stupid and a waste of time. Bring your own abilities into the classroom and start from there. Even if you have no idea what you can bring to the class, start anyway. Nature will begin communicating with you using your personal combination of avenues even if you are not aware they exist. You just need to be open to options and not block the hints and hits that start flying at you.

I may not have had to learn the fine art of barking in order to converse with nature, but I did have to pick up new terminology. In the beginning, I relied on a couple of terms from the Findhorn books. The founders of the Findhorn garden divided nature intelligence into two distinct entities or forces: devas and nature spirits. These terms have been used for centuries to refer to nature, and the Findhorn founders continued to use them.

(I later learned that "deva" and "nature spirit" actually refer to two different functions within one intelligence and not two separate forces or entities. We have something similar going on with our brains. We have one brain, but it is divided into different lobes with different functions centered in each lobe.)

"Deva" refers to the creation and design functions within nature. I like to think of this as the center of nature's architectural planning. When thinking about what makes a carrot a carrot (its taste, color, shape), we are thinking about nature's devic function. "Nature spirit" refers to the action and implementation functions within nature (its planting requirements, growth cycle, nutritional requirements). What action is needed for the development of a strong, vital carrot that reflects all the aspects of its architectural plan?

Perhaps this will help: Picture the inside of a shoe factory from the 1940s. See its gears, belts and boxes moving, all tended by the workers. The devic level designs the factory in detail. It determines the structure that is needed for performing the job and accomplishing the goal. It's why our factory doesn't include a horse racing track in the middle of the main floor. That would be ridiculous and useless. The nature spirit level operates the belts, oils and gears to ensure that the factory and its workers do everything needed to accomplish its goals.

When I began working with nature, I accepted how Findhorn used the terms "deva" and "nature spirit" and thought of them as separate entities. It made thinking about nature's intelligence easier and the simplicity it provided in those early days made learning about working with nature more efficient. I knew exactly where to focus my attention when requesting information. If my question was about design, such as the layout of my garden, I knew to focus on the Deva of the Perelandra Garden. If I wanted information about how to plant beans, I focused on the nature spirits connected with my bean seeds. In return, nature used my early understanding and referred to itself as deva and nature spirit. As far as nature was concerned, this ancient terminology was perfectly acceptable and a good starting point. Nature and I knew what I meant when I said "deva" or "nature spirit," and this was critical for successful communication.

3. Learning About Nature's World

One of the things that has stayed with me all these years from C. S. Lewis' book *Perelandra* is the main character's difficulty describing what he has never before seen or experienced after he arrives on the planet. How could he describe a color that bore no relationship to any other color he had ever seen? There were no words. He had no frame of reference, no foundation on which to set the colors, shapes and textures that made up the landscape sitting right in front of him. He had to accept that it was there and it was real. And then he had to step forward, trusting that he would be safe as he moved into this new reality.

My first year working with nature gave me a similar experience. From the winter months to the next fall when I closed down that garden, nature showed me different aspects of its reality that were well beyond anything I had known or experienced. I could have simply said that a bunch of really weird things happened and dismissed them. But I was already clued into the idea of a classroom and understood that nothing was to be dismissed. Weird though events may have been, I was experiencing them for a reason.

One evening I was talking to Clarence about devas when I saw a four-foot high, four-inch wide arc of white light off to his left. At first I thought my mind was playing tricks on me. After all, it was late in the evening. I tried to concentrate on our conversation and ignore this "thing." But it kept pulsating its light at me. I wasn't seeing the arc from within a meditative state or with inner vision. I was completely present in the room—and so was it. I didn't feel Clarence and I were in danger nor did it seem like this was some lost space alien who had dropped in for a little company. And since I didn't drink alcohol or take drugs, I was fairly confident that I wasn't hallucinating. After a few minutes, I gave up and started laughing. I told Clarence that I would not be able to continue the conversation with this thing pulsating at me. As I described what I was seeing, the light brightened and danced around a bit in the air beside him. To me it seemed alive. Clarence said he had been feeling something next to him but couldn't see anything.

Quite frankly, I did not know what to do with the light. So I offered it a cup of tea. The thing pulsated brighter. I blinked several times to make sure my eyes weren't playing tricks on me while Clarence left the room to make tea—for the two of us, not for our guest. I gave my full attention over to the arc of light. It got brighter still, and with great gentleness the light's energy flowed out from the arc, crossed the room and touched into me, giving me a soft physical sensation. A sense of awareness washed through me. It identified itself as devic and said it was there to verify to me that devas were a reality.

When Clarence returned, we continued our discussion with the arc still off to his left. I didn't say anything to him about what had just happened. To be honest, I didn't think I could adequately put it into words. As we talked, the arc slowly removed itself from my awareness and from my sight. This was my first visual devic connection.

In February, I was told to go into the woods at midnight, sit by a specific white oak tree and lean my back against the tree. There was snow on the ground and a biting wind. At the appointed hour, I bundled up and trudged out to the tree. I set a stool next to the trunk and leaned back against the tree. (I knew how to follow instructions.)

In less than a minute, I felt a strange energy from the tree flow into my back. The energy began to fill my body, so to keep things from getting "clogged and crowded," I used my breath to move my own energy into the tree, creating an exchange. It was a variation on my Going Home experience. But instead of intensifying during the exchange, the exchange with the tree felt gentle, comforting and stabilizing. My body got so warm that when I returned to the tree the next night (at midnight as instructed), I didn't bother wearing a coat.

I continued this routine for about two weeks, until nature told me to stop. I think had I not felt the warm energy from the tree, I might have considered that sitting coatless in the woods in the dead of winter was nuts. At least I hope I would have arrived at this conclusion. But feeling the comforting warmth verified that something was going on—and that I didn't need a coat.

During the same period, we were running low on wood for the stove, and Clarence had to find some suitable trees to cut for our supply. Nature told me where to find a dead, perfectly seasoned, thirty-foot tree that would be ideal for our needs. I was also told that we would have to enlist the help of the tree's nature spirits in order to get it down without damaging the surrounding trees.

Sure enough, the tree was sitting deep in the woods right where I had been told it would be. It was leaning, which meant that the angle of the fall was limited to that one direction. If the tree fell exactly straight, it would do no damage. If it fell no more than a foot to the left or right from this straight line, it would damage a number of healthy trees.

I talked to Clarence about what I was learning concerning the role of nature spirits. I suggested that when he was ready to fell this tree, he ask for its nature spirits to help in the process. He should state very clearly how he wanted the tree to fall.

Early the next morning, Clarence headed for the tree. I was just waking up when I heard a tremendous shout from him, "No! No! Four feet to the left!" A few seconds later, there was a crash that shook the house. A few seconds after that, I felt a gentle kiss on my forehead. A clear, precise kiss. No mistaking it for a fly or a breeze. Nature said that we now had our nature spirit connection. My energy experience with the oak tree had been my preparation for this moment, and a nature spirit was the bearer of the kiss.

Clarence came into the house with a stunned look on his face and explained what had happened. He asked for the nature spirits' help just as I had suggested, then sawed the tree as carefully as he could so it would fall properly. As it came down, he saw that it was falling way off course—in fact, it was falling four feet off to the right. His instant reaction was to shout exactly what needed to happen. In mid-air, this thirty-foot tree moved four feet to the left and came down exactly on target. No other trees were damaged.

I had read that at Findhorn there was a wild area set aside for nature spirits. Humans weren't allowed to enter. In light of the kiss and tree experience, I felt that I should do the same at Perelandra. I picked a spot in the woods next to the garden and roped it off as a gesture, a gift for nature spirits. When I was finished, I stood in the middle of the area and invited the Perelandra nature spirits to this special place that I now called the "Elemental Annex." Instantly I felt a heightened energy and heard, "Finally! Now we can get down to business!" Feeling very much out of place, I gingerly stepped out of the area. The Elemental Annex was now the base of operations for the nature spirit activity at Perelandra.

That winter while these unusual and unexpected events occurred, I still had to find out what nature's plans were for the new garden season. Each day I requested to enter the classroom and felt a shift of energy indicating that I was in. My first question was always the same: *What do I do today?* I let nature decide the curriculum—the subject, the focus, the activity, the order of activity, the timing and rhythm. I continued to make the assumption that I knew nothing. Besides, I was always curious. I wanted to know what nature would say when I asked, "What do I do today?" As far as I was concerned, this was nature's show and I was there to learn.

During my first days in the classroom, I thought it would be impossible to forget anything. Each day felt like a special event. How could I forget this extraordinary thing nature was telling or showing me? Or the next extraordinary thing? It only took a few days of receiving the extraordinary before I started forgetting what was said to me two days ago, even a day ago. Trying to make sure I remembered everything became a constant weight on my mind. Time to start writing it down. I began making detailed notes during and after each class and after each out-of-the-ordinary event. Thank god because it gave me something to refer back to when memory failed me (which was often) or I got confused (which was also often). And writing provided an additional perk. Nature used it as an opportunity for me to transcribe a more extensive body of information. Neither one of us was relying on my somewhat questionable memory once I began transcribing what I was hearing.

The focus for these early classes was the preparation and planning for the new garden. It became a master class in how to make a complex reality (my garden) with its many moving pieces and parts manageable. One important key was to reduce each step of gardening to a single question. A simple question called for a simple answer. Then, in light of the information I was just given, I'd ask the next logical question. By relying on logic and common sense, I was able to maintain a flow of questions and record nature's answers. I was accessing nature intelligence.

Because it was still January and the ground was frozen, all the planning was done on paper. We started from square one. I asked if I was to plant a garden that year. I had considered that nature might want time to repair any soil damage caused by my use of Sevin®, even though it had been nearly two years since my last application. I had been thinking about spreading fertilizer over the entire garden and keeping it covered with 6 inches of hay while the soil simmered for the season. Perhaps this was the way to go. (A fine example of "human think.") When I asked, nature enthusiastically responded, "Let's plant!"

Once nature greenlighted the garden, I didn't assume anything I had done up to that point would remain the same. I asked about the basics: location, size, shape, number of rows, row orientation. Was I to continue mulch gardening? (Yes.) Luckily I didn't have to relocate the garden or change its rectangular shape. (That would have required taking down a bunch of trees.) And the rows remained in straight lines.

Instead of using all-purpose fertilizers, I now needed to use several organic fertilizers, each providing different nutrients. When I asked if I needed to have the soil tested (so I'd know what the hell I was doing), I was told that wouldn't be necessary. Nature would give me the information for the needed fertilizers and how much I was to add. (Nature provides its own soil testing lab!)

The obvious next questions: Plant what? Where? How? Like most gardeners, I received an array of seed catalogs each winter, all filled with photos of flawless vegetables that would never be duplicated in a real garden. Nature and I used the catalogs as another communication bridge. They told me which catalogs to work with. (I ended up with four.) Considering that I was now working with nature, I assumed I would need some pretty exotic catalogs from "nature-approved" seed companies. (Human think.) The collection nature wanted me to use included Park Seed and Burpee, two large U.S. companies who, at the time, offered mostly regular and hybrid seeds. (An early lesson: Nature doesn't consider all hybrid seeds to be crappy, worthless, dangerous seeds used solely by lazy, stupid people who don't care about the planet.) Smaller companies offering organic seeds filled out the rest of the chosen catalog collection. I was then told to choose between the Park Seed or Burpee catalogs for my primary list of what's available and the options. I chose Park Seed—for no other reason than the catalog's page size was easier to work with.

Most garden catalogs contain the same list of vegetables, flowers and herbs. They differ when we have to choose the plant variety we want in our garden. That's when we get into the battle of the hybrid, the organic and the heirloom options. For example, Park Seed lists the following tomato options: Park's Whopper CR Improved Hybrid, Big Beef Hybrid, Celebrity Hybrid, Better Boy Hybrid, Early Girl Hybrid, Cherokee Purple Organic, Black Krim, Rainbow Blend Heirloom...See what I mean? And this is only about 5 percent of tomato varieties they offer.

Starting with artichoke and continuing through the entire list, one vegetable at a time, to zucchini, I asked, "Do I include ______ in the garden?" Whenever nature said "yes," I recorded the name on a sheet of paper. On this first pass, I ignored all the available hybrid/organic/heirloom seed variety options and just concentrated on finding out what I was to include in the garden. After asking about zucchini, I asked, "Is there a vegetable not listed in Parks Seeds that needs to be included?" If they answered yes, I asked which catalog(s) had the missing vegetables. Then I read through the list of vegetables not included in the Parks Seed catalog asking, "Do I include ______ in the garden?" When I had the full vegetable list, I moved on to flowers and then herbs and repeated the same process.

For the second pass, nature and I concentrated on identifying the regular/hybrid/organic/heirloom seed variety options for each vegetable/flower/herb on my list.

Did this seed routine take time? You bet it did. Nature slowed the selection process because I needed the information to be broken up into bite-size pieces. Nature was perfectly capable of downloading all the information for my entire garden in one chunk. But once downloaded, what was I going to do with that massive chunk of interwoven, detailed information? It's a lot faster to leaf through a catalog and choose the vegetables and varieties that tickle our fancy for whatever reason. Often it's because of those photos! Sometimes it's because of past success and experience. But no matter, maintaining human control and allowing our choices to be driven by our desire or experience is a faster process than breaking it down and carefully finding out what nature recommends for creating a balanced garden. From what I learned that first season, our human control gives us a weaker garden that is vulnerable to more problems.

By mid-February, I had a fully planned garden laid out on paper. I knew what I was to do to prepare for planting, what varieties I would be planting and where, what seeds to use and how much space to allow for each variety. With just a handful of new additions, the vegetables pretty much remained the same as in previous years. But many more flowers and herbs had been added. This garden was going to look very different.

My next questions had to do with garden timing: when to prepare the soil, when to spread the hay and when to plant. I put aside the charts the Myers had given me with the lists of vegetable planting times in our area. Nature was giving me a different timetable for everything. Sometimes the timing was so different that I would have to step over my own doubt and just go do it.

I was constantly concerned about "hearing" nature's information accurately. Let's face it, the information I was getting included a high degree of weird, and this caused me to raise questions about my accuracy. I was a lot braver when it came to planning the garden on paper where it was easy to correct a mistake. Just erase it and start over. It wasn't going to be that easy to correct mistakes in the garden. Eventually I would have to buck up and start moving those plans off paper and into soil.

In late February, nature said to go out to the garden and stake the new row locations. Starting at one end, I paced along the garden's border. I pounded in a stake wherever nature told me to stop and added a label listing what was to be planted in that row. In previous years, using the string method, it took me a full afternoon to lay out the rows. With nature, the process took about a half hour.

As soon as we finished identifying the garden's seeds, nature gave me a list of seeds to start in flats in the house—tomatoes, green peppers, broccoli, cabbage, Brussels sprouts and cauliflower. I planted according to nature's new instructions on timing and seed depth. Then for each variety, nature told me to call on the deva and nature spirits connected with the vegetable to fuse its full energies into the seed. The response was astounding. No seeds took more than two days to germinate. The tomatoes germinated and had their first set of true leaves in less than two days. The seedlings then grew twice as fast as what I had observed in previous years. The quality of color in the plants was vibrant. There is a difference in the shade of green between broccoli, cabbage, Brussels sprouts and cauliflower. Now these differences were more pronounced. When I touched the plants, the leaves had a different quality to them. It was almost as if the leaf could barely contain the life that was now held within the plant and touching the leaf caused that life to spring out from it.

What I was observing with these seedlings was beyond any previous experience. It was my first validation that what I was doing with nature as a gardener, insane though it may seem, was leading me in the right direction. The plant growth, the colors, the feel, the obvious strength and health were sitting in flats right in front of me. I couldn't deny what I was seeing. It wasn't my imagination or some kind of vision-altering meditative experience. It was real. Friends and neighbors who visited commented on the differences they saw, as well. (Interestingly, no one asked me what I was doing that could account for the differences.)

Speaking of insanity: While I was in the classroom with nature, I was learning about a new logic and a new reality. The information and my understanding felt strongly sane and deeply stable.

But when I stepped outside the classroom and traveled beyond Perelandra, what I was learning and experiencing when placed within the context of the world that surrounded me looked and felt different. I'd see other people's gardens and remember the helpful instructions I had received over the previous three years. Within this broader context, what I was experiencing with nature felt like pure insanity. When I reentered my world and stepped back into the classroom, everything that had seemed insane in the broader context became sane again.

In early March, a full month ahead of my previous year's schedule, I was told to transplant everything but the tomatoes and green peppers into the garden. I was also told to begin the transplanting at 10 P.M. on a specific day. As instructed, I spent the days prior to that getting the plants ready for the big move by hardening them off (taking the flats outside every day so that the plants could get used to the cold and wind). This is when I questioned nature's sanity. I felt protective about these young plants and it seemed too soon and too cold to plant them in the garden. (Human think.) Despite my doubts, I forged on and did everything nature directed me to do. It was one of those "let's see where this leads" moments.

On the specified evening, the moon was full and bright, enabling me to see what I was doing without the aid of a flashlight. I carried the flats of young plants into the garden and began working.

Nature gave me instructions on how to plant without causing the plants to go into shock. I was told that the energy of the plant at night was in the root system, making transplanting at night preferable. During the day, the energy was in the stem and leaves. In human terms, at night the plant was in a quiet state similar to sleep. If I worked carefully and slowly, the transplanting could be done without disrupting that state. The plants could settle in quickly and their growth rhythm wouldn't be disturbed.

So there I sat on the mulch in the moonlight with my winter coat, hat and gloves on, transplanting in slow motion. I pulled back the hay and made a hole just large enough for the root ball, careful not to stir or disturb the soil unnecessarily. It felt more like I was gently slipping the plants into the soil and not digging them in.

As I worked, I felt a penetrating air of peace surround me. It was how I imagined the Leboyer Nonviolent Birth Method would be. I was working in gentle moonlight. No artificial lighting. No noise. Careful, quiet movements. And I could sense that the plants were not being disturbed.

I completed the transplanting by 3 A.M. I left the garden feeling a deep peace and inner quiet that I was able to duplicate in this first-year garden only one other time.

Despite the bitter March cold and wind, the little plants grew at a rapid pace. The hay that had been pulled back formed a protective wall around the plants. On the nights when a heavy freeze was expected, I asked if I should cover the plants for protection. (Human think.) Instead I was told to ask nature to provide protection for the young plants. "Okay. I'm asking you to protect these young plants from tonight's freeze." Then I spent the evening holding my breath and hoping for the best. The next morning I walked outside expecting to find a bunch of freeze-dried plants. Instead I found a heavy frost sitting everywhere except on those plants. They continued growing as if nothing had happened.

AS THE PLANTING SEASON continued through April and into May, nature gave me information on when to plant specific seeds. I then prepared each row as directed, planted the seeds, asked that the devic and nature spirit energies be grounded in the seeds and welcomed each new energy into the garden. With every planting, I could feel the overall energy of the garden building.

I noticed different dynamics, different sensations, with each new garden energy. But nothing really surprised me until the Onion Deva. That deva communicated with me with a force that was stronger than anything I had felt up to that point. I didn't think I was going to have many arguments with an onion. And if I was dumb enough to start one, I knew I wasn't going to win.

While working with nature to plan the garden, I wondered if it might be good for the garden's overall balance to include carrots. At the time, my garden soil was mostly clay—Virginia is famous for its brilliant red clay. During the previous years, I had worked on the soil, adding mulch and nutrients. Eventually I made it acceptable to most vegetables, but I still couldn't get carrots to grow. Actually, it was more like coaxing carrots to drill through brick. But this year, I decided it might be good to include carrots for their energy and the garden's balance and not worry about harvesting the stubby little roots for food. I asked nature about this and got an immediate and resounding "yes."

In hindsight, I suspect that I had picked up on a hint from nature when I felt moved to ask about the carrots. But no matter, it seemed like nature was pleased that I had considered something solely for the sake of the garden's balance rather than the garden's harvest. They decided to have a little celebration and show their pleasure. After planting the seeds, I asked that the carrot devic and nature spirit energies be grounded into the seeds. Nature grounded it all right—in every row in the garden! I had closed my eyes during my request and nature's energy download into the seeds. It only took maybe fifteen seconds. When I opened my eyes and looked into the garden, I saw three-inch-high carrot plants sticking up everywhere. Not just in the row where I had planted the seeds. Carrots were now growing in every row. I looked at this for a few minutes. Did I do or say something wrong? Was I seeing what I was seeing? Why were there carrots everywhere? This wasn't the plan. Finally I got it. "It's a joke. Right, fellas?!"

Not really wanting a carrot garden, I decided I'd call nature's bluff. Recalling some of my old lessons from the monk, I used my focus to collect the carrot energy from all the rows and direct it into the one row where the seeds had been planted. Then I said, "No. No. I meant ground the devic and nature spirit energy in the carrot seeds in this row only, thank you." After about fifteen seconds, the three-inch tall carrot plants in the seeded row were now six inches tall—approximately ten minutes after planting the seed—and the carrot plants in the other rows had fallen over on the mulch. (Nature can be such a show off.)

I came away from this experience feeling that my garden might get a little slippery and that there was no guarantee that what was planted or growing in spot X was going to stay in spot X. Was the entire garden going to start walking around? I also came away saying to nature, "Alright. What else can you do?" And "What rules are you playing by?" I now saw that nature had the ability and power to work with form in ways I could not yet imagine. I was having enough trouble wrapping my head around the carrot event, and that had just happened right before my eyes.

In early spring, as part of my effort to break down the clay and have friable soil, I asked nature to bring in more earthworms. When it came time to prepare the rows for planting, I discovered an enormous amount of earthworms everywhere I cultivated. That was the good news. The bad news was that it was impossible for me to work the soil without chopping earthworms. I wanted them, I got them, and now I was chopping them up into little pieces and back to practicing genocide. Becoming frustrated and angry at the situation, I stopped cultivating, walked out of the garden and announced out loud, "I'm going to have a fifteen-minute tea break. When I return, I want all of the earthworms that are in this row (I pointed to the row) to be out of the row. You can be on either side of the row, but not in it." Then I stomped off, fully expecting nothing whatsoever to come of my request—which even to me sounded nuts.

I returned fifteen minutes later as promised (or threatened!), picked up my cultivator and began working in the same row. The earthworms were gone from the entire row. I was surprised—and a little spooked by this turn of events. (Cue the *Twilight Zone* theme.)

When I finished working the soil, I wondered, *If I can "order" earthworms out, can I invite them back in again?* It was worth a try, so I said, "OK. The coast is clear. I now invite you to come back into the row. I'll give you ten minutes." I sat down, waited the ten minutes, then went back to the row, picked up several handfuls of soil and found them filled with worms again. New questions: What the hell kind of power did *I* have? And how were these worms able to deal with the concept of time?

The worm experience gave me an idea. Moles had taken over our lawn. I sat down on the lawn and asked to be connected to the Deva of Moles. I felt a considerable shift but no response. Trusting that the connection was made, I laid out my case about why I'd like the moles to leave the lawn area. I explained that I didn't want the moles to leave Perelandra, that I understood they were integral to the life cycle at Perelandra. But would they consider living in the woods or in an open field area about two hundred feet away? In either place they could live without being disturbed. Then I suggested that they leave the lawn area around 9 P.M. Just in case moles couldn't tell time, I changed that to sunset so that they could move to their new areas without being attacked by our two cats and two dogs—who happened to enjoy killing moles. At sunset our animals would be in the house sleeping off dinner.

Still nothing from the Mole Deva.

Assuming my efforts had been rejected, I returned to the garden. (It had been worth a try.) About a half-hour later and well before sunset, I heard leaves rustling in the woods. I looked up and saw a herd of moles—at least a hundred in number—scurrying along the woods' edge, heading for the open field area. Each of our animals ran toward the commotion, and seeing that there was absolutely nothing I could do to get our four hysterical animals out of the way, I shouted to the moles, "I thought I told you sunset!"

Well, the sight of a hundred moles overloaded our animals' circuits and they stood frozen in one spot, making noises and scratching themselves out of frustration. The moles ran right by them unharmed en route to the open field.

New lesson: My intent to provide safe passage for the moles was appreciated, but my human-think solution didn't provide the best answer. What I had watched was nature's better solution.

4. *Developing an Equal Partnership*

In late May, Clarence and I attended a workshop given by Peter and Eileen Caddy, two of the co-founders of Findhorn. I received two important bits of information from the Caddys that day.

First, they talked about a three-month program the Findhorn Community was giving that winter called the "Essence of Findhorn." As they spoke about it, I knew I had to go to Findhorn and be a part of that program. I assumed like-minded people would be attending and we'd have a chance to swap experiences and ideas about working with nature. I desperately wanted to be around people I could openly speak with about my garden. At Perelandra I often felt isolated. When I tried to describe what I was experiencing with friends, I was met with a mixture of skepticism and boredom. When we joined friends for dinner, they made a point of not including me in the conversation. I was the crazy woman. My day and what I had to say about it seemed to annoy them. They wanted me to sit there quietly and eat my meal. The idea of being with others who wouldn't wall me off was appealing.

Second, I asked Peter what one could do if she has already made a connection with nature and was being run ragged from trying to do everything nature said. (Since connecting with nature in January, I had made it a point to do everything they suggested as soon as I possibly could. Surely this was my job as the student. As a result, my day was completely at their mercy, and I was exhausted.) Peter gave me a one sentence answer. "Remember, *you* are the creator of the garden."

All the way home, I kept thinking, "I am the creator of this garden...*I* am the creator of the garden..." By the time I got home, I was beginning to believe that I was the creator of the garden. But I wasn't sure what this meant. What did Peter Caddy mean by "creator"?

That evening I brought the issue up with nature and asked them to explain my role in the garden from their perspective. They said I was never meant to be in the role of the servant. The student is not the servant. Rather, I was to function in an equal partnership with nature intelligence. *Equal* partnership. That meant I had to face my own power, my own intelligence and my own abilities. I was not to see myself as someone less than nature intelligence. I was different. Not less. The relationship they sought with me was an equal, co-creative partnership.

Up to this point, I had thought I was giving nature free rein to decide the day's subject, focus, activity, the order of activity, timing and rhythm. In reality, nature and I were in a constant give-and-take and, in a way, deciding these things together. All along, I had been encouraged to describe what I was seeing and what changes had occurred as a result of some action or passing of time. I had not realized how important my side of the conversation was to nature. Instead of thinking I was chattering on about something that I assumed nature already knew and could see, I had been providing valuable information back to nature that had to do with what *I* was observing and what *I* understood.

The partnership was, in fact, a profound partnership between nature and me that was being played out in a garden. Every step forward with nature required a full response and readout from me. I had to be fully engaged, not just physically but intellectually and emotionally as well. If nature told me to dig a hole one foot deep, I wasn't just to dig the hole and leave it at that. What did I see? How did it feel to dig the hole? Did the shovel cut through the soil easily or with difficulty? What did the soil look like? How did the soil feel? Was it warm? Was it cool? How did it change as I dug deeper? How did it compare to other holes I had dug in the garden? What insects, worms and other crawly things did I find? Did I have any questions about what I was seeing or thinking?

I was participating in an information loop. Nature projected information to me and I acted based on that information. In turn, I projected back my perception of what I was doing or thinking. Nature then adjusted the flow and substance of the next information I would receive based on my input. Together we were developing and fine-tuning our language and action. I was not a passive student sitting in a classroom like a lump listening to nature lectures. I was an engaged student who was actively participating in determining the scope and timing of the lessons. And nature was not some bored teacher mindlessly tossing pre-packaged lessons at me. My teacher constantly adjusted the information so that I could hear *and* understand it. This give-and-take reminded me of the love-energy flow in the Going Home experience and the warm-energy flow with the oak tree that winter. Now it was an education flow. I now understood that the continuing development of our partnership depended on the quality and content of our give-and-take. I needed to do my part better.

I arrived in the garden the next day with a different attitude. I came prepared to assume my position of partner—and I came prepared to learn what that meant. First, I felt I needed to address my 24/7 work week. As it stood, I was doing any and everything at all hours of the day. I did not think I could make it through the rest of the season if I continued to keep this rhythm and pace. I announced that I would no longer be available at three in the morning. I needed a solid eight hours of sleep and I needed time for relaxation, so after leaving the garden at sundown, our "office" would be closed for the day. And I would not be available in the morning until after ten. (I'm a late-morning girl.) We were now on a 9 hour/7 day work week. I have to admit that I needed to summon courage to articulate these changes. Who was I to make such demands? (Oh, right. An *equal partner* in this partnership.) The response I received was one of gratitude. Nature is not human, and it was clear that they had been waiting for me to take responsibility for myself and define my needs—my working conditions. *(I am the creator of my garden.)*

In my newfound capacity as "creator of the garden," I led a ceremony at Perelandra. I declared all of Perelandra (not just the Elemental Annex) a sanctuary for devas and nature spirits, a sanctuary where they could function in partnership with me in peace and together we would work toward balance—whatever this meant. With that, I invited to Perelandra any devas or nature spirits who wished to join.

As soon as I finished my declaration, many different wildflowers popped up in the woods, and empty flower pots that I had prepared for outdoor annuals were now filled with blooming annuals. My declaration and invitation had obviously been accepted. The potted annuals lasted the entire season. Every time I walked by those pots I would eye them suspiciously. I often thought they would disappear just as "magically" as they had appeared.

By mid-June, I had developed a daily garden routine. Each morning (at ten!) I sat on my bench beside the garden and requested to enter the classroom. Then I would run down a list of every plant variety growing in the garden and ask the deva of each variety, "Does ________ need attention?" If the answer was yes, I continued the questions to find out what was needed. It didn't take long to create the day's to-do list because most days only a handful of varieties needed attention.

I would then focus on the nature spirit level, and we would work together in the garden accomplishing the different tasks. I asked what we needed to do first. Whatever popped into my mind, that's where I headed. With each task, I asked the nature spirits how best to do the work. As I worked, I would be given insights about what I was doing and why. In turn, I kept up a running commentary about what I was seeing, sensing, feeling and thinking. Once completed, I'd ask, "What's next?" I continued rolling through the to-do list this way each day.

It took a few years before I understood I was working with one united nature intelligence containing separate functions and not separate nature entities. Obviously it didn't matter that I was dicing up nature intelligence in the beginning because I was still focusing my attention on and getting the correct information from the correct "lobe." For example, I didn't ask devas to provide nature spirit information and assistance. I had a good working understanding of their job descriptions. Devas: architects. Nature spirits: action and implementation.

Reconstructing My Foundation of Logic

Even though I wasn't a knowledgeable gardener with twenty years' experience behind me, I still came to this new garden with a certain amount of foreknowledge based on my woefully short three years' experience combined with the reading I had done on gardening and ecology. This information had automatically become part of my foundation of logic. If you had asked me, "Are you willing to let go of that logic for something new?" I would have said without hesitation, "Yes. Of course." But stating my intent didn't magically wipe away that old logic. Those foundations are developed from years of experience and exposure to available information. They are strong and deep, and the individual pieces are tightly hooked together. They don't just float away with the swipe of a hand and a few spoken words. How we perceive reality and make judgments about the reality that constantly swirls around us is drawn from our foundation of logic.

The logic that I came into this partnership with in January limited me in what I saw, sensed, experienced and understood. Everything that had happened since the beginning of the classroom had served to challenge and dismantle the old logic and then replace it with the new, piece by piece. Many of the events were startling and, through the element of surprise, resulted in large—sometimes seismic—adjustments in my foundation. What I believed to be illogical and impossible in the beginning eventually became reasonable—and logical. But I still had elements of the old logic that interfered with my ability to perceive fully the new reality. This needed to be dismantled if I was going to really learn from what lay ahead this gardening season.

One afternoon nature told me to harvest a yellow squash and hold it in my hands. I was told to just watch it sitting in my hands and not to do or think about anything else. I had been looking at it for about five minutes when the yellow squash began to gradually turn green and change into a cucumber that was slightly larger in size than the squash had been. The switch took less than a minute.

I have to tell you—holding a squash that turns into a cucumber is the kind of experience that can stop you in your tracks. Particularly if you haven't been forewarned. Somewhere along the line, I had been taught that if you pick up a squash and hold it in your hands, chances were good that it would remain a squash no matter how long you held it. It was one of those handy assumptions that readily sprang from my foundation of logic and provided a comforting predictability. I "knew" the squash was not going to just start slip-sliding around and become something else. That day in the garden was a brain-freeze moment. I had to stand still and slowly take in what had just happened. "Hold on. Nobody move. Let me get this." I even accused my partner of not playing by the rules. Of course, that was the point. Whose rules were we talking about here?

This didn't feel like I was witnessing a delightful magic trick. I stared at the cucumber for a good half hour, slowly gathering my wits about me. I sniffed it more than once. It definitely smelled like a cucumber. It looked and felt like a cucumber. I turned it over and around every which way looking for any evidence that perhaps the squash was hiding underneath some Halloween costume that made it look like a cucumber. (I have no idea why I thought this would be a more reasonable explanation than what had actually occurred. I was grasping at straws.) I knew I had started out holding a squash because I was standing next to the squash plant I had harvested it from. The cucumber plants were at the opposite end of the garden. Also, the cucumber I was now holding was larger than the other cucumbers still on the plants.

Just as I was getting used to that cucumber, it slowly changed back to the yellow squash. (I never ate the squash nor did I taste the cucumber. I didn't know what was going to end up in my mouth. I'm not that brave.)

I wasn't sure what I was going to do with this experience. Nature showed me that form could change dramatically and relatively quickly. And nature could change the form of anything it wanted—at any time. With that, my foundation of logic had made a seismic adjustment. The reality I had come to expect all these years was no longer nailed down.

IN MID-JUNE, the federal government announced that the entire eastern seaboard of the United States was suffering under severe drought conditions, and several states (including Virginia) were declared agricultural disaster areas, making them eligible for government assistance. I was concerned about the plight of the farmers around us whose fields were turning brown.

However, the Perelandra garden was covered with more than six inches of mulch and, according to what I had read about mulch gardening, it was protected from drought. When a neighbor called to tell me her mulch garden had burned out, the drought became personal. I now knew I was working under adverse conditions, and my new acid test was whether or not nature and I could keep this garden thriving. As the summer months pressed on, the drought worsened. But the Perelandra garden continued to grow lush and green. (By the way, because of the mulch, I didn't have to do any watering. The moisture in the soil held.)

About this same time, the cabbage, broccoli, cauliflower, kale and Brussels sprouts plants became heavily infested with my old friend and source of frustration, cabbage worms. It was the worst infestation I had seen, and it seemed to explode overnight. There had been light cabbage moth activity and I had spotted just a few clusters of eggs here and there on the leaves. (Moth eggs become worms.) The activity had been so light that I wasn't concerned. The garden seemed to be naturally controlling the moths. During the previous three years, when cabbage worms had shown up on plants, I shifted my counterattack from Sevin® to organic methods. But this year, I used neither. I felt a dead bug was a dead bug, whether killed organically or otherwise. I had to consider another solution, and according to my daily to-do list, it was time to pay attention to cabbage worms.

Given my earlier success with earthworms and moles, I thought I'd try this approach again and connected with the Deva of the Cabbage Worm. In my role as creator of the garden, I stated that I wished to give one plant at the end of each infested row over to the cabbage worms. Then I requested that the worms remove themselves from the other infested plants.

The next morning, the plants that had held an army of cabbage worms the previous day were now clean—except for the one designated plant at the end of each row. Now that was utterly amazing. I even muttered "wow" about fifty times. What surprised me most was the number of cabbage worms on the designated plants. Each plant only had the number of worms it could support. The rest of the worms—the sheer number of which would have completely eaten the designated plants in no time—were gone. Vanished. I found no evidence of them anywhere.

In less than seven days, the chewed leaves of the non-designated plants had mended, leaving no evidence of worm activity. As a bonus, the designated cabbage plant formed a perfect four-pound head later in the summer. Its outer leaves of the plant had been completely eaten by the worms and only the central ribs and veins along with the head of cabbage remained.

Observation, Experiential Learning and Courage

As we moved along together, I was learning that just because I carefully observed something did not always mean I understood what I had observed. A lot of times the act of doing something had insight built into the action, and I knew what I was doing and why. For example, when transplanting, digging a hole the size of the root ball was simple and self-explanatory. Placing the root end of a plant into a hole large enough to comfortably surround its roots but not so large that it swallowed the entire plant carried with it reason and was probably a good planting practice. However, transplanting small plants into the garden in late winter fell outside reasonable planting practices.

This is when I learned not to question what nature was telling me—just do it and watch. (It didn't stop me from accusing nature of being nuts!) If it was beyond my currently held reason and if it was not self-explanatory, I knew I was to observe the results of what I had done over a period of time. Watch how the plant responded. Sometimes a day or several days would go by before I reached some understanding. Sometimes the observation period would last weeks or months. And sometimes it would last years, with one year's work layering on top of the previous year's work. At some point, I would come to an ah-ha moment. Finally the last piece was in place and I could now understand what was going on. I could see the goal we had been aiming for and why. Had I gotten impatient and shortened or stopped the observation period, I never would have come to that ah-ha moment nor would I have been able to reach an understanding. I can't tell you how many remarkable changes occurred in the garden solely because I had the courage to wait and watch. And there were plenty of times when it did take courage not to interfere or mount some kind of misguided human driven rescue mission.

Sometimes nature provided a body of information that would help me understand, but not always. I learned that understanding something required a certain amount of pre-knowledge and experience. If our slate is blank and there is nothing to draw on in our foundation of logic, the new thing we are trying to understand would then require some preparation, some pre-knowledge, before we could understand it. It's very much like landing on the planet Perelandra and not knowing how to describe a color we had never seen before. There are no words. There's no preexisting knowledge or experience that this new thing can be linked to. We can't say, "It's kinda green," when, in actuality, it's not kinda like any green we've ever seen before. There is no recognizable base color. Is it even a color? Or is it something else?

Nature did not rely on feeding me blocks of information when I needed to understand something. Preparing to understand could not be an intellectual exercise—at least, not for me. It was not a matter of listening and transcribing what I heard. Because we were dealing with something new, I would not have been able to hear the words with the correct meaning, nuance and depth. Instead, nature's preferred way to lead me to understanding was to provide a string of experiences, small steps, that led me forward to an eventual larger understanding and insight. And it did this in the context of my garden. As long as I stayed in the moment and fed back to nature only what I was seeing and sensing from the one small thing from each day's to-do list, we were able to maintain our give-and-take information energy flow. By the time I got to the ah-ha moment, I had a body of experience, observation and information that, when put together, led to the ah-ha. I could understand what we had been doing and why. This led to more changes in my foundation of logic.

Of course I write this after over forty years' experience working with nature. My understanding and insight now can make what I'm writing about the garden's first year sound logical and reasonable. The height of grace. *Au contraire.* There were so many times when I didn't know what the hell I was doing. Sometimes it sounded so crazy that I'd stand in the middle of the garden and accuse nature of "losing its mind"—again. (It seemed like nature rather enjoyed when I didn't stand on ceremony and treat it as some god on high. It was my friend as well as my teacher and partner.) Or I'd stare blankly at something, scratch my head and mutter, "Whatever." I often wondered if I was doing the right thing, if I was hearing properly, if I was skewing what I was hearing because I didn't think I could or would want to do something.

In short, I can't say I was graceful about this, especially back in those early days when I rarely understood what was going on or why. I often left the garden at the end of the day feeling confused. What always pulled me forward was curiosity and the courage to come back to the garden the next morning, throw away everything in my head that didn't make sense, regroup and just refocus on that day's to-do list. I refused to remain swamped by my own confusion and the larger picture. Instead I reminded myself to concentrate on the small stuff. I could handle the small stuff.

Nature's Manifestation Partnership with Humans

Very soon after this, the intensity of my education was stepped up. One morning, as I was putting together my to-do list, nature said that it was important for me, if I wished to continue learning, to gain insight and understanding regarding various dynamics of manifestation. If I were to continue to develop in my position as an equal partner, I needed to understand what was happening around me in nature's world and the role I, as a human, played in it. The only thing I knew about manifestation was the word "manifestation." I had not read anything about it or heard anyone talk about it. When nature used the word, I didn't understand what they were talking about—but that didn't matter. Without question, I wanted to continue.

Over the next ten weeks, I experienced three different dynamics of manifestation.

#1. THE DRIVE-BY DROP: (My name, not nature's.) The first one is something many of us have experienced and can be used in everyone's daily life. In fact, it's the go-to manifestation process to use in partnership with nature. We need something. We state our need. Lo and behold, a big truck rumbles down the road and, just as it passes us, the very thing we need falls out of the truck and the driver continues on unaware or unconcerned. Or somebody walks up to us and says, "I think you should have this," and hands us the needed item or information. Or, we need a new car and only have $500 to spend. We check the car listings online and find the perfect car that someone needs to sell quickly—for $500. At this time, I needed hay for mulch. Due to the drought, the farmers around me had lost their first cutting of hay and were holding on to every available bale to get the cattle through the next winter.

The biggest breakdown in this common form of manifestation revolves around clarity. What we humans request is what nature provides. As far as nature is concerned, there is a vast difference between our stating, "I need some mulch" and "I need one ton of grade B hay for keeping my 30x50-foot garden mulched six to eight inches deep during this entire growing season." The trick is to state precisely what is needed and the job or goal we're addressing. Don't overstate it and don't understate it. If we understate it, nature ends up not knowing what we really need. (I say: I need some mulch. Nature responds: What kind? For what? How much? For how long? When?)

If we overstate it, we use many more words than necessary. This only serves to narrow nature's flexibility for providing the best options for meeting our needs and goals. I'm not kidding when I write "many more words than necessary." I was once asked to read a mission statement that was being proposed for a community. It was about ten typewritten pages long and listed details for every thing and every contingency they could dream up. It was their herculean effort to provide clarity and they were leaving nothing to chance. But what I saw was a massive, unfocused wish list. They had thrown all their wishes and desires for the community and for themselves living in that community into one big pile. In the process, they had completely clouded over their community's goals and removed nature's ability to maneuver in response to those goals. If there was a better and easier way to draw together their needs, nature was not going to provide it because the overly worded statement had eliminated all options but the one that the community members themselves had come up with.

Nature explained that clarity in manifestation extended beyond words to include imagery. If we can perceive it, if we can imagine what we want, we can provide an important layer of clarity. In return, clear imagery assists us when attempting to define or describe something using words. We can see in the visual what we missed in the worded statement. When clear imagery is combined with a clear statement, we provide nature with the full package needed for manifestation in partnership.

One other point: In order to provide clarity, we need to be able to focus. Although the Drive-By Drop is the manifestation most easily and readily available to us, nature said we generally botch (my word, not theirs) the process by both our lack of clarity and our spotty focus. If we don't know what we want or what goals we wish to accomplish, we can't hold a focus, we slide our attention all over the place and we become too easily distracted. (Oh, look. A chicken!) When partnering with nature to set up a Drive-By Drop, distraction can disperse clarity and we end up with a problem—a drive-by drop of chickens.

For two weeks, I worked with nature to develop clarity in words, clarity in imagery and undistracted, disciplined focus. The monk had already helped me develop these skills and I came into nature's classroom with a decent foundation. However, in order to work in partnership with nature for manifestation, I needed to fine-tune those skills. Every day (often while nature provided a sudden and crazy string of noisy and visual distractions for focus training), I'd write a statement about some item or action. It didn't matter if I wanted or needed it. This was an exercise in writing clear statements. Nature assured me we weren't going to trigger an actual manifestation, so I was free to let my imagination fly. I used newspaper clippings and magazine photographs for ideas. After writing a statement, nature would point out the weaknesses that were embedded in my sentences or by the use of certain words instead of other words. They'd draw my attention to where I was unclear or misleading or where I had not provided enough information, leaving a hole in the statement. I'd try it again and again until nature indicated that I had a strongly worded statement for using with manifestation.

I found it easier to start with crafting the statement and then adding the imagery. If the statement was solid, the imagery was easy to visualize. But there were times when the imagery revealed something that was missing in my statement. I'd adjust the statement and try it again. I found that the more closely my statement and imagery accurately reflected one another, the easier it was to hold my focus on what I was doing.

It was easier to visualize an item (a bucket, hoe, lawn chair) than to visualize purposeful action (a protest march, my role with nature). For purposeful action I had to include a clear list of goals in the statement, visualize the goals being met and stay away from the journey leading to the goals. Nature would provide the best journey for reaching the goals. In general, I learned that it was always smart to give nature a "free hand" to respond with the best option for accomplishing a goal and for setting up for a Drive-By Drop to occur.

It was time to apply what I was learning to real life in real time. I still needed that hay. My statement was simple: "I need grade B hay for keeping my 30x50-foot garden mulched six to eight inches deep during this entire growing season." Next, I was given nature's magic decoder ring and secret handshake for activating a Drive-By Drop: Contact the deva directly involved with what is being requested. Then read the statement aloud and visualize what I'm requesting. That would activate the manifestation.

I asked to be connected with the Deva of Hay and felt an immediate energetic connection. Really. This is all I did. I simply asked to be connected with that deva. Over these many years, I've watched people try to make working with nature appear complex to prove that only they, one of the enlightened and special ones, are able to form this partnership. Don't buy their routine. Working consciously and directly with nature intelligence requires common sense and clarity, not complexity and specialness.

Once I read my statement aloud, the Deva of Hay said that I would need hay for *two* growing seasons and not just the one season because the drought would cause a hay shortage next year as well. With this information, I modified my statement and read it out loud again: "I need grade B hay for keeping my 30x50-foot garden mulched six to eight inches deep for two full years, beginning with this current year's growing season."

With that stated, I was told to release from the process by requesting that I be disconnected from the Deva of Hay and to let nature handle it from there. I was not to be anxious or worry about whether my request had taken effect. I was to continue my usual daily routine *assuming* that this particular need would be met. I was to relax and, especially, I was not to try to figure out where the hay might come from, for that would only interfere with and place limitations on the manifestation process. (I continued on with my day, feeling that I had been given the hard part of the bargain.)

Within a couple of days, a neighbor called and gave us the name and telephone number of a local farmer who had a huge pile of damaged hay sitting in the middle of his field that he wanted to get rid of. He wasn't interested in charging us for the hay. He just wanted it removed from his field.

It was a beautiful mound of hay. Perfect for mulch gardening. Our only way of moving it to Perelandra was to load what looked to be over a ton of hay into our van. It took us nine days to complete the job because of one little thing I had not included in my Drive-By Drop statement. I did not request that the hay be in bales held together with twine. In fact, I had visualized the hay already spread on the garden. Had I thought to include a stack of hay in bales, our transporting job would have been much easier and less time consuming. The hay had originally been stacked, but over the two years it had been sitting in the field, the twine had rotted. We had to move this mound of wet, partially decomposed hay into the van, one heavy pitchfork full at a time.

The hay lasted exactly two years.

#2. THE DOWNLOAD: In July, nature moved me into an entirely different area of manifestation.

One afternoon, I was told to sit on the ground and to verbally request and visualize one cubic foot of cow manure. (What did one cubic foot of manure look like? I had to get a ruler so that I could accurately imagine a cubic-foot-size "box" sitting on the ground in front of me.) Having lived four years across the road from the Myer's pasture with their herd of cows, I had a good idea of what cow manure looked like. With my eyes closed, I visualized filling the box with manure, one cow plop at a time. I now had a tightly packed invisible box of imaginary cow manure sitting in front of me. What next?

Nature then gave me a series of steps to follow. First, I was to connect with the Deva of Cow Manure and state that I wished to manifest the cubic foot of manure I had visualized in front of me. Right away I felt various energies come together and mix. Once the different energies had commingled, I was told to connect with the nature spirits of the cow manure energy in my "box" and follow their directions. By now you know how I did this: I asked to be connected with the manure's nature spirits.

Once connected, I felt myself lift (vibrationally) to a level that I immediately recognized from my time with the monk. It was the vibrational level where astral traveling occurs. There the nature spirits and I waited. At least that's how it felt. Like we were standing on a street corner waiting for something to happen. After what seemed like ten minutes or so, I felt a third energy join us. It was the energy of my "box" of cow manure. Just me, my nature spirit friends and a box of manure standing on a street corner. What more could a girl ask for? What now?

I was told to focus on the manure and imagine holding it with my hands. The "box" ceased to be a container and I now had a cubic-foot block of manure in my hands. (It felt solid, not icky.) Once I visualized my hands comfortably supporting the manure, I felt a shift as we three slowly moved "down" in vibration together. Nature spirits reassured me that I wasn't alone and they were with me every vibrational step of the way. I didn't have to try to figure out what to do. I only had to focus my attention on experiencing what was happening in the moment.

The descent, although something I had experienced many times with the monk, now occurred much more slowly. (Or perhaps it had more clarity than I had ever experienced and just seemed slower.) As we moved from one level to the next, I could feel the manure energy change. For a few levels, I felt the energy change as a dynamic but it still remained energy. Eventually, it started to take on what I recognized as physicality. I could feel atoms moving, then molecules and cells forming. What I would call "form" was establishing itself within the manure's energy field.

We continued to slowly descend (in vibration). All this time I had my eyes closed so that I could focus on what I was experiencing. Eventually, I picked up a slight clean manure smell and the block became weighty. When I felt the manure was now a recognizable form resting in my hands, nature told me the process was complete. I opened my eyes. My hands were resting on the ground in front of me and holding a cubic-foot block of manure. Real manure complete with bits of undigested blades of grass and an array of crawly creatures. Mission accomplished. What now? Nature reminded me to disconnect from the Deva of Cow Manure and the manure's nature spirits now that the manifestation process was completed and could be closed.

I'm not going to say that I took this experience casually. But I also didn't freak out, as they say. My summer had been filled with one exceptional, out-of-the-box experience after another. By this time, these crazy experiences created a mutually supporting context and took on an air of normalcy. My foundation of logic was clearly changing. Be that as it may, that block of manure sitting in front of me was still definitely weird.

For some time, I just stared at it, thinking about what had happened, what I had felt and sensed during the process and what I experienced. For a few minutes I was afraid to touch the manure. (Would it bite me? Would it yell? Was it radioactive? Was it really real?) When I finally touched it, I found it was a perfectly rotted, finely textured block—with not much odor, a testament to its well-rotted state. I poked at the pile until I was totally convinced that there was indeed a real pile of manure sitting on the ground in front of me. But what was I to do with it? Was I to publicly announce a "miracle event" and sell tickets? No one would believe me. Should it be encased? Or bronzed? Was it safe? Was I to treat it like the weeping wooden statue of Christ at The Pilgrimage Church of Wies in Bavaria? (Did anyone know where I could find a Rococo architect?) Finally I asked, "What do I do with this manure?" Nature told me (rather casually) where to top-spread it on the garden. (Of course. Use it. How silly of me. Cancel the call for the architect.)

Manifestation in its "natural state," shall we say, occurs in less than the proverbial twinkling of an eye. This manifestation process took about two hours. It had been slowed for my benefit so that I could experience as much of the process as possible. The point of the lesson was for me to experience how reality became form so that I could perceive it with my five senses. Subsequently, whenever I was invited to join in a Download manifestation, it always took as long as I needed to experience and learn new things about the process, and never was it the same amount of time.

For a week, I was invited to practice the Manure Download. I must have downloaded about six blocks of manure and spread each in different areas in the garden. The garden was looking good.

THE DOWNLOAD VARIATION: After a week of this, I experienced a variation of the Download Drop. We agreed to materialize one squash seed. I then connected with the deva of the squash variety I had chosen and read my statement and visualized that variety's seed, once again activating the manifestation process. I then connected with the nature spirits of that seed. We moved to the same "astral traveling" level and waited for the seed energy to arrive. Once there, the nature spirits, seed energy and I moved as usual through the first levels of the process while the seed remained in energy form.

As the seed took on atomic structure, I felt the nature spirits release from my awareness. I was now on my own. My initial impulse was to strengthen my focus to "hold" and stabilize the seed energy.

On the atomic level, I could feel different energies commingle and magnetize together more strongly. The package of individual energies that were part of the seed was becoming a unified whole. As we moved through the process, the unifying and magnetic sensation that was drawing the energies together became even stronger. I also found that for me to properly stabilize the seed energy, it was important that my own vibration match the vibration of the seed. In essence, I couldn't assist or support the seed reality on the atomic level if my own vibration was geared to the level for astral traveling. The seed and I had to be vibrationally synchronized, something I was able to do with my focus on the seed.

At the very end of the process, just as the seed was about to become fully physical to my five senses, I had to intensify my inner vision's focus and once again visualize the actual seed in its physical form sitting in my hand. That's when I felt the final sensations of form taking hold within the seed. I opened my eyes and there, sitting in my hand, was the seed.

This experience gave me an appreciation for how much is packed inside one seed. It held the full devic package that covered the entire life cycle of the plant. As we moved together through the levels, I could feel the presence of the many elements of the squash plant in its full vibrancy—including its mature shape, growth and production. It felt like the universe was tightly packed in that small seed. I saw that germination was the controlled explosion of this universe from the confines of the seed. After this experience, I would never again look at another seed the same.

I was invited to continue working the Download Variation process for a couple of weeks. Each day nature and I agreed on something that was needed in the garden or around Perelandra—seeds, fertilizers, plants, tools…anything. And then we'd go to work. The quality of focus—the intensity of focus—required from me during the process needed to be exceptionally strong, clear and unbroken. Sometimes I got sloppy with my focus and the process came to a halt. Sometimes I lost the focus altogether, and the energy package would release from the process, move back to the devic level and disperse into its individual components once again. Sometimes if I wasn't able to pull together the exact amount of intensity needed just prior to the thing becoming physical, I would open my eyes only to find it sitting twenty-five feet or so away.

Tools were an interesting manifestation lesson. First I had to get over my prejudice against tools actually being under the domain of nature. But I soon found that each tool contained nature intelligence. After all, a tool, no matter how simple or complex it is, is made up of a combination of natural elements. We may not find plastic handles growing in the wild, but we will find hydrogen, oxygen and carbon (the combined elements needed for plastic). I also had to get beyond my assumptions and accept that along with a tool's intelligence came the opportunity for the tool and me to converse. (My quiet, bucolic, rural life away from the city was becoming quite noisy.) To manifest tools, we kept things simple—a hand trowel, a hoe, a wooden basket.

As I descended through the levels with a tool's energy "package," I could feel a distinct change in how the package drew itself together. Although there was still the feeling of life in my hands, its activity felt more restrained than with manure or a plant or seed. In the beginning I had a little trouble synchronizing my own vibration to that of a trowel because the shift between levels was more subtle than I was used to. After a couple of afternoons of practice, I began to recognize those changes and could move more easily with the tool as we descended the levels together. Aside from this, the manifestation process for a tool remained the same as the process for a seed.

While learning about tools, nature included the demanifestation process—a reverse action that removed the tool from its five-senses form sitting in front of me and returned it to its energy state. I found the *ascent* through the levels with a tool easier to recognize and hold than when we were descending. I'm not sure why this was the case except to point out that with demanifestation I started with five-senses form, an easier dynamic for me to start the synchronizing.

Due to Clarence's work schedule, he was rarely present at Perelandra during my classroom times. As the summer progressed, I spoke to him less and less about what I was experiencing. To talk about it felt like I was dispersing the experience. I also discovered that talking about what I was doing was exhausting. By the time Clarence returned, I had had the day's experiences, talked to nature about what I had picked up from the experiences and made extensive notes. Describing it to someone else wasn't something I yearned to do. During the manifestation lessons, I hardly spoke at all and the sketchy descriptions I had been giving him were now sketchier. Luckily, Clarence didn't press.

One weekend while I was working on demanifestation, he was in the kitchen fixing something and had his tools spread out on the floor. I walked by on my way to the bathroom and, without thinking, flicked my hand in the air and thought, "Let's get rid of that hammer." Instantly, the hammer disappeared. Out of all the things I had experienced up to this point that summer, the thing that shocked me was the disappearance of that hammer. What the hell just happened? At the time, Clarence didn't notice it was missing and I wasn't sure what to do to get the hammer back. What level was it on? Had I accidentally nuked it out of existence on all its levels? And, if so, how did I manage to do that? I needed to retreat to the bathroom and figure out what to do next.

I decided that the best course of action was to say nothing. Maybe he would think it was misplaced (which, in a way, it was) and just purchase a new hammer. I don't know why I was so reluctant to tell him what happened. Perhaps it was because I didn't know what happened. Surely a simple swipe of my hand was not equal to the precision and focus needed during the demanifestation process. I remember feeling embarrassed by this incident. I felt I had made a terrible, careless mistake and I was not sure how to fix it.

When I walked through the kitchen on my way back out to the garden, Clarence said, "Hey, have you seen my hammer? I thought I put it here [pointing to the spot on the floor]. I swear it was there a minute ago. Did you take it?"

I was caught. It was either lie and make him think he was crazy or confess and let him think I'm crazy (which could not have been that much of a leap for him to make). Here's an idea of how that conversation went:

> "I'm sorry. I think I demanifested it. I didn't mean to. I was just walking by."
>
> "Ahhhh...okay. What are you talking about?"
>
> "I flicked my hand over the hammer on my way to the bathroom and it disappeared."
>
> "Okaaaay...Can you get it back? Or do I need to buy another hammer?"
>
> "I don't know. Let me go talk to nature about it and see what I can do."
>
> (Picture my quick escape here.)

In the garden, I explained what had just happened and asked what I needed to do to get the hammer back and repair any damage I may have done. I apologized if I had broken some natural law. Finally, I admitted that I knew I had been too casual when I walked by the hammer but, other than this, I was not sure what I had done.

Nature pointed out that I needed to experience human power and what can happen when unleashed without considering the ramifications. The disappearance of the hammer was not an accident. It had occurred because of my focused thought, "Let's get rid of that hammer," coupled with my hand swipe. My intent at that moment had been sharp and clear, and the two actions (thought and swipe) had been well focused. Nature said I needed to see and experience this part of human power if we were to have an equal partnership.

About five minutes later, Clarence poked his head out the kitchen door and said, "It's back! Thanks." For the remainder of the summer, if Clarence misplaced or lost something, he'd first accuse me of making it disappear. I, on the other hand, said that if he didn't stop saying that, I was going to swipe my hand over him and make *him* disappear.

I thought a lot about the hammer experience and what it was saying about my power as a human being. At the same time, and as a result of the disappearing hammer, my partnership with nature changed again. I was beginning to feel that I was not nature's little delicate snowflake that needed protection. I had power. Well, at least I was hell on hammers. Now I had to continue learning about and recognizing my power, and I had to learn how to synchronize my power with my nature partner's power.

By the end of July, I was feeling fairly confident about what I was learning and experiencing in the classroom. I was once again in control of myself and nothing else had disappeared by "accident." Of course, I wasn't allowed to remain in that quiet, confident state for very long. There was a third stage of manifestation yet to come.

#3. Creation and Manifestation: I was sitting on the bench after finishing the day's garden work when nature told me I was ready for the final step in our manifestation lessons. If I wished to continue (of course I said yes), I was to set up as usual and request to be connected with nature's devic level. This was the first time I was connected to a generic, all-purpose deva rather than to a specific deva like the Deva of Carrots.

Once I was on the astral traveling level and had settled in and synchronized my vibration with the all-purpose devic dynamic, I felt myself gently "rising" to a different level. In short order, I tipped into the Void, a state I had experienced years earlier with the monk. Now I was back in the indescribable state of Oneness. I don't know how long it lasted. (They still didn't have clocks, or even time, in the Void.)

At some point I realized I was out of the Void again and was now experiencing what seemed to be the level just "below" it. I felt and saw a lot of swirling energy around me. Eventually I could sense countless magnetic pockets forming as different energy swirls were being drawn closer together and toward the pockets. Nothing was distinguishable. I couldn't point and say, "Oh look, there's my hammer." But I could tell there was a lot of action and attraction going on. The All-Purpose Deva explained that if the Void is where nothing can be distinguished from anything else, yet all that exists, has existed and will exist is present, then the vibrational level just below (or outside) the Void is where individuation begins and forms start to take on their characteristics and properties. All reality's individual components come from the Void. In essence, all that is, is created from Oneness.

The magnetic attraction I was feeling and seeing was the force that drew together the different energy dynamics and elements to create unified, balanced "packages" that, when downloaded in vibration would become recognizable form—a chair, a jacket, a plate, a car. Nature, on the devic level, provides the magnetic force that attracts and draws together a package's elements. All the elements and dynamics needed for the blocks of cow manure that we had manifested had been drawn together by the Deva of Cow Manure just outside the Void. The source for creation is the Void, Oneness. And the starting point, the wellspring for what we call "life" is on the vibrational level just outside the Void where nature's devic operation functions. The Download process that I had participated in was to simply shift the already organized manure "package" from one vibrational level to the next until its vibration became synchronized with Perelandra's. Now, from just outside the Void, I was experiencing and literally observing nature's devic architectural work as it was occurring and I saw where that manure's creation had begun.

The next day the lesson continued. Nature said that on the level just outside the Void I could apply focus and intent and personally experience becoming something else. On this level where the devic packages are created, this shift from one form reality to another is simple and easily accomplished (said nature). If I raise myself to the vibrational level outside the Void and I use the power of my intent and focus to declare that I wish to experience something else, a shovel for example, this would happen.

I had a few questions:

1. Why would I want to do something like this?
Why would I want to become a shovel?

2. What's the point?

3. What are the chances I, as an individual human being with my own set of characteristics and properties, can get lost in the swirling primordial goo of space and never be seen again?

4. Again, why do I want to become a shovel?

Nature assured me I would be safe if I wanted to experience this. Up to now, nature had proven itself to be a responsible partner who cared about my well being. It was time that I either relied on nature's intent to do no harm or I say no to the experience. I decided to take the leap and rely on nature. Other than spending the rest of my life as a shovel, what could go wrong? With that, I said, "Let's do it."

From the level outside the Void, I declared that I wished to experience the reality of a shovel. With that, I felt a gentle "dismantling" of myself, as if I had been released from my own gravitational field and pull. When I was no longer aware of myself or the surroundings I had already experienced on that level, I experienced a new vibration, a new gravitational pull, a new reality that included the Deva of the Shovel. I felt the different properties of the shovel—its shape, weight, size, strength. I stayed within this awareness for a while (I don't know how long because shovels also don't wear watches) and discovered that being a shovel was actually comfortable. The connection with the Deva of the Shovel felt different. It was more immediate, more intimate. It felt like the deva and the shovel's elements were a family with strong, stable ties. There was a simplicity to the connection, and I was able to experience balance from nature's perspective as that shovel. I wasn't just some inanimate object hanging out in the cosmos. I had links and connections to a community of elements that had come together to create the shovel. I had awareness of what I would call "belonging." And I could feel the stabilizing gravitational pull that was holding everything together. I had life.

At a certain point, I felt myself as the shovel begin to weaken gravitationally and myself as a human take on strength. It was a gentle switch that reminded me of watching the squash/cucumber change in my hands. With the switch complete, I felt "settled" into myself. Then the All-Purpose Deva, nature spirits and I began our vibrational descent together. I came out of the experience with a smile. (I have to say that in describing this to you, I have not been able to find the words that capture the fullness of the experience. But hopefully what I've written gives you the idea.)

For the next few weeks, I worked with a new manifestation process that combined all that I had experienced and learned up to that point. Once there was agreement on what to materialize, I would then connect with my new friend, the All-Purpose Deva, and shift to that space just outside the Void. From there, I stated what I wished to manifest and why. Then I requested that I become what was to be manifested. This occurred with the help of a second deva, the deva of the item to be manifested, and I'd feel the gravitational pull draw me to and include me as part of that item. After spending time experiencing the item's reality, the All-Purpose Deva would assist me as I returned to my human self. Then I could reflect on what I had learned from the experience and, after considering how I planned to use the item, I could make the decision as to whether or not this particular item was well-suited for the purpose I had intended. Remember, in my role as "creator of the garden" and in my co-creative partnership with nature, whatever I described and visualized was manifested. Sometimes I made dumb decisions. Up to this point, we'd go through the whole process and, at the end, I'd find that my original decision had been faulty (like the hay with no twine) and what I now had before me was not perfectly suited for the job. This is when demanifestation came in handy. However, by first becoming the thing, I was able to know beforehand if my decision was correct before we manifested it.

Once I made my final decision and activated the process, I watched the various energies of the package draw together on the level outside the Void. The All-Purpose Deva, the item's deva and I then descended together through the different vibrational levels until we got to the astral traveling level. There I felt the shift to the nature spirits who were working with the thing we were manifesting. It felt like the package was being handed off. We continued through the descent process and at the atomic level we had another handoff. I took sole responsibility for the energy and its descent until it was vibrationally synchronized with Perelandra and became visible.

I probably worked with this full manifestation process two or three times a week for the remainder of the garden season. I made sure that whatever was manifested was something that I could use in the garden. I also made sure that my requests were simple rather than complex—a hand trowel and not a tiller. Just the thought of a tiller with all its moving parts and technology gave me a headache. Could it be done? Certainly. But I was not the person to do it.

MY EXPERIENCE WITH MANIFESTATION is not something I take lightly. It is a complex, deep, intense experience on every level. I felt nature had provided me with a gift by showing me how life and form came to be. And I was honored to receive their gift. Because of manifestation, I now felt closer to nature—and to life. I had been drawn into the heart of nature's family and experienced how it operated from the inside. This had a big impact on how I communicated with nature, how I saw my role as nature's partner and how I interacted with nature. It changed how I thought about nature and how I perceived the life around me, whether it was in an easily recognizable living form like a plant or what we call "inanimate objects." Everything that I had experienced prior to the manifestation lessons certainly altered my understanding of nature. However, after the manifestation lessons, how I saw nature and how I understood nature expanded and deepened dramatically. When I said the word "nature," it had a much deeper meaning than before. Life came more into focus and took on a sense of greater intimacy. It was a comforting place to find myself in.

It's important that I say that I never manifested anything without first being *invited* to participate. I also got an agreement from the devic level on the item to be materialized. To make these decisions on my own would have amounted to human manipulation. Could I have used the power of my intent to override nature's role in manifestation? Sure. We humans dink around with life and creation all the time. But if I was to understand how nature and I were to live in mutual harmony and balance, I could not take on the role of the manipulator. Our partnership had to be cooperative.

From the beginning, I knew I wasn't experiencing manifestation as a tool to enrich myself. Nor was it meant for me to use as a parlor trick to razzle-dazzle friends. I have been the recipient of every psychological pressure imaginable, designed to try to get me to do "just one trick." But their efforts fail. I've learned over the years that there are three categories of people:

1. This is the group that will read what I have written about manifestation and it will simply hit the right chords. They'll know that manifestation as I have described it is part of reality and they will learn from it. If I manifested an elephant for them, they would consider my action unnecessary, frivolous and perhaps even disrespectful to the elephant and the process.

2. These are the fence sitters. They won't make a decision one way or the other unless they see just one more piece of evidence. After manifesting the elephant, they would say, "That's fine. But let's see you manifest a Sherman tank." They're never satisfied.

3. Then there are the confirmed skeptics. They are particularly adept at pressuring and can be nasty and insulting while they're at it. Their argument boils down to this: If I do it just one time for them, they'll believe. Well, they're full of crap. After seeing the elephant in the room (so to speak), they would accuse me of dabbling in Las Vegas magic, brand me a charlatan and take out a scathing ad in *The New York Times* accusing me of animal cruelty. They will never believe—until it's time for them to change their foundation of logic around this. In that case, their journey will lead them to their own ah-ha moment and they won't need a demonstration from me.

Waging Peace with the Japanese Beetles

In late July, the corn began to tassel, attracting a horde of Japanese beetles. Over only a few days, they had eaten the pollen from the tassels and demolished the corn silk. With the normal process, pollen, aided by wind, falls from the tassel on top of the stalk onto the silk flaring out from the top of the corn ears. Each strand of silk is connected to a tiny kernel nub on the corn ear. When the strand is pollinated, the kernel is fertilized and fills out. Without pollen and silk, we end up with an ear of corn with no edible kernels. If I wanted to salvage any corn, I had to deal with the Japanese beetles.

I talked to nature about the situation and asked if there was something I could do to save the corn. Nature told me to first connect with the Deva of the Japanese Beetle. Much to my astonishment, I touched into an energy that I can only describe as that of a battered child. It was an energy of defeat, of being beaten into submission. Yet it still had mixed in with it anger and a strong desire to fight for its life.

Japanese beetles are not indigenous to North America. The beetle larvae entered North America in a shipment of iris bulbs prior to 1912. They are not very destructive in Japan, where they are controlled by natural predators, but in North America, they can do serious damage to about 200 species of plants. They have become a problem for our agricultural industry as well as for gardeners. Consequently, we wage chemical and biological warfare in an effort to control Japanese beetles. What I experienced when I connected with the deva was the result of that long war. The deva explained that the energy of defeat, of being beaten and the strong desire to fight for its life were not part of the beetles' original devic pattern. I had tapped into a layer of energy that had attached to the devic pattern as a result of being under constant attack from humans. I needed to have this experience in order to understand what our relationship with the beetles had already done before I made any requests on the devic level about removing them from the corn.

Under the circumstances, I felt I had no right to ask anything of the beetles. So I simply asked that they recognize Perelandra as a sanctuary and invited them to join us so that they could begin to heal. I stated that I would not damage or destroy the beetles and would make every effort to enhance their healing process. To seal the bargain, so to speak, I stated that I would leave an area of tall grass that was a proven favorite of the beetles untouched.

I then addressed the issue of the corn. Still hoping to salvage some of it, I decided (on my own) that I would try to raise the vibration of the individual stalks—perhaps the ears would fill out in spite of the Japanese beetles. (Pitiful human think.) I spent three days placing my hands on each stalk and transferring an energy of love to the corn. At the end of three days, nature had had enough of this nonsense and I was told to leave the corn alone and not return to it "until further notice."

I was now to learn something about nature's preference for pragmatic love in action. Nature does not respond to what it called "static love" (gooey, sentimental love). Our partnership revolved around action and purpose—love in action and with purpose. Once while giving a workshop, I was asked to accompany several of the community leaders to a bush. It was a rather large bush, and it didn't take a horticulturist to see that it was dying. They told me they had recently transplanted the bush, and, as part of their transplanting process, about fifteen community members would form a circle around it each evening, join hands and send the bush love...*LOVE.* The bush had the nerve to start to die on them anyway. They asked me what they should do. I walked up to the bush, looked at the soil around it, checked the leaves, then turned around and said, "Try watering it." That's love in action. Not to be confused with love*less* action. Love in action is appropriate action done in a conscious, caring spirit.

I stayed away from the corn for three weeks. When I was told to return, I discovered that every ear of corn was half filled out—like someone had drawn a line and only the kernels on one side of the line were allowed to fill out. Nature said that the corn's devic pattern had been temporarily adjusted, making it possible for these ears to mature without using the normal pollination process. They wanted me to see how nature can operate with endless available options in the level below the Void and override or adjust a set devic pattern. They explained that half the ear had matured because this planting of corn was to be fed to the birds at Perelandra that winter, and only the amount that was needed had matured. A later planting standing right next to this corn and not yet damaged by the beetles would fully mature using the natural pollen/silk process and could be harvested for our use exclusively.

A month later, the second planting matured untouched.

In the years since making the agreement with the Japanese beetles, I've noticed that they have increasingly become more calm and fewer in number. There have been seasons when I didn't spot any beetles around Perelandra. That's when I get concerned about the well being of the beetles and wonder if something drastic has occurred in the environment causing their demise. But the next season they return and I always make it a point to welcome them back. Because of the shifts and changes on the part of the beetles and within me, I've not had reason to request anything special from them. Their presence here changes from year to year but still feels in balance.

IN MID-AUGUST, my days became quite difficult to manage. I received word from Findhorn that I had been accepted into the Essence of Findhorn program. I was to report the first week of November. That gave me a little over two months to can vegetables for the winter, prepare for my trip to Scotland and put the garden to bed.

With these pressures, I changed my attitude toward the way I approached the garden. I no longer had time to do everything that was being suggested on my daily to-do list. So I tended to enter my morning meetings with nature much like a drill sergeant. "OK. What needs to be done?" (Listen.) "Fine. I'll do this, this and this, but the other stuff will have to wait."

One morning I arrived to find that the row of Brussels sprouts plants—that had grown to stand a perfect three feet tall—now hosted a horde of bugs, leaving the leaves badly damaged and the plants looking weak.

I couldn't believe what I was seeing. I connected with the Deva of Brussels Sprouts to find out what was going on. I was told:

> *When you look at the garden now, you see a half-empty glass. You focus on the negative. You deal with only the work to be done. You no longer see the beauty and what is being accomplished here. The insects are showing you something. Your change in attitude has unbalanced the energy of the garden, leaving it vulnerable. Since you have altered the balance, it is important for you to re-establish the balance. You must understand the power contained in thoughts and attitudes and the integral part they play in the balance of the whole.*

I needed to return to the garden, but more importantly, I needed to recapture the attitude that I had had throughout the summer. It wasn't easy. I found it difficult to drop all else and refocus exclusively on the garden.

I wasn't sure what to do to rebalance the garden and asked nature for help in understanding what was needed. For three days while I worked with the plants, I focused on seeing the garden in terms of our accomplishments and its beauty. At the end of the three days, the bugs had vanished from the Brussels sprouts plants, and the plants had started a healing process.

Now I saw that a major key to maintaining the garden's balance was human attitude, specifically *my* attitude. It wasn't the reduced amount of work that had thrown the energy off, it was the attitude with which I was working: Pressed. Concerned. Worried. Anxious about the trip. Now when I left the garden to spend more time with my other responsibilities, I made it a point to leave with a clear, settled, quiet mind. With this, the garden balance held.

I now have assistants working in the Perelandra garden and I frequently warn them about what I call "checking off a list." This is when they have disconnected their presence from the life and vitality of the garden (as I did back in 1977) and are mindlessly moving through their tasks as if checking them off on a list. When this happens, their focus has switched from caring for and about the garden to a task list to be checked off and completed by the end of the day. Just walking into the garden area, I can feel a change in energy that alerts me to someone working in check-list mode. All I have to do is point it out and they switch their focus back to the garden.

I also watch out for an assistant who might be going through a difficult patch and, without realizing it, use their garden time to think about and through the situation. The Perelandra garden is my research garden, and it's important that it not become a dumping ground for staff problems. Healing and balancing are certainly two benefits of gardening, but the staffer needs to use their own garden at home for this and not the Perelandra garden. If the person needs time to settle out their problems, I'll reassign him/her to another job outside the garden until they feel able to refocus on the garden work.

One of the issues that had become a worry and had helped lead to the problem with the Brussels sprouts was money. The Essence of Findhorn program cost $900, and I didn't know how we were going to come up with that money. I believed that I was to go to Findhorn that winter, but I had no idea how I was going to get there. So I wrote and activated a Download Drop for the $900.

Enter Isadore. He was still living in New York City and was now divorcing his third wife. He usually called us a couple of times a year just to see how we were doing. Now he was calling to offer us a five-day, all-expense paid vacation to the MGM Grand Hotel in Las Vegas. In light of everything I had to do, I was not overly excited about his offer. But he had not made that kind of gesture before and I didn't want to hurt his feelings. (I can't believe I just typed that. But it's true. Ugh.) He was a frequent visitor to Las Vegas, and the MGM Grand Hotel labelled him a "high roller." So his time there was complimentary of the hotel, as long as he gambled. For some reason, the MGM Grand extended their generosity to high-roller guests. We accepted Isadore's offer and his plane tickets and flew to Las Vegas for five days of free lodging, free meals and free headliner shows. We only had to pay for tips.

I'm not sure there were two more opposite spots on the planet than Perelandra and the MGM Grand Hotel at Las Vegas. We stayed in a fancy but over-the-top decorated room complete with round bed and ceiling mirror. We ate fancy meals. It was about 120 degrees during the days, so we didn't walk outside the hotel except to take a taxi to another hotel for a show or to look at their rendition of Vegas weirdness. After three days of this, we were bored and decided we couldn't take any more of the lifestyle of the rich and famous. So we headed back to Perelandra. About a week after we got back, we received a check from the MGM Grand Hotel for $900. It was a refund for the two days left on our vacation. I called Isadore and told him that I would be sending him the check since it seemed obvious that the money was a reimbursement to him and not us. He said, "Just deposit the check in your account." And that's the weird story of how I got the $900 for my trip to Findhorn.

IT WAS FALL, AND I was raising questions about when and how to put the garden to bed. Nature said that it was important to wait until after the first heavy frost before closing down for the winter. I waited and waited for that frost.

Finally, in late October, the frost hit and I moved into the garden to do the work to complete the season's cycle. What I had assumed would take one or two days actually took seven days. It was an extraordinary experience, similar to the demanifestation process I had experienced earlier. Throughout the summer, I saw and felt the garden as one environmental unit or biosphere and the plants as individual elements within that unit. Now, instead of building the unit piece by piece as I had done with the garden planning and planting in the spring, I was dismantling the unit and preparing it for winter.

I spent the seven days connecting with each plant variety, thanking it for its presence and releasing its energy from the garden by removing its physical form. I did everything gently and slowly, respecting the fact that this growing season was over and we were going into a period of rest and peace. The atmosphere around me was calm. Every move I made was deliberate and precise. I found that even if the frost had already killed a plant, the energy and its intelligence had remained a part of the larger garden biosphere until I removed it. Whether what I removed was dead or alive, I could feel its energy release from both the biosphere and from my awareness.

As with manifestation, it's difficult to find the words to adequately describe this experience because of its depth and its extraordinary mixture of peace, gentleness and supportive love. I had a lot of feelings about that garden classroom and everything we had been through together. It wasn't easy to release it, to let go, even knowing (hoping) that in spring the classroom would resume.

That summer, my new partnership with nature had touched my life and my heart. I had learned something about the life around me, whether it was inanimate or growing. I had learned something about power—my own and that which is contained in all life. I began learning about equality, balance and teamwork. Nature had become my dear friend and my teacher. With nature I had touched truth, experienced creation and learned something about universal law. I now understood that truth and universal law course through all reality—including my small garden. And I had a whole new respect for a certain shovel.

Chapter 21

Findhorn, Scotland

ONE WEEK AFTER CLOSING down the Perelandra garden, I arrived at the Findhorn Community, a small spot located on the northeast coast of Scotland, just a stone's throw away from the North Sea and well off the beaten path (as they say). I took a transatlantic flight to London, an overnight train to Inverness, Scotland, and a short connecting train to Forres, Scotland. At Forres, an elderly woman walked up to me, introduced herself as Joanie Hartnell-Beavis, and said she was there to drive me to Findhorn. This was an unexpected surprise. So I traveled my last leg of the trip, Forres to Findhorn, in a car. I had no idea who Joanie Hartnell-Beavis was nor did I realize that I had been met by one of the elders of the community and a good friend of Eileen Caddy. But I was grateful.

Back in May when I had met the Caddys in Virginia, I spoke briefly with Eileen about my Going Home experience. She asked me to write it in detail and send it to her. Thinking that she could help me understand the experience, I sent her the letter. When I didn't hear back from her, I figured she didn't have anything more to add.

Joanie explained that Eileen had received my letter and had passed it on to several others to read. (My first lesson about Findhorn: Nothing is private.) They were meeting that afternoon at Findhorn Park, and she invited me to join them for afternoon tea. Of course I accepted and thanked her. From our conversation, it was obvious that, based on what I had written in the letter, these people had assumed I was an elderly woman. Several times Joanie said, "You're so young." By the time we got to my destination, I was starting to feel bad that I was just thirty-two. She dropped me off at Cluny Hill, the large hotel where the Essence of Findhorn group would be staying and said she'd be back after lunch to take me to the meeting.

Cluny Hill is an old, stone hotel that had been built originally as a summer spa. It had thirty-six large bathrooms, each with a wonderful, extra long clawfoot tub where a person could stretch out for a luxurious yet uninviting brown water bath. The hotel had been known for its "restorative" peat bog waters. And because it had been a summer facility, it wasn't insulated. There were radiators in each room and bathroom, but there were days when they seemed nothing more than decoration. And the luxurious brown baths were hot only if you knew exactly when to time your bath before all the hot water was gone. I quickly settled into my assigned room, then joined 125 community members and guests in the huge hotel dining room for lunch. Several members were already sitting on the radiators.

Joanie picked me up as planned and off we drove to Findhorn Park, the trailer park where the Caddys and Dorothy Maclean resided in the early 1960s and planted their first garden in sand with the help of devas and nature spirits. Joanie led me to one of the older caravans and there we were greeted by six more men and women, including Eileen Caddy. It didn't take long before I realized that these people were the elders of Findhorn, the people who had been drawn to the Caddys and Dorothy at the very beginning, before Findhorn became a community. They were the core of Findhorn, the keepers of its history. I remember feeling a strong, quiet stability in that living room. I also felt honored to be meeting them.

They reminisced about the early days and talked about how they, along with Peter Caddy and Dorothy Maclean, would meet weekly in that same living room to talk things over, plan and share ideas. (Dorothy was now living in Canada but was coming back to Findhorn for a few weeks around Christmas. Peter was touring Europe and the U.S. giving his Findhorn talks. He, too, would be back around Christmas.) They pointed to a chair and told me that was where ROC (Robert Ogilvie Crombie) would sit and talk to them about nature spirits. ROC (1899–1975) was a Scottish scientist and writer whose work with nature spirits was included in the two Findhorn books. His insights and descriptions led me to include nature spirits in my garden classroom. He had died just two years prior to my arrival, but I swear I could feel his presence in that room. The others must have felt it also because no one was sitting in ROC's chair. I suspected that whenever the group met, ROC was still with them.

They asked me to talk about my Going Home experience. The comments they made had to do with how young I was. I wasn't sure how to take this except to think that it probably meant I was a little ahead of the game, whatever that meant. When they turned the conversation to my garden, I explained how I used what they had written as a starting point and how I moved forward from there using what I had learned from the monk. I didn't give them details. I just wanted them to hear where the Findhorn books had led me and to thank them for opening that door.

After a couple of hours, it was time for Joanie to take me back to Cluny. As I was leaving, they gave me a warning. They felt that Findhorn might be challenging for me. If I had any problems, I was to feel free to contact them. And for one last time they made sure I understood I was young. It felt like they were sending their child out into the wild to face a pack of wolves. I had no idea what these people were talking about and they seemed reluctant to provide clarification. But I was grateful to know they had my back, if I needed them.

I spent my first week participating in the Findhorn Experience program, a requirement for anyone new to the community who was enrolled in the Essence of Findhorn program. It gave us a good introduction to the place. We met for talks and lectures in the mornings and dispersed among the community to work in different departments in the afternoons. I chose to work in the gardens and publication departments.

I spent two days in the Cluny gardens. We day laborers were assigned various weeding, transplanting and general maintenance tasks. I was just happy to be working in soil again. Actually, it was sand. Compared to my garden with its clay that I could squeeze into a ball and bounce off the side of a building, Findhorn's soil was a treat.

We began the afternoon with an attunement. We stood quietly in a circle holding hands and "attuned." What this accomplished, I didn't know. What were we attuning to? If it was not with nature, then with whom? The leader? The others standing in the circle? Was this Findhorn's way of creating teams? Why would we want to attune solely to other humans when working with nature in a garden? I used the time to connect with nature. Now I was back on familiar ground. Because I was at Findhorn, I expected the connection to feel different, perhaps stronger, than what I had experienced in the Perelandra garden. (Human think.) But it felt exactly the same. Apparently we were working with the same nature.

As I began my assigned task, nature gave me information that was counter to what the garden focalizer (leader) had given me. When I said something to him about certain plants possibly needing a different approach, I was told to go back, do what I was told and shut up. (That's loosely translated.) This was followed up by a look of exasperation. I tried to explain that I had a little experience working with nature but he didn't want to hear it. He looked weary. His job as a focalizer was tough enough and now he was faced with this American chick who thought she knew something. He needed to slap her back into place. So I returned to my task, explained to nature what I was being told to do and asked them to help me help the plants as much as possible, considering the circumstances. So much for my dream of freely sharing ideas with like-minded gardeners.

I returned to the Cluny garden a second afternoon and again connected with nature during the attunement. While weeding, I thought about my experience so far in the garden and decided I would keep a low profile during my stay. Although this made no sense to me, it was obvious that the Findhorn gardens were not the place to speak freely about working with nature in partnership. I would not talk about the Perelandra garden or what I had experienced unless someone specifically asked me about it. (Was this what the elders were warning me about?)

I spent the rest of my Experience Week working in the publication department. Because it was in a newer building at The Park, it was rumored to be well heated. The rumors were correct. As with the gardeners, publication always started with an attunement—to whom or with what I still didn't know. By this time, I was convinced it was a way to indulge in organized hand holding. There were about thirty people in the department, all pressing to get David Spangler's book, *Revelation: The Birth of a New Age* printed and ready for release. They were already months behind schedule. The book binding machine was large, impressive and old. Also touchy. (Someone needed to attune that machine.) It seemed to prefer the female touch and would break down whenever a man tried to operate it. If a button needed to be pushed, they'd call a woman over to do the pushing. The machine would then continue happily spitting out books. If a man pressed the same button, the machine would stop—for hours. I sat quietly at a corner desk trimming pages, basking in the warmth and getting a little high from the glue fumes that wafted around the room.

My Findhorn Experience was a week of fun with an exceptionally happy group of people. About half the Experience people were also there for the Essence of Findhorn, so I had a head start meeting my soon-to-be fellow Essence-ites. With such a friendly and enjoyable week under our belts, we were looking forward to the longer program. But the Essence of Findhorn that year turned out to be a completely different and less fun-filled experience.

Our Essence program was poorly organized, overbooked and staffed by two well-meaning members who had been "guided" to run it, even though they had no prior experience leading an intense, international group of thirty-five adults. Our two focalizers (leaders) argued the first week and spent the rest of the program not talking to one another. Terrible mistakes were made and the atmosphere was full of angst. After about two weeks of this nonsense, our non-speaking focalizers decided that the way to solve their leadership problems was to bring on two more equally unqualified but well-meaning people who had been "guided" to help. It was a study in how not to run a large group. I have to admit that it was sometimes interesting to watch the daily debacle unfold. There were lessons to learn but we participants seemed to be the only ones who were open to learning them. The four focalizers just stumbled on. It was difficult for us to suggest changes to the program because, at that time, any suggestions or feedback were seen as negativity—and dwelling on negativity was forbidden at Findhorn. Hugging was preferred. The focalizers liked addressing problems by hugging them away. Our group included two professional group leaders, one from the Netherlands and the other from Iceland. Each had years of experience running programs and leading groups large and small. They were willing to help straighten out the mess, but their efforts were rebuffed by our focalizers. So most of us who had taken time out from our lives, traveled to Findhorn and paid for these three months ended up experiencing the Essence Debacle.

Like any experience, even this one wasn't completely awful or useless. The mornings were spent in discussions led by our non-speaking leaders (they would talk with us but not with one another) or playing games and listening to lectures given by different members of the community. The topics revolved around the "New Age," a term I had not heard about prior to Findhorn. Talks about arcane spiritual theories and meditation were also thrown in. Some of the lectures were quite good and thought provoking; others were bad and boring. To get through the bad and boring ones, several women in our group began knitting. Now our lectures included the background sound of clacking knitting needles.

Eileen visited one morning and talked about meditation and following the voice within. She also led my first experience with a guided meditation. It had something to do with seeing ourselves walking up a mountain trail to a cave. She told us that inside the cave we would find someone special who would give us important information. When I entered my cave, I was surprised to find my monk sitting on the floor beside a small campfire. I had not "seen" him in several years. We two old friends greeted one another with warm smiles and I sat down beside him. As usual, he didn't speak and I didn't say anything to him because it felt like there was nothing to be said. It was comforting to be with him again.

When Eileen instructed us to leave our caves and come down the mountain, I was reluctant to leave. For one thing, thanks to the campfire, I was the warmest I had been in weeks. But the monk encouraged me to carry on with the meditation and assured me that I would be fine. (He didn't tell me I was too young!) When I finally left the cave, I got confused (or perhaps dyslexia got me) and took a wrong turn. To descend the mountain I should have turned right. Instead I turned left and continued up the mountain. I knew I was walking further up but since this was my first guided meditation, I didn't think it mattered. I was happy to enjoy the mountain's beauty and the vista. It reminded me of the two afternoons I spent in the Alps near the summit of the Aiguille du Midi.

But while I was walking up, Eileen was talking everyone else *down* the mountain. I don't know what caused it but I began to physically shake and cry—a soft cry, not a wail that would have scared the others in the room. I was lost and knew I needed help. But once the meditation was over and I asked for help, it was clear that Eileen did not know what to do. As my shaking got worse, our Icelandic professional group leader took control of the situation. She sat next to me, held my hands and "talked me down" in a most efficient manner. She had me count backwards with her, starting from ten. As we slowly descended through the numbers, I could feel my body gradually settle and the shaking lessen. By the time we got to one, I was back in the room and no longer shaking or crying. Looking back on it now, it seems like an obvious and simple solution to my situation. I was a rookie at all this Findhorn stuff and I had made a rookie mistake. (Was this what the elders were warning me about?)

When the Essence program began, I was assigned to work in the Cluny Housekeeping Department. Each afternoon, housekeeping vacuumed Cluny's miles of hallways and cleaned the thirty-six bathrooms. My first week I was assigned the task of making signs with the new names chosen for each of the bathrooms. It was a lot easier to say, "Daffodil needs six rolls of toilet paper," instead of "Take six rolls of toilet paper to the bathroom on the second floor in the east wing down the far hallway past the closet next to room 36." (It was also easier to shout, "The toilet in Sage is stopped up and running over!") The bathroom names may have sounded like a New Age nicety but, in the name of efficiency, the housekeepers needed those names.

On Saturday mornings it was all hands on deck to clean the rooms used by the departing Experience Week participants (who had to be out of their rooms by 8 A.M.) and get ready for the new Experience Week group (who were due to arrive at noon). My room-cleaning buddy was Long Tall John. He was a trained psychotherapist from New England who was now living at Findhorn as a member. We used to have interesting discussions as we changed sheets, vacuumed, cleaned bathrooms, dusted, removed candle wax from the furniture and cleared out the empty wine bottles, used condoms and tampons that had been tossed under the bed. (We could have used a pair of tongs with our cleaning supplies.)

John was not yet allowed to practice as a psychologist because the community had a hard policy about "rough edges." It was assumed everyone arrived with rough edges and were given work assignments unrelated to their expertise or training while the edges (mythical or real) got sanded down or chiselled off. I never completely understood what was meant by "rough edges" or what removed them. From my observation, it seemed like something that annoyed another community member was tagged "rough edge." Emotions and, I assume, rough edges were flying everywhere. Not a day went by without someone "going through their stuff" or melting down. It was especially evident at Cluny because everyone was living under one large roof. There was no escape. It wasn't unusual to walk down the hall and hear someone screaming and wailing in his or her room. At first I was alarmed and wondered if the person needed help, but I was told they were okay. They were just going through Scream Therapy. We Essence-ites began referring to Cluny as an institution for the emotionally disturbed. Long Tall John was needed as a therapist, not a housekeeper.

Going through one's "stuff" presented a problem that we housekeepers had to address while I was there. It started with a woman who was participating in an Experience Week. A couple of days after she arrived she began feeling depressed and deeply saddened. When she described it to her focalizer, she said it felt like she was experiencing grief. But she didn't know why she would be feeling this way because no one in her life had recently died. The next day her depression and her grief worsened. We housekeepers heard about it and decided to investigate. Was there something about the way we were cleaning the rooms that gave this woman such a reaction?

After a little digging, we discovered that the previous occupant in her room had to leave his Experience Week early because he learned that his father had died unexpectedly. While he made travel plans to return home, he stayed in his room, experiencing deep sadness and grief. It seemed clear that the energy of his heightened emotions was still present in the room, and this is what the woman had stepped into. She was going through his grief, not her own. Somehow we needed to figure out how to clear the grief out of the room. Smudging and burning incense were discussed but I didn't think they would address the problem adequately. I offered to talk to nature and find out if there was something better that would do the job. We suspected that more than this one woman had experienced a previous occupant's "stuff," and we might be dealing with a much larger problem. By this time, Long Tall John had told several people in housekeeping about our Saturday morning discussions and the Perelandra garden, so my focalizer gave me the go-ahead to give nature a shot. What did we have to lose?

Two days later, I came back to the group with a new process from nature for clearing out a room, a building or an environment—the Energy Cleansing Process. The next Saturday, after our morning blitz through the rooms, we housekeepers met up in the Cluny sanctuary and I led them through the first Energy Cleansing Process with the room in question as our target. The process provided the framework for us to work together with nature in partnership and included a white sheet of light moving through the targeted area, collecting darkened and inappropriate energy as it rose. Once the process was completed, we sat in the sanctuary and hot washed it. Everyone of the twenty-five housekeepers saw pockets of darkened energy collect in the sheet as it rose. And everyone agreed that the Energy Cleansing Process was the perfect thing for the Cluny housekeepers to do at the end of our Saturday blitz. It was the final touch.

We go back to my first lesson about Findhorn: Nothing was private. It didn't take long for word to get out about what we housekeepers were doing in the sanctuary. A few days after that first Saturday, we were asked to include the entire hotel in the Process.

I had to think about that a bit because I wasn't sure I could "stretch" the white sheet to cover something the size of Cluny. (Human think.) I asked nature if the process needed to be adjusted to take into consideration larger target areas. I was told that the process as set up with nature held. The sheet of white light could be any size. It was energy and could be created easily to fit the job. All I had to do was define the target area. During the process, my challenge was to keep everyone focused on the same sheet that covered the same target area and to help everyone maintain their focus as the sheet moved up through the hotel. My dubious experience with Eileen's guided meditation gave me some understanding about the importance of keeping everyone moving in the same direction. Luckily, my ability to feel energy helped me to recognize when the group's focus was getting a little soft (someone was dozing off or had become distracted) and areas of the sheet were beginning to sag or lag behind. At these points, I would ask nature to stop the sheet from rising, recollect everyone's focus with a gentle word or two and get them to use their focus to even out the sheet before we continued to raise it. (Look at me. I'm leading a Process!)

Each Saturday after completing the energy cleansing, we housekeepers would go down to the dining room to join everyone for lunch. We heard people talking about suddenly feeling something pass through them, starting at their feet and exiting their heads, as they were walking to lunch. That was right at the time we were doing the Process in the sanctuary. They described the sensation as pleasant but weird. Had anyone else felt anything? Several others said they felt it, too. This verified for us that the Energy Cleansing Process was real and working. I checked with nature to see if we needed to add some kind of protection for humans when the sheet was passing through them. Again, no adjustment needed. Based on my description and goals for the Process, nature had already included the necessary safety nets. Everyone was safe. Those who were sensitive to energy and energy movement would feel the sheet. Others would not.

A few weeks later after a particularly rancorous Essence discussion (heated discussions were not unusual for us), I sat in the meeting room after everyone else had left. It felt like a battleground. The others had just gotten up and walked out, paying no attention to what was left behind. It was a Friday and we would not be returning to that room until Monday morning. I wasn't sure who would be using the room over the weekend so I decided to make the room safe and also to try an experiment with the Energy Cleansing Process. Working with nature, we moved the white sheet through the meeting room. But this time, we stored the darkened energy wrapped in its sheet in one of the ceiling corners of the room. It was a large room with high ceilings so I was sure no one would accidentally walk through the stored bundle—not even Long Tall John. The next day, when we housekeepers did the Energy Cleansing Process for the entire hotel, I made sure the bundle stored in the upper corner of the meeting room remained untouched.

Monday morning I told my fellow Essence-ites what I had done and why. They didn't feel that our Friday discussion warranted my actions. And besides, the room had the weekend to clear that stuff out and settle down on its own. I said, "Let me show you what I'm talking about." With that, I asked nature to release the darkened energy from the bundle and return it to the room. The change in the room was palpable. The Essence-ites may have had the weekend to relax and distance themselves from Friday's discussion, but the energy that had been discharged in the room had not changed. Everyone could feel the raw energy settling around them. After a short discussion, they requested that I lead them through the Energy Cleansing Process to clear the room properly. From that point on, we cleared out the room after every, shall we say, spirited discussion. It helped. There were fewer tears and fewer people felt attacked. (But our two stubborn focalizers who had argued that first week in a location outside Cluny continued to not talk to one another. What the hell, you two?)

In January, our morning schedule included one week devoted to nature and gardening. It was to be led by members of the gardening group. Finally. Perhaps now I'd be able to ask some questions. Just prior to the nature week, one of our focalizers asked me if I'd like to talk to the group about my gardening experiences. I said, "Sure." It was a casual offer and an equally casual acceptance. She suggested that I write an outline of the things I wanted to talk about and she'd be happy to go over the outline with me, if I wished. She said I should plan to speak for about an hour.

What in the world would I talk about for an hour? I wasn't sure I had enough to say. I wrote a general outline of the things that had happened with nature and in the garden that previous year. It was only one page long, but when I saw everything written out on paper for the first time, I was overwhelmed by the depth and extent of the experiences. It also showed me I had enough to talk about for an hour.

As suggested, I met with the focalizer to go over my outline. We sat on the floor of a large broom closet because she was a smoker. Smoking was prohibited everywhere in Cluny but the bar—and, apparently, broom closets. We wanted more privacy than the bar could give us. I don't know what she had expected to hear but it quickly became obvious that it wasn't what I was telling her. As I moved through my list, filling in some details along the way, she smoked with more intensity. She kept saying, "I can't believe I'm hearing this." After over two hours, we stumbled out of the closet, surrounded by a thick cloud of smoke. She told me I would probably need three hours or more for my talk, and that I could have the whole morning of the first day of nature week to present the Perelandra garden.

I was quite nervous the morning of my talk but, after stumbling around a bit at the start, I launched into the adventure of my garden. I wasn't able to finish that first morning, so they insisted that I continue the next morning. On the second day, I arrived to find a number of the gardeners sitting in with our group. They wanted to hear what I was saying. (The Cluny garden focalizer was sitting there, as well.) After the second morning, I still wasn't finished. In fact, I had only gotten through manifestation, so I was given a third morning. This allowed for more gardeners to join us. In all, it took nine hours to describe what had happened in my garden classroom. When I got to the part about putting the garden to bed, I couldn't go on. It had been just eight weeks since I had that remarkable experience with nature. I said softly to myself, "Why am I here?" Then I got up and left the room. I had to be alone.

Once I spoke publicly about the Perelandra garden, I became a "nature expert" and was invited to just about every departmental and group meeting imaginable. I was even asked to give my garden talk to the full community. (The Essence folks attended en masse for support and to cheer me on.) I felt the responsible thing to do was to accept all invitations and to share my experiences and lessons as openly and honestly as possible. After all, nature had given me this tremendous gift. It seemed only right to give something back by sharing what nature had given me.

In actuality, I needed a business manager—some cigar-smoking guy from Brooklyn named Sol who would take me under his wing and say things like, "Listen, doll. Ya can't keep goin' through life respondin' to everybody else's beck and call. You'll end up killin' yourself." Instead of Sol, I was rescued by Dorothy Maclean. She was visiting the community for a few weeks and was aware of what I had been talking about.

One day at lunch I was walking through the dining room looking for a quiet place to eat. A bunch of members sitting at different tables were calling out, urging me to join them. That's when I spotted Dorothy sitting off to one side by herself. She nodded when I noticed her, giving me the encouragement (and courage) to ask if I could join her for lunch. *Yes. Of course.* After the initial pleasantries, I told her that I felt the community's sudden embrace of me was over the top and I didn't know what to do about it. She smiled and quietly said, "Always remember, the people who put you up on a pedestal are the same people who will kick the pedestal out from under you. Don't get lost in the highs and don't pay attention to the lows." She encouraged me to stay true to myself, no matter what. It was a key piece of advice given me by a wise woman who had seen it all. That lunch was the start of my friendship with Dorothy that has lasted forty years.

As if picking up on the inevitable, a couple weeks after that lunch with Dorothy, the Findhorn members at Cluny began chipping away at their pedestal. Dorothy's warning buffered me from the personal pain I might have felt and instead allowed me to back away and observe the actions of an unorganized, mildly angry mob. I was no longer the Cluny darling. Now I was too big for my britches. I needed to be knocked down a peg or two. I needed to chisel off my rough edges. I was still invited to meet with different groups, but the dining room was a different matter. Instead of urging me to join them, they would turn away and ignore me as I walked by. At first I couldn't believe what I was seeing. (Was this what the elders were warning me about?) Their shunning was as ridiculous as their initial over-the-top response had been. But thanks to Dorothy, I was prepared. What they didn't seem to understand was that I wasn't sitting on their pedestal and eventually, as they chipped away at it, that pedestal was going to fall over and smack them on their heads. Bottom line: Thank you, Dorothy.

The meeting that was most special to me was the three hours I spent with the Findhorn gardeners. As we sat together, I could feel that I was with "my people." Because the timing and rhythm of the many gardens that were scattered around The Park, Cluny and the auxiliary houses were different, as each group normally met separately. When I met with them, it was the first time all the groups had gathered together in one room. There must have been over forty people there.

As they arrived, I noticed something about the gardeners that I had not seen elsewhere in Findhorn. It was a little thing, yet meaningful to me. They were concerned about the comfort and well-being of one another. They weren't "I" oriented. Rather, they were "you" oriented. They knew if someone had had a strenuous or tiring day in the garden and made sure that person got a soft chair with pillows. They made sure everyone had tea. They took care of one another. Elsewhere I had observed people choosing their seats in a group setting based on the clothes colors or types of gemstones the person next to them was wearing. I saw people reject seats solely because the person they would be sitting next to was wearing the wrong colors and would cause them to have an energy drain (so they said).

With the gardeners, I finally had the kind of informal give-and-take nature/gardening discussion I had hoped for when I made the decision to come to Findhorn. Nothing was planned. We just talked. They explained that because they were required to make room for a continuous daily and weekly flow of guests (some who had gardening experience and some who had never gardened before but wanted the Findhorn experience), it was challenging to find their connection and rhythm with nature. I could see that because I didn't have similar disruptions at Perelandra, I could maintain a continuous flow with nature that stretched over many days. Each Findhorn gardener had his own style and strengths, which made it difficult when working together as a group to "hear" nature. Mostly they used intuition—and hoped for the best. No one had had experiences like what I was describing and they suspected that they would not have similar garden experiences with the current Findhorn setup. How was it possible for different people with different levels of experience and understanding to function as a unified group with nature in the same garden? I didn't have any answers for that. But I did suggest they might want to look at their attunements and restructure them *with* nature so that people weren't just standing in a circle holding hands. The day laborers needed more instruction.

They talked about the pressure they felt from the community to produce food—and more food and more food. The gardens were there to provide for the community and the nature focus that had started the gardens (and the community) was secondary. (Remember, I'm writing about early 1978 Findhorn. I have no idea how their gardens fit in with the larger community now.) I explained that Perelandra's garden harvest was secondary and the nature classroom was primary. But I had to admit that the harvest had been more than enough for two people. As I listened to them, I realized that Perelandra and its garden were set up for me in the most advantageous way and needed to be protected. I would lose my classroom if I allowed a community to form around me.

A young woman who had been sitting quietly finally spoke. She said that when she was in the garden, she always felt she was working under a blanket. To everyone's surprise, most of them admitted they had the same experience. And then suddenly all the talking stopped. For maybe five minutes there was quiet—a deep, sad quiet. When they resumed speaking, they expressed their determination to keep moving forward and to find answers. They also admitted it had been helpful to hear their different experiences and decided to meet regularly in the larger group.

I met with the gardeners one more time, in the Cluny sanctuary. They had asked me to lead them through the Energy Cleansing Process for all Findhorn's gardens. *All* of them. The gardens at Cluny, the ones at The Park and the ones at all the auxiliary locations, including an island off the west coast of Scotland. Per nature's instructions, I had each of the gardening groups focus as a team on the sheet in their own gardens. Then we slowly raised all the sheets simultaneously. There must have been twenty sheets moving through twenty different gardens. It was a little tricky, but we pulled it off. We were one happy, proud bunch when it was over. We sounded like a sports team that had just won a championship.

Clarence joined me my last two weeks for his own Findhorn Experience and work week. I was busy taking care of loose ends while he got absorbed into his group. We barely saw one another. I needed to finish the bathroom signs, a task I had somehow managed to stretch out over my entire three-month Essence time. The quiet afternoons spent in my room making those signs was a welcomed contrast to the hubbub going on around me. My housekeeping focalizer had shown terrific patience with me. During the afternoons I spent working on the signs or visiting other groups after the nature thing busted open, I was not helping the team clean Cluny. There were some complaints but overall they seemed to understand.

At their request, I needed to train the housekeepers to lead the Energy Cleansing Process and make sure everyone had a copy of the steps. Several years after I returned to Perelandra, I found out that someone who had joined Cluny housekeeping after I left had played around with the process in an effort to streamline the steps and shorten the process. Not too long after the changes were made, the process stopped working. I suspected that in their zeal to "improve" the steps, they had unwittingly dismantled the embedded safety nets. Nature would have shut down the process at that point since it was no longer aligned with the original description and goals. The housekeeping focalizer had to dig out the original steps to get it back on track. Lesson: Don't screw around with another person's work. Come up with your own process that reflects your own definition and goals.

On the last day of the Essence Program, our two non-speaking focalizers admitted to us that they had not been speaking to one another throughout the entire three months and perhaps, as a result, the Essence Program may have suffered. (Ya think?) They apologized and said they were now dealing with their issues together. We Essence-ites just stared at them. What do you say? For our last Essence task, we were asked to write down our thoughts about the Program and include feedback on how we felt it could be improved. Then we were each handed a box of crayons and a long strip of paper, about three inches wide and twelve inches long. We were told to go ahead and write down our thoughts. Again we just stared. By this time, I was becoming well-versed on what constituted a poorly run group and couldn't believe what an obvious, manipulative dis this was. On my skinny strip of paper, I wrote (in red crayon):

> If you are serious about reading and considering my feedback, you are going to have to provide me with a normal-size sheet of paper and a regular felt-tip pen. I'm an adult, not a child. Based on what you have provided us for this exercise, I can only conclude that you don't care about what we have to say. If I'm wrong, let me know and we can discuss it.

Our leaders did not follow up with us, so a small group, including myself and the two professional group leaders, asked to meet with the focalizers of the community. We didn't go in with guns blazing. But after about ten minutes of calm discussion, it was clear that these two people didn't want to hear anything from us. They just said, "Thank you for your input," which was Findhorn-ese for "You're dismissed. Now go away." We thanked them for their time and left. Someone in the group said, "That's okay. They'll figure it out." Someone else responded, "They're going to have to before someone gets hurt."

By late February, my fellow Essence-ites had left Findhorn to resume their lives and Cluny felt like a ghost town. I made the rounds to say goodbye to the people I had met. I caught up with Eileen and Joanie and, after telling them a little about my Essence experience, I assured them I had survived. Dorothy had already returned to Canada, but before she left we agreed to meet up again, especially since her travels frequently brought her to the Washington, D.C. area. I was eager to get back to Perelandra. I wanted to go home.

Chapter 22

The Classroom Continues

Sophomore Year: 1978

When I returned to Perelandra, I was completely exhausted physically and emotionally. I literally couldn't look at the garden. I couldn't even look at it out the window. I felt strangely disconnected. I stayed inside the house for two weeks and worried. Had I spoken too much at Findhorn? Were my first-year garden experiences meant only for me and not to be shared? Even though it made no sense to me, I wondered if nature preferred I had kept my mouth shut. I even questioned if my actions had violated some trust and, as a result, my connection with nature had ended.

When I was asked to talk about the garden during the Essence Program's nature week, it didn't occur to me to clear it with nature first. When I said yes, I had no idea what my little talk would lead to. I assumed I'd spend an hour describing what had occurred and that would be it. I didn't realize what I might be jumping into until after I looked at my outline. And even then, I still assumed I would speak for maybe a couple of hours, and that would be it. What caught me completely off guard were the nine hours it took to describe my first year and the response from my fellow Essence-ites. From that point on, I simply rolled with the fallout.

Of course, while sitting in my living room at home worrying about all this, I wasn't talking with nature about how I was feeling. That would have been too reasonable and too easy. Instead, I sat and stewed. But even though I was ignoring nature, nature was not ignoring me. After two days of staring at logs burning in the stove, I began to feel support, nature's support. It was as if a small platform had formed beneath my feet. Wherever I moved, I could feel that platform. And there were no strings attached with this support—no demands, wishes, hopes or urges for me to talk with them. Nature was just there for me.

I began seeing a wholistic chiropractor who had been recommended by a friend. He introduced me to flower essences (Bach and Flower Essence Society) and to kinesiology, the muscle testing procedure I needed for self-testing the flower essences and determining which ones I needed to take. I was drawn to flower essences right away. I liked their efficient but gentle effect on the human body. When it came to helping the body repair, it made more sense to work with something that provides a positive healing dynamic and not something that attacks or damages the body. A body in need is already down. So why kick it again, all in the name of healing? I purchased the Bach Remedies and FES sets right away, determined that I was going to learn how to use them. And each day I practiced kinesiology and tested the essences. By the time I was ready to plant in May, I was pretty proficient and I had a new tool for maintaining my health and balance. I was going to need it.

I finally walked outside into the cold late-winter air, sat on the bench and looked at the garden for the first time. Yep, it was still there. After about an hour I said, "I'm ready. Let's do this thing." And with that, I re-entered nature's classroom.

I now have over forty years' experience gardening in partnership with nature, and I know how different the garden can be from season to season. It's my classroom as well as a research laboratory, and all sorts of patterns and rhythms are built into each season that would never be included in a family kitchen garden. But in 1978, I only had one year's experience under my belt and fully expected the second year to be just as remarkable—and orderly. However, once everything was planted, nature told me not to do anything else for the garden for the rest of the season, except harvest. Every day I was to walk down each row, observe, talk about what I saw and keep a record of it. Once again, I thought nature had lost its collective mind.

For three months, I watched a semi-disaster take place. Cabbage worms and Mexican bean beetles were all over the place. Some plants just keeled over and died. Others, like the tomato plants, went totally berserk and took over half the garden. It was a strange thing to watch happening, especially when comparing it to the previous year.

The "chaos" caused a problem. Starting in early summer, we had visitors from Findhorn nearly every weekend. Some came for a vacation that they assumed would include free room and board. Others stayed a week or two and used Perelandra as a halfway house to reintegrate back into the larger society after spending years in the Findhorn bubble. But most came to see the magnificent garden I had talked about. They'd take a look at the new garden and then look at me as if I were a crazy fraud. They'd say things like, "Gee. I know a fellow who is a really fine gardener. Maybe you'd like to talk to him. I'll give you his phone number."

I responded by trying to defend the garden. But instead of simply telling them that I trusted there was a reason behind what was happening and that the reason would become clear to me once the process was completed, I tried to give them a logical explanation based on what I thought was happening. Of course, at that point I hadn't a clue what was going on and my conclusions were way off the mark. When I asked nature for a hint, I'd hear, "You'll see." By the end of summer, I learned to ignore outside opinion and not let it influence me or interfere with the process in my own garden classroom. I also learned that not only was Perelandra not to be a community, it was also not to function as a halfway house, if I wanted to continue the classroom uninterrupted. (I had to do an Energy Cleansing Process for the house and garden nearly every day just to unload the "stuff" the guests felt free to release at Perelandra.)

Actually, it wasn't until the following year that I found out what was going on. The second year's garden turned out to be a fact-finding mission and an environmental impact study. During the winter planning, the garden had been designed devically. (Remember, it was designed on that vibrational level just outside Void.) What I laid out on paper represented that devically balanced garden. But once it was growing in soil, it was bombarded by man-made pollutants and disturbances. Now the devic balance was severely challenged. That second season I was observing what plants were able to maintain strength, what plants broke down, which ones died and what insects and how many were attracted to which plants.

To guarantee that I not fret over or fiddle with the "garden of chaos," nature gave me an assignment. I was to prepare and erect the Native American tipi that we had just purchased. It was an eighteen-foot-in-diameter, canvas Sioux tipi in kit form—meaning that I had to sew the pieces together and prepare sixteen poles. You haven't lived until you've sewn fifty-six-foot-long zigzag seams through three layers of heavy-duty canvas. I sat with my sewing machine on the kitchen floor and opened the kitchen door so that, as I sewed the seams, the canvas would slide across the linoleum floor and out the door.

White pine trees make the best tipi poles. Our woods didn't include white pine trees, so we had to use young oak trees. They needed to be four to six inches in diameter at the base and about twenty-five feet long. Once cut, cured and stripped, I had to sand them smooth. Did you know that the circumference of a tipi pole that is being stripped and sanded is eternity?

The entire job took ten weeks. In September, Clarence and I raised the tipi together. I had read that the Sioux nation of old could erect their tipis in twenty minutes. It took us days. I set up the interior in the traditional manner, complete with a liner, rain channels and a fire pit. I cheated by including a small mattress and sleeping bag.

Each day during the summer, I'd take a break from the Great Tipi Project and stroll along the rows in the garden. I dutifully kept detailed notes just in case there was to be a test at the end of the season. By fall, I was happy to put this garden to bed. As winter approached, I still didn't know what it was all about. But I was at peace in my tipi, diligently learning how to make a smokeless fire in the pit. I slept in this magical, beautiful, quiet, peaceful place every night during that fall and winter.

Junior Year: 1979

It has been written that the shape and structure of a tipi creates a space that generates an unusually strong power. I think the poles are the key to a tipi's power. When they are placed in position, they create a bottom cone that sits securely on the ground. The tipi cover is then stretched around this lower cone. But the Sioux poles are twenty-five feet long. Where they meet and cross at the apex of the lower cone, they are tied together. Another eight feet or so extend out from where they are tied, forming a second cone with its wider opening facing up to the sky. The Sioux say that the upper cone collects universal or cosmic energy that then travels down the upper cone's poles to the lower cone and grounds, literally.

From the moment I first entered the tipi, I could feel a deep sense of peace. But I had some pretty unusual experiences in that special space, as well. One morning, Clarence was calling—actually yelling—to me from outside the tipi's front door flap. I asked what he wanted and why he was yelling. He said he had been calling me for a good twenty minutes and I wasn't responding. (I guess he thought I was dead and had been screwing up his courage to enter the tipi and check.) I had not heard him even though I'm a fairly light sleeper. I realized that I had been "off someplace," but I had no idea where that was. I had no memory of images or meeting anyone or having a conversation. But I could tell I had not been in that tipi. And apparently I had been beyond the range of Clarence's yelling. The whole incident scared me a little, but I already had a catalog of strange experiences in my life and felt that I just needed to move forward and get on with my day. At some point I would discover where I had been and why.

Then there was the night I was lying in the tipi watching the stars through the smoke hole. (If you ever get a chance to enter a tipi, take time to lie down and watch the sky through the smoke hole. Day or night, it's magical.) All of a sudden I was consumed by deep fear. It just landed in and around me like a dark cloud. It wasn't connected with anything personal, so there wasn't any reason or logic to it. The fear quickly intensified, and I spent the entire night wide awake, huddled in my sleeping bag. I was shivering from fright and sweating at the same time. The odd thing is, I knew I was okay and that this was something I just had to get through. In the morning, I was drenched in cold sweat. I went on about my day as usual, believing that at some point I would discover what the hell was going on with my Night of Fear.

(As of yet, I haven't figured out what the two incidents were about. Someday.)

Despite these two strange experiences, I loved spending the fall and winter weeks in the tipi. Of course, I had the best of circumstances. Each evening I ate dinner in the house, watched a little television and took a hot shower. Then I'd run out to the tipi, set the fire for the night, hop into my sleeping bag, jam a wool cap on my head, watch the stars and drift off to sleep. I wasn't exactly roughing it. But I have to admit that after those two experiences, I would head into the night with a little flicker of apprehension. I just never knew what was going to happen next.

As winter moved into spring, I could feel the tipi atmosphere shift from a Native American experience to that of a Perelandra nature sanctuary. Once nature verified what I was feeling, I changed the interior layout to reflect the shift by bringing in specific rocks and driftwood from the woods and placing them according to nature's instructions.

During the garden planning, I saw that a number of changes were being made and realized that I was seeing the adjustments resulting from the environmental impact study from the previous year. There were changes in the seeds and planting rhythm. The rows now had a more complex interplanting of flowers and herbs along with the vegetables. The row layout itself had changed. Instead of straight rows, they were now curved around a center of natural quartz rocks. Despite all the changes, I sensed the garden was back to having a familiar order and, once it was planted, I resumed my familiar gardener's rhythm, turning my attention to the daily to-do list.

By now, I understood that the primary focus for this garden was balance, and I could tell how well the balance was holding by looking at the condition of the plants. If a plant looked weak, or the color, texture and quality of fruit were off, or the plant attracted more insects than it could comfortably support, I knew its balance was being disturbed. But once I checked with nature about adjusting the soil, water, temperature and nutrients, I didn't know what else to do if the plant still didn't respond.

Enter Cosmic Chess: Nature said that in order to achieve a stronger, more stable balance, I could no longer look at a plant or its energy as an isolated entity. I had to think of the individual plant in terms of its relationship with the whole. That's where Cosmic Chess came in. This was one of the more enjoyable, challenging and amazing lessons nature has given me.

The game board was any garden at Perelandra—flower or vegetable. It was my choice. The first garden I chose was a small flower garden in front of the house. The point of the game was to determine what was needed to achieve balance on the game board. To start out, I had to consider the proper shape and size of the garden. I was told to mark a border that "felt right" to me. Since I wasn't sure what that meant, I simply marked a border that appealed to me. Then I was told to "feel" the energy that was now contained within that border. I still wasn't sure what I was doing, so I just tried to sense something—anything. Then nature told me to go away and return later that day.

When I returned, the border I had marked with timbers and a rock had been slightly adjusted. The space was a little larger and the shape a bit different. I was told to "feel" the garden's energy again. Now I had something to compare it with, and I could actually feel a change—a greater sense of stability, a smoother sensation. And this was just from simple changes in the shape and size.

The board was set. I was told to plant one flower plant anywhere I wished within the garden and, once it was planted, I was to feel the shift in the garden's energy. If I didn't like the feel of the energy, I could change the plant's position. When I was happy with my "move," I was to leave and return the next day.

The next day, I found two plants in the garden—mine and a "stranger." I was told to again feel the energy shift and that, if at any time I felt nature's move created an unstable energy, I was to change their move. I admit I had to get used to nature's magical adjustments, additions and disappearances that went on during

Cosmic Chess. However, by the end of summer, nature's "magic" was my new normal.

We went on for a couple of weeks like this. I would make a move, then nature would make a move, and each time I felt the shift in energy. A plant's variety and flower color had to be considered. Shape, size, color and type also had to be considered when placing a rock, pebble or piece of driftwood. Once, I placed a beautiful, large rock beside one of the plants. It shifted the energy balance drastically, but I thought the shift was in balance. The next day I discovered a much smaller but better quality quartz rock where mine had been. I could tell that the smaller rock created a higher quality balance and provided greater stability.

There were times when I had to "correct" a nature move—even times when my correction was corrected, only to have me correct their correction. (The plants that were being moved around had to have been confused.) I was becoming more confident about this energy thing, and nature was getting more crafty with its moves. The game didn't end until I felt the garden was balanced and strong and nature agreed. If I was wrong—which I was four times in the first game—I would return the next day to find a position changed, an addition made or even something removed. Once we agreed that the garden was balanced, the game was called. I'd take time to think about and admire the game results, then we'd move to another garden and create a new board.

After a number of games of Cosmic Chess, I became more open to options when it came to the task of establishing balance within the garden. My to-do list shifted to reflect my development. I was no longer just considering a single plant or row of plants. Now I saw the garden area as a large bubble, a biosphere, with its own atmosphere and collection of plants. And I was also taking into consideration any destabilizing effect coming in from outside the biosphere.

At some point in the middle of the summer, a local real estate agent knocked on our door. The ten-acre wooded lot next to Perelandra was for sale. Did we want to purchase it? When we moved to Perelandra in 1973, we were told that the lot next to us was owned by a fellow who worked for the CIA and that he had purchased it for retirement. We had been a little spooked by this news. What the hell were we going to do with a CIA agent living next door? As soon as the realtor told us he wanted to now sell the lot, Clarence and I put our heads together and figured out how to buy that ten acres. Our future spy issue had evaporated and Perelandra was now twenty acres.

Shortly after purchasing the land, nature let me know that I was to move the garden from its present location beside the house to a small patch of open field that came with our new land. The original garden was bordered by trees on the east and north sides, and the tree limbs were now reaching out over much of the garden causing a shade problem. I figured nature would address this problem at some point, but I did not expect relocation to be the solution. As if this wasn't enough, nature said it would be best if the new garden site was ready for the next gardening season! (Oh, sure. No problem. Love that deadline. By the way, what do I have to do to move the garden 400 feet to its new location? Can you get me a rototiller?)

Time out for a quick trip to New York City. One morning I awoke with a crystal-clear awareness that I now needed to tell Isadore what happened to me after I left Upperco. It was time he knew. As far as I was aware, he knew very little about my post-Upperco life. If he was ever going to deal with his role and face what he was responsible for, I would need to give him the information. So I called him in New York and made an appointment.

We met in his apartment. It took about two hours for me to tell him the painful story. He didn't challenge what I was telling him, nor did he try to defend himself. He just sat there. When I finished, he said, "If this had happened to me, I would never speak to my father again." I looked into his eyes and calmly said, "I'm speaking to you because I'm a better person than you are." His reply: "Yes." This was my moment of triumph over Isadore.

We never spoke about my post-Upperco experiences again. His wife (#4) told me later that he said he didn't believe me because, if it were true, I wouldn't be speaking to him. His rules in life were still the only rules that mattered—to him. But I think he did believe me. After that meeting, he acted differently and spoke to me differently. An edge had disappeared. I had taken a stand and he now knew he wasn't going to be able to roll over me.

Back to Perelandra. Moving a garden is a chore. (That's the diplomatic way of saying it.) I didn't know how I was going to break the news to Clarence (I'd need his help), so I didn't say anything for several weeks. Then one day, as we were returning from a walk, Clarence looked right at the "proposed" new site and said, "You know, that's a much better location for the garden." Well, I'm no fool. I know an opportune moment when I see it. I said, "Funny thing…" Then told him about the garden move.

By fall I had staked out the new site with nature. Clarence called a neighbor with a big fancy tractor for help. The fellow suggested we disc the area instead of plowing it so that the soil would be less inverted. But our field just laughed at his fancy tractor with its big disc. He could not get the disc blades to cut into the soil. That's when I knew this new garden was going to present new challenges.

Fred Garrison came to our rescue. While Clarence and I sat in the field waiting for Fred's arrival, we could hear him lumbering down the gravel road on his old—really old—tractor. When he got to the garden site, he surveyed the land and said that if he could get his plow to make the first cut into the soil, he'd be able to plow the whole site. (There's nothing like years of experience and expertise. Go for it, Fred.) His equally old plow had just one tine, so this was going to take some time. He placed two huge rocks that he had brought with him, one on each side of the plow, to add the weight needed to cut into the soil. Then he lined up the tractor and slowly started down the center of the proposed garden site. The tine sliced into the soil right away. By the time Fred was finished, I had a newly plowed garden. It was to sit untouched for the winter.

That fall after the new garden site was plowed, and just to make sure I didn't get bored, nature brought up another project—a sanctuary built on the tipi site that would be modeled after the tipi design. It was to have eight sides, an octagon, and the wooden walls were to be six feet high. Using this as a base, we were to build an octagon roof made from eight triangular-shaped fiberglass pieces that joined together at a point eighteen feet above the floor. The top point was to be a copper two-foot high cone cap, with copper wires running from the cap down the seams of the fiberglass pieces and to the ground. The structure was to have a wooden floor. The tipi fire pit that was ringed in white quartz rocks was to remain unchanged beneath the floor. On the floor directly over the fire pit, I was to place five eighteen-inch square slate pieces in the shape of a celtic cross. Nature then gave me a list of what was to go on each slate slab. The new sanctuary was to be completed by and activated on the following summer solstice. (Geez. What's with these damn deadlines?)

I hesitated and winced when I gave Clarence the news. He winced too. Clarence had shed-building skills and had never taken on a project this large or complex. Even though neither one of us understood why we needed to build a sanctuary, especially since we considered the whole of Perelandra to be a sanctuary, we agreed that this project felt important. We started making plans for the new sanctuary right away.

Senior Year: 1980

In early spring, I could feel a next step sitting in front of me, and I needed to decide if I wanted to take it or not. It seemed like I could continue on in the current classroom level or move forward to a new level. It didn't take long for me to make my decision. So one afternoon in the tipi sanctuary, I connected with nature and announced that I wanted to continue on to the next step. It was as simple as that. No clues were given about what that next step was.

With the next step, my garden shifted from a classroom for learning about nature from nature to a classroom/laboratory where nature and I would work together to develop solutions to problems and disseminate information about the human/nature partnership to others. But as I've said, I didn't know any of this when I stated that I wanted to go on.

My first job was to close down my original garden next to the house. I removed the straw, fertilized the bare ground and then seeded it for grass. It felt like I was leaving an old friend, one who was happy to see me moving forward.

My second job was to get the new garden in place and settled. As I moved through the late winter/early spring planning with nature, I discovered that not only had the location changed but the size and shape, as well. It was to be a circular garden measuring one hundred feet in diameter. (More than three times larger than the original garden.) Starting at the midpoint of the circle, I was to mark the rows—eighteen concentric circles three feet apart.

Before I could set the rows, I had to get the guy with the fancy tractor back to disc the plowed soil. Then I spread fertilizers. Clarence rented a rototiller to work in the fertilizers and to smooth the soil for the final prep. Only then was it time to mark the concentric rows. I hammered in a tall pipe at the midpoint of the circle, tied a fifty-foot long string to it with tags taped three feet apart along the string. I held the first tag, the one that was three feet away from the pipe, and walked in a circle around the pipe sprinkling a line of white flour as I walked. (Had I used something like lime to mark the rows, the fertilized balance in the rows would have been altered. We all know white flour is fairly benign nutritionally!) When I was finished, I had eighteen concentric circles marked. In the center where the pipe had been, I set the large quartz rock that I hauled over from the center of the original garden. Lastly, I spread three inches of straw between the rows. All of this took over three weeks but, when I finally stepped back to look at my efforts, I saw that I now had a new, mulched garden with set rows. For me, that was a huge accomplishment. When I had looked at the plowed clay soil with its deep furrows throughout the winter, I wasn't sure I would be able to get the garden established to this point. (Note to nature: Do not make me move the garden again—ever.)

Clarence built a small shed/office, giving me a work center. We also hauled over the cinder blocks and board I had used as my bench at the original garden. I was now set. I worked every weekday from the time he left Perelandra in late morning until sundown—sometimes longer. (I also began a summer-long obsession with Entenmann's chocolate chip cookies. I needed something to get me through those summer days with my new, big garden.)

On weekends, Clarence and I worked on the sanctuary together. It was a difficult structure to build because of its unusual shape. I had the singular joy and added excitement of nearly losing my life during construction. We had the roofing framework up and, since I was the lighter person, I needed to go up the ladder to the apex to slip on the final top piece that would hold the timbers in place. While trying to get the piece in place, the entire roof framework collapsed. So there I was swinging in the wind on a ladder about eighteen feet in the air. Clarence was at the bottom of the ladder struggling to keep the thing from tipping over the six-foot wooden wall and slamming me to the ground. After I resumed breathing, I slowly and carefully climbed back down while Clarence continued to hold onto the ladder with all his strength. The framework was set up again, only this time more securely. After talking it over, we decided it was best to have Clarence at the bottom of the ladder in case of another snafu. (I may have been lighter, but he was stronger.) My second trip up the ladder was a success. (Note to self: Next time, hire a professional builder. And stay off ladders!)

With a great deal of work and effort, we met our deadline and finished the sanctuary in June in time for the summer solstice. It just so happened that Peter Caddy was in the Washington area that week. I had already met up with him a couple of times as he traveled through Washington and over time we had become friends. So I called him and asked if he would like to "officiate" at the activation of our sanctuary. (It felt like the right thing to do.) He not only eagerly accepted but also showed up with a couple of friends to help witness the moment. As we walked into the sanctuary, Peter stopped at the door, turned and said to me,

"This is where the Pan/Christ energies
will come together."

I had no idea what he was talking about. (It was one of those moments when I just mumbled to myself, "Whatever.") I didn't understand what he meant by "Christ energy," but if it came with a rototiller, it was welcome. At the time he said it, I had the sneaking suspicion that he was hinting that Perelandra was about to become a Findhorn-like community. In the doorway that day, I had two choices: Either ignore him or pummel him to death. I decided to ignore him.

> Note: "Christ energy" is the ancient metaphysical term used to describe the evolutionary dynamic of moving forward. "Pan" is nature's involutionary dynamic for grounding and coming into form. "Evolution" or "christ" also are terms used to describe the White Brotherhood. (More on this later.) "Christ energy" does not refer to the historical figure Jesus Christ.

THAT JULY, ISADORE DIED. He was sixty-one years old and he died of stomach cancer.

We had struck an uneasy truce that was facilitated by our not seeing one another more than once a year. I knew he would never understand my life and I wasn't going to try to help him understand. (I hadn't told him anything about my nature work.) To him, I was still an unmarried, liberal, tree-hugger with long hair (long hair drove Republicans mad) who lived with Clarence in the woods. We didn't even have air conditioning or a garbage disposal, for god's sake. It was just too much for him to deal with. I also knew that I would never understand his life or what he called "the good life." When he died, he was preparing to divorce his fourth wife, and he now had a total of five minor children (the youngest was six months old) from his last three marriages. I couldn't help but wonder, "Have you ever heard of condoms?" Admittedly this is an odd thought for a daughter to have about her father, but it was a valid question.

I did not make it to Connecticut for his funeral. Instead, I was at his office in New York City following his written instructions and trying to open his safe. (Once again I was struggling with a combination lock.) Michael Slater, his accountant, was with me and couldn't get the safe open either. Neither could the random passersby we had hauled in from the hallway. After over an hour of failed attempts, we called a professional safe-cracker. Michael had to leave and I was left in the office to deal with the safe-cracker, the safe and Isadore's instructions.

A half hour later, in walked "Slim the Safe-Cracker," pulling his bag of magic tools on a dolly. At first he didn't want to touch the safe unless Mr. Small was present. That was reasonable. (But Mr. Small was dead and would not be joining us.) I had to convince Slim that Mr. Small wasn't feeling well and was in the bathroom. Finally Slim decided he couldn't wait any longer and it was okay to proceed. It took him less than two minutes to open the safe. Had I blinked or sneezed, I would have missed the moment. When he opened the door, a large stack of musty smelling money fell out and spread all over the floor. Slim and I just looked at one another. It was $42,000 in old $20 bills. (I later counted it.) I don't think either one of us knew what to do, except it was obvious Slim wanted to get out of there fast. He explained that the lock had broken the last time Mr. Small closed the safe and the tumblers weren't working properly. We'd have to get the lock repaired before closing the safe again. Then he handed me a bill for what I considered an exorbitant cost for his two minutes of service. With all this money on the floor and Mr. Small still not back from the bathroom, I had a feeling Slim was trying to take me for a ride. I took his bill and went into the outer office to call Slim's office to verify the charge.

I wasn't being taken for a ride. The going rate for safe cracking in Manhattan in 1980 was over $300. When I returned to Isadore's office, Slim looked like he was in shock. All the color had drained from his face. I had left him alone with all that money laying around his feet. Clearly I wasn't following protocol. I picked up enough money from the floor to cover his bill and handed it to him. Before he left, he asked if I wanted to search him. You know, like do some kind of a police pat down. I told him no, that wouldn't be necessary. (Since he was freely volunteering for a pat down, I didn't think he had taken anything.) I told him if there was a problem, Mr. Small would be contacting his company. With that, Slim the Safe-Cracker left. As I watched him roll his tool bag out the door, I thought, "There is no safe in all of Manhattan that this guy can't open." I wondered what Slim did on weekends.

The point of getting Isadore's safe open was so I could retrieve his safe deposit key. According to Isadore's instructions, I was to go to the bank (his office was in the Empire State Building and his bank was on the first floor) and empty his safe deposit box before the bank heard about Isadore's death and froze his accounts. (A year prior to his death, Isadore had made Michael Slater and me co-trustees and I was a co-signer on his box.) Isadore died on a Friday. I was standing in his office getting his safe cracked open on Saturday morning. I had to get to the safe deposit box before noon. Monday would be too late. I was to divide whatever was in the box equally and give each of the three wives (my mother was excluded) their share to cover the children's expenses while the estate was being settled.

By the time Slim left, it was too late to get to the bank. So I sat in Isadore's office and counted the money from the floor, then called Michael and asked what I was to do next. He told me to shut the safe (they'd fix the lock later), stuff the $42,000 in my bag (oversized to accommodate the anticipated contents of the safe deposit box), take it back to Virginia and deposit it in my bank to keep it safe. We'd disperse it once Isadore was buried and everything settled down. Michael knew there would be problems with the three wives who were already jockeying for Isadore's money and issuing vague threats aimed mostly at me since I was one of the trustees and the easier target. Most of what these women knew about me had come from Isadore. Apparently they thought I was going to steal the money and head off to Tahiti. Michael warned me that I now would be learning something about greed.

While I dealt with Slim and the $42,000, Clarence was in Connecticut attending Isadore's gravesite funeral along with a handful of assorted family members and several gentlemen from the Mafia—Isadore's golfing buddies. In all, there were about twelve people present, including the rabbi. When the hearse arrived, there were no pallbearers. So the golfing Mafia and Clarence volunteered their services and hauled the casket to the gravesite. As part of the Jewish burial ceremony, the rabbi approached the daughter from marriage #2 to cut the black ribbon she had pinned on her dress. (It's tradition for expressing grief at the loss of a loved one.) She panicked because no one told her he was going to do this and, when he approached with scissors, she thought he was going to slay her and offer her up as a sacrifice. Honest to god, this is what she thought. Crazy wife #2, who was raising her two kids Catholic, must have been telling this poor girl some pretty interesting stories about Jewish traditions. A cousin I had not seen since I was five years old had flown in from California for the funeral. She added to the ceremony by raising a screaming, crying ruckus because she wanted her "Uncle Izzy's" casket opened at the cemetery. She wanted to see him one last time. (The casket remained shut.) Wife #3 and her daughter never got to the funeral because wife #4 deliberately gave them the wrong directions to the cemetery. On top of all of this, it was one of the hottest days that summer and everyone was sweating profusely. Clarence later told me it was a good thing I wasn't there.

Isadore's estate was divided equally among his children. His "good life" and gambling had eaten through a good portion of the money. But the five younger children now had enough to cover their education and living expenses. (Picture the irony here.) Clarence and I celebrated our modest windfall by buying a lawn tractor and a rototiller. We were in heaven.

By the way, when we finally opened the safe deposit box, we found a bunch of empty envelopes, rubber bands and paper clips. One of Isadore's pals told me that at one time the box held $1 million, but apparently Isadore had gambled it all away. I dutifully divided the envelopes, rubber bands and paper clips into five equal piles, one pile for each child (I donated my share of trash to them) and gave each of the warring mothers their children's share.

About six months after Isadore's death, I had a vivid dream. I saw a pedestal with a black dial phone sitting on it. The phone started ringing and wouldn't stop, which annoyed the hell out of me because I hate ringing phones. Finally I walked over, picked it up and said, "Hello?" I heard, "Machaelle. They healed me. They healed my heart." It was Isadore, and his voice was as clear and real as could be. I thought, "Crap. He's not dead. How could he still be alive?" As he kept repeating "they healed me," I was frantically trying to figure out how I was going to tell him that his fourth wife had cleared out of their apartment and moved to California, taking everything in the apartment with her. And over the six months, Michael had dismantled and closed down Isadore's entire world, personally and professionally. His material life no longer existed. How in the world was I going to break this news to him? After a few minutes of panic while Isadore kept repeating something about healing his heart, I just said, "Okay." And hung up the phone. (Was I going to have to get an unlisted number to get rid of this guy?)

A couple of weeks later, I realized what he was talking about. Isadore had told me about his cancer right after he was diagnosed. I went up to New York and tested him for flower essences (Bach and FES). I put together an essence solution in a four-ounce bottle. When I handed it to him, I said, "If you're smart you'll take this twice daily. I'm not going to check up on you and ask if you are taking them. It's up to you what you want to do. If you run out, call me and I'll send you another bottle." Two months before he died, he called to tell me he had run out of the solution and needed more. I was surprised. I hadn't expected him to take something he had never heard of before. I sent a new bottle right away. When I was in his apartment the weekend of his funeral, I found the second bottle unopened in his medicine cabinet. That was weird. He had taken the first bottle but had not touched the second one.

Back to the dream. Apparently Isadore wanted me to know that his cancer was gone and that the flower essences were a major factor in his healing process. Wife #4 had told me just prior to his death that the cancer had spread and the cells were now also surrounding his heart. This would explain why he was saying "they healed my heart." It's not easy for people who have recently died to make a clear contact with someone still living. Actually most people don't even bother trying. It takes discipline and training to bridge between levels. But Isadore used the mechanics he knew best—the phone. He ran his business almost solely over the phone and was famous for his take-no-prisoner negotiating business calls. So how better to contact me than by phone. I was surprised he felt it was important to do this. His "phone call" gave me another verification about the effectiveness of essences post-death.

By the way, I didn't need to get an unlisted phone number. Isadore hasn't called me since that one time. Thank god.

I WAS RELIEVED TO GET back to the garden. In my absence, the garden took on some interesting refinements to its shape. It was still a round garden with eighteen concentric circular rows. But now three spiral paths cut through the rows leading to the center. Grass had grown up through the mulch marking the spiral paths and, much to my amazement, they were equidistant from one another. (Nature had a ruler.) The garden was now divided into thirds. There was also a wide band of grass separating the outer three rows from the rest of the garden. I checked to make sure what had formed in my absence was, in fact, to be considered permanent. Clarence placed a timber border along the new paths and I mowed their grass to set in and solidify the changes.

I had one more thing to do to complete the job of moving the garden. I needed to shift the Elemental Annex from its original location to a spot close to the new garden. I marked the new location in the woods next to the garden and invited nature to shift its nature spirit headquarters to the new spot. Again I felt the energy build, indicating the shift had occurred. (This time I wasn't standing in the middle of the Annex during the shift.) With the move, the original Elemental Annex was deactivated and returned back to the woods. The whole job took about a half hour and, more importantly, it didn't involve hauling any rocks or timbers.

A couple of months after returning from Findhorn, I began receiving invitations from my Essence mates to give workshops. They would set up the gatherings and all I had to do was travel to their homes. I'd get a little money for my efforts and to cover my travel expenses. Since I wasn't the one initiating the invitations, I took it as a sign that I was to continue what I had started at Findhorn and speak publicly about nature. It didn't occur to me how absurd this was in light of my having only one year's experience working with nature under my belt. By 1980, I had accepted a total of six invitations, and in the summer of 1980, I had just one scheduled week-long workshop that was to be held in the Netherlands. It would be my longest workshop and I had a lot of anxiety about it. I wasn't sure I had a week's worth of information to talk about with those thirty people. On top of this, Isadore had died just three weeks prior to the scheduled start of the workshop. I had spent most of that time in New York City with Michael and the attorneys shutting down Isadore's life and dodging the bullets coming at me from the warring wives. What I really wanted to do was hide out in my garden, not travel to the Netherlands.

To my surprise the Netherlands workshop went well, and I discovered that when it came to nature and my garden classroom, I had enough information to speak on and on for a week. But the trip really drained me. I didn't realize how depleted my reserves were from Isadore's death and my time spent traipsing around New York City. In the Netherlands, I was determined to hang on and complete the job I had committed to. But by the time I got back to Perelandra, I knew I could not travel and, at the same time, continue my work in the garden. For one thing, traveling took too much time and energy. I also saw at Findhorn what could happen if I let workshops overtake the garden, and I was determined not to let that happen at Perelandra.

I needed to find a workable balance between learning from nature and sharing what I learned with others. The only thing I knew was what I saw others like Peter, Eileen and Dorothy doing. They were year-round world travelers. Since I couldn't haul my garden around the world with me, I needed help finding a different approach. I told nature how I felt about the traveling. And I talked about my feelings about wanting to share what I was learning. I felt deeply that this was something I could do to give back to nature for what it was giving me. I said, "To balance these two goals, I'm going to have to operate differently from the traditional workshop approach. How do I accomplish this? I need your help." No response came right away so I disconnected and returned to the garden, sure that eventually I would get an answer.

From that point on, I accepted no more traveling workshop invitations, but I did accept special guests. Dorothy Maclean was in the area and she wanted to visit for a weekend. You know that sense of relaxation, even relief, we get when we are talking with someone of like mind and we don't have to explain what we're talking about? They just know. That's how it was for me that weekend with Dorothy.

Of course she understood what was happening in the garden and moved through it with gentleness and respect. I told her how I was working with nature and what I was doing in the areas that had needed help. When I showed her the kale, I told her I was getting some really odd information from the Deva of Kale. I was to top dress *one cup* of dolomite lime around each plant. I was hesitating because I thought I wasn't hearing this correctly. Any gardener would say that this amount of lime would kill the plants. I even asked some local gardeners about it and they agreed. But every time I checked with nature, I got the same "squirrelly" information: top dress *one cup of dolomite lime around each kale plant.* Dorothy's response: "The devas told you to do it. What are you waiting for? Just do it." I got the kick in the ass I needed, and I received it from sweet, gentle Dorothy Maclean, of all people! With that, I applied the lime. The plants thrived.

In the fall, I had another visiter from Findhorn. This woman talked on and on about a space soul she was connected with. She sounded pretty goofy, but the space soul sounded kind of interesting. She asked if I'd like to get hooked up, too. I shrugged and said, "Sure." I could not have been more casual about this. I had no idea what I was going to do with a space soul. She said she'd have to ask him if it was okay to make a connection with me and, if so, she'd assist him as he inserted a gold disk in my forehead. (Wait. Insert a what? You didn't say anything about a disk.) This was getting weirder by the minute. But despite this strange, yakking woman, I had a feeling I'd be okay. Apparently when she asked about the connection with me, he said, "yes," because in less than five minutes, we were in the sanctuary and I was getting an invisible gold disk energetically implanted in my forehead. (Was I now going to start setting off airport security alarms?) I actually felt something enter my forehead, indicating that the fifteen-minute operation was a success. The woman then drew a simple line pattern on a piece of paper and told me that I could connect with him any time by visualizing the pattern. (My very own secret code!) The pattern activated the disk. The space soul's name was Hyperithon (pronounced "hi-pear'-eh-thon").

For about five days, I couldn't stop thinking about that pattern. You know how someone can say, "Don't think of the word 'chocolate,'" and all you can think of is chocolate? That's how it was for me and that damn pattern. Every time I pictured it, I'd hear this cheery voice saying hello to me. I'd apologize for the disturbance—again—and he'd laugh. Then we'd disconnect. I never said anything to him beyond my apologies. I just couldn't think of what to say. (Really. What in the world does one say to a space soul? How's the weather?) Eventually, I stopped accidentally dialing his phone number, and I forgot about him and the disk and the secret code—for two years.

Nature's Post-Graduate Classes Begin: 1981

Relatively speaking, 1981 was a calm year for me. Clarence continued working the second shift at Xerox so I still had the major part of my day at Perelandra alone. There were no major construction projects facing us. No one was dying. The warring wives settled down and stopped shooting at me. I didn't have to travel anywhere for workshops. I had a lawn tractor and a rototiller. The new garden had settled into a nice rhythm, and life was good.

During the winter months, I spent a lot of time in the new sanctuary going over the notes I had made about the 1980 garden. I described the different plant and soil difficulties I had observed. And with this information, nature began developing new processes for us to use together to address the different issues.

But first, I needed to learn how to set up something called a four-point coning. Nature said it was an inter-level energy vortex that contains balance between the involution (nature) and evolution (human) dynamics. (Huh? I didn't get it.) Nature went on to explain: It was like creating a balanced nature/human team that was specifically set up for a particular issue or focus. The coning vortex had four points: two representing nature and two representing humanity. For nature, the coning included the deva of whatever I was working on and Pan, the big-deal coordinator of the nature spirit level of nature's intelligence. (This was when I "met" and began working with the Pan dynamic of nature intelligence.) For the human side, I was to say, "I'd like to be connected with the appropriate members of the White Brotherhood." (Whoever the hell they were.) Finally, I was to ask to be connected to my higher self (whatever that meant). Once I activated the four points of my first coning and felt the difference it made in the sanctuary, within me, with my ability to participate in the session and with my ability to clearly and accurately hear nature, I began to activate four-point conings for all my nature sessions.

That winter with conings now part of my routine, we developed the Soil Balancing and Stabilizing Process, the Atmospheric Balancing Process, Plant Triangulation Process, Flower Essences Foliar Feeding, Insect Balancing Process, Insect Triangulation Process and the Calibration Process. Since Findhorn, I had been working frequently with the Energy Cleansing Process, so that was already included in the garden. I now had too many options to remember, so my daily to-do list morphed into a Troubleshooting Process that listed all the options and was designed to identify only what was needed in the garden, where and when. This magnificent bit of organization inspired me to refer to the Troubleshooting Process as "Machaelle's Suicide Prevention Process."

As I introduced each process into the garden, we worked together to smooth out the steps both from my perspective as well as from nature's. I needed the process to be laid out seamlessly so that I could move from step to step effortlessly and not have to try to remember any information or instructions nature had given me along the way. I couldn't work with a process that bumped and banged around in my head. Nature needed for the steps to unfold and build according to nature's laws, its rhythm and its timing. In short, we aimed for a process that would do the work that was intended while, at the same time, remaining true to the laws of nature. Finally, each process had to be set up to enable nature and me to work it together as a team. It was a summer-long exercise in fine tuning and tweaking until each process felt smooth and there were no holes in the steps. In some ways, it reminded me of Cosmic Chess.

I also worked in a coning while getting the plans for the new season. The garden's shape, size and row orientation remained the same—thank you. But there were some changes with the vegetables, herbs and flowers that were to go in. And they included okra. I hate okra. In my early twenties, I pledged not to eat anything that is hairy or slimy. But this is the Perelandra research garden and not a family kitchen garden. So I didn't whine about the okra. In fact, I discovered that the okra plant and flower are actually gorgeous and, if I delayed harvesting, I'd end up with a foot-long okra that could be used as decoration or as a child-safe sword.

The garden's center changed, as well. Over the next couple of years, new items were added to the simple quartz rock that was sitting in the center. As each year progressed, adjustments were made. Older items changed position or were removed altogether. As in Cosmic Chess, everything had to be in just the right position. And with this careful construction, the garden's power center gradually developed. By the time we were finished, the very center of the Perelandra garden consisted of a Genesa® crystal sitting over a slab of clear quartz crystals that was sitting on four slate pieces that, in turn, sat on a layer of marble chips covering a tensor energy poster (Cheops pyramid energy). This was surrounded by a mineral ring comprised of different stones, a circular herb garden and a circular slate and marble chip walking path.

The Calibration Process, the final process we developed in 1981, was for me, the gardener. I was experiencing strong feelings of sadness and loneliness that kept descending on me like a depression, and I couldn't figure out how to shake them or where they had originated. I tested flower essences often but that didn't eliminate the problem. I wasn't sure what to do. During one of my sanctuary sessions, I talked to nature about it. (What did I have to lose?) I explained how I felt and asked what to do. Nature instructed me to describe my feelings and thoughts in detail. When I finished speaking (about twenty-five minutes later), I was told to sit quietly for half an hour. During that quiet time, I didn't feel anything happening nor did I have any insights. But when it was over and I stood up to leave the sanctuary, the weight had been lifted. It was remarkable. For the first time in weeks, I felt unburdened. Nature explained that my internal ability to process thoughts, feelings and emotions had become jammed. As I described how I was feeling, nature followed how I was processing what I was saying inside my body. It identified where I was jammed and it simply unjammed me. That's all it took. I immediately set up with nature to develop this miracle into a new process.

Along with the Calibration Process came two important insights that strengthened my partnership:

1. The peer relationship: In the garden classroom, nature normally took the lead and taught me about nature's reality. I was clearly the student, which was appropriate since I knew nothing. With the Calibration Process, *I* had taken the lead. I had initiated its development. The emotions I had been experiencing had backed me into a corner and I needed to step forward and ask for help. I brought the problem to nature and nature provided the solution. And with that, I clearly saw the foundation of our new working partnership. My relationship with nature had begun to shift in a significant way, and I was no longer just the student.

2. The scope of the partnership: Up to this point, except for the development of the Energy Cleansing Process at Findhorn, my focus with nature had been the garden and its environment. After working with the Calibration Process for several months, it was clear that my partnership could extend beyond the garden to include human health. I struggled with this insight because I had assumed and accepted that my job was to work with nature within the context of a garden and its environment. I didn't think human health was part of that package. Besides, the world was drowning in healers, alternative and otherwise. They didn't need me to join in. It was the natural environment

> that was in trouble and I didn't think there were enough people working in this area.

Over time, I came to realize that I didn't understand what nature meant when it used the word "garden." I knew what *I* had in mind by it but I had a feeling it wasn't the same as what *nature* meant. And it was nature's understanding of "garden" that was driving the Perelandra classroom. Finally, in a classic "duh" moment, I asked nature how it defines a garden.

> *From nature's perspective, a garden is any environment that is initiated by humans, given its purpose and direction by humans and maintained with the help of humans. For nature to consider something to be a garden, we must see humans actively involved in all three of these areas. It is the human who calls for a garden to exist. Once the call is made, nature responds accordingly to support that defined call because a garden exists through the use of form.*
>
> *Humans tend to look at gardens as an expression of nature. Nature looks at gardens as an expression of humans. They are initiated, defined and maintained by humans. When humans dominate all aspects and element of the life of the garden, we consider this environment to be human dominant. We consider an environment to be "nature friendly" when humans understand that the elements used to create gardens are form and operate best under the laws of nature, and when humans have the best intentions of trying to cooperate with what they understand these laws to be. When humans understand that nature is a full partner in the design and operation of that environment—and act on this understanding—we consider the environment to be actively moving toward a balance between involution (nature) and evolution (human).*
>
> *As a result, the nature-friendly environment supports and adds to the overall health and balance of all it comprises and the larger whole. It also functions within the prevailing laws of nature (the laws of form) that govern all form on the planet and in its universe. In short, when a garden operates in a balance between involution and evolution, it is in step with the overall operating dynamics of the whole. The various parts that comprise a garden operate optimally, and the garden as a whole operates optimally.*

> *Nature does not consider the cultivation of a plot of land as the criteria for a garden. Nature considers a garden to exist wherever humans define, initiate and interact with form to create a specialized environment. This is the underlying intent of a garden and the reason behind the development of specialized environments such as vegetable gardens. Nature applies the word "garden" to any environment that meets these criteria. It does not have to be growing in soil. It only needs to be an environment that is defined, initiated and appropriately maintained by humans.*
>
> *This is what nature means when it uses the word "garden." The laws and principles that nature applies to the co-creative vegetable garden are equally applicable to any garden, whether it is growing in soil or otherwise. The principles and processes that have been developed for the Perelandra garden apply across the board because all gardens are operating with the same dynamics—only the specific form elements that make up each garden have changed.*

My work with nature and our developing partnership had blown wide open. But it took me a while to wrap my head around what nature was saying about gardens in this session. To keep from feeling like I was spinning out into space, I turned my attention back to my garden—the one growing in soil.

In May, my friend Gloria visited. As I showed her around the garden, she stopped, looked at me, and said, "You ought to write a book about this. You could call it 'Behaving as if the God in All Life Mattered.'" As soon as she said this, I knew exactly what was to be included in that book. I was to introduce myself to the reader, describe the first year garden and end with a series of lessons and exercises I had learned from nature since 1977. With Gloria's words, all the information dropped into my head, and I was now walking around with a book inside me.

I didn't take this moment too gracefully. The last thing I wanted to do was write a book. Other than those who choose to be professional writers, who in their right mind would want to write a book? One of my issues was time. When would I have time to write a book? Besides, I felt people were reading too much about this kind of stuff and not bothering to act on the information. I did not want to add to the prevailing couch-potato syndrome. But really, the idea of writing a book felt like a daunting task that no sane person would take on. I looked at Gloria and said, "You are not allowed back in my garden!" We had a good laugh, but I could tell she wasn't letting go of that book idea. I, on the other hand, avoided the idea by keeping my focus on the garden. (What book?)

To prepare for working with the Flower Essences Foliar Feeding Process this first season, nature said I would need to put together essence solutions for each vegetable variety. I had to test them as the seeds germinated. (In a misguided attempt to impress you with the enormity of this task, allow me to tell you that this involved kinesiology testing a total of 110 bottles for each of the forty-five vegetable varieties. By the time I was finished, I was an expert in kinesiology speed testing.) I needed to mix the essence drops in a water/brandy solution in separate containers and store the labeled containers on a shelf in my garden office. My office was beginning to look like a laboratory, except for the ever-present box of cookies. When the Flower Essences Foliar Feeding Process popped up in the daily troubleshooting, I had the needed solutions ready to go and could do the foliar feeding that day.

While making the solutions, something surprised me. The essences that were needed for each variety were extensive, many bottles and many drops. And they were for variations of extreme emotional situations: deep depression, fear, exhaustion and panic. I didn't normally associate these feelings with a head of cabbage. (Did I need to put these plants into therapy?) Odd though the testing results may have seemed, it was clear that the plants benefitted from their essence applications.

Another oddity: Tomatoes had not been included in the new garden. However, during the winter planning, nature said we'd need a new smaller garden that was to be set up about fifteen feet away from the outer edge of the main garden. It was to be circular, measuring twenty feet in diameter. Tomatoes were to be planted in this garden, but not this year. Instead of tilling, I was to mark the garden's border with timbers and spread twelve inches of straw over the entire area. The grass was not to be removed and the soil was not to be touched. I would be leaving this smaller garden undisturbed for a year before establishing its center (several minerals sitting on cedar driftwood) and planting. I have to admit, out of all the garden prep over the years, this was the easiest—by far. But I couldn't imagine how these steps could possibly prepare the soil enough for planting. My garden's clay soil had already beaten a fancy tractor with its big disc attachment.

As fall approached, I could feel the garden winding down. It was/is my favorite time of the season. The garden was thriving. The flowers were going nuts with the shorter days and cooler temperatures. I had successfully kept up with my work with nature and I was still breathing. The number of tasks that I needed to do each day was also winding down. An air of peace and quiet settled in. Fall was my time to sit back, observe, enjoy—and eat more cookies.

I had a new friend, a groundhog, who came into the garden each day around 2 P.M., climbed the mulberry tree and sat there for a couple of hours watching me. I think he wore a watch because he arrived at the same time every day. At the end of his day, he'd climb down and return to the woods. Dottie's cows and horses stood next to the garden fence and watched, as well. Deer would pass through the garden, but they always walked along the mowed grass paths and not through the planted rows. We put up bird feeders, per nature's instructions, and the birds coming to the feeders were joined by raccoons, skunks, chipmunks and squirrels.

The biosphere was turning into a wild kingdom, a peaceful wild kingdom. I had tithed ten percent of the produce to the wildlife, but it didn't seem like they ever took their ten-percent share. As my fears about their potential damage dissipated, they increasingly interfaced with the plants in gentle, non-destructive ways. The garden was at peace and I was at peace with the garden.

I had even softened my concerns about insects. Instead of seeing them as invaders buzzing around looking for plants to attack, I saw them as my first line of communication when something was wrong. I think it's fair to say that the insects became my first garden assistants. Wherever they were especially active and causing plants to suffer became the insects' way of pointing and shouting to me, "Hey! A little attention needed over here!"

Someone had suggested we incorporate Perelandra as a business. This way we could deduct gardening expenses. However, I couldn't see how we would operate as a business. Maybe a nature research lab could be seen as a business. Gloria tried to persuade me to register as a non-profit for tax exemption. But the idea of trying to explain Perelandra and my work each year to some guy in a three-piece suit made my eyes spin. I didn't want that headache. So in September 1981, we became Perelandra, Ltd. For company assets we listed eight metal trash cans used for storing the different organic fertilizers, a bunch of timbers used for borders and a garden shed/office. I tried to include the groundhog and the cookies, but the lawyer said I was stretching it a bit.

Chapter 23

The Path to Pivot Three
1982

As I moved into 1982, I could feel something different coming down the pike. Nature gave me two instructions (1) Create an "official" office, something with a roof, heat and electricity. And I was to include a filing cabinet. My first thought: "Why? I don't have enough stuff to warrant a filing cabinet." (2) Take an R&R. The ease with which I would face the near future depended on my doing these two things during the first six to nine months of this new year. My focus in the spring was to remain on planting the garden. I was not to think beyond this.

Setting up an office was fun. I loved creating work spaces. But I had no idea why I was creating another office. I already had two offices: the garden office for the growing season and the sanctuary for the winter months. It wasn't heated and could get chilly, but I wasn't complaining. I converted our small spare room in the house into the new office. The Meyers gave me a four-foot-square wooden table they had been storing in a barn to use as a desk. I bought a small electric typewriter and a two-drawer filing cabinet. I pulled out the boxes of notes and papers I had stored in my closet and garden office. Once I got the papers filed, I was close to needing a second filing cabinet. Which raised another question: How come nature knew how much paperwork I had stored away and I didn't? (Cue the *Twilight Zone* theme again.)

The R&R was more challenging, but I diligently worked on being laid back. I slept late, read spy novels, walked around the woods, watched TV and visited with a few friends. I think if I had been graded on my R&R, I would not have gotten a very high grade. Maybe a C or C minus.

Around March, my relationship with Clarence became a concern. He was still supportive of my work, but over the previous four years we had gradually changed our relationship to what can best be described as brother and sister. Twenty years later, in 2001, we found out that Clarence falls on the high functioning end of the autism scale, which makes social interaction, intimacy and nonverbal communication challenging for him. He hasn't been "officially" diagnosed but he kept scoring high on different checklists. For me, this explained a lot about why we had drifted apart. Between his autism and my continuing focus on my nature work, I think it was only natural that our personal relationship shift. At the same time, as my work intensified, my need for emotional support also intensified. We had friends, but none of them ever wanted to hear about what I was doing. I think they were afraid my craziness might rub off on them. As a result, I felt alone and lonely.

It was a painful time for me. I reached out to nature, but that never fully solved the problem. (Note to self: Nature's love is not the same as human love.) I seriously considered ending my ten-year partnership with Clarence but I kept sensing that, even with the changes, we still belonged together. I just didn't know why. (Clarence also felt we belonged together and he, too, didn't know why.) I even thought about filling the emotional void by having a clandestine affair or two, but this seemed too complicated, too potentially annoying and like too much work.

I felt my heart was breaking. I said nothing to Clarence about what I was thinking because it seemed to me this was my issue, not his. Finally, I made a decision. I would continue my work with nature while also maintaining a non-intimate partnership with Clarence. Peggy Townsend's prediction back in 1973 was correct:

> There would come a time in my psychic growth when my relationship with Clarence would need to become secondary if I was to continue moving forward. At that time, I would need to decide carefully if I wanted to continue my development.

In 1982, I made my choice.

The pressure I had been feeling for weeks lifted immediately, and I was able to turn my attention back to the spring garden. The more I focused on the garden, the more my life made sense and the more I strengthened and stabilized emotionally.

IN LATE APRIL, I ATTENDED a Feldenkrais "Awareness through Movement" workshop given by one of the top Israeli teachers. I didn't feel like going, but this man's reputation was so special and his presence in our area was so unusual that I couldn't pass up the opportunity. I was lucky enough to get a private lesson with him, as well. On the day of my appointment, I drove with several friends who also had appointments to the house where he was staying.

> Note: The Feldenkrais Method was developed by physicist, judo master, athlete, mechanical engineer and educator Moshe Feldenkrais, D.Sc. It is an educational method for improving the function of the body and the state of mind. It is a unique approach to feeling better, moving better and performing better.

The years of garden work had been wearing on me physically. All the deep knee bending and crouching caused knee and lower back pain. And that spring I severely strained a tendon in my back. I had been taking regular Feldenkrais lessons for several years, but wanted to see if the Israeli teacher could help me further. When I met him for the private lesson, I told him that gardening was my profession and not my hobby. I had a feeling that this information would make a difference in how he approached the lesson. And it did. His work was not gentle, but I could tell that he respected my profession and wanted me to continue with it for many years to come. (If only I could get the rib cage on my left side to move.)

Something else happened that day that was equally extraordinary—if not more so. The Israeli teacher gave his private lessons in the home of friends with whom he was staying during his Washington visit. Those of us who arrived for the lessons waited on a balcony.

At one point, I was alone on the balcony, reading a book and enjoying the beautiful early spring day, when Gerta, the woman whose house we were in, joined me. I didn't know her, but before we could engage in small talk, she sat next to me, held both of my hands in hers, looked me in the eye, and said quietly, "I am a camp survivor." I was so taken off guard that at first I had no idea what she was talking about. Honestly, for a few seconds I thought she was talking about some terrible Girl Scout camp. Then, from the look in her eyes, I realized she meant she was a concentration camp survivor. She continued speaking softly: "They don't know what to do with us. They don't know how to help us." She continued, "Our experience has moved us beyond any therapy they have to offer, and none of the doctors know how to help us. They can't even hear what we tell them."

She held my hands a little longer. I said nothing, but I continued looking into her eyes. Finally, she gave me a little smile that made me feel completely connected to her, squeezed my hands, then left to go back into the house.

I sat quietly, thinking about my moment with Gerta. First of all, I wondered how she knew I was Jewish. I didn't think a survivor would say these things to a non-Jew. Then I thought about *what* she said. Gerta was telling me that there were some experiences a human can have that are beyond the ability of anyone else in society to comprehend or assist with. That it is possible for us to experience something so outside the realm of prevailing reality that the experience itself effectively distances us from that society.

Gerta's words have stayed with me for more than thirty-five years. And many times over that period, I have thought of what she told me that spring afternoon, smiled and said, "Thank you." Without either one of us knowing it, she had provided much-needed ballast for the upcoming changes in my life.

IN MAY, CLARENCE AND I were having lunch at a local diner with our friend Wayne. We started talking about Paris and that got me thinking about how much I missed Paris. When I mentioned this, the two men said almost in unison, "Well, why don't you go back?"

I hemmed and hawed a bit, and they continued urging me to take a trip back to Paris by myself. I started laughing at the absurdity of resisting a trip to Paris coupled with the absurdity of taking time out to take that trip. Finally I said, "All right. I'll do it!" Right there at lunch, the three of us decided I would go to Paris in the fall for ten days—alone. (I had no idea how I would make this happen. First, I needed to renew my passport.)

In late June, I scanned the TV Guide for something semi-decent to watch. I had spent a long day in the garden, and I wanted to be entertained—even mildly—while I ate dinner. My attention was drawn to a miniseries based on Dwight Eisenhower's war years. It was a three-parter and a repeat. The first time it aired, I could not have been less interested. Now, despite the fact that I didn't think a show on Eisenhower's war years could be entertaining, I felt compelled to watch.

I had an odd reaction to this cheesy, grade-B movie. I kept shouting at the screen things like, "That isn't what happened! You've botched the story!" The program infuriated me. Yet, each night, I diligently watched—and each night I ranted at the TV. I was beginning to question my sanity. I had never reacted so viscerally and vocally to a TV program before. (Or since.) Plus, I was getting into a flap about a historical period I knew nothing about. (I thought D-Day was the end of World War II.) How in the world did I know they were taking faulty creative license in this program?

For you to understand just how ridiculous my response was, I need to confess the somewhat amazing relationship I had with history. Grasping history—attempting to memorize all those dates, names and places, and figure out the significance of events—overwhelmed and bored me.

In my high school world history class, the teacher gave us a test at the beginning of the year to discover how much we already knew about the subject. I scored 23 on the test—the lowest mark in the class. At the end of the year, he gave us the same test to see how much we had learned. I scored 67. Despite the fact that I had failed the test again, he gave me a B for the year and announced to all that I was the person who had learned the most because

I had improved my score more than anyone. (But I still thought D-Day marked the end of World War II.)

So, here I was, telling this TV screen that it was screwing around with facts and misrepresenting historical events. At the end of the third evening, I noticed in the credits that the miniseries was based on a book. I copied down the title and author, and asked Clarence to pick up the book at the library on his way to work the next day. I was determined to rectify the misconceptions of the program and prove my gut instincts to be correct by reading this book—even though I didn't know what the hell I was talking about.

Clarence handed me the book the next evening, and I stayed up all night reading. When I finished, I couldn't say I was now an expert on World War II, but I did have another odd reaction.

When I closed the book and put it down, I saw an old, arched wooden door inside my chest—just like the door I had seen when I learned about reincarnation. Only this time, the door didn't open slowly. Instead, it blasted open, as if someone with a great deal of strength had kicked it open. The sensation startled me, and I felt a physical ripping in my chest as the door bolted open. It was not pleasant, by any means. Instantly, I began to think about Eisenhower. It was as if I suddenly knew him (which would have surprised my high school history teacher). The whole experience was scary, and I backed away from it fast, choosing to focus on my day instead. When in doubt, return to the garden.

I couldn't get Eisenhower out of my mind, no matter how hard I tried. It was another one of those "don't think of chocolate" moments. Instead of addressing the situation head on to discover what was happening, I resisted it. I didn't know what all of this was leading to, but I sure didn't like it one bit. I didn't have much respect for people who claimed they were connected with famous dead people and then used this connection to further their own status. To me, it was a cheap trick to gain fame and fortune off someone else's accomplishments, and no one could prove or disprove the claims. This was exactly the kind of situation I wanted to avoid. Whenever anyone asked me about my past lifetimes, I always told them I was a peasant street sweeper or a goat herder. Not everyone can be a king, high priest or master guru.

The constant flow of Eisenhower thoughts combined with my efforts to resist them were so shattering and set up a tension that was so deep that I began crying every time I was alone. There was a battle going on inside me and not only wasn't I sure which side would win, I wasn't sure which side *should* win. I did not stop crying for three weeks. Finally, I realized that this situation was not going to resolve or dissipate on its own, nor was it something I would be able to wait out and cry through. If I was going to get on with the rest of my life, I was going to need help.

That's when I remembered Hyperithon, the space guy with the golden disk. I had not talked to him in two years, so he couldn't accuse me of pestering him. Maybe he could give me some insight on what was going on. I felt a little shy about "dialing his number" after all this time, but he "answered" with that same cheerful "Hi!" I had grown accustomed to two years ago. I reintroduced myself, just in case he had forgotten me. He assured me he knew who I was, and then, to my surprise and before I could tell him why I was calling, he said he could help me with this Eisenhower situation. He'd be glad to answer any questions I might have.

I first asked him if I had lost my mind. He stated flat out that I had not. So, there I was, asking some invisible space soul with a weird phone number if I was sane—and I actually felt comforted by his answer! (Thank god. Hyperithon says I'm not nuts.)

I asked him if what I was perceiving about Eisenhower was accurate. He agreed that both the TV program and the book had been full of inaccuracies. (How the hell did he know about a TV show and a book?) I then gave him a brief description of my perceptions. He listened and said I was picking up on things well. That meant I had some past connection with this dead, famous fellow—exactly the thing I wanted to avoid.

Hyperithon asked if I'd like him to give me an overview of what was happening. I said "yes." He confirmed that I had been linked with Eisenhower as an aide and assistant in several lifetimes, the last being World War II. I did not have special military knowledge, nor did I have extensive military training. Our connection was not that of military peers. I had been a minor aide and, eventually, a friend who functioned as part of his military support staff during those different lifetimes. I didn't give him the benefit of expertise. Instead, I was someone who could listen and someone with whom he could relax, trust and bat around ideas.

Hyperithon ended by saying:

> *Your relationship in World War II with the soul you know as Eisenhower was one of clarity, closeness and strength. As you have touched into his life through the TV program and book, it is natural that these things be remembered by you. Dynamics between people—more accurately, between souls—are not lost or forgotten. But it is only his high accomplishments as the military leader that attract you, because that is the part of his soul journey you have most recently experienced. His presidency and his relationship with his family are all experiences outside your relationship. Therefore, they sound none of your chords.*

This was all I could absorb for the moment, and I wanted to know nothing more. At least it was enough to stop me from crying. However, it wasn't enough to stop the flow of Eisenhower thoughts. And I still felt uncomfortable about what I was remembering.

Five days later, on July 28, I screwed up my courage again and asked Hyperithon for more information.

> *I understand the difficulty you are having with what you are presently learning. It is never easy to significantly expand one's working knowledge about life. Some of the emotions you feel are your reactions to suddenly moving within life on a more expansive level. You are not consciously used to balancing and absorbing so many aspects of life at one time. But you must realize that you are capable of doing this. You have been trained. You have evolved into this. Again, your discomfort has to do with seeing various aspects of life consciously come together into one whole. The sense of inner stretch you feel comes from consciously dealing with the interrelationship of the past, present and future in an experiential, grounded manner. In essence, you are experiencing the grounding of a higher, more complete, spiritual concept, and finding out that the more conventional, seemingly more "grounded" way of looking at relationships (i.e., in a linear manner within the context of one's present lifetime) no longer applies and is no longer appropriate.*

Finally, he suggested that I relax as much as possible and allow my memories to surface at their own pace. If I let this happen, I would release a lot of the stress I was presently feeling. (I left this session thinking, "Easy for you to say.")

I didn't fully understand what Hyperithon was telling me. But I decided to follow his suggestions to relax and let things surface on their own. I would not try to force anything nor would I try to understand anything (even if I could). I trusted that eventually things would come together, and I'd know what was going on—just like so many of my experiences in the garden. Or, things would not come together, and I'd fall apart and start crying again. (Note to self: Should this occur, purchase stock in Kleenex.)

THIS WILL GIVE YOU AN IDEA of how intense that time was for me. To divert my thoughts and attention from one insanity, Dwight Eisenhower, I embraced another insanity, writing *Behaving as if the God in All Life Mattered.* Since Gloria's visit, I had not been able to toss that book out of my head. In short, the book won.

At this point, the garden was now planted, had settled in nicely and was hitting a good rhythm. I still continued to work daily with the troubleshooting list, fine-tuning the new processes as I went along, but not much needed my attention. It was obvious that it didn't need me staring at it. Damn. I couldn't use the garden as an excuse to avoid the book.

I bought a ream of paper, sat down at my desk in front of the typewriter and essentially plunged off the deep end into writing a book. First, I activated a simple four-point coning: the Deva of *Behaving* (good lord, the book had a deva), Pan, the appropriate member of the White Brotherhood (Who are these guys?) and my higher self. I didn't know how we were all going to work together but I knew I'd need all the help I could get to write that book. By September, just two months later, I had finished the first draft of *Behaving.*

On September 16, I wrote a letter to a friend from my old Findhorn days.

> I am now on the last leg of what looks to be a four-year cycle. I knew I was coming out of something and going on to something different when I was "told" in January to go on a sabbatical this year and basically rest at Perelandra until the fall. I was to pay attention to the quality of my rest because the next stage depended on it. So, like a good kid, I hid out at Perelandra doing my nature spirit and deva thing and tried to relax. To complete the process, I'm leaving Monday (September 20) to spend ten days alone in Paris—an entirely different environment and one that I love—where I can't expect to function as a nature researcher. I feel that these ten days will be the icing on my "sabbatical cake." Then I will return to Perelandra and move into the new.

I HAD JUST ENOUGH TIME to close down the garden for the winter, and on September 20, I boarded a plane bound for Paris. I had announced to Clarence and our friends that I was going to take full advantage of my solo trip and not contact anyone. I also didn't want anyone to contact me. No postcards, no phone calls, no nothing. I wanted to experience and think only about Paris.

I stayed at a small hotel in the 7th arrondissement near the Eiffel Tower. I walked all over Paris, sat at cafes and watched traffic roll by on busy streets. One afternoon I sat in a cafe near the Arc de Triomphe where twelve major streets converged into a massive circle and watched tourists and traffic somehow magically manage to avoid one another.

I visited my favorite museums and went to the Louvre to make sure Michelangelo's *Dying Slave* was being well treated. I sat in the Rodin Museum gardens and ate lunch. I stared at the Seine and watched the boaters. For some inexplicable reason, I window shopped. I didn't buy anything, just looked. I discovered a huge, complex brass perpetual motion machine on the main floor of one of the larger department stores and spent about an hour watching it operate—perpetually. I found a tiny restaurant near the hotel. Each night I'd arrive for dinner and, after the third night, they showed me to a small table by the window that they had already set for me. The restaurant and its staff made it feel like home. I sat there reading my international spy novel and blissing out on Paris food. One afternoon, as I was stuffing my mouth with my day's ration of Paris' perfect pastry, I said aloud, "I'm really having a good time!"

I had one piece of business to take care of. The fall equinox fell on September 23, at 10:30 A.M. This is nature's "new year," and each year, at the moment of the equinox, I call in the new cycle for Perelandra and for me. On the morning of the 23rd, I set out to find just the right spot in a Paris park to experience the equinox. I ended up at a park right off the Avenue des Champs Elysées. It just so happened that there was a dahlia show going on. Consequently, every garden was filled with blooming dahlias. Dahlia colors are especially vibrant and clear, and this park, in the midmorning sunlight, was literally pulsating with color.

I found one garden that was more secluded and stood in front of it waiting for the equinox moment. Out of habit, I happened to look down at my feet several times. I wasn't looking at anything in particular—it was just something to do while I waited.

At the moment of the equinox, I looked at the huge dahlia display in front of me and quietly called for the next cycle for both Perelandra and me. That was all I said. I felt the equinox energy pass through me.

I stood quietly for several minutes longer, then looked down at my feet again. Between them was a chestnut. I knew it had not been there a few minutes ago. I figured it was nature's verification that the equinox "took," so I picked up the nut and put it in my jacket pocket. Then I headed out to find the perfect pastry shop for my New Year's celebration.

I didn't think about Eisenhower the whole time I was in Paris. While I couldn't keep him out of my head at Perelandra, the thoughts about him never even tried to enter my head in Paris. However, on the September 30 return flight, Eisenhower thoughts crept back into my mind. Over the Atlantic Ocean, I resolved to settle the Eisenhower thing one way or the other so that I could get on with my life.

PIΛOT THREE

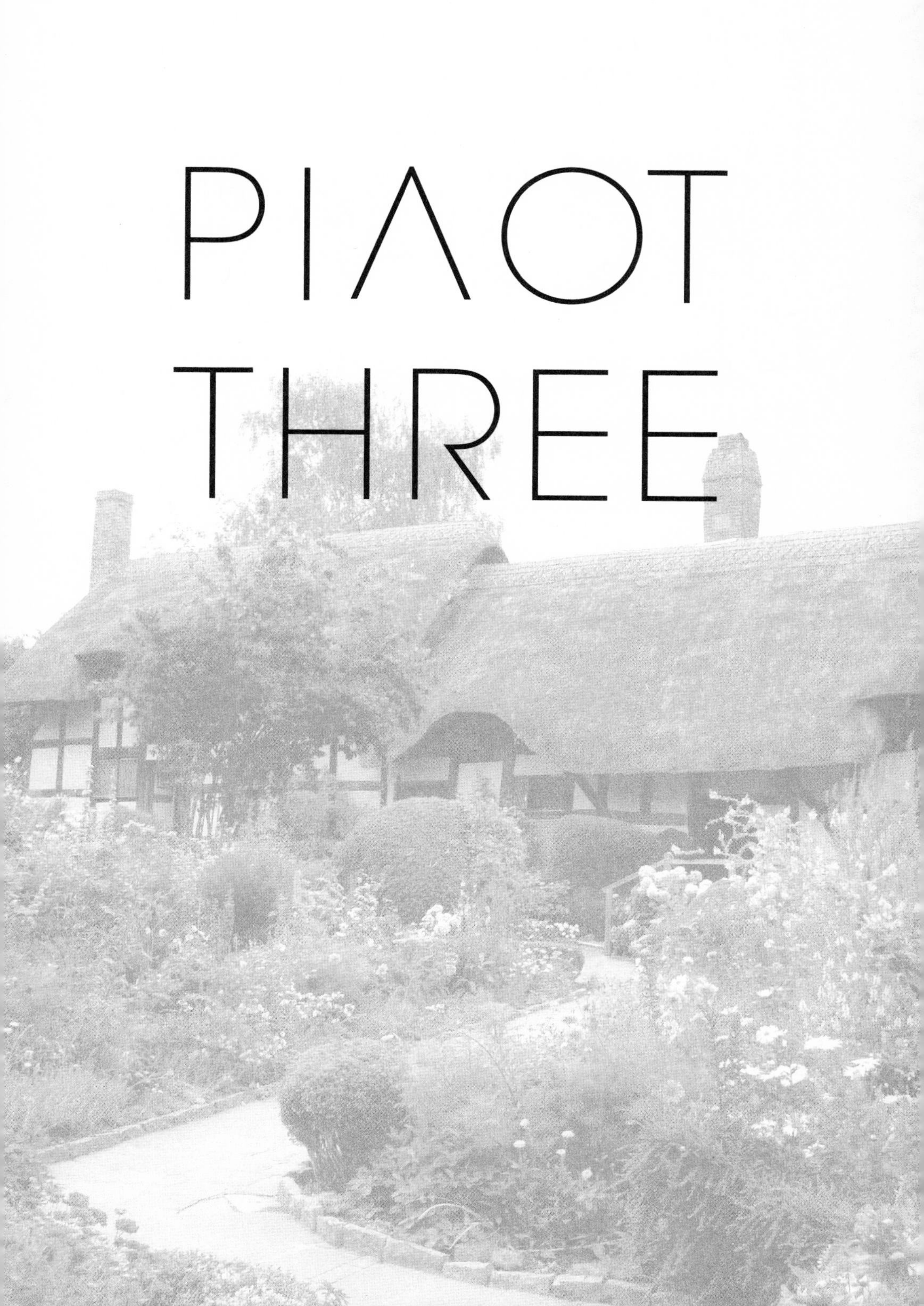

Chapter 24

A Divine Release of the Soul from the Yoke of Custom and Convention

Socrates

Prelude to Pivot Three

On October 12, I screwed up my courage and marched into the sanctuary determined to find answers. I wanted the cards put on the table. If I was crazy or if I was delusional, I wanted to know it now.

Hyperithon seemed like a good place to start since he had provided some answers before I had left for Paris. I dialed his number and he answered right away with that same cheery "Hi!" I had thought about different ways to approach my original pre-Paris question: Am I crazy? Maybe I was missing something, and if asked differently, I'd get a different answer that would indicate I needed to get help. I understand that using an invisible gold disk that was activated by a weird line drawing to speak with an invisible being was plenty of evidence that I might be dancing on the edge. But I had nowhere else to turn, and I felt that the best thing for me to do was to continue moving forward with this situation and see where it was leading. I'd remain alert for any signs of trouble but I'd continue moving.

Using what I learned from nature about how to ask a solid question that didn't include holes, I began by asking Hyperithon if the experience I had been going through the past four and a half months around the Eisenhower situation was one of growth and correctness, or did it impede growth and balance for either me or

Eisenhower. Using my own words, Hyperithon verified that my experience was one of growth and correctness. Then he went on to say that the opportunity before me was mutually beneficial to both me and Eisenhower, and that Eisenhower was creating a professional family in which he (Eisenhower) hoped I would participate. (I was being hired? Really? What the hell did I have to offer?) My response: "Are you sure you have the right person?"

After assuring me he was talking to the right person, Hyperithon continued:

> *Social mores and expectations that have nothing to do with a person can interfere with development. When a person takes on patterns that are established and passed down by others whose development is different from their own—mores and pressures that have nothing to do with them—it is not only inappropriate, but it can render that person impotent. The energy one absorbs through incompatible social mores and expectations surrounds the individual with a debilitating fog. The key to functioning as a fully potent human being with his own sense of balance lies in the individual's ability to shed inappropriate mores, expectations and energy. In order for you, Machaelle, to move with the opportunity before you, you will have to cast off all such discordant patterns.*

He said that Eisenhower and I were "soul friends" and that we had a strong bond that had formed over several lifetimes. It was this bond that drew me to his funeral, for I was one of the souls there supporting his transition. We had worked together a number of lifetimes and now, if I so desired, we could reconnect in areas concerning work and "soul development."

> *Your knowledge of various disciplines—your astral traveling, your Void experiences with the monk and your manifestation lessons with nature—allow you to transcend levels easily and well. This enables you to move forward by utilizing more options than what is normally available to others. You have not gone into this Eisenhower experience blindly, even though it presently feels that way to you. Your reconnection, which began at his funeral, had been unconscious until the television program and book opened the door and allowed it to flow into your consciousness.*

The things that Hyperithon said that day resonated strongly. I knew with every fiber of my being that I was hearing truth, even though I didn't understand much of what he was talking about. The fog brought on by my fears, caution and doubt was moving out and now I could see a straight path before me. But I would still remain alert and look for any signs that I was crazy.

Hyperithon suggested that I "speak" with Eisenhower directly, since he had been present with Hyperithon during the entire session. That startled me. Luckily, I did not have time to think about it, or I might have refused the invitation. I said yes.

Eisenhower spoke first. His voice was strong and clear. He addressed the difficulty I was having with this whole situation. In fact, he commiserated with me, saying that if he were in my shoes, he would have dismissed everything as being too nuts to seriously consider. Right away we had something in common.

While Eisenhower spoke, I "saw" myself standing in a room with a door. I couldn't see him, but I could clearly feel his presence in the room. After a few minutes, the realization of who I was talking to so disconcerted me that I asked to speak to Hyperithon again.

I had my hand on the door knob and was about to bolt, when I turned and said, "Wait. Do I call you 'Eisenhower'?" That got us into a short discussion about names. He explained that he chose to use the name David, which was the name he had been given at birth: David Dwight Eisenhower. His father's name was also David, so to avoid confusion everyone in the family called him Dwight or Ike. Now he preferred David.

By the time we finished this discussion, which felt more like a friendly chat, the ice had broken, and I had warmed up to this man. He was no longer Dwight Eisenhower, former Supreme Allied Commander, former U.S. President and present dead guy. He was now David, the friendly fellow who just happened to be dead.

After about five minutes, we ended our conversation, and I refocused my attention back on Hyperithon. That's when I brought up my fears that I might be fantasizing this whole thing and that I might be confusing fantasy with reality. I once again talked about my fear of losing my mind. I said, "This is crazy. You must know that." He said no, he did not know that. In fact, for him the opposite was true. This was not crazy, it was an opportunity and it was real.

Then he reminded me that he and David were looking at this opportunity from a broader perspective than I was. Should I decide to continue, more pieces would come to me to assist with my shift and pattern re-alignment. (Wait. What shift? What pattern re-alignment? What's a pattern re-alignment?) This would allow me to function in a more expanded and effective manner. He assured me that I would be able to deal with the changes, that thanks to my training with nature I would do so with balance and care, and that this re-alignment would give me a new dimension of operating.

By this time, my head was spinning. I asked Hyperithon what advice he could offer to help me more fully understand and participate in what was happening. He said my most unfavorite word in the English language—relax.

He also said that I needed to trust. Although what was happening to me was not the "average" occurrence (there's an understatement), it was, nonetheless, reality. And it was an opportunity to explore life on a level far beyond what I could presently imagine. I also had the opportunity to free myself from any remaining unnecessary limitations. The more I understood about human potential, the more I would be able to function as a spiritualized soul in form.

In one final effort to make sure I was moving forward on the right path and wasn't wandering around in the weeds, I asked: "Does this experience with David disrupt or remove me in any way from the purpose and path I came into this lifetime to experience?" Along with my sanity issues, I was deeply concerned that accepting this opportunity might require me to step away from my nature work. I knew I was not prepared to drop my partnership or nature's classroom. Hyperithon told me that the opportunity with David was part of that path and purpose. And, as if he had read my mind, he added, "Your work with nature is an important part of your path and purpose. The Eisenhower opportunity will expand your nature work."

I could think of no other questions, so I closed the session feeling fairly satisfied that by continuing, I was doing the right thing, even though I barely understood what was happening. I decided to fall back on what I had learned from nature when looking at something I didn't understand—wait. Give it time to play out, to unfold, to complete. With time would come understanding.

OCTOBER 13

I met with Hyperithon again. I still had no questions but I wanted more information. He began by addressing my drive to "do well" in my life and spoke about it as a dynamic I needed to understand more fully.

When an individual has a balanced drive to do well, he uses it to help propel himself along in his journey, even during those times when he finds it difficult to move. Also, that drive to do well helps keep him alert and reflective about his own evolution. When this dynamic, this drive, is unbalanced, it can be used as a catalyst to do risky, splashy, even extraordinary things in order to be recognized by others. The motivation for movement shifts from inside the individual to someone or something outside him. For example, he may link his desire to do well with his fear of not being accepted. This will cause him to shift his actions to do well in a way that will ensure that people around him acknowledge his efforts in a positive and accepting way. He has stepped over the line and shifted his motivation to strive for quality to striving for bringing outside recognition to himself. In order to maintain balance, a person must be clear about his motivation to do well. As a person remains on course, striving to be the best he can be, he will automatically draw to himself quality, sincere, encouraging, nurturing recognition.

Hyperithon then went on to talk about my spiritual development over the past two and a half years:

Spiritual potential lies in one's horizontal and vertical actions. It is not just how much you affect others around you (horizontal), it is also how well you connect with and operate in multilevel communication and connection (vertical). Spiritual potential relates to both "directions." Over the past two and a half years, you have trained and disciplined yourself to connect with and to receive clear, usable information from various

> *vertical levels. Horizontally, you have developed your writing, your ability to translate and transcribe inter-level material, kinesiology and the conings. For you, "all systems are go." You have grounded yourself and established the necessary tools needed for the opportunity that lay before you: Perelandra, the sanctuary, your close communion with nature that includes supporting and strengthening your physical systems, your adjusted partnership with Clarence, your stabilized sources of finance. You cannot possibly look around and not see the evidence of readiness—and of achievement.*
>
> *You are experiencing being on the threshold of change. It is quite difficult to relax during these times because the "threshold of change" means that one is still living out old patterns but has vision into and is moving toward new patterns. This makes you eager to leave the old in order to fulfill this vision of the new. The resulting anxiety takes you out of step with the present and lessens the quality of the intermediate steps one needs to move through in order to enter the vision of the new. Again, relax.*

With this session, I started to feel more confident about moving forward. I now knew something about how to watch for potential problems and how to maintain balance so that I would not get snared by the problems in the first place. Hyperithon had given me an overview of what I had done to prepare for this change, and now I felt less like I was hanging in space by my toes. And he also gave me more insight about the difficulties I was experiencing in just dealing with the information I was presently facing. Now all I needed to do was learn to relax. Sure.

OCTOBER 14
I practiced relaxing. Marginally successful.

OCTOBER 15
When I opened the next session with Hyperithon, I asked him to address my confusion about overlapping lifetimes. Hyperithon had told me that the person I was in my lifetime with David during World War II did not die until the 1970s. I, Machaelle, was born in 1945. That meant that for twenty-five years we were both alive and living in the same country on the same level. Hyperithon said:

See yourself as the sun. A bright, vibrant, pulsating light sphere that continuously sends out individual rays to gather experiences. Each set of experiences travels from the ray back to the sphere, where it becomes part of the total reality of the sphere, part of its memory bank. All the rays going out are equal in their connection with the sphere. No ray is more distant than the next. They are all equi-distant, all "equi-close."

Understanding this phenomenon by allowing yourself to accept the two rays that function within the same time span and understanding that both rays are but individual reflections of your soul will free you further from the limitations of time and space. This, in turn, will enable your many rays to function with more agility.

By time and space limitations, we don't mean the escape from physicality. Rather, it is a different reflection of physicality. Our preconceptions of time and space are directly reflected in the physical reality around us. The broader truth of time and space does not demand that different lifetimes on Earth occur linearly. Once a person releases such notions, nothing is left to stop him from having lunch with another reflection or ray of his own soul—two simultaneous experiences, one might say.

He then added:

As you relate to David, you need not strive in any way to take on or effect any characteristics or mannerisms that you have discovered belong uniquely to your ray in the World War II life. To David, you are all the reflections the two of you have shared in other lifetimes. He recognizes each of these individuals in you. The reverse is equally true. You are not responding only to the Eisenhower part of his soul. You recognize the other reflections you have experienced with him, as well. You both have strong soul connections that have played out on Earth in various lifetimes, and it is the recognition of this closeness that draws you back together consciously at the present.

One final thing: Think of the individual soul rays as part of the larger soul sphere and not limited to a specific lifetime of character traits or patterns. The information each ray experiences is not restricted to that ray. Rather, it flows freely through the soul sphere as one organic whole becoming available to all the other rays. An individual has in his conscious memory bank twelve lifetime experiences or rays. They did not occur in linear time, making the most recent ray—in your case, the

> *Machaelle ray—the only receiver of benefits of these twelve lifetimes. They are occurring simultaneously and flowing to and from you at all times through the larger soul sphere. You also have benefit of all the other rays, though they are not consciously fixed in the Machaelle memory bank. Be that as it may, they are still a part of you and you, as Machaelle, are a part of them. It is just that to fully live out the Machaelle ray, you need the specific patterning of the twelve lifetime rays you have chosen to be a part of your* conscious *memory bank. You do not lose all else that is being fed into your soul-center.*

I thought about this session for most of the day. While translating Hyperithon's words onto paper, I physically experienced what he was saying. I could feel the energy of the words. Consequently, I felt this simultaneous lifetime concept more than I intellectually understood it. And as a result, I was more comfortable with the notion that I (as one of my conscious soul rays) died when I (as Machaelle) was in my mid-twenties.

OCTOBER 16

I talked with Hyperithon about a bad head cold that had descended on me overnight. I thought I'd find out if he knew anything about medicine and health.

> *The cold you are experiencing is a clearing out and cleansing as a result of what you are learning and experiencing with the Eisenhower opportunity. It is not a manifestation of blocking, which has been your concern about this cold, and will quickly process through you. Note that you are releasing mucus easily, not "holding" on to it. When a person's reality expands, there comes with it a certain amount of de-crystallization, re-arranging and cleansing. The old is making way for the new. The opportunity facing you is settling in nicely. The cold will not be severe, only inconvenient. It is moving through your body quickly.*

He continued:

> *It is not your fantasy that you now sense David with you constantly. Every time you open or direct your attention, or your consciousness to him, you will find him there. This is not a new phenomenon to you. Every time you direct your consciousness to me, or to any of us who*

make up your conings, or any specific individual, soul or spirit, you will find us. The only difference now is that you have personal knowledge of David. You are able to visualize him in physical form, even see pictures of him and read about him. You remember him from his speeches on television when you were young. But these things do not change the rules or the circumstances. Those who open their consciousness to us and allow us to connect with them will always "hear" us in some fashion.

October 17

As promised, the cold dissipated quickly—overnight, in fact. Somewhere between blowing my nose again and sneezing one more time, I began to feel that I was entering a new phase of the Eisenhower opportunity. This is all I could figure out on my own, so again I looked to Hyperithon for help.

I can verify that you have entered a new stage and that you are standing on an exciting edge of reality. I have already picked up from your thoughts that you wish to meet with David, face to face. It is this stage that you are now entering.

You are to link initially by using your connection with him during World War II. This is but a framework upon which you can establish a mutual starting point. It is something upon which both of you can lock in your respective focuses. But once the focus is comfortably established, you will both note a clear and distinct desire to change the framework. You are each to allow that to occur. Although you both are reconnecting within a familiar framework, it is as two more expanded souls and not the two individuals who worked together during World War II. Changes will need to occur.

Pivot Three

October 18

I opened this session with Hyperithon determined to move forward—whatever that meant. He had already indicated that a face-to-face meeting with David was possible, and I was interested in doing just that. However, I did not believe that "face to face" meant two people physically standing in front of one another. I assumed it meant that I would sense or feel David's presence and see him through my inner vision. So far, I had only heard him through my inner hearing. Hyperithon asked if I still wished to meet David directly. Without hesitation, I said, "yes." Although I was curious about the chance to join his professional family, I did not think this required a "personal interview." I wanted to meet him because of the strong connections I had felt with him over the past four and a half months. I believed that if I met him face to face, I would be able to better identify and understand these connections.

Hyperithon told me to go into the sanctuary and lie down. He gave me the list of who I was to connect with for opening a new coning. As soon as the coning was opened, I felt a strong shift of energy inside my body, like someone had just shifted my gears.

After about ten seconds, I sensed that I was no longer in the Perelandra sanctuary. I could hear sounds of people talking and feel activity bustling around me. When I opened my eyes, I found myself standing in the middle of a busy city sidewalk. I figured I was astral traveling again, so I just stood there calmly for a couple of minutes while I tried to determine where I was and what I was supposed to be doing. I had been through this astral traveling drill many times before. However, this time I noticed that people were skirting around me to avoid bumping into me. It was as if they could see me. This was different.

A man wearing a tan military uniform was walking toward me. As he came closer, I had a deep feeling that I knew him. He looked no more than fifty years old, and he walked with the energy, ease and grace of a natural athlete. When he smiled, I knew exactly who he was. I had seen pictures of that famous smile before.

"Machaelle Wright?"

"Yes."

"I'm General Eisenhower. Come with me. I have a car waiting for us."

I asked, "Where are we?"

"London. Be careful, they drive on the left."

People continued to step out of our way as we walked down the sidewalk. I could hear the sound of our footsteps—his and mine.

We stopped alongside a parked car. For some reason, I recognized it to be a 1942 Packard. A younger military fellow snapped the general a salute and opened the back door. I didn't know what the protocol was about who should enter a car first—a general or a woman—so I hesitated. General Eisenhower gestured for me to get into the back seat first. Then he climbed in beside me.

I looked at him and said, "You know, they think you're dead."

He smiled. "Well, those press boys never get anything right!"

I looked down at myself and saw that I was wearing a woman's military uniform, a dark olive-drab jacket with brass buttons, a tan skirt and a pair of brown leather "sensible shoes." From the look and feel, the uniform seemed well tailored. I assumed that this must be part of the World War II framework, like we were acting out a play and wearing well-made period costumes, so I did not question it. However, the irony wasn't lost on me. In a million years, I never thought I'd be wearing a military uniform, costume or not.

"Can other people actually see me?" I asked.

"Yes, of course."

"Well, that's unusual. I've not experienced that before when I astral traveled."

"Actually, you've not previously experienced what you are now doing. You're not astral traveling." Changing the conversation, he said, "We can only spend a few minutes together, then you will have to leave."

With that, the younger fellow got into the car, started it and pulled away from the curb. We drove less than ten minutes. In fact, we only went a few blocks before stopping in front of what looked like an elegant hotel. The fellow opened the back door, and both David and I got out.

He said: "You need to leave now. If you wish, we can meet here tomorrow morning at 6:45. I have a meeting I must attend in the morning, and you are welcome to come along on the ride. We can talk along the way."

"Fine. I'll be here." Then reality hit me in the face, and I asked, "How do I get here?"

"Open that coning and tell them that you want to meet with me. I'll be in the same spot as today. That'll do the trick. Now, you have to go."

I started to walk away, then turned around and asked, "How do I get out of here?"

"Walk down the street. It's all arranged. They tell me you'll just make a switch."

"Okay. See you tomorrow." And with a quick wave, I added, "Nice meeting you."

I turned away and walked down the street. I'd say I walked no more than two minutes, when I felt the same internal sensations I had felt while lying in the sanctuary. Within seconds, I could sense the sanctuary around me. I opened my eyes and found that's exactly where I was.

I had no idea what had happened to me. I made notes about the experience, recording what I saw and sensed along with our conversation. I didn't supply reason, meaning or purpose since I was in the dark about all that. When I was finished, I left the sanctuary and continued my day.

It was a perfect fall day at Perelandra. Sunny and comfortably warm. The trees were just beginning to show their fall colors. I walked out to the garden and spent time tucking it in, then finished closing down my garden office for the winter. Afterwards I walked around the woods. I kept reminding myself that I had been in London that morning. I didn't dwell on what my ten-minute adventure might mean because I had already decided I was returning to London the next day.

As I walked around the woods, I could tell that *everything* around me had changed. How I perceived what I was seeing had changed. I was thirty-six years old and once again my life felt like it was making a big shift. Perelandra and nature had shown me a larger reality, a reality that I had become deeply comfortable with. With my morning London trip, that reality had busted open and now it included something beyond anything I had previously imagined. Something had clearly happened, but I didn't understand what. I knew I had been in some London somewhere and had met David Eisenhower. As a result, it was impossible for me to look at Perelandra's trees, soil, sky, our house and the animals the same way. Everything at Perelandra was now part of this new expanded reality. All I knew for sure was that I felt comfortable with what had occurred, and, to my surprise, I felt quite at ease with David.

OCTOBER 19

Early the next morning, 6:15 to be exact, I connected with Hyperithon to get set up for my appointment with David.

> *We begin this session, prior to your second formal meeting with David, with a few more insights that might help you move through the experience with more clarity.* (Now we're talking. Let's have more clarity.)
>
> *You will not be acting out World War II, even though you are using the framework you experienced together during that time. The motivation for your current working partnership is not war. This time it is mutual growth in another context—a context that will become clearer to you shortly as you work together. We don't wish to spell it out because it is important that you allow it to flow naturally, rather than try to stuff purpose and clarity into the experience based on your preconceived notions.*

I asked if the area of our working partnership would be comparable in intensity to World War II.

> *Yes, but on a different level. We see destruction as a force with a wide range of definitions. World War II demonstrated one area of destruction. There are others of equal intensity that are positive rather than negative phenomena. All aspects of World War II may be present to you again, but you may not recognize them since their dynamics will be so completely different. You will not be facing the horrors of war. You have already done that. But because of your discipline, you require life experiences and growth to encompass a certain quality and intensity. Consequently, you can take on life from a broader vantage point. Don't expect this present situation to be different. This is what we mean when we answer yes to your question comparing your present working partnership with that of World War II.* (Wow. I didn't feel this added much clarity. It was time to trust as I moved forward.)

I was told to lie down in the sanctuary and open the same coning I had activated the previous day. I "arrived" back in London just about a half block from the hotel where I was to meet David. Once again, I was wearing a military uniform. I saw him come through the door, so I walked quickly toward the hotel. As soon as I got to him, we exchanged greetings. He said he was glad I had decided to come. I told him I was too curious about what was happening not to come.

The car pulled up, and the same driver jumped out to open the door. I settled in the back seat along with the David. He explained that we would be driving about two hours to a place just outside a small town named Hamet-on-Raven. His meeting would be short. He suggested that I might be more comfortable if I waited in the car during the meeting. I agreed.

On the ride there, we talked about our names again. He insisted that I call him David, then he asked me about the unusual spelling of my name. I explained that it was the Hebrew spelling of the French name, and that I had been born into a Jewish family.

I spent a lot of the ride looking out the window. Once we got out of the city, the landscape looked similar to what I had seen during my travels in England. Although I did not specifically recognize anything, I had no difficulty believing that I was in England. The fields, the beautiful fences, the small herds of sheep and cattle, the stone cottages. It reminded me how much I had loved England back in 1967.

David's meeting took no more than half an hour. The driver, who up to that point had not exchanged any words with me directly, accompanied David inside. I stood outside the car for a bit and felt the firmness of the ground beneath my feet and the sensations of the cool breeze against my face. I heard birds chirping in nearby trees and saw a few fly overhead. I watched clouds move across the sky. I looked at my reflection in the side of the car to see what my uniform looked like. I wasn't thrilled with the color, but the style wasn't too bad. My hair looked a little shorter, but other than this, I appeared to be the same Machaelle. When I got back into the car, I was convinced that I was as physically present in England as I normally was at Perelandra. I just didn't understand where *this* England was located.

David and the driver returned to the car not long after I had gotten back in. He asked if I'd like to go for a walk along a nearby river with him before returning to Perelandra. I didn't want to leave yet, so I quickly said yes.

While walking, he offered me one of two apples he had swiped from the meeting. At first he was concerned about my stamina and how long a walk we should take. I assured him I was fit. Then I said something quite unusual: I told him I jogged five miles every morning. This wasn't true. I've never jogged. However, my body felt strong and fit, like I did run five miles daily. The news seemed to surprise him also, but he quickly said that he had forgotten about my jogging. (Forgot? Now I was confused.) He was surprised that I jogged in the mornings, since we had already established on the ride out that mornings were not my best time of day. I was beyond confused. I was lost and had no idea what we were talking about, so I dropped the subject.

He asked me about my childhood. I gave him a thumbnail sketch, choosing not to go into detail. I told him that Isadore had served in the Army during World War II, but I thought he was stationed in New Mexico. This was where he met Dorothy. I briefly described my parent's marriage. As I spoke, I saw (in my mind's eye) a cube. The walls were the facade that faced out to the world where my parents put their energy. They made that facade appear normal to others, and everyone saw it as a "regular" marriage. Inside the cube was nothing but black—a darkness that was created by the secrets they kept from each other in the marriage. Into that darkness, I was born.

I told David what I was seeing but quickly changed the subject by asking him about his childhood. (I didn't want to lose my chance of being hired because of my crappy childhood and parents.) He talked a little about his brothers and life in Abilene. He remembered his family as strict and strong, and his childhood as a lot of fun.

I began to tire—not physically from the walking, but mentally from the focus I had to maintain while listening to David and taking in my surroundings. David suggested that I leave for Perelandra right away and not wait until we got back to London. I agreed. He asked if I wished to come back. I said "Absolutely." So we decided on the time (near noon) and place (along the same river) to meet the next day. He then urged me to walk away from him. As I did, I felt myself shift—and when I opened my eyes, I was in the Perelandra sanctuary again. It was after 11 A.M., and I needed a nap.

OCTOBER 20

I met David by the river. This time, he had driven there by himself. We walked for quite some time, talking about normal, insignificant things. It seemed like he was deliberately keeping the conversation light, so I followed along. What I noticed most was our ease together. There didn't seem to be a male/female barrier between us. I also felt that I was safe with him. We were just two old friends who enjoyed being together. Even the occasional silences were not awkward. I found that if I relaxed and said what popped into my mind that I could recall small pieces of past lifetimes when we had known one another. But I had to really relax to do this and just go with whatever came into my head. It made the conversation somewhat disjointed because I kept dropping into completely different memories. He had no problem going along with whatever I was saying and kept encouraging me not to hold back.

He asked how I was doing with understanding the situation I was now in. I told him I had no idea what I was doing, only that I was somewhere in England walking around in a military uniform with a dead guy. Because there were no screaming headlines in the newspapers back at Perelandra about Eisenhower coming back from the dead and residing in England, I had to assume that the country I had visited in 1967 and the one I was presently walking in were not one and the same, although they had a similar feel. David laughed at my blunt description of things. He also verified that the two countries were not one and the same but cautioned me not to press this point yet.

He brought along two more apples, in case we got hungry. When he got them from the car, I joked, "Are apples all this country has to offer for food?" He took it as a challenge and invited me to his "center" where I could have a decent meal and meet the others on his staff. They were eager to meet me. I took this as his challenge to me and accepted.

We decided that I would meet him the next day by the river. He said we were only about an hour's drive from his place, and he thought "arriving" in this more serene setting by the river as opposed to the streets of London might be less disconcerting for me. By this time, I was becoming concerned about accidentally "landing" on top of someone's head in London. The river made a fine meeting place. (If I landed in the river, at least I knew how to swim.)

I asked him why no one in London seemed surprised by my sudden appearances out of thin air. It seemed to me people would faint or run away screaming or something. He said that one of the easiest places for a person to "join in" is a busy city street. No one thinks that a person just suddenly appeared out of nowhere. There's so much activity and movement going on that they all think they simply had not noticed the person before. (I was going to have to pay more attention the next time I walked down the streets of Washington or New York City.)

OCTOBER 21

We met by the river at 4 P.M. and went for a short walk before driving to his place. Once again he drove the car, and, as promised, the trip only took an hour.

I couldn't see the center from the road, and when we arrived, David had to get out to open a gate at the entrance. The cobblestone driveway snaked through a small woods. When we stopped in a parking area, I noticed that there were a motorcycle and several cars that were quite a bit more modern looking than our 1942 Packard. The center was a gorgeous stone, two-story house with a steep, sloping roof. I said to David that it reminded me of an old English cottage. He explained that actually the house was only a little over ten years old, but that they had it built to look like an older English house. The front door was a work of art in itself. It was a large, beautifully preserved wooden door with medieval-looking, black wrought-iron hardware—and it was arched.

David asked if I was ready to meet the others. Actually, I was quite nervous about meeting new people but said, "Yes. It would be silly to back out now." Even though the door looked like it would need three men and a horse to move it, it opened easily and quietly. I walked into a large, light-filled room with warm-white walls, dark wooden floors upon which lay several oriental rugs and, at the other end of the room, a huge black grand piano.

Almost immediately, a familiar fellow with dark hair, dark eyes and dressed in a military uniform walked over and greeted us—our "chauffeur." David introduced him as Butch. We shook hands and small-talked a little bit. I didn't know what Butch, or the others for that matter, knew about me, so I assumed the more "normal" role of a woman meeting a few people and put aside the fact that I had just appeared by a river from Perelandra, whose location in relationship to that river I wasn't sure of. At one point Butch asked me how my trip had been. I didn't know what he meant by that. What trip was he referring to? I covered my bases and said, "It was just fine."

Shortly, we were joined by two other men, also in military uniforms. David introduced them as Mickey and Tex. I was invited to take off my jacket, if that would make me more comfortable, and join them by the fire for a cup of coffee. I had trouble getting the brass buttons on my jacket unbuttoned, so I gratefully accepted a little help from stronger fingers. They said something about buttons on a new uniform sometimes being a little stiff to work at first.

We sat in an area not far from the piano. It had two full-size sofas, three overstuffed chairs and a large coffee table—all of which were positioned around an enormous stone fireplace, complete with a crackling, comforting fire. Mickey brought in a tray with a silver coffee pot, china cups and saucers, all the accoutrements one might need for coffee and a plate of small pastries. The coffee was really strong—the kind that curls your teeth. So I put my cup down and planned to let it sit for a while. Maybe once it cooled down a bit, it wouldn't taste so strong. But Mickey noticed and asked me right away if the coffee was too strong. I tried to answer as diplomatically as possible—I didn't want to offend anyone, especially over a lousy cup of coffee—but when I hesitated, he announced, rather gleefully, that he was going to make another pot and rushed off before I could stop him. The others began kidding David and telling me that they had been waiting for someone with a little clout to complain about that coffee.

Apparently, David insisted that the coffee be strong—like a Turkish espresso. They kept referring to it as "David's sludge." To get it the way he liked it, the coffee had to be boiled. No one else liked it, but he ignored their protests. It was obvious that they felt confident that he would not ignore me. I was a guest and a woman. I had the necessary clout. Before I knew it, Mickey was back with another pot of newly brewed, perfect coffee and four clean cups, which he gave to everyone but David.

I asked who played the piano and was told no one. Then David and Butch confessed to dinking around a little on it, but it was nothing that any sane person would call "playing." They explained that they all felt that a home should have a piano in the "parlor" just in case someone should come by who knows how to play. This struck me as a little on the nutty side. And they had it tuned regularly. Obviously, these men were full of hope.

It might sound to you that this living room was stuffed with furniture. But the room was so large that the piano and the seating area looked dwarfed. It was actually an open, airy room with just enough comfortable furniture to maintain a homey feel. The only thing I thought was missing were pictures. There were no pictures on the walls.

The evening could not have gone more easily for me. There was a strong sense of family among the four men, and they seemed to have no difficulty including me. The conversation was easy. I learned that the motorcycle belonged to Butch, and that it was a classic BMW that he had restored and kept in mint condition. We shared my scooter and his cycle tales with everyone. I suspect that we both embellished our stories a little.

The dinner was incredible. It was served in the dining room just off the living room. Although the room was considerably smaller, it was still large enough to easily fit maybe fifteen people at the table. I found out that Mickey was the "king of the kitchen." He did all the cooking and would not allow anyone to mess around in his domain. For our meal, he had cooked a large roast, potatoes au gratin and fresh green beans. For dessert, he had baked one of the most decadent chocolate cakes I had ever experienced. (He also baked the pastries that had been served with coffee earlier.) David had promised a decent meal, and he—and Mickey—had truly delivered.

By around 10 P.M., I began to feel drained. I assumed that I would have to go back to the river in order to leave, but David suggested to me privately that we go for a walk around the garden and that I leave from there. My exit from the evening with these men felt as graceful and "normal" as my entrance had been. I struggled back into my jacket, said goodbye, thanked them twenty or thirty times (and I meant it) and walked out the front door with David as if we were heading back to the car.

Instead, we walked down a narrow, winding path through a large garden with a lot of tall evergreen bushes that looked like boxwoods. A couple of times we passed stone benches nestled in among some bushes just off the path. I realized that we had circled around the house and were now in the back. From this vantage point, the center did not look at all like an English cottage, as it had from the front. Actually the place was very large and now looked more like an English estate. I mentioned to David that, despite the real size of the house, I still liked thinking of it as a cottage, which had been my initial impression when I first saw it. He suggested that I call the place "the Cottage." That sounded more in fitting with my evening's experience than calling it "the center" or "David's place," so I agreed.

When I told him how much I had enjoyed myself, he asked if I'd like to join them for dinner the next evening. Mickey would be cooking, of course. I accepted his invitation. He then suggested that I plan to "come in" at the spot where we were now standing. It was private, he assured me, and I could just walk around the path to the front door and come right on in. They'd all be inside. I said I'd be glad to try it, but he better give me the Cottage phone number in case I screwed up and ended up wandering around London or along the river. He laughed and said that I'd be just fine. I took him at his word.

I walked down the path away from him still wondering what kind of job they had in mind for me. I have to admit that I was reluctant to leave, but in less than a minute, I felt the shift occur, and then I felt the Perelandra sanctuary around me again. When I checked my watch, I noted that seven hours had passed since I had "left" Perelandra.

For so many years, I had wondered what people did once they died. Did they live a life? If so, what kind of life? I was now learning something about the post-death mysteries and its practicalities. They laugh, drive cars, eat apples, eat finely prepared meals together and argue good-naturedly about coffee. Oh, yes—and they keep a grand piano in tune just in case someone comes along who knows how to play it.

OCTOBER 22

I departed Perelandra at 5 P.M. for my second Cottage evening.

Much to my relief, I arrived at exactly the spot David had recommended the evening before. All I had to do was open the coning, state my intention to shift to the Cottage and picture the spot. The whole process had to take less than thirty seconds. I arrived once again in my uniform. Actually, I was becoming rather fond of the thing. It gave me a sense of stability knowing what I'd be wearing when I "dropped in." I stood in the garden for a while and collected myself. This was the first time I had arrived without someone meeting me.

I noticed that the sun would be setting shortly, even though it was only 5 P.M. (Each level's planet has its own unique relationship to the sun. As a result, the Cottage weather is more moderate and not as rainy as our England. Also, the time zones on our planet, where London time is five hours ahead of Perelandra time, are not the same as those on the Cottage level where the Cottage is just one hour ahead of Perelandra. To coordinate our schedules more easily, the men have set their clocks to Perelandra time. To not add confusion, I keep my home clocks at Perelandra on Eastern Standard Time. I ignore the switch to Daylight Saving.)

I found my way along the path to the front of the house. All the cars and the motorcycle were in the parking area—including that 1942 Packard. Once I got to the front door, I hesitated because I wasn't sure I'd be able to open it. David had made it look easy the evening before. I decided nothing ventured, nothing gained—so I grabbed the handle and turned it. I heard a solid clunk, and the door began to swing open. (A well-balanced magic door.) I walked inside and said, "Hello?"

David walked around the corner, "Hello. You're right on time." I managed to get my jacket unbuttoned myself this time and after hanging it for me on the coat pegs on the wall next to the door, David asked if I'd like a "formal" tour of the place. At about that time, Mickey appeared with a mug of coffee for me, suitable for safely carting around on a tour. He also let me know that it was the "good stuff" and not the "sludge."

I was first taken into David's office, located just off the "piano end" of the living room. It was about the size of the dining room. Three of the walls were lined with floor-to-ceiling bookcases. I noticed that most of the books were about the military, especially military history. He had a huge mahogany desk that sat on a big oriental rug. There were a few things on top of the desk, each (I felt) placed with precision. It struck me as an exceptionally well-ordered office. Just to the right of the door was a small wooden table with a chess board set up on it. The pieces were moved around the board leaving the impression that a game was in progress. David explained that a game was always in progress. He and Tex played one another in ongoing games. Mickey told me that they never sat down together, neither one of them had enough patience for that. They'd just stop on their way in and out of the office, look at the board, figure out whose move it was and make a move if it was their turn. To give the games a little twist, they sometimes made small wagers.

I was next led to the kitchen, Mickey's domain. I had the feeling that I should be more honored to be in the kitchen than in David's office. It didn't look like it lacked anything. It had a dishwasher, large refrigerator, deep double sinks, a beautiful gas stove, double ovens, a microwave (or something that looked like microwave) and plenty of counter space. It was a chef's dream. Although all the appliances looked similar to what was on the Perelandra level, I had a feeling the internal makeup and how they functioned was quite different. Mickey proudly showed me two coffee makers—one, obviously brand new. He said that he had picked it up in town that day so that he could make a pot of the good stuff for all of us. David announced that he was glad to have his "quality" coffee to himself.

We went through the kitchen into Butch's office. This one was about twice the size of David's. Three of its walls were lined with four-drawer filing cabinets. Butch and Tex were at Butch's desk working on something when we walked in. They explained that this was the information center where they kept all their records, files and necessary information. They also showed me a long hallway off this office where additional information was stored in filing cabinets. It was pretty impressive, but I had to wonder why a group of men who were modern enough to have a microwave didn't have their information computerized. I put my observation in my back pocket and saved my question for later.

Before it was completely dark, the five of us walked back through the living room and out french doors just behind the piano to a large stone patio. The patio steps led to the gardens. From there I could see that the Cottage sat on a hill. Beautiful fields stretched out before us, and there were no houses in sight. David pointed out the public golf course beyond the gardens to our left. I asked if he still golfed, and he enthusiastically said "yes." But he could only get Tex to go out with him. Butch and Mickey both hated the game. He asked if I played golf, and I quickly said "no." I had the feeling that had I not been emphatic, he would press me into a golf game at some point.

When we walked back into the Cottage, I noticed for the first time that the entire living room wall next to the piano was clear pane glass and that the french doors were a part of the glass wall. I had not noticed that wall as glass before this. I wondered what else I wasn't seeing.

We were then joined by another man, a younger man who looked to be in his late twenties. David introduced him as John and explained that he worked with them from time to time and periodically stayed at the Cottage for several weeks when necessary.

Once again we sat around the fire. They asked if I would like some wine. When I declined, Mickey brought in an entire pot of coffee for me. The others had the wine. We quickly settled into a casual conversation that revolved around what had occurred since I had left the evening before. I was struck by how much and how quickly I felt a part of this group. They were each quick-witted, quick to tease one another and quick to laugh. As the evening went on, I noticed my guard coming down.

I had been there for about an hour when there was a knock at the front door. David got up to answer, and I had the impression that no one was surprised by the knock. The visitor was an older man in his late sixties. He was short and a little stocky, and as he walked with David over to where we were sitting, I thought I recognized him but I couldn't place him. David introduced him to all of us, and as everyone was exchanging greetings and shaking hands, my recognition grew stronger. By the time he shook hands with me, I knew exactly who he was—my father. Not Isadore, but a completely different man named Max.

I had been seeing him in my mind's eye for a few days while I was doing my chores at Perelandra, and I had gotten insight that he was my father from another lifetime. I hadn't paid too much attention to this because the experience didn't seem to be "going anywhere." It was just a mildly interesting tidbit of information about some man from another lifetime.

Now here he was standing before me. He must have noticed that I recognized him, because he stopped shaking my hand and wrapped me in a huge bear hug. He kept calling me "Katie." From somewhere inside this man's hug, I took a shift and I dropped into Katie's life. I was now Machaelle, operating within the memory of another person's life, a person named Katie.

When we let go of one another, we started talking about the "old days" with all the familiarity of two old friends who had not seen one another for awhile. I was so taken off guard by the moment, that the only way I could figure out how to get through it was to suspend my intelligence, relax and just float along with what was going on. Yet every fiber of my being felt at ease and grateful to be with Max again. His presence made me feel safe.

Max was quite the talker. He clearly had an Irish storyteller's streak in him. As I listened, I realized I knew these stories. We were not really father and daughter—at least not biologically. Katie's father died when she was five. She had been daddy's girl, so the death was an especially deep blow for her. The once bubbly little girl became withdrawn and shy.

When she was six, Katie accompanied her mother to the local ice skating rink to pick up Seamus, her older brother, who was having a lesson. She was sent inside the rink to get him while their mother waited outside. Without thinking, she walked across the ice to her brother who was half-listening to some pointers being given by his teacher—Max. He insisted that Seamus try a movement several times before leaving the ice and, while Seamus skated, Katie stood next to Max, as instructed. When Seamus left the ice to change to street shoes, Max talked to Katie about skating and asked if she would like to learn. She whispered, "yes."

Max walked the two children to where their mother was waiting and talked over the possibility of Katie joining his beginner's class. He also suggested that Seamus be allowed to stop skating because his heart wasn't in it, and Max felt it was a waste of time and money to try to force a child into a sport that they didn't want to be in. The next week, Katie started skating classes and Seamus was freed from them.

Katie was a natural on ice. She loved everything about it and quickly became one of Max's star pupils. She developed a strong bond with him, and he became her "new father." At the same time, Max opened his heart to her. Underneath her shyness, a determined, spunky little girl gradually surfaced as the months went on.

Katie's mother suffered numerous financial setbacks after her husband's death. Within the first year, she told Max she needed to remove Katie from the skating program. Max would not hear of it. Katie had potential, and as much as he disapproved of forcing a child into a sport they didn't like, he believed in providing all the opportunity that a child could handle for a sport he or she loved and showed promise in. Max suggested that he take over Katie's training exclusively, at no charge. Skating and Max had so clearly benefitted her daughter that she agreed.

By the time Katie was seven, she was living with Max, attending the local school and skating during most of her free time. She blossomed. Katie's mother, who had always understood and gotten along with Seamus better than she did with her daughter, gratefully deferred Katie's upbringing to Max. With that, Katie officially had a new father whom she clearly loved.

As Max regaled everyone at the Cottage with his Katie stories, I found myself chiming in when a detail was missed or to add my own comments. I had no foresight about what I would say at any given time. Everything was just right there on the tip of my tongue. No one in the room questioned my seemingly endless knowledge about Katie and Max. This most "unnatural" scene was enfolded in "naturalness."

The men asked if "I" became any good as a skater. Max was shocked that they didn't know. "I" was a world class pairs skater and won the Olympic gold medal for England two consecutive times. Katie had presented Max with her second medal, which he happened to have in his coat pocket and took great pride in showing to everyone in the room. When I held the medal, I recognized it and felt I could remember the routine I had skated with John, my partner (not the fellow I had just met that evening), to win that medal. It felt like a long mathematical formula with numbers and movement had dropped into my head.

By the time we were eating dinner, Max was insisting that I get back on the ice. He was completely focused on my physical condition. David assured him that to do what I was presently doing, I had to be in top condition and that I had resumed a physical training program in preparation for this. I wanted to interrupt and ask, "What training program?" But the conversation galloped right on. Besides, I also wanted to ask, "What was I doing in this training program?" I wasn't aware of any training program. But I had a feeling that if I didn't interrupt, I'd find out. Sure enough, Max turned to me at the table and asked, "How many miles are you running?"

"Five to seven."

"Daily?"

"Six days a week."

"Sit-ups?"

"Four hundred."

"Pushups?"

"One hundred."

"Daily?"

"Yes."

While I was answering him, I was thinking, "This is nuts. I don't do any of this. What the hell am I talking about?" That's when several of the others at the table said they wanted proof and challenged me to do twenty pushups right then. Without thinking, I got on the floor in the dining room and knocked off twenty pushups without any strain. I figured I was in the midst of a miracle!

Max left about an hour after dinner after nailing down a promise from me to join him on the ice at the rink soon. (This was a brave promise since I, Machaelle, did not know how to ice skate. I had been pretty flashy on roller skates as a four-year-old kid in Baltimore, Maryland, before moving out to Upperco, but I didn't think that was going to get me through this ice skating thing.)

Not long after Max left, I needed to leave as well. I was feeling drained again. As David walked me out to the garden "landing and launch pad," he didn't say anything about the occurrences of the evening being unusual. Instead, he raved about what a great fellow my dad was—and I agreed whole-heartedly. He asked if I'd like to join them for dinner again the next night. I accepted without hesitation.

I opened my eyes in the Perelandra sanctuary and checked my watch. I had been gone six hours. I lay there for a while wondering who I was and who the hell was Katie. How did Max, Katie and ice skating figure into the mix? I assumed that she was probably one of the soul rays that Hyperithon had spoken about but I didn't understand why she and her life were such a dominant element at the Cottage. And why did Max see me as Katie? Where was Katie? Was she free-floating around the cosmos body-less? I couldn't get a handle on these multiple mysteries—so I tried a pushup. I struggled through one, then left the sanctuary completely confused but determined to return to the Cottage the next day.

October 23

I arrived back at the Cottage garden at 5 P.M. and stood there for a few minutes collecting myself. The sky was overcast, and I could tell there was a distinct fall nip in the air. I remember loving the feel of the cool breeze against my face.

Our evening was a continuation of the night before, with one exception. Max again joined us, but he brought along my (Katie's) brother, Seamus. I found out later that the men at the Cottage had encouraged Max to do this. When I saw Seamus, I immediately spotted a family resemblance. We looked like brother and sister. He gave me a hug and asked me what in the world I was doing in a military uniform. I told him I wasn't sure. He seemed to accept that as a reasonable answer. He called me Katie, too.

Just as with Max, I "knew" Seamus once he hugged me. I knew he was a musician and had his own band. He had hated skating, but he sure had a passion for music. He gravitated toward the piano in the living room right away—"just to check it out," he said. He pronounced it a "beautiful instrument" and, after a little urging (actually hardly any urging at all), he played several songs he had recently written. They had a Billy Joel flavor to them—or perhaps it's more accurate to say that Billy Joel's music has a Seamus flavor. At this point, I wasn't sure which was more "accurate."

Seamus was as focused on his music as Katie had been on skating. His band rarely toured anymore, choosing instead to remain the house band to perform year-round, five nights a week, at the largest pub in a nearby village. In a tribute to absolute simplicity, the pub was named "The Pub." The band was so famous that people traveled to The Pub from all around to hear them. Reservations had to be booked three to four months in advance. This allowed all of the band members to stay in one place and have a life, while maintaining their musical standing with the public. To my surprise, we weren't talking about some distant village on another planet. The village and pub in question were a fifteen-minute drive from the Cottage.

Max, Seamus and I entertained everyone through dinner with more family tales. At one point, Seamus talked about how Katie had been quite the source of income for him when she was eight years old. That piqued everyone's interest, so they got him to disclose all, over Max's objections. This led to Max's famous pencil-and-donut lecture—the world's worst talk on human sexuality.

It seems that, in his zeal to be a responsible father, Max decided that Katie needed to learn about the birds and the bees when she was eight. He admitted to putting much thought and research into the task before talking to her. On the Big Day, he held her in his lap while he showed her medical book pictures of the differences between men and women. Katie had showered with the boy skaters quite often, so this didn't surprise her at all. Then he moved on to the "female section" of the talk. For this, he relied on another medical book that had the female reproductive organs drawn on a series of color transparencies.

Katie didn't give a hoot about female organs, but she was fascinated by those transparencies. She had never seen anything like that before, so she spent much of this part of the talk flipping the transparency pages back and forth and watching the picture change. It was during this time that Max explained the woman's menstrual cycle, and all Katie caught from what he had said was that at age twelve she would start bleeding from "down there"—"down there" was appropriately pointed out on a transparency.

Finally, Max moved on to the "sex section." For this he used a donut and a pencil as props, both of which had been carefully placed on his desk beforehand. When we got to this part at dinner, Seamus insisted that we could not continue without the right props, which Mickey cheerfully provided. In keeping with the tone of the entire talk, Max chose to describe the sexual act to Katie in the most straightforward terms he could. Katie listened intently, watching the pencil and donut movement.

When it was over, she decided that this was the most absurd story she had ever heard. Nothing like this could ever happen. Max had to be lying to her, and this broke her heart. He had never lied to her before. Max said, "It was terrible. Here she was on my lap with big tears rolling down her cheeks, and I could not figure out what was wrong. She wouldn't say anything and just stood up and walked out of the office."

Katie then went to Seamus and told her big ten-year-old brother about the talk. After she got it out, she asked Seamus what he thought. He said he wasn't sure about all of it, but it sounded about right. Actually, he was quite happy about what she had told him. He had been trying to figure things out with his pals, and here was his little sister describing the whole thing.

That's when Seamus developed his ingenious money-making scheme. He tricked Katie into telling his pals what she knew, saying that they might know better if what Max had told her was right or not. Unbeknownst to Katie, he then charged his pals an "admission fee" to hear the real facts.

By this time, the men were roaring with laughter while at the same time completely sympathetic about little Katie's pain. They razzed Max unmercifully, which he took with a fair amount of grace. Even though we were all having a great deal of fun with this story, I sensed the men around me moving emotionally closer. I suddenly felt protected by them.

The evening ended with Max pressing me to set a date and time when I would come to the rink and skate. I agreed to October 25 at 3 P.M., the day after the next. I didn't think any amount of time would be sufficient for me to learn to skate in, so I might as well get this over with and prove to everyone that Machaelle Wright did not know how to skate. Maybe then I would learn just when I was doing all this jogging and physical fitness stuff.

The evening ended for me about 11 P.M. Once again I was invited back for dinner. When I told them that I was becoming a little suspicious about who they were going to introduce me to next, they assured me that it would just be the Cottage team.

When I got back to Perelandra, it was a little after 11 P.M. I tried another pushup—again, unsuccessfully. My ice skating debut was going to be a disaster.

OCTOBER 24

As promised, we had a relatively quiet dinner with just the Cottage "family." It had only been four days since I first entered the Cottage, but already I was feeling very much a part of this routine and every day I looked forward to my evenings there. An ease and familiarity had settled around us as a group, and I liked it.

No one had yet asked me about my work, and I had no idea how David planned for me to fit into the Cottage team. I still didn't know what they did. It seemed like the important thing for me to do at that point was roll with the reality that was playing out around me.

I asked a couple of questions about Max and Seamus—nothing that would explain how they fit into the picture. I just wanted to know if they lived close by. Seamus lived in the village close to The Pub and Max lived on the far side of the village, a half-hour drive. The rink was about forty-five minutes from the Cottage.

While we were talking, I realized that I had a lot of questions about Max and Seamus when I was at Perelandra. But at the Cottage, I seemed to easily fall in and out of Katie's life, and those questions disappeared.

After dinner, as I was preparing to leave, David suggested that I arrive at the Cottage the next day at 2 P.M. Someone would drive me to the rink for my 3 P.M. appointment with Max. I was curious what they would do once they found out I couldn't skate, but I did not say anything. (Was this a test? Part of my job application?) I was about to disappoint everyone. I didn't even have ice skates.

OCTOBER 25

When I arrived at the Cottage, I was met at the door by Seamus. "Hi. I'm driving you to the rink. The others will follow shortly." Before I could say anything, he had me turned around and headed in the direction of his car.

Our time together during the trip was enjoyable and relaxed. I slipped into Katie's life and found myself laughing about old times with him.

When we pulled into the rink parking lot, I recognized the building. I knew exactly where to enter and where the locker rooms were. Seamus told me that he would see me down at the rink, and I headed off to change clothes.

I walked into the locker room and straight to locker number 1622. Across the locker door was a strip of masking tape with the name "Allison Brown" on it. I realized that 1622 had been Katie's locker, but it was now assigned to someone else. I turned around to look for a locker with my name on it, and that's when I spotted a gym bag on the bench just to my right with "Machaelle Wright" handwritten on a piece of paper that was pinned to the bag. I recognized the writing to be Max's. He had written "Machaelle

Wright" and not "Katie." He knew something about what was going on. In the bag was all that I needed for ice skating—including skates. Everything was in good shape, but it was obvious that the clothes and the skates were not new. They had that broken in, comfortable look to them.

While I dressed, I felt a deep sense of familiarity about everything. I knew what to do, how to dress and where to go. As long as I didn't try to think about it, I could function effortlessly. It felt like I was two people. One knew exactly what to do. The other observed and was fascinated at what was being played out. It seemed to me that the trick was to allow the feeling of familiarity to dominate and keep the feeling of wonderment and questioning in the background. If I did this, I might be all right. I have to say, at this point I was not working myself up to being on the ice. My focus was on the immediate challenges—getting properly dressed and finding the rink.

I walked out of the locker room with skates in hand, turned to my left and headed down a hallway that led to double doors. I walked through the doors, down some steps, turned to my left again and walked through another set of double doors. In front of me was an entrance that cut through rows of seats and led to the ice. Max was sitting on the right, waiting. With hardly a word between us, I sat down in front of him and began putting on my skates. We had done this together a thousand times. As I was lacing my boots, fear gripped me and I said, "I'm not sure I can do this."

"Of course you can. It's like riding a bicycle. It'll all come back to you as soon as you get out there."

"No. You don't understand. I can't skate."

"Don't be ridiculous. Lace up your skates and get out there."

I just looked at him. I decided I had gotten this far, I might as well keep going. The worst thing that could happen was that I'd fall as soon as I stood up on the skates. And if by some miracle I made it to the ice, I'd quickly prove that I was a woman who had a pair of ice skates on for the first time in her life. I felt certain that I wasn't going to be able to bluff my way through this.

Max began giving me instructions about what he wanted me to do to warm up. I listened to him as if I was actually going to get out there and do what he said. When he finished talking, I found myself standing on the ice. I had been so focused on what he was saying that, without realizing what I was doing, I had gotten out of my seat, walked to the ice, taken my skate guards off and was now standing on the ice. When he pointed for me to move out, I did just that.

I slowly circled the rink while getting the feel of the ice beneath my skates. It was an incredibly joyous, freeing feeling that, for a short while, left me with a lump in my throat and tears in my eyes. I gradually picked up speed as I felt my whole body move across the ice. Max let me circle the rink quite a few times, then began telling me what he wanted me to do. By this time, I was completely focused on the feeling of freedom that I was experiencing and Max's instructions. Nothing else existed, not even my doubts and questions.

Max gradually increased the degree of difficulty, and my body operated with a strong, familiar coordination with each new move. I had never before felt such clarity and organization in movement. At least, not with the body I had at Perelandra. I now realized that the body circling on the ice was Katie's body, not Machaelle's, and it was operating on many years and many hours of experience that had left a deep cell memory.

Before I knew it, three hours had passed. I didn't especially feel physically tired, but I was beginning to have difficulty holding my concentration and was having a problem completing some of the moves. Max stopped the practice and handed me my skate guards.

For the first time, I looked into the seats and noticed all five men from the Cottage sitting next to Seamus. It looked like a military invasion. They were pretty intense. I assumed it was because they were in shock. From their serious expressions, it was clear they weren't there just to enjoy some figure skating. They were there to *observe* me skating. After talking to me for a few more minutes, Max joined the others while I removed my skates. I told them I would be back shortly, then headed to the locker room to shower and change clothes.

When I left the locker room, I ran into David, literally. He was waiting for me just outside. He told me he had been sent to get me because they would be driving me back to the Cottage. Seamus needed to get to The Pub, and Max needed to stay at the rink to work with another skater. Several of the others had already left in one car. I was to ride back with David and Butch.

In the car, we got into a discussion about how it felt for me to be out on the ice again. I told them what an emotional experience it had been and how I was grateful Max had been there to talk me through it. I didn't bring up my feelings of fear, shock and surprise, nor did I talk about my questions about being able to skate in the first place or my suspicions about Katie's body. For the moment, I simply allowed myself to sink into the joy of the experience. They said I seemed confident and content while skating. They also talked about my physical strength a lot.

After dinner, David asked me to have coffee with him in the living room. I didn't think much about the invitation until I noticed that the others were not joining us. We settled in front of the fire with our coffee—two separate pots.

About halfway through my first cup of coffee, I began to feel all of the fears and questions surface that I had about everything that had occurred since returning from Paris. I talked to David about my confusion. I told him about trying the pushups at Perelandra and not being able to do one. I talked about how much the Cottage meant to me, and that I was beginning to have the urge to cling to the Cottage for fear that it might disappear from my life.

As I spoke, my fears overwhelmed me, and I began to cry. I worked very hard to describe each fear I was experiencing, but my words were halting and inadequate. Every time I formulated a fear, I'd quickly see how ludicrous and inappropriate it was and throw it out before David could say anything. Then I'd address the next fear and go through the same process. David listened intently to everything I said and spoke little himself. Basically, I was having this conversation with myself. One by one, I addressed my fears.

In the end, I resigned myself to the fact that whatever would be, would be. If my time at the Cottage was to soon end, I'd somehow be prepared for it. I would trust. This didn't make me happy; it just gave me more peace of mind.

When I finished the conversation with myself, David looked me squarely in the eyes and said, slowly and carefully,

> I promise you here and now, that you will remain personally connected with the Cottage for as long as that connection enhances your soul's growth.

Without hesitation, I said,

> I promise *you* that I will remain personally connected with the Cottage for as long as that connection enhances the Cottage's and your growth and direction.

Instantly, I sensed that something important had occurred. And it felt so big that I actually scared myself.

"Did I just officially become a member of the Cottage team?"

"Yes. You did."

That's when I heard applause coming from the patio. I looked out the doors, and there on the patio was a group of about thirty people—wispy people that looked like you could walk right through them—applauding enthusiastically about my new membership into the Cottage. I looked at David, who was at the time looking at these people and smiling, so I knew that he was seeing them also and that I wasn't hallucinating. Or we were both hallucinating. After about five minutes of applause, they disappeared.

I said, "Friends of yours?"

"Yes. Yours, too. Come on, let me show you to your room. You must be a little tired."

With that, he took me upstairs for the first time. At the top of the steps was a long hallway that veered off to the right. I estimated about eight or ten closed doors, which I later learned were bedrooms, that lined the hallway. He led me into the first room on the left—a large room (about 20x30 feet) with wall-to-wall off-white carpeting, a high ceiling, a fireplace at the far end, a bed, nightstand and lamp, dresser, several chairs and a small sofa that created a seating area and a desk. The bed was already made up and the covers were turned back. (There were no chocolates on the pillow.) There was also a small bathroom and walk-in closet that had another uniform just like the one I was wearing and assorted casual clothes—all in my size. I looked at David suspiciously.

He didn't give me time to put any questions into words. Right away, he took me to the room next door. "This," he said, "is the shower room." When I walked inside, I could barely believe my eyes. Before me was a large, sunken, serpentine-shaped pool that I estimated to be about 15x20 feet in size. I said, "It looks like a lagoon." Around three of the sides were steps that led into the water, which looked to be about three feet deep. The wall opposite where we were standing was natural rock. David pointed to a button that was recessed into the rocks on the right and told me that all I had to do was push it to start the water flow coming out from the rocks, if I preferred a shower. Except for the rock wall, the room was white. To my right were several stacks of towels, and hanging on white pegs along the wall were six, white terry-cloth robes, each with initials monogrammed on the pockets in navy blue. The last robe had the initials MSW on the pocket.

I turned to David in amazement, and said, "You've known all along this would happen tonight!"

"I hoped. We weren't absolutely sure. You've always had the freedom to say 'no.'"

He asked if I ever drank champagne. When I told him that I drank a little bit for special occasions, he suggested that perhaps this was just such an occasion and asked if I felt like having some champagne to cap off the evening. We went back downstairs. On the coffee table was an ice bucket chilling a bottle of champagne and two glasses. (Mickey was indeed a magical man.)

We toasted the occasion, and that's when I admitted that I wasn't exactly sure what we were toasting. David said that in order for me to accomplish what was now before me, I had to make a commitment to the Cottage from the heart and soul. A commitment made through understanding and intellectual knowledge would not provide the strength, stamina and dedication I needed in order to address what now lay ahead. He also explained that the heart and soul commitment had to spring from inside me, and, to this end, it was crucial that no one at the Cottage do or say anything prior to the moment that would directly result in my commitment. It had to come from within; I could not be encouraged from outside. At the right moment, only he could extend the "invitation" for me to join.

I asked if the skating had anything to do with this. "Yes. You will need all the physical strength you can muster. By activating Katie's skating, you've activated the physical strength that you'll need. But I don't think we should go into that now." I agreed. I could tell I was too tired to listen. Questions about Katie and her body would have to wait.

After a few sips of champagne, I needed to go to bed. "Am I spending the night here?" I didn't want to assume this. David told me that now, as part of the team, I would be spending each evening and night at the Cottage, and that I would return to Perelandra in the mornings. I couldn't take in any more, so I excused myself and went upstairs to my new room.

David had said to let them know if I needed anything, but, after a quick check of both closet and dresser, I couldn't think of anything that they missed. I was impressed. Who bought all these clothes for me? How did they know my sizes? Or my preferences? In the immortal words of Scarlett O'Hara, I said aloud, "Tomorrow is another day."

I walked into the lagoon room, locked the door, undressed and sat down in the water. It was warm and comforting. I discovered that if I sat on the bottom step, the water came up to my neck. It felt strange to be in that large lagoon by myself, yet it also felt like I had come home. I *was* home. Before I drifted off to sleep, I got out, dried off, put on my very own monogrammed robe and returned to my room. By the time I hung up my uniform and finished getting ready for bed, I was exhausted. I think it must have taken all of three seconds for me to fall into a deep sleep.

October 26

When I awoke, I was surprised to see that I was still at the Cottage. I more than half expected to be looking at the Perelandra sanctuary. I noticed a small clock on the night table that read 9:15. I had no idea what the Cottage morning schedule was, so I quickly dressed in my uniform and rushed downstairs, assuming I was already late for something.

Mickey greeted me in the living room and invited me into the dining room for some breakfast. I kept him company by holding up the kitchen doorjamb as he prepared eggs and toast for me. By the time I sat at the table, the others had joined us and had poured themselves coffee. I was embarrassed to be late for breakfast, but they insisted that I should be getting as much sleep as possible and not worry about their schedule. Their main concern this morning was my comfort. Was the lagoon all right for me? Was the bed comfortable? Did I know there were extra blankets in my closet? Was the room too warm? Was it too cold? I felt like I had dropped into a gaggle of Jewish mothers. I assured them that I could think of nothing I needed, and I thanked them for everything they had already done. This last bit they waved off as if a bunch of men making sure a woman had everything she needed was nothing unusual.

By 10 o'clock, I felt certain I should be doing something. David suggested that I leave for Perelandra from my normal spot in the Cottage garden. He showed me a short cut through the living room and off the patio to the location, then told me to feel free to enter the Cottage through the patio door when I returned. Since I had been at the Cottage for such a long period of time, I wasn't sure if the departure process was going to be "normal," or if I'd have to do something extra. David said that he felt there would be no change. In any case, I should try it and see if it still worked. I turned away from him and walked down the path into the garden. In less than a minute, I felt the shift.

When I sensed the Perelandra sanctuary around me, I opened my eyes. My watch read 10:20. Since it was daylight, I assumed that was A.M. and not P.M.

I LEFT THE SANCTUARY to find Clarence and to let him know I was still among the living. He was used to my being off by myself, but this had been an unusually long period of time.

As of September 1, Clarence was no longer working for Xerox. He wanted time to be at Perelandra, work on some small construction projects around the place and decide what he'd really like to do with his life. The commute had become tedious, and working on copy machines had become boring. The earnings on the money I had inherited from Isadore gave us enough to cover our basic expenses if we were careful.

I wasn't used to having Clarence around. In fact, I was used to having my afternoons and evenings to myself. I had developed an intense and focused daily schedule that didn't accommodate another person. So when he began staying at Perelandra all day, we quickly discovered that we bumped into one another a lot. The thing that saved us was our separate bedrooms. This gave me the privacy for my schedule at the Cottage.

As usual, Clarence was putzing in the kitchen when I found him. As I chattered on about nothing in particular, I realized two things: (1) It really was the morning after the night before, and (2) I was hungry. Clarence offered to fix me breakfast. As he prepared it—eggs and toast—I kept thinking about how I seemed to be surrounded by men making me breakfast. I wondered if I was going to start gaining weight.

While I ate, I told Clarence that I was going to need a lot of time to myself for a while. I didn't give him any details about why, because I wasn't sure how long I would be going to the Cottage, and I wasn't sure how much I should tell him about the situation. In the past, he had never questioned my need for privacy, and he was patient about my not talking about what I was doing. He knew that eventually, when I was ready to say something, I'd let him know what was going on. This morning was no different. I was relieved, because I had told him nothing about my struggles with the Eisenhower memories over the previous four months and I wasn't sure how I was going to work Eisenhower and the Cottage into the conversation.

My major focus at this point was to see if it was appropriate and possible for me to leave for the Cottage from the comfort of the bed in my room rather than from the sanctuary. I called Hyperithon and he "cleared" me for doing the shift from my room. That's all I wanted to ask him, so I cut the conversation short, saying that when I had a little more time, I'd like to talk with him again. I had some questions. He didn't seem to take offense—in fact, he was his usual pleasant self.

By the time I finished doing my Perelandra work and eating an early dinner, it was 5 P.M. and time to leave. I settled in my bed, opened the coning and visualized the Cottage garden. In just a few seconds, I felt the shift.

I stood in the garden for about ten minutes while I acclimated to my surroundings. When I got to the patio door, I found David standing there, obviously waiting for me. He steered me into his office where a coffee tray was set up—with two pots, of course. I settled into a big chair, and he sat at his desk while he asked me questions about my day at Perelandra. We had talked for about an hour, when he looked at his watch and announced it was time for dinner. I admitted to him that, even though I had already eaten an early dinner at Perelandra, I was now actually hungry again.

"I'm going to weigh 800 pounds in a month, if I keep this up."

"Don't worry about it. You're probably not eating enough." I looked at him as if he were crazy.

When we entered the dining room, everyone was standing there waiting. The lights were off, and all I could see was candlelight, the sparkle of silver and the fresh white of a linen tablecloth. It was a special dinner to celebrate my joining the Cottage.

There were people in the room that I didn't know. Quite frankly, I couldn't see very well because the lighting was so dim. So I sat down where told with Tex to my left and David at the head of the table to my right. John was sitting across from me, and to his right was Butch. Beyond that, I couldn't really see too well. I was mostly struck by the festiveness of the candlelight, the silver and the linen. It was a beautiful visual combination.

Champagne was poured. I had never been in a situation such as this and I wasn't sure what to do. I thought I was in a 1930s movie and Bette Davis would be swooping in any minute. Then it hit me.

I stood and restated the commitment I had made to David the night before. Only this time, it was for everyone's benefit. Everyone applauded in approval. Then each man from the Cottage stood, one by one, and welcomed me, each in his own words. I had never experienced anything like this before and was deeply touched.

A fellow at the other end of the table got up, and I thought I recognized him. But I knew I had to be wrong, so I waited for him to speak. Sure enough, as soon as he spoke I knew it was Clarence. And it wasn't someone dressed up to look like Clarence either. I knew this because of a little habit Clarence has. When he is in public and he gets nervous, he starts talking and won't shut up. At our partnership Mass, he gave the world's longest welcoming speech. Here he was, sounding just like Clarence. Finally, he got to the core of his toast.

> May we find the courage to free ourselves to have the expanded life Machaelle has chosen. May she continue to teach me so that someday I can open up more aspects of life to myself. (Then he raised his glass to me.) To our partnership.

Before I could raise a question or say anything to Clarence, everyone took a drink of champagne, and the man who was sitting at the other end of the table opposite David stood to give the final toast. I did not recognize him—except for the fact that he had that wispy look about him and I felt I could walk through him, if I wished. Maybe he had been one of the wispy folks standing on the patio and applauding the previous night.

He raised his glass and said,

> A toast of gratitude for the sparks of energy created by your commitment to this new life. May they continue to spread joy throughout the universe and serve to energize the points of creativity existing in the universe.

As soon as he finished, I knew who he was—Hyperithon. I leaned over to David and he confirmed my hunch. I was so surprised at Hyperithon's presence and so taken by his toast that I forgot all about Clarence for a while. Actually, what Hyperithon had said hit me between the eyes. He was indicating that what I was doing with my life affected the bigger picture. Now, that was a surprising thought. I spent the first half of the dinner quietly thinking about his words and letting them sink in.

I spent the rest of the dinner watching Clarence, who was having a great time at the other end of the table and didn't seem to want to pay any attention to me. I was also watching Hyperithon. I wanted to see what it was like for a wispy person to eat. Could I see the food go down his throat and into his stomach? Weird stuff like that. (By the way—no, I couldn't see the internal workings of his digestive system. I guess once he put the food in his mouth, it became wispy, too.)

Shortly after dessert and coffee, Hyperithon and Clarence got up together and began saying their goodbyes to everyone. Clarence and I still had not had a chance to say anything to one another, and here he was leaving.

I said, a little surprised, "Well, see you back at Perelandra."

He cheerfully tossed off a "Yea" and left the room with Hyperithon. So, there they were—Clarence and some wispy space guy going off together. Everyone else in the room was acting as if this were the most normal thing that could be happening. I asked David what I should say to Clarence when I got back. He told me that Clarence would not remember anything. But he would probably be a little tired.

I said, "Was he aware he was here?"

"Not consciously. But we knew you'd want him here for this dinner, so we extended him an invitation, which he accepted, and then we arranged it."

He told me not to say anything about the evening to Clarence. When he was ready to know about such things, he would either ask me a question about something relating to the dinner or simply remember the event on his own. Since I couldn't pursue this in any direct manner with Clarence, I decided just to find out how he was feeling when I returned to Perelandra in the morning.

By the time I got into bed, it was quite late. My final adventure for the night was the shower. I decided I'd push that recessed button and see what happened. Water streamed out over a rock ledge. It looked like a waterfall and nothing like a regular shower. The water temperature could be adjusted by a small handle just left of the button.

As I stood under the water, I felt an energy move through me. When I stepped away from the streaming water, the sensation stopped. As soon as I stood under it again, the sensation returned. It felt like my shower included some kind of a body balancing. Since there were no bars of soap sitting around, I suspected that I should not use soap if I wanted the full benefit of this balancing and cleansing. I rinsed my hair without shampoo under the waterfall. When I finished, my hair had never felt cleaner. I made another mental note to check with the others in the morning about the practical matter of soap use in the shower.

October 27

I was up and dressed by 8 o'clock so that I could join the others for breakfast. They teased me royally about not sleeping until noon and, once again, told me I needed all the rest I could get. I was not to feel any pressure about their schedule. I accused them of pampering me to death. They informed me that they planned to ignore my protests.

By the time I got to Perelandra, it was 9:30—and I was hungry again. (This was nuts.) Over breakfast, I casually asked Clarence how he was feeling. He complained about being a little tired and said he didn't feel like he rested last night at all, even though he knew he had slept.

Chapter 25

Integration

When considering the Cottage, there is an obvious and undeniable bottom line: I'm functioning with two separate bodies. The human soul has an intricate and tightly woven relationship with its body, like that of a hand to a glove. The soul is the hand, the body the glove. There is a familiar and broken-in fit between them. For the Cottage, my soul needed to fuse with, acclimate to and learn to function with a second body, a different glove that had been broken in by a different hand. Although Katie and I were connected through our soul rays, we were independent people with separate life experiences and different development.

Physically, if you stood us side by side back in 1982, we would appear to be twins. At the Cottage, we have photographs of me (Machaelle) at three-and-a-half years and Katie at six. They look like they are the same child. But this physical resemblance only indicates that the basic makeup of Katie's soul and character reflects through her body in ways that are much the same as the reflection of Machaelle's soul and character through Machaelle's body. (We're both stubborn and have a high degree of determination!) With Katie's body, my Machaelle soul would feel a relationship and not feel it is residing in an alien "container."

Despite the similarities, it took almost two years of work, change and adjustments to integrate my Machaelle soul comfortably with the Katie body and establish a smooth operating unit that included one soul and two bodies. It wasn't easy. When I made my commitment to join the Cottage, I set off a chain of events that took on an intensity that, at times, I wasn't sure I was capable of enduring. In short, my commitment was the easy part. What I had to go through in order to settle in and fulfill that commitment was the challenge.

I've learned that I had easier options available that I could have worked with, had I chosen them. But somewhere along the way (most likely before I was born), I decided that the most effective and advantageous way to do what I had to do (whatever that was) would require two bodies and two levels. Or, knowing me, I could have looked at the list of options and thought, "Hey, this one looks challenging and nearly impossible to pull off. I'll try that one." As it turns out, my decision to work with one soul/two bodies/two levels made me valuable as a Cottage team member, but I didn't understand any of this in the beginning.

Spasms and Shatterings

For the first order of business, I had to stumble my way through a bunch of weird, painful and challenging adjustments. Luckily, I had my gaggle of Jewish mothers surrounding me at the Cottage to help. But no one knew for certain what I would need to go through. It had been a very long time since someone tackled the one soul/two bodies/two levels hat trick. I was starting as someone from a new era with a body composed of many new variables. So we were all flying by the seat of our pants (as they say). Soon after the celebration dinner, the reality of my two bodies began to set in. While the Machaelle soul and the Katie body got used to one another, I experienced multiple physical problems in both bodies that had to be addressed. The three major issues were spasms, "shatterings" and cranial realignments.

Spasms occurred exclusively at the Cottage with my Cottage body. The best way to describe a spasm is to say that I would suddenly and without warning feel like I was vomiting. Really. I'd be doing something or talking and all of a sudden I'd get hit with a spasm. Picture the last time you projectile vomited and that's what a spasm felt like to me. In actuality, the spasm was occurring within my electric system and nothing was shooting out of my mouth. At first I was embarrassed and would look around for the mess I needed to clean up. But there was never any evidence of a mishap. After several minutes of riding out the spasms (they often came in groups of two or three) and drinking a cup of Mickey's tea, I'd be okay again.

As unpleasant as spasms were, shatterings were worse. Each body's electric system needed to function together as a synchronized unit. A shattering occurred when the two electric systems suddenly experienced a massive short-circuiting. It felt as if my internal environment suddenly shattered (hence the name), and electric sparks were flying everywhere. I couldn't focus on anything, I couldn't remain seated in one place for more than two minutes and I couldn't finish a sentence. It usually took the Cottage men one to two hours to pull me out of it and for me to fully regain my ability to hear, see, relax and focus.

ON OCTOBER 29, four days after I made my commitment, I experienced my first shattering. When I left the Cottage, I felt I should stay in the coning all day and not close it down while at Perelandra, as had been my usual custom. Luckily, I followed my instinct.

Clarence and I met a close friend of ours for lunch. Elizabeth had been out of town for five months and, of course, knew nothing about the Cottage or what I was doing. (At this point, I hadn't even told Clarence. He just knew I needed more time to myself.) When we were in the parking lot and about to leave, Elizabeth asked what I had been doing lately. I told her I was going to spend the afternoon recording the progress of some sanctuary work. That explanation seemed innocuous enough and I expected the subject to be dropped. Uncharacteristically, she asked what it was about.

"I've made some serious shifts in my awareness that are as challenging to my life and how I see it as when I first began working with nature. It's been going on since July, and I'm now seeing some important patterns. That's what I'm recording."

I figured this was still vague enough. I did not offer her any more information because I felt a time-and-place constraint—we were standing in a parking lot. Instead of letting it drop, as had been her pattern during the seven years we had known each other, she was now fascinated. She said she was headed to the Sherwin Williams store just up the street to check out wallpaper samples and, if I felt like it, I could go with her and fill her in while she looked through sample books. Sitting in a paint store looking at wallpaper samples while I talked about the Cottage felt as inappropriate as standing in a parking lot. But then she made a suggestion that overrode my initial hesitation. I could follow her in my car (Clarence and I had driven separately), which would give me time alone to decide if I wanted to talk to her about it. If I pulled in behind her, fine. If not, she'd understand that I wasn't ready to talk about it yet.

I pulled in, deciding that I could give her a sketchy idea of what was going on without letting her know details or the whole story. Up to this point, Elizabeth was not someone who seemed particularly interested in this side of my life so I didn't feel inclined to explain the Cottage. But I felt like it might be good to bounce something about what I was doing off a third party. If I was crazy, she'd spot the signs and tell me. I still had misgivings about doing this in a paint store but thought I'd give it a try.

It was a Friday afternoon and the store was nearly empty. Elizabeth and I had the wallpaper section to ourselves. We sat side by side at a table while she looked through large, sample wallpaper books and I talked. I mentioned that this scene was crazy, but she suggested it was a good sign that she was looking at beautiful patterns—lots of creativity—while I talked. This sounded so much like Elizabeth. And as usual, I didn't have a clue what she was talking about, but it sounded hopeful.

I started rather clumsily. I was concerned about how she would react. Before long, she wanted the names of those involved. She said it was frustrating for her to deal with so many unknowns while listening. I gave her the names of the men at the Cottage, including Hyperithon, Max, Seamus and Eisenhower. She was surprised that out of all people, I was talking about Eisenhower. We both agreed that our memories of him were that he was old, boring and dead.

The fact that she hadn't fainted or brought the conversation to an end at this point gave me encouragement to continue. For two hours, I spun out the story. She asked a lot of questions. All the while, she continued flipping pages and looking at wallpaper samples. She rarely made eye contact with me, yet I could tell she was listening intently. She seemed to fully comprehend the space/time thing I was dealing with. I told her about the Cottage in England and about my daily schedule. I ended by telling her about my commitment to the team and the big celebration dinner. Her immediate reaction surprised the hell out of me. She was disappointed that I had not invited her to the Cottage dinner.

Finally she said, "Well, you've certainly had a busy time. I'm not sure what to say now."

I said, "You'll probably just put this on the back burner and forget about it."

"Oh, no. I want to be invited to the Cottage for a weekend."

I was floored, but the possibility of this happening made us laugh. We spent the rest of the time looking at wallpaper samples and joking about her spending a weekend at the Cottage in the English countryside.

When it was time to leave, Elizabeth continued on to another wallpaper store in a nearby town. She told me later that she was followed all the way to the second store by a fellow in an old car with a bumper sticker on the front bumper that read "Dwight David Eisenhower—I like Ike." While looking at more wallpaper samples, she saw a pattern that intrigued her, so she turned the page to read the information on the back. That wallpaper pattern was from the boyhood home of Dwight D. Eisenhower. Later when she told me about these two incidents, she said she felt they both verified what I had told her that afternoon.

I headed back to Perelandra. As I was driving, I began to feel nauseous and extremely exhausted. In fact, I wasn't sure if I was going to make it back to Perelandra and considered pulling over. Once I arrived, I felt I had to get to the Cottage right away. I already had the coning set up and activated so all I had to do was state my destination. Just doing this small thing took all the determination and focus I could summon. I felt the shift activate and in less than a minute I was standing in the Cottage garden.

As soon as I walked into the Cottage, I was met by David, who seemed to be anxiously waiting for me.

"Are you okay?"

"I feel fragile and exhausted. I don't know why."

He led me to a couch. "Here. Sit. Let me look at you. This has been difficult for you. You've done a courageous thing."

I was confused. I didn't know what he was talking about. And I didn't understand how he knew what had happened with Elizabeth. But I knew I was not in good shape. I felt weak and my mind was flying around the room at 100 mph. I kept replaying disjointed bits of my conversation with Elizabeth as if I were an out-of-control crazy person. At one point, I asked David if he minded that I had said so much to Elizabeth. I kept wondering if I had done the wrong thing. He said, "Of course not. You were supposed to talk with her."

I still didn't understand. His entire focus was on me—he kept talking, telling me to focus on his voice and insisting I relax. (Relax? Really? While body parts were shooting around the room? Sure, I'll relax.) He seemed deeply concerned about my condition. For the most part, he refused to let me replay what had happened. I had a terrible time hearing and seeing him. All the while, my mind and my focus continued to race. At first I could only keep my attention on him for a short period of time before my whole body would start to feel jittery—like all my nerve endings were crackling with electricity. I also had terrific head pressure and pain. Each time I tried to ask him what was going on, he'd say that we'd talk about it after I was feeling better. When he'd see me get physically restless, he'd insist we change rooms, go for a short walk, change seats or change positions.

This went on for about an hour, I think. I don't know if he knew what he was doing or if he was simply trying every trick in the book to help me, but he went through a progression of things that eventually restored calm to my sensory systems. Now whatever he said to me was said almost in a whisper. This forced me to focus on his words more. Every time my mind jumped away, he would bring me back. Finally, I felt myself relax. The pressure was leaving my head and I could stay in one position longer. My vision had improved and I could see David again. That's when Mickey joined us with a pot of tea. (Mickey's special blend of tea proved to be a godsend as I struggled through these events over the next couple of years.)

"How is she?" He was obviously concerned, too.

David said, "It drained her and she experienced some shattering. But she's okay. She wasn't damaged."

Mickey turned to me, "You did an amazing thing. We were all concerned." Then he softly touched my head.

I asked, "What did I do?"

David quickly said to him, "We're not discussing it until she's fully revitalized."

"Right. I'll tell the others she's fine. They're waiting now."

David turned to me, "What you did today was important, but I don't want to get into details now. I just want you to know you're strong and gutsy."

"I don't understand."

"Because of the physical state you are in with the two bodies, you were the only one who could do what you did today. We could not help you."

I could begin to feel my body relax more as we were joined by the others who wanted to see for themselves that I was still in one piece. They agreed that I looked tired, but good. David said he felt I was "coming back nicely." It seemed everyone knew what was going on except me. But whatever I had done had resulted in my first shattering. I noticed that my torso felt exposed and vulnerable, but being surrounded by my Jewish mothers gave me a strong feeling of protection.

After about two hours, I felt much better and needed to go for a walk. My mind was calm, my body wasn't jumpy, my head didn't have pressure, and I was no longer trying to replay the afternoon. Everyone accompanied me and as we moved through the gardens, they decided now was the time for me to learn how to hit a golf ball. I received a half-hour lesson, given by all. It resulted in several lost balls and a lot of laughter. I did not show promise as a golfer.

When they finally explained what had happened, they said that up to October 29, my new life that included balancing the Cottage and Perelandra realities had grounded only in the Cottage body. Everything that had occurred prior to October 29 had occurred with and through the Katie body. They pointed out that the Katie body was already adjusted to the Cottage level since this had been Katie's home level. The Cottage reality needed to physically move through Katie's electric system into the Perelandra body's electrical system in order for synchronization between the two levels and the two bodies could begin. Because of the coning I had left open that day, synchronization between the two bodies began as I told Elizabeth the story. While the two bodies and their two systems hooked up, all hell broke loose as they attempted to mesh. No one at the Cottage was sure how either body would hold up as the new reality moved into and through the Perelandra body. They could only speculate.

My two-hour conversation with Elizabeth not only dumped a massive load of information on her but I also dumped it on myself. Luckily, Elizabeth was just hearing words. I understand that must have been challenging for her, but a bumper sticker and a wallpaper sample was all she needed to consider that what I had said did not spring from the fantasy of a mad woman. A bumper sticker and some wallpaper weren't going to do the trick for me. I had more to deal with as my two bodies started the work needed to establish a functioning unit.

The spasms and shatterings went on for the first eight months, but they were especially prevalent during the first six months. Without exaggeration, I can say that I dealt with spasms and shatterings three to four times a week during those early months.

Cranial Adjustments

During the first year, I worked on the Perelandra level with my chiropractor, B.D. Salvesen, and received frequent cranial adjustments. The challenges for the Perelandra body included learning to fully release the soul all at once during the shift, rather than in quick stages, and dealing with the enormously heightened energy the Cottage experience was infusing into the Machaelle body. This created the need for cerebrospinal fluid (CSF) pulse balancing and structural realignment, especially with the cranials. All ten major cranial plates had to settle in a new, more expanded position and learn to contract and expand on the inhalation and exhalation in the new position. While I banged around with this problem, I experienced terrific head pressure and pain from time to time, which indicated that one or more cranials had jammed and were in need of adjustment. I ended up visiting Salvesen about every two weeks this first year.

I had my first appointment on November 30, five weeks after I made my commitment to the Cottage. I had been experiencing a strange head pain at Perelandra for about three weeks. I rarely get headaches so just having any kind of pain drew my attention to my head right away. It felt like someone was pumping air into my head, and I was feeling the pressure of too much air. I seemed to be missing a relief valve.

I had to explain to Salvesen a little about the Cottage if she was going to help me in any real and useful way. To my luck and surprise, she didn't blink. I think knowing me for over three years helped her not write me off as a lunatic. It also helped that we had established my Machaelle-body baseline and the pattern of what I usually needed when I visited her. Normally I went to her every few months for a periodic maintenance check and generally walked away with no more than a minor adjustment. On the whole, we both knew my body was strong and able to easily maintain its balance.

However, for this visit she had to adjust all ten cranials. Then I needed an essence for stabilizing the cranials after the adjustment. She felt that the strain of translating everything that was happening to me took four times more energy than normal and resulted in my need for the essence. My thyroid tested balanced, which indicated to her that my perceptions and translations surrounding my new reality were accurate. My adrenals and liver tested balanced and strong but my pituitary, heart, pancreas and pelvis all tested weak. She said my pelvis couldn't maintain alignment under the strain of the commitment's intensity. She did a pelvic adjustment that also balanced and strengthened the heart/pituitary link. She felt the heart/pituitary problem showed the intensity of my heart and soul commitment. Lastly, the pancreas was strengthened with three supplements.

I told her about the trouble I was having with the shattering and what I had to go through to come out of it. She suggested that I see her within seventy-two hours after a shattering, before the trauma crystallized in either body. And she recommended that I take Rescue Remedy when a shattering occurred. (If only I had ETS—Emergency Trauma Solution—for Humans available back then. Oh well. Sigh.)

In her opinion, all the adjustments pointed to a shifting of my internal gears to a new balance. The cranials needed to realign to handle the new intensity and flow of energy that I was experiencing. She said I looked like I was trying to catch six balls with my hands, but was only able to snag four of them as the other two flew by. The effort was creating a "spasm" in the cranials, hence the need for essences. She felt that with the adjustments, I would be able to catch all six balls in a basket with ease. She assured me that she was doing only what my body was "asking for," and that she planned to let me take the lead in this. I was clearly operating in an area well beyond what was taught in chiropractic school, so she was going to follow my lead and not try to dictate a direction of her own. She felt that needing just one minor spinal adjustment and one essence (for the cranials) indicated to her—beyond a doubt—that I was dealing with very strong energies from outside myself. Because of this, she had no trouble accepting the idea of the Cottage, and she was excited about what I was learning about the human body from my Cottage experiences.

In June, Salvesen asked if I could shift to the Cottage from her office. I said I'd try. It would be the first time I attempted the shift outside Perelandra. She held the CSF pulses in my head while I did the shift. I stayed at the Cottage for about five minutes, then came back. She was still holding my pulses when I "arrived back." She said that while I went through the shift, I had no discernible CSF pulses. As soon as I got to the Cottage, the pulses returned strongly and in a different rhythm than they had been prior to the shift when I was just in the Machaelle body. Once I got back fully to the Machaelle body, the pulses returned to their original "Machaelle rhythm." She also said that, by far, my pulses were stronger while I was at the Cottage. "It's very clear you're working with two separate bodies."

In September, she asked if I could get someone at the Cottage to work simultaneously with my Cottage body while she worked on my Perelandra body. By then the two bodies were well connected electrically and communicating with one another. An adjustment on one body now needed the support of a corresponding adjustment on the other body. I immediately thought of Max. Because of his work as an athletic trainer, he knew how to give needed adjustments, including cranial. Salvesen discovered that when I had my Cottage body activated, she could surrogate test it using its electrical connection with my Perelandra body. She could tell me to tell Max what was needed for the Cottage body and, if needed, talk him through the adjustments. My appointments now consisted of Salvesen, Max and two bodies on two levels. (Salvesen only charged me for one body on one level!) Together we achieved stronger results that held for longer periods of time.

Split Molecular Process (SMP)

At some point during these early months, I decided it was time to understand the mechanism I was using for the shift between the two levels. While at Perelandra, I asked Hyperithon to explain what I was doing. He called it the "Split Molecular Process."

> *Each shift that a soul or life force moves through on its path to form, as it is experienced on Earth, is done through the use of the Split Molecular Process. The life force does not "leave" any one level for the next. It does the equivalent of the SMP from one level to the next, then does the process again, from the new level to the next—and so forth, until it reaches full form as you know it. In this way, all life force, no matter what level, maintains its link with all other levels it has experienced.*

The SMP is, therefore, a fundamental reality within all life force. [Unbeknownst to me, I had been experiencing and participating in the SMP during my work with the monk and my experiences with the Void and during my work with nature and with my manifestation experiences.]

Now, with regard to the Cottage, there is an unusual twist to the process. You are shifting your life force or soul force horizontally from one dimension to a fully compatible sister dimension in another reality. The pairing of your two bodies was tricky. You have two complete and independent systems that, although related within the same individuated soul system, needed to be as complementary with one another as possible. The two forms had to be close to identical. This is because the physical appearance of the body is directly related to and aligned with the makeup and expression of the soul force. Your soul or life force would not have found the form of a short, old, male acceptable. In fact, the soul would have been repelled by that form and remained within the Machaelle body as you attempted the SMP the first time. It is not that one is better than the other: It is simply that they are not compatible to the same soul-ray expression. So your two bodies had to relate physically in similar and compatible ways, thus creating a harmonious field between them.

There is nothing I can use to measure or define the field between your two bodies. [Picture two dots that are three inches apart. The space between those two dots is the field that Hyperithon is referring to here.] *Nonetheless, it is an important physical reality that had to be addressed. Usually, measurement refers to time, distance and space within one dimension, and is not easily transferable between dimensions—unless they are sister dimensions. You are physically present on two sister dimensions that, like your two bodies, are related but separate and independent. However, that connecting field between the two bodies had to contain a high degree of balance. As you have integrated the Katie body with the Machaelle body, that field's stability has strengthened and improved.*

One other important issue with the physical bodies is that one body had to be the "power plant" during the process. This is because you do the SMP daily rather than infrequently during times of major transitions. So, one body had to maintain the physical power necessary to move through the process on a regular basis, plus the relative power of the two bodies had to be compatible. Had the power been too different, too unequal, it would have destabilized the bodies and the connecting field between them. Although your conditioning at Perelandra is inferior to the Katie body, it is still within the compatible range of the Katie body's condition. It was not difficult to pair the two bodies, and because of its athletic conditioning the Katie body assumed the power-plant role.

The SMP itself is activated by an individual's intent. Consequently, it is activated from within the individual's life force or soul. Within the physical body, that life force is anchored in form both electrically and molecularly. Just as all molecular systems contain DNA, they also contain life force. The electrical system also includes an individual's life force. The electrical system functions as a bridge between the soul's life force beyond form as you know it and the soul's reality within that form—specifically, the molecules. An individual's intent registers first within the electric system. It then registers as direct action within the molecules.

Life force, on any given level, can be equally divided once. Just as a person intends to take a step and then the corresponding muscles follow, a person can intend for the life force to equally divide and it will follow, as long as the intent includes the facility for receiving that life force once it is split. In your case, this is the second body. The split does not include the molecules. It only involves the life force contained in molecules. It is called the "Split Molecular Process" because the split or division itself originates from the individual's molecules, not the electrical system.

The life force in your electrical system in the Machaelle body remains "untouched," which allows you to have a continuing connection and relationship between the two bodies whenever you are at the Cottage. When it is time for you to enter the death process, the life force will first split from the Machaelle body molecularly and then follow electrically. Once the life force has split electrically, the Machaelle soul now contained within the Katie body will be separate and independent.

Regarding the Katie body: You draw the physical power for the split from this body every time you do the process, no matter which body you are moving into. When coming from Perelandra, the life force is received first by the Katie electric system. Prior to activation, this body is in a suspended state within the Cottage dimension, but cannot be discerned by the naked eye. It is most closely aligned to the electrical level within physicality. Once your life force moves into Katie's electric system, it activates that body and shifts it into "naked-eye" form as your life force reunites with the molecules. As you know, this only takes ten to fifteen seconds. When you leave the Cottage in the morning, the reverse is done, and the Perelandra body is reunited with the incoming life force.

The Katie body shift to its electrical state at the Cottage while you are at Perelandra is simply an option in the process that was deemed by all concerned, including you, to be the most efficient way of integrating and co-existing with the expanded reality of two bodies. Once you are at Perelandra, it is not necessary for you to pull double duty by keeping both bodies "up and operating," as it were. It would add more complication to an already complex situation. In the preliminary meetings held with you (beyond your consciousness), it was agreed all around that maintaining the Katie body in a suspended state on the electrical level while you were at Perelandra was preferable. It was also preferable to maintain the Perelandra body in a quiet, but fully physical state, while you were at the Cottage. Both states facilitate the demanding and complex situation you took on with the two bodies.

> Note: They tell me that these preliminary beyond-my-consciousness meetings were held in 1981 to discuss the possibility of my doing this kind of SMP. The meetings did not make my October 1982 decisions automatic.

Does this clear up the questions you have about the technical elements of the SMP?

Machaelle: *Yes, I think. However, if I talk about this with others on the Perelandra level, what is to protect people from trying it and getting into trouble?*

Hyperithon answered: *Mostly their ability, training and quality of intent. You never questioned the SMP because of your training with the monk, with nature and with manifestation. For you, the process was a logical step that you only needed to trigger through intent. Others do not have this intimate training and experience. Their intent has built into it limitation based on lack of experience. Desire alone will not move them through the SMP.*

To be honest, back then I didn't understand all that Hyperithon had said. But what I could understand made me feel more confident about what I was doing. The SMP was an actual process that could be described, and I felt safer knowing that I was using a process that was well structured. It contained order and organization. It wasn't chaotic, nor did it occur by happenstance. It included controls. I wasn't just flinging myself around the cosmos.

ELIZABETH ONCE SHARED something she was told by a teacher: If you learn or experience one completely new thing each month, you are living a vital and active life. I responded, "What if we learn or experience something new daily? Or two or three things daily? What kind of life is that?" This was my new life, especially the first few years.

My principal focus early on was to continue the task of integrating, synchronizing and adjusting. It involved every part of my life. Simple things like getting out of my uniform and wearing the clothes that were hanging in my Cottage closet. I discovered that I needed to wear coordinated colors each day to help stabilize the field between the two bodies, so I pinned small colored ribbons to the inside of my clothes at Perelandra and the Cottage. At first the colors for each body were different (such as ivory and heather green), but gradually they became a matched pair of the same color (yellow and yellow). Finally, after five years, I ended up needing just ivory ribbons for each body. About fifteen years ago I stopped needing any ribbons. (I guess that's a graduation of sorts!)

I met Max at the rink a couple of times a week to ice skate. I found out that the impressive conditioning routine that I listed off the first time I met Max was the routine Katie normally kept during her skating years and not something that was occurring when I arrived at the Cottage. In short order, I stopped skating altogether. The strong physical conditioning was "locked" into the Katie body, and I didn't need to work to maintain its level of strength.

When I asked if Katie was floating around in space in search of her body (that I was now inhabiting), I was told that Katie had died a natural death and had made the independent decision to return her soul to her/our soul source (the central source from which our two soul rays extended). She had voluntarily relinquished her body to service. I had not evicted her. It was a decision that I am deeply grateful to her for. The technical issues around her decision to return to the soul source so that her body could be synchronized to my soul remain a mystery to me because I haven't asked for this to be explained yet. I will someday. I have time on my side. In a hundred years when I have nothing better to do, I'll ask for all of this to be explained. (Until then, thanks Katie.)

The Information Policy

This leads me to the Cottage-imposed Information Policy. Within the first twenty-four hours after my commitment dinner, David let me know that they were instituting an Information Policy. They would give me information about what I was experiencing *only when I specifically asked for it.* In short, I needed to take the lead. This meant I had to ask a direct question, and then I'd only be given the information that was needed to answer that question. We did this so that I would not be overwhelmed by information that merely served to satisfy an intellectual itch. It was—and still is—critical that I move through the integration process at my own rate and in my own timing. The only way we could assure that my timing was being fully adhered to was to address only what I could articulate in a question.

Actually, it was more complex than this. The issue revolved around the information I was ready to integrate. This didn't just hinge on my asking any direct question that came to mind. I could override my ability to integrate information by asking questions for purely intellectual curiosity. I had to need the information.

For this, I had to learn the difference between an intellectual question and an integration question. When we ask a question just for the sake of asking the question, and have no intention of doing anything practical with the answer, this is an intellectual question. It springs from our curiosity. An integration question is one in which the answer is received in right timing, and we are able to integrate into our life the information we receive from the answer. It can change the way we think, how we perceive the reality around us, how we act and how we move through our daily schedule. It is a question whose answer moves through a complete experiential grounding process. It is information we *need.*

There is no general, hard-and-fast formula for discerning an intellectual question from an integration question. What is intellectual for one person is integration for another. But here is what I did to learn to distinguish between the two for myself:

1. I stopped asking questions that did not apply to whatever I was experiencing at that moment. That automatically cut out a lot of questions.

2. When I mistakenly asked an intellectual question, I paid attention to how the answer affected me. I noticed that when I could not integrate the answer, it would bounce off me as a rubber ball off a brick wall. I could physically hear the words, but my body felt "hard," and the word energy was bouncing off it. As a result, I had difficulty comprehending or retaining the answer. I wasn't ready to absorb it. Whenever I felt an answer bounce, I would disregard my question and the answer. If I could discern the bounce fast enough, I would stop the person who was answering, tell him I wasn't ready to ask that question and apologize.

3. After a while, I could anticipate the effect an answer would have on me by thinking out a question I had doubts about ahead of time and feeling whether the answer's energy would be absorbed or bounce off. Even if I didn't know the answer, I could still feel an "answer energy." Once I felt the impact, I could decide whether or not to even open my mouth.

In my office at the Cottage (yes, I have an office), I keep a running list of the questions I think I'll want to ask when I simplify my current situation and get there full time. There's another way to say this: Once I die and reside full time in the Cottage body, I might want to ask these questions. For now, they're not important to what I'm doing. (Timing is everything.)

The Cottage Level

The Cottage was built especially for David and his team, and is based on architectural sketches drawn by David. It is situated in England—the "England equivalent" on that planet. Its currency is English, not like our Euro. (If Brexit goes through on the Perelandra level, the two currencies may once again match.) Its customs and social structures are very like our England. The general population speaks with what we would recognize as an English accent. David (who maintains a Kansas accent) and the others in the Cottage are considered guests of this country and not citizens. David has a personal history that began with his association with our England during World War II that drew him to locate the Cottage in its present setting. (It helped that the English weather on the Cottage level is better than on the Perelandra level.)

The Cottage level is on a planet that is as large and as complex as Earth, but it is not our Earth. I once asked David why he chose to continue his existence in form. He said, "I believe there is a truth in form, and I am determined to fully discover it." After death and after his subsequent healing process, he chose to set up his headquarters on the Cottage level, once again aligning himself to form as we experience it on Earth. All who work and live at the Cottage have the same commitment to this form. (Thank god, because if they weren't on a level that was compatible with our Earth, I'd have the additional challenge of switching back and forth between two different vibrational realities. I'm not sure I could deal with that on a daily basis.)

It took a while for me to get used to the idea that the form that I experience on the Perelandra level (natural elements, inanimate objects, people) is equivalent to the form I experience on the Cottage level. I kept assuming that there had to be a difference between the two. For some reason, the group of wispy people on our patio applauding the evening I made my commitment made more sense to me. But they were the anomaly as far as the Cottage level is concerned. To wrap my head around the Cottage's twin-like reality, I had to step beyond my own doubts. After a few weeks of living and functioning on that level, I began to more easily accept what I was actually experiencing.

There is an entire population of about 3.5 billion people living on the Cottage level. Most of them, like us on Earth, are born into and die out of the level. But there are about 550 people, like those at the Cottage, who live beyond time and age, and simply materialize into the level for a specific, and sometimes lengthy, amount of time. David once explained to me that the differences I felt between how people live life on Earth and how they live it on the Cottage level are due to one basic fact: The population, the civilization, that comprises the Cottage level is more mature. Their human existence spans more years than ours. Consequently, they have already addressed many of the problems that are currently occurring on our level, solved them, learned from them and moved beyond them.

My experience of the people—the drop-in visitors like those at the Cottage as well as the born/die population that surrounds us—is one of genuine warmth, openness and friendliness. Whenever I'm at the Cottage, I feel surrounded by a calm energy as opposed to the static, crackling, intense energy of the Perelandra level. For me, it is an honor and pleasure to live among the surrounding Cottage population.

They comfortably recognize and welcome drop-ins—people who associate with that level as visitors. Consequently, the Cottage team is looked at as a special addition to the community and not as some carnival freak show. At the Cottage itself, there is a fairly constant flow of short term drop-in visitors. If anything like this happened openly on the Perelandra level, we'd either create a religion around these people or declare them aliens from space and lock them up before they got out of hand and poisoned our water supply or something. These kinds of interference can just wreck a drop-in's schedule. They'd never get anything done.

Those who are born into and die out of this level relate to money in much the same way you and I do on the Perelandra level. They do something to earn it. They make and sell things or they work in businesses and receive salaries. They pay mortgages and rents. They purchase food, clothes and supplies in shops and stores. In our area at the Cottage, everything is local and there's a sense of pride among the locals about that fact. (I don't know if other countries have something like Amazon.com. So far, I haven't needed to look beyond the village for anything I've wanted to purchase.)

The drop-ins, people like the Cottage team, relate to money differently and the Cottage level openly accommodates those differences. The drop-ins don't earn a salary as such, but through the banks they have access to an infinite flow of money. Every drop-in has a bank account that maintains a balance constantly. They exchange that money for goods and services as needed. When I asked how one gets into the infinite money dynamic, they explained that it had to do with a person's sense of self-worth, and that this is a different inner journey for everyone. Once an individual truly understands his self-worth, he automatically shifts into this infinite-flow dynamic and experiences having money as needed.

The bank in our village provides services similar to banks on the Perelandra level. They have checking and savings accounts, they offer bank cards and credit cards, they cash checks and provide loans and mortgages. But the banks on the Cottage level also accommodate both the finite and infinite money flow. There are separate finite and infinite teller windows in the bank's lobby. (They don't call them "finite" and "infinite." Those are my names. It seems like everyone just knows which windows to go to.) Most of the windows serve the finite accounts. The people with the infinite accounts go to the windows at either end of the row.

The men at the Cottage all have simple checking accounts from which they can draw any needed funds. They don't have complex bank accounts for maximizing earnings because their money does not have to earn more money. Whatever is needed is there for them to draw from. They keep a record of what checks they have written, but that's just to keep themselves informed about how they are moving money. They don't bother subtracting amounts, and they use the monthly statement they get from the bank for making sure the bank records of all their transactions are in order.

You're probably wondering about the source of the infinite-flow money for these banks. Where does the money flow from? I don't know. (Maybe Warren Buffett's company is more expanded than we realize!) It's one of those questions I have on my "when I have time I'll ask these questions" list. Right now I know enough to operate my own little infinite-flow account that Butch set up for me. I don't need to know how the banking system itself works.

Everyone who lives at the Cottage pays local and national taxes. The men feel strongly that they are guests of this country and choose to participate in its governing structures whenever required by their hosts. For example, they each have a valid driver's license (I don't have one yet) and pay into the national medical system, even though they will not personally need this sort of medical assistance. They do not vote, however, because they say it is important that the people for whom the social and government systems were created—the born/die people—determine their own timing and direction.

About technology, we're not computerized out the yin-yang at the Cottage or in the village. Computers are part of the Cottage level but are strategically placed for more targeted functions and goals. In comparison, the Perelandra level seems to be in the midst of a massive, competitive computer movement. Let's see how many different devices in how many sizes for how many tasks we can make—and sell. The Cottage level moved through something similar a long time ago and backed away from that pervasive kind of computerization. As I said, it's an older civilization and they have lived through many different waves of development before us—and learned from those experiences. What I see from them now is the result of their decisions about how best to computerize.

At Perelandra I have three computers and one iPad, each for specific jobs. (I do not have or need an iPhone.) Because we're out in the country and surrounded by cow fields, it surprises people how computerized and technologically advanced the Perelandra business is. But this is what allows my staff to function efficiently.

So I'm not opposed to computers—or technology, for that matter. I'm just describing the different computer uses on each level.

Because I use computers for much of my work at Perelandra, I also have a computer in my Cottage office that is linked to my main computer at Perelandra. The information I enter on the Perelandra computer is synchronized with the Cottage computer so that I can refer to any file while I'm there. The synchronizing doesn't work in reverse. I can't type something on the Cottage computer and have it appear on the Perelandra computer. I could have two-way synchronizing had I wanted it. But I chose to control my work habits and limit myself by closing down the Cottage-to-Perelandra syncing. It's a cheap trick I play on myself, but it works. Besides, what's important to me is to have everything synchronized onto my Cottage computer and ready to go once I commence working after death. (I'm planning to take a few weeks off for a well-earned vacation!)

One interesting thing that I find on the Cottage level is their overall sense of simplicity. When we think of advanced civilizations or see them portrayed in movies, they often wear odd clothing (usually made out of aluminum foil) and stand just four feet tall with big heads and one oversized eye. I think this says something about how we on the Perelandra level perceive the future and the changes ahead of us. There's a comfortable simplicity on the Cottage level. It's not the exterior that reflects evolution and technological development. Rather, it's the interior. Kitchen appliances look similar to ours but operate more effectively and efficiently. Cars appear normal in design but they operate on fuel chips that don't require refueling or batteries. Housing is designed to function with better technology such as heating and cooling, but the architecture is similar to our housing. Appliances and vehicles last a lot longer than we are used to. In the last thirty-five years, the Cottage has purchased two new cars.

The Cottage Members

The men at the Cottage are peers and members of the White Brotherhood (explanation to come shortly). They have lived many born/die lifetimes in form and have a deep experiential knowledge of living through form as we know it. They appreciate form and agree with David about wanting to discover the truth in form. This is why they also have chosen to operate from the Cottage level.

The Cottage team doesn't physically age. They each chose the age when they functioned with the most strength, maturity and intelligence and that's the age their bodies reflect. It serves each man as a strong base upon which to continue evolving. As members of the White Brotherhood they are looking at a future that spans the rest of time. Going through a physical aging process, something they have already experienced in other lifetimes, would not serve them well now.

Until I came to the Cottage, they went by the names David, John, Eric and Stephen. In order to recreate the necessary World War II environment into which I was to be received during those first weeks, John, Eric and Stephen each took the nicknames of original members of David's personal World War II SHAEF staff: Tex, Butch and Mickey. Now, thirty-five years later, we still call them Tex, Butch and Mickey, mostly out of habit.

DAVID (real name David): David heads the Cottage team. He sets the pace and timing and makes the final decisions on direction. He functions in an intricate and equal weave with everyone at the Cottage, and I would characterize his leadership as open and flexible. He has an energy that I would describe as peaceful power—a power that promotes stability and confidence. If I had to choose one word to define him, I would say "integrity." He's still an avid but self-proclaimed lousy painter. He loves golf, the outdoors and nature.

TEX (real name John): Tex has a sharp mind (and sometimes a sharp tongue) that he says he honed to a fine edge during a previous lifetime as an attorney. At the Cottage, he is particularly valued for his fearless ability to ask the right questions and to poke holes in ideas, discussions, strategies and plans. He loves golf and chess—and hot discussions. With Tex, conversations can quickly become debates and differing opinions require strong and logical presentations and defenses. I had to learn how not to get sucked into his intellectual traps. Rather quickly I realized that all I needed to do was tell him I didn't give him permission to pull that kind of stunt with me.

BUTCH (real name Eric): Butch handles the office information flow. He has complete photographic recall. The reason they have not computerized, so I am told, is because of Butch. A computer can't give them what Butch and his photographic recall can. After all my years around him, I can say they are right. If he sees something or hears something, it's carefully filed somewhere in his head and can be recalled at a moment's notice. It's certainly more efficient than searching for some hardcopy report or booting up the right file on a computer. (There is a complete collection of paperwork at the Cottage, as well. It's like a backup system for Butch's memory—just in case.) It's fair to say that he and I are polar opposites: I have a lousy memory and he has total recall. I've accused him of stealing my memory chips. He has a passion for his BMW motorcycle (which he still has) and spends just about every evening at The Pub, enjoying friends and the music. He is not a golfer.

MICKEY (real name Stephen): Because I don't like to cook, I consider Mickey to be a culinary genius and magician. Aside from getting a cup of coffee or tea, we're not allowed in *his* kitchen. He's lucked out with me because I am not going to get into an argument with him about kitchen rights. He loves guests and holidays so that he can unleash his talents. Sometimes I'll look at him and say, "There is something seriously wrong with you." I have no idea how he does all that he does for us. He makes the Cottage our home and not a glorified office building. He keeps us together and moving forward. On top of this, he's a brilliant and valued thinker who gets pulled into meetings when they need extra ideas. He has a strong, creative mind and, intellectually, he is closer to my style of thinking than the others. He loves to run and garden. He declares forcefully that he hates golf.

MACHAELLE (pronounced Michelle): Even after all these years, I still feel I'm the new kid on the block. I'm there because of my partnership with nature and my ability to work well within that partnership to develop processes and address problems. When I first arrived, I had a slight physical resemblance to Katie. Now that has changed and I resemble Machaelle 100 percent. Because what I'm doing on a daily basis requires power from the Katie body, that body is locked in at age thirty-six. And like the others at the Cottage, I don't physically age. It's a little side benefit. Jack Benny would be jealous. (If you didn't get this, ask your parents who Jack Benny was.) I struggle with golf and the game's fine points elude me. File me under the "not a golfer" category. But I walk, hike and bike ride. Once I get there full time, I'm going to learn to row a boat so that the damn thing goes in a straight line and not in circles. I'm hopeless.

Newer Members of the Cottage

JOHN (real name John): When I arrived at the Cottage, John was introduced to me as a consulting member of the Cottage team who was still alive and living on our Earth level in the United States. He had a position and an already developed expertise that made him a valued member of the team. On Earth, he was not conscious of his connection with the Cottage. His agreement to participate in the team on the Cottage level was made by him during a series of discussions about options that were available to him. He spent about six months out of the year in a "split" existence. During this time, he maintained his normal daily schedule and was completely unaware of his activities at the Cottage. At the Cottage, he was unaware of what he was doing on the Perelandra level.

In 2013 he died (on the Perelandra level) and joined the Cottage team full time. The day he died he joined us for dinner at the Cottage and handed me a £10 note to pay off a long-standing bet between the two of us that I had just won. He slept a lot during the first week after his transition, but after that week he was back to being the John I had become accustomed to. Because of his predeath time at the Cottage, his death and transition were nearly effortless. He already knew the drill and he knew where he was headed. He's lukewarm about golf but will play if pressed. He enjoys joining Butch and Seamus at The Pub.

HYPERITHON was first introduced to me by the woman from Findhorn as a "space soul." I later learned that this means he has the ability to easily navigate between many vibrational levels within form. Sometime after I received his gold disk and before I arrived at the Cottage, he visited Perelandra to look at what I was doing. I was unaware of that visit. I never saw anyone walking around the garden. (The fact that I had accepted the disk opened the door for his visit. Without that, he would not have felt he had permission to enter Perelandra.) In his role as the head of the White Brotherhood Department of Science and Technology, he was interested in the work I was doing and the co-creative science I was/am developing. He and I have collaborated on a few projects for the Cottage, and I expect to work with him more frequently after I get to the Cottage full time. Hyperithon, nature and I make a good science team. He is a close friend of David's (which is how David found out about what I was doing in the first place) and a consulting member of the Cottage team. In 1995, he moved to the Cottage and now leads his Science and Technology Department from that location. He and David tell me that the move made a lot of sense since government and science/technology are so closely connected. Hyperithon loves to laugh, he still greets everyone with a perky "Hi!" and he especially loves good conversation over an enjoyable meal with fine wine.

LORPURIS heads the White Brotherhood Medical and Health Department, a massive department staffed by top medical personnel and researchers. Since 1984, he has been my primary physician. My two-body life is considered an anomaly, and I am both his patient and his research guinea pig. We're also good friends. He makes sure I stay standing and don't fly off into the sun. In 1995, he also moved to the Cottage. As with Hyperithon, Lorpuris' move made sense because of the governments' role in personal and public health on the Perelandra level as well as all other compatible levels. Lorpuris and I have collaborated on a number of health-related projects for Perelandra and will continue to do so once I get there full time. Out of all of us in the group, Lorpuris is the soft-spoken one. But he likes a good chuckle. Golf bores him.

Frequent Visitors

MAX AND SEAMUS continue to visit the Cottage several times a month. Max still trains young figure skaters and runs his own state-of-the-art rink. He likes to escape to the Cottage from time to time just to be with us. I'm always glad to have my dad around. Seamus has become close friends with Butch and John. As a trio, they play off one another and egg each other on. It seems like the people in the village enjoy these three when they are together. (They haven't been arrested yet.) Both Max and Seamus love golf. (Have you noticed that the description of our recreational activity revolves around how everyone feels about golf? It's a key issue, thanks to David.)

THE WHITE BROTHERHOOD AND THE COTTAGE WORK

The White Brotherhood is a huge umbrella organization that transcends time and space and includes experts in every field of human experience, such as medicine, science and technology, education, religion and philosophy, finance and government/military. It also happens to have the world's most unfortunate name that can rattle many people's sensitivities on the Perelandra level in this current era of racism, bigotry, sexism, white supremacy and hate crimes committed in the name of religion. It's just not a good time for the name "White Brotherhood." But this group did not choose that untimely name. Prior to being tagged "White Brotherhood," I don't think the members thought about naming their group. They simply knew who they were and what they were doing.

We on the Perelandra level love to name everything, including groups. A gaggle of people get together for some common purpose and the first thing they do is come up with a name. The bottom line is, *we* gave this group the name "White Brotherhood" hundreds of years ago. At the time, "white" represented all colors, the reflection of all colors. And "brotherhood" represented all of humankind, male and female. The people who came up with the name knew that "White Brotherhood" was the most accurately descriptive name and would signal to others that the group was inclusive, not exclusive. But times have changed. I tell people who have a problem with the name to just change the group's name. The members don't care. As long as they know who you mean when you use your special name to link with them, they are fine. You just need to let them know ahead of time that when you say, "I wish to be connected with the Order of the Roundtable of Nose Bleeders," you are referring to the White Brotherhood.

Out of respect, I prefer to continue to refer to them as the White Brotherhood. This is an ancient name that, when used, eliminates confusion. When I say "White Brotherhood" or connect with them in a coning, everyone involved knows who I mean. I also use the name as a small act of defiance. I'm still a bit of a rebel at heart and I'll be damned if I'm going to allow a bunch of nutballs—racists, bigots, sexists, white supremacists, general haters who like to commit crimes against humanity in the name of religion and others who are frightened when they just hear the name and want to lash out—sully the name "White Brotherhood," a name that represents the opposite of all those people.

Over the years, I've had the pleasure of meeting a number of the members when they have come to the Cottage for meetings. They don't wear ID badges or carry business cards. (Hi! I'm Harriet Hofnaggle, proud member of the White Brotherhood since 482 A.D.) They dress according to the style of the Cottage level (no aluminum foil couture) and they drink coffee, tea and wine. They also like *anything* Mickey fixes for them. I've always found these people to be humble, intelligent, gracious and graceful. They are deeply aware of what's happening on a number of reality levels. They have a broad vision and connect events to ancient and recent history as well as the present time and the projected future. From their discussions, it's immediately clear they have a high degree of expertise and experience in their respective fields, as well as a high degree of respect for one another. And they are fearless. They are not afraid to challenge one another. (Can you understand why I feel I'm the new kid on the block?) What they have in common is their dedication to and respect for evolution along with a profound sense of caring for the current state of civilizations and the people living in them as they seek to progress. At a certain point in their personal evolution, they chose to continue their work and help others. They became members of the White Brotherhood.

The central dynamic that drives the White Brotherhood focus and work is evolution. Its goals are to keep everything and everyone progressing according to the timing and rhythm of all involved. Each area of human experience has its own department or unit within the White Brotherhood. In each department there are two main subdivisions: consciousness raising and action. David and his Cottage team head the action division for government/military. (Government and military remain linked because the military is an extension of government and is still its major implementation arm.)

A different White Brotherhood team addresses government/military consciousness-raising. We can identify consciousness-raising activity when there are public events that draw lots of publicity and the attention of multitudes of people. A good example is the protest marches against the war in Vietnam in the 1960s and '70s. Those of us carrying signs and marching in the streets during that war did not directly change policy. We didn't have the expertise nor were we in a position for doing that. But we knew how to walk and carry signs and shout and persist. Our demonstrations showed public demand and support that led to change. Consciousness-raising events can cause people to think, argue, learn, debate, discuss and, eventually, shift their beliefs and positions.

Once we reach new understanding, how do we effect change and create structure to accommodate that understanding? The Cottage team assists us with these changes in government/military. Unlike the consciousness-raising activity, the Cottage work does not attract large groups of people or publicity. The Cottage work is done behind the scenes with individuals who are in positions to create structure and set policy changes in motion. The quiet doers. The creative thinkers who are capable of picking up new ideas seemingly out of the blue and who are in positions to push them forward into action and change.

The Cottage division now consists of over 450 government/military experts—men and women from different countries, different levels and different eras, each with training and experience in different areas of government and military. They do not work out of one huge center but, rather, reside and work from many different levels. (Their communication setup is beyond words! It's how David and his staff who live at the Cottage can oversee and coordinate this large team that is scattered everywhere.) Their work is global, and it is multilevel to include government/military transitions that are occurring on other related levels of reality. Sometimes the members function alone, but more often they function in small teams consisting of individuals with related expertise.

Cottage information doesn't get dropped on the Perelandra level in some special hand-tooled, leather-bound book titled *Mighty Important Information from the White Brotherhood that You Now Need to Pay Attention To.* The teams identify problem areas, establish plans and design strategies that will help people understand what's happening and give them solutions and the tools for moving forward. They download these options and answers directly into the planet's leyline system—an electrical gridwork that surrounds and stabilizes each planet, each level, and is used for, among other things, receiving, sending and moving information among levels. The Cottage information is specifically designed for targeted individuals and can be picked up by them using their intuition and creative intellect. It is up to that person or group to utilize the information as they see fit in order to establish needed solutions and the path forward. It does not come with a loud-speaker announcement telling them this information is brought to you by the Cottage. It enters an individual's decision-making process as an idea or plan that just crossed their mind. As an added perk, as the targeted individuals institute the changes, they will feel the Cottage wind at their backs and this will help propel them forward.

Perhaps it would be more helpful if people did receive leather-bound books full of plans and memos from the Desk of the Cottage Team. That would surely get people's attention and maybe move things along more quickly. It took me a couple of years before I understood that the Cottage team did not operate as a typical military command. They didn't issue a bunch of orders for others to follow. When I first arrived and was told what they do, I called them "the Pentagon of the White Brotherhood" and assumed they operated, at least in some areas, according to military structures and traditions. I wanted those orders to be given. I wanted more direct action and solutions put into place more quickly. I wanted them to speed things up.

However, the Cottage has one rule that they will not violate. This has to do with free will. They will give us options, plans, ideas, warnings and opportunities. They may do things to attract our attention, but they will not *force* us to pay attention to what they've put together, and they will not interfere with our responsibility to make decisions about how best to proceed with the information. The bottom line: *We are always the masters of our own garden.* The White Brotherhood and the Cottage teams will give us the benefit of their expertise, insight and experience, but they will not make decisions for us nor will they do the required work for us. For our part, we must decide to be open to their assistance and then we must decide the best ways to apply what is given. This is one reason why the Cottage teams spend time identifying the most open, creative, intuitive people to work with. (It's also why they all seem to have an exceptional amount of patience.)

Because of free will, there is a fluidity about the Cottage teams and their work. Their information isn't carved in stone. They don't download a solution and then expect us to follow it step by step. Granted they are working with strong individuals on the Perelandra level who have their own training, experience and self-discipline and can recognize a good idea when they see it. There's not much chance they will grab onto new insight and then run off half-cocked to Crazy Land. Still, who knows what we free-willed humans will do. The teams watch how individuals receive the information and what they are doing with it. At different points along the way, a team may download a course correction—new options and clarifying information that will add power and a greater chance of success. While the situation in question moves forward, different members may join a Cottage team to provide additional expertise and insight. In short, when something needs to be addressed, we are not given information and then cut loose to figure it out on our own. We have help every step of the way, if we want it. It is a true give-and-take collaboration.

One example I can give you about how this give-and-take works is to point to my own experience in the summer and fall of 1982. During the early years at the Cottage when I thought about my journey to that level, I would have said that David, Hyperithon and the Cottage team had been in the driver's seat. That they told me what I needed to do. But if you look carefully at how it unfolded, they weren't in the driver's seat at all. *I was.* I could have said no at any point along the way. (I still can say no, should I go mad and wish to back away.) I could have chosen to not ask the next question or request the next bit of information. I was the one who said, "This is what I need now." Everything that Hyperithon said to me leading up to October 18 fell within the range of information I was asking for. And I was the one who said yes before each step I took. They couldn't even tell me that I needed to initiate and state a commitment in order to join the Cottage. I had to do this on my own. Sure, David first responded to my moment of pain on October 25 and told me how the Cottage could commit to me. But he gave me no indication that I should respond back. Yet I immediately responded and said the words that were needed. It had been a long trip to get to that point, one that actually started back in 1969 when I felt compelled to go to David's funeral. But it was *my* journey and they were *my* choices that allowed me to move forward. The Cottage's support provided the wind at my back as I moved along, making the journey feel right to me.

When the men have talked about my trek to the Cottage, they've explained that they could not do or say anything that would have influenced, pushed or encouraged me to take the next step. I had to be the sole initiator and my movement had to be based on my own decisions. Even when I met Max, they couldn't introduce him as my (Katie's) dad. I had to get this intuitively. The same with recognizing Seamus. As each approached me, I had the opportunity to recognize who they were. I guess had I chosen not to recognize them, they would have just been a couple of visitors who came for dinner. I'm sure the dinner conversation would have been different.

Up until the moment I made my commitment to the Cottage, the men were never sure what I would do or if I would choose to continue the journey. They knew something about the obstacles I would face and that it would be challenging for me. They tell me that there was a lot of pacing going on when I got back from Paris. Would I or would I not continue? As they describe these days, it sounded to me like they all had been holding their breath. This might explain why, when I made my commitment, it felt like something had been released and there was a sudden eruption of applause by the wispy group on the patio. Perhaps everyone was breathing again.

PIVOT

MY PERELANDRA / COTTAGE LIFE

Chapter 26

Lacing Two Realities
1983–1984

FOR THE NEXT TWO YEARS, I clinched my jaw, grit my teeth and hung on. Sometimes it was a bumpy ride. At other times the ride was relatively smooth. But always the ride was surprising. Mind you, just because I had met the Cottage team and was living on the Cottage level did not mean I knew what I was doing—or why. I kept hoping for a plan to drop into place. Something I could read and refer to that would lay out the big picture and provide the road map for me to navigate my way through that big picture. No such plan existed.

On top of that, the Cottage team was almost as much in the dark as I was and also did not know how my integration journey would progress. They had an array of options based on what was already known about similar situations, but there was no guarantee that I would pick any of those options. They had to wait, watch and jump in whenever they could help. It felt like I was in a jungle, hacking my way with a machete and creating my own path.

I dealt with my new life by keeping the two levels and two realities separate in my head. I organized and compartmentalized my day. I left the Cottage at 9 A.M., had a quick fifteen-second commute to work, spent the day at Perelandra dealing with my nature work and Perelandra life. Then I left for the quick commute back to the Cottage at 5 or 6 P.M., spent the evening at the Cottage with everyone and retired around 11 P.M. My schedule made life feel manageable.

Of course, my day wasn't always this organized. The Cottage team made sure my schedule was not interfered with from their end. The conversations, meals and guests all fell within my Cottage hours. If I needed to meet someone, it wasn't going to happen at three in the afternoon. I'd be meeting that person after I returned home for the evening. However, there was an abundance of interference on the Perelandra level. Life just stumbled on, and I had to figure out how to fit in lunches or dinners with friends, appointments, meetings, errands and my Perelandra work within the Perelandra hours.

Some of this was my fault because I wasn't saying much about what I was doing. Except for Elizabeth, most of the people around me knew nothing about my Cottage life. I briefly talked about it with my closest friends because I felt that if we were going to continue our friendship it was important that they know who I was and what I was doing. It was my truth-in-packaging moment. Some of them listened, looked confused, mumbled "okay" and never mentioned the subject again. Others stopped talking to me altogether.

My moment of honesty was painful and I have wondered from time to time, if I had to do it over, would I do the same thing with these people. I've always come to the conclusion that I would. If they had not known about this essential part of my life, any friendship would have been shallow, even fake, because it would not have been founded on truth or based in reality. The friendship would have been an illusion.

The handful of people who did accept this new part of my life went in the other direction and leaned towards making me a "star." Their push to hear the newest stories from the Cottage made me feel like a trained circus act who was expected to perform on cue. With these people I was no longer "normal." I could not sit with them over a cup of coffee and discuss the current drought or the upcoming holidays or an interesting article I had read. Nor could I casually talk about my life at the Cottage. (Hey, I went into the village this morning and spotted the nicest sweater. I'm thinking about buying it.) I'd see an expression of eagerness, as if they were about to grab me by the neck and shout, "Tell us more!" Clearly I had become the in-house entertainment. Sometimes I didn't mind talking about the latest Cottage discussion. But overall, their over-the-top enthusiasm got tedious. I didn't want to be a star or a circus act.

I remember one evening early on at the Cottage when I was sitting on the couch in front of the fire. I was alone and it hit me that I was sitting there just as me. I was not a teacher. I was not expected to teach anyone anything. I was not a circus act. I was not expected to entertain anyone. I was just sitting there. My life may have been different from the members of the Cottage team, but at that moment it was clear that I fit in with these people and they had given me something precious. They allowed me the feeling of normalcy. I was just a girl enjoying the crackling warmth of a late-fall fire.

Max reminded me that, from the Cottage perspective, my life at Perelandra could appear pretty strange, as well. On November 1, three days after my discussion with Elizabeth in the wallpaper store, Max initiated a similar experience, except now it was from the Cottage end of things. He had joined us for dinner and during the evening's conversation he began asking questions about Perelandra and the garden and what my life was like there. It was a repeat of my moment with Elizabeth, only in reverse. By the time I finished answering his questions and explaining things the best I could, a couple of hours had passed and I had given a mini-tutorial on nature, Perelandra and life on the Perelandra level.

What I found charming about the evening was Max. He had as much difficulty wrapping his head around my Perelandra life as Elizabeth had with my Cottage life. We tend to think that the reality we are most familiar with is the reality everyone is most familiar with, but that's just not the case. For the first time, Max was hearing about a new dimension with its own population. There were times when he would ask a question and the others would jump in and say to Max, "Why don't you join us for lunch tomorrow and we can fill you in more." (It was Max's question, not mine and it was too soon for me to deal with the answer.)

That evening was the first time I had talked about Perelandra and my work while at the Cottage and it led to a mild shattering. I found out later that my silence had led Tex to question if I was the correct person for their team. David assured him and the others that I would be opening up and talking soon. That evening, spurred on by Max's questions, I unleashed. It felt good to be talking about Perelandra and nature.

By the end of the evening, I had activated the Perelandra reality into and through my Cottage body's electrical system. This act strengthened the connection between the two systems, and they were able to operate back and forth more freely. Unlike my first shattering that had my electrical systems short-circuiting all over the place, this one only left me exhausted to the bone and a bit light-headed. After my Jewish mothers made sure I was okay, I retired upstairs with a cup of Mickey's tea. It didn't take me long to sink into a deep sleep.

At Perelandra, I spent the winter writing—a lot. Recording what happened at the Cottage each day helped anchor my complex life. I also spent time with Elizabeth and talked freely about the Cottage with her. But it was more than just feeling free to speak. I felt *compelled* to speak. I don't think I could have stopped talking, even if I had tried. (Poor Elizabeth.) I dominated our conversations but she seemed to understand my need. Every once in a while she would tell me that she felt like she was listening to a good adventure story. I didn't like hearing the word "story" because it carried a strong connotation of "fiction" when used, but that slight bump to my sensitivities was unimportant. I still needed to talk. This went on for over a year. (Poor Elizabeth.) As we neared 1984, I noticed that my drive to talk about the Cottage was easing up. We were talking about other things now, along with a quick update on Cottage news.

One afternoon, Elizabeth asked me to make a promise. I had to promise that I would not commit suicide in order to get to the Cottage early. And if I was contemplating suicide, she made me promise to talk to her before acting on it. Her words surprised me. Suicide could not have been further from my mind. But she could see how much I cared about my Cottage life, and she was afraid I would cut short my Perelandra life in order to be there full time.

As surprised as I was about her concerns, I understood. For me, life at the Cottage was interesting and appealing beyond words.

I didn't have any trouble making the promise. Here's what I knew that Elizabeth didn't understand. I was determined to stay with my Perelandra/Cottage life all the way to the end. Why? Because I wanted to see how this thing was going to play out. Including the Cottage into my life's mix added a complexity that challenged every detail, every projection into the future—even death—and I had no idea what was going to happen or when. I was thirty-seven years old and I was determined to not interfere with the timing.

Committing suicide would have been a monumental interference—free will run amok. I wanted to find out how I was going to pull off a Perelandra/Cottage life. I wanted to know why I was being given this opportunity and why the Cottage team wanted me to join. When I'm facing a mystery, it's my habit to say, "Well, let's see where this leads." Then I step forward. That's what I was doing with the Cottage. I *really* wanted to see it through to its conclusion. Once I experience my death in real timing and I'm living just a Cottage life, I want to be able to look back and say, "Well done, Machaelle." Suicide would take that moment away from me.

On the morning of December 3, 1982, I felt a heightened energy around the Cottage and no one was telling me what was going on. I left for Perelandra thinking it was probably something I didn't need to know about.

As I went about my day, I received insight that the two French visitors the Cottage men had been expecting were arriving that afternoon. I was to aid one of them, and I would know what to do once I met him. (Okay. Whatever.)

When I returned to the Cottage, David met me in the garden to tell me the guests had arrived and were upstairs resting before dinner. I told him I already knew they had arrived. He asked if I knew who the visitors were. I said no, but I had "gotten" that I was to help one of them, and I would know what to do once I met him. David suggested I might want to rest before dinner, as well.

When I came down for dinner, I found Charles de Gaulle sitting in the living room in front of the fire with David. They stood when I entered, and I walked over for the introductions. I have to say, I could not have been more surprised or nervous. Really, who expects to find Charles de Gaulle in their living room? The first thing I noticed about General de Gaulle was his height. He's a very tall man. He looked exhausted and aged—about eighty years old, I'd guess. I could tell he had an air of power, but it was combined with the fragileness and vulnerability of a broken man.

David introduced us and we made eye contact for the first time. In fact, we couldn't seem to release eye contact. I recognized his expression. It was the same shattered expression that he had had the day of David's funeral. And I realized that when David's coffin passed before de Gaulle on the Capitol steps, the general received a shattering insight that had to do with his role and service to his beloved country. Now David and the Cottage team were giving him the opportunity to address those issues.

I don't think he consciously remembered seeing me the day of David's funeral. Perhaps if I had been standing in front of him with a bicycle, it might have jogged his memory. He surprised me by saying in strongly accented English, "You know, don't you."

"Yes." Yes, I knew he was in a private hell.

Tears came to his eyes and he sat down, staring into the fire. I sat next to him.

David said nothing, but I could tell that he was quietly urging me to do whatever I had to do.

"I've been told I'm to ask you for help," said the general. "But I'm not sure what kind of help or why."

Up to that point I would have replied, "Well, that makes two of us." However, as soon as he talked about my helping him, I understood that I was to stabilize his electrical system using flower essences right away and continue testing him regularly throughout his entire visit. I excused myself and got my sets of essences from my room. (I had used the Split Molecular Process to shift my sets from Perelandra to the Cottage.) When I returned, I said, "I think I can help you, if you wish."

"Please."

I explained flower essences to him and told him I felt they would help stabilize and support his electrical system as he goes through his process at the Cottage. Much to my continued amazement, General de Gaulle was open to both my help and the essences. He kept saying he knew I was to help him. (I never asked him how he knew this. I was content to let that mystery remain.) He tested for six bottles in all, including Rescue Remedy, one time daily for his entire stay at the Cottage. When I administered the essence drops to him, I could feel a dramatic shift in his body. Then I suggested that he might wish to have a quiet evening and dinner in his room. He thanked me, kissed me three times on my cheeks and left for his room.

At dinner, David and I told the others about the essence testing. They thought it was quite possible the essences solved the major problem they had anticipated with the general—how to get him to feel confident and to open up. I felt the essences would support that process and take the pressure off the Cottage team to have to deal with the general on this more personal level. They could now focus on the government/military matter at hand.

The Cottage men called the work they were doing back then "flipping the coin." Using World War II as the foundation, they were reviewing every decision and each action taken by those in government or the military during the war. They explained that each government/military decision and action that went into making up what we call World War II had a coin. On one side of the coin was a battle-related act and on the other side of the coin was the related non-aggressive alternative. World War II had been global. It had touched nearly everyone. It was the playing out of humankind at its very best and its very worst.

For years the Cottage team had studied each detail of the war, one piece at a time. When they identified the non-aggressive alternative that could accomplish the same goals, they declared that the coin was flipped. With each flip, they were reweaving World War II as a unified non-aggressive action. Using the flipped coins, the team could create new government/military strategy to address problems and design opportunities for us to use as we move forward. Because World War II has already played out, the new strategies and options would feel familiar and not alien to people. This would give people the confidence to step forward with the new strategies.

They said that they had nearly completed this mammoth task and had just a few more coins to flip, including the coins connected with Charles de Gaulle. His strong ego combined with his keen intelligence and sense of privacy had added a layer to his wartime activity, and the team had been unable to satisfactorily pierce through it. They needed to see "clean" action and "clean" decisions in order to identify the correct non-aggressive options and flip the coin. They wanted to go through his part of the war with him in person so that the right questions could be asked that would lead them to the core of his role.

Anticipating that he would be a tough nut to crack, they had estimated that they would need a month to work with General de Gaulle. But to their surprise, they only needed eleven days. Some of those days were rough on everyone because they had to challenge and press through his resistance in order to get to the heart of the matter that they were reviewing. On those days when I returned from Perelandra, I could feel the electricity in the air. I tested everyone each evening for essences, at their request. It seemed to keep them clearheaded and standing.

On the evening of the eleventh day, it was announced that all of General de Gaulle's coins had been successfully flipped and that the general and his assistant François would be leaving the Cottage after dinner.

After they left, Mickey served a special celebration cake. David toasted our teamwork, especially the guts and courage it took to cut through de Gaulle's resistance. I asked if I had stumbled onto my job at the Cottage and with the team as in-house essence practitioner. David said they hoped it would be my side job. With General de Gaulle, they saw how valuable a tool the essences could be. But, as they said, it was my side job. My main job was my partnership with nature. This was as much as he was willing to say about it. For now, I needed to continue integrating my Perelandra/Cottage life and working with nature at Perelandra.

In January (1983), I turned my attention to the Perelandra garden to find out what was needed, when and where. With my day-to-day Cottage challenges from all the new stuff swirling around me, I have to say that returning to the classroom with my partner was a relief. There's a certain element of mystery when working with nature to establish a season's balanced garden. Everything in the natural world is constantly changing, and this includes co-creative gardens. After gardening with nature for six years, I was used to dealing with its mystery and magic. Each January I may not have known what was in store for the garden (or myself) the coming season, but I had built a calm confidence in the process. With this first garden after my Cottage commitment, it and its mysteries became my anchor.

One of the things that the Cottage team provided was support. The men surrounded me in a circle of support. Unlike most of my friends and acquaintances on the Perelandra level who expected me to *not* talk about what I was doing, the Cottage team expected me to talk about everything I was doing at Perelandra each day.

I made the typical mistake that so many have made by assuming that if someone is in the White Brotherhood, they know everything. So in the beginning, I didn't feel a need to talk about fertilizing and planting rhythm. But after my first few evening debriefing sessions with the team when they asked questions and pressed me to say more, it hit me. Even though each man had a deep appreciation and respect for the natural world, their expertise, experience and knowledge did not extend to nature intelligence and the nature partnership. These debriefings weren't just some kind of job they had to perform in order to help me settle into the Cottage. They actually wanted to hear about my day and encouraged me to talk. In turn, their questions and comments gave me ideas about new ways to approach any number of things with my nature partner and my work at Perelandra. I now had that much-talked about wind at the back and because of their continuous support, I began to rapidly leap forward with nature.

Besides the garden, I had two new projects that I was able to complete in 1983, thanks to the team's unending encouragement.

Behaving was published and my cabin was built. Both had their own set of challenges.

Before coming to the Cottage in October, I had finished writing *Behaving* and had sent copies of the manuscript to twenty-five publishers. In short order, I received twenty-five rejections in the mail. At that point I wasn't sure what to do and put the manuscript on the shelf while I dealt with the hectic early days at the Cottage. After New Year's, Clarence mentioned that he was working with a fellow whose mother worked at Harper and Row Publishers (now HarperCollins Publishers). Clarence spoke to her son, her son spoke to her and she said she'd be happy to have someone at Harper and Row look at my manuscript. Ah-ha. Now I had an in, a connection. A few weeks later, the manuscript was returned along with another rejection letter from some editor and a gift from the mother, a book on self-publishing. I took this as a hint.

Today, self-publishing doesn't carry a stigma. But back in 1983, they were called vanity books and people made jokes about them. They were usually written by people who would not take "no" for an answer and had lots of money to pour into vanity publishing houses. Once I read the book on self-publishing, I softened on the idea, especially since I didn't seem to be getting anywhere with regular publishing houses. I had a discussion with the men at the Cottage about *Behaving* and, after reading the manuscript, they began pushing me to self-publish. I told them my concern about where I would get the money to do it. They urged me to just move forward with the project and assume the money would be there when I need it. (Easy for them to say.) With that, *Behaving* was again on the front burner.

One of my friends from my early days in Washington worked as a book designer at National Geographic. I called her and asked if she would help design my book and point me in the direction for getting it printed. We met over a weekend, reminisced about our time in Washington (I had not seen her in fifteen years) and talked about the book.

After I described the book, my friend took a weird turn and launched into a speech about birds being the *real* people, and people being the most destructive creatures on Earth. She accused me of putting man above nature and asked me what the difference was between me and any other religious fanatics who believe they know the truth and believe they never make mistakes. Somehow, I was able to diffuse her accusations and calm her down by telling her how important mistakes are in my work and how much I learn from them. She asked me to leave the manuscript with her, and I drove back to Perelandra feeling that her professionalism had kicked in and overridden her personal judgments. With her help, I now had the book ball rolling.

About two weeks later, her professionalism had been overtaken by her personal judgments again. She returned the manuscript along with an amazingly nasty letter telling me she would have nothing to do with the book. She felt the subject matter was too explosive to release to the public and people would only misuse the information. (The book is about my life and my work with nature.) There were already too many instances of this kind of misuse throughout history. She wrote, "the most destructive and goriest moments in history" were merely for the sake of a civilized-sounding philosophy. She concluded her attack by likening me to Adolph Hitler and James Watt (Ronald Reagan's Secretary of the Interior who was described as an "anti-environmentalist"). Wow. With friends like this…I was deeply hurt. It felt like I had been stabbed in the chest with a long knife multiple times.

But at the end of her letter, her professionalism had crept back and she included a list of steps I would need to go through to get *Behaving* printed. She even included the name of a printer that National Geographic used. So along with her attack, I now had the information I needed to move forward.

I sent her a letter thanking her for the information and letting her know that all she had to say was "no thanks" about helping me. She didn't have to kick me in the balls (metaphorically speaking) and accuse me of being a potential mass murderer or destroyer of the planet. (God, what a girl has to go through to get a little help.)

Behaving was published three months later. I think it was the final three months in printing history before computers revolutionized the industry. As it moved through the old process, *Behaving* proved to be a charmed book. The first spell was cast on the galley machine that printed out the book's text on a never-ending length of paper. (Like printing on a big roll of toilet paper.) *Behaving* was scheduled next in line for galley printing behind another book. But the printer kept breaking down and that book wouldn't print out. The guys decided to change books and try *Behaving*. Success! (No one could explain how this happened, but they all began to eye me and my nature partner suspiciously.)

Once edited and the changes were made, the final galleys were printed out and sent to a guy with scissors, an exacto knife and a pot of rubber cement. He cut the galleys into page length and pasted them onto boards. Essentially, he designed the pages and it was obvious to me that the job required expertise and years of practice—and patience. Galleys have to be tweaked just so to fit on the boards properly. Getting small strips of paper with one line of text to stay in the proper position on the board could be challenging. *Behaving* had one such rogue sentence about the Deva of Carrots that kept falling off, causing the guy to scream threats at the Deva of Carrots if that line didn't stay in place.

They had a designer who helped me design the cover using a photo of Mo, the rescued baby possum that I had hand raised. This was the era when color photographs had to be sent to Hong Kong to be separated into four-color transparencies. (We've come a long way since then!) Just when we thought we were ready to print the book, they told me that someone had dropped the ball and my cover photo had not been sent to Hong Kong. They shipped it out air express that morning but said it would take another three weeks before they would receive the transparencies.

Less than a week went by and we had the transparencies in hand. They said this had never happened before. (They were eyeing me even more suspiciously now.)

Several people read the text as it moved across their desks. They loved the book. One young woman was inspired after reading it to get a new job in the field she had always loved. As painful as my former friend's letter had been, my experience with the folks at the printer was pleasant and equally healing.

On September 29, I drove my truck to the printer to pick up 3,000 copies of *Behaving*. Everyone who had worked on the book threw a little party—soft drinks and cupcakes. I gave them each a copy and they embarrassed me by asking for my autograph. Then I surprised them by asking them to sign my personal copy. It was a high school yearbook party! I returned to Perelandra feeling like I had accomplished something big and had given birth to a book. I placed my copy on the seat beside me and every few minutes I would glance down just to make sure it was still sitting there. I had actually written and self-published a book! And in the process, I discovered that I enjoyed "talking to others" through the written word. (By the way, I got the money to pay the printer from the settlement of Isadore's estate.)

My next hurdle was how to sell the book. I knew I did not want to advertise *Behaving* in the traditional ways such as print advertisements. To me, advertising was a form of manipulation and that felt like the wrong thing to do in light of nature's emphasis on non-manipulation. I believed that if what I had to share rang true with others, they would talk to their friends about it and the book would move on word of mouth. If what I had to say *did not* ring true, no one would buy the book, there would be no word of mouth and the book would die a quiet, dignified death. I was prepared to accept that outcome.

As it happened, right after the book was printed I was asked to give a weekend workshop at the home of a couple we knew. I accepted the invitation because they had just moved into an earth house and I wanted to see the house. The house was great, the workshop went well and I sold my first six copies of *Behaving*. In the back of each book, I had inserted an order form. With just six copies and six order forms, the book spread out from there. A year later, I received a copy of a magazine from South Africa that included a glowing review of *Behaving.* (I have no idea how the book got to South Africa. It's one of life's little magical moments.)

THE IDEA OF BUILDING A CABIN grew out of a conversation I had with Wayne, the friend who had encouraged me to travel to Paris back in October 1982. He built and restored cabins. One evening he showed me a book with photos of restored cabins while talking about wanting a cabin in the woods as a get-away for himself. With my latest life expansion, I had been wishing for more solitude and fewer interruptions. But these had just been idle thoughts drifting aimlessly around in my head. Now Wayne was talking about a cabin in the woods. As he flipped through the photographs, I spotted "my cabin," a beautiful one-room cabin with a porch and sleeping loft. I asked how much money it would take to build such a cabin and, after a few moments of thought, he said, "About $19,000." Suddenly a picture flashed in my mind—a one-room cabin with a loft out by the garden. It faced the garden and included a view of rolling farm land and open skies. I asked him how soon he could start building, which surprised everyone present, including me. That evening when I returned to the Cottage, I told them about the cabin. They cheered me on. They could see how it might help me balance and juggle my two-level life more easily.

The next day I awoke with my mind still on the cabin and asked Clarence how he felt about it. He agreed with the Cottage men and also said having my own place might help me juggle my complex life. We walked out into the woods to locate possible sites. I did not want to assume it would be located in the garden area. I connected with nature, and we were led to a location right on the edge of the woods, facing the garden. It was the mind-picture I had seen the night before and the spot was perfect. The cabin would sit directly in line with the middle of the garden. The site looked as if it had been waiting for my cabin to be built there. It was mostly clear of trees except for three young saplings.

The team felt certain the cabin was being "urged on me" by my influential friends (nature), and that I had nature's full support for this. Later when I talked with nature about the cabin and the proposed location, they verified the team's pronouncements. They formally invited me to include the cabin in the garden biosphere and become a permanent part of the garden environment. This change would signify a new level in our partnership. I could tell that their invitation was special and I felt deeply honored.

On June 18, Clarence and I went to our bank to talk about a loan for the cabin. The male loan officer totally disregarded me throughout the entire time we were there. He didn't even shake hands with me. As far as he was concerned, I might as well have been a potted plant. There was a photography show by a local National Geographic photographer set up around the bank. Every time I looked over Clarence's shoulder, I looked right at a photo of David sitting between Kennedy and Truman at some formal function. I recalled the discussion we had that morning at the Cottage about reality and illusion. I looked at the idiotic loan officer and then at the photo and wondered, just what was reality and what was illusion here? Despite the loan officer's foolishness, we (or should I say Clarence, accompanied by his "little lady") got the loan. Construction on my 20x20-foot cabin began in early July.

THE SUMMER OF '83 was an odd summer for me, but I learned a lot about juggling projects and maintaining focus. I oversaw the construction of my cabin and drove the hour and a half to the printer two to three times a week to help move *Behaving* through its many steps to publication. I also continued working in my idyllic garden that now included the activity and sounds of a construction zone. Luckily, nothing new or different needed to be introduced in the garden and I was able to keep up with the maintenance tasks each day.

However, I did stumble onto something new—a two-week flower essence process. I hadn't planned to do something so intense. It started with one essence test that resulted in a solution (multiple essences mixed together to form a solution) that I was to take daily for two weeks. As soon as that solution's dosage period ended, I'd retest and a new solution would start that lasted the next two weeks. This two-week rhythm kept up for several months, until finally I tested clear. As a result, I unloaded a lot of internal baggage that I suspected had been interfering with my goal to live a smoothly integrated Cottage/Perelandra life. By the end of the summer, the Two-Week Flower Essence Process was "born." (This process was updated in 2011 in *The Perelandra Essences.*)

In the evenings I was debriefed by the men at the Cottage on how everything at Perelandra was progressing. If someone had said to me that, along with everything else, I would be talking to these men each evening about what was happening at Perelandra, I would have said, "You're crazy. I don't have the time or energy to go over the day's events." But that summer I learned about the benefits of bouncing what was happening off the men and how it made juggling Perelandra's schedule easier. It kept everything from building up to a screaming crescendo in my head. (That and the Two-Week Flower Essence Process!)

On November 19, three weeks after *Behaving*'s publication, I moved into the cabin. That first night I noticed a clear improvement in my SMP commute. I don't know why but the process felt smoother. (It was probably a combination of the cabin and all those essences I had taken.) The cabin served as my primary residence for the next eighteen years.

IT SOUNDS LIKE I PUSHED the Cottage off to one side while I attended to the projects at Perelandra. That wasn't the case. Every day at the Cottage there was a steady stream of discussions, insights, guests and meetings I could sit in on. I was also busy internally as I continued the long process of integrating my two bodies/two levels/one soul existence. Sometimes I'd wake up sick, like I was getting the flu, but it would only last twenty-four hours or less. I continued to need cranial and structural realignments and would set up appointments with Salvesen and Max. My dreams were so vivid that I found I couldn't ignore them or the insights they were giving me. I was passing milestones that I didn't understand but were understood by the men and celebrated. (Mickey would never allow an opportunity for a celebration to pass.) My daily colors were changing and new colors were popping up. (By the way, each morning at breakfast the men would tell me what colors I would be wearing that day. They could see the day's color in a glow around my head that they claimed only they could see. Sometimes they would debate among themselves what color they were seeing. But most of the time, one of them would casually look up when I sat down at the table and say, "Heather green.")

How I approached my day at the Cottage and at Perelandra was very different, and I think this is what helped me deal with the complexity. At Perelandra, I was the one who drove the day forward. I took the lead. I created and initiated my schedule, I made the decisions, I (along with nature) initiated the day's rhythms. The only things in my Perelandra day that I did not personally take the lead on were dinner and grocery shopping. Clarence was kind enough to help me out by cooking dinner each evening, and I was not going to argue with him about it.

I didn't take the lead at the Cottage. If there was a discussion, I'd listen and join in if I had anything to say. The schedule for meetings and visitors was also out of my hands. The day was set by the men and I only needed to follow the crowd.

This wasn't because they liked to dominate women. I've never felt any instance of masters lording over the little lady from them. Instead, they took charge because they knew I was under enough pressure and it was their way of helping. They were always on the lookout for ways to assist. Most of the time I was smart enough not to argue with them about it, even though I would sometimes accuse them of going overboard. There were numerous times when I felt I was effortlessly racing down a highway on a bicycle because I was drafting behind the men. They knew where we were going. To be honest, it was a relief. I was on a major information-gathering mission and, at some point, I felt confident that I would figure out what I was doing and why. For now, I just needed to sit on my bike and follow along.

1984

When I think back to 1984 and how that year rolled out, I tend to remember it as a fairly calm year that included two or three important developments. But when I read through my journal notes covering that period, I was amazed at the non-stop events, changes, challenges and intensity that wove around the big developments. That year I had to start learning when to say "no" and to stand my ground when it came to others impacting me, Perelandra and my work. But it was a slow, sometimes painful process.

First of all, I felt it was impolite to say no. (I was a girl. We're taught to be polite.) I needed to get over that fast. And I needed to learn which situations required me to stand my ground. This was not something I could learn from a book. I tend to think of myself as someone who can withstand a lot of pressure. So if I was going to learn the No Lesson, I had to experience pressure that was one ounce beyond my pressure threshold. I needed to see it, hear it, feel it and reel from it. I needed to buckle at the knees. It takes a lot for me to cry uncle. (Cue the pressure parade.)

Behaving's sales were picking up nicely. Book stores were starting to place orders and the book received another glowing review, this time from a magazine in Great Britain. (Do not underestimate the magic of word of mouth.) That good news meant that each day I had to take time out to fill orders and respond to a growing number of letters. (Success is such a bitch.) Now I had to develop a functioning small business. Isadore knew how to set up a business, but he taught me how to ride horses, not how to create a small business. Like so many other women faced with developing a business, I had to use common sense combined with my life experience and then wing it.

Since moving to the cabin and joining the garden biosphere, I had felt that parts of Perelandra's sanctuary had come along with me and were now part of the garden. To reunite all the parts, nature and I needed to go through an official sanctuary-moving ceremony, which sounded a bit like this.

Machaelle: Hey, can we move all the sanctuary energy and intent to the garden biosphere?

Nature: Sure. Do you want to do it now?

Machaelle: Yes, let's do it.
(A shift that lasted thirty seconds occurred here.)

Afterwards, nature gave me the go-ahead to convert the former sanctuary into the new Perelandra office. We added electricity, shelving, counters, desks, chairs, filing cabinets, waste baskets, a scale for weighing packages, a handmade ceramic pencil holder from my Garrett days and all the supplies from Office Depot that are needed for office activity. I did not install a phone. If people wanted a copy of the book, they needed to request it by mail. I had a box of padded shipping envelopes and a cigar-size box full of postage stamps. I got tired of licking stamps so I added a sponge and a bowl of water. Each customer had a 4x6-inch file card (filed alphabetically and neatly stored in a metal card box) with a record of what they ordered and abbreviated notes on any correspondence. And voila! We had Perelandra's first business office. Everything was done by hand and had that personal touch.

There was one more switch to make. I moved my personal files out of the house and over to the cabin. The old office was converted into a guest room. (This may have been a mistake.)

ALONG WITH THE INCREASE in book sales came an increase in the number of people who wanted to talk to me and visit Perelandra. They would begin by stating that they would like just a few minutes of my time to discuss something important about working with nature. Could they *please* come to Perelandra for a talk. It would take a half hour at the most. I would say yes because I thought it was important to help people develop their own working partnership with nature. However, once they got to Perelandra, their agreed-upon few minutes stretched into a full afternoon. After they sat down, I knew they were going to remain parked in that spot for the afternoon and my day was shot. Also, their conversations had nothing to do with nature. They wanted to tell me about their life (starting from birth), their pain, suffering and hopes. They wanted me to solve their problems and carve out the path leading to their life's work. They assumed that if a person can talk with a tree, they can also straighten out another person's life.

Some of the people were crafty and pushy when it came to busting into Perelandra. I guess they felt self-important and entitled. These folks would just appear unannounced.

One guy from New York hired a cab from the airport and showed up at the Jeffersonton post office. (That was one expensive cab ride.) They called Perelandra and asked me to come get him. His cab was gone and he was now stuck there. When I arrived, I found a disheveled guy wearing torn jeans and a shirt that hadn't been washed in a while and, as would be appropriate, he had a major case of body odor. He was one of those highly intelligent men who just couldn't be bothered with personal hygiene. He wrote poetry, which he insisted on sharing with me, and owned a rock shop in New York. Actually he was a good conversationalist once I got past the poetry and the smell. When Clarence returned home after work, he drove the guy to the train station—with the car windows rolled down.

A few weeks later, I received a large box from New York full of rocks, crystals, petrified wood and petrified dinosaur dung (this is what the label said). It was a miracle we got the package. The guy had wrapped an old grocery produce box with masking tape (not strapping tape) in lieu of a strong rope, and when the box arrived, it had busted open and was in several pieces. The UPS driver carefully set down what was left of the box and handed me a handful of cardboard pieces and a bunch of loose rocks that had been rolling around the back of the truck.

My safety became a concern, and Clarence and I had discussions about what we could do to discourage gate crashers. I suggested a moat containing a herd of hungry alligators. The post office people agreed to not give anyone directions to Perelandra. But people just drove around until they found us, which I found amazing because we are so far off the beaten path. And I was equally amazed that people assumed that taking time out to give them a guided tour of the garden, serve them tea and crumpets and listen to their life stories was the thing I wanted to do that day.

In my effort to be considerate, I actually tried to help them with their problems and discover their path, but that was crazy on my part. I certainly didn't feel qualified to be dispensing advice, but I had a level of common sense I could draw on that they seemed to be missing. Unfortunately, I could tell some people placed far too much value on what I was saying. (The guru speaketh.) The bottom line: I found the whole situation confusing, time consuming and annoying.

I tried to place some structure and control on the people who called for an appointment by charging $25 for an hour of my time. But that was too cheap and didn't deter anyone. So I upped the price to $50 for an hour. That lowered the number of people requesting my time, but it gave the ones who paid the fee the feeling that they owned me and could stay as many hours as they wanted.

Finally I had to buck up, get over my concerns about appearing impolite, take control and tell them flat out that their time was up and I had other things I had to tend to. That may seem like an easy, reasonable thing for a person to do but, for me, it felt rude. I actually had to screw up my courage to make that announcement. To their credit, when I took command of the situation, they would thank me for my time and graciously leave. (Oh, *that's* what you're supposed to do, Machaelle. Just be clear. Duh.) Eventually I decided that being expected to solve people's personal problems was not a good or appropriate use of my time, so I stopped accepting visitors altogether.

In January 1984, I had one of my vivid dreams. In it, I was seated in a room with Peter Caddy and I was telling him about the unusual change my life had taken. In my dream, I started by saying, "I'm working in the Pentagon of the White Brotherhood." I went on from there. I described the Cottage team and their work, at least as much as I understood about their work. By the time the dream ended, I was exhausted.

At dinner I shared the dream with everyone. Then David asked me to describe my relationship with Peter Caddy. I explained that I had seen little of Peter when I was at Findhorn, but we had reconnected during his numerous trips to the United States and that he had come to Perelandra to help activate our sanctuary. Over time, we forged a loose friendship. (Stick a pin here. More on this later.)

In January, I sensed a change concerning my translation process that would link me with a new intelligence. Not knowing what any of this meant but feeling it might be an important development, I followed my gut instinct and had my first coning session from the Cottage. It was a trial run to see if I could do this work from there with that body instead of with the Perelandra body.

When I first activated the coning, I experienced vertigo and nausea. To my surprise, I received a "fine-tuning" adjustment during the session that I assumed came from the coning members, feeling a shift in my head. It felt like the parietal bones at the top of my head opened wider.

After some experimentation, I discovered that the session and my equilibrium worked best when David was in the room with me and functioned as my anchor—a job he seemed eager to perform. It was awkward translating the session in writing, so I thought I'd try oral translation next time.

David suggested I use a dictaphone. (For you folks who are now shouting that I should have recorded the sessions on an iPhone, remember it was 1984.) He also thought it would be easier on me if I translated simultaneously into two dictaphones—one at the Cottage and the other at Perelandra. This way, I wouldn't have to unnecessarily drain myself switching tapes and transcripts between levels. That week, Clarence and I purchased a dictaphone and Butch picked up something comparable for the Cottage.

On February 2, I began a new series of translation sessions from the Cottage. I still didn't know who or what I would be linking with. Apparently David knew something about what was going to happen because he told me several times that I could refuse this step, that I could say no. He assured me it would be fine if I decided I wanted to hold off. I told him he had to be nuts. After all this fanfare, I couldn't imagine saying no. It felt right and I felt ready. I plunged ahead, ignoring my high level of nervousness.

With David serving as my anchor and sitting to my left, I opened the coning as instructed and asked to connect with the intelligence I was to translate. Immediately, I felt a major shift in energy unlike anything I had felt before. I sat for a couple of minutes adjusting to the intense energy.

The session lasted for two hours, and when I was finished, I had met Universal Light, the nature intelligence of the outermost barrier surrounding our universe. This barrier monitors and controls the inflow and outflow of reality, information and activity flowing in to us from beyond our universe and flowing out from within our universe to the beyond. Its protective function is a critical element within our reality. Its intelligence truly was different than any I had experienced up to that point. If I had to choose one word to describe Universal Light's function, I would say "survival." The survival of all that exists in our universe and beyond. Despite Universal Light's vast significance, its energy also felt deep and caring.

When it was over, both David and I were drained. I also felt down, depressed. I didn't think I had translated Universal Light well. I wasn't sure I felt comfortable with oral translation. The process of marrying the right words with the energy felt too fast and I thought it was too easy to make mistakes. David said he didn't agree. From his perspective, he felt the translation went well and that the information was clear. I decided I'd continue working with the dictaphones to see if I could smooth out the process and feel confident about it.

We joined the others for a quick lunch, then I left for Perelandra. Butch said he would transcribe the session tape that afternoon.

I arrived at Perelandra famished and had something to eat right away. I continued to question the quality of the work I had done. When I returned to the Cottage, I was still depressed, so I took a long nap. I dreamed about flying angels doing precision drill practice over Perelandra. I also had an elaborate dream about a singing, dancing, technicolor commercial for a new beer. Actually, it was an old beer packaged in a new can that had a new technique for sealing the seam. I consciously decided this dream was nuts, and it was time to wake up. When I did, I was no longer depressed. (Thank you, weird beer commercial.)

At dinner the men told me that Hyperithon had called that afternoon to give his congratulations for a job well done and to let David and me know that we needed to increase our protein intake on session days to counterbalance Universal Light's drain on us. (Hyperithon had been included in the coning.)

Maybe the session wasn't a failure after all. In fact, when I read Butch's transcript, it read much better than I had remembered. The only parts I could recall were the bumpy or difficult ones where I ran into problems finding the right words. I had no clear memory of the session as a whole. I decided I needed to have another session as soon as possible to get over my case of nerves and to settle down. We agreed to reconvene in four days. In an effort to relax and feel comfortable about my new friend, I decided that Universal Light was male and I would call him "Igor." (There, that's better.)

During February and March, I had a total of four sessions with Igor and my confidence around oral translation improved. He covered topics such as the Law of Triangulation, Horizontal Healing and Timing. With the increased protein, my strength increased and held up throughout the sessions. And I didn't experience an energy drop at the Perelandra end. However, both David and I still felt seriously hungry afterwards. I left these sessions with a deep appreciation for Igor. I could see that his insights were laying a new foundation of information for me. At the same time, I had to admit that I seem to have a knack for coming up with some pretty weird friends.

My work with Igor raised one problem at Perelandra that led to two new additions in the Perelandra office—a desktop computer and a daisy-wheel printer. While Butch was transcribing the sessions off the dictaphone at the Cottage, I was transcribing them at Perelandra using an electric typewriter and correction tape. If my session with Igor lasted an hour, the time I needed for transcribing was four hours.

I excelled at speaking into a dictaphone, but transcribing something off a dictaphone was not my forte. I didn't know how to use a computer but from what I had heard about it, this was bound to be more efficient and less time consuming. I took the leap into the world of computers—and we can blame it all on Igor. I named my first Microsoft computer "Butch" in honor of my Cottage transcribing partner. And, as they say, I never looked back. Now my one-hour Igor sessions only took three hours to transcribe. Transcribing off a dictaphone was still not my forte.

BACK IN THE SPRING OF '83, I had raised a number of questions with the men at the Cottage about the effect a battle might have on nature at the battle site. Does nature withdraw from a battlefield? What happens to the soil on a battlefield? Does the battlefield heal? They told me I'd have to find out those answers from nature. So I tossed the questions in my ever-growing mental to-do file.

That fall I had a conversation with Salvesen. Out of the blue, she asked me about some nature work I was doing with battlefields. (I had spoken to two mutual friends about my battlefield questions and they, in turn, talked to Salvesen about it.)

Right about then, she said she thought David was trying to get in touch with me. I linked with David and, sure enough, he was waiting for me to finish talking before "ringing through." He wanted to join in on the battlefield discussion. In fact, he wanted Salvesen to go to the Gettysburg Battlefield with me to do the battlefield work that I had been talking about. He also wanted to be included in the coning once we were at Gettysburg so that he could work directly with us. He planned to function as tour guide with Salvesen, while I concentrated on doing nature processes.

This development was a surprise to me as much as to her. My battlefield questions were still in my to-do file and I had not yet talked with nature about them, although I had planned to have a session after putting the garden to bed. I also didn't know anything about a special process that might result from my session.

David seemed to be assuming what my questions were leading to. He suggested we travel to Gettysburg sometime in February or March when the "ungodly cold weather" would assure us there would not be many other people around. That's when Salvesen informed me that she happens to be a Civil War buff (another surprise) and that she would be pleased to be a part of this adventure. We chose March 7 as the date for our appointment with the Gettysburg Battlefield.

Three months later, I had a session with nature that addressed my battlefield/soil questions in ways I could never have imagined and it led to the development of a remarkable process called the Battle Energy Release Process.

The Relationship Between Nature and War

You have been correct in that there is a connection between nature and military history. There is a healing role that must be addressed where military action touches nature.

Remember the concept of horizontal healing: like healing like, form healing form. When war is waged, it is not simply a matter of moving form (e.g., weapons), of creating strategy of form against form (e.g., battle strategy), man against man, equipment against equipment. When war is waged, corresponding energy is moved on all levels. The many sounds of war (we use "sounds" figuratively and literally) are echoed throughout the universe on all its levels. Up to this time, the movements of mankind through the instruments of war have been appropriate. It has been one structure in which humans can grow, change and move forward. It has not been the only structure available to humans, but surely it has been the most widely used.

Nature serves as a buffer for mankind on Earth in regard to the universal energies that naturally flow to Earth. Were it not for nature, those energies would hit humans directly, shattering them. Universal energies, by nature, are more homogeneous than the energies of Earth. This, of course, relates to the fact that Earth is of five-senses form: Its energies are in their most differentiated state. Consequently, it is essential that nature serve as the intermediary, as it were, between the souls who reside on Earth in a state of individuation and the larger, more encompassing, homogeneous energies of the universe that are available to them.

We do not indulge in a value judgment of war. As a foundation, as a framework, we do not see war as wrong; we see it simply as a framework. However, war—as a framework for progression, change and growth—is no longer effective or appropriate. The developments in warfare in recent years have unbalanced the relationship of negative creating positive. They now result in negative creating negative.

When regarding nature in light of war, one must look at several levels, aspects, elements, functions and roles that nature has played. Since we have mentioned the role of nature as the buffer between universal energies and humans, we will go on and talk about a role that nature plays of which humans are not aware: the buffer between man and universal energies regarding mankind's impact on the universe—war being a particularly prime example of the need for this buffer.

War on Earth is, as a framework, not alien to change and growth processes in the universe. Wars on other levels have been created in similar ways. However, because of the differentiated form that war takes on Earth, it is, in its impact on the universe, extremely powerful in its most dense, most intense way. Consequently, it has been important that nature serve as a buffer between Earth and the universe so that the universe's balance would not be unnecessarily tipped due to the intensity of the Earth's individuated warfare.

We speak here of the specific power that is created when one takes the whole (e.g., a war or battle) and clearly separates it into all its parts, coordinates those parts and moves them as one unit (of its many different parts) in one direction for one cause. World War II is an example of this principle on its broadest level: It was not just one country against another; it was countries against countries—and the whole was larger than ever before. There were more individuated parts than ever before, and the Allies were successfully (albeit not easily) brought together as a unit and moved forward for one purpose.

The impact of World War II beyond Earth was great. Without nature's buffer, the universe would have indeed tipped. By this, we mean universal balance would have shifted to such a degree that its sense of natural timing and rhythm would have been thrown off, and it would have needed a period of time to regain its balance. Nature absorbed the intense energy released by the battles of World War II and, in turn, released it out to the universe as a less intense and more easily absorbed energy form. Not only was the universal balance not tipped, but the knowledge, information and growth experiences occurring within the framework you know as World War II were picked up and used simultaneously in various situations throughout the universe.

One could look at what we have been saying as the vertical role between humans, war, nature and, ultimately, the universe. In general, man has not understood the impact of war on the energy around him. All action, all intent, moves energy. This is a law mankind is only beginning to understand. Consequently, he has gone through thousands of years of battles without understanding its implications.

When war is waged, a release of intense, basic emotions occurs. It is an eruption of emotion. Humans cannot sustain their lives within that kind of intensity, for when the battle is over, the intensity of the battle remains. We are dealing with the very same principle you deal with in the Energy Cleansing Process: how emotions remain within a room after grief, or after an argument between spouses. Multiply that by five hundred thousand, and you can begin to imagine the intensity we are dealing with in war. In order for humans to survive, to continue living, to move out of the framework of battle and continue moving forward, they must be buffered from this intensity.

As you know, nature absorbs energies but, on the whole, will not transmute them. Consequently, this enormous body of intense energy created in battles throughout history is being held by nature. It has always been meant to be a temporary assignment, but as one well knows, "temporary" (in terms of time) on one level can mean quite a different thing on another level. Humans have the ability to transmute or change energy from one level to another. However, the process that we will develop for you to use for transmuting these war energies places you as the representative of mankind back into the field of battle to connect with nature and to release battle energies that have been held for the sake of mankind. You will then release these energies from nature, call for them to be transmuted, release them from Earth's biosphere, and allow the energies to take their balanced, healthful position within the context of the universe.

Once that is done, this specific battle will become useful to, and usable by, the universal whole.

By confronting these battle energies that have been held by nature, you are not acting in the role of the absorber. In fact, you are not acting in the role of the transmuter. Instead, you are acting in the role of the conductor, the orchestrator with nature. You will facilitate the release of these energies. You will facilitate the transmutation process and the release of these energies into their rightful place in the universe. This work will go on outside you. You will neither move the energies through your body nor serve as the absorber. That has already been done by nature. Consequently, you will be fully protected. Your understanding of the dynamic of energy will allow you to facilitate what must happen without, shall we say, getting in the way of the process. The new Battle Energy Release Process is a technical process within the laws of nature.

Once these battle energies have been released from an area of battle, it will then be appropriate to facilitate the rebalancing and healing process within nature in the battlefield area using flower essences. We recommend that you complete the Battle Energy Release Process, then test with nature concerning the area to receive insight on the essences needed to complete nature's healing process.

Of course, simply left alone, nature would eventually achieve balance; but by facilitating this process, you once again step into the role of humans taking responsibility for their own actions and working co-creatively with nature for the healing of Earth. Not only will these actions actually facilitate the healing process within the realm of nature, but they will also symbolically sound a note of humans taking responsibility for the destruction that they have created within nature. So instead of it taking years for the rebalancing of nature within the area, you will leave the battle area having cleared the energy that has been held within nature all these years and released (in the form of flower essences) to nature precisely what it needs for its own rebalancing—and that is a good day's work.

It's not unusual for me to come out of a translation session and think, "Well, that was interesting." Or "That's different." This time I thought, "Well, I never could have imagined this." It's one of those moments when excitement and amazement crash into one another and I came out of this session muttering, "Holy crap."

A few days later, I opened a second session to get the steps for the new Battle Energy Release Process. To do this work, nature also instructed me on how to set up a four-point coning that would ensure the proper balance, strength, clarity and protection needed for the process. As I looked over the session transcript and process steps, I couldn't help but sit back again and say to myself, "Wow. Who knew?"

The new process was an important development for the garden. You see, soon after we moved to Perelandra in 1973, the previous owner of the farm visited and told me that the farm's fields had been used by Confederate soldiers during the Civil War as a staging area prior to the Battle of Manassas. Most of the fields and open land in our area of Virginia had been touched by the Civil War, so I didn't think too much about the significance of this information for Perelandra's land.

But I began to connect some dots when I mixed all those flower essence solutions for the plants growing in the new garden. Each plant variety's essences addressed extreme emotional stress, fear, panic or pain. I had no idea how or why plants would contain such intense human emotions. Now I knew that the plants were growing in soil once used as the soldiers' staging area prior to battle and the essences had provided a window into the soldiers' minds. These were the emotions that had been released as they prepared for battle thirty-one miles away in Manassas. With the Battle Energy Release Process, I now had some understanding about what I was dealing with and a process in hand for tending to Perelandra's field.

Had I known how to do it in 1984, I would have high-fived nature. This felt like a huge moment and a giant step forward. It takes the idea of land restoration and reclamation to a new level. I was eager to do the process right away for the garden and Perelandra, but nature told me to wait. (Ugh. Stopped in my tracks.) While waiting, I had two more sessions with nature that advanced my growing understanding about battle energy and land. Each evening I returned to the Cottage and shared the transcripts. (All the battle transcripts and the process steps are included in *The Perelandra Garden Workbook.*)

On February 25, just a week and a half before Salvesen and I were scheduled to go to Gettysburg, nature gave me the go-ahead to do the Battle Energy Release Process. As soon as I shifted to Perelandra, I settled in front of the cabin's double doors facing the garden, collected myself, took a deep breath and opened the coning. I set up the process for Perelandra's twenty-one acres. Then I carefully moved through the steps as nature had instructed.

As it turned out, it was a simple process that flowed easily. But I was surprised by the intensity of the release of the battle-related energies. It was as if steam jets had been opened all over Perelandra, and white energy shot out and up from the fields and trees for about twenty minutes, forming a white cloud about thirty feet thick above the tree line of our woods. When I called for the energy to move on to its next higher level, I watched the cloud move up and away from Perelandra and felt it being received and absorbed into the universe.

As the energy released, I had a physical reaction—a clear and dramatic increase of what felt like electricity in my body. I checked to see if the battle energy was somehow moving through my body. Nature said no, I was responding to all the activity going on around me, and I was fine. My system would settle in a few minutes. (And it did.)

I returned my focus back to the garden and checked for any essences needed to stabilize both Perelandra and the garden now that the energy had been released. Using a glass bowl, I mixed a solution made up of four different essences and walked the bowl out to the Genesa® crystal in the middle of the garden for a natural release from that location. I set the bowl on the slate, then turned around to go back to the cabin.

That's when I spotted a three-foot-long gold satin ribbon in the spiral grass path that I had just walked on less than two minutes earlier. It looked like it had gently drifted in with the breeze and was lightly resting on the grass. As soon as I saw it, I knew it was a gift from nature. The process had worked, and nature was giving me their version of a high five. I smiled, picked up the ribbon and carefully tucked it in my coat pocket.

Before returning to the cabin, nature told me to look at the garden soil. I walked out into the middle of the planting area, pulled back the winter layer of mulch and scooped up some soil in my hands. Its consistency had changed from heavy, red Virginia clay to black loam. At this point, I'd say it had been a half hour since I finished the Battle Energy Release Process. How in the world could soil change so significantly in that short period of time? I checked the soil in the other two garden sections and found the same results. I needed to think. I needed a cup of coffee.

I sat quietly in the cabin that afternoon, staring out the window at the garden for a long time and thinking about what had just happened. I had transcribed the battle sessions and read them several times. I had gone over them with the men at the Cottage. I was experienced when it came to working in partnership with nature and observing what looked to be miracles as a result. Yet, with this, I was flabbergasted.

First, I was surprised by the amount of energy released. I had not expected anything like that from a 120-year-old battle-staging area. This wasn't where the battle was fought. This was where soldiers rested and prepared for battle. Obviously I had not understood the scope of what the Battle Energy Release Process would be addressing.

As I thought about the sheer volume of energy that had collected above the trees, I wondered if I was going to get a call from the neighbors asking if I knew anything about a strange cloud over Perelandra. Since no such call came, I assumed I must have been seeing the process play out with my inner vision.

That evening, when I told the men about what happened, they expressed concern that I had done this alone. I just looked at them and laughed. "But I always do my work alone." (Oh, right—Jewish mothers. For a moment I had forgotten.) I explained it was important to do a new process alone so that I'm not interrupted and can feel and see how the steps are progressing. As part of my responsibility in the partnership, I could catch any steps of the process that need shoring up for my benefit.

The men showed no surprise at how much energy had been released because they knew first hand what happens both in battle and when preparing for battle. That made me think about the depth of the trauma soldiers take away from a battlefield. No wonder it's so hard for them to talk about it—and so hard for us to hear what they are really saying. How do you put that experience into words? With this kind of intensity, PTSD seems like the reasonable and correct response to have in war.

Later that spring, when I tested the garden for fertilizers to add, there were dramatic changes in what was needed. Before the process, it seemed like the plants had been drawing their nutrients through a screen or a barrier that was made up of battle-related energy. This spring the barrier was no longer there. With unfettered access, the soil's nutrients were more easily available to the plants and fewer fertilizers were needed. After the seeds germinated, I tested to see if any plants still required their own essence solution. They did not. That raised new questions: What are we ingesting when we eat plants that have been grown in old battlefield or battle-related soil? Over the span of human history, were there any areas on the planet where battles had not been prepared for or fought?

Gettysburg Battlefield: Phase One

On the morning of March 7, Salvesen and I arrived at Gettysburg. I can't think of a better person in the world to do this kind of work with than Salvesen. She's game for just about anything. She's fearless and she loves adventures. She has a great sense of humor and she loves chocolate. (I brought along a generous supply of chocolate for the day.) As it turned out, we both needed all of this to get through the afternoon.

This was my first trip to the battlefield and I didn't know what to expect. The handful of people who knew about our trip said, "You'll never be able to do that work. The Gettysburg Battlefield is too big." When I told David about their comments, he said matter-of-factly, "Ignore them."

David knew every square inch of that battlefield and every detail of the battle. Salvesen was remarkably well versed about the battle, as well. Of the three, I was the undisputed dummy. I knew nothing about Gettysburg or the battle. I only knew how to drive my little truck and how to do the Battle Energy Release Process. I looked to Salvesen and David to lead me through the day, one manageable step at a time.

There were "Eisenhower" signs all over town. David's retirement farm, which is now the Eisenhower National Historic Site, is located next to the battlefield. Salvesen led me to the Visitor Center parking lot. It was empty, except for us. David was right about the time of year to schedule our trip. The temperature was barely above 30 degrees Fahrenheit and we had a stiff breeze to make it feel even colder. We definitely weren't going to have any problems with crowds of tourists.

I swear I didn't plan this next thing. When I turned the engine off, I looked up and right in front of us was a sign, "Eisenhower Tour Starts Here." I said to Salvesen, "This must be where we start." And right next to the sign was a wooden map holder mounted on a post. I went over and found one map. When I looked around the parking lot, I saw that the rest of the holders were empty. (Let the magic begin.) I got back into the truck and handed the map to Salvesen.

David had given each of us specific jobs. Salvesen was to work with him as he directed us around the battlefield, and I was to concentrate on working with nature and doing the Battle Energy Release Process. She and I still didn't know how we were going to approach a battlefield that was feeling larger by the minute.

We also didn't know how Salvesen was going to "hear" David as he gave her directions for driving around the battlefield. But as soon as I opened the coning we were to have activated for the day, which included all the members I would need for the Battle Energy Release Process work, plus David and Salvesen, they became connected and could communicate with one another. After a few "Can you hear me now?" moments between the two of them, David started giving her directions.

Our first glitch occurred as I pulled out of the parking lot. Salvesen told me to turn right but David wanted us to turn left. We drove around for a bit, making right and left turns according to what he was saying, and ended up close to where we had started.

(David caught our mistake and looped us around to get us back to where he wanted us.) By the time we got to our destination, he and Salvesen had worked out their communication kinks. (Had we turned left out of the parking lot, we would have arrived at our first spot in about two minutes.)

We stopped in front of the Eisenhower Observation Tower and immediately Salvesen declared David to be brilliant. He was going to have me do the work from the observation towers situated around the battlefield. This way I would be able to work with large swaths of land in several directions just by standing on the tower platforms. So much for all the comments about this battlefield being too big for me to do the work.

The Eisenhower Observation Tower was tall—very tall. I had a backpack with six boxes of essences in glass bottles, spoons, paper towels and a notebook. It had a little weight to it. I stood at the tower base, looked up, and I remember thinking, "Shit." I took a deep breath and lugged myself and that backpack up 100 steps.

When Salvesen and I got to the platform, we were treated to an amazing view. It would have been perfect if the temperature had been higher than 30 degrees and the wind had died down a little. I was relieved but not surprised to find no visitors on the tower platform.

David asked me, as a favor to him, to start by doing the Battle Energy Release Process for the Eisenhower Farm. Salvesen pointed me to his farm. He explained that this would fulfill a promise he made many years ago, when he first bought the property, to do everything in his power to restore the land and its soil to its original state of fertility. I felt it would give me a good warm-up before tackling the battlefield and told him I'd be glad to do that work.

Focusing on the Eisenhower Farm, I went through the steps as I had done at Perelandra. After a substantial release of battle energy, I tested the property to find out what essences were needed as stabilizers. Because I wasn't going to be able to leave glass bowls of essence solution around the battlefield, nature set up with me earlier to shift the energy from the essence drops placed in a spoon, expand that energy as needed for the area and immediately infuse it into the soil—in this case, the Eisenhower Farm. The process for the farm moved smoothly and, including the Battle Energy Release itself, took only about ten minutes.

With this, I felt ready to get down to battlefield business. David told Salvesen I was to focus on Big Round Top first and gave us the landmarks needed to identify the large land area surrounding it that was to be included. Salvesen pointed out Big Round Top. It was all the way on the other side of the battlefield to our right. Together we identified the landmarks. I focused the coning on that area and did the process.

David then told Salvesen to point me toward Little Round Top, which was also on the other side of the battlefield but more directly in front of us. Just as I was about to start the process, we heard footsteps. Someone was slowly climbing the tower. I figured I had time to complete the process before this person reached the platform. I set up, moved through the process and tested essences. As I held out the spoon with the needed drops for nature to do the shift, the stair climber joined us on the platform. I couldn't back away from the work at this point, so when he arrived, he saw two women, one holding a spoon out in front of her and the other humming the theme from the television program *The Twilight Zone.*

The guy didn't say a word. He walked over to the platform railing, looked out over the battlefield for maybe three seconds, then went back down the steps. I think we scared him.

David told Salvesen we were finished at the Eisenhower Tower. Our next location was the observation tower at Oak Ridge. To my relief, this tower was not as tall, but it was closed. That didn't bother Salvesen. She climbed over the closed gate at the base and headed up to the platform. I followed behind with the backpack.

We got halfway up the tower steps, and guess who pulled up in a car? The Eisenhower Tower guy! He took one look at us. We looked at him. And he just continued driving on down the road. (He couldn't shake the two witches of the Gettysburg Battlefield!)

From the Oak Ridge Tower, I did the process three times, facing in a different direction for each process. Again David gave me landmarks that laid out the full area for each process.

Before getting arrested, we climbed back down the tower and over the gate. David led us to the third stop: Barlow Knoll. There was no tower. But there was a small and obviously old cemetery. I said to Salvesen, "We're going into the cemetery."

There was a car parked on the road next to the cemetery, and a young woman was sitting in it eating her lunch. Now, there are many other more scenic spots around the battlefield, and I wondered what in the world would make somebody choose this cold, windy spot.

When we entered the cemetery, I asked Salvesen to walk around and look like she was interested in old tombstones while I stood to one side and found out what I was to do there. I had a feeling it was going to be different. Nature told me to do the Battle Energy Release Process for the cemetery, which I did from a spot that the young woman in the car couldn't see.

Once completed, I was told to call for the release of any souls still connected to the cemetery. I hadn't done this before, so I decided to take a stab at it and just say the obvious, "I call for the release of any souls still connected to this cemetery." It worked. I could see and feel a lifting of energy from different spots around the cemetery. It was strong and distinct enough that it caught Salvesen's attention as well.

When everything was clear, she pointed to one particular gravestone and said that there was a problem there. I walked over to a small gravestone that was cemented in a line with about twenty other gravestones. Only the cement connecting this one stone was cracked through, and the gravestone had separated from the line of stones. It belonged to someone named Johnston who had died in 1882.

I stood in front of the stone waiting for some clue as to what I was to do. Within thirty seconds, I saw a gold rope-like band of light rise from the stone. It shot out at a 90-degree angle and connected to the young woman who was still sitting in her car eating her sandwich. I sensed that somehow Johnston and the woman were linked, and I was being asked to uncouple them by cutting the gold band. I checked my hunch with the coning members and found it was correct. I used intent and my two fingers as scissors and successfully cut the band straight through.

As soon as I finished the cut, a soul rose from that stone and the young woman started her car and drove away. I looked at Salvesen and said, "She could have said thank you."

WITH THAT, DAVID SAID we had done good work and could head on home. We decided that we needed to catch our breath first and eat chocolate. Salvesen directed me to another empty parking lot that faced Evergreen Cemetery, a large, more formal cemetery than the one at Barlow Knoll. So, there we were, sitting in the truck eating chocolate when Salvesen said, "Is there a reason why that door over there keeps getting bigger?" I looked and didn't see anything, not even a door. She pointed it out again, and I realized that the big tree in front of the truck was blocking my view.

Before I could declare her delusional, she was out of the truck and heading toward the cemetery. I grabbed my backpack and followed. To get into the cemetery from the parking lot, we had to climb over a fence, something that didn't phase Salvesen in the least. As we walked toward the door she was pointing to, I still didn't see any changes occurring.

The door was part of an underground crypt (which we dubbed "the bunker") that belonged to Dr. James Warren. Salvesen told me to test the crypt door for essences. (Really, Salvesen. The door?) I didn't have a clue what this was all about, so I followed Salvesen's lead and did an essence test. The door needed one essence. Why, I didn't know. Nature and I shifted the essence from the spoon to the door. Then Salvesen asked me to test her, and she needed the same essence.

She turned away from the crypt and pointed to an observation tower near the cemetery. I needed to do a Battle Energy Release for the land area between the crypt and the tower. I did this and released two different essences to the area.

Next, I had to test Dr. Warren (who was still hanging out in the crypt)—and then Salvesen again. They each needed the same two essences.

Finally, she told me to do a Battle Energy Release Process on the observation tower itself.

Right at the point when I began to think she was messing with me just to see how many tests I would do before protesting, Salvesen was contacted by none other than Dr. James Warren, honored resident of the bunker. He asked to accompany her to her office, where he could observe several techniques she worked with that he needed in order to assist others who had died during the Gettysburg Battle. He had been a physician then, working at a "MASH unit" that had been set up near where the cemetery's observation tower was now located.

It would probably be another one of those understatements to say that Salvesen and I were a little surprised by all of this. But she invited him back with her. We even suggested he might like to ride along in the truck with us. Which he did. Luckily, we couldn't see him. I think we would have needed a lot more chocolate had that been so. But we could clearly *feel* his presence. We held the door open for him and made sure he was comfortable before heading out of Gettysburg.

It took two and a half hours to do all the battlefield work. When we left Gettysburg, we both felt that this was only the first stage of the work and that I might need to return to complete the job.

As we drove south and as we passed the High Water Mark and the Copse of Trees, Salvesen wondered aloud why that area had been missed in our work. She explained that this was where the climax of the Gettysburg Battle had occurred and that it was a particularly fierce battle leaving bullet shells six inches deep on the ground. I didn't say anything. I was still the undisputed dummy, and I wisely figured nature and David knew what they were doing.

En route, we suggested to Dr. Warren, who seemed perfectly happy to be wedged between Salvesen and me in the front seat of a pickup truck, that we stop at McDonald's and give him a real modern-day experience. We didn't sense that he was particularly excited about this, so we didn't stop. Besides, it might have been a little too much experience for him. (We forgot that just riding in a vehicle and speeding down a highway was giving him a modern-day experience.) By 5:30 P.M., Salvesen and Dr. Warren had been dropped off at her home, and I was headed back to Perelandra.

I spent the evening at the Cottage, laughing and talking about my Gettysburg adventures. The men were pleased about what was accomplished. It was clear to me that they were celebrating something I was not yet aware of. David was personally pleased that his hookup with Salvesen had worked so well. Other than that first right turn/left turn mistake, his directions to her were clear and unmistakable.

Before drifting to sleep, I thought about the day in all its wacky, wonderful detail. Did this day really happen? On one hand, it was total insanity. Traipsing around a battlefield following directions given by a dead guy. Hauling a heavy backpack full of little bottles up observation towers to do a process with nature. Releasing one or two essence drops from a spoon to be picked up by nature, expanded and infused into acres upon acres of soil at one time. Really? Releasing souls from an old cemetery and, while at it, setting free a girl sitting in her car eating a sandwich. And to cap off the day, collecting a long-dead doctor and driving him back to Virginia. It was all utter madness.

On the other hand, it also felt "normal." By that time, I had been living my two bodies/two levels/one soul life for a year and a half. Events that would have seemed beyond the pale prior to my coming to the Cottage were now feeling like my new normal. My day at Gettysburg with Salvesen showed me how much I was integrating into this new life. Yet, I still had to admit the day was weird. How much further could life stretch?

But I also felt honored to have been able to do the work at Gettysburg. I felt that I, as a representative of mankind, had returned to the battlefield, taken responsibility for the trauma that had been left behind and helped clean it up for the benefit of humanity and nature. That was deeply gratifying. And I felt a closeness that one has with an old friend as nature and I functioned together in our partnership to do the Battle Energy Release Process. I fell asleep thinking, "Yes."

The next day I checked in with nature about Gettysburg and found out that they wanted me to return in May for another phase of the work—if I agreed to continue. Of course, I agreed to return. Was there a question about that?

Salvesen took Dr. Warren to her office the day after we returned from Gettysburg. Six weeks later, I talked with her and asked how she was doing with the good doctor. She said that originally she had felt he might be there to assist her, but now she knew he was there to learn from her so that he could help those men from the Gettysburg Battle who were still in need of release.

He was especially interested in her cranial work. She felt him standing beside her intensely observing what she was doing every time she worked with a client's head. So she helped him by describing aloud what she was doing and why. Her clients thought she was talking to them and wondered why she had suddenly become so chatty about cranial adjustments.

In May, Salvesen told me that Dr. Warren had left her office on his own about a week earlier, two months after we had driven him from Gettysburg. In her mind's eye, she saw him back at the battlefield administering cranial adjustments to one soldier after another. After he adjusted each man, the soldier disappeared from the picture. To us it seemed like Dr. Warren was finally able to complete his work as a battlefield physician.

AT PERELANDRA, THE THING I yearned to do more than anything was turn my focus to the garden. In March, nature told me that the garden's center was to be changed. Per instructions, I now set a topaz on top of the quartz crystal slab. Nature explained that this gem would connect with the devic dynamic that is present on other levels of form beyond Earth, including the Cottage level. David felt I was having a shift at Perelandra comparable to the one they experienced in their work as a result of what happened at the Gettysburg Battlefield. Whatever was happening at Perelandra felt right even if I didn't know what it meant.

I had gotten the season's plans over the winter and I needed to move the plans off paper and into soil. I had pulled back the straw earlier and now the soil was ready for tilling. The tilling took me five hours, and I have to say I could not have been happier to be doing something simple, mundane and physical. It was like taking time out from the Cottage world to take a deep breath. While I worked in the garden that spring, my world once again felt manageable in size and scope.

On the evening of April 10, I received insight at the Cottage to change the outer ring of the garden. Instead of planting annual flower seeds, I was to plant rose bushes—a 300-foot ring of roses—all different colors. The men thought this change might be part of the earlier change I made to the center of the garden. Intriguing as that may have been, I ignored it and focused on the task of planting a bunch of roses.

I had never planted a rose bush so this was bound to be an adventure. Using catalogs, I tested with nature for the bushes I was to order. On April 23, fifty-two rose bushes arrived. They were bare-rooted, so I soaked them in buckets of essence-infused water while I got everything prepared. For the next two days I dug fifty-two large holes around the outer ring. I divided the roses according to the section where they were to be planted and started planting. By April 27, all the roses were safely in place—and I was exhausted. Good lord.

In the midst of dealing with the roses, I dealt with two outside interruptions. The first was from two women who had read *Behaving* and wanted to discuss the book with me. They presented a reasonable and compelling case for a discussion, so we set up a lunch. To my confusion and annoyance, at lunch, the two women didn't mention the book at all. They chatted. (I don't chat.) After an hour, they left the restaurant saying they had other things they had to do, and I left muttering, "What a waste of time."

The second distraction occurred during another lunch with Elizabeth and her husband. He kept telling me I should feel free to discuss the Cottage in front of him and that I should be the one to bring it up and not wait for him to raise the issue. (He would flunk the Information Policy test.) So I decided I'd call his bluff to see if he showed any interest. I told him who David was and talked about the Cottage work. He didn't pick up on any of it. From his expression, it was as if the words coming out of my mouth could not have been more boring. Or perhaps I was speaking in a foreign language that he didn't understand. He showed no visible interest, his eyes glazed over and he asked no questions. Elizabeth was no help. In the midst of my explaining about the Cottage work, she announced (1) that a woman sitting near us was eating a huge lunch yet was so skinny, and (2) that it was interesting how the topic of nuclear power and war can put such a damper on a discussion. I just stared at her.

Instead of blaming myself for causing two useless lunches, I saw what happened for what it was—crappy, stupid lunches filled with feigned interest, insensitivity and resistance. I was able to return to the garden without carrying the two experiences with me. This was a big change for me.

By the end of June, the full garden was planted and humming along, and the roses had leafed out and were blooming. I'd love to be able to say that things settled down into a gentle summer rhythm, but I can't. I travelled back to Gettysburg three times in May and June to do more work. (More on this in the next chapter.) Acquaintances and friends were still insisting that I meet this person or that person. Each time they insisted that it was important. In fact, it was more like Charlie Brown, Lucy and that damn football. The meetings were always trivial and time-consuming.

In July, I demonstrated that I was perfectly capable of shooting myself in the foot, thank you. At my invitation, a friend from Holland visited for a week. She wanted to hear about the Cottage, and I was looking forward to sharing that part of my life with her. But after the third afternoon of discussions, she wanted to talk about something else, and she indicated that I needed to start acting like an honest-to-god hostess and show her the sights. Extending an invitation during this time was a dumb move on my part. I didn't have the energy to play tour guide. I was deeply focused on the garden and the Cottage. Stepping outside my "small world" was disorienting.

I was hanging on by my teeth as it was and her visit just made matters worse. She resisted the Cottage information and began tossing off cutting remarks aimed at me. One morning I awoke furious at what was happening and talked over the situation with the men. Without hesitation they said, "Just ignore her. You stand your ground and make her adjust to you." I laughed and asked, "How do I ignore a house guest?" They just kept repeating their advice until they felt I was catching on. I left the Cottage feeling freed and paid no attention to my friend's resistances for the rest of her visit. We were both a lot happier.

FOR THREE MONTHS, my appointments with Salvesen had occurred every three to four weeks rather than every two weeks. She said I was rewiring, whatever that meant. When I experienced head pain, I knew it was time to see her. But in July, the head pain increased. Besides the cranials, she made several other adjustments and I needed several essences. I also needed to step back, take an R&R and sleep ten hours each night.

I had no idea how I was going to accomplish any of this, but I forgot about what could happen if my Jewish mothers were unleashed. Hearing what Salvesen had to say, they jumped into action right away. They even called Max in to help with the mission. We went for walks, we talked about nothing significant and somehow they made sure I slept each night for ten hours. (I accused them of drugging my tea.)

At the end of July, the head pain returned with a vengeance. It was going to be a week before I could see Salvesen and, quite frankly, I didn't think I could wait. Besides the intensity of the pain, I was becoming annoyed with all the trips back and forth to Salvesen's office. It was over an hour's drive into the Virginia suburbs with its accompanying traffic. Up to this point, I think I had been so deeply grateful for Salvesen's help that I ignored the travel time and traffic.

And if this wasn't enough, one of our neighbor's cows ambled through Perelandra en route to eat my garden. Our dogs, Jesse and Elsa, raised a raucous over the intrusion and cut the cow off before she could reach her destination. As I was running to aid in the chaos, I saw Jesse nip at one of the cow's legs and get kicked in the head. The kick stunned her, but she was still conscious. I carried her to the house, gave her a strong dosage of Rescue Remedy, then called the vet. He was concerned about a concussion and brain swelling. I drove her to the vet right away and he kept her overnight for observation.

BY THE TIME I RETURNED to Perelandra, I needed help with my own head pain. I didn't want to wait a week for Salvesen and I didn't want to make another trip into the Virginia suburbs. But mostly, I didn't think I was going to have the patience to live with this any longer. So I opened a coning and asked Hyperithon for help. I had decided I would do whatever I was told. (At this point, I was open to head amputation.)

Hyperithon instructed me to lie down on my bed in the cabin at Perelandra, with my essences by my side. Then I was to split to the Cottage and lay down in the lagoon room with David seated to my left and the essences by my side to the right. David's presence would assist and stabilize me. I was to let Hyperithon know when I had all this arranged and was ready.

David was still in Jewish-mother mode and accompanied me to the lagoon room right away. As soon as I gave Hyperithon the go-ahead, he explained that he was connecting me to the White Brotherhood "medics," and that all I had to do was lie still and let them work with me. (I was certain I could manage lying still and doing nothing.) They would be working with both bodies simultaneously.

I felt the medics begin by gently holding my head for a few minutes. It was a comforting experience, and I could feel myself relaxing. Then I got an image of Jesse returning from the vet and being back to her usual active self. That relaxed me even more. I realized that wherever my focus was directed was where they were working. I felt things happening in my head, then diaphragm, under my sternum, the pelvis, the diaphragm again, my head again. The right femur was rotated in, and the pelvis shifted down toward the floor for a second time. I felt emotion rising when they worked on my diaphragm. While they rotated the right femur, emotions rose again and I cried a bit. They rotated the left femur gently inward, holding the rotation in place as I cried deeply. Once I relaxed, I sensed that they wanted me to give them "permission" to continue, so I did. That's when they worked on my head one more time.

When body parts stopped "moving around," we talked—for the first time. They said that this was the medical procedure I could use from that point on and that it could be done with or without Salvesen's presence. For this procedure, I must be split at the Cottage and Perelandra simultaneously so that both bodies are activated in full form and can be worked on together. David was to be present at the Cottage to stabilize and balance me. I was to open a full coning including both bodies, David and Salvesen, if she's present. From that coning, I was to request to be connected with my Brotherhood doctors, tell them what's bothering me and pay attention to what they're doing. If Salvesen was present, she was to pay attention and only do whatever was requested of her by the medics. By observing their work, she would learn new directions in her own work. I could open this process from any location on the Earth and Cottage levels. (For me that meant I could travel between levels and not be concerned about my bodies possibly "going off track" and becoming stranded in space.)

Right away, I realized that the implications of this procedure were enormous. They recommended that I work with them frequently and urged me not to hesitate contacting them any time I felt pain or just out of sorts. They told me how to close the coning and that, after this first session, I was to go for a short walk (one-quarter mile, to be precise) at Perelandra and the Cottage simultaneously.

David accompanied me and as we walked along, I noticed that I no longer had any pain in my neck or pressure in my head. My hip sockets were operating smoothly, and there was a deeper lumbar arch that made me feel more balanced and stable. I also felt the walking was "greasing" me structurally and pumping the cerebrospinal fluid (CSF) more strongly.

I spent a quiet evening at the Cottage letting this experience and the changes settle in. The shifts felt different—deeper—from when Salvesen worked with me. And I felt freed. I had dropped into a new world of medicine that addressed my situation better. It was also a little scary. What had I gotten myself into? I was leaving the comfortable world of the familiar and entering the unknown. Was I being irresponsible by taking this step? No question about it: I knew this was a *big* step.

I didn't cancel my appointment with Salvesen, just in case. When I got to her office, I told her about the new medical process and said I wanted to show her what I was doing and get her impression of the work. She was curious and she was game. I split from her office to the Cottage and was joined this time by David, plus Max and Hyperithon, who wanted to observe the process as well. (It felt like I was lying on a gurney in a multilevel observation theater.) After I opened the coning, I was told to have David seated at my head at the Cottage and Salvesen at my head at the other end. Then Salvesen tested both bodies to see what condition they were in before we started. The Perelandra body was fine. The Cottage pelvis was out. No adjustment was made.

When we were ready, I told the "Company docs" to start. While they worked, I kept a running commentary going for the benefit of my "theater observers." My entire right side was being gently tilted, then lowered. This was relaxing—especially the lowering part. They did this three times. Then they did the same thing twice to the left side. My focus shifted to my head, and I felt electric-like energy moving from one side of my brain to the other—mostly right to left. It felt like some kind of balancing procedure. Salvesen cupped her hands on each side of my head, holding them about two inches away, and she felt the energy shifting. They worked on the diaphragm area again, this time to the left of the sternum. My focus returned to the head.

While I concentrated on that area, Salvesen saw two "supports" forming from the left leg to the right shoulder and the right leg to the left shoulder. It created an X, with the supports crossing at the diaphragm. My left side felt like the left foot was plugged into an electric socket. The left side of my neck relaxed, then the right side. The whole left side of my body dropped toward the floor, then the right side. The sensation of the X felt stabilizing. The light that I saw when my eyes were closed changed from dark lavender to white. Salvesen said that usually signifies a clearing.

She was instructed to test me for essences, and I needed three for the Cottage body only. The Perelandra body was clear. She was asked if she understood the relationship between the X stabilization, the point at the diaphragm where the supports cross and the head balances. She said she could feel it, but she wasn't understanding it intellectually. They assured her that she'd understand after observing further sessions as they work on the X.

Lastly, she checked both bodies again. Neither one of them needed adjustments, supplements or essences.

I closed everything down, and Salvesen and I just looked at one another for a few minutes without saying a word. We both knew we were onto something. It was like one of those rare moments in medical research when a researcher realizes she just stumbled onto *the answer* and thinks "Is that what I think it is?" For me, this could not have come at a more perfect time. Besides freeing me, it gave me flexibility. If I needed help, I could get it immediately, no matter where I was. No waiting, no appointments needed and no driving necessary.

Afterwards at the Cottage, I had coffee with Hyperithon and David to review what just happened. Hyperithon told me these medical sessions were a first for the Brotherhood, as well as for me. Up to this point in time, they had not been able to transcend and stabilize different realities well enough to work effectively with individuals. The coning setup that included nature added the missing piece. They have also not worked with a two bodies/two levels/one soul setup before. (This surprised me. I had assumed there were hundreds of us and that someday soon I'd receive my invitation to the class reunion.)

Hyperithon pointed out that my medical team had kept up with my progress with Salvesen through Hyperithon and his gold transistor. They felt it was important that I go through the series of shifts and changes that had occurred over the past couple of years before opening to this new level of work. He said that what was now happening was a bona fide breakthrough for all participants, not just me.

Over the next two months, I had more than fifteen medical sessions. I took them at their word when they told me to not hesitate contacting them if I felt any pain, no matter how slight or severe. At first I felt like a whiny hypochondriac, but eventually I noticed that it was easier for them to fix a problem in the early stages rather than wait until the problem had seated into either body.

Some of the sessions were relaxing and simple. Others were excruciatingly difficult, to the point where I thought I would pass out from pain. I understood it all had to do with my continuing development and integration process, and this belief was what kept me going. Over time, my partnership with my medical team improved, and I could give them better input about how I was feeling. Also my confidence in both them and the process grew. The bottom line: I was relieved and grateful to have their help.

In late August, the men surprised me with a trip—a two-and-a-half-hour drive to a seaside resort. They had rooms reserved for us at the Oceanside Hotel, a grand old, elegant hotel that was right on the beach. Someone had packed a suitcase for me with everything I would need for the day. All I had to do was get into the car. (A regular car and not the 1942 vintage Packard, which had been returned to an antique dealer not long after I arrived at the Cottage in '82.)

We spent the afternoon walking along the shore, eating hot dogs on the beach and swimming. I threw a shilling into the ocean to seal my wish to return. Then we changed clothes and had a late dinner together in the hotel dining room. We arrived back at the Cottage around 2 A.M. It was the first time I had spent the entire day at the Cottage level, and I survived. There were no spasms, no shattering, no head pain. It was just the break I needed.

In October I had another surprise. I met Lorpuris in the flesh. He's my height (5'9") and looks to be about forty years old. He's also soft-spoken and has an air of gentle dignity. When we were introduced, I felt like I was greeting an old, dear friend. It turned out that my medical "team" consists of just Lorpuris. He heads the White Brotherhood Medical Division and I could tell from watching how the others at the Cottage showed warm respect for him that I probably couldn't do better than have him as my physician. Meeting him face to face and talking to him about what I had been experiencing with the new medical work changed how I functioned in the sessions. I was more relaxed and open. He was no longer some guy in the sky.

October 25 was the second anniversary of my commitment to the Cottage. I worked with nature to place fourteen single white roses around the Cottage for the men to find throughout the day. I wanted them to know that I was grateful for their help and that they meant a great deal to me—especially on this day. That evening the men presented me with a gift that they claimed had my name all over it. Naturally, I expected something with my name on it. Instead, I unwrapped a beautiful crystal fawn.

AFTER PUTTING THE GARDEN to bed that fall, I spent time thinking about how I could set things up better at Perelandra so that I wouldn't feel so pressed. My work in the garden with nature and my Cottage life were nonnegotiable and needed to remain unchanged. What was negotiable was housekeeping, cooking and other simple but time-consuming maintenance chores around the property that I no longer had time to do. Clarence was back to working full time. His months at Perelandra had not given him any clues into what he wanted to do so he took a job with another copier company. Consequently, his time was limited when it came to working around the property. I needed help.

About this time, I had a conversation with Beatrice, a young woman who had read *Behaving* and was keenly interested in coming to Perelandra to work. She was working in a similar job in California and came highly recommended by her employers who also happened to be friends of mine. There were two glitches. She would need plane fare to come to Virginia. Also, she was in a relationship and Hank, her partner, wanted to work with her at Perelandra, as well.

As much as I needed help, adding one person to Perelandra felt like a massive leap to me. Now I'd be adding two people. Hank also had excellent references from my friends and had the outdoor maintenance skills we needed. Beatrice would cook and clean while Hank worked around the property. (I explained that neither one of them would be working with me in the garden.)

Clarence and I discussed the matter and we decided to give these two a try and hire them on. Because we would be providing room and board, their salary would be manageable. The *Behaving* sales would pay for their salaries and expenses, but we would need to personally pay for their travel from California. We rearranged our finances and wired the money for the plane tickets.

The arrangement turned out to be a flaming disaster. Beatrice arrived at the airport sporting red velvet high heels, striped ankle socks, a red mini dress, a nose ring and red hair. (Actually the red hair was lovely.) Her appearance screamed "California," but I figured the East Coast winter and Virginia's conservative mindset would encourage her to tone it down a bit. Hank arrived looking like a lost hippie.

We had to drive two vehicles to the airport to deal with their luggage. Hank rode with Clarence and Beatrice rode with me. As I drove to Perelandra, Beatrice told me that she thought she was pregnant. She didn't know what she wanted to do about the pregnancy, but she knew she no longer wanted to have a relationship with Hank. She said she wanted to be upfront and let me know what was going on. I, on the other hand, was silently screaming. *Why did you accept this job? Why did Hank come with you? Why did you fly all the way across the country just to dump this mess in my lap? What did you expect from me? Did you not catch that I was really busy with my work?* I was barely hanging on as it was.

Instead of screaming at her, I collected myself and calmly told her that we had planned for them to come as a couple and we only had one spare bedroom. She said that would be fine. They would not mind staying in the same bedroom. I felt I had just landed on Mars. What the hell was going on?

I talked to Clarence about the turn of events, and he said that it was clear from his conversation in the car with Hank that he knew nothing about a pregnancy or Beatrice's desire to end the relationship. We decided to continue forward and see how this was going to shake out. Beatrice wasn't sure about the pregnancy and maybe it was a false alarm. Anyway, it was possible that she and Hank would reunite, if given a little time. (Of course, that may mean another pregnancy that wasn't a false alarm.)

The other issue for us was their travel expenses. We had stretched our resources to get them to Virginia. We didn't see how we could manage covering their return expenses at that moment. (What we wanted to do was drive them back to the airport the next day.) Lastly, I was a little panicked. I *really* needed help. Now I also had to deal with this mess.

We should have taken them back to the airport the next day. It went from bad to worse. Clarence and I put out time and effort to accommodate Beatrice and Hank and to make them feel at home, but there wasn't a reciprocal effort coming from those two. They informed us how many hours they wanted to work each day (5), how many days a week (5), and that they expected to have access to our car on Sundays so that they could get away on their own.

I don't know what happened in their previous job with my friends, but it seemed like they felt they had been taken advantage of and they were not going to let that happen again. It didn't matter how we treated them. The thing is, when Beatrice got around to cleaning and cooking, she did a good job and I was grateful. But I had to put up with her snide remarks while she did the job. And Hank was working well around the property, when he felt up to putting out the effort.

I was still hoping for the best and wanting to be fair, but it was hard to determine what was fair with two people who had already decided how things were going to be. I kept thinking, "Let's give them a bit more time to settle in and get used to their new jobs and life."

My breaking point finally happened on December 25, seven weeks after they arrived. Clarence was busy cooking Christmas dinner for everyone when he received a phone call from his family telling him that his father had died in his apartment the night before. They thought he had had a stroke. Clarence needed to drive to Roanoke, Virginia, right away.

I helped him pack and spent time talking him through his shock before he started the drive. He told Beatrice what she needed to do to finish cooking the meal. Then he left.

Both Beatrice and Hank were miffed that Clarence had left. They claimed it spoiled their Christmas Day and the dinner. They kept making comments about how inconsiderate it was to throw the dinner preparations in Beatrice's lap. I had to keep reminding them that Clarence had a valid reason for leaving.

At the Cottage, I had been discussing my situation with Hank and Beatrice since their arrival. About two weeks into their stay, David said, "They're goldbrickers. Get rid of them." The Christmas Day debacle convinced me that they were goldbrickers and no amount of time was going to improve the situation.

But I still couldn't just kick them out. (I'm such a putz.) I gave them a new list of the work they were expected to do that included new hours. After Hank got drunk and drove our car into one of our flower gardens, I took away their car privileges. If they wanted to leave the property on their day off, they'd have to walk or rent a car with their own money. I also told them I wanted to know if they agreed to the new job requirements. And I wanted a commitment from each of them by January 1.

Beatrice left in January. Hank said he wanted to stay on at Perelandra. He seemed sincere and he stayed for another ten weeks. Without Beatrice around, Hank was easier to get along with—at least at first. David kept telling me Hank was still a goldbricker and I needed to send him back to California. It took me ten weeks to finally say "Enough!" and send Hank packing.

Clarence and I had held onto the situation longer than we should have because of the money it would take to send them to

California. But when it came time to get the two of them back on their respective planes, we found we had the money for their air fare. We just had to stop hesitating and take a firm, clear stand within ourselves as well as with Beatrice and Hank. (Oh, *that's* how it's done, Machaelle.)

Chapter 27

The Mount Shasta Mission
1984–1985

WHILE I WAS DEALING with intruders in 1984, setting up Perelandra's first office, filling book orders, meeting and working with Igor, developing the Battle Energy Release Process, traveling to Gettysburg, upgrading the garden's center, planting the rose ring, sort of entertaining a guest from the Netherlands, developing a new medical procedure with Lorpuris, and working hard to constrain myself from inflicting bodily harm on Beatrice and Hank, the Mount Shasta Mission fell from the sky and clobbered me on the head. It wasn't a small thing.

The Mount Shasta Mission was a massive, intricately coordinated operation led by David and his team involving over 40,000 people, 15,648 spacecraft and their crews, one mother ship, ten dead historical government leaders, Hyperithon, Lorpuris, Universal Light, nature and yours truly, the nature girl. Its goal was to shift the planet's government/military leyline system in its entirety from a configuration that supported Piscean dynamics to the new configuration supporting the emerging Aquarian dynamics.

Let me unpack that paragraph a little for you. The leyline system is a complex electrical gridwork that surrounds and weaves through each level's planets. It stabilizes and supports the planets and their populations (if planets are inhabited) as they move through their countless stages of evolution. For the inhabitants, the leyline system also supports all societal development—its systems of government, its education, its medical development, its scientific and technological advances, its philosophy and religion, its artistic expressions. The leyline system is also used for shifting, releasing and making available information and assistance from the White Brotherhood.

The Piscean era has covered a period roughly 2,000 years long, out of which our planet, the universe and all its populations are presently about to pass. During this era, we have functioned within a specific framework of universal laws that have Piscean dynamics as their moving force. It was an era that explored, developed and demonstrated the parent/child, the higher/lower and masculine-dominate relationships. These principles were expressed in each society's decision making, actions and social structures.

The Aquarian era, the era we are moving toward, emphasizes equality, cooperation and teamwork. I don't think anyone knows how long the Aquarian era will remain in play before we require a new roadmap for our next evolutionary era. I suspect the timing depends on us. How long will we wish to operate within the Aquarian dynamics and follow its roadmap? When will we feel ready to step forward into the new?

We are currently in a transition period that is expected to last 200 years (so David tells me). During the transition, the old Piscean structures, actions and traditions that had at one time been appropriate break down and are replaced by Aquarian structures, actions and traditions. When David described the government/military transition to me (which began when we dropped the bomb on Hiroshima and Nagasaki), he said it was going to be messy. In general, people don't like change and will resist it with every ounce of energy they can muster. (I can't tell you how many times I've said to David, "You didn't tell me it was going to be *this* messy." To which he replies, "Patience. It's moving along well." Machaelle: "Define 'well.'") As long as the leyline system remained in its Piscean configuration, an overriding desire to hold on to the old would dominate our development. With a new Aquarian leyline configuration in place, dropping the old and embracing the new, which reflects equality, cooperation and teamwork, would become easier and would be embraced by more people around the planet.

The Mount Shasta Mission was planned to provide us with the new government/military leyline configuration. David's goal for the mission was ambitious. He wanted to move the entire government/military framework into its new configuration all at one time, something that had not been done before. I'm told that leylines usually shift gradually, piece by piece. But he and the team felt the time was right to attempt a full shift. If they succeeded, we on Earth would have the best, most complete and comprehensive assistance for moving forward in the areas of government/military, especially during this difficult and messy transition period.

In order for a mission of this size and scope to be successful, a million pieces had to come together and be set into place at precisely the right time. I didn't know anything about the mission until it was time for me to make a move, and even then I didn't know why I felt compelled to make that move or what it meant. If there is one thing I can say about the Cottage men, they know how to keep poker faces and they don't telegraph anything. They were not talking about a new project while I was around, yet it was something the Cottage team had been working on for quite some time. The right events had to start unfolding and in May 1984, things started happening. The Mount Shasta Mission was moved to the front burner and there it stayed for over a year.

For me, the Mission started simply. It was that dream I had in January 1984 when I told Peter Caddy that I was working in the Pentagon of the White Brotherhood. I had had a number of vivid dreams since joining the Cottage so this one wasn't unusual. When I shared it with the others, nothing was said except for David's question about my relationship with Peter Caddy. I recorded the dream in my journal and forgot about it.

At Perelandra, it was business as usual and I focused on the tasks that paraded in front of me, one by one. In February, I started working with Igor. During February and March, I had the sessions with nature that resulted in the Battle Energy Release Process. In March, I worked with the process at Perelandra and then at the Gettysburg Battlefield. I made changes to the garden center and added the topaz that linked the garden with the devic dynamic throughout the universe. By the end of April, there were fifty-two rose bushes growing in the outer ring of the garden. I still didn't know anything about a mission and had not connected any of the garden's dots. As far as I was concerned, they were just the usual kinds of changes and developments that I needed to set in place. (I use the word "usual" loosely.)

But ignorance cannot remain blissful forever. In May, thanks to Peter Caddy, I was catapulted right into the middle of the Mount Shasta Mission.

May 20, 1984

Albert Townsend, a friend of mine from my Findhorn days, called to tell me that Peter Caddy was in town. He met with Peter that afternoon, and Peter had specifically asked Albert to invite me to some potluck dinner and talk he was giving on Tuesday evening. To me, this was the invitation from hell. For one thing, I was busy planting the garden. I didn't have time to go to some Findhorn gathering. When it came to these events, I usually ended up bored, annoyed and/or disgusted. In his world, Peter was a star, and he was treated like a star. Wherever he went, adoring fans would cluster around him—especially women. It wasn't a pretty sight. So during Albert's call, I was silently screaming, "No! No!" But instead of declining, I told Albert I'd think about it. What made me even consider the invitation was that Peter had specifically asked Albert to call me. That had never happened before because Peter knew how I felt about these gatherings.

At the Cottage, I told the men that Peter was in town and trying to get me to travel into the Maryland suburbs for one of his Findhorn evenings. They urged me not to put myself out unless I really wanted to see him.

The next day, Albert called again. Peter was urging Albert to persuade me to come see him. Albert told me that Peter had two hours free the next day before the potluck dinner, and we could speak privately then. Now I was puzzled. What did he want to talk to me about? Peter had never pressed like this before so mostly out of curiosity, I said yes. That's when I decided I'd tell him about the Cottage. I would begin, just as I had begun in the dream, by saying, "I'm working in the Pentagon of the White Brotherhood."

The next afternoon at the appointed hour, I arrived at the home where Peter was staying. I was nervous about how he would react to what I was going to say. After we settled in the living room, I looked at him, took a deep breath (here goes nothing) and said, "I'm working in the Pentagon of the White Brotherhood." Immediately, he jumped up. "Wait a minute. I'll be right back." He rushed out of the room, opened a door that I assumed led down to the basement and called to whoever was down there to come up right away.

When Peter returned, he introduced Bob (owner of the house), told Bob to have a seat, then asked me to start from the beginning. I said again, "I'm working in the Pentagon of the White Brotherhood." At that point, Bob shot Peter a look and Peter urged me to go on. I had no idea what was happening, but I continued.

When I finished describing the Cottage, the team and my understanding of what they were doing with governments and militaries around the world, Peter explained why he asked Bob to join us. At lunch that day, Bob spoke to Peter about a problem with his job. Bob worked at…(drum roll, please)…the Pentagon. And he was a member of the Pentagon's meditation group. (Who knew the Pentagon had a meditation group?) Bob explained that there was a meditation room in the Pentagon building where civilian and military staff met regularly to meditate for peace and to infuse Aquarian consciousness into the Pentagon and its activities. My delicate and lady-like response to this was, "Are you shittin' me?" The meditation group was not a secret, but they were a quiet bunch and their activity was not generally known.

It turned out that Bob was currently working on a sensitive project that, if successful, could advance peace in one area of the world. But his boss was threatening to move Bob to another office. This would remove him from the project, and he would not be in a position to effect or assist the peace effort that was going on. Neither Peter nor Bob gave me details, and I wasn't asking. Bob felt that without continuing in his present position, the effort would likely fail.

At lunch he asked Peter for ideas on how to get beyond these seemingly insurmountable walls. Peter said he had no idea, but he felt the answer would come to them. In I walked a couple of hours later. And there we all sat, a little amazed at what was happening.

Peter was a no-nonsense, we-can-do-this kind of guy who hated idle chit-chat and wasn't a fan of wasted time. So he turned to me straight away and asked if I could get in touch with David and ask him for his thoughts on the matter. His sudden request caught me off guard and, without thinking, I said I'd give it a shot and see what happened. After over two years of practice, it was easy for me to "phone" David while I was on the Perelandra level. Second nature, actually. But other than with Salvesen, I had never done it in such a public situation. Now my main concern was whether I could hear David accurately while these men were staring at me. Would their focus, combined with my nervousness, create an interference, a cloud of static, and cause me to distort what David was saying? I connected with David, described the setting I was in (to give him a heads up) and told him about Bob's situation. He suggested that he talk with Bob right after my meeting with Peter.

Since I would be returning to David later, I left my connection with him open while I continued telling Peter and Bob about the Cottage. When we finished and were about to start David's conversation with Bob, I stretched out on the floor. By distancing and lowering myself a little from the men who were sitting, I thought I might avoid some of the energy their focus was creating in the room. I was doing everything I could think of to buffer myself and create an undisturbed link with David.

The conversation between David and Bob went well. To my relief, I could hear David clearly. This was important since the two were conversing in military-speak about a situation in which I had no knowledge. I had to make sure I passed along precisely what each said because I couldn't risk inserting my uninformed interpretation. First of all, David was well aware of the work Bob was doing and spoke with clear knowledge of Bob's situation. David gave him advice about priorities and presentation. The only other thing I remember from their hour-long conversation was David telling Bob that he needed to discover the power of his own integrity and learn to stand his ground in his job. If he tried to appease or compromise in an effort to keep his job, he was going to create problems for himself. And with that, the conversation was over. Bob seemed pleased and made comments that sounded like he understood everything David had said regarding Bob's project.

While I was still hooked up with David, Peter asked me to ask him if he got the report Peter sent him back in the 1950s. (A report back in the 1950s? Are you kidding me?) Without hesitation David said, "Yes. I have it right here." Clearly Peter had not expected that response. He was beyond surprised. I remember thinking that he was literally close to falling off the couch and that I had never seen such a strong reaction from him. David said that he wanted to meet with Peter about that report. Peter told him he had a free day on September 24, when he would be returning to the area, and offered this as a meeting date. David asked for a preliminary meeting to be held sooner, if possible. Peter's only other free time between May 22 and September 23 was the next day. He had three hours in the afternoon. David asked him to pencil us in and told me I had to be there to act as middleman again.

After I disconnected from David, I asked Peter what that report was about. He told me that back in the 1950s, he and several others did some "planetary work with space brothers." At the conclusion of their work, Peter wrote a report, *An Introduction to the Nature and Purpose of Unidentified Flying Objects*, and sent copies to twenty-six prominent scientists, world leaders and spiritual leaders that were on a list Peter's wife, Eileen, was given during meditation. The list included Winston Churchill; Air Chief Marshall Lord Dowding, the Deputy Director of Intelligence at the Air Ministry who was responsible for the study of UFOs; and His Royal Highness Prince Philip. Peter was to verify that each person on the list had received their copy. Getting the report to these people was not simple because they each had layers of staff around them who could divert the report before it got to the right person. Peter had wonderful stories about the unusual, outrageous, even magical things that occurred that enabled him to get those reports into the hands of each person. He had been able to verify that twenty-five of the people had indeed received their copy. However, he had never been able to verify one report—the one sent to President Dwight David Eisenhower.

After giving me a thumbnail description of the report, Peter asked some more questions about the Cottage and my life there. He didn't blink at what I was saying. In fact, it all made sense to him—including my involvement with their work. I said I was glad it made sense to one of us.

That evening at the Cottage, everyone was upbeat but I was still confused. I asked David what the next day's meeting would be about, but he would only tell me it had to do with Peter's report.

May 23, 1984

During breakfast, I talked to the men about my anxiety around my unexpected new role as the translating middleman for the Cottage and especially about my concern for accuracy. They assured me I was doing fine, but I wasn't sure they were picking up on the depth of my fears about this. As a middleman, I had been suddenly thrown from my safe hiding place at Perelandra into a more public role representing the Cottage. Wasn't this above my pay grade? After all, I was just their nature girl. After they assured me that everything was fine, I decided that the only way to deal with my concerns was to keep moving forward and give it my best shot.

I drove back to the Maryland suburbs and arrived precisely at 3 o'clock, just as a thunderstorm started that looked like the end of the world. Lightning was flashing all around, loud thunder was rolling overhead and a car-wash rain was pelting down. At least I wasn't going to be pummeled with hail when I got out of the truck. Peter met me at the door, gave me a towel and led me upstairs to a small attic room where we had privacy. The attic amplified the storm's racket and we had to speak over its competing sounds throughout the entire meeting. When I connected with David, he was with Hyperithon and Butch (who was there to record the meeting). On our end, it was Peter, me and the thunderstorm.

David got right down to business. He said he was planning a mission, and this meeting was to see if Peter wanted to do more multilevel work that would build on what he did in the 1950s. In a nutshell, he explained that he wanted to activate the new Aquarian leylines for the global government/military arena. The mission would involve a large group of spacecraft, plus a major landing attempt at Mount Shasta in California. It would be a coordinated action designed to shift the full Piscean government/military leyline grid to the new Aquarian grid. (As I translated back and forth, I was hearing about this mission for the first time along with Peter.)

David continued. Peter's job would be to locate a suitable site on Mount Shasta that would serve as ground zero from where the leyline shift would be triggered. David felt that this would be relatively easy for Peter to accomplish since he was now living in Mount Shasta, California, and knew the mountain well. Peter was also to get the right people to that site to function as witnesses. My job would be to work with nature to prepare the site for the mission and to act as liaison between the Cottage and those chosen to witness the mission at Mount Shasta.

After he finished giving us the overview, David asked if we would like to participate. Peter agreed immediately, both to the plan and the goal. I don't think it occurred to him to say no. I was a bit overwhelmed and surprised that I was being given a job in the mission. (What was it that David said about a bunch of spacecraft?) I agreed to it anyway. Overwhelming or not, it sounded like the most important thing I'd ever have a chance to be a part of.

David told Peter to make sure he penciled us in for that open date on September 24, when we would all meet again. Then he told me I needed to go to Mount Shasta and begin my preliminary nature work at the site Peter found before the September 24 meeting. Peter and I both said fine, and that was it. By this time, I was in a daze and probably would have agreed to capturing killer whales using just my bare hands and teeth. Luckily what I had agreed to did not sound that dangerous, just odd—very, very odd.

The meeting completed, David, Peter and I continued talking. It was the most normal-feeling conversation for me to be a part of, like a group of friends sitting in a cafe catching up—only we were talking about some pretty beyond-normal things. David spent a fair amount of time explaining to Peter how I was getting to the Cottage and about the Split Molecular Process I was using to accomplish it. Again, Peter didn't blink. Finally, David and Peter said they were looking forward to working together. With that, I disconnected from David.

Peter commented that he was pleased that his earlier "space brother work was not for naught." He had no problem accepting any of what David had said. It seemed like it all fell in with his life-long experiences and training. I, however, felt like I had fallen down a rabbit hole and couldn't believe this was happening.

After more discussion about the SMP and my life at the Cottage, it was time for me to leave and for Peter to get ready for yet another evening with his devoted fans. He gave me his address and phone number at Mount Shasta and told me he would let me know as soon as he found the mission site. It was a large mountain, and it might take him some time to locate the right spot. When we parted, I joked that since neither of us had anything else planned that summer, why not work on a major global mission? In that understated English way of his, he said, "This kind of thing keeps life from becoming boring."

By the time I left, the thunderstorm had passed. I got into my truck and started the trip back to Perelandra in rush hour traffic. What usually took two hours stretched out to four hours. I probably should have stopped somewhere for coffee because I was still a bit in a daze and having a little difficulty locating reality. I simply could not believe what had just happened and what I needed to do—go to California this summer to prepare for...what? Some spacecraft landing? Don't say "spacecraft" to me. This was exactly the kind of language that drove me 'round the bend. I hated terms like "spacecraft" and "space brothers." I always thought that people who talked about this stuff were a bit hare-brained and needed to eat meat. I had successfully kept them at arm's length—until now. And now I was one of them!

On top of this, I couldn't believe that as a result of my middleman translation between Peter and David, Peter was going to tell a bunch of people to come to a mountain in California to witness something. My god, what if I had made a mistake, gotten confused about what David was saying and said the wrong thing to Peter? (Like make a right turn instead of a left turn.) It was one thing to alter my own actions and life based on my ability to perceive inter-level communication accurately. But now I would be impacting others' lives and plans. The notion made me deeply uncomfortable. At that moment, I felt frightened and very, very nuts.

That was when I got stuck in a major traffic jam on the Washington Beltway. I turned on the radio and learned that traffic was backed up for over ten miles on both loops of the Beltway because some guy was jogging down the median strip—naked.

I had two choices at this point: Either sit in traffic and think about David's meeting or think about the naked man. I chose the naked man. I wondered what in the world would make a man decide to jog down the median strip of a major highway at rush hour minus all his clothing. Granted it was a warm day, but I didn't think this warranted a public trot in the buff. Surely he must be nuts.

But what about all these people sitting in their cars barely moving because everyone wanted to get a look at the naked jogger? Whether he was a well-toned specimen or a complete physical disaster, it didn't seem to warrant a major traffic jam in the heat of the afternoon just so people could gawk. After all, it was only a naked man. I decided the gawkers were also nuts.

All of a sudden, in my mind's eye, I saw the naked man walking beside my truck. He looked right at me and said, "Don't worry, Chickadee. You're not the one who's nuts. No one really understands sanity anyway." Well, that made me smile. This monster traffic jam caused by a naked jogger and a bunch of gawkers managed to make David's meeting seem reasonable—and sane. I didn't think that could happen. Sitting in my truck thinking about David, Peter, Mount Shasta, spacecraft and leylines was the sanity in the midst of everything else going on around me at that moment. And that's when I felt a gentle peace settle over me—over my mind, my thoughts and my very being. Sure, I would be honored to participate in the mission at Mount Shasta.

I never actually saw the naked jogger. By the time I got to his location, he had either exited the Beltway's median strip or had been carted off. But I continue to have a soft spot in my heart and warm memories of him.

When I returned to the Cottage that evening, the men were sky-high. (Pardon the implied pun.) David told me this operation was coming together as they had hoped and that they had officially named it the Mount Shasta Mission. (That seemed reasonable.) I told him that during my trip back to Perelandra, once I got out of that traffic backup, I had gotten some ideas about what I was to do at the Mount Shasta site. It looked like I would be working with nature to discover the environmental impact such a landing might have on the site.

Later that evening, I told them about my adventure with the naked jogger. After a lot of laughing, jokes and comments, they explained that I had been kept in the dark because it was important that Peter and I make our initial movements that brought us together for the meeting based on our free will decisions and not be influenced from outside. Would Peter insist that I meet with him when he arrived in the area in May? Would I say yes? Would I tell Peter about my Cottage dream? Would I be willing to act as their middleman? Would Peter bring up his report to President Eisenhower? Would we both agree to a meeting as soon as possible? We had to say "yes" to every step along the way. Bottom line: The White Brotherhood doesn't manipulate. Our being in the dark allowed us to freely make decisions that led us to the moment when we agreed to participate. At that point, we were enfolded into the Mount Shasta Mission and would now participate in its planning and execution.

(Asking David if he received that report back in the 1950s is a testament to Peter's long years of training in a principle called "faithfulness to the job." It's an important concept that boils down to this: If we accept responsibility for doing a job, we also accept responsibility for completing that job. Even if it means waiting thirty or forty years—or longer—for an opportunity to finally come along that enables us to complete it.)

The next day the activity around the Cottage picked up dramatically. Phone calls were made, meetings were scheduled, planning discussed—all for the Mount Shasta Mission. It was on.

To duck the hubbub, I left for Perelandra early. I decided that, on this day after finding out about the mission, I needed to put my hands in soil and not think about anything but the Perelandra garden. This is like saying, "Don't think about chocolate." And of course, I couldn't stop thinking about the two meetings with Peter and the mission. It was the Mount Shasta Mission's version of chocolate.

That day I realized that the garden was now a multilevel laboratory for working out the processes needed for the mission. I was starting to connect some dots. Working with Igor, the Battle Energy Release Process, Gettysburg, adding the topaz to the garden's center, planting the roses and working with Lorpuris were all to be used for the mission. And I felt that I was to return to Gettysburg and plant comfrey somewhere in the battlefield. I didn't yet know where, when or why. I also had a gut feeling that it was more important than ever to maintain the garden's schedule, timing and rhythm. However, it felt like the Mount Shasta Mission had thrown a major monkey wrench into the middle of the garden's season. Thinking back now, I remember that I didn't get my first garden assistant until 1991, so I can't explain how I managed to keep that garden's rhythms during the Gettysburg/Mount Shasta Mission time that stretched from May 1984 to July 1985. But I did.

For the next few days, I thought about my concerns surrounding my role in the mission. Once again, I did not feel up to the task. David said these feelings were normal and that the apprehensions would lessen as I got more involved with the mission's work. A healthy dose of nerves at critical times keeps a person honest and on their toes. In short, he seemed to not be bothered by my lack of confidence. I just needed to keep moving forward.

Gettysburg Battlefield: Phase Two

On May 29, I had a session with nature to find out when I was to return to Gettysburg for phase two and what I was to do. I already knew that this was not going to be a repeat of phase one and the Battle Energy Release Process work, and that planting comfrey was somehow involved.

> Pan: *There are three phases to the completion of the work at the Gettysburg Battlefield. Phase one, completed by you, David and Salvesen in March, was the initial clearing, release and rebalancing of the battlefield*

area. This has set the stage for phases two and three. The battlefield has now begun its movement back to its nature balance and, if you so choose, you could consider the Battle Energy Release work complete. However, because of the significant role Gettysburg played in the destiny of the United States—and the rest of the world, when one takes into account the impact post-Gettysburg United States has had on it—there are two additional stages to complete if all of the ramifications surrounding the battle are to be dealt with. In light of the Mount Shasta Mission, these last two stages are now essential.

Between the completion of phase two this year and spring of next, certain souls will be drawn back to Gettysburg to experience an internal shift and release regarding their personal connection to that battle. Besides freeing themselves, that will also free the battle from the bonds the battle's participants hold. This will allow the energy of the battle to move fully onto the level of its higher intent and restore it to its higher purpose. [Flipping the battle's coins.] *It is that restoration that will be key to the Mount Shasta Mission. The energy of the higher purpose played out upon the Gettysburg Battlefield will have a direct bearing on the Mount Shasta Mission. (Just how, we suggest you leave for later.)*

Phase two, the planting of comfrey, is to facilitate the internal shift of those who will be drawn to the battlefield. Comfrey essence assists the healing of soul damage that may be the result of this lifetime or another lifetime. The "call" has not gone out yet to these individuals and will not go out until the comfrey is planted. Your concern that any delay on your part in planting the comfrey at Gettysburg might be hindering what is to occur there with these people has been misplaced. The timing for your return is quite fine. We fully recognize your desire to complete phase two, and we are cooperating with you.

When you arrive at Gettysburg, David will tell you where the comfrey is to be planted. Open the coning (as you have today) and include in it the Overlighting Deva of the Gettysburg Battlefield. The combined insight of this deva, along with the intent of the phase two framework held within the White Brotherhood, will feed into David, and he will intuitively know where to direct you. This teamwork (you, David, nature and the White Brotherhood) is also setting the tone for the Mount Shasta Mission. So although there may be a number of ways to approach phase two, this particular way has been set up for a specific purpose and will be referred back to in the future.

> *As for phase three, we can only tell you at this point that you will need to return to the battlefield in the spring of 1985. By this time, the Battle of Gettysburg will be released from all ties and can be fully raised to its higher purpose. The co-creative and cooperative nature of that phase-three shift will hold great importance. We suggest that next spring you open this coning and receive full insight into phase three. You will be directing that phase's shift.*

Planting comfrey for phase two was going to be a snap—except for the fact that it is illegal to plant anything in the battlefield, a national park, and I might get arrested. What surprised me in this session was to learn that the Gettysburg Battlefield work itself was going to link with the Mount Shasta Mission. But it didn't seem to surprise David and the others at the Cottage.

Salvesen couldn't return to Gettysburg with me, so I asked Laura Townsend, Albert's wife, if she'd like to accompany me. She said yes right away.

On June 1, I drove into Gettysburg knowing exactly where I needed to go and how to get there. I was no longer a stranger and the battlefield was now my turf. I headed to the Eisenhower Tower, sensing that this was where I was to begin. Things were a little different now. It was a beautiful, warm, sunny June day, not a bitter cold, windy March day, and there were busloads of kids all over the place, many scampering up and down the Eisenhower Tower. Laura and I climbed the tower steps. (We did not scamper.)

At the platform, I found a relatively private spot, opened the coning, connected with David and told him (silently, so as not to frighten the kids) where I was and that I was going to check the battlefield to make sure phase one had held. I then connected with the Deva of the Gettysburg Battlefield and tested that, due to the Battle Energy Release Process work, the battlefield only needed one essence. Other than this, the work was holding well. I put the essence drops in a spoon and held it out as nonchalantly and inconspicuously as possible. (During this trip, I discovered something important: If you appear only *slightly* loony, people will give you a wide berth, ignore you and not call the cops.)

Once the drops were shifted, I asked David where the comfrey was to be planted. He told me to go to the Copse of Trees and plant the comfrey in a triangle configuration—not *in* the Copse, but *near* it. With my marching orders in hand, Laura and I headed back down the tower and drove over to the planting site.

The Copse of Trees is a circle of trees, approximately 100 to 150 feet in diameter. The Copse is part of the High Water Mark where Pickett's Charge was halted on July 3, 1863. It was also the climax of the battle at Gettysburg. The bus and tourist activity at the Eisenhower Tower was nothing in comparison to what was going on at the Copse of Trees. As soon as we arrived, I realized it was a good thing I didn't have to plant the comfrey *in* the Copse because it was surrounded by a tall, lethal-looking pointed iron fence. I felt certain that David had remembered that fence, and I also felt certain that he made a point (pardon the pun) of telling me not to plant inside the Copse because he could visualize me climbing over the fence and impaling myself. This turn of events would be counterproductive to my goal for that day.

Laura and I strolled around the Copse area among the crowd looking for a good place to plant comfrey. I had three small plants, a hand trowel, a gallon bag of potting soil and a quart bottle of liquid seaweed (fertilizer) mixed with water in a picnic basket. Laura had brought along a towel and a jug of lemonade so that it would appear we were looking for a picnic spot—something that was not illegal. We found an area among some boulders and honeysuckle close to the copse where the grounds keepers obviously could not mow. We sat on the towel and drank lemonade. All the while, I was stabbing the ground around me with the trowel to find three spots in a triangle alignment where I could dig small holes and not hit rock. Did I say planting the comfrey was going to be a snap? I was wrong.

I finally dug the three holes, quickly planted the comfrey and watered them in with the fertilizer mix. When I looked at the finished results, the plants looked like they belonged. Just to make it official, I told nature the plants were in. Then I put out a silent call to all who needed to return to the Gettysburg Battlefield for a release and healing. Back in 1984, the Copse of Trees was the first stop on the tour map, and I felt certain most visitors would make it to that spot. For those who were there because of phase two, nature would surround them with comfrey energy from the plants, thus making sure they had the support they needed for a comfortable process.

And that completed phase two. I was relieved. I had had no idea how much phase two had been weighing on me. Now I felt light, even giddy. (Me? Giddy? Why, yes!) Before leaving Gettysburg, we stopped at one of the diners to celebrate with coffee and pie.

When I returned to the Cottage that evening, David told me that Hyperithon had called to confirm that phase two was complete and in motion and to give me his heartiest congratulations. I know the words "in motion" begged for a question or two, but frankly, I was too tired to ask or to care. My part of the job was successfully completed. I went to bed.

The Summer of '84

David was right when he said that my apprehensions would lessen as I got more involved with the mission's work. Obviously the Mount Shasta Mission moved my partnership with nature up to the next level and beyond the borders of the Perelandra garden. This was a new classroom, a new project with new goals, new issues to address, new problems to solve, new preparations to be made. But the foundation for my mission work had already been established in the Perelandra garden. The Mount Shasta Mission became a collection of variations on the themes that I had been working with for seven years.

In mid-June, I finished developing the Post-Death Process. (This made me a little nervous. Were we going to need the Post-Death Process on the mountain?) The process was a holdover from my work with the monk. When I had developed the steps earlier, I realized that this was something that would benefit everyone as they moved through their death process. But, as we all know, *everyone* dies. Did that mean I needed to hang out a shingle and become a Post-Death Process practitioner in my spare time? How in the world was I going to accomplish that? I discussed this at the Cottage and they came up with an easy solution that I had not seen because I was busy feeling panicked: Work with nature to make the process user-friendly and offer it to those who want it for their own loved ones. Apparently, now was the time to finish the job.

Salvesen came to Perelandra in July because she had requested her own gold disk that would give her a direct hookup with Hyperithon and facilitate their back-and-forth communication. I needed to assist with that procedure and, in the process, I got to see a gold disk for the first time. It was about one-quarter the size of a dime and paper-thin. Once the procedure was complete, I gave her Hyperithon's "phone number," which she tested right away. They could hear one another well and the migraine headache she had been battling for several weeks magically disappeared. A couple weeks later I had my first medical session with Lorpuris. Salvesen's disk allowed her to observe what Lorpuris was doing during the sessions I had in her office.

By August most of my work in the garden was Mount Shasta related. I was especially concerned about soil testing because, all of a sudden, I wasn't getting clear test results. I was using the same testing process I had used for years without any problems—until now. I needed to talk with nature to find out what was going on.

> *Your concern is the preparation of the Mount Shasta site and how to accomplish this in a co-creative manner. The key here is not simply adjusting the Mount Shasta ecosystem to bring it into a balance. You are also seeking to prepare the ecosystem to support a specific event—the Mount Shasta Mission. This intent is key and must remain clear in your mind in order to get the accurate information needed for the site preparation. Nature has the information ready for what you will be doing. But two aspects must come together before this information can be unlocked for your use as well as ours as we proceed into the co-creative adventure that lies ahead.*
>
> *Our suggestions: Go to the mission site. Fully define the site—allow it to integrate into your sensory system and knowledge bank so that it can be easily recalled. Then, acting as a connector, open a four-point coning that includes the relevant devic levels, Pan and Hyperithon. Allow Hyperithon to shift the actual vehicle they wish to land at the site in imagery and energy through you. Allow the image and energy to marry with the site, and hold that marriage of the two realities for us while*

we register what will be needed to prepare the site for a successful mission landing.

We suspect that some preparation work can occur during this fall's visit. But you will most likely have to return to the site just prior to the event in order to finish the work. It would not do the Mount Shasta mountain's ecosystem any good to have to hold an extraordinary, but smaller, ecosystem (that of the site) within its larger whole. You are not seeking to impact or adjust the evolutionary process of the mountain. You are seeking (1) to guarantee that the mountain's evolutionary process isn't disturbed while using the site for an extraordinary event, and (2) to learn what this type of event demands from nature in order to be fully stabilized and grounded. In the process, we all learn. However, should current conditions change, we may reverse ourselves and separate the mission site from the mountain in order for it to establish its own rhythm and timing earlier than presently expected. We will inform you of this should it be needed.

We suggest you put the soil tests away for now. You are "jumping the gun" by trying to break down the soil work on the mountain this early. The confusion in today's test results is due to the many options available to you and us [nature] *for accomplishing the needed goals. We need more precise input from you—i.e., the location of the site and the marrying of the two realities at the site. Once you return from California, work with the soil tests again. The confusion will be cleared up.*

We suggest you take the full soil balancing kit and the full array of flower essences to Mount Shasta in the fall so that you'll be prepared for any work that might occur then. The important thing for all concerned is that you identify the site and marry the vehicle to it so that we can get the precise information of what will be needed for the mission.

This session is a perfect example of what I'm talking about when I say "variations on the theme." My work with the Soil Balancing and Stabilizing Process had been in the Perelandra garden where all the elements are in place and the goals had long ago been set. At Mount Shasta, we would be introducing a new goal and new elements into an already established mountain environment. When I finished this session I thought, "Oh right, all the mission elements need to be included in order to get an accurate readout on the soil testing."

On August 16, Peter Caddy called with good news: He had located the Mount Shasta Mission site. He said he verified that it was the site with two "sensitives" who were friends of his. I didn't think their input was going to matter since I knew the Cottage team and nature would be giving the final okay, but I didn't say this to Peter. He added that getting in touch with the potential witnesses was proving effortless and that everyone he had spoken to was eager to participate. David wanted me to tell Peter that St. Germain (another member of the White Brotherhood whom Peter had worked with for years, including the 1950s project) was now involved with the mission. Peter responded, "I'll say he is!" St. Germain was the one who gave Peter the list of witnesses he was to invite.

Peter called back a few days later, and we settled on the dates for my California trip—September 10 through September 16. I wasn't sure how many days I'd need to do the work at the site, so I gave myself a week.

On August 27, I received surprising news from nature: I was to develop a set of flower essences—the Perelandra Rose Essences—from the rose bushes growing around the outer perimeter of the garden. I would need them for the mission. To my relief, I didn't have to worry about making the Rose Essence tinctures until the following spring when the roses would be in early bloom. That would give me time to find out from nature how I was to make these essences, locate and purchase bottles and droppers, create labels, design a box and find a box manufacturer. There were fifty-two rose bushes, and I have to admit I hoped all fifty-two would not be needed for the Perelandra Rose Essences. Lordy. (As it turned out, only eight roses were needed for the set.)

Even though I was now deeply engrossed in the mission work, feelings of concern crept in from time to time. It was one thing to be working with nature with new processes in the garden and have a broccoli plant drop dead because of a mistake on my part. It was quite another thing to work in the Mount Shasta Mission and have a mistake cost us global peace or some such thing. Let's face it, the stakes were a lot higher. The closer I got to the California departure date, the calm I had felt throughout the summer receded and was replaced by a fairly constant low level of stress, like background noise.

Around this time, I had another vivid dream. I was trying to help a spacecraft land into our physical level, but I was having difficulty. The craft was stuck and just "sitting" in the night sky. It finally landed when I worked with nature to supply the craft with four times more phosphorus than was available in the site's soil. While working, I experienced a tremendous physical power surging from my chest, as if the power to get the craft to land came primarily from my sternum. I awoke with the residue of the surge and a constriction in my chest.

At breakfast, I told the men about my dream and said flat out that I was not sure if I could take it if the mission failed as a result of my role in it. I was convinced I was their weak link and that I wouldn't be able to step around my fears. Surely this in itself might adversely affect the mission. As I spoke about these things, I realized I was describing a pressure I had been experiencing in my chest the past several days—and the scream I felt building up inside me the past few weeks. I had held the pressure inside, not wanting to burden the rest of the team.

None of the men seemed concerned about anything I was saying. In fact, they were downright calm. Again they reminded me that what I was experiencing was natural and that they would be worried if I didn't have those feelings. David said he was confident that the mission would succeed and reminded me that they had the benefit of a broader perspective about the mission that I didn't have. He urged me to unload the pressure I was feeling by talking with them about it. They pointed out that they were the ones who could understand what I was going through because they were the only ones out of everyone I knew who understood the scope of the mission and why I would be so concerned.

In retrospect, I think I was still expecting them to figure out that I wasn't up to the task, then fire me (nicely), give me my consolation prize and bring in the real expert. Especially in this early stage of the Mount Shasta Mission's preparations, I felt overwhelmed by the other team members' expertise and experience. In comparison, my qualifications seemed to be lacking. What I didn't understand or appreciate was the value of my previous seven years of work with nature, my two-and-a-half years with the Cottage, my experiences with the Split Molecular Process and my proven ability to function between different reality levels. I also didn't appreciate the value of my still being alive on the Perelandra level. It was clear they were not going to fire me. (I was a little bummed I wouldn't be getting a consolation prize.)

In early September, I prepared for my trip to California. Hyperithon came to the Cottage for a series of meetings and to go over how he and I would work together on the mountain. He also let me know that a mother ship (not a spacecraft) would be landing at the site for the mission and that the mother ship was more complex than a spacecraft. (We all knew that, right?) Nature and I may have a few extra challenges while addressing the balance of the site with the ship.

The Cottage team, Hyperithon, Pan and I put together the Mount Shasta Mission four-point coning. Up to then, I had been using the Perelandra garden coning when I did mission work.

1. Devic Point: Deva of the Mount Shasta Mission, Deva of Mount Shasta (mountain), Deva of Perelandra

2. Nature Spirit Point: Pan

3. White Brotherhood Point: David, Hyperithon, Lorpuris

4. Earth-level human point: Machaelle and her higher self

I had my pre-trip medical session with Lorpuris and was declared ready for the trip. Then I had a final preparation session with Pan.

Note: For all the Mount Shasta work, I partnered with the part of nature intelligence that has been traditionally called "Pan." In nature intelligence, Pan is the name of the area where the devic and nature spirit elements come together and are linked with the heart of nature. Pan was included in the coning and all my testing and questions were directed to Pan, as well. From nature's perspective, by focusing my partnership with Pan, I had the benefit of one-stop shopping and did not need to address nature's intelligence by its separate devic and nature spirit parts.

Pan: *We, like a number of others, are waiting for the results of our work at Mount Shasta. What you fail to realize is that we are not leading or guiding you through this. Rather you, through your work with Hyperithon, are giving us the direction that must be taken for the needed preparations and successful completion of the mission next year. So, the next move is not ours. It is yours.*

As you've speculated, we would like you to work within the new Mount Shasta Mission four-point coning. There will be no issue of "holding" us in the coning while you do your work. The activated coning will remain "in place" until you close it down after the work. If there is to be specific input from us, you will either receive it directly through your intuition or via the suggestion of any of the others present in the coning on any of the levels. So you see, you will not have to enter the Mount Shasta work with concerns regarding your connection with us.

After the initial work has been completed and its results have been registered with all concerned, add the Deva of the Mount Shasta Mission Site to complete the mission's coning. We suggest that there be a meeting prior to your leaving California that includes you, David, Hyperithon, Lorpuris, us in nature and any others David feels would be important to the proceeding. Set this meeting up within the Mount Shasta Mission coning. The purpose of the meeting is to establish whether there is any follow-up work you should do while you are still there. This can only be determined after the initial results are reviewed by everyone. We also suggest that time be given during that meeting for nature to express its views and suggestions. There might even be the need for a question-and-answer session between the participants and nature. Again, this is to establish and verify that all the necessary information has been received from the trip. It is not to move into different areas of planning. For this trip, you are our liaison through whom we can gain clear access to new and necessary information.

With this said, we will close. Know that many are with you as you leave Perelandra and go to Mount Shasta. We truly look forward to being a part of what will happen this week.

I can't say the session wiped away all my concerns, but it helped. I left Perelandra focused and determined.

Mount Shasta, California

Peter Caddy and Karen, his new, young, Texan-tall wife, met me at the airport and drove me to their home in Mount Shasta. (Okay, here's where you may need a little help: Mount Shasta, the mountain, is in the town of Mount Shasta, California. And all of this is not to be confused with Mount Shasta, the mission.)

After dinner with the group who lived and worked with the Caddys, I retired to the guest bedroom in the basement. I showered, got into bed and shifted to the Cottage. It was especially critical for my two-body system that I continue spending the required number of hours at the Cottage while I was in California. I hooked up a medical session with Lorpuris for calibrating my bodies to the time-zone change, thus eliminating any lingering jet lag, and he made sure the two bodies were well synchronized.

As soon as the session was over and I closed down the coning, something strange happened. My body at Mount Shasta curled up in a tight fetal position and I began to shiver uncontrollably. I was also hit with intense feelings of insecurity, and my mind was racing all over the place. It was impossible to go to sleep, so I re-opened the medical session. Lorpuris checked my two bodies again and said everything was okay from his end.

I still couldn't get to sleep. As soon as I started to drift off, I hit some internal trampoline and would bounce back up to a state of alertness. Plus I was still freezing and continued to shiver. I took another hot shower, but as soon as I got back into bed, I started shivering uncontrollably again. By morning, I think I had managed to get maybe two hours of restless sleep, and I was annoyed. We were scheduled to go to the mountain that day, and I was going to have to do my work there after the trip and almost no sleep. On top of it all, no one at the Cottage could figure out what had happened that night. But I could tell they were concerned.

As soon as Peter saw me at breakfast, he cheerfully asked how I had slept. I decided not to say the usual, "Oh, fine," and told him what happened. Without missing a beat, he said that they had had trouble with that room before. Over a hundred years ago, there was a massacre of Native people in the area, and Peter had been told by one of his psychic friends that the guest bedroom was located where a mass grave connected with that massacre had been. He had three local medicine men work on clearing the souls out of the grave, but it didn't solve the problem.

I wanted to pummel Peter for not giving me a heads up about that room. I would have to deal with the situation after we got back from the mountain, if I was to get any sleep—or move to a motel.

The Site

That afternoon, Peter, Karen and Edith Laming, an old friend of Peter's and another one of his "sensitives," headed off to the mountain. (Peter had a long history of collecting psychics, like they were baseball cards.) He had planned for Edith to join us, mainly because Edith said she had gotten guidance that she was to join us. I was skeptical. It seemed to me that if she was to join us, someone at the Cottage would have said something to me about it. I knew what I was to do at the mountain and decided I would just have to cut through any extraneous distractions to get my job done.

On September 11, I saw Mount Shasta for the first time. It was and is magnificent. After all the discussions and work surrounding the mission, the mountain was finally right there in front of me. It is not especially tall, not like the Alps, but it is majestic and stately, all the same. This beautiful mountain was now my new office.

After we parked, Edith wandered off on her own. Peter and Karen surprised me by saying they had *two* sites to show me. Peter and Edith had picked out the first spot together—a huge, open, flat area called Sand Flat that included a stone "altar" that someone had erected at one end. Peter liked this site because it was easy for people to get to (in fact, you could drive to it) and because he was concerned about the older witnesses. I guess on paper this site looked perfect—for a rock concert or a soccer game. But everything about it rang wrong for the mission. Among other things, I didn't think it had the privacy that was needed. I opened the mission coning and tested if this was the site. "No." I asked the question several different ways to make sure I was getting an accurate response, but I still got a big fat emphatic no. I told Peter this wasn't the site. Karen said she knew where the site was and led us to the one she had picked out that was near the first rejected spot. I got a negative test response there, too.

Houston, we have a problem. I had flown from Virginia to California to work with a mission site that didn't exist. Should I meet with the Cottage team that evening (after dealing with my mass grave) to find out what I was to do next? Should I just fly back to Virginia and wait for Peter to call again?

Before I had time to panic, Karen said, "Follow me." And off she and I went on a trail that led further up the mountain, leaving Peter to find Edith. Eventually Karen turned off the trail, and we began a more strenuous climb up the mountain over big rocks and large fallen trees. I will always remember Karen during this hike. I don't know why, but she chose to wear high heeled sandals that were held on her feet with skinny straps. I, on the other hand, was wearing hiking boots. She didn't let those high heels slow her at all. She was in front of me the whole time and I figured if this woman could trek up the mountain in those silly shoes, I could follow her without complaining.

At one point, I looked up and saw a small bump or hill jutting out from the side of the mountain. In unison and out loud, we said, "There it is!" Karen estimated the bump was at least at the 8,200 foot mark. Once we got there, we climbed over an enormous fallen tree that was laying at the edge of the bump, and once again in unison we said, "It's full of trees and rocks!"

I couldn't imagine how this could be a site for anything except one camper with a small tent. Because it jutted out from the mountain, it was relatively flat. Fallen trees that were about three to four feet in diameter fenced in the flat area in a near-perfect circle. I estimate that area to be 200 feet in diameter. But there was a forest of enormous live trees and large rocks in the site itself. Despite this, I knew we had found what I was looking for. I reopened the Mount Shasta Mission coning, asked the question of the hour, and the site tested positive. I asked the question in several ways to make sure my gut feeling wasn't throwing the test results. Every variation of the question tested positive. This was it.

But how in the world were they going to land a mother ship in this mess? Then it hit me. For a successful landing, they needed the rocks' minerals to stabilize the craft. Besides being too exposed to the public, the other two sites were sand. Nature went on to tell me that during the mission they were going to shift the trees and rocks from five-senses form to an energy level beyond form, which would allow the ship to land through the trees and settle into the site as if it had been cleared. Once the mission was over and the mother ship left the site, the rocks and trees would shift back to five-senses form, returning the site to its pre-mission state. Now that was brilliant. Based on my experiences with manifestation and shifting between different levels, this highly unusual plan actually made sense.

The First Nature Work at the Mission Site

We didn't know where Peter and Edith were at this point and I didn't want to wait for them, so I got down to business while Karen stood to one side and watched. First, I walked the outer circumference that was marked by the fallen trees and took time to visually spot the perimeter. Then I spent time taking in as much detail as I could. I looked, I smelled the air, I touched things and I listened. (I didn't lick anything.) I focused on the coning again, and asked once more, "Is this the site to be used for the Mount Shasta Mission?" Yes.

I pulled out seven boxes of essences, two boxes of soil balancers, paper and pen from my backpack, refocused on the coning and began working. Before leaving Perelandra, Pan and I had put together an outline of how I was to proceed with the testing, but now at the mountain, I quickly saw that I needed to allow for flexibility in that outline. In short, nature and I would need to wing it a bit. This was when it really got interesting.

1. My first question: Did the site need an energy cleansing to prepare for today's work? No.
2. Did I need to clear the site with essences? Yes.

Here was a change. I had to do *two* tests, each with a different focus:

Test A–To prepare for the day's work.

Test B–To clear out a "glamour" problem that was attached to the mountain. (I didn't know anything about the history of the mountain so this test surprised me.)

Pan told me to always administer whatever was required for one testing focus before I went on to the next question or test. I shifted a drop of each needed essence for Test A to the site using the same procedure we used for the Gettysburg Battlefield. Then I did Test B and shifted those drops.

3. Pan confirmed that the mountain's site was ready for the day's mission work. I lay down on the ground and shifted to the Cottage so that I could be present at both locations. I was joined at the Cottage by David, Hyperithon, Lorpuris and Butch. Then Pan told me to expand the Mount Shasta Mission coning to include Universal Light (my new BFF, Igor).

4. Next, I needed to test Karen and myself for essences. I also got the intuitive hit that her adrenal glands were weak. We each took our essence drops.

5. I tested the site using the soil nutrients I put together at Perelandra—my first Expanded Soil Balancing Kit.

Deficiencies: iron, magnesium, calcium, chlorine, boron, sulphur, aluminum, sodium, molybdenum.

(Wow. And this was the strong site?)

Pan said not to supply any of the needed balancers to the soil. I was just to get a readout of the soil to establish a baseline prior to the mission's work with Hyperithon.

6. I shifted my focus to the Cottage. When I indicated I was ready, Hyperithon held my left hand, created a miniaturized energy mother ship that was identical to the one that was to land on the site, and shifted that energy through me at the Cottage and into me at the site. He then moved the ship's energy through me and into the ground, which

was pretty easy since I was already lying on the ground. When the ship's energy settled, the mother ship expanded in size to cover most of the site. I didn't move for about thirty seconds to make sure the shift was complete. In my mind's eye, I could see what seemed to be a full-sized mother ship sitting in the site. But since the trees and rocks were still present, I assumed the ship wasn't in full five-senses form.

7. I sat up and retested the site for changes. Deficiencies: magnesium, potassium, potash, phosphorus, sulphur, aluminum.

   No longer deficient: iron, calcium, molybdenum, chlorine, boron, sodium.

I re-checked Karen and myself. Karen had a serious potassium drain and her adrenal glands were still weak. But she did not need any essences. I tested clear; nothing was needed.

8. I waited about fifteen or twenty minutes while Hyperithon got the information from the site that he needed. Then I laid down again and he reversed the process by miniaturizing the ship, removing it from the site through me, then through me at the Cottage and back to him. He told me to tell Karen that she needed to take a potassium supplement that day and to have her physician check her adrenal glands.

I came out of this experience thinking, *Is there anything more interesting than this!* I wasn't in the garden but I was still in my world. What I had been learning in the garden was being stretched and expanded beyond anything I could have imagined.

I now understood more clearly what I would be doing with nature on the mountain. It had to do with what happens when we introduce one biosphere (the ship) into another biosphere (the site). From the testing, I saw there was a natural exchange that occurred between the mother ship and the landing site as the ship settled in. The readout of what deficiencies were in the site's soil prior to landing gave us a baseline and defined the playing field we were working with. Then Hyperithon introduced the mother ship, an alien reality with its own environment, its own biosphere, its own makeup. When it settled into the site, the iron, calcium, molybdenum, chlorine, boron and sodium that had previously been deficient were no longer so. These elements had been drawn *from* the mother ship and introduced into the soil. However, the mother ship drew elements from the site's soil: magnesium, potassium, potash, phosphorus, sulphur, aluminum. So now we had an idea of what kind of exchange would occur between the site and the ship, and what the site still needed in order to physically support the landing. (This may solve the mystery of the UFO sightings reported by some old drunk in a row boat floating in a southern swamp. Maybe the combination of the swamp, the battered row boat and the drunk provides all the elements those UFOs need at that moment.)

You'll notice that potassium was not deficient in the soil prior to the ship's landing. However, after it landed, potassium was now not only deficient in the soil but in Karen, as well. Karen said that in her mind's eye, she saw the mother ship sitting in the site. As far as she was concerned, it was physically present and she had received a full sensory experience. This told Pan, Lorpuris and the Cottage team that a high level of potassium would be needed by the ship itself for a successful landing and, if necessary and as part of a natural give-and-take, it would not only be drawn from the site's landscape but also from the people present. Therefore, the witnesses might experience a potassium depletion during the mission. (I have no explanation as to why I did not have a potassium drain during the landing. But I didn't. Maybe it had something to do with my life-long passion for bananas.)

After more than an hour, I finished the work, pulled myself back together into one body, closed down the coning and was just telling Karen to eat lots of bananas when Peter came walking up to the site. He took one look at the area and declared that it had too many trees and rocks. He told us that Edith was angry that I had ignored her guidance about the first site and that she had just gotten new guidance to tell Peter to go find us because she had found another site. (Lord save me from psychics and their "guidance.") As proof that her new site was the "true" site, two birds had landed on her outstretched arms. Edith was proving to be a problem, so to keep things from getting out of control, I agreed I would look at her new, bird-approved site.

Peter led us to a path located on the other side of the mission site, and our trek down the mountain was a lot easier than the trek up had been. On the way, I silently contacted David and told him about the new developments. He told me the site I just tested was the mission site and, to keep peace, I was to reopen the coning and do the soil test for Edith's spot. He felt that once she saw the test results, she would know that (1) we tried her site, and (2) it didn't hold up in the testing. After my night with the slaughtered Indians and my two measly hours of sleep, I wasn't thrilled about doing more testing. But the peace-making diplomatic approach made sense. It made more sense than thumping Edith over the head and burying her on the mountain. I didn't have a shovel with me.

We met Edith at her site. It was another large, sandy, wide-open space that was conveniently close to a road and perfect for a gathering of 20,000 old people and their walkers. After I set up the coning, switched to the Cottage and started the testing, Edith became increasingly agitated. She left us and began furiously pacing off a *huge* five-pointed star in the middle of her site. This old woman was literally stomping. I felt like I was being slammed with a tsunami of angry energy and was having difficulty holding my focus. Hyperithon, sounding alarmed, told me to ask Karen to stand quickly between me and Edith (who was still stomping around) so that I could switch out of the Cottage and close down the coning safely. When Karen stood between us, she commented that she could feel the waves from Edith pelting her in the back.

I was furious at Edith and her rudeness. I was also stunned that someone who had been "in the trenches" for many years could act so irresponsibly. I felt that she had to know that her stomping around was going to cause a problem for me. I suspected she was angry that I was the one working with the mission and not her. She was older, and she certainly did not miss any opportunity letting me know she was more experienced. Who the hell was I, this unknown young twit that even the birds refused to land on? Now I understood why I needed to clear out a glamour problem that was attached to the mission's site. As we drove back to the Caddy home, an icy air hung between Edith and me. I could not and would not speak to this woman.

When we got back to the house, I contacted the Cottage to assure David and Hyperithon that I was fine. I told them that I felt good about the testing at the mission site, that it felt clear and accurate. David confirmed that the site I tested was the one they were going to use. With that, I added the Deva of the Mission Site to the mission coning. It was now complete.

The Mass Grave

That evening, I retired to my mass grave to deal with the dead Indians. Having developed the Post-Death Process, I had an idea about how to approach the situation. But this would be different because I was now working with people who had died over a hundred years prior rather than within the three-day window needed for the process. I was going to have to set it up, start the ball rolling with the first step and see where it led.

I opened the four-point coning for the Post-Death Process and asked if people from the mass grave had tried to contact me the night before. I got a strong yes, so I asked to be connected with these people. Immediately, I felt a clear, tangible connection, and before me stood twelve gentle, grateful looking people. With them, I ended up having one of the most extraordinary experiences of my life.

Pan told me they needed flower essence testing so that they could balance, detach and move on. They quietly stood in a line, and one by one, I worked with them. I'd finish working with one, he/she would fade out of sight, and the next one would stand before me. I had each put a hand on my knee (I could feel the warmth from their touch) to connect their electrical system physically with mine. Then, I tested. I placed a drop of each needed essence in each person's mouth. I saw no drops fall to the floor, so I assumed the drops were administered successfully.

Some of them reached out and touched my cheek; some had tears in their eyes. Some quietly said what I thought was "thank you." There were adults and children, including a set of twin boys I thought to be about seven or eight years old. I must say, working with these people was healing for me, as well—especially after my experience that day with Edith, the site stomper.

When no one was left in the room, Pan told me to balance and stabilize the grave-site area. That was easy since the room was in the basement and I was actually sitting in the middle of the grave. He explained that this work would permanently "close the door" so that no other souls would be drawn into the site. The medicine men that Peter had gotten to deal with the grave helped some souls release, but the site itself was still functioning as a mass grave. It was acting as a magnet drawing more souls to it. Balancing and stabilizing the soil would eliminate the magnet effect and balance the grave with the environment surrounding it, thus keeping the grave site clear.

Pan then explained that what I experienced the night before was the result of these Indians trying their best to contact me. They knew what help they needed and they knew I could provide that help, but they had not meant to cause problems or discomfort when they tried to contact me. The simple explanation is that they didn't know how else to get to me without my first linking to them. Because their situation was thwarting their evolutionary development, they had only the most rudimentary skills for connecting between levels. What I experienced from them the night before was the result of giving me their best shot: extreme cold, emotions of insecurity causing me to ball up in a fetal position and mental disruption. Then it was up to me to figure out what was happening and say something like, "May I help you?" This would have activated a link. Once I called them to me, the coning provided a stable environment in which to connect with me and I experienced them in the "normal" fashion.

After two hours with the Indians and the grave, I finally completed the work. I remember feeling honored to have met these people and to be given the opportunity to help them. Dealing with Edith on the mountain had been...well, let's just say unpleasant.

Dealing with the Indians in the mass grave was special, rewarding and comforting. I took a shower, returned to the Cottage, had soup with the men while we talked over the day on the mountain and my time with the Indians. I slept peacefully.

While still at Mount Shasta, I had the scheduled Cottage/nature meeting and was told that the September 11 work at the site was holding and I did not have to go back to the mountain that trip. I returned to Perelandra on September 16 and refocused my attention on the garden while the Cottage men did whatever it was they were doing with the information collected at the mountain.

The September 24 Meeting

We held the September 24 meeting at Perelandra. Before getting started, Peter gave us an update on Bob's progress at the Pentagon. Everything David had stressed to Bob when they met in the spring had worked out perfectly. He used David's advice and stood his ground. Instead of being fired, he was transferred to a more advantageous position that allowed him to continue working with that peace project.

For the meeting, we had in attendance on the Perelandra side of the "table" Peter, Salvesen (David had asked that Salvesen join us) and me. On the Cottage side of the table, we had David, Butch, Tex, Hyperithon and Lorpuris. I opened the coning and that connected everyone. David conducted the meeting.

First, he gave an overview of the purpose and goals of the mission to make sure everyone was clear about what was planned. He told us that it would be beneficial for all concerned for the leylines that have supported the Piscean government/military structures and activities throughout its 2,000 year history be deactivated en masse. And it would be equally beneficial to immediately activate en masse the new leyline grid supporting the Aquarian structures and activities. The mission would be an unprecedented undertaking. But if successful, it would give everyone the opportunity for an exceptional level of efficiency and effectiveness when establishing the needed government/military changes that reflected Aquarian principles.

As I understand it, leyline changes normally occur piecemeal, covering a span of years within a transition period. But this creates an "evolutionary lag time" for us, and progress is more challenging. David felt he had the right team, and it was time to attempt the en masse changes for the government/military leylines. He explained that to do this, *thousands* of spacecraft would be positioned beyond Earth's atmosphere in a pattern mirroring the layout of the current government/military grid. Once the spacecraft moved into the Earth's atmosphere, they would link to the leylines magnetically. When ready, the call for the shift would be made by David at the Mount Shasta site.

Another of David's goals, and one that would create an additional challenge, was to make sure the ship at the site and the people aboard the ship (David, his team, the crew and the invited guests) were fully in five-senses form so that each of the witnesses could experience what was happening using their five senses. The issue about having the Mount Shasta Mission in five-senses form was an especially critical one. David wanted their information to be fully accessible no matter what sensory range a person might function with. Everyone is different. So to cover the widest range of sensory perception, there would be a group of witnesses and not just one witness.

He then announced that the mission date would be between July 14 and July 17, 1985, with the target date July 15. They would be landing at the mountain site at dusk. And he confirmed that the site's privacy, size and natural stabilizing support had been checked and approved.

Peter asked if a mother ship would be landing. When David told him yes, Peter said he thought the diameter of the site was too small for a mother ship. (At this point, I just let the conversation roll. They were seriously talking about mother ship sizes. How often does this come up in conversation? But then, how often does any of this come up in conversation?) David responded, "You're thinking of the older ships. Like Japanese cars, the new ones are smaller, more efficient and technologically superior." (And I'm thinking, "Well, of course. Makes sense. Why would we want some big old clunker with a rebuilt motor, retreads, missing windows and faded vinyl upholstery?")

David then turned to the mission's medical issues. My work at the site and Karen's reaction to it confirmed that medical preparation would be needed for Peter's witnesses and David's invited guests. Lorpuris would work with the invited guests. Then David asked Salvesen if she would join the mission and provide the medical work for the witnesses. To my surprise, rather than just saying yes, she said she would give a definite answer by the end of four weeks, but that she felt it would be yes.

David explained that it was critical that everyone at the Mount Shasta site be physically stabilized so that their sensory systems functioned well throughout the mission. To this end, Lorpuris and Hyperithon put together a simple process based on what we had done on the mountain that could be used to prepare the witnesses prior to the mission.

1. Salvesen would get an initial readout of each witness, establishing their medical baseline: What essences, structural alignments, supplements and cranial adjustments were needed? She would do any needed work, thus balancing their bodies.

2. Hyperithon would shift the mission's mother ship as a miniaturized energy package through my Cottage body and into my Perelandra body. Then the energy package would be transferred into the witness's system. (I would need to be present at the Cottage and at Perelandra for the full transfer of the package to occur.)

3. Salvesen would get another readout. The results would show her how each person's body reacted to and processed the ship. With that information, she could shore up and strengthen their weak spots prior to the mission.

4. Finally, Hyperithon would remove the ship from the witness's system, shift it through me (my two bodies) and transfer it back to himself. Salvesen would check the person again for any aftereffects of the procedure or of the ship's removal.

Peter volunteered to go first. Salvesen found he had a tight left psoas that was pulling his pelvis out of alignment, a weakened solar plexus, and he needed one essence. He also needed a cranial adjustment. She did all the work, checked him again and said he was ready.

Hyperithon shifted the mother ship package from my Cottage hand, through my Cottage electrical system and into my Perelandra electrical system. He then moved it into my Perelandra hand, transferred it into Peter's hand (that I was holding) and, finally, into Peter's electrical and nervous systems.

We waited about twenty seconds before Salvesen checked him again. Remember, he had just tested clear and balanced less than five minutes prior to the ship's package hitting his system. Now his left psoas was tight again and his pelvis was out again. He had a potassium, phosphorus and B-vitamin drain. He needed no essences. After Salvesen restored his balance, Hyperithon moved the ship out of Peter's body by reversing the trip through my two electrical systems. When Salvesen tested Peter again, his balance had held and he tested clear.

Lorpuris suggested we wait an hour and do the procedure with Peter once more. He suspected that after this first experience, Peter's body was already learning how to process a mother ship and would respond better to a second procedure.

The second landing went more smoothly for Peter. Still, he had another B-vitamin and phosphorus drain, his thyroid was now weak, and his left pelvis was out again. But it was obvious that the more he experienced the process, the more his body learned to identify and successfully sort the experience. We suspected that we would have to do a landing process for each of the witnesses three times before they could respond to the ship on the mountain without misaligning, draining or short-circuiting. For this, everyone would have to be at Mount Shasta several days prior to the mission so that Salvesen and I could work with them. We also decided that Salvesen and I would try to work with any witnesses living on the East Coast that winter and spring so that we could make the work load at Mount Shasta more manageable. (We really needed Salvesen to say yes to the Mount Shasta Mission.)

David asked Peter about the people he was inviting to the mission. Peter explained again that he had been getting the "witness list" from St. Germain and felt there would be a total of about twenty to twenty-five witnesses present on the mountain. David warned him about not including any press people because this was not to be some "glitzy publicity show."

David concluded by asking if we understood the mission and what we were each to do. Peter restated his understanding of what was to happen on Mount Shasta, and after making a few minor clarifications, David okayed Peter's understanding. When we ran out of questions, we ended the meeting and I closed down the mission coning.

Right away Peter jumped up and called six people on his list. All six answered their phone—which he pronounced a miracle. His conversation went something like this (to be read with a cheery British accent):

> *Hello,* [name inserted]. *Peter Caddy here. Dwight Eisenhower is planning a mission to shift the government/military leylines around the planet next summer. Are you busy between July 14 and July 17?* [Wait while the person checks his calendar.] *No? Good. He will be landing a mother ship at Mount Shasta sometime during this period. Would you like to come and be among the witnesses?* [Listen.] *Good. We'll get in touch with you shortly with the details. Goodbye.*

Everyone responded to Peter's phone call as if they got this kind of call every day. They each stated that they would be happy to witness the event, and two even agreed to meet with Salvesen and me the following Wednesday at Perelandra for their first round of the landing process.

After the first two landings with Peter, I could tell that doing the process multiple times for over twenty witnesses was going to put a lot of strain on me if I had to be in both locations for each procedure. Hyperithon, Lorpuris and I decided to try streamlining it using Hyperithon's transistor in my head for shifting the ship's energy to me at Perelandra. I would then move that energy from the transistor into the person's body. If that worked equally as well as the first procedures had with Peter, it would make life a lot easier for me. (The new and improved process proved to be a success.)

Salvesen said it was important to establish a strong neurological foundation for each witness, as well as their general health baseline, providing her with the level of health and structural balance they had prior to the mission. This way, she would know how to respond to them on the mountain during the mission. Based on what she was seeing, she also felt they would need a strong pelvic foundation or they would "blow out" during the mission. This was going to be a major experience for these people, and she was concerned about who we might have to carry off the mountain. (Those were her words. I didn't tell her about the Post-Death Process.)

During the September testing on the mountain, Karen had a potassium drain as the ship's energy shifted into the site. Many of the people Salvesen and I worked with experienced a similar response along with a B-vitamin drain during their landing procedures. Salvesen explained that these elements are basic nutrients for the nervous system, and when the nervous system is working overtime, it quickly draws them down. In this case, their nervous systems were scrambling to identify, process and sort a completely new experience—an actual mother ship. Hence, the drain. It did not matter how many times they had seen *Close Encounters of a Third Kind* or how many discussions they had had about UFOs and space travel. Seeing a mother ship in a movie or talking about it was not the same as experiencing it in five-senses form. Our electrical and nervous systems aren't stupid. They know the difference between art and reality. But we were finding out that with practice, the two systems could learn.

Shortly after the September 24 meeting, Salvesen officially committed to the mission. She told me she had been concerned initially about several changes that were going on at her office and the fact that her daughter's second birthday was right at the time she would have to be at Mount Shasta. A few years ago, I asked what made her say yes to the mission. She said, "The mission was important." And that was that.

The Gold Protection Dome

On the evening of October 15, I had a strong gut feeling that I needed to do something with nature that night to protect the mountain site. When I told David what I was feeling, he suggested I check it out right away and said he wanted to sit in while I did the check.

I opened the mission coning and Pan stated that I needed to activate a dome over the site that would function as protection. It was to cover the entire landing area plus twenty-five feet beyond the site's outside perimeter that was ringed with the fallen trees. I was also to link David, Hyperithon and myself to the dome, and the three of us would remain connected to it until after the mission was completed in July. This way, if something happened at the site that needed attention, nature would be able to quickly contact any of us directly.

Following the steps that Pan laid out for me, I watched a dome of golden light form and cover the entire area, rising well above the tree tops. Once this was complete, I offered my assistance for any maintenance or repair the dome and site might need during the preparations and the mission. Immediately, I saw a gold beam of light connect the site with the topaz in the center of the Perelandra garden. Then I saw three beams of light move out from the topaz. One beam connected to David, one to Hyperithon (he was present as one of the coning members) and one to me. Finally, Pan told me that within three days after the landing, I was to work with nature to release the protection dome and the three gold-beam connections with the Perelandra topaz.

I came out of this session convinced that nature had just separated the site from the mountain. That was a change from the information Pan had given me before my trip to Mount Shasta. At that point, there was to be no separation of the site from the mountain's rhythms and timing until the week before the mission. Now, with our work in September, combined with the mission's ongoing preparations, Pan decided it was time to create the site as a separate, mission-focused biosphere with its own rhythm, timing, balance and stability.

ENTER IGOR

On October 17, just when I was beginning to wrap my mind more comfortably around this thing called the Mount Shasta Mission, I received a clear hit to open an Igor session and set it up as a meeting that included David. (So much for comfort.)

Igor: *Well, hello. The preliminary work that has been done regarding the Mount Shasta Mission has now been completed by all those concerned. That preliminary information has also been received on our level so that we are aware of the dynamics of the mission, its balance, its direction and its projections. Until this time, what we had to say about the mission was minimal because we had to wait until the preliminary period was complete.*

What we would now like to propose is a series of meetings. We suggest that not only David and you, Machaelle, be present, but also Tex, Hyperithon and Lorpuris as well. You will function as the translator for us. David will function as your session stabilizer and also conduct the meetings in which a free flow of information and ideas can be expressed among us all.

The Mount Shasta Mission has ramifications that go beyond Earth itself, and it is now time that a broader picture be considered. We foresee the need for three meetings and suggest that they be held fairly close together. There might be a need for a fourth meeting, but that won't be known until the third is completed. We perceive that you, Machaelle, will not have difficulty in holding focus during this more intense meeting process.

We recommend that the meetings begin as soon as possible, for we see you are now entering the next planning stage of the mission. There are broader opportunities you might wish to take into consideration, and it would be best to discuss them before you get too far along in this next planning stage. With that said, we simply recommend that the meetings be held as soon as possible.

Are there any questions regarding what we've said or the meetings themselves?

David: *Is there any issue in having others present beyond those you've suggested?*

Igor: *We leave additional participants up to your discretion. There is not a number issue here. As we get into the meetings, you might see that some might need to be present for one of the meetings but not for any of the others.*

Machaelle: *What am I going to need in order to stabilize myself during these meetings?* [Previously for my Igor sessions, I needed to eat 90 additional grams of protein and double my intake of carbohydrates in order to remain stabilized throughout the session because Igor's presence created a strong drain of those nutrients.]

Igor: *Because of your position as translator and David's as your stabilizer during these sessions, only you two need be concerned about the additional protein and carbohydrate requirements for the meetings. This coning may tire the others slightly, but it will not throw them off balance physically or drain them. It may even energize them. The key issue here, in terms of nutritional support, is that no one other than you and David need be concerned, and your regular protein and carbohydrate intake for our sessions will hold you for these next meetings, as well.*

David: *I think we should have the first meeting here this coming Wednesday.*

Igor: *We agree. Please don't misunderstand—this is not an emergency situation. We feel strongly, however, that you will want the information we wish to give you and you will want to think about these ideas before you proceed any further with the mission planning.*

We have nothing more to add at this point. We will assume, along with you, that we will begin the meetings next Wednesday. We'll see you then.

With that, I closed the coning and looked at David for a clue as to what was going on. Either he didn't know, or he wasn't talking.

Meeting #1

At Wednesday's meeting, Igor proposed that the Mount Shasta Mission be expanded so that the government/military frameworks that exist on other levels, including those levels beyond our solar system and universe, can benefit from and reflect the underlying intent behind what was to occur on the mountain. Igor, speaking for those involved with the proposed expansion, said:

> *Our primary focus, at this point, is the new government intent. We have not had the opportunity to participate in and experience a shift of intent so clearly grounded and fully expressed in five-senses form within the area of government as this. We would like to link with the Mount Shasta Mission for the purpose of using its energy, intent and dynamics, and connect this with the larger government/military frameworks that are beyond the scope of the current mission. Of course, at this point we would like to say (in case there's any question) that our support for this mission is fully with you, whether or not we participate actively. What we are proposing is an expansion of your mission to include the universe and beyond. If you'd like a moment to discuss it among yourselves, please feel free.*
>
> David: *First I'd like to know how you're planning the expansion.*
>
> Igor: *The most important thing is to maintain the integrity of the intent of your mission. You have set an ambitious scope of clarity. In order to maintain that clarity and the power of that clarity, we would have to work with you with the same intent. In essence, although there may be more than one equally successful approach to this mission on Mount Shasta next July, it would be disastrous if, after choosing your intent, we participate with a different direction. Although they may be equal, their two energy fields would collide, and the Mount Shasta Mission would experience such an inflow of abrasive energy that the chances for success would be minimal. We say this so that you will understand that our suggestion is to join with you, not create a different mission of our own.*

With that, everyone, including Igor, had a two-hour discussion aimed at understanding what the expanded mission would mean for the Cottage's primary mission. What were the benefits? What were the pitfalls and drawbacks? How did Igor propose for the expanded mission to be set up and woven in with the primary mission? If the expanded mission was included, would the protective dome need to be enlarged or changed?

Igor was proposing a gigantic expansion of the Mount Shasta Mission by recommending that they mirror the setup planned for the primary mission. Along with the 7,834 spacecraft for the primary mission, the expanded mission would add another 7,834 spacecraft. We're now talking about a total of 15,668 craft. Each expansion craft would be paired with a primary craft, and together as a unit each pair would position itself over the government/military leylines around our planet. Then when David gave them the go-ahead, each pair, acting as a unit, would shift the leylines to the new configuration. It was obvious that the expansion would add a significantly heightened impact to an already heightened situation.

> Igor: *There are issues to consider about the spacecraft themselves. One is the different systems and designs used in craft technology and their working together in a balanced pairing. We feel that there is going to have to be an extensive coordination effort between representatives of our craft beyond this universe and representatives of your craft within the universe so that the spacecraft can be paired in such a way that the two craft create their own balanced energy field. Pairing two different craft (which would resonate two opposing energies) would create disruptive waves within the atmosphere as they move together. We have representatives on standby who have full knowledge of our available craft, their capabilities and their energy output. One of the reasons we suggested these meetings now is so that, if you wish (and so choose) to allow us to link up with you in the mission, we may get about the business of pairing the craft.*
>
> David: *From your perspective, do you see any impact on our mother ship and the actual activity planned at the mountain site itself?*
>
> Igor: *There cannot be any impact on what will occur on Mount Shasta. It is vitally important to all that what occurs there goes as planned and be experienced solely by the team and the participants that David has brought together.*
>
> David [to Hyperithon]: *Can you meet with these fellows tomorrow?*
>
> Hyperithon: *I can meet with them any time they can get to me.*
>
> Igor: *We anticipated that you would want to meet prior to making your decision. We have members of our group positioned and ready for a meeting with whomever you please at any time. Just give us a time.*

Hyperithon: *Can we meet on the Cottage level?*

Igor: *Yes. We've provided for that.*

Tex: *Would the expanded mission's second tier of craft affect the energy on the mountain site itself beyond what is already anticipated?*

Igor: *We took that into consideration. But you have already addressed the issue yourselves. The protection that Machaelle and nature placed over the site will stabilize the area in such a way that the impact of our being present in the mission will not be felt by those present at the site. There will be a heightened energy in the atmosphere, but we do not perceive, in any way, that this will present a problem or danger to Earth or its atmosphere. We would suggest that the question be dealt with by representatives from both spacecraft groups and that between now and July—to assure that what we consider safe is, indeed, safe—some test runs within Earth's atmosphere of paired craft be completed. It will be essential that the protection dome that Machaelle has placed over the landing site remain activated and be maintained until the entire mission is over. We recommend that the protection be lifted from the site no sooner than twenty-four hours after the mission has been completed.*

Hyperithon: *Can we be assured that the energy created by the double spacecraft will be safe to all, whether on the mountain as part of the mission or not?*

Igor: *The information that we will gather between now and July from the paired craft test runs will be enough to assure us about the safety.*

Tex: *Should the existing protection dome be enlarged?*

Igor: *At this point, we don't see the need to broaden the protection. But as time grows near, if any of us feel that it should be enlarged, we feel that can easily be accomplished and need not be an issue. The present protection is fine for maintaining the stability of the site until July. If the protection is to be enlarged or adjusted, the appropriate time to do it would be in July when Machaelle goes to the mountain to do the final preparations of the site for the physical landing and mission.*

Hyperithon [to Machaelle]: *If it needs to be heightened, can this be done?*

> Machaelle: *Yes. If you give me the specifications, I'll have nature expand the protection to your specific requirements.*
>
> Lorpuris: *I have felt all along that it is important to protect those whom Peter is inviting as witnesses prior to going into the mountain area. Now it might be doubly important with this expanded mission.* [To Machaelle] *Can that be done?*
>
> Machaelle: *Yes, I think. I can work with Pan to protect them prior to their going to the mountain with the same energy that's protecting the site itself.*
>
> David: *We're going to need to think about this proposal. Do we now have enough information to make a decision?*

With no further questions, the meeting ended and I closed down the coning. Hyperithon would be meeting the following afternoon with representatives from the expanded spacecraft group, and we would all come together in three days for the next full meeting. David said he would announce his decision about the expanded mission then.

(Dear God, please, *please* don't let me return from Perelandra tomorrow and find little green people sitting in the living room drinking coffee and discussing spacecraft pairing problems, saying things like, "Oh Cedric, I don't think we should pair the turquoise Ford Pinto craft with the Buick craft with the orange racing stripe. It's just not a good match. It'll look like a Howard Johnson's.")

Besides my deep desire not to see green people, I had two other reactions to this meeting. First, I found the discussion remarkably logical and reasonable. After each outlandish point was explained, I kept thinking, "Of course. That makes sense." It was an advanced class in reality and energy dynamics. To say it was amazing to hear and consider these things is a gross understatement.

My second reaction: "Oh crap, I can hardly get a handle on the size and scope of the primary mission, and now they are talking about doubling its size! Thanks a lot...By the way, where is the universe and beyond? And what kind of government systems do they have? Do they pay taxes?...Wait a minute. Did they just say we might blow up the planet? Bummer."

Meeting #2

Meeting #2 was held on October 27. David announced his decision to expand the Mount Shasta Mission with one proviso. At any point, if the expanded mission jeopardized the primary mission, David would declare the expanded mission cancelled and the expanded mission would immediately uncouple, detach and pull back. It was understood that the expanded mission was an opportunity that could not occur at the expense of the primary mission. Everyone agreed.

The rest of the meeting was spent discussing how best to assure the stability, safety and well being of everyone who would be present at the site—David's ten guests who were arriving on the mother ship and Peter's witnesses who would be arriving on foot.

David's ten guests were chosen from the group of leaders who had participated in the different Piscean governments throughout its 2,000 year history. As key members of this group and acting on the group's behalf, they needed to release their guardianship, responsibilities and connections to the old governments in order to disconnect their hold on the old leylines. Their release would unlock the grid. Only after that was done could the spacecraft hovering above the old leylines shift them to the new Aquarian configuration. (This was similar in principle to what occurred at the Gettysburg Battlefield when people were called back to release their karmic connections. Only when they had detached could the battle move to its higher purpose.)

The personal challenges the ten leaders faced revolved around returning to the Earth's level of reality and adjusting to its five-senses form. Like the witnesses they had to remain focused and alert. And there were health issues to consider. No one was sure what impact the descent through the different levels and into the site's environment would have on these people. Lorpuris and his teams were already working with the leaders to strengthen and stabilize them. (They tell me my experiences and problems adjusting to the Cottage gave the medical teams additional information to work with.)

The other group was Peter's witnesses. The final count of those who said they wanted to participate was twenty-two. These were people who had known Peter for many years, and it was expected that they would have previous experience in events involving multiple levels. But it was also assumed that they hadn't experienced anything like what was to occur on the mountain and would need to be prepared.

Salvesen's work was a major part of their preparation. Her goal was to keep everyone from becoming overwhelmed and shutting down. No one was to black out or faint—if it could be helped. To be effective witnesses, they needed to remain conscious, alert and focused on what was happening and process it through their sensory systems. St. Germain said their training and development in these areas were taken into consideration when he provided the list to Peter. As witnesses, they would automatically ground everything that they processed into the new leyline grid. This would make the Aquarian government/military information more easily accessible to others. No psychics or guides needed. No information would be left dangling in midair.

Grounding is such an important part of an operation like the Mount Shasta Mission that St. Germain contacted David as soon as it became known that a mission was being planned. He wanted to infuse the mission's grounding setup into his own leyline operation that occurred back in the 1950s when he worked with Peter and others to move portions of the grid to support the coming Aquarian dynamics. The grounding process had not been completed and the usefulness of the information provided by those leylines had been more limited. Now he wanted to be included in the Mount Shasta Mission and finish the job.

Over the next eight months, there were three more major meetings with Igor and each one resulted in an expansion or refinement in the mission. Opportunities were presented, considered, tossed out or woven in. To me it was fascinating to watch how David and the Cottage team allowed the Mount Shasta Mission to expand (with much thought and care) to include wider opportunities.

GETTYSBURG AND THE MOUNT SHASTA MISSION

In November, Igor suggested another expansion. This time it had to do with my work at Gettysburg. I already had phase three scheduled for April. I didn't know what I would be doing, but I figured it would be a mop-up job signifying the completion of the battlefield work. In this November meeting, Igor had different ideas and gave us the final piece (from his perspective) of the expanded Mount Shasta Mission.

We now want to switch to the subject of Gettysburg, to give information in order for you to understand the importance of Gettysburg and phase three. From earlier discussions, we know that the Gettysburg work is going to tie into the mission. As you gentlemen know, that which has occurred on Earth in the form of battle has in energy and intent occurred on all other levels throughout the universe and, we might add, beyond. Although there haven't been great cosmic wars within the universe, there has been intensity equal to that of the intent, emotions and energy that were released in five-senses form through the battle known as Gettysburg. We would like to add to the insight of Gettysburg at this particular point because, from our perspective, this is the last piece of the Mount Shasta puzzle to come into place.

In the spring, Machaelle will return to Gettysburg. At that time, Gettysburg will be fully detached from its karmic links. Those souls who still have karmic attachments to Gettysburg will have been called back by that time and will have gone through their release of that connection (and we might add, the healing process that will accompany the release).

The precise framework for this third phase need not be discussed at this point, and quite frankly, it is too soon to discuss those details. But the results of the third phase will raise the Gettysburg Battle to the level of its higher intent and purpose. This level has always existed and has been a part of the Gettysburg Battle from its moment of conception. The highest intent and purpose was never lost. Rather, it was made complicated by a multitude of karmic connections that wove a pattern of intensity and complexity, separating the Battle of Gettysburg from its higher purpose.

That weaving and that separation is what is being removed this year as each person is called back to Gettysburg to go through their release. Each will release his karmic link and his part of the weave, so what you will have in the spring is the echo of the battle that occurred and the superimposition of the higher intent of the Gettysburg Battle. These two will mesh. The battle itself, in energy, will take on a new identity. (In order for this identity to be achieved, we needed to erase that middle ground, the karmic links.) The higher level and the level of the historic battle will come together to create the new identity; this has been referred to at the Cottage as raising a battle to its higher purpose, its higher intent. [Flipping the coin.] *When that occurs, all the corresponding levels within the universe and beyond that have, in any way, been connected to the Battle of Gettysburg will shift to their higher identities, as well.*

The full and complete shift of the battle into a new identity with a new vibration is what will be linked with the Mount Shasta Mission. The battle's higher purpose will infuse the energy that will be grounded into the leyline system around the world and, with the expanded mission, be released into the universe and beyond. It will sound the note of the new direction and new intent of the framework known as "government"—government around the world, beyond the world and beyond the universe.

One result of this shift will be with the work at the Cottage. At the moment of the Mount Shasta shift, when the new leyline system is activated, the work that has gone on at the Cottage—what you call "flipping the coins"—will also be activated and infused with the new intent that the raising of the Battle of Gettysburg will initiate, thus aligning the battle with the heart and soul of the country. After this activation, that Cottage work may be successfully used to create, formulate and move Earth within the framework of government into the new, which, up to this point, without that particular activation, has not been appropriate to use.

The meeting ended with one final question.

John: *If the Mount Shasta Mission is anything less than five-senses physical, what do we end up with?*

Igor: *There will be a degree of difficulty on all levels regarding the activation and accessibility others will have with the information moving*

> *through the new leylines should the mission not be fully five-senses physical. If this were not true, then St. Germain would not seek to align with this mission the entire Aquarian leyline system, which currently does not have incorporated in it five-senses form. He fully understands the importance of grounding these things through the five senses. This is important not just to Earth, but to all other levels.*

IGOR JUST MOVED GETTYSBURG'S phase three to a whole new level of importance. I couldn't help but think about how this all started with my developing the Battle Energy Release Process and David asking me to go to the Gettysburg Battlefield. It was a simple little process that I wanted to do for nature and the battlefield. Who knew it would lead to this? (Probably nature...and Igor.)

There wasn't any question about David and the Cottage team including the Gettysburg Battle as part of the mission. The range of possibilities this provided was too important to pass up. After the meeting, there was much discussion about what this meant for the Cottage work. David brought the conversation back to the matter at hand and reminded everyone to not lose focus on the primary mission. Everything hinged on the success of that mission.

The completion of the Gettysburg Battle phase three work hinged on me—and my partner. I was more than a little worried. I wasn't sure what was going to happen if I screwed up the third phase. And what was I going to be doing at Gettysburg? Wasn't it something about activating the very work the Cottage men had been doing all these years? No pressure there. It was clear that opportunity was knocking and intergalactic office doors were springing open. Very looooong communication lines were being laid. Information would be flying everywhere. You know, I don't mind the fate of the Western world resting on my work...well, I don't mind much. But I have some serious problems with the fate of the Cottage, the planet, the universe and beyond resting on it.

In January 1985, the work at the Cottage stepped up to a new level. Except for an occasional discussion with the men about the nature work at the mountain, I wasn't involved in their planning.

I was busy dealing with Beatrice and Hank and, frankly, I just wanted them to disappear. That whole situation with those two felt peripheral yet, at the same time, their intrusions could not have been more annoying. To maintain sanity, I turned my attention to nature's information for the 1985 Perelandra garden. (When in doubt, plant a garden.)

In February, I was talking to the men about how the garden work was coming along and described the progression of the planning and the processes I used with nature each season for putting together garden information. The men suggested I make notes on what I was talking about. When I finished, I immediately recognized that it was a list of chapters, and that these chapters were for a book—a book that I suddenly wanted to write. I wanted to help others forge *their* partnership with nature within the context of their own garden. I wanted to pass on what I had learned from nature. It was time. I decided that I would not start writing until August of that year, after the mission, and it would be called the *Perelandra Garden Workbook.* Thus, in the midst of the mission's madness, my second book was born.

In March, I had an appointment at Perelandra with four women who wanted to talk to me about something—I wasn't sure what, but they said it was important. They would be driving from Baltimore, Maryland, so I figured I'd give them some time for their effort. As it turned out, they only stayed about a half hour, and I never did figure out what they wanted from me. As they were leaving, one of them offered me a gift. She said it was a Hopi paho. I had never heard of pahos before and knew nothing about them. Through the lens of ignorance, all I could see in my hands was a large feather, obviously a special feather, with a long string tied to one end. The woman explained that the Hopi Indians are the guardians of peace on our planet, and wherever a Hopi planted a paho, peace was grounded. I accepted the gift and thanked the women. Then they left Perelandra.

Even though I had no idea what this paho thing was all about (the Google web service wasn't launched until September 1998), the comment about grounding peace caught my attention and I felt that somehow it was going to be used for the Mount Shasta Mission. Since at the time I thought I was quarter Navajo, I assumed that perhaps now *any* Indian could bury a paho. (I would not find out that I was actually quarter Hopi for another four years.) I opened the Mount Shasta Mission coning and asked if I was to take the paho to the mountain. The answer was yes, but we wouldn't know if or how it was to be used during the mission. I would be told what to do on the mountain. Terrific. Now I had a mystery in the form of a feather attached to a string. Like everything else, I felt certain the addition of the paho hinged on the success of the primary mission.

Meeting with Pan

In March, I had a lengthy session with Pan to get nature's perspective on how the mission, its preparations and Hyperithon's practice landings at the site were progressing and how the dome was functioning. Below are excerpts from that meeting's transcript. I know it's a bit lengthy, but as fascinating and exciting as Igor's meetings were, this one with Pan took it over the top for me. I wrote earlier that the Mount Shasta Mission was a master class. This meeting with Pan was the master class within a master class, covering advanced energy dynamics and principles, biosphere building, domes, protection, establishing balance, maintaining balance, multilevel teamwork and the importance of clarity and attention to detail. Similar to my first year garden, the meeting was a unique window into the reality around us and the profound partnership we can have with nature. With that said, I just had to share my favorite meeting with you. We began with Pan discussing Hyperithon's practice landings that have already been going on at the mountain site.

> Pan: *Each time there is a practice landing, even though it is out of the five-senses range, we are able to further fine-tune and adjust the environment within the protection dome for the mission. We would like six more landings to complete our process. If you, Hyperithon, need more landings beyond the six we have requested, there's no issue as far as we're concerned. Just as you were able to receive data regarding the actual landing and the ship when Machaelle went to the mountain in*

September, we have been able to receive valuable data on how best we may support this mission every time the ship is married to the site.

The next issue was the dome.

We perceive the next question to be about the protection dome having to do with whether the protection needs to be broadened in area or intent. At this point, the dome need not be changed, either in size or intent. It is set up and functioning in a manner that responds completely to the site's preparation needs between now and July. This "mission preparation" intent must be shifted prior to the physical landing, and that would be the purpose of Machaelle going to the mountain prior to July 15. She can do this work one, two or three days before—whatever she feels comfortable with. At that time, because of the actual physical landing to take place, the ceremony and the work that's to occur, the site will have to change from an intent of preparation to the "mission go" intent. No one need concern themselves with the framework for that shift at this time. When Machaelle gets to the mountain in July, we will have spoken to her and she'll know precisely how that shift is to occur. In essence, she will be the representative of the mission at the site and will be the person to shift the dome to "mission go." Now, if she's feeling uncertain about her position in that role, in terms of representing the mission itself, she can come to the mountain as liaison for the mission and connect with David when activating the coning. His understanding of the mission and his intent will initiate the shift to "mission go."

Machaelle: *I would prefer that I work with David because of his position in the mission. His understanding and knowledge about this mission is far greater than mine. My focus is primarily on nature, so I am deliberately not paying attention to information that I'm not directly involved with.*

I'm a little out of my area here, but what about the people who are coming in by mother ship? Does their reality need to be entered into the protection as well?

Pan: *When you connect with David for the shift to mission go in July, you'll need to allow their reality as a group to move from him into you and, finally, into the dome's biosphere. Get an essence readout for the dome environment once this group is added. We will then accommodate their presence as well by infusing the biosphere with the essences this group needs. We recommend that this shift occur* prior *to your introducing the witness group. That will allow the energy reality of David's group to interact and commingle with that of the witnesses. Whatever trauma or imbalance that might occur when these two groups actually meet face to face will show up at that time. We recommend you test for and introduce essences into the environment that will accommodate their initial face to face, shall we say, shock. The witnesses will be dealing with, for lack of a better term, a crisis of faith. Most likely they will not be convinced of the mission and its goals until it actually unfolds in front of their eyes. The group coming in by ship already understands what will be happening and will not be dealing with that crisis of faith.*

Machaelle: *I don't need to know the makeup of David's group as long as he has it in his mind, do I?*

Pan: *No. Just move his information as energy through you. You will function (as you functioned in September) as the conduit.*

Machaelle: *Since you've not mentioned this, I take that it's not important one way or another whether Salvesen goes with me to the mountain prior to the landing for the mission-go shift.*

Pan: *It's not important. It's your choice. I suggest strongly that you take whomever you feel comfortable with and that whoever goes understands that they are not to press you in any way in terms of timing. Shifting the protection dome to mission go is going to be critical and shouldn't be interfered with by anyone who doesn't understand the importance of what's going on.*

Machaelle: *The question arose a while ago about whether or not I could include in the protection dome different elements such as the sensation of an enclosed, protected environment so that when the witnesses enter the site they would have a sense of enclosure and protection. What do you think?*

Pan: *Again, there's no issue here. That would be an ingredient you can add in July, if you so wish. The domed site already has within it the characteristics of an enclosed environment. When you get to the mountain in July, the kind of detail and refinement you are now considering can be added easily just before you shift the environment to mission go.*

Machaelle: *I'd like to switch the topic to the actual landing on the mountain.*

Pan: *That's fine.*

Machaelle: *We want to make sure that the people coming to the mountain both by ship and on foot maintain a strong stability throughout this entire landing, and the question arose as to how nature might help facilitate this. We thought of creating a team with nature and myself, for the express purpose of responding to any needs during the actual landing. What we need is your input on this.*

Pan: *I have already taken that situation into consideration. Remember, when the question of the expanded mission first arose, I was part of the coning. Therefore, I understood the situation from nature's perspective. What I've been devising throughout this particular meeting addresses those needs. When you add both group realities into the protection dome prior to the landing itself, their stability will be met by the infused essences that you will be introducing into the environment. What we will be doing is maintaining those essences as part of the biosphere of the protected site. When they enter this environment, the groups will automatically receive the assistance they need for their stability. That's one of the beauties of this type of isolated and protected environment: We can create, and have been creating, something completely separate and apart from the mountain specifically to address the needs of the Mount Shasta Mission.*

Machaelle, you can have complete confidence that each group assembled at the mountain will have available to them what they need for their stability as a group. That is one reason your trip to the mountain prior to July 15 is important. This is also assuming that Salvesen will have done her work with the witnesses prior to their coming to the mountain so that this group will be entering into the site already having had their individual needs met. As a group dynamic, their needs will be met within the dome itself. Don't forget that in terms of energy, a collection of individuals is very different than a unified group. Therefore, it will be equally important that Salvesen meet the witnesses' individual needs prior to coming to the mountain for the mission.

Machaelle: *Okay, that took care of that situation. I take it I'm to bring the Perelandra Rose Essences.*

Pan: *They will be the primary essences used on the mountain. Most likely the need for Bach and the FES essences will show up in the individuals during their work with you and Salvesen.*

Machaelle: *With everybody coming to the mountain for this landing, it seems important that nature somehow be represented by something other than the actual physical location of the mission site.*

Pan: *Let me interrupt here because you're jumping the gun and getting into our next order of business, which has to do with the grounding process of the mission. I recommend that your Mount Shasta Mission coning be another element added into the dome's biosphere prior to the landing. This includes the Deva of Perelandra, the Deva of Mount Shasta (the mountain), the Deva of the Mission Site and the Deva of the Mount Shasta Mission so that there will be four devas representing the devic point of the coning. I will be happy to continue to represent the nature spirit point. I suggest that David, Lorpuris and Hyperithon together represent the White Brotherhood point and that you, Machaelle, continue to represent the Earth-level human point, the connection that bonds the entire coning. By including the coning, you add a unique nature/human balance and grounding dynamic into the environment.*

Machaelle: *Is there anything else that you see now that I need to add to the coning or site?*

Pan: *Yes. This is most likely going to be our last suggestion in terms of the site shift to mission go. Your position as liaison with nature has to be taken into consideration because you will be entering the mountain not just as a representative of humanity, but in the role of nature's liaison as well. In this particular mission, that's been a key role from the beginning in terms of your work and your understanding. Also your presence on the mountain during the landing will represent, among other things, man and nature come together. You are the bridge between the intelligence of nature and the intelligence of man. You are the one who has brought man and nature together in this mission.*

I recommend that when you shift the site and dome to mission go, you enter the gold dome as Machaelle, the human. But at some point early on, shift your presence in the site to that of nature's liaison. At this point, activate that connection within you and add it as an element into the site. That addition will give more stability to those coming to the mountain, particularly those coming on foot.

But there is another side to this: You will be coming to the mountain with these people and be functioning in this mission as nature's liaison. By virtue of your having added your reality to the protection, the people entering the site will sense its presence and be relaxed around you as you work. You will not strike an alien note in them because your unique working reality will already be present in the environment.

I have one more suggestion regarding grounding—not the grounding in the site, but the grounding within the mother ship as it comes in. I recommend placing Perelandra's crystal/topaz in the mother ship in a prominent position and using it for the purpose of grounding during the ship's positioning and descent into the site. [The crystal/topaz from the center of the Perelandra garden had been shifted to the Cottage several months prior to this session using the Split Molecular Process.] *Now, "using" does not mean doing anything in the ship other than recognizing the crystal's position and its function. You need not tell the historic leaders who are participating in this mission the crystal's purpose, but the ship's crew, those involved with planning the mission, certainly Hyperithon and David, should understand what that crystal/topaz is doing. During this mission, the crystal/topaz will be returning to Earth—the same level as the Perelandra garden. Because of that, it will function as a honing device. It will help move you into the site, physically ground you, and connect the reality of the ship and the group of leaders on the craft into the site. Another way of saying this is that the crystal/topaz will function as a fusion device.*

David: *Is there a specific area of the craft in which the crystal/topaz should be placed?*

Pan: *We'll leave that up to you.*

Hyperithon: *I think I know where it belongs. Am I allowed to borrow the crystal/topaz out of the Cottage between now and July for the practice landings?*

Pan: *Yes, as long as it is in the Cottage for the coming summer solstice, its removal from the Cottage is fine. However, I recommend that the crystal/topaz not be taken out for a long period of time.*

Hyperithon: *I can have it back to the Cottage within the same day.*

Pan: *That is best. Machaelle physically feels the crystal/topaz presence in the Cottage, and it would be good not to remove it for any long period of time.*

David [to Hyperithon]: *Then you'll have to have it out and back within a day.*

Hyperithon: *Would you recommend that we continue our simulations with the crystal/topaz present?*

Pan: *I recommend that the shift of the crystal/topaz be synchronized with the ship's descent into the site. If the ship is just beyond five-senses form, then the crystal/topaz should also be just beyond five-senses form.*

Hyperithon: *There's not a problem with that. In fact, I can possibly use the crystal/topaz energy without removing it from the Cottage.*

Pan: *No. Remove the crystal/topaz form, have custody of the form in your presence and then shift it to the site as part of the ship.*

Hyperithon: *Fine.*

David: *Should the crystal/topaz be kept in its wooden box?*

Pan: *Not while it's being used for the mission during preparation and mission go. It must be exposed to light on the spacecraft.*

Hyperithon: *Need it be natural light? We're going to have difficulty with that.*

Pan: *No, it must simply be exposed to the craft's interior light.*

David: *Just to be clear, are you saying we need to transport the crystal/topaz back and forth in the box?*

Pan: *Yes.*

Hyperithon: *I had a feeling that crystal/topaz was coming with us.*

Pan: *You'll find that the crystal/topaz is going to make quite a difference not only because of its function as a crystal/topaz combination but also because the topaz itself links with the universal devic realm in nature. The other important aspect is that because the crystal/topaz originated from Perelandra's garden, it has been infused with the Perelandra-level energy, which is the level you're coming into at the site.*

Hyperithon: *Yes, I understand. It makes all the sense in the world.*

Machaelle: *I'm finished with my list of questions. Is there anything else we can think of at this point?*

Pan: *I am also finished with the information I held for this meeting, unless you have specific questions.*

Hyperithon: *No, I think I have what I need for now.*

David [to Pan]: *I think we should have another meeting with you just prior to Machaelle going to California to make sure we have all the information we need at that point.*

Pan: *That's not a problem. At that time, we can give Machaelle the steps she will be using for the site's shift to mission go. We're available at any time, as you know.*

David: *That sounds fine. Do we feel it's a wrap?*
[All indicated yes.]

Gettysburg Battlefield: Phase Three

I received word from nature in mid-April that it was time to go to the Gettysburg Battlefield for phase three. In a surprise move, I found out what I was to do from Igor and not Pan. He said that phase three consisted of two steps. The first step would be done at the battlefield. I would do the second step at the Mount Shasta site just prior to shifting to mission go.

> Igor continued: *The many souls who have had karmic ties to the Battle of Gettysburg have answered the call to return to the battlefield this past year. Once there, they either consciously or unconsciously experienced a shift that allowed them to free themselves from the battle. For the most part these souls experienced a change in insight either around war in general, Gettysburg specifically or their relationship to their country. As this release occurred, their karmic bonds to the battle were broken. Not only were they set free from the battle, but the battle was set free from them. That was vital if we were to continue forward with phase three.*
>
> > Note: A few days prior to doing the phase three work, I read an article in a local newspaper about a surprising increase in visitors to the battlefield during 1984 and early 1985. No one could explain the sudden influx.
>
> *For Step 1, go to the area where you planted the comfrey. You will be working with the Copse of Trees and the High Water Mark areas. In each, you are to conduct the final "mop-up" phase of the karmic release process the souls have been going through over the past year by infusing each area (Copse of Trees, then the High Water Mark) with the Comfrey essence that will be released to you from the plants. Infuse the entire area with the Comfrey essence (you'll see the area to be included for each spot in your mind's eye once you get there tomorrow), then do an Energy Cleansing Process and use the comfrey energy to form the cleansing sheet starting at five feet below ground level. This will clear both areas of any karmic energy that may still be present.*
>
> *Next, do a Battle Energy Release Process for each area. That will release the final energy of the Gettysburg Battle held in custodianship by nature for over 100 years. Once released, test each area for essences.*

This will complete the job in those two areas and bring you full circle with the job you began in phases one and two. The battle will be fully released from the battlefield.

There's more to do, however. I suggest you do this last part from the Eisenhower Tower. Once on the platform, connect with the Overlighting Deva of the Gettysburg Battle and ask for a balancing and stabilizing readout to facilitate the final healing of the Gettysburg Battle. For that work, test the battlefield using your flower essences and your full Soil Balancing Kit as both your balancers and your stabilizers. Each needed element is to be administered to the battlefield by nature, which will be poised and ready to infuse them throughout the entire battlefield area as a single unit. Once completed, the Gettysburg Battle will be raised to its higher level and ready for linking into the Mount Shasta Mission's protection dome this July.

And finally, there will be a gift given to you from nature. You and Salvesen will be directed from the Eisenhower Tower to the gift. You are to take the gift with you to Mount Shasta and physically place it at the protected site just prior to the shift to mission go as part of the linking of the battle to the mission.

Machaelle: *Who should be included in the coning for this work at the Copse of Trees and High Water Mark?*

Igor: *The coning you have been using for the Gettysburg Battlefield work plus David, Hyperithon, the Deva of the Copse of Trees and the Deva of the High Water Mark.*

To answer your thoughts about the gift: The gift should be kept in your cabin at Perelandra until your trip to Mount Shasta. It should be kept with you during travel and in your custody once you arrive in California. It will be carried to the mountain by you, and you will place it at the protected site area. Nature will "guard" (if you will) the gift the entire time it is in your custody. Once placed into the site, nature will receive its presence and assure its clarity. You need not be concerned about the gift absorbing any inappropriate energy—especially during the trip to Mount Shasta.

On April 22, Salvesen and I travelled to Gettysburg one last time. We first headed to the Copse of Trees. There were buses and people everywhere. This was not going to be easy. We walked over to where the comfrey had been planted the previous June and, lo and behold, much to my relief the three plants were still there. While trying to look as inconspicuous as possible, I opened the coning. Almost immediately, an area stood out to me visually, and I knew I would be infusing the Comfrey essence into an area that included the Copse of Trees and the land extending some forty-five feet beyond the circular copse fence.

This is where you insert "And a miracle occurs here." Everyone cleared out. There were no people, no children running around, no buses and no cars. Salvesen mumbled something about the extraordinary clout I must have. I, on the other hand, felt that out of the many amazing things that had occurred during the Gettysburg work, this had to be the most amazing of all. I walked over to the copse to begin my work.

First, I worked with Pan to infuse the area that I could see in my mind's eye with the essence from the comfrey plants. According to Pan's instructions, I only needed to wait fifteen seconds while this infusion took place, and, as it occurred, I could feel a change in the atmosphere.

Once the infusion was completed, I set up the area for an Energy Cleansing Process. I asked Pan to add the Comfrey essence to the energy sheet used for clearing. The Comfrey essence ensured that the Energy Cleansing Process focused only on the karmic issues we were working with. In comparison to the countless other Energy Cleansing Processes I had already done, this one moved exceptionally quickly and smoothly. The whole process was over in about three minutes.

As per instructions, I did not test the area for essences after the energy cleansing. Instead, I set up for the Battle Energy Release Process, which moved as easily as the Energy Cleansing Process and was completed in about three minutes, as well.

With those two processes finished, I tested the area for needed essences to stabilize the work. Here's where I hit a snag. None of the essences I brought with me tested positive. But I kept testing that something was needed. Then Pan told me to test for the new Rose Essences. Because it was early in the season and the roses had not yet bloomed (something that had to happen before I could make the essences), I did not have a Rose set in hand. Luckily, I remembered the names of the eight roses and I was able to test a mental list. Royal Highness tested positive. Here's how nature described this essence:

> *Final stabilization. Royal Highness relates to the full stabilization a person (or environment) must experience when an evolutionary step or movement has been completed. In gross terms, one might say that this is the mop-up essence. Royal Highness helps insulate, protect and stabilize the individual (or area) and the shift during this period when both are vulnerable.*

Pan said he would create the essence from the Royal Highness bush growing in the Perelandra garden. After stating he was ready, I gave the go-ahead and Pan shifted the new essence into the Copse of Trees area. That's when Salvesen, who was sitting about forty feet away, said she saw a cloud of soft pink light envelope the copse and land. The Royal Highness rose is soft pink, something Salvesen didn't know.

Next I was told to go to The Angle, just north of the Copse of Trees and right next to the road, to work with the rest of the High Water Mark area. Still there were no people, cars or buses. This time, I infused the Comfrey essence and did the two processes for a larger area that extended south past an obelisk. And again everything went smoothly—and fast.

That area also needed Royal Highness. But just as I was about to call for the release of another "batch" of the essence, a Wilson Tour Bus pulled up and parked right next to us. (I knew my luck couldn't hold out much longer.) Salvesen quietly announced, "Here come the troops!" But to my amazement, my luck still held. The people were facing away from me, the door remained shut and there were no sounds coming from inside the bus. The people just silently sat there and paid no attention to me. That was spooky. I finished the work, and Pan infused the area with Royal Highness. This time, both Salvesen and I saw the pink cloud.

Immediately after the infusion was completed, the bus pulled away. On the back of the bus was a huge mural of a bald eagle landing on a ridge not unlike The Angle and High Water Mark area. I said to Salvesen, "The eagle has landed." With that, three more buses pulled up, a bunch of tourists got off and strolled around, and cars started driving down the road.

THE EISENHOWER TOWER: Going back to the Eisenhower Tower was like returning to an old friend, although I wished my friend were shorter and had fewer steps. We made the climb to the top and—you guessed it—no one was there. In light of the traffic and activity at the battlefield that day, there should have been fifty people on the platform. I mean, really...what is there to say about these little magical moments? I got down to work and added the Deva of the Gettysburg Battle to the coning. I now did the final essence and soil kit tests for the entire battlefield to facilitate its healing process. The battlefield needed Royal Highness essence, and the soil needed nitrogen and greensand. Pan infused Royal Highness first, giving the entire battlefield a beautiful pink glow (in my mind's eye) and then applied the two soil amendments to the battlefield soil.

THE GIFT: With that accomplished, I was now faced with finding my mysterious gift from nature. Let's see...where in this big battlefield was my gift? It felt like we would be hunting for the proverbial needle in the haystack. We were leaning against a tower railing facing the battlefield and discussing what we should do next, when Salvesen said, "I wonder why those trees over there are glowing." She pointed to something across the battlefield that looked to me like a short line of Redbud trees in bloom. I could barely see them, but I checked with Pan and found this was where we were to begin our search: Little Round Top.

At Little Round Top, Salvesen told me to sit on one of the handy humongous boulders while she walked down into the overgrown field just in front. Hey, she found where we were to start the search. Why would I start arguing with her now? The field was filled with more monster rocks. It was definitely not a field for farming or for tourists to tromp around in either. She moved slowly and headed further down the field and out of sight. I just sat there enjoying the view—for half an hour or so.

When I finally caught sight of her, I felt I was to join her. She had tried to move back up the hill toward me, but she told me that the snakes crawling around near her feet stopped her. She figured they were hinting that she was moving in the wrong direction. I thought, "She said snakes. Great." (I'd rather deal with the tour buses.) So I walked slowly and carefully down the field to meet her while listening for any slithering sounds. We continued moving wherever the snakes weren't moving. I guess you could say we were taking the path of least resistance.

Eventually we climbed over some more rocks and came upon a huge, hidden boulder that sat low to the ground. It had a large hollowed out circular "garden" in its center—maybe six feet wide and ten feet long. The garden had beautiful, healthy wild plants growing in no more than an eighth-inch of soil. In some places I couldn't see any soil at all and the plants were just growing out of the rock. (Ten years later, I learned I had been looking at the miracle of chelation.) In the very center of the garden were some small stones and a small piece of wood. It was clear that no human had placed them there because the arrangement looked too natural, almost random.

As I looked at this amazing garden, I heard Pan telling me that this was the fairy ring of the Gettysburg Battlefield—nature's center and office for the battlefield. True to the tradition of fairy rings, the boulder, its garden and the center arrangement were extremely powerful—powerful enough that the hair on my arms stood up when I first saw it. Salvesen leaned down and carefully picked up the piece of wood from the center, held it in her hands and said, "Here's the gift." I checked with Pan and, sure enough, it was.

When receiving a gift such as this, it's important that the recipient not reach out to *take* the gift. The recipient must *receive* the gift. So when Salvesen placed it into my hands, I made sure I didn't make any move toward it or her.

The gift was a piece of weathered wood measuring five inches long and shaped like a long-barreled Civil War gun. (At least, that's what it looked like to me.) After carefully examining it, I wrapped the gift in clean paper for protection and put it in my backpack where I knew it would be safe. Actually, I didn't want to let the gift out of my hands, but I was afraid I might damage it if I didn't protect it for the rest of the trip.

We stayed at the fairy ring a little longer, mostly because I was reluctant to leave. After all the time and work I had done at the battlefield, this moment by the garden rock felt like I was being given a big thank you, like I was being received as one of theirs. Finally I silently thanked nature and said we had to leave. And guess what? We didn't have any problem with snakes as we walked through the middle of the snake area and out of the field. *Magic.*

By the time I got to the Cottage that evening, David had already received confirmation from Hyperithon that the Gettysburg work was successfully completed. Everyone was pretty elated about it. Personally, I was just relieved that everything had gone so well. I told them about my gift and that I had placed it in my cabin at Perelandra next to the paho.

It was now spring, and I returned my attention to the Perelandra garden. On May 4, I received word from nature that I was to add several items to the mineral ring that encircles the crystal/topaz sitting in the center of the garden. On top of specific quartz rocks that formed the circle, I laid an agate, a malachite, an azurite, a piece of amber, a small piece of coral and a piece of petrified wood. When I got everything in place, I felt a shift, and for the first time in many months, I felt tension free and my body relaxed.

That evening when I told David about the garden changes, he asked me to find out if the additions to the mineral ring were to be split (using the SMP) for the Mount Shasta Mission. The answer: yes. They were to be placed in the wooden box with the crystal/topaz at the Cottage. My assumption, based on what I felt when I added them to the garden center, was that these new items would enhance and stabilize the grounding effect of the crystal/topaz on the ship.

On May 16, David said it was time for me to contact the twenty-two witnesses who had confirmed to Peter that they were coming. I wrote the following letter.

Dear ________,

Peter Caddy has informed me that you have been invited to witness a mission that is scheduled to take place on Mount Shasta in California this July. I am the liaison for those of you who are coming to the mountain by foot and those who are coming by craft.

The purpose of this mission is focused on the global government framework and its shift from the Piscean dynamic to the Aquarian dynamic. Part of what will occur on the mountain is the creation of the global leyline system for the Aquarian government framework as well as the activation of that new system. The leyline shift and the entire thrust of the mission, is being planned and organized by those working in the government/military "branch" of the White Brotherhood.

Undoubtedly, Peter mentioned several things about this mission to you. One is that a mother ship will land at the mountain site between July 14 and July 17, with the primary target date as July 15. Two: the landing will be attempted on the physical plane rather than the etheric. Work has been going on this past year for the purpose of assuring in every possible way that the meeting be experienced by the witnesses through their five senses. As part of the preparation, you are asked to contact me at Mount Shasta (Finlandia Motel, 916–555–5555), on July 13 or 14 in order to go through a body balance. It is a painless twenty-minute procedure and will be done by a holistic chiropractic physician and myself. For the success of the mission and your own well being, this work must be completed prior to going to the mountain site.

We are asking that you come prepared with a flashlight (the ship's arrival will be around dusk), a bottle of water, hiking boots or good walking shoes, and cool weather hiking clothes. We also ask that your physical condition be such that you can easily walk two miles.

I am requesting that we meet as a group in my room at the Finlandia Motel on July 14th, at 3 P.M. At that time, I will be able to give you the details of the mountain meeting, its purpose, timing, etc.

I am also including information about the motels in the town of Mount Shasta in case you need to book a room. If you were planning to stay with the Caddys during this time, perhaps I should say (if you haven't heard), that they are now living in San Francisco. I will be in Mount Shasta at the motel by July 11, if you wish to get in touch with me. Prior to then, you may contact me at Perelandra: 703–555–5555.

Looking forward to seeing you at Mount Shasta.

Sincerely,
Machaelle Wright

I printed twenty-two copies of the letter on Perelandra stationery and mailed them two days later

ON MAY 18, I MADE MY FIRST Perelandra Rose Essence: Gruss an Aachen. The other seven bushes had buds, and I would be able to make those flower essences shortly. By June 19, all the Rose Essences were produced—except Ambassador. There were new buds on that bush, but I couldn't tell if they were going to pop open before my trip. However, on July 7, I found a perfect flower on the bush and I was able to make the Ambassador essence! Finally. The Perelandra Rose Essence set was now complete. I was one happy, relieved, grateful camper, believe me. Lorpuris surprised me by asking me to split several sets to the Cottage for him to use with those arriving on the mother ship. The first Perelandra Rose Essence sets travelled to the mountain in my backpack and on a mother ship.

> How nature describes the Rose Essences: *The Perelandra Rose Essences function with one another to address the electrical circuits that support us as we proceed through evolutionary process. As we move forward and address new situations, learning curves, challenges and ideas, there are mechanisms within us that are set in motion to facilitate our periods of growth. The Perelandra Rose Essences balance and stabilize those circuits that support us and our process mechanisms.*

During this period, the Cottage was a proverbial hotbed of activity, and every day it seemed to me that the intensity increased. In early June, David sat down with me for a "little" talk. First, he told me who would be coming to the mountain on the mother ship. Up to that point, I only knew ten dead historical leaders would be joining the Cottage team. I had been curious about who the leaders were, but I knew David would tell me when it was important for me to know. Now he gave me the full roster. Besides the crew of about thirty-five and David, there would be Hyperithon, Lorpuris, John, Butch, Tex, Mickey and St. Germain. Then he told me the names of the ten leaders who would be participating in the mission: Winston Churchill, Franklin Roosevelt, Harry Truman, Charles de Gaulle, Joseph Stalin, Cardinal Richelieu (Armand-Jean du Plessis), Mao Tse-tung and three eighteenth-century political advisors whose names were completely unfamiliar to me. One advisor was American, one Egyptian, and the other was French. They had operated behind the scenes and were considered inconsequential at the time. As a result, they were lost to history. But in truth, they had been important to their governments.

David explained that the ten leaders had been selected to represent the group of Piscean leaders on the mountain. When they released their guardianship of the government/military leylines, they would be releasing the guardianship of everyone in the larger group, as well. He pointed out that it was an honor for them to have been chosen. As he spoke about it, it hit me what an extraordinary honor this really was. And what an exceptional moment it was going to be when they relinquished their guardianship and responsibilities on the mountain. It was an historic moment that only a few of us would be privileged to witness.

I had some questions about Stalin and Mao. After all, they were responsible for the death of millions during their most recent reigns. I wondered why they were included in the honored group of ten. David pointed out that there is a difference between the actions of a person's mind and personality and the quality of his consciousness. If I understood him correctly, he was saying that the level of consciousness in each of these men was great and they functioned as two of the guardians of government for our planet throughout the entire Piscean Era. But like us, each was responsible for his individual conduct and remained personally responsible for whatever occurred during their respective periods of leadership. David pointed out that the ten leaders, including Stalin and Mao, now embodied the broader consciousness of their souls, not just their personalities. I was not to see any of them solely as personalities with troubling histories. To be honest, I didn't really understand everything David was saying, but I assumed it meant no one would be going off the rails at the mountain and mounting a last-ditch coup. We were all going to be safe.

By using the physical bodies the ten had already embodied on Earth while functioning as leaders, they would be able to move into the Earth level as if pulled by a magnet. Although coming to the mountain was still an extremely tricky exercise for them, it was felt that returning to the familiar would help ensure their stability and balance during the mission and while on the mountain.

Finally, David let me know that there would be 7,834 spacecraft positioned around the planet for the primary mission and another 7,834 spacecraft paired with them for the expanded mission. (This was the first time I heard the actual number of craft included in the mission.)

The summer solstice arrived at 6:44 A.M. on June 21. Since beginning the co-creative garden and my partnership with nature in 1976, I have diligently observed the precise moments of each solstice and equinox, no matter what ungodly hour they occurred. These moments also fuse me with nature's rhythms and the seasonal rhythm of the garden. My conscious intent heightens the impact of those energies, making them especially strong and supportive. Each summer solstice, I have received a color from nature that best reflected the tone and intent of the solstice for that year, and I placed bows in that color in the center of the garden and on each of Perelandra's buildings. As you can see, it was and is an important time for me.

I felt this summer solstice heading into the Mount Shasta Mission to be especially important. After all, the summer solstice is a celebration of the fusion of energy and form, which coincided with the mission's intent. The only problem: I slept through it. In fact, the solstice had completely slipped my mind. I woke up several hours after the moment, and before I even got out of bed, it hit me in the gut. I missed the solstice. I couldn't believe it!

I opened a coning right away and set Perelandra up for the solstice, as I would normally, to see if there was anything I could do to rectify my mistake, but I was told there was nothing for me to do. Around noon, I opened another coning and asked Pan what happened. I was especially interested in knowing if I should do something to reverse what I felt was an obvious and potentially serious screw-up on my part. (You know, like throwing my body off the nearest cliff as a sacrifice to nature or something like that.)

> Pan: *We realize that this is an unusual summer solstice for you and one that would evoke questions. As you have noted, there are no solstice colors displayed at Perelandra for the first time in eight years. And you were asleep for the actual moment of this solstice. One other obvious difference you have noted: When you attempted to open the Perelandra coning several hours after the solstice moment, thus attempting to make the grounded solstice energies available to Perelandra, you were not able to accomplish this. We point out all of this to verify your sense that this is indeed a most unusual summer solstice for you.*
>
> *This solstice is going to be a key element at the Mount Shasta Mission. The solstice energies were grounded into the Perelandra garden center at 6:44 A.M. and shall be held there by us until you go to the mountain for the landing in July.*
>
> *As you know, the summer solstice is the celebration of spirit and form fully come together and made visible as one unit. It is the celebration of nature within five-senses form. This is what is being held within the garden center at Perelandra and what will be released by you at Mount Shasta at a specific moment as the ship is moving through its time and space zones. At that moment, you will focus on the crystal/topaz in the center of the Perelandra garden, and from this point of focus, you will call for the release of the solstice energy. You will then direct the energy from the center of the Perelandra garden into and through the crystal/topaz in the mother ship. From that point, you will direct the energy to expand beyond the ship and release it to the universe. It will then be made available to all the other craft involved in both the primary and expanded mission, as well as to the universe at large. What you will be directing will be similar to what you have already done at Perelandra*

when you receive and ground the solstice/equinox energies and direct their release through the garden crystal. The same principle is involved. Only this time these specialized grounded nature energies will be released from Perelandra by you at the mountain to the advancing mission and ultimately into the universe. This action will not only infuse the mission with nature's solstice energy that celebrates the coming together of spirit and matter, but it will also release to the universe a strong five-senses form ingredient that will enhance the environment surrounding the mission, thus enhancing the mission itself.

We feel you need take nothing from Perelandra to the site in order to accomplish the release from Perelandra. However, check with us just prior to leaving for Mount Shasta in case there is a change and there is something for you to take along to assist this particular work.

You also need not move the solstice energy into the site itself as you release it from Perelandra to the mother ship. This solstice energy will automatically become part of the site's environment once the energy is available to the universe. The principle focus of your action, the energy release, is the marriage of the solstice energy to the incoming mother ship, the surrounding mission craft and their environment.

We suggest that David be informed of what you will be doing and that he brief those in the expanded mission so that they will adjust their actions accordingly in order to receive the solstice energy. You need not concern yourself once the energy is released into the universe. Your job, as it were, will then be over.

We wish we could be exact about the timing for this work at Mount Shasta. We understand that it would ease your mind. But you will have to receive that timing on the mountain. We can say now that this action will be directed by you at the site the evening of the landing, not before. You will receive a clear indication from us that the time for the release of the solstice energy has arrived. Do not worry. We will not let it slip by you.

As for your concerns about "missing" the solstice this morning: Hopefully you now understand that you missed nothing. You did exactly what you were supposed to do. If any questions arise once you share this information with David, we'll be glad to expand on what we've said here.

LATER THAT DAY, I MET with David and told him about this new development. That led to a discussion about how I was going to set up to hear/receive these kinds of multilevel directives. He expanded the discussion by asking how I might facilitate receiving information from each of the mission "department heads" while I was in California, in case they needed me (and nature) to respond to any incoming x-factors. For an answer, I consulted Pan, who said that any time I went to the mountain, whether I was working or not, I was to open the Mount Shasta Mission coning. That coning would allow each of the mission leaders to have direct communication with me. Pan also told me the signal to activate the summer solstice energy movement from Perelandra would come through the coning. In short, the Mount Shasta Mission coning provided me with an intercom system that included a connection with nature, the other coning members and each of the mission department heads. (I hoped they wouldn't all be talking at the same time.)

The day after the summer solstice, I got a call from Gary Dunlap, one of Peter's invited witnesses. He wanted me to explain the mission to him. After I talked to him about the primary mission, he informed me that anything Peter Caddy was connected with was a disaster because of the glamour he brought to it. Gary also told me that he had gotten "guidance" (oh god, here we go again with the guidance) that the mission would be attacked on the mountain by "dark forces" and that it would fail. Well, that thrilled me. Let's all just flush years of work down the toilet and go to the beach in July instead. It definitely added a new wrinkle to things, and now I wondered if I needed to pack my handy-dandy imaginary laser six-shooters for the Mount Shasta Mission.

Really, there was nothing I could say to Gary. Besides, it was clear that he considered me inconsequential and was flicking me off. He wanted to hear from David himself. I told him that I would pass along his information to David. Gary said he and his partner had not made up their minds about witnessing the mission because, he reminded me, they had serious concerns about Peter's involvement. He ended the conversation by telling me he would get in touch with me when I arrived in California. (I so looked forward to the moment.)

That evening I talked to David about Gary's phone call. Here's all that David said: "Don't listen to him. He's a fool." And with that, I took my laser six-shooters out of my suitcase and put them back in my underwear drawer.

It was as if Gary's call carried a warning: "Attention. Things are about to spin out of control." I began getting odd phone calls from strangers from all around the country. It had to do with the twenty-two letters to Peter's witnesses that I sent out in May. No one had bothered to contact me directly. But most of them had some pretty unexpected and unusual responses to that letter. A few xeroxed their letters and posted them on community and college bulletin boards; some witnesses sent copies to friends; some "conveniently" left their letters in books that they then loaned out to others; and some actually announced the mission, giving names, dates and phone numbers from the letter, in classrooms, workshops and meetings.... I kid you not.

I couldn't see how anything I had written in that letter had inspired the witnesses to conduct themselves in such a reckless manner. In keeping with the same outrageous conduct, the calls I received from the uninvited people were jaw dropping. Not one of them asked me if they could participate. They just informed me they were to be there, that they were "guided" to be there. And they each made it clear that they, and they alone, would be the one responsible for the success of the mission. They didn't want to hear about the mission. Each said they already knew about the mission from their "guides." No one would admit that the little they knew actually came from my letter and not their so-called guides. One of them said she was the walk-in for Benjamin Franklin and, of course, "he" had to be at the site. Each of them, including "Ben Franklin," had been told by their "guides" that, for the mission's success, they were to do such things as toss programmed crystals into the site and conjure up energies to be released at the site during the mission.

Now, as someone who had been working with nature for over a year to develop the balance of the site, the thought of these fine, "well-guided" maniacs lobbing crystals around and unleashing who knew what into the site made my skin crawl. Let's just say I got concerned. It was obvious that I was still going to need to pack my laser six shooters. (Hmm. Do you think these people were the "dark forces" that were going to attack us on the mountain?)

And who were those witnesses Peter had invited anyway? Those well-disciplined, knowledgeable, experienced, mature ones who were passing their letters around like a bunch of silly teenagers? Out of all the options they could have chosen to take with that letter and the mission information, being discreet and keeping their mouths shut apparently wasn't one of them. I had to wonder, were these people morons?

While I was jumping up and down, ranting and essentially demonstrating my own version of a maniac, David calmly told me to say nothing to the intruders. Let them blather on. I was to go to the mountain and see who showed up. He felt most of them would not put the effort or the money into getting to the mountain, and we'd figure out later what to do with any who did make it.

Obviously, I wasn't prepared for this. Working with nature at Perelandra and at the Cottage had insulated me from this kind of New Age crap. I was livid. I was angry that these people could be so arrogant and disrespectful—to the mission and to those who were planning the mission. As for myself, I was being written off as an irrelevant twit. I couldn't believe that despite the fact they didn't know what they were talking about, it didn't stop them from considering that their presence alone was required for success. And I was embarrassed. What kind of crackpot level was I living on? I don't know about the others at the Cottage, but just the idea that we might be invaded by a bunch of out-of-control "experts" in nothing added additional pressure on me. I concluded that the only way I could function was to concentrate on the mission and let the intruder chips fall where they may. Hopefully David was right and none of them would show up.

By now, everyone at the Cottage (myself included) was busy taking care of the final preparations. I put together a notebook with copies of my notes, mission sessions, the Gettysburg work and any other information I would need for the work I was to do at the mountain.

At Perelandra I was still getting odd phone calls from people who felt they were "guided" to take over the mission. But, out of all that insanity, one phone call stood out as different. It was from Sarah Wheatley. What caught my attention was her demeanor. It was completely different from the others I had talked to. She was polite, soft-spoken and willing to listen to what I had to say. She explained that she had been told about the mission by a friend who heard about it in Colorado and who had recently traveled to visit her in…(insert organ music here for suspense)…Gettysburg, Pennsylvania. Sarah asked if there was anything she could do to help the mission. Now, that was a different approach. I told her a bit about my nature work at the Gettysburg Battlefield and about David's work at the Cottage. Then I gave her my brief, scrubbed-for-public-consumption description of the primary mission. For a few seconds, Sarah was quiet. Then she said, "I'm in my office and you'll never guess who I'm looking at right now." When I asked who, she said…(more organ music)…"President Eisenhower." She worked for the U.S. congressman from the Gettysburg district and kept a framed picture of Eisenhower on her office wall. There were so many "coincidences" with Sarah that I told her, "Look. I don't know what you can do to help. But I'll talk to David about your offer and get back to you." Unlike the other calls that often left me with a creepy feeling of alarm, Sarah's call made me feel comfortable…and safe.

I presented her offer that evening. David liked what he heard. He suggested I tell her to go to the Gettysburg Battlefield while the mission was going on in California and just stand there to hold the presence of the mission at the battlefield. I called her back the next day and asked if she would be willing to do this. She was thrilled to help. I gave her the projected touch-down date in July and any other details that might help her. As we talked, it was clear to both of us that she would know where on the battlefield to go once she got there. I said it was certainly a quiet job that she was being given, but she replied that she was glad to do whatever we needed. I told her I'd call her once I got back from California and we'd exchange tales of our respective adventures. Sarah gave me hope for Earth's humanity. (Not once did she mention anything about guides!)

Just before leaving for California, I had been seeing in my mind's eye an ivory satin bow, similar to the bows I had used in the garden as part of the summer solstice celebrations. Well, I can take a hint. I asked Pan: Was an ivory bow to be placed at the site? Pan said yes. I was to place a bow when I did the shift to mission go. And I was to use the bow as the focal point for grounding the solstice energy into the site after it was released through the mother ship and into the universe.

To end the session, Pan told me to make sure I did an Energy Cleansing Process for my motel room when I arrived. And finally, I was to have a medical session with Lorpuris the next evening to prepare my two bodies for the time zone changes and trip. The coordination between the two bodies while at Mount Shasta would be especially critical. Throughout my trip, I had to continue splitting my day at both locations—Mount Shasta and the Cottage—so that each body could maintain its strength and energy.

The next day, I met Elizabeth for lunch. Over the previous months, I had talked to her several times about the mission and the mountain. At this lunch, she gave me a gift. She said she didn't know why she chose this thing to give me, but she felt I was to have it. It was a beautiful, small, hand-carved spoon made from cherry wood. I didn't know why I should have the spoon either, but I told her I would take it to the mountain anyway—just in case. Besides, it was small and light.

That night, after the medical session with Lorpuris, the pressure around the mission hit me full force, and I had a good cry. Then I pulled myself together and packed for the trip.

My "site kit" backpack included a box of the Perelandra Rose Essences, the four boxes of Bach Flower Remedies, two boxes of the FES Flower Essences, my soil balancing kit (two boxes), pens, a binder notebook with my work notes and records, a regular tablespoon, a wooden "gun," a feather on a string, a small wooden spoon and a yard of ivory satin ribbon. The kit was weighty—and definitely weird. I decided I would take the backpack on the plane with me. I was not going to let that thing out of my sight.

AND THIS IS WHERE I LEAVE YOU with a cliffhanger. I've written a book titled, *The Mount Shasta Mission.* It describes what happened on the mountain. It includes the complete meeting transcripts with Igor and Pan, plus it reveals who showed up and who didn't. It also includes minute by minute details on everything that happened, including how the wooden "gun," the paho, the small wooden spoon and the yard of ivory satin ribbon were incorporated into the mission.

If you'll remember, for me the Mount Shasta Mission started with the dream where I was telling Peter Caddy I was working in the "Pentagon of the White Brotherhood" and with the naked jogger who insisted I wasn't crazy. From that point on, I kept putting one foot in front of the other and saying "yes" at every key juncture along the way. And look where it led.

I'll give you one final bit of information, and it's what I call "the Mount Shasta Mission spoiler alert":

> *It happened! On July 16, 1985, the government/military leyline gridwork was successfully shifted en masse to its new Aquarian configuration and fully grounded. And the expanded mission remained part of the mission. It was a very big deal—for us, our universe and beyond.*

Chapter 28

Building Foundations

The Cottage Foundation

The Mount Shasta Mission was just the beginning of a new phase of work for the Cottage team. When the leylines were activated, it was as if someone had plugged the system into a big electrical socket in the sky. But the leylines themselves were "in neutral"; that is, they had yet to be programmed beyond the overall intent that this system operate with the Aquarian government/military dynamic and principles. Nothing specific had been introduced into the system.

For nearly a year after the mission, the Cottage team worked to put the finishing touches on the first Aquarian government/military "software program" that was to be seated into the leyline system. I use the term "software program" because this is what was used when the Cottage team described it to me. And like a comprehensive new program, it is massive and it is deep. It serves as the foundation for the Aquarian government principles and, as with any good foundation, the program is solid, strong, broad, clear, clean, inclusive and capable of supporting the movement and variables the future might require. (At least, that's what they tell me.) Thanks to the mission's emphasis on grounding, the program opens every conceivable five-senses door so that no matter how an individual or group addresses their governing setup and principles, there is information, support and assistance for the new structure and direction of that government.

Once the foundation program was built and finalized, it had to be seated into the new leylines. That's when nature girl and her partner jumped into the mix. I worked with Pan to conduct a series of steps that were a continuation of the Mount Shasta Mission work we had done together. I was back in that world and my master class covering how reality works continued. It felt pleasantly familiar.

To prepare for seating the program, I first had to do a little house cleaning and clear out debris from the leyline grid. David told me that the 1985 deactivation of the old Piscean leylines and the activation of the new Aquarian grid created a strong protective reaction throughout various government/military areas where Piscean principles were dominant. This had been expected, and I now needed to clear out the debris caused by that reaction from the Aquarian grid so that it would not function as a "computer virus" in the new foundation program.

My work with the new grid was done from the center of the Perelandra garden where several government/military leyline circuits intersect. This gave me direct access to the system. I don't think that was planned when they shifted the grid. There are intersecting leylines all over the place. I know some people like to make a big deal about this and call these locations "power points," but really, they're quite common. I suspect someone took a look at the new grid after the mission and said, "Hey, look! Some of the circuits intersect under the Perelandra garden! We can take advantage of that."

Sweeping Out the Debris: June 20, 1986

Once I told Pan what David wanted to accomplish, he gave me the following five-step house cleaning process.

> 1. I had to shift the intent of the Mount Shasta Mission coning, thus creating a new coning, because the mission for which the coning was originally set up was completed and any leyline work we did now was beyond the mission's parameters.

By using the mission coning as the foundation for the new one, rather than creating a new four-point coning from "scratch," we maintained a link with the Aquarian grid from the moment of its creation. This would add continuity and stability to the new coning and to any work done from within that coning.

> Note: Conings, coning construction and coning management are essential components of my work and for setting up my partnership properly. For any work I do at the Cottage and at Perelandra, I look at the coning first and ask, "Is this the proper coning for the job?" If needed, I'll adjust the coning right away. Once I activate a coning, I feel I've got my team around me and I'm ready to work.

I opened the original coning, and David stated that its focus was now to be for the programming and maintenance of the Aquarian government/military leyline grid and the ongoing Cottage work with this system. When the intent changed, four members of the original coning were no longer needed: the Deva of the Mount Shasta Mission, the Deva of Mount Shasta (mountain), Universal Light and Lorpuris. And a new member was now required: the Deva of the Aquarian Government/Military Leylines. The new coning was given a name: the Cottage Leyline Coning. (I lobbied for something a little snappier like "Dragon Toes" but got outvoted.) With the statement of the new intent, the shift occurred automatically, and I was now operating from within the Cottage Leyline Coning. (It actually felt a little different.) It looks like this:

> Devic Point: Deva of the Aquarian Government Leylines, Deva of Perelandra
>
> Nature Spirit Point: Pan
>
> White Brotherhood Point: David and Hyperithon
>
> Earth/Cottage human point: yours truly (this includes my higher self and my two-body system)

2. I tested the Perelandra garden to make sure it was balanced and fully prepared for the leyline debris sweep. Nothing was needed and the garden was ready.

3. I activated both of my bodies so that I could be present at the Cottage while simultaneously present in the center of the garden. (I was getting good at this Split Molecular Process thing!)

At the Cottage, the heads of several mission departments had gathered. For this part of the work, they used their focus to recreate the intent and complexities of the Mount Shasta Mission from each of their perspectives. The energy from what they recreated was shifted to Hyperithon who, in turn, infused it into a small golden, energy spacecraft, about a foot in diameter. (Was this the precursor to drones?) The spacecraft was visible to everyone present and gave us something concrete to focus on. Hyperithon placed the infused craft into my hands. I expected it to weigh a good fifty pounds but it was actually light as a feather, as they say. It was smooth to the touch and pleasantly warm. I moved the energy spacecraft from my hands and into my body. Then I shifted it from my Cottage body to my Perelandra body and, finally, into my Perelandra hands. It was still light as a feather, smooth to the touch and pleasantly warm. As instructed, I gently placed the spacecraft on top of Perelandra's crystal/topaz sitting in the center of the garden.

By recreating the intent of the Mount Shasta Mission, they recreated the situation on the mountain that had caused the Piscean reaction to begin with. Only now, the recreation attracted the debris that was enmeshed in the leylines and pulled that debris out of the grid and into the spacecraft. The infused spacecraft acted as a decoy with a big vacuum cleaner attached to it.

For about fifteen or twenty seconds, I watched energy bubble up from the leylines located under the garden's center and quickly disappear into the craft. Once completed, Pan informed me that the debris-laden spacecraft was now throwing off the garden's balance. So I tested for balancing and released three drops of liquid seaweed to Pan for infusing into the garden soil.

4. Using the Energy Cleansing Process, I cleansed the debris from the spacecraft. Pan activated the white cleansing sheet about five feet beneath the craft and extended it

five feet out from the craft. We moved the sheet up to and through the craft, coming to a stop about ten feet above the garden. I could see that we now had the debris in the cleansing sheet. I asked Pan to form a bundle with the sheet, move it out of the Earth's atmosphere and release the contents appropriately and safely. I saw the bundle form and slowly lift up and out of my sight. Then, to be sure, I asked Pan to do a final sweep of the entire leyline system. After about ten seconds, I was told the grid was clear.

5. We had a newly cleansed leyline system and craft. Pan suggested I set up another protection dome, this one over the center of the Perelandra garden where the craft was still sitting. He explained that the garden center was now an open portal to the grid and needed to be protected until we completed the work with the foundation program. As soon as I called for a protection dome, a gold dome of light about ten feet in radius and eight feet tall formed over the garden center. The day's work was completed, and I moved out of the dome leaving the little spacecraft sitting in the center of my garden. (Of course. Isn't this what everyone has sitting in their gardens?)

The Summer Solstice Infusion: June 21, 1986

Pan gave me the next step. I was to infuse the spacecraft and the garden's crystal/topaz with the summer solstice energy in order to prepare them for use during the seating of the foundation program. I don't know if this was taken into consideration for the timing of that step, but on the summer solstice in 1986, we also had a full moon—a lineup that I'm told is pretty rare.

At 6:34 P.M., the moment of the solstice, I stood inside the dome and directed the summer solstice energy to infuse the crystal/topaz. Once this was done, the crystal/topaz in the garden lit up. Within a few seconds, I saw the solstice energy from the crystal/topaz expand to envelop and infuse the small spacecraft sitting on top of it. I requested that the energy in these two objects be held "until further notice." Mission accomplished, I closed down the Cottage Leyline Coning, and David told me he'd let me know what day we would be shifting the foundation program into the grid.

Pan's Plan for Programming the Leylines: July 2, 1986

David said we would be programming the leylines on July 3. On July 2, we had a meeting with Pan to find out what procedure we would be working with the next day. The men provided the details for what they wanted to accomplish and Pan provided the details for how to accomplish it. What struck me during this session was the procedure's meticulous precision. All movement was to be done quietly and carefully. My balance, the Perelandra garden's balance and the program's balance were to be checked a number of times throughout. Every action, thought and focus was to be kept clean, sharp and clear. I had done a lot of precise work for the mission but I felt that this programming procedure took the concept of precision a major step further.

> Pan: *First, let me say that everything is ready for tomorrow's programming. There is no additional preparation that needs to occur prior to July 3. The mission energy and the leylines that were cleared on June 21 have remained clear. There was a possibility of picking up additional debris between the solstice and the programming, but with the dome in place this has not occurred.*
>
> *To explain, the leyline system, although cleansed and protected, is currently in a state of vulnerability until the programming and its activation. The vulnerability was minimized, however, due in part to the fact that the process utilized by David on the mountain was well within the range of five-senses form. This resulted in greater strength for these leylines. Had David's work been carried out on a level beyond five-senses form, we would have had a far different situation facing us now.*
>
> *The steps I'm about to give you are based on the current conditions at Perelandra and on the planet. The fact that you will be initiating the process from the Cottage and completing it at Perelandra will give you*

an advantage regarding the necessary synchronization between the two levels—the Cottage and Earth levels.

Machaelle, you are already experiencing this Perelandra/Cottage connection because of your two-level life and your two-body system. I point this out because had you not had this linkup already in place, you personally would have had to deal with a synchronization issue prior to shifting the foundation program into the Earth's leylines. At Mount Shasta, David dealt effectively with this issue by coming into the Earth level in five-senses form. That took care of his synchronization challenges during the mission.

1. *Before Machaelle opens the coning at the Cottage, the Cottage crystal/topaz should be placed in a prominent position within the room where all of you will be assembled during the procedure.*

2. *Have all present at the Cottage as you begin the process. This includes Machaelle. It will be essential for her to be present at the Cottage and make her shift to Perelandra while, at the same time, shifting the foundation program to Perelandra. That combined action will assure an automatic and full synchronization of the foundation program with the Earth level and its leylines.*

As a side note to Machaelle—If we do not synchronize everything tomorrow, the foundation program and its activation would be as if you were trying to play a 45 rpm record on a 78 rpm player. You can discern the sound and perhaps even identify the song, but its distortion would be terrible. [What Pan is describing here is similar in principle to the synchronization I learned about and experienced when moving from one level to the next during manifestation. I don't know how Pan would explain it today using DVD technology as the metaphor instead of the old vinyl records. Just thinking about that makes my head hurt.]

3. *Activate the Cottage Leyline Coning from the Cottage and include everyone who is present in the coning.*

  3A. *Check the coning's balance once everyone is included.*

  3B. *Check everyone's individual balance.*

This will give you the balance of the parts as well as the balance of the whole.

4. *David, hand the entire foundation program as an energy package to Machaelle while she is present at the Cottage.*

She should not be physically present in the Perelandra garden at this point. It is essential that her focus be fully at the Cottage.

4A. *Once she has custody of the energy package—which can be verified by both Hyperithon and myself—her balance should be checked by Lorpuris for any needed essences.*

Her attention should be fully on that which she has in her custody and not diverted to an additional task such as testing for balance.

David: *Lorpuris will be present and ready to assist her.*
Pan: *Good.*

5. Pan: *Machaelle, do a two-body Split Molecular Process. This will activate your Perelandra body.*

5A. *Move slowly and as quietly as possible to the center of the Perelandra garden.*

At this point, you will be physically present on both levels simultaneously. However, you will need to keep your focus primarily at the Cottage and on the foundation program. Once in the center of the garden, take a moment at the Cottage to re-establish full focus on the foundation program you are holding. (David, you may wish to symbolize or name the foundation program for her so that she can use that for re-focusing. This would simplify the process for her.)

6. *Lorpuris, link with Machaelle's Perelandra body before the foundation program shift and do a balance check on her there.*

This will assure her protection when she receives the program into the Perelandra body.

7. *Machaelle, shift the program, as you did the different Mount Shasta Mission energies—first into and through your Cottage body system and then move the program package into your Perelandra body.*

This movement will also assure the automatic synchronization of the program with Earth's leylines.

7A. *Lorpuris, check Machaelle's Perelandra balance again once she has shifted the program and is holding it within her Perelandra body.*

8. *At this point, with the foundation program stabilized within her, Machaelle is to request that the protection dome be released.*

All she need do is state the request. That will indicate to us that she is ready and we will immediately release the dome. She need do nothing else.

9. *Machaelle, when everyone is ready, infuse the foundation program, thus releasing it from your personal custody, into the interior of the golden spacecraft currently sitting within and on the crystal/topaz in the center of the Perelandra garden.*

To infuse the program, you need only to breathe the program energy from within yourself into the craft interior. Since it will be better that this part of the process be as unencumbered as possible, only I will assist to assure complete and full transference.

10. *Once complete, I will verify the fusion and report that to David through Machaelle. Hyperithon will be able to verify the fusion from the Cottage level, as well. As soon as she has completed the transfer and it has been verified, we need to stop for another balance check for her.*

The seating and activation of the foundation program into the leyline system will take place from the spacecraft sitting in the Perelandra garden.

11. *Machaelle, once the craft interior has been infused with the foundation program energy and your balance has been checked, you will add an additional infusion of the crystal/topaz energy that is also holding the summer solstice energy.*

To do this, use the energy from the crystal/topaz at Perelandra, not the Cottage. However, everyone will see a change in the crystal/topaz at the Cottage when you finish this step.

12. *Machaelle, call for the release of the craft from the crystal/topaz and "allow" it to expand to the size of the outer-most ring of the Perelandra garden. The craft will then be 100 feet in diameter.*

12A. *Check the balance of the garden biosphere using both essences and soil balancers.*

Once this is accomplished and the craft is stabilized into its position in the garden (touching the ground fully), you will be ready for the program seating and activation.

It is my understanding that a number of those who will be present at the Cottage also wish to be present at Perelandra for the seating and activation.

David: *That's true. There are also a few who wish to be present solely at Perelandra for this, but I haven't discussed it with Machaelle yet.*

Pan: *It is my opinion that there should be complete freedom for whoever wishes to be present at Perelandra. I realize that this is Machaelle's decision, but their role as witnesses would greatly benefit the activation, especially this particular activation.*

Machaelle: *I have no issue about who is present. I wouldn't mind the company at that end. As long as they don't step on me or scare the bejeebers out of me.*

David [laughing]: *You'll be safe.*

13. Pan: *David, you will call for the release of the new foundation program from the ship and its activation by making a statement, the same procedure you used to call for the leyline shift at Mount Shasta.*

Do this after everyone is in position at the Cottage and Perelandra. Once you make the statement, the program energy from the craft interior will release and move instantaneously into and throughout the full government/military grid. As you had thousands of craft in position to assist in the creation of the new grid at Mount Shasta, we of nature will be present throughout the entire leyline system to assure the seating and activation of the new foundation program. In Earth time, this should take no longer than thirty seconds.

13A. *I will inform Machaelle of its completion, and you may begin your verification and checks at any time after that. The activation of the program should register on all appropriate levels the moment this step is complete. At that time, you will see another change in the crystal/topaz at the Cottage.*

14. *Machaelle, check the balance of the garden environment again just to be sure it held during the seating and activation of the foundation program.*

14A. *Connect with the Overlighting Deva of Planet Earth and check the balance of the planet using essences and soil balancing.*

What I am referring to is that part of the planet's balance that is directly linked to the new government/military leylines. Do not attempt a full environmental balance of the planet. Although that can be done, the planet would only stabilize for a second before shifting back to imbalance due to the prevalent consciousness and habits of the planet's inhabitants. Instead, focus on the balance that pertains only to the government/military leylines. You need not do a planetary check of the grid prior to this time because that is what we have already verified as clear and ready to go. The check we are discussing is to verify that everything held after the activation. If not, we can re-balance it immediately. Leyline balance will greatly assist the new foundation program and will allow the program's impulses to "go right to work" without a lag time.

15. *Machaelle, after step 14 is complete, call for the craft energy to disperse so that it will no longer be present at Perelandra.*

16. *Lastly, the Perelandra visitors will need to shift their focus to the Cottage to remove themselves from the Perelandra level and the garden.*

17. *Close the coning.*

The Cottage crystal/topaz will maintain its light to signify full activation of the leyline system. I recommend that it be placed in David's office and remain there for however long he wishes. The quality of light within the Cottage crystal/topaz will enable David to monitor the stabilization and power of the leyline system and any programming that it contains. This pertains to the foundation programming and any future "update" programming.

David: *Do you have any suggestions regarding the timing for tomorrow?*

Pan: *From the standpoint of the planet, translated into linear time, I suggest the process begin at 8:32 P.M. tomorrow night. I also suggest the program's seating and activation occur no later than 10:10 P.M.*

David: *Thank you. You seem to have covered everything.*

July 3, 1986

As you might imagine, this was an important moment for the Cottage. (It was a nerve-wracking moment for me.) Standing with David to witness what was about to happen were eleven Mount Shasta Mission leaders, along with Hyperithon, Lorpuris and fifteen other members from the White Brotherhood, including St. Germain. I was more than a little nervous because so much was riding on getting that program safely to Perelandra and installed into the leylines. I had visions of sneezing or dropping the program or tipping it over and having all its bytes fall out in a big pile at my feet. In my pocket, I had a cheat sheet with the steps I was to take. That morning, as if to announce this was the day and the leyline programming was on, David and Hyperithon moved the Cottage crystal/topaz into place in the living room were everyone would be gathered.

Precisely at 8:32 P.M., I opened the coning and included everyone standing with me at the Cottage individually and as a group. I checked the coning's balance while Lorpuris checked the others for balance. All tested clear.

I then proceeded to do everything as laid out by Pan the day before. When I had to make a move, I made sure I made it slowly and carefully. When I had to shift my focus, I checked to make sure my focus was fully on target before moving on to the next step or, in some cases, the next breath.

When David shifted the foundation program to me as an energy package, he announced the name of the program for the first time: *Overlord*. This was the focal point we were all to use during the procedure. I understood that he was using the name of the operation he had led for the Normandy invasion during World War II, and I thought, "Well, that's interesting." However, when he made the announcement, the others in the room broke out in applause—enthusiastic applause. Now I was lost and knew I didn't understand the true significance behind naming the program *Overlord*. But it didn't seem like the right time to stop the proceedings and ask for clarification. I didn't mind being the dumb one in the room and I still had work to do.

All the shifts, my movements and my focus changes went well, thank god. When I infused the energy from the crystal/topaz into the spacecraft, I could tell that the grounding dynamics of the summer solstice had become a permanent part of *Overlord.* With this, the craft expanded to the larger size, just as Pan had described. It now sat on the entire garden, and once again, I found myself enveloped in the energy of a spacecraft. It was becoming old hat for me, and I didn't experience any of the discomfort I had felt on the mountain the first time I found myself in the mother ship.

At this point in the proceedings, I noticed about twenty-five people standing in a circle around me in the Perelandra garden, watching as I worked. Their focus felt gentle and supportive. They were a bit wispy in appearance so I was unable to recognize anyone, but they all felt friendly. I said "hello," and went on with the work. Their presence was comforting.

When it was time for David to call for the release of the program to the leylines, he said simply,

I call for the release, seating and activation of Overlord
to the new government/military leyline system
in the name of peace.

I felt a dramatic motion in the air and saw a thick layer of energy quickly drop from the craft and disappear into the soil. The ground beneath my feet moved slightly. I assumed I was feeling the program seating into the leyline circuits. Either that, or I was experiencing my first earthquake. And that's when the crystal/topaz at the Cottage lit up.

We waited quietly for about thirty seconds, and then Pan let us know the seating and activation were complete. It seemed like a perfect moment for some kind of celebration to break out but, instead, Hyperithon immediately got down to business and started receiving a series of verifications and checks. Once completed, he confirmed that *Overlord* had seated successfully and was fully activated in the leylines. Lorpuris checked my balance and everything again tested clear.

The work with the spacecraft was now completed. I directed my attention to Pan and called for the craft to disperse. And that's exactly what it did. Millions of tiny flecks of gold light shot up from the garden and floated out into the night sky. I watched this beautiful and dramatic sight for a few minutes, then did a balance check for the garden. All tested clear.

Finally, I connected with the Overlighting Deva of Planet Earth and, along with Pan, checked the balance of the full government/military leyline system and the planet's environment that the system impacts. The planet's soil needed three drops of liquid seaweed. I placed the drops in a spoon and held it out for Pan to shift to wherever it was needed. This took ten seconds. And with that, the crystal/topaz at the Cottage became brighter.

Overlord was seated and my work was done. I thanked everyone who was present in the garden and told them I'd see them shortly back at the Cottage. (What else do you say at such moments? I was just happy they weren't expecting me to serve beer and pretzels.) Within a few moments, I could no longer see or feel anyone around me, so I closed the coning. It was 9:43 P.M. We had gotten everything done well before the 10:10 P.M. deadline.

By the time I got back to the Cottage, the celebration had commenced. After formally meeting the people who were at Perelandra and sharing what we had each just experienced in the garden, I asked about the name *Overlord*. David wanted to use this name because of what it meant to him personally and what it signified historically. But in order for the name to be used for the foundation program, the Cottage team first had to flip all the coins and shift the original Operation Overlord to its higher intent and purpose. The applause was not just out of respect for Operation Overlord and what it accomplished in World War II, but also for the fact that now its coins had been flipped, and the higher intent and purpose for that operation, an operation that had turned the tide for us all in 1944, now resonated throughout the universe and beyond.

The Globe

On March 6, 1987, I worked with nature to activate the Globe, a twelve-foot in diameter globe of our planet that was specially designed for the Cottage team. It presently resides in its own room at the Cottage, which we've cleverly named "the Globe Room." Its operation and capabilities have expanded since 1987, and currently two sides of the room contain long consoles filled with lines of red and black buttons and grey levers. The planet's continents, countries and topography are delineated in remarkable detail. But when certain buttons are pressed on the console, the government/military leyline system appears as it is laid out on and in our planet. It's quite impressive. With other buttons, they can highlight specific elements and aspects of the system. The levers highlight different active non-government/military leylines (such as the science and technology grid) and provide the Cottage leylines with more context. The team can see a larger picture. And then for an even larger picture, there are levers that highlight corresponding government/military leyline systems on other planetary levels (and beyond). They all relate to and impact one another. It looks like a massive macramé project in space.

The leylines move information in two directions: from the Cottage to Earth (and beyond) and from Earth (and beyond) to the Cottage. The Cottage team downloads and seats information into the system in response to our current actions and needs. The Globe's leylines are never static. In fact, they're quite active. Different circuits light up, different colors appear, and they will light up in ways that show what combination of circuits have been activated by a particular situation. Using this technology, the Cottage team can identify what is happening in the arena of government and military well before it becomes a crisis, oftentimes before it is recognized as a problem by those involved, and provide an array of options to be considered for resolving the situation. It's not unusual for members of David's team who live outside the Cottage to arrive just to observe what is happening with the Globe's leylines. More often than not, if I'm looking for someone at the Cottage, I'll find him in the Globe Room watching circuits.

There isn't a separate grid for nature because nature, its environmental development and its evolution are part of the science and technology grid. What is important for me and my work is that nature is part of all the grids. Nature provides the matter, means and action needed for the grids to exist. This gives me automatic access to any grid, even though my focus is primarily on the Cottage grid. Any balancing and stabilizing I might need to do with the Cottage grid is done from the Globe Room rather than from the Perelandra garden. It gives me more flexibility, and I do not have a spacecraft sitting on my zucchini plants.

A Note on Current Politics

I am writing this in June 2018. With all the careful work that was done for the Mount Shasta Mission and the programming of the new leyline grid, I think a major question is left hanging in the air: How the hell did we end up with Donald Trump as president? At first blush, I might say, "Hey, these snappy-dappy leylines aren't working!" But I would be wrong about that.

So why *are* we left to deal with Trump? First of all, the Cottage team did not choose Trump. Nor do they choose anyone in any election. Those choices belong to us and us alone. (Remember that White Brotherhood rule about not interfering with our free will.) Once a choice is made—whether by the citizens or as a result of outside intrusion—the Cottage teams deal with the positive and negative consequences. They provide us with what is needed for our movement forward in the direction of the Aquarian principles while taking all the variables into consideration. So first, it behooves us to express our free will and vote intelligently. (And yes, I do vote.)

David has said that transitions can be messy, even ugly. I think it's been borne out historically that when faced with change, Americans tend to first burn down the house and then eventually build the new out of the ashes. Subtlety doesn't seem to be our strong suit. (Winston Churchill once said, "Americans will always do the right thing—after exhausting all the alternatives.") Trump is an exceptional house burner. Destruction doesn't seem to bother him, so he careens around destroying whatever he can get his hands on. For most people, watching him crash about, leaving everything and everyone burning in his path, has been painful. So many people's lives have been damaged. So much environmental havoc has been wreaked.

This leads to the second major question: How the hell do we get out of this mess? I've thought about this a lot. When I've talked about it at the Cottage, they always tell me Trump is doing a fine job digging his own hole and self-destructing. Have a little patience. But I need more than that. For one thing, I don't think he's self-destructing fast enough. Finally, it hit me. Trump and the actions taken by his people may actually *facilitate* us as we seek to move toward the new Aquarian government/military structures. *He may force us to move faster.* By the time he's finished bulldozing through everything, we may find ourselves further down the road than we thought was possible. And once we get through this transition and look back, we may see that he has shortened our messy, ugly time.

As I've said, his election was not planned by the Cottage team, but that doesn't mean there isn't a silk purse to be made out of his sow's ear mess. Lousy coins can be flipped because there is always a positive underside. Trump's actions (and those of leaders like him) are full-bore destructive. He is so over-the-top outrageous and such a loose cannon that he's quickly burning the house down and forcing many, including the traditionally non-engaged folks, to think, to act, to organize and to unite.

I lived through the Civil Rights and anti-war movements in the 1960s and early 1970s. It was an extremely active time. But I have never seen the level of citizen activism I'm seeing now. And if we look at it carefully, this is activism leading to change that reflects Aquarian principles—equality, cooperation and teamwork. It's happening all around us—the huge Women's March after Trump's (tiny) inauguration, the many women who said they've had it with lousy politicians and are running for public office (and winning), the #MeToo Movement and #TimesUp Movement announcing that women and their bodies are not public property, the Parkland kids and the other teenage shooting victims fearlessly rising up and taking on gun violence and the NRA, the public's outrage and its quick multifaceted response around the plight of immigrants and their children, and the long overdue uptick in voting. It's true that some folks are stomping around and noisily holding on to the old Piscean ways with all their might. But every time the "Pisceans" try to destroy or shut something down, I'm seeing an even stronger Aquarian response.

So the simple answer for getting through this mess is to look for, align ourselves to and, when inspired, create action and change that reflect *equality, cooperation and teamwork.* The rest is debris. It may be destructive, cruel and inhumane, but it's still debris. It's not an easy or even graceful way to get through a transition and it takes constant vigilance, courage and action. But this is how we can align to the new government/military leylines. And this is how we open ourselves to the information and assistance that is being provided by the Cottage. When we do that, we will feel the wind at our backs as we move forward.

Perelandra's Foundation

Almost from the moment I arrived at the Cottage, the men said, "You don't realize how lucky you are to be so aware of these things before you die." They were referring to my two-level life and what I was learning from nature. Maybe they wouldn't say this to me daily, but I'd hear those words at least once every few days. At first I'd respond, "Yea, yea. Easy for you to say." (As I bounced off the walls and blew around the room in a fit of shatterings and spasms.) I didn't think much about what they were saying because I assumed they were talking about the limitations of their personal awareness prior to *their* deaths. There was always a wistful touch in their voices and I tended to re-translate their statement to, "Think of what we could have accomplished had we known about life's larger picture earlier."

No matter how much I tried to blow them off, they continued to say these words to me—for years. As I've moved through my thirty-six years (and counting) at the Cottage, I've gone through a gradual evolution around their statement. I'm now seventy-three years old and I have to admit they were right. (But I'm not going to tell them that!) The surprising revelation for me is that the sentence "You don't realize how lucky you are to be aware of these things before you die" is the underlying driver behind Perelandra's post-Mount Shasta development and why I decided to write *Pivot.*

ONCE THE MOUNT SHASTA MISSION was finished, I felt lost. I missed the meetings and the discussions about leylines and spacecraft and feathers on a string. I missed the beauty of the mountain and the quiet work my nature partner and I had done there together. As weird as all those things had seemed at the time, not having them as part of my day now felt even weirder. In an effort to get my bearings, I turned my focus to the garden but, in my head, I was still floating around unmoored.

The team encouraged me to start developing Perelandra's foundation so that the work I was doing with nature could be made available to all who wanted it. I would still keep my daily schedule—working at Perelandra until the early evening and then returning to the Cottage until the next morning—but my primary focus would be on developing Perelandra. They would let me know whenever they needed my services as the in-house nature girl (like when they needed to download *Overlord* into the leylines). But they made it clear that it was important I concentrate on Perelandra and continue my work there. They also made it clear that they wanted to hear about what I was doing and, with this, the daily debriefings resumed. Even though I decided to take this on, I have to admit that in 1985, I had no idea what creating Perelandra's foundation would entail. But I had a starting point—the *Perelandra Garden Workbook.*

In August, I dug out the list of chapters I had written down while we were still in the midst of the Mount Shasta Mission, opened the coning that I set up especially for that book and began writing. In less than five months, I had broken down and written the entire process nature and I went through each year to create and maintain the Perelandra garden. My intent was to encourage people to use the *Workbook* as a guideline for creating their own garden and establishing their own partnership with nature.

While writing that fall and winter, several things occurred that pushed me in a trajectory that I would stay on for the next thirty-five years whenever I was working on a book.

First, an editor from a small independent publishing house contacted me and said they were interested in carrying *Behaving.* They would redesign the book, copyedit the text (which was needed) and distribute it more widely. At the time, saying yes seemed like the right thing to do for *Behaving.* I signed a contract and they went to work sprucing up the book. Their book designer was a fellow named Jim Brisson, and he laid out *Behaving*'s pages and photos in a way that made the book not only more attractive but also more readable.

I ran into a snag when the editors got hold of the text. This publishing house carried a lot of New Age books and they wanted to add more New Agey language to my text. I resisted. But their push for one change shook me out of my reluctant willingness to compromise and made me take a firm, immovable stand. In *Behaving,* there is a section titled "What's This Crap about Fairies?" The section title page includes a photo of one of the Meyers' cows. Her expression said it all. You could imagine her staring skeptically at someone and saying, "Hey, what's this crap about fairies?" I received letters from people telling me how much they loved that page and that they had cut it out of the book and framed it.

My new publisher didn't love that page. It was too sharp, too harsh, too rough. Never mind it was accurate. It wasn't New Agey. They wanted to change the title to "What's This Malarky about Fairies?" That cow did not look like she was the type to utter the word "malarky." The editors tried to convince me that their way was better by telling me that they asked their printers what *they* thought of the page. The consensus was that using the word "crap" made it seem like I was a lousy writer who just didn't know a better way to say it. (Thank you for the insult.) I still said no. The editors said they'd have to get back to me on this.

About a month after that kerfuffle, they still hadn't gotten back to me. That's when I learned that the company was filing for bankruptcy. (I guess I could make a false claim and say, "You shouldn't have messed with me, people." In actuality, the company went bust because of their own poor business decisions and their inter-office fights. Welcome to the New Age.) I jumped into a "protect *Behaving* mode" and let it be known that I wanted my contract returned with a letter stating that I was no longer bound by said contract. I also wanted everything pertaining to *Behaving* mailed to me. It took three months to navigate through their insanity but, eventually, they complied with everything I wanted. I now had a beautifully laid out book with text that had been professionally copyedited. I just needed to get it printed.

My reward for persevering and coming out of this somewhat unpleasant experience was Jim Brisson and Beverly the copyeditor. Together we became the Perelandra publishing team. (A couple of years later Beverly retired from the publishing world and I had to find someone to pick up the mantle. Jim steered me to Elizabeth McHale and we've been a team for over thirty years.) We put the final touches on *Behaving* and Jim helped me find a printer. *Behaving's* second edition proudly included the photo of the cow with the title, "What's This Crap about Fairies?"

I now had a bad taste in my mouth about publishing houses. I did not want to deal with these people (they were a waste of my time), and I especially did not want them trying to overlay their uninformed opinions on my books. I wanted to present my work cleanly. And I didn't want some publishing house sitting between me and the reader.

Enter the second big event. That December, Ventura Publisher, the first desktop publishing program, was announced. I can't tell you how much the newspaper article about that new program excited me. It wasn't just that I immediately saw desktop publishing as the way to circumvent my publishing challenges. I also saw it as a development that would revolutionize the publishing industry altogether. It meant freedom. No longer would information and stories be blocked by faceless editors and their pink rejection slips. Now people who weren't established big-time authors could say what they needed to say, whether good or bad, and publish it themselves without being forced under the thumb of a publishing house intent on making content decisions driven by questionable marketing practices. And with Ventura, small town residents who had lost their only newspaper could easily and inexpensively launch a new paper that carried the local news that was important to them. Everything inside me screamed "Yes!" (Picture a fist pump.) I ordered Ventura Publisher right away and, in the process, became part of the first wave of desktop publishers.

There was just a minor glitch. I had to learn about book publishing and how to use Ventura Publisher. From the beginning, Jim Brisson was a remarkably generous man when it came to sharing what he knows. To get started with Ventura, he taught me about page layout and book design. I told him what I wanted to do with the *Perelandra Garden Workbook* and he said, "Let's do it." He explained the importance of line length and spacing, right and left page balance and vertical justification. He gave me the publishing rules and then told me how to break them. He introduced me to scholar's columns, a handy catch-all column for all kinds of tidbits and information. He designed the *Workbook*'s right and left facing pages and then sent the specs that I needed for setting up those pages in Ventura.

Here's where Jim had more faith in my ability than I thought I deserved. He told me he decided to design the pages according to the best presentation for my book and see how much I was able to translate into Ventura. It was a complex book with lots of instructions and steps, and I needed a lot of options for laying out the pages. I took on his design as a challenge. After a couple of weeks of trial and error and some well-placed curses and screams, I had set up the facing master pages and was ready to pour in the book's text, chapter by chapter.

As streamlined and speedy as working with Ventura felt at the time, it still had some new-program clunkiness in certain areas. For example, to insert a left quote mark, I had to enter a multi-digit HTML code. And the code for that quote mark was different from the code for the right quote. There were HTML codes for every "special" character other than periods and commas. That slowed things down a little. But prior to Ventura, I had been preparing material for public consumption using the word processor Wordstar for the body text and hand-applied stick-on letters for headings and titles. Compared to that, Ventura and its HTML codes were a *major* leap forward.

And then there was Chapter 18. This was my longest chapter in the *Workbook*, running thirty-six pages. Following the procedure I had used for the previous chapters, I poured the text from Wordstar into Ventura, inserted all the layout refinements, HTML codes and spacing, then hit "Save." The screen went blank. My thirty-six pages were floating around somewhere in cyberspace. I stared at the screen in disbelief for a few minutes. Finally I stood up, stomped around a bit and got a cup of coffee. I returned to the office and repeated the work I had just done on Chapter 18. I hit "Save," and the chapter disappeared again. When it happened a third time, I gave up and called Xerox, the company that sold Ventura. A wonderfully pleasant woman told me that Ventura could not save a thirty-six page file. It was too big. (Now you tell me.) I would need to split the chapter. She let me know that they were coming out with an update for Ventura shortly and recommended I get that update. (No kidding.)

Boy, looking back now I realize just how far we've come with desktop publishing. A few years after publishing the *Workbook*, Jim let me know that the printing industry standard had changed and printers preferred working with a different desktop publishing program—Quark. I figured if I didn't fight the industry, I'd end up with a better printing job. (A happy printer is a good printer.) I learned the new desktop publishing program and fell in love with it. No more HTML codes. More flexibility. They changed the industry standard again a few years back but still were happy to work with Quark files, so I haven't budged from my beloved Quark.

AFTER THE *WORKBOOK* WAS SENT to the printer, I turned my attention to the garden and its new season. I found out that there was a second essence set I could produce—the Perelandra Garden Essences. These tinctures would be produced from the garden's vegetable and flower plants. A year later, nature let me know that there was another set of essences I could produce from the rose ring—the Perelandra Rose II Essences.

What drove me to say yes every time nature informed me about a new set of essences were the descriptions Pan gave me about what the essences would address. Once I understood what they would give us, I couldn't say no. I couldn't say, "Sorry. I don't have time to produce any new essences. I need to practice my bowling skills."

> The first Rose set, the one I took to Mount Shasta, provides support as we proceed through our normal evolutionary process and address new situations, learning curves, challenges and ideas. These essences also facilitate our periods of growth.
>
> The new Rose II essences support us during a deep expansion experience when we are required to function in new ways, and with patterns and rhythms yet to be experienced.
>
> The Garden Essences balance and repair our body's electrical circuits that are needed to address the issues that we face in our day-to-day life in today's world.

I became a finely tuned essence production expert. Initially, I produced five gallons of tincture, which raises the question: Why in the world did I produce five gallons when a gallon or two would have lasted several years? The quick answer: I was busy and my time was pressed. I was looking at the long picture. I didn't want to make the same tinctures over and over. I already knew that taking essences as a tincture rather than as a concentrate (when the tincture is diluted) was safe because I had been taking the undiluted Rose tinctures since first producing them. It was easier and more time-efficient to bottle the essences as tinctures than to go through the extra steps needed to dilute them into concentrates. So for the first two years, a half-ounce of tincture went into a half-ounce bottle of Perelandra essence. When I got some bottle-filling help, we started bottling the essences as concentrates. I needed to add just a few drops of tincture (Pan told me how many drops were needed) to the preservative solution to make a half-ounce of essence concentrate. Now five gallons of tincture could last maybe twenty years. Sigh.

With each new set of essences, bottles and droppers needed to be bought, labels needed to be made, information needed to be written, box wrappers needed to be designed and boxes needed to be constructed. You know what the worst part of all this was? Deciding the colors for each set's box. I wanted the sets to have their own color so that they could be easily discerned when sitting next to one another. And I didn't want the colors to clash. I felt that over time that would annoy the customer when looking at the boxes sitting together. (Well, it would annoy me.) And they couldn't look "too feminine." I didn't think men would purchase something that looked like a tampon box.

AS *BEHAVING* CONTINUED to sell, I was able to build a mailing list. Actually, my list was a collection of carefully alphabetized 3x5 cards. Every year I sent out a catalog announcing old and new products. (The first year's catalog was on a single sheet of paper.) So when people found out about the Perelandra Essences, they ordered them. That may sound like a classic "duh" statement, something that business school graduates would point to and say, "Yes, dummy. Selling your products should be your goal!" I was always surprised when my work was well received, but the success of the essences also tended to annoy me. I'd fill, label and box thirty sets, stack them on the shelf and think, "There. That ought to last a month or two." In just a few days I'd be down to a couple of boxes and think, "What the hell?" (Success really is a bitch.)

On top of that, people began pressing me to give a workshop on how to work with essences. Well, that seemed reasonable. How could I say no to that? I knew that the essences were an amazing health aid and, if I could help people tap into what the essences could give them, I wanted to do that.

I gave my first workshop at Perelandra in the spring of 1987. We set up chairs under the trees. It was a warm day but we had a nice breeze. It was very pleasant. I think about thirty people attended, which also surprised me. (I have got to be the most astonished teacher and business person who ever existed.) But the other thing that amazed me was the amount of information I had stored in my head that I could give these people that day. It was similar to being told to create an office with a filing cabinet and then asking, "What am I going to put in that filing cabinet?" Throughout the years I had worked with Pan to develop numerous essence processes to better address different health issues. Until this first workshop, I had no idea how much we had developed. It was unavoidable: Another book was staring me in the face. That summer I started writing *Flower Essences: Reordering Our Understanding and Approach to Illness and Health.*

IN 1988, I COULD NO LONGER do the nature work and the business by myself. My first staffer was Clarence. Initially he handled all the business-related stuff. After about ten years, he got "promoted" to the job he really wanted—garden assistant and chief Perelandra putterer.

At this point, things developed rapidly. Phyllis Atwater, a writer who had read and loved *Behaving,* contacted me and asked for an interview. She wanted to write several articles and help get Perelandra known. I knew I could use some help in that department and agreed to meet with her. She wrote three excellent articles and got them published in three very different types of publications. One article was published in *Acres U.S.A.*, a well-established newspaper that carried alternative farming information. I received letters from farmers saying things like, "I've been a farmer for over thirty years and have always felt the presence of those nature spirits. But I didn't know how to describe what I was sensing and I was too embarrassed to try. I didn't have the words until reading about what you are doing. Thank you." I still treasure those farmers' comments and stories.

Phyllis' efforts blasted Perelandra open and within a little over a week after the articles ran, our orders more than doubled. One would think that this would be a moment of blissful celebration. But exploding a business to that degree in that short period of time meant that I needed to quickly improve the business structure I had already established to handle the old level of activity. Everything needed to be upgraded or enlarged, even the waste baskets.

Now twice the amount of trash was being generated. Clarence no longer had the time for the daily trip to town to take the packages to the Sherwin Williams Paint Store for UPS pickup. (You read that right. The UPS desk was in a paint store.) We made arrangements for UPS to come to Perelandra each day for our pickup. I also needed to add more staff. We became a small business with two staffers, then three, then four and so on.

People started requesting more workshops. This wasn't an easy development to say yes to because I'm one of those people who goes through stage fright hell for about two weeks prior to the event. I'm totally convinced that I'll stand before a group of eager listeners and go blank. I would have no words to say. But I found that once I start talking, I'm fine. Then it's a matter of shutting me up. In 1989, I put together a summer workshop series: Nature (introduction), Flower Essences, Gardening with Nature, the Mundane-Fantastic Workshop (about my Cottage life), Mount Shasta Mission and an Open House. The schedule was daunting but, if I didn't have to spend time working in the business, it was doable.

SIX DAYS PRIOR to our first open house, I received a phone call from Dorothy's husband letting me know that my mother was dying of cancer. After some urging from her husband, Dorothy spoke to me during that call. (I suspect he had insisted she speak to me and that's why I got the call.) I couldn't tell if she was sober because she really sounded like a person who was dying. Her voice was flat and her words mumbled. She couldn't hold a focus and her sentences tended to ramble. I told her that I had a big open house scheduled in a few days and would come see her the day after the open house. I don't think she believed me about the open house or that I would come see her. But it seemed like the right thing for me to do. I never did get to see her one last time. She died three days after that phone call.

I did the Post-Death Process for her and then spent the next few days thinking about her life as my mother and my life as her daughter. I had often wondered if she would say something or make some kind of gesture at the very end of her life that would somehow demonstrate that she actually cared about me. If ever there was going to be a time, I figured that would be it. But she made no such statement and no such gesture. To be fair, I made no such statement or gesture to her. She died and that was it. There was no memorial service or funeral. She was cremated and I have no idea where her ashes were spread.

THAT SAME YEAR, Peter Tompkins, co-author of *The Secret Life of Plants*, contacted me and asked to interview me for his new book, *Secrets of the Soil*. My time with Phyllis had been such a success that I said yes to Peter Tompkins. We spent the afternoon together. Instead of interviewing me about Perelandra, he talked about himself and hit me with a long list of conspiracy theories that he had collected over the years. I thought the whole afternoon was weird. But he came to the Gardening with Nature workshop, which gave him enough information to include Perelandra in his new book. I ended up as chapter 23 in *Secrets of the Soil*. It was hard to get all puffed up about being included in a famous author's book because there were so many errors and misstatements in my chapter. He even got my name wrong.

But a few months after the book came out, I got a handwritten letter that began, "Dear Chapter 23." The writer then explained that he was Chapter 10 in that book and that he had read the chapter on Perelandra and was most intrigued. Could we talk? Along with his charming letter, he included a sheet listing his many scientific accomplishments (including the fact that he had discovered Streptomycin, the first effective treatment for tuberculosis), his international medals and his awards. The list took up the entire sheet. Albert Schatz (Chapter 10) definitely caught my attention.

This was the start of a friendship that lasted seven years. By the time we met, Albert was retired and in his late sixties. He was spending his time exploring alternative science and health practices. He was one of funniest people I have ever met, and he had a beautifully brilliant and creative mind. I loved corresponding and discussing my work with him. He was enthusiastically supportive. He urged me to remain independent so that outside corporate funding and government agencies would not force me to compromise my work. Keep it clean.

He also answered two major questions that had weighed on me for years: Would it be helpful to go to college and get a degree in soil science? Would more people take my work seriously? Albert was the perfect person to ask. He was a recognized microbiology and soil scientist, and he had been a professor of Science Education at Temple University for eleven years. His answers to both questions were succinct: "No." He said that getting a degree would be a waste of my time and, in the end, I'd have to forget most of the information I had been taught. I needed to continue as I was.

Over our seven years, Albert and I had an ongoing argument that would morph into a spirited debate, only to morph back into an argument. He felt (strongly) that I should press my work onto key scientists and educators. I needed to publish in recognized scientific journals. They *needed* to hear about co-creative science. How were they going to hear about it if I didn't get the information out to them? On the surface, that seemed like a reasonable and logical approach for me to take. But I countered by saying it would be an utter waste of my time. It was my experience that those who were open to my work somehow found me on their own. (Like you, Albert.) There was the issue of an individual's timing involved here, and the only person who could break down barriers caused by timing was the person himself. Certainly not me. It would be a fool's errand. Besides, I didn't speak their language (they like to use all those Latin words), and they could and would use stupid stuff to make mincemeat out of me in five minutes. They would have to find their way to me on their own. Albert and I never arrived at a resolution or even a compromise about this. I still maintain that my side of the debate was the winner.

Not long after we met, Albert called and, like any good teacher, gave me an assignment. "Machaelle, you *have* to get nature to define some words!" He said he had a feeling that when nature uses these words, it didn't mean the same as when we use them. He then gave me a list to present to nature: form, nature, devas and nature spirits, consciousness, soul, basic sensory system perception, energy, reality, perceived reality, balance, life vitality, grounding, intent and intuition. I didn't know what nature would say, but I took the assignment on as a challenge. And as Albert suspected, nature's understanding and use of these words turned out to be quite different from ours. These definitions have become an important component in Perelandra's foundation.

Let's take the word "reality" and I'll show you what I mean. According to the Chambers Dictionary, reality is "the state or fact of being real. It is that which is real and not imaginary." Here's what nature means when it uses the word "reality":

> *From our perspective, reality refers to all levels and dimensions of life experience within form and beyond form. Reality does not depend on an individual's perception of it in order to exist. We call an individual's perception of reality his "perceived reality." Any life system that was created in form (which occurred at the moment of the Big Bang) has inherent in it all dimensions and levels that exist both within five-senses form and beyond. How we relate to an individual or object depends on our present ability to enfold and envelop an individual's many levels. The scope within which one exists, the reality of one's existence, is truly beyond form, beyond description. If one understands that the evolutionary force that moves all life systems forward is endless—beyond time—then one must also consider that it is the continuous discovery of these vast levels inherent in all life systems that creates that evolutionary momentum. Since this dynamic is beyond time as expressed on any form level or dimension, reality is endless.*

IN 1990, I KEPT FEELING that I needed to expand the four-point coning I had been working in to one that would more accurately reflect my current life. It was still a four-point coning, but the number of members for each point increased.

My original four-point coning looked like this:

> Devic point: Deva of Perelandra, Deva of the Perelandra garden
>
> Add to this the deva of the project or focus I was working on.

Nature Spirit point: the nature spirit level connected with whatever I was working on

White Brotherhood point: David and Hyperithon

My higher self

Here's the new "MSW Foundation Coning":

DEVIC POINT

DEVA OF THE PERELANDRA PROJECT:

The full project being researched and developed by MSW on the Perelandra and Cottage levels.

MSW functions within the Perelandra Project with this deva and in partnership with Pan as the co-creative research scientist. Together they create the lab's intelligence base.

DEVA OF PERELANDRA, LTD.:

Moves the Perelandra Project information and products out into the world

Develops and works with the outreach dynamics that drive and shape the business

Provides the full financial support for the business and Perelandra

Perelandra, Ltd.—a corporation that reflects involution (nature)/evolution (human) balance

DEVA OF WIZBANG (MY PERSONAL COMPANY):

Receives and works with MSW's intellectual property and royalties

Creates the partnership between nature/Pan and MSW in the world of finance

Provides personal financial freedom and support

DEVA OF THE COTTAGE:

Provides a stable Cottage/Perelandra connection

The Cottage: MSW's home base

Supports her life and work

DEVA OF MSW'S CONTINUING EDUCATION AND TRAINING:

Addresses her knowledge and understanding of her role within the Perelandra Project

Addresses the internal structure, action and function required when working in partnership with Pan

Opens MSW to the breadth and depth of her training and the knowledge gained from past experiences

Connects MSW and gives her access to reality as it applies to her continuing work, education and growth

Note: For any project or focus I wish to address, I start with my Foundation Coning and add to it the deva of the specific project or focus. For example, for this book I added the Deva of Pivot *to my Foundation Coning.*

NATURE SPIRIT POINT

Pan: the heart of nature and my partner

Functions as MSW's bridge into the heart of nature and nature's intelligence

Pan *is* the heart of nature. Pan *is* nature's intelligence.

Ensures that the heart of nature and nature's balance is present throughout my work and life

WHITE BROTHERHOOD POINT

HYPERITHON: the head of the White Brotherhood science and technology division

Links MSW with the science and technology division within the WB

Hyperithon plus the Deva of the Perelandra Project, Pan and MSW create the full co-creative research team within the areas of science and technology for the Perelandra Project.

LORPURIS: the head of the WB medicine, health and medical technology division

Lorpuris plus the Deva of the Perelandra Project, Pan and MSW make up the co-creative research team within the areas of medicine, health and medical technology for the Perelandra Project

MSW's primary physician

ELYKIAS: MSW's Hopi grandmother

A healer and medical researcher

A strong woman who adds dynamics to the coning mix that are unique to women

Functions in a personal supportive capacity with Machaelle

Adds her medical knowledge to MSW's research and information

Provides a woman's wisdom, strength, understanding, support and love

DAVID: The central stabilizer and support for MSW

MSW HIGHER SELF WITH TWO BODIES

Creates, initiates and drives the coning

The two bodies comprise the range of MSW's life activity.

The two bodies open the coning range and allow it to fully function.

The Perelandra body is the lens through which she works when focused on the Perelandra level, making her work accessible to the Perelandra level.

The two bodies combined function as the bridge that connects two distinct levels of reality.

Note: You may have noticed a new character—Elykias. She appeared in my consciousness one afternoon, introduced herself and told me about our connection. When I told David, he already knew who she was and encouraged me to develop our relationship. She is a direct, no-nonsense woman who knows how to cut to the heart of any matter. She shows me a level of womanhood that, with her help, I hope to achieve someday.

When I activated my Foundation Coning, it was as if twenty doors had suddenly blown wide open. My understanding of the direction, definition and purpose for Perelandra and my work was greatly expanded. Now when I'm setting up the coning for any new development, I'm not the only one defining, providing direction and giving purpose to whatever I'm doing. That alone expands the scope of the development. The Foundation Coning links, unifies and coordinates everything and everyone I am connected to and working with on the two levels. I went from working with a small team to a large team.

> By the way, *don't* try to set up my Foundation Coning to use for yourself. It's a personal coning that relates to my life and reality. It doesn't translate to another's life or needs. I recommend you set up your conings based on the less complex one that I started with and used for many years. If you are to expand your coning at a later date, it will be for a good reason and you'll be told when and whom to include.

With my Foundation Coning, I felt like I was shot out of a cannon. That summer, while I tended the garden and prepared for the summer workshop series, I wrote four major papers ("Co-Creative Definitions," "The Calibration Process," "Miasms" and the "Body/Soul Fusion Process") and two new books *(Perelandra Garden Workbook II* and *MAP: The Co-Creative White Brotherhood Medical Assistance Program).*

I introduced the "Co-Creative Definitions" paper at the Nature workshop, the three remaining papers introducing new flower essence processes at the August Flower Essences workshop, the *Perelandra Garden Workbook II* at the September Gardening with Nature workshop and *MAP* at the October Mundane-Fantastic workshop. I put everything through the desktop publishing process but couldn't get the books printed in time for the workshops. So, like a crazy person, I xeroxed and collated book pages, inserted them in folders with metal clasps and handed out copies to each person attending the workshop. (Every once in a while, someone will call and mention they still have their "original" book or paper from 1990.)

The *Perelandra Garden Workbook II* included the gardening energy processes that I had developed with nature but were not ready in time to include in the first *Workbook*. The complete *Workbook* became a two-volume set.

MAP was especially close to my heart. It was/is the culmination of seven years of work with Lorpuris to develop a comprehensive and effective medical program that would connect a person with his or her own White Brotherhood medical team, using nature as the conduit. Once we saw how efficiently the setup with nature and Lorpuris was working for me, Lorpuris decided this was the answer for providing a new White Brotherhood medical service. After seven years of trial and error, we had a proven ironclad program. The good news: *Anyone* could get hooked up with their personal medical team and they didn't have to be sporting two bodies on two levels to accomplish it. In 1990, Lorpuris' medical teams were ready to open their doors. They hung their shingles and I handed out the book.

With the publication of the two books that fall, I announced to my staff that *MAP* was going to be a slow seller because the name "White Brotherhood" in the title would scare everyone except the brave and slightly whacky Californians. (God bless the fearless Californians.) Undaunted, they would buy the book first, begin the program, experience success, and then through word of mouth, the book would start moving beyond California. It would be a gradual and slow process. I would know *MAP* was finally mainstreamed when some little old white-haired lady rocking on her porch in Kansas bought a copy. Prognostication isn't my strong suit. (I think I'm a dyslexic prognosticator. The opposite always occurs from what I think will happen.) In less than a month after publication, we got a call from a woman in Canada who had gotten a call from her friend in Texas to tell her to get a copy of *MAP.* It wasn't exactly the scenario I had pictured but it was close enough. *MAP* was now off and running.

After my 1990 summer of insanity, I was forced to admit that I was tired. I was willing to step back from everything but the garden and the Cottage. I was willing to slow down on writing books and papers for publication, but not the research notes. At the same time, the garden was starting to take a toll on my body. I was forty-five years old and thirteen years of constant deep-knee bends, tilling and hauling heavy bags was wearing me down and sometimes causing pain. The men at the Cottage pressed me to hire an assistant, but I couldn't stand the idea of having another person in the garden, especially one who didn't know anything about co-creative gardening. I mounted all kinds of resistance, yet the men kept pressing.

One day I was tending to the roses and my knees buckled. I collapsed on the ground in pain. I had finally done one too many deep knee bends. Luckily my knees didn't suffer permanent damage but they were clearly tired. I had to yell "uncle." A young woman who was already on staff asked if I needed help in the garden. It didn't take long for me to recognize how much an assistant could help, especially with the routine mundane tasks requiring deep knee bends. Even I had to admit that with help, I was freed up to do my main job—nature research. She was the beginning of a long line of garden assistants, some really good and some not so good.

With an assistant to take care of the winter garden maintenance and a staff to keep the business operating, I was able to take a break—the first since moving to Perelandra. My good friend, Elizabeth, had been spending the summers on Cape Cod for years. She saw I needed help, put her house-hunting hat on and found a house that I could rent for the winter that overlooked Cape Cod Bay. After arriving in December, I discovered the depth of my exhaustion. For the first three weeks I did nothing other than eat, stare at the bay and watch the tides come in and go out. It's an understatement to say it also helped to get a break from Perelandra as the business continued growing and the activity increased. Our quiet little place in the country had become a bustling business that included more staff, more office space, delivery trucks dropping off supplies and a daily arrival from UPS to pick up the packages. I returned to the Cape each winter for the next thirteen years.

Once I was able to do something other than watch the tide roll in and out, I developed a gentle rhythm that included walks on the beaches, Cape exploration, writing and thinking. I loved the cold winter winds, the storms, the snows, the hearty winter residents, the restaurants and the solitude. I loved stopping at my neighborhood gas station and asking the attendant for the day's goat report. Her goat was widely respected for its uncanny ability to predict storms. It was all based on how far up a hill the goat climbed each day. There were quite a few of us who stopped in for the daily (and accurate!) goat report. Thanks to email, I was able to keep up with what was happening at Perelandra. Thanks to my Foundation Coning, I was able to move back and forth seamlessly between the Cape and the Cottage.

IN 1993, I HIRED two young women to add to my staff. It was an ordinary moment that turned out to be serendipitous. Over the next few years they blossomed and have become part of Perelandra's foundation as well as Perelandra's future.

Beth was a twenty-year-old secret geek when she was hired. One winter I returned from the Cape and asked her,

> "Have you ever looked at a website?" (At the Cape, I had just seen my first website.)
>
> "I glanced at one once."
>
> "Do you think you could build a simple website for us?"
>
> Pause while thinking. "I think so."
>
> "Do you think you could do it in three months?"
>
> Pause again while thinking. "I'll give it a shot."

Three months later our first website went live. It was simple, clean and did the job. I've since learned how outrageous my request was, but Beth dove into the challenge and triumphed. (Our website has been redesigned and upgraded several times by teams of geeks who took a year or more to finish the job.) She has become my top person in our Publication Department, managing our huge website, paying attention to all our computers, installing software updates, designing and sending out email announcements to our customers, creating the e-books and helping me with book publication. She's self-taught, delightfully eccentric (as any self-respecting geek should be) and I don't know what I would do without her. She could leave Perelandra tomorrow to join a top-notch company (several companies have tried to steal her away) and earn a ton of money, but she stays. (Thank god.)

The second fortuitous hire was Jeannette. Like Beth, she also came with a secret, but it had nothing to do with computers. She had been a special-education teacher with experience in putting together teams, as well as evaluating staff. I was interested in having the Perelandra staff function as a team, but I didn't know how to put that together. Sometimes I was successful but mostly I just caused frustration for myself and the others. And I *hated* firing people. To be honest, some staff just needed to be fired. The first week after Jeannette came on board, I asked,

"Have you ever fired anyone?"

"Yes."

"Would you mind firing those three people over there and hiring new people to fill their spots?"

Pause while thinking. "Okay."

She once joked that the thing you most want to do in a new job is fire a third of the staff and become the target of everyone's hate! She soldiered on back then and has been soldiering on since. She has become the top dog in the business (just below me, of course, and her own dog, Luna). She deals with business problems, staff problems, hiring and firing, outside vendor issues, contracts, the company's finances and everything in-between. In her copious "spare time," she's one of my three garden assistants. She's taken an enormous burden from my shoulders and gives me the freedom I need to continue my work.

That was twenty-five years ago. If you've called our Question Hot Line, you've spoken to Beth or Jeannette. Both of these women will anchor the Perelandra business after I leave for the Cottage full time. (Two more important planks were added to Perelandra's foundation.)

IN 1994, I GOT WORD that there were two more sets of essences to be added to the Perelandra collection: Nature Program and Soul Ray. I can't say this news excited me. But again Pan let me know what these two sets would address and how much they would add to the Perelandra essence mix.

The Nature Program Essences address and re-establish our body's electrical system balance in two ways:

> They strengthen the system in relation to the body's bacteria, virus and fungus populations. These microbial populations are a vital component when addressing the healthy function of the human body.
>
> Sobopla, Moon and Bowl Essences address the balance of the body's electric system in light of its relationship to the larger environmental and planetary picture.

The Soul Ray Essences balance and stabilize the body's electrical circuits that are connected with and support an individual's soul-level activity. They also address the circuits that support an individual's development towards conscious awareness of this activity, as well as the circuits that support the integration of the soul-level activity with our physical, emotional and mental levels.

Well, how could I say no to these two sets? So it was back to tincture production and box colors. This time I had a staff, and together we went through the pain of choosing the two new colors. It took us a week of spirited debate to make the final selections.

The tincture for the Nature Program and Soul Ray Essences was produced differently from the others. Plants and flowers growing in the garden were not used for these new patterns. The new process came straight out of my Mount Shasta Mission experience, only now I wasn't carefully building a domed energy biosphere on a mountain. Instead I was building a domed biosphere of electrical patterns to be contained in a quart tincture jar. As usual, I worked with Pan. (Of course.) For each new essence, Pan collected electrical patterns derived from dozens of specific natural elements located all around the planet (and beyond), moved them through a process that coalesced the many individual patterns into one complex, expanded and completely new pattern. The final unified pattern was then "downloaded" into its quart jar of water. After that, the jar was set in the sun and put through the regular finishing essence steps. The individual patterns that Pan had drawn from wide-ranging locations introduced a global (and beyond!) dynamic with these two sets and greatly widened the scope of the entire five-set collection of Perelandra Essences.

The coalescing procedure for creating the Nature Program and Soul Ray tinctures led to the creation of the Perelandra Solutions. Over the course of the next few years, nature and I developed the MBP Balancing Solutions that balance and strengthen each of our body's systems (cardiovascular, immune, digestive, etc.), the assorted Perelandra Solutions for human and animal health issues, and the ETS Solutions (Emergency Trauma Solutions).

Up to this moment in 2018, I've written or developed:

ten books (nineteen books, if we count the updated publications, and second and third editions),

six different medical programs and approaches,

five sets of Perelandra Essences (with beautiful color-coordinated boxes),

a set of fourteen MBP Balancing Solutions,

nineteen Perelandra Solutions for humans and animals,

seven ETS solutions (Emergency Trauma Solutions for humans, animals, plants, soil, atmosphere, water and soil-less gardens),

two Soil Balancing Kits (basic and expanded),

an annual summer workshop series and open house,

six DVDs taped live during my summer workshop series and open house,

six audio CDs of different talks I've given,

the Nature Cards

and a Perelandra mug.

As you might imagine, the Perelandra business has changed a lot since I started it in the early '80s. I used to handle the whole operation myself and became quite good at keeping all the plates spinning in the air at one time. But now, with the addition of computers and technology and lots of fiber-optic cables, I would not know where to begin. We have twelve full-time staff and four to six part timers. Our production department has taken over the original house and the production women pump out an average of 12,300 bottles of Perelandra Essences and Solutions each month. (So much for my whining about the measly thirty sets—240 bottles—of Rose Essences *I* filled and thought would last a few months!) The tipi/sanctuary/office building has been taken down and replaced with a naturalized garden. The mailroom and customer service are now in the converted loft of our business barn. We no longer lick postage stamps. The whole postage operation has been computerized and, even if I wanted to, I wouldn't be able to figure out how to post a package without first receiving some serious training from the mailroom staff. The only thing left from my original office is the handmade pottery pen holder that I keep displayed in a safe spot in the mailroom for sentimental reasons. The garden assistants have taken over the cabin and turned it into the garden office. I live in a house that I had built on the property. (Clarence is living in his own home next to Perelandra.) The Perelandra property has expanded from its original ten acres to seventy-seven acres. The business takes up just a small portion of the land and the rest is a combination of woods and meadows that have been posted, protected, conserved and returned to their wild state. Our twenty-two deer, along with our numerous bears, coyotes, wild turkeys, skunks, rabbits, groundhogs, foxes, possums, raccoons, birds, honey bees and other insects, snakes, lizards, turtles and a gazillion other wild animals are happy.

As for me, I'm Perelandra's CEO and I hold its definition, direction and purpose. Thanks to my staff, I've been freed from the day-to-day business responsibilities to focus on research and development.

And with that—Houston, we finally have ourselves a Perelandra foundation. Whew.

Chapter 29

The Linen Closet Between Two Realities

WITH THE PERELANDRA FOUNDATION set in place, our activity and outreach increased. The annual workshop series was always filled to capacity, sometimes over-capacity. The open house attracted hundreds of people who traveled to Virginia from all around the country and from around the world. We've had visitors from as far away as Brazil, Great Britain, France, New Zealand and Japan. One year a group from Japan flew in to Dulles International Airport, boarded a bus and arrived at Perelandra for the day's open house. (We had arranged for Naoko, the leader of their group, to translate my talk into Japanese as I gave it. I'd say a few sentences and then she would translate. Only the Japanese could understand the translation, yet everyone there was mesmerized and stared at Naoko from beginning to end. There wasn't one sound, no one moved in their seat, no one got bored and left the talk. At one point I laughed and teased them, "You people think that if you stare at Naoko hard enough you'll suddenly understand Japanese!" I have to say, her voice was soft, soothing and lilting. It was easy to become transfixed.)

Then a series of outside events forced (inspired?) me to adjust or replace some of the foundation planks.

IN 2006, THERE WAS A SERIOUS outbreak of Avian Flu that many, including the World Health Organization, were watching carefully as it spread out of Asia, into the Middle East, Africa and Europe. There were concerns that if this virus started jumping from birds to humans, we would be facing a pandemic that would lead to global disruptions and widespread death that would rival the 1918 pandemic. I watched this development closely. I needed to know when to act and how to respond. The virus had been identified—H5N1. I worked with Pan to develop a solution to address possible exposure and infection. I read up on past pandemics, including the Spanish Flu pandemic of 1918 that resulted in 50 to 100 million deaths worldwide. I wanted to know what to expect and to find out what people did back then to successfully avoid infection. I found three reports of success in the U.S.—one from a sanatorium in New England, another from a small town in the West and a third from a naval base on an island off the West Coast. The secret to all three successes and the thing they had in common was strict sequestration. No outsider was allowed in. If anyone left the sequestered area, they were not allowed back in because of possible contamination.

Taking my cues from the success stories and what health officials said about Avian Flu, I made the decision to cancel the 2006 workshop series and open house. Flying birds and traveling humans were rapidly spreading the virus around the world. I did not want Perelandra to participate in this viral spread.

About the same time, reports were coming out stating that the planet's temperatures were rising faster than scientists had anticipated. A lot of it had to do with the continuing buildup of manmade carbon dioxide, largely from manufacturing and car exhaust. Just for the hell of it, I did a little math and discovered that the *average* number of people coming to just one of our open houses by bus, plane and car added the same amount of carbon dioxide into the atmosphere as one Humvee (notorious for its lousy gas mileage) traveling around the equator *three* times. I did not want Perelandra to participate in the destruction of the planet's ozone and climate crisis so I cancelled our annual workshop series and open houses altogether.

The workshops and open houses had become a major part of our outreach activity, and my decision had a major impact on the business. I asked Pan, "What do we do now that I've closed down these annual events?" Essentially Pan said, "Go virtual." With that,

I set a new plank into place. We had already taped the workshops and those were made available as videos. Our on-site open house morphed into our *virtual* open house. We were able to move most of the normal open house activity online. We established a new annual open house rhythm and set aside several Saturdays each year so people could call our Question Hot Line, place orders, look at special slide shows of the Perelandra garden and submit questions to me using our forum. (That way no one had to miss my words of wisdom and weird, smart-ass comments.) To provide folks with the experience of walking through the garden and feeling its balanced energy, Pan and I created EoP, Essence of Perelandra. Its pattern isn't just produced *in* the garden but created from the elements in the garden biosphere that create its unique balance. Now people could benefit from this balance any time they wished and not depend solely on one afternoon's journey to Jeffersonton. Sure, it's not the same as actually visiting Perelandra but at least we're not helping to destroy the planet.

THE NEXT MAJOR CHALLENGE occurred closer to home. One of our neighbors left a packet of information at my door about using "Biosolids" as a fertilizer on his fields. He asked for my thoughts about this. I had no idea what Biosolids were, so I asked Jeannette to do a Google search and find out something about it. She got back to me right away and explained that Biosolids was land-applied Class B sludge—Class B *toxic* sludge, actually. Our neighbor would be making a seriously bad and dangerous move.

I put together a team of six staff and organized an Erin Brockovich-like investigation to find out what was going on with land-applied sludge. We spent several weeks tracking down and reading state and federal regulations. We located government offices to ask questions. Taking my cue from Erin, I kept saying, "We need to follow the money." That led us into a statewide and national scandal that is still set to explode one day, but not before a lot of people's health has been compromised, livestock killed and land destroyed. You see, sludge is offered as a fertilizer to farmers and ranchers *at no cost.* Back in the 1950s, farmers refused the free fertilizer offer as soon as they heard the word "sludge." They instinctually knew that sludge was the wrong thing to add to soil. So a Manhattan marketing firm had an in-house contest to come up with a new, more palatable name for sludge. They chose "Biosolids." The new brochures made it sound like it was safe enough to spread on your breakfast cereal and land owners began to accept the free offer—as did golf courses, schools, athletic fields, public camping areas and national forests.

If it's free, who is making money on this scheme? First of all, there is a legitimate problem to be solved around how we deal with the massive amount of sludge that comes out of water treatment plants. They used to dump it into rivers, lakes and oceans but found that it destroyed those rivers, lakes and oceans. The 1972 Clean Water Act stopped this practice. So they started dumping it on land instead. Right now, treatment plants and state governments are paying Biosolid companies to remove the sludge and get rid of it. Individual states are also *receiving* money to accept sludge from other states for spreading as land-applied fertilizer. This "solution" works only as long as farmers keep accepting the free sludge and providing their land as a sludge dump. Virginia imports sludge from other cities along the East Coast—New York, Philadelphia, Baltimore and Washington, D.C. The state is paid for providing that service. A multi-billion-dollar, profit-motivated service industry has sprung up to address the country's expanding sludge disposal problem.

What's in this stuff? The industry likes to emphasize that Biosolids are processed human waste. They are even pushing hard to get Biosolids classified as organic. This would allow organic farmers and gardeners to receive their fair share of free fertilizing. But over the years it has been tested by a number of facilities, including Cornell University, the National Academy of Science and the CDC. Here's what they found: Class B sewage sludge is filled with PCBs; chlorinated pesticides such as DDT, aldrin, chlordane and lindane; chlorinated compounds such as dioxins; heavy metals such as arsenic, cadmium, chromium, lead and mercury; asbestos, petroleum products and industrial solvents; radioactive material flushed down the drain by hospitals, businesses and decontamination laundries; and significant concentrations of infectious-disease-causing viruses, bacteria, protozoa, parasitic worms and fungi.

According to the CDC, the parasites in Class B sludge can cause typhoid fever, dysentery, gastroenteritis, diarrhea, abdominal pain, cholera, hepatitis, meningitis, pneumonia, paralysis, encephalitis and severe respiratory problems. Just the odor alone (and this stuff stinks beyond words) can cause nausea, vomiting, stomach cramps, migraine headaches, flu-like symptoms, asthma attacks, abscesses, tumors, cysts, allergies and sudden illnesses caused by microbial pathogens.

You can come into contact with Class B sludge if a gardener, farmer or rancher within a mile of you has spread it on their land. There are documented cases of children and adults dying after exposure to sewage sludge. Also entire herds of cattle. And there are sludged land areas where nothing has been able to grow in that soil for many years. The land is barren.

I wrote a lengthy report based on the information that we gathered and made it available on our website to help make people aware of this issue. I condensed the report and included it in the latest edition of *The Perelandra Garden Workbook.* We've passed out copies of the report to as many people as possible in our surrounding area. Some of those people didn't appreciate our efforts and reacted with a smidge of hostility. But I'm pleased to say that a number of people have backed away from spreading sludge. All they had to do was say "no" to the companies who were pressing them to accept the free "fertilizer."

I still had the problem with my neighbor to deal with. This was a serious situation and an equally serious threat to Perelandra's existence in Jeffersonton. We had several people on staff who had health conditions that would be compromised, and they would have to quit their jobs in order to avoid sludge exposure. Spreading sludge isn't a one-time event. It can occur semi-annually or annually. So the threat would be constant.

I had other important issues to consider. There was the condition and balance of the Perelandra garden itself. Would we be able to eat anything that was harvested from that garden? There was also the health and balance of all the wildlife that interfaced with and were a part of the garden. How would they fare? Then there were the Perelandra tinctures that are produced in the garden. Could they be produced safely in a sludge-enveloped atmosphere? My work, my business and my home were at stake.

I turned to Pan, laid everything I knew about the problem on the table and asked, "How do I solve this problem? How do I stop this neighbor from spreading sludge and how do I protect Perelandra, the staff, the garden and the tinctures?"

When it came to stopping the neighbor, time was an issue. It was getting close to the spring fertilizing season. After discussing the problem with people who knew him, I found out that he was known to be a bit on the hyper-frugal side. (This explained why he wanted the free sludge.) That small piece of information led me to my next move. Armed with the sludge information, I paid my neighbor a visit. I talked to him about what we had discovered about "Biosolids" and its dangers. I gave him a copy of my report. (He didn't know anything about sludge except what the Biosolids company had told him. He was under the impression that it was safe.) To seal the deal, I made a business offer. I would pay for half his fertilizing costs if he did not spread sludge. It was a fair deal from my perspective because I was saving my company and protecting my staff. The offer surprised him, but he accepted. For the next seven years, we shared the cost of fertilizing his fields. In the end, I paid a little over $13,000. But when you put that number next to all that could have been lost, it was worth it.

The agreement with my neighbor bought us some time but it didn't make the sludge problem disappear. You see, during our investigation, we learned that the #1 state in the country for importing sludge was Virginia. And the #1 county in Virginia for spreading sludge was Culpeper County. Perelandra is in Culpeper County. This was a problem that was not going away, and I needed to do something to protect the garden and our tincture production. I turned to Pan again, "How do I protect the tincture patterns and keep them 100 percent clean?"

The answer was nothing short of brilliant. Pan created the Perelandra Tincture Bank, a protected repository for all of Perelandra's electrical patterns that are used for producing our tinctures. It does not exist in five-senses form but it functions as if it were in five-senses form. Without realizing it, I was already halfway down the road that led to the Bank. My work with nature for the Mount Shasta Mission and the work we did together to create the tincture patterns for the Nature Program Essences, the Soul Ray Essences and the Perelandra Solutions had already laid the groundwork I would need for the Bank.

Here's how it works. Each Perelandra tincture pattern has an account in the Bank. When I see it in my mind's eye, it's similar to a wall of safe deposit boxes. Every pattern has its own labeled, seamless box (to protect the pattern from cross-contamination). Working with Pan to set the Bank up at the start, we went through a series of steps similar to the process I described for the Soul Ray and Nature Program Essences to create the electrical patterns for each of our tinctures. Once a pattern was created and checked, we moved it into its box. The Bank currently holds eighty-nine Perelandra electrical pattern accounts.

When I develop a new tincture, we add a new box to the Bank. We balance, stabilize and label the box. Only when this is completed do we develop the new electrical pattern and transfer it into its box. I then activate the Bank's protection system by shutting the box's self-locking door.

When a tincture is produced in the garden at Perelandra, I give permission for the corresponding account in the Bank to open and for Pan to download the electrical pattern directly into the beaker of water sitting on the table in the garden. In order for this to continue working over the years ahead, Pan included the dynamic of infinity as an added element in each electrical pattern. A pattern can be downloaded from its box and used as often as needed for as long as needed. If this is ringing a bell for you, it's the same concept used for our personal infinite bank accounts at the Cottage. Apparently, this infinity notion is a part of natural law and the dynamic is there to be used when needed.

The Bank solved several problems that I was facing and provided a number of benefits that I had not expected.

1. The electrical patterns held in the Bank are pristine and will remain in that state no matter what environmental

disaster crops up on the Perelandra level (such as spreading land-applied Class B sewage sludge).

2. The Bank tinctures were developed from electrical patterns that were/are at their cleanest, strongest, most balanced state when banked. Downloading them from the Bank adds clarity and consistency to the patterns and the tinctures. All the elements that create the patterns' unique qualities are transferred into the tincture beakers at the garden and again into the concentrate bottles.

3. By downloading the patterns directly from the Bank, we are not locked into the garden's timing for producing the flowers needed for the Rose, Rose II and Garden Essences. Nor do we have to be concerned about droughts and storms. The patterns for those three flower essence sets are the same quality as patterns produced from perfect flowers growing in perfect weather.

4. By creating the Bank, my concerns about maintaining the quality of tincture production once I've moved to the Cottage full time have been addressed. (Some of our customers have similar concerns. They ask what's going to happen with the Essences once I die? Some call and ask about my health. It's the indirect way of asking the same question.) I have provided detailed instructions and trained a team of staff to produce our tinctures. They operate with great care and precision, and will continue this work once I leave. Well, that's fine for the first post-Machaelle generation. But I'm setting up Perelandra for the long game. When looking at generations down the line, it's quite possible that some fool is going to say, "Hey, I have a better idea. Let's make the tinctures a new way." And with this, the quality of our tincture patterns would be compromised. The Bank solves that problem. No matter how many iterations of tincture teams we have, the same quality of electrical patterns from the Bank will be used. It will always be the original patterns made by nature and me.

5. The Bank, its accounts and the deposit boxes are protected to the hilt. I did not want *anyone* breaking open the boxes and screwing with the patterns. We've set it up so that only I can open a box and only Pan can download a pattern for tincture production. The download happens *after* I give the go-ahead for which box is needed for the download. Without my nod, Pan won't "touch" the box. So if you ever hear someone say they are downloading their electrical patterns from the Perelandra Bank, *ignore them.*

With the addition of the Perelandra Tincture Bank, another new and very special plank was set into Perelandra's foundation.

IN JUNE 2014, WE WERE HIT with a fourth outside challenge when we were contacted by the FDA (Food and Drug Administration). They asked us to meet with them at their Baltimore office at our earliest convenience. They had been reviewing our website and had some issues with our product descriptions. Jeannette and Beth traveled to Baltimore for the meeting. The first thing they discovered was that the FDA didn't know how to classify Perelandra's products. We weren't a food, a supplement, a drug or homeopathic. We were their headache. They knew something needed to happen from their end, but they didn't know which regulations applied to us. After listening to Jeannette and Beth report on the meeting and seeing where the FDA was headed, I set up our approach to the FDA situation.

1. Jeannette and I constructed a coning and wrote a DDP (direction, definition, purpose) for dealing with the FDA. Then it was activated with nature. Here's our DDP:

> To work cooperatively with the FDA staff and whoever else is involved in order to:
>
> • obtain the information needed to comply with FDA regulations without compromising the integrity of Perelandra's information,

• get a clear understanding and approval of the specific wording we are permitted to use to describe Perelandra products on our website and in our catalog,

• develop a positive relationship with the FDA that will be supportive of Machaelle's and Perelandra's work now and in the future and that will not impede the work,

• describe Perelandra products clearly and accurately to the FDA and in a way that ensures Perelandra products will not be classified as drugs or put in any FDA category that will impede Perelandra's business, and

• establish a position with the FDA to minimize the time and effort required of us by any FDA reviews in the future.

2. I removed myself from the mix for any FDA meetings or direct communications. I did this because I knew I would have to restrain myself from taking a flying leap over the table and strangling someone. (I was in major lioness "protect Perelandra" mode.) I was certain that impulse was counterproductive.

3. I asked Beth and Jeannette to function as the Perelandra point team. They wouldn't inflict bodily harm and with them we had our best chance for establishing a cooperative relationship. I stayed in the background where I couldn't injure anyone. Jeannette and Beth always reported back to me, and I would add my two cents about the next steps we needed to take. At Perelandra, we divided the massive FDA job—Jeannette spoke to and corresponded with the FDA team, I rewrote all the product descriptions and written material, and Beth made all the changes on the website, on our labels, in our catalog and in our printed brochures.

4. We hired an attorney who was well versed in the FDA world. He was there to help us understand and navigate that world if we needed help or had any questions. (We hardly used his services and he was always surprised at how much the folks at the FDA were willing to help us and cooperate with us.)

To make the changes they were requiring, we estimated that we would be dancing with the FDA for two years. Our attorney told us that normally the FDA requires companies to comply within a couple of months. To the FDA's credit, they accepted our timetable once they saw the number of changes we'd have to make and our willingness to cooperate.

Our website descriptions were changing daily, and I needed to explain what was happening to our customers before they started thinking they were losing their minds as the text changed in front of their eyes. I sent the following email.

As some of you know, we have been working with the FDA for the last eight months in order to make adjustments that meet their requirements. We passed their physical plant inspections with flying colors. They were a little surprised at just how clean, careful and organized our departments are. But their sticking point is our bottled-product descriptions. Here's the crux of the FDA regulations that we are dealing with:

> *In the FD&C Act, a "drug," in part, is defined as an article that is intended to diagnose, cure, mitigate, treat, or prevent disease, or affect the structure or function of the body of humans or animals. The "intended use" may be shown by the circumstances surrounding the distribution of the article; this may be established through claims found in, for example, catalogs, brochures, audio and videos, graphic images, internet websites, testimonials, other marketing materials, and even in the product name. Furthermore, a claim that may imply/suggest that a certain product may diagnose, cure, mitigate, treat, or prevent a disease/condition can also be considered a "drug claim."*

Overall, working with the FDA folks has been a mutually pleasant and respectful experience. They are being as helpful as their rules will allow. (Just don't offer them a cup of coffee. They can't accept it. Should we all end up in a courtroom, the coffee offer may come up as an attempted bribe. I'm not making this up.)

I became aware of some FDA regulations thirty-five years ago when I developed the Rose Essences. Since then, I have tossed out pieces of helpful information in order to provide product descriptions in FDA-friendly terms. While Perelandra was operating on a small scale, it was pretty easy to "fly under the radar." Now that we've become more widely known nationally and internationally it's impossible to fly under that radar.

The bottom line: We now have to eliminate anything in our bottled-product descriptions that touches on what is covered in the FDA paragraph above. In the coming months you may notice more and more of our descriptions becoming, shall we say, succinct. Surprisingly, we actually have room for finding some common ground with the FDA. But there are areas where our two very different logics will never meet. For example, I believe in the intelligence of the individual and feel it is important to give the customer as much information as they need in order to make a good decision about whether to purchase and use our products. The FDA folks are zealously protecting senior citizens, the vulnerable, the innocent and babies from snake oil salesmen and sure death. Sometimes it boils down to you being able to legally buy our products but we can't tell you what they do. Honest to god, there are times when I feel like I've fallen right into the middle of the Mad Hatter's Tea Party.

With this, I have some very fine news to give you. As I mulled over the FDA regulations, I asked Pan the question, "How in the world can Perelandra convey full and complete information in our bottled-product descriptions when surrounded by a world of regulations that don't apply to us, make no sense, and appear to be never-ending?" Because of the wonderful answer I received to this question and the resulting Perelandra development, I just may have to send flowers and several boxes of chocolate to the folks we're working with at the FDA. (I'll risk a bribery charge.) In their zeal to reduce our descriptions to cryptograms, they have actually freed us all. Stay tuned for more information coming shortly and get ready to smile.

With best wishes from the person who really knows
how to make a silk purse out of a sow's ear,
Machaelle

Pan's answer to my question was the Perelandra Information Center (PIC). For six months, I worked with Pan to develop and set up PIC. Like the Bank, it is not in five-senses form but it operates as if it was in five-senses form. It eliminates all limitations placed on information about the Perelandra bottled products and puts the individual back in the driver's seat.

In November 2014, I announced PIC to members of the Perelandra staff who volunteered to be the beta testers for this new program.

> You have been chosen out of tens of thousands of eager wannabe "applicants" for beta testing the new Perelandra Information Center (PIC). The Center is now open and fully

stocked with all the information about any of the Perelandra bottled products: the five sets of Perelandra Essences; the ETS collection for humans, animals and environment; the MBP Solutions; and the Perelandra Solutions for humans and animals. Enter the Center and you will have the answers to any of your questions and access to the full range of information behind each bottled electrical pattern of your choice. And if this wasn't remarkable enough, the information you seek will be tailored to you personally according to *your* timing and current needs. No longer will you have to sift through a bunch of generic coded crap just to find something that may apply to you. It will all apply to you personally.

About PIC

The Perelandra Information Center "holds" the complete body of information that is connected with each Perelandra bottled pattern. The PIC may be accessed by any individual who wishes to learn about a particular Perelandra bottled product and whether it is right for them to purchase and include in their health regimen.

You will find that each Perelandra Essence and Solution has its full description and all relevant information stored in PIC. This includes relevant health issues and conditions, as well as the specific health benefits each Essence and Solution provides.

Anyone who shows an interest, has questions or wonders about a Perelandra bottled product, who wants more information than is given in the guidelines we can provide publicly, and who is in need of or open to the Perelandra bottled products has immediate and automatic access to the PIC and that product's information.

Immediately the information they request is released to them to be received and made accessible. What is released is based on the range of details an individual needs or wants and is compatible with that person's stage of development and timing. In short, the information is given in balance with the individual.

The information is transferred by nature to the individual on his or her PEMS levels (physical, emotional, mental, soul) and by any and all communication avenues and sources that are available to and used by him or her.

As a person uses the product and is ready to expand his/her understanding of that product, a new range of information will automatically flow to them. PIC, the Perelandra Information Center, provides an individualized classroom for continuing his or her education and understanding about the Perelandra bottled product(s) being taken.

The PIC information is automatically translated into the individual's native language and will include the breadth, depth, spirit and nuances of PIC in their language.

No matter what language, the information is expressed in words, insights and visuals that are easily understood by the individual. The information is personalized and it "speaks" directly to the person.

Protection: The integrity of the Perelandra Information Center and the body of information it holds is fully protected from any intrusion by outside, unauthorized individuals, organizations or activity. The information is kept clean, clear and untampered with as it remains available to all. This information is for personal use only and is not to be misrepresented by anyone for private or public gain.

How to Work with PIC

To receive the full benefits of the Perelandra Information Center, you only need to state:

"I'd like to be connected with the Perelandra Information Center."

The connection will occur instantly. No waiting needed.

To organize requested information, work with one bottled product at a time. Once connected to PIC, state the name of the first solution you wish to receive information about. For example, state "I'd like information on ETS for Humans." Then ask your questions one at a time or describe the information you would like.

- You may ask specific questions about specific situations.
- You may ask for a better understanding of an Essence or Solution.
- You may ask for a list of areas in your current life where using a specific Essence or Solution will benefit you.
- You may ask questions about dosage as it applies to you in a particular situation or in general.

Once you are finished asking questions or requesting information, move on to the next bottled Essence or Solution you wish to have information about.

Before you "leave PIC" and return to your day, disconnect from PIC by stating:

"I'd like to be disconnected from PIC."

You will be disconnected instantly. There is no waiting and you don't need to test for stabilizing or take ETS. Just move on with your day.

If you did not receive any answers while you were in PIC, that information will come to you as you move about your day. If after two or three days you have not received the information you requested or you are having trouble understanding it, reconnect with PIC and ask them to resend or clarify.

PIC List Testing for Specific Situations

(Or the answer to the question, "What do I take for ____?"):

- PIC removes the walls and limitations that occur when only one set of Essences is tested or one Perelandra Solution is taken for a situation. There are times when it is important to remove the walls and test the full range of eighty-nine bottles to see what *combination* can work together to address a specific issue.
- For this, you will kinesiology test (or intuit) the PIC List, the handy checklist that lists all our Essences and Solutions. The bottles that test positive are needed to create a wide,

broad platform of interwoven electrical patterns that best get to the heart of the situation and return the individual back to health. This is an exciting development because it removes the restraints and allows the Essences and Solutions to function in a coordinated, connected way.

• If you are diagnosed with an illness or condition, you may also address the timing, sequence and dosage that is tailored to you for this issue using the PIC List.

• If you are dealing with a chronic condition, you may address the full range of patterns the same way as described above to get the combination you need.

The Perelandra Information Center is now open and waiting for you to come through its doors.

THE BETA TESTING WAS A HUGE SUCCESS. We plugged a couple of holes, and I wrote a thirty-four-page PIC manual that explains how best to work with each aspect of the program. We announced it to the public on February 20, 2015.

Announcing!
The Grand Opening of PIC,
the new, state-of-the-art
Perelandra Information Center

We invite you to enter PIC—it's open 24/7—and learn about what PIC offers and how to use its services to enhance your life and your health. To say that with PIC the sky is the limit is an understatement. There's no registration fee, membership or purchase requirements. You don't even have to travel to get to PIC. It's there to serve you any time you'd like, no matter where you are. All you have to do is come on in and enjoy this new world.

Everything—every book, program and product—I have introduced over the years has been well-received. But *nothing* has been received by the public as well as PIC. I was stunned by the response and the reactions. It's as if everyone had been waiting for something like PIC. (Who knew?) Apparently I needed the FDA to push me in the right direction, and I needed Pan to create PIC's structure and function to get me there.

It took a little under two years to complete the changes to our newly encrypted FDA-friendly information. By then, the FDA folks felt like family—but we still couldn't offer them coffee. As for me, I left our FDA adventure with PIC. I don't think I can adequately express how much it has meant to me to have the information surrounding the Perelandra bottled products set totally free with PIC. I always wanted to provide everything people needed. But ill-informed people with faulty opinions and government regulations kept getting in the way. Hell, even I was a block because I knew what I couldn't say and kept truncating the sentences I wrote. With PIC, *nothing* stands between the person and the information they want. All middlemen have been eliminated.

The Linen Closet Appears

In 2015, I celebrated my seventieth birthday. One of my first thoughts that day was, "I made it." I have survived, even though there were times I wasn't sure I was going to make it. I carved a path forward from Upperco (and Pivot One) that was non-traditional but it worked for me. I did not have formal education beyond high school, but I was smart enough to catch invaluable lessons along the way from life, my community, my country, my world and especially from nature. In short, I have received the finest, most relevant education a person can obtain. I've lived an honest life (at least I have tried to) and I've experienced the pleasures one receives when caring about others. I built a successful business that reflects my life—non-traditional, honest and caring. With Perelandra and the Cottage, I finally found where I belong. At the Cottage, I found my family. I discovered I have a dad, a brother and a grandmother who actually care about me. I even answered the questions I had raised in my late teens around life after death. (If there is life after death, what is that life like? What do people do? Do they work? Do they eat? Do they have wings and fly around?) And I realized that I had lived a life that reflected who I was. It had not been bent out of shape by the society around me. I managed to stay true to myself and to hold a steady course. Then it hit me: Boy, what a girl has to go through to put together one little life!

On that day, as I sat on my deck, looking out over Perelandra's meadows and thinking, I saw myself walk through a beautiful, arched country-garden gateway and enter the final phase of life. In my earlier years, I sometimes looked ahead to the older years and saw them as a repository for old people who were waiting to die or fighting against gravity not to die. But at seventy, when *I* walked through the gateway and entered the last phase, I experienced something quite different. I was greeted by a large group of elderly people who were smiling at me and indicating that I had now been received into a secret society, and I had earned my right to be there. It was a society where everyone had time to think, converse, appreciate, enjoy, create and continue to develop in new ways. They didn't have to schedule time to stop and smell the roses. Appreciating the roses was a normal part of their day. Everyone standing before me had a unique lifetime of experience and had lived through their own sliver of history. And they each had a story to tell.

This group is secret not by design but because those who are younger ignore them, except when providing physical assistance. For many, the elders don't exist. They are inconsequential. They are invisible. Yet every elder standing before me on my birthday was a walking treasure. I felt honored to be part of this group and once again I thought, "I made it."

Prior to my birthday, I looked at my death as the moment when I would formally detach from Perelandra and shift to the Cottage full time. Over the past few years I've prepared Perelandra for a seamless change over that included setting up the proper legal and financial frameworks and training key people. My goal has been for Perelandra to continue rolling along on its own steam once I depart. I'm even working with nature to begin to move the garden into the new post-Machaelle phase. Of course the R&D department will be closed down because I will be taking that with me and continuing my work with nature at the Cottage. When I considered my death, I had created a clear division: pre-death when I would be living my Perelandra/Cottage life and post-death when I would be living a Cottage life full time. That's what made sense. That's what seemed logical.

Then "the linen closet between two realities" showed up and the pieces of a new logic began to move into place.

I saw a "prototype" for this linen closet back in 1983, when I visited an earth house to give a workshop. It was a floor-to-ceiling closet that was built through an interior wall of the house and extended about fourteen inches beyond the wall on each side. The two sides had their own set of doors. One side opened into a laundry room where fresh towels and sheets were folded and stacked on the shelves. The other side opened into a common room where folks could take needed clean towels or sheets from the shelves. I thought it was the height of efficiency.

In 2015, I saw something similar in my mind's eye—a closet sitting between two realities with one set of doors opening out to the Cottage and Cottage level and the doors on the other side opening out to Perelandra. Instead of sheets and towels, the shelves held the Perelandra products, processes and developments that I could still continue developing from the Cottage. The other side of the linen closet would make those developments available to staff and folks on the Perelandra level. In short, because of the linen closet, I will not be detaching from the work I have set in place at Perelandra. And because of the linen closet, I will not be required to be physically present at Perelandra in order to continue this work. It was clear that the logic I had previously constructed around my death and departure had to change.

Here's how the closet between two realities works. Let's take for example, the Perelandra Tincture Bank, which is included in the linen closet. From the Cottage, I can open the closet door to access the Bank, to monitor the patterns, to provide needed adjustments for tincture patterns and to create entirely new patterns to be included in the Bank. The doors on the Perelandra side of the closet are opened whenever tinctures are produced at Perelandra by the tincture production team.

But there is a problem when it comes to new patterns that I create post-death. The tincture team won't know something new is available. Sure, we could set up some prearranged system or signal that I could give to the tincture team that would let them know there's a new pattern. But that kind of setup has too much room for error. They wouldn't know what to name it or how to describe it. And someone could easily misread the signal. Then it dawned on me. We already have a much better solution in place that would be air tight and have no holes: MAP. From the Cottage, I can tell the MAP teams directly that a new pattern with its new name and description has been banked and is available. They, in turn, would work with Pan to download the new pattern from the Bank and release it to anyone on the Perelandra level whom they are working with and who needs it. I realized that MAP as a program is an early "folded towel" that had already been placed in the linen closet because it functions between two levels: the Cottage-level MAP teams and the Perelandra-level MAP. Nature provides the conduit between the two levels. Problem solved.

Besides the Bank (which holds all the tincture patterns) and MAP, the linen closet also contains PIC. On the laundry room side of the closet, the PIC structure has already been set up to allow Lorpuris, Pan and me to expand how PIC operates. The PIC user doesn't need to do anything except open the user side of the closet and move through the program as currently written. Any future expansion will automatically be woven into PIC's information and function. Another problem solved.

Of course, the closet includes the Aquarian government/military leylines. I have access to that grid at the Cottage with the Globe. When needed, I work with nature to balance and stabilize the leylines. That directly impacts the physical leylines that are a part of our planet on the Perelandra level.

There are a number of things I work with on at the Cottage level that impact what's happening on the Perelandra level and are included in the closet. For one thing, there's the Dolphin Project. (I gotta tell you, it's utter hell stuffing thirteen adult dolphins in that linen closet.) This is a project that was set up for me by Pan. For the past thirty years, I've been working with a pod of wild dolphins that I meet with at the sea each year in the fall. On their way to their summer grounds, they stop by our meeting area that's located out in the ocean not far from the hotel. I test them for Perelandra Essences, Perelandra Solutions and ETS. After the first few years when they each tested positive for ten or twelve bottles, they settled down to an average of one or two bottles. It didn't take long for them to learn to open their mouths to receive the drops. In fact, there are some years when they have tested clear (nothing needed), but I give them a couple of drops of EoP, ETS or Royal Highness (Rose Essence) to keep them happy. They like the drops. What can I say?

We started with six adult dolphins and over the years they have added seven calves. They remain healthy and strong (and it seems ageless), but when I questioned why they reproduced so sparingly (seven calves over thirty years), I was told some of their history. The dolphin population on the Cottage level is still recovering from a long period of distress that was caused by ocean pollution when the Cottage level was dealing with their environmental breakdown generations ago. (With much work and global effort, the ocean condition has greatly improved. But it has taken many decades to turn that around.) The drops my pod receives "magically" benefit the dolphin community as a whole on the Cottage level, as well. (Don't ask me how. That's more information I'm waiting until after I die to get.) But all of this activity occurs on the laundry room side of the linen closet. The dolphins on the other side, the ones on the Perelandra level, *also* receive benefits from the drops I give to the pod on the Cottage level. (Again, I don't know how. I just do my job. I'll ask questions later.) It's clear to me that the Dolphin Project was set up by nature to address similar types of distress on the two levels. All I can say is that it seems to be working, at least with my pod, and I'll continue the work with them until the drops are no longer needed. I've grown quite fond of these creatures.

The dolphins have taught me that the linen closet between two realities doesn't have one set of rules carved in the wood on the inside of the doors. We're not just opening the doors on the Cottage side to put something in and opening the doors on the Perelandra side to take something out. With the dolphins, I can open the Cottage doors to provide drops of essences that benefit the dolphins swimming around in front of me, the dolphins swimming in the oceans on the Cottage level *and* the dolphins swimming in the oceans on the Perelandra level. It seems like the rules for animals have more flexibility when it comes to these levels.

I've had to install a dog door in the linen closet. My last companion animal at Perelandra was Toby, a magnificent dog who was the best at this companionship business. He went with me everywhere. He loved being at Perelandra, getting to know each person on the Perelandra staff and jumping into the garden pond. Wherever I was, Toby was right there with me. He died of old age in August 2014. It broke my heart to lose him. Two days after his death I had to walk from the house and across the field to attend a meeting at the business. When I got to the gate leading to the field, I stopped. I couldn't continue on because it was the path Toby and I had taken together every day. I just couldn't get myself to walk down that path. Instead, I walked the long way around the field. It took two weeks before I could walk Toby's path again.

On the morning of Toby's death, I spent time with him talking about the Cottage and my life there. When he was with me at Perelandra, he seemed to understand a lot of what I said to him but I never knew how much he actually understood. On this day I spoke to him as if he could understand it all. I said if he wanted and if the Cottage was where he was to be, he would be welcomed by all, especially by me. I set it up with Pan to receive Toby as he left Perelandra and to move him in the right direction. He had a peaceful, quiet death later that afternoon.

That night at the Cottage, David told me that Toby was with Henry, a veterinary doctor who was part of the White Brotherhood. Toby was now sleeping and he was fine. Henry was going to move him through the final stages of his death and healing process, which Henry estimated would take two to three months. Then he would determine Toby's next best move. Now all I had to do was wait (my favorite pastime) to see if I was going to be his next best move.

Henry gave us updates on Toby's progress every few days. For three days Toby was "sleeping it off." Then gradually he came out of it. He began drinking water, then liquid food, then solid food. Mostly he slept. After about a week he began to move around a little. He got up and explored the room he was in. But mostly he slept. Henry took him for short walks outside and Toby began to regain his strength.

From what I understand, Toby's soul/devic level holds all the patterns for his body, mind and spirit at its prime. Those were the circuits that had supported Toby when he was in his strongest, healthiest and most alert years. These circuits are triggered after death and provide what is needed for full repair and restoration. Since Toby wasn't on medication when he died, the circuits were able to "flow" freely. Consequently, his repair time was quick.

Henry said that Toby was aware that he was "coming back to me" at the Cottage. Apparently he understood quite a bit of what I had said earlier. According to Henry, Toby knew he was "going home." After discussing it, we decided that Henry would bring Toby to the Cottage on Friday, August 29, just three weeks after he died. But early Wednesday morning (August 27) he called to say that Toby was ready and eager to come now.

At 4 P.M., David and I were sitting outside when I got a strong feeling to turn around. I saw Henry walking across the lawn toward us with Toby on a leash. Toby spotted me and Henry quickly took him off leash. I sat down on the ground and called my friend. He sprinted over to me. I don't know who was more happy—Toby or I. He had no difficulty recognizing me. Maybe my Cottage body was a little different from my Perelandra body but, as far as Toby was concerned, I still had the same familiar soul. I made it a point to say and do things with him that had been our habit together at Perelandra to confirm to him that it was really me. As Janis Ian sang, "Silly habits mean a lot."

I introduced him to David and the two became buddies right away. All those times at Perelandra when I was focused on David while we were talking—well, now Toby was meeting the "other end of those conversations," and I dare say it felt familiar to him.

Henry stayed with us over the weekend to monitor Toby's progress. He said that Toby needed the benefits of belonging again. Physically he was 100 percent. No hip or joint problems. His two lumps were gone. His breathing was normal. His vitality and energy were high. He had clear eyes again, he was alert and curious. Clearly he was a dog in the prime of his life. And he was very happy. Actually, the two of us were very happy.

Later that first evening, David said to me, "Every friend of nature needs her own nature friend." When I thought about it, I realized he was right. I had my nature friend back.

OBVIOUSLY WE ARE ALL going to die, whether we want to or not. (I don't think that's a spoiler.) Imminent death is a major factor in the lives of the secret elder society. I could die any day now. I'm in life's final phase where death is unavoidable and something I expect in the not-too-distant future. In my earlier years, death used to sit far ahead into the future. Now it sits just in front of me. Because I can honestly say that I realize how lucky I am to be aware of certain things before I die, I have some very different feelings about the inevitable. I'm not looking at the end of my life and closing down. I'm not looking away from the horizon, waiting for death. Instead, I'm looking up at the horizon ahead, and I'm actively preparing for the future and the continuation of an active, vibrant life.

Like most sane people, I'm hoping to die quietly in my sleep—just after finishing a good international spy thriller and polishing off a box of Fran's chocolates. I once asked Pan for nature's take on human death. He said that the trigger for our death comes from our soul. When that triggering occurs, nature immediately provides the matter, means and action required to accomplish the person's "powering down" and death. I'm lobbying my soul for the good thriller/chocolate/sleep scenario. We'll see how far I get with that.

One More Loose End to Tie Up

Dear Miss Moore,

I doubt if you remember me. I was a student in your tenth grade English class at Stephen Decatur High School in 1960. You gave us an assignment to write a paper on how we imagined our lives would be fifteen years down the road. What were our goals? Where would we be living? Would we be married? Did we have children? Did we go to college? What did we study? What was our profession? Our politics? Our religion? Essentially, you asked us to map out the blueprint for our future. At the time I could not think a day ahead, let alone fifteen years. I handed in a page and a half, describing how I wanted my mind to be like a mound of sculptor's clay that was shaped by my life's experiences as I went along. I ended with the hope that my mind—my clay mound—would never become glazed and would remain forever soft and workable so that it could continue to be shaped by my experiences throughout the whole of my life. For this, you gave me an A+.

To complete that assignment from fifty-eight years ago, I now submit this book. I'm sure you will agree that I never could have imagined back then all the twists and turns my life would take. It has been a most unusual trajectory. I would be honored if you felt I deserved another A+.

Your grateful student,
Machaelle Small Wright

P.S. My clay-mound mind has remained soft, and life continues to shape it.

Contact Us

Website: perelandra-ltd.com
E-mail: email@perelandra-ltd.com
Question Hot Line 1-540-937-3679
(Wednesdays: 10 A.M. to 8 P.M. Eastern)

We're here to help you with any questions you might have about Perelandra, our products and about establishing and working with your co-creative partnership with nature.

Phone Order Lines
U.S. and Canada: 1-800-960-8806
Overseas and Mexico: 1-540-937-2153
Fax: 1-540-937-3360

Perelandra, Ltd.
P.O. Box 3603
Warrenton, VA 20188

Special Note to *Pivot* Readers

We have posted photographs for *Pivot* on our website. Had we included them in the book, they would have added quite a number of pages to an already big book and increase the price considerably. The *Pivot* Gallery on our website is our way of getting around this. Be sure to go to:

perelandra-ltd.com/pivot

More Books by Machaelle Wright

Behaving as if the God in All Life Mattered

Co-Creative Science:
A Revolution in Science Providing Real Solutions for Today's Health and Environment

Dancing in the Shadows of the Moon

The Mount Shasta Mission

MAP:
The Co-Creative White Brotherhood Medical Assistance Program

The Perelandra Essences:
A Revolution in Our Understanding and Approach to Illness and Health

Perelandra Microbial Balancing Program Manual

The Perelandra Garden Workbook

Perelandra Soil-less Garden Companion:
Working in Partnership with Nature in Your Home, Job, Business, Art Project, Research and Profession

Excerpt from

MAP

The Co-Creative White Brotherhood Medical Assistance Program

How MAP Can Help You

To give you an idea of how MAP came into my life, I have talked about a somewhat exceptional development that most people would not encounter in their lives, but that was responsible for leading me into MAP. However, I don't want to leave the impression that MAP is only for exceptional times. It is not. MAP is for those who feel that their present medical support—whether traditional or alternative—is not enough. For years, you may have felt absolutely comfortable with your medical support, and then suddenly, without a shadow of a doubt, you know you need more. To function well you need more input, more support. Yet, when you look around and try alternatives, none feel right. MAP is then your answer.

Because the MAP team includes nature, MAP is a physical program (not a spiritual program) that works on your well-being from the physical, emotional, mental and spiritual perspectives. Because of the unique position of the MAP team, it works on strains, pressures, pain and conflict being felt on all these levels simultaneously. When it comes to our health issues, these four levels interrelate. Normally we go to professionals who are experts in one level or one area of a level. It is up to us to put a team together that addresses the different aspects of the problem. And, when we put these teams together, they rarely consult with one another. So we don't have a sense of a united and coordinated medical approach. The MAP teams work on all levels simultaneously and function as a coordinated unit. Consequently, a MAP session is more comprehensive and its results are deeper than those we experience with other health systems.

We can initiate MAP during times of illness and injury, or it can be initiated during times of relative health when we feel we are capable of a better level of health and balance—and we want it. MAP is a comprehensive health program that you will use throughout your entire life. It is not a one-time program only for emergency situations. We are constantly changing and developing throughout our lives. MAP helps us maintain a high level of balance and function throughout all our changes and shifts. In short, it gives us a chance to experience an exceptional quality of life.

We can begin MAP at any stage in our life and at any age. We do not have to be healthy to begin (some have thought this was necessary), and we do not have to be sick. We do not need to abandon any medical support we have been using in order to begin MAP. If you are combining other health practices with MAP, this is fine. Just tell your MAP team what other things you include and how. MAP will accommodate them. As I worked with my team and experienced the depth of their work, I gradually dropped the other health practices I had been using, one by one. Before I felt comfortable switching my medical needs to MAP exclusively, my confidence about MAP had to grow. However, if I had a serious illness or injury that needed quick medical attention, I would not hesitate to get it. The difference is that I would work with my MAP team throughout the "repair" and recuperation period, as well.

It is important that you understand one thing about working with a White Brotherhood MAP team. They will not, under any circumstances, circumvent your timing on any issue. You are in complete control and command of your timing and rate of development. They will not circumvent your timing, because it would be wrong to do so. This would, in effect, remove you from the driver's seat in your own life and place you in the position of a child being catered to by the almighty parent. Your team will simply not participate in such activity.

In MAP, you control your timing and development in an interesting way. You will note in the instructions that you are urged to talk to your team. Tell them everything that comes to mind that is bothering you on any of your PEMS levels (physical, emotional, mental and spiritual). You aren't going through this exercise because your team is stupid and can't see you are in trouble. The troubles or situations you can articulate to your team tell them what you are ready to work on. And the extent to which you can describe the situation tells them the extent to which you are ready to change what is bothering you. You are your own barometer. They will not work in areas beyond those you recognize and describe. Consequently, your team will never put you in a position of facing and dealing with something for which you are unprepared. In the MAP sessions, you are your own master, and your team assists you in achieving your goals of health and balance in ways that are beyond belief. You are simply demonstrating your wisdom by choosing the best team with which to work.

FROM LORPURIS

I would like to add a bit to what Machaelle has already written. In short, I would like to assure you that we are eager to assist you in your quest for health and balance in any way you see fit. There will be those who will gravitate to MAP and wish to establish themselves in the program, but they will hesitate because they will feel unworthy of such an expanded approach or feel inferior, believing that we would consider it bothersome to work with them. It is this situation I would like to address.

I would like to point out that it is not a sign of good health and balance if individuals refuse help despite the fact they have gravitated toward the very help they are refusing. You might feel that I am stating the obvious. But we see the greatest stumbling block in establishing the kind of medical assistance that so many are presently seeking, either consciously or unconsciously, as being this issue of feeling unworthy of the help. It is a vicious cycle—and one we cannot step in from "out of the blue" and release a person from.

We suggest that if the concept of MAP feels right to you, yet you are feeling hesitant because you can't believe something "so good" could come to you, that you temporarily put aside your hesitancies for the purpose of entering the program. As we have said, feeling unworthy—and I use the word "unworthy" to cover feelings such as inferiority, weakness, fear and lack of capability—is a sign of being in need of help. Once you have entered the program and have discussed with us the reasons for your hesitancies, we will then be able to work with you to obtain a new level of balance that will effectively adjust your sense of self-worth and thus take care of the very reason you might not have entered the program.

In the MAP workshops I have given at Perelandra, this issue of self-worth has come up often. Invariably, someone will say he or she simply can't understand why a medical team from the White Brotherhood would choose to work with them. And, if that team does this kind of work with them, doesn't it mean that they are being chosen by the Brotherhood to then do something significant—like save the world or something? Surely you can't remain "just a housewife" or a car mechanic if you have a MAP team.

In the overall picture, the White Brotherhood is focused on shifting all that exists on this planet from a Piscean dynamic (parent/child) to an Aquarian dynamic (teamwork). Everything must shift. And all of us are involved in this shift. No one is exempt. We are responsible for catching on to what's happening and doing the work needed to make this shift. The MAP medical teams are not doing something extraordinary for a handful of "chosen" people. This program is for everyone who wants it. By working with us individually, the MAP teams assist us in living life with a better balance and getting on with the changes that are needed. Everything that is involved in the work of a housewife or auto mechanic must go through this shift, as well. The last thing a MAP team wants you to do is throw away everything and go off to "save the world." MAP wants you to do what you are meant to do, do it the best you can, and take responsibility for shifting your piece of the life puzzle from the Piscean picture to the Aquarian picture. It's all important to MAP. No one is insignificant.